Marketing Channels:
A Management View

Second Edition

Bert Rosenbloom
Drexel University

The Dryden Press
Chicago   New York   Philadelphia   San Francisco   Montreal   Toronto   London
Sydney   Tokyo   Mexico City   Rio de Janeiro   Madrid

To Pearl, Jack and Robyn

Acquisitions Editor: Karen Emilson
Project Editor: Ruta Graff
Managing Editor: Jane Perkins
Design Director: Alan Wendt
Production Manager: Mary Jarvis
Cover design by Margery Dole
Copy editing by Terry Fertig
Indexing by Jennifer Gordon

Composition by G & S Typesetters, Inc.
Text type: 10/12 Trump Mediaeval

Address orders to:
383 Madison Avenue
New York, New York 10017

Address editorial correspondence to:
One Salt Creek Lane
Hinsdale, Illinois 60521

Library of Congress Catalog Card Number: 82-72312
ISBN 0-03-058996-7
Printed in the United States of America
  5-039-9876543

CBS College Publishing
The Dryden Press
Holt, Rinehart and Winston
Saunders College Publishing

Foreword

The literature and practice pertaining to marketing channels has blossomed in the last decade through the contributions of many individuals and firms. Within this context, today's student needs a comprehensive and insightful exposure to this increasingly important area of business and marketing. This revised work by Bert Rosenbloom certainly helps provide this exposure.

Marketing Channels: A Management View represents a second edition of a most successful channels text. The book is characterized by its managerial perspective, focusing on the channel decision maker's design and management of the firm's marketing channels. This perspective provides a common thread to the text and results in a well-organized, highly readable book.

Marketing Channels: A Management View is also distinguished by its comprehensiveness and currency. Additional depth is provided in the revised edition, and many topical issues and developments are integrated into the discussion. From a student's and instructor's perspective, the book also offers an excellent infusion of illustrations and examples and provides twenty-five cases for additional pedagogical benefit.

Professor Rosenbloom is to be commended for this significant contribution to the channels and marketing literatures.

Stephen W. Brown
Consulting Editor
The Dryden Press and
Professor of Marketing
Arizona State University

Contents

The Dryden Press Series in Marketing
Stephen W. Brown, Consulting Editor

Principles of Marketing

Boone and Kurtz
Contemporary Marketing, Fourth Edition

Kurtz and Boone
Marketing

Rice and Smith
The Marketing Experience

Talarzyk
Cases for Analysis in Marketing, Second Edition

Talarzyk
Contemporary Cases in Marketing, Third Edition

Advertising

Dunn and Barban
Advertising: Its Role in Modern Marketing, Fifth Edition

Consumer Behavior

Blackwell, Engel, and Talarzyk
Contemporary Cases in Consumer Behavior

Block and Roering
Essentials of Consumer Behavior, Second Edition

Engel and Blackwell
Consumer Behavior, Fourth Edition

Retailing

Marquardt, Makens and Roe
Retail Management: Satisfaction of Consumer Needs, Third Edition

Rogers and Gamans
Fashion: A Marketing Approach

Salesmanship

Hise
Effective Salesmanship

Young and Mondy
Personal Selling: Function, Theory, and Practice, Second Edition

Sales Management

Futrell
Contemporary Cases in Sales Management

Futrell
Sales Management: Behavior, Practice, Cases

Marketing Research

Churchill
Marketing Research: Methodological Foundations, Third Edition

Zikmund
Exploring Marketing Research

Sciglimpaglia
Applied Marketing Research

Zikmund, Lundstrom, and Sciglimpaglia
Cases in Marketing Research

Advanced Marketing Research

Green
Analyzing Multivariate Data

Channels

Rosenbloom
Marketing Channels: A Management View, Second Edition

International Marketing

Terpstra
International Marketing, Third Edition

Industrial Marketing

Hutt and Speh
Industrial Marketing Management

Preface

Since the first edition of *Marketing Channels: A Management View* was published in 1978, the field of marketing channels has grown substantially. More research is being done on marketing channels, the literature is accumulating rapidly, and more and more collegiate schools of business have added marketing channels courses to marketing curricula at both the undergraduate and graduate levels. This dramatic increase in interest in marketing channels reflects the growing importance of this area within the larger field of marketing. Further, with the increased emphasis on strategic planning in marketing in recent years, a fuller understanding of marketing channel management has become even more important. Marketing channel management as one of the key strategic areas of the marketing mix offers great potential for improving marketing management through strategically planned and effectively managed marketing channels.

Given these developments, the managerial approach to marketing channels pioneered in the first edition of *Marketing Channels: A Management View* is more relevant and timely than ever. Thus, the second edition continues to be consistent with the original objective of the first edition—to provide a *managerial focus to the marketing channels literature within a comprehensive and integrated managerial framework*. The content of the second edition continues to emphasize the kind of knowledge needed to make more effective channel decisions. While the text still covers all of the important aspects of channel theory and research, it avoids drawn out and esoteric discussions of this material and instead stresses *managerial implications*.

The basic approach and style used in the original text have also been maintained in this edition. Every effort has been made to present material as clearly and concisely as possible, and carefully chosen examples and vignettes have been used abundantly throughout the text to add concreteness and interest. Even though this second edition presents some rather sophisticated material, students are likely to find it one of the most interesting and easily understood of any upper division marketing text. The only prerequisite necessary is the basic marketing course which virtually all students will have taken before enrolling in the channels course.

Although the basic objective, approach, and style of the first edition have been maintained, substantial changes and additions have been made to the content of the text. These changes and additions are discussed in the next section.

Organization of the Second Edition

Part One, Marketing Channel Systems, lays a basic foundation of marketing channel concepts within a managerial framework. Chapter 1 has been greatly expanded. The relationship of channel management to the marketing mix and strategic marketing management is discussed in depth, the distinction between channel management and physical distribution management is carefully examined, and the concept of channel flows is introduced explicitly and discussed in detail from a channel management perspective. Other marketing channel concepts introduced in the first edition have also been refined in this chapter. Chapter 2, which deals with marketing channel participants, has also been greatly expanded. The material on manufacturers and wholesale and retail intermediaries is treated in much greater depth, and all data have been updated using the latest census figures available. Chapter 3, which presents an analysis of the environmental setting of marketing channels and discusses the implications of environmental change for channel management has been entirely rewritten to reflect the many environmental changes that have occurred since the first edition was published. The section on the legal environment has also been greatly expanded. Also, this material has been placed within the chapter rather than being divided between the chapter and an appendix. Chapter 4, dealing with behavioral processes in marketing channels, has been updated to incorporate the substantial amount of behavioral channel research that has taken place since the first edition was published.

Part Two, Developing the Marketing Channel, beginning with Chapter 5, presents a comprehensive discussion of channel design. The seven-phase channel design paradigm introduced in the first edition has been retained but new examples and refinements have been added. Chapter 6 offers a detailed discussion of the last phase of channel design (selection of the channel members). New illustrative material has been added and more emphasis has been given to the problem of recruiting prospective channel members. Finally, Chapter 7, dealing with how various market dimensions influence channel design strategy, has been refined and updated.

Part Three, Managing the Marketing Channel, discusses the administration of existing channels. The first chapter in this part (Chapter 8) discusses the problems involved in motivating the channel members to perform their tasks effectively and efficiently. The revision of this chapter places more emphasis on learning about channel member needs and problems and provides an expanded and updated discussion of distribution programming for motivating channel members. All of Chapter 9 in this edition is devoted entirely to product issues in channel management. It has been substantially expanded to include a comprehensive discussion of the relationship between strategic product management and channel management. The material on pricing issues in channel management comprises a separate chapter (Chapter 10). Much new material on pricing in relation to channel management has also been added. Chapter 11, which deals with promotion in the marketing channel, has been revised to treat the distinction between "pulling" and "pushing" promotional strategies more explicitly than the first edition. Tighter organization was also achieved by placing this chapter directly following the pricing chapter rather than following the physical distribution chapter. Part Three concludes with Chapter 12 on physical distribution and channel management. This chapter has been thoroughly revised to provide a fuller discussion of the interfaces between physical distribution management and channel management.

Finally, Part Four of the text, Appraising the Marketing Channel, begins with Chapter 13 which tackles the issues involved in evaluating channel member performance. While the basic substance of this chapter is the same as in the first edition, some important refinements have been made to provide a stronger basis for performance evaluation in marketing channels. Chapter 14, the final chapter in the text, provides an updated discussion of the influence of vertical marketing systems on channel management.

The second edition of *Marketing Channels: A Management View* also has longer and more detailed chapter summaries than the first edition, and many of the discussion questions have been revised and new ones added. Finally, the case section, Part Five, has been substantially expanded. There are now a total of twenty-five cases. Almost one third of these are new to this edition, and most of these new cases are longer and more challenging than the cases they replaced. Thus, the section now has a good mix of short, medium, and long cases. A matrix relating the cases to relevant text chapters can be found at the beginning of the case section.

A Note on the Use of the Term Channel Manager

As in the first edition, the term "channel manager" continues to be used throughout as a way of referring to anyone in the firm involved in making channel decisions. Such terms as "decision maker," "marketing manager," "manager" or "marketer" could have been used in place of the term channel manager. But I chose to continue using the term channel manager because I believe it provides a sense of focus for referring to the important role of channel decision making within the firm. Regardless of what the individual's actual job title is, when that person is involved in making channel decisions, he or she is filling the role of channel manager even though such a position may not formally exist on the firm's organization chart. In other words, anyone in the firm who is making channel decisions is, while involved in that activity, a channel manager.

Acknowledgments

This revision effort was made much easier because of the excellent input provided by a fine group of reviewers. I would like to express my heartfelt thanks to the following colleagues for the excellent and painstaking job they did in providing ideas, comments, and constructive criticism which were invaluable to me in revising the original text:

William Black, University of Arizona (Tucson)

Raymond W. Knab, Jr., New York Institute of Technology

Charles W. Lamb, Jr., Texas Christian University

Orville C. Walker, Jr., University of Minnesota

Kaylene C. Williams, University of Delaware

I would also like to express my continuing thanks to the original group of reviewers who played such an important role in helping to shape the first edition of the text: Boris W. Becker (Oregon State University), M. Bixby Cooper (Michigan State University), Donald J. English, Jr. (St. Mary's College), Joseph P. Guiltinan (University of Kentucky), Stephen K. Keiser (University of Delaware), and Charles W. Lamb, Jr. (Texas Christian University).

The high level of professionalism displayed by the Dryden staff in the development of the first edition continued unabated in the second edition. I would especially like to express my sincere appreciation to Karen Emilson, Nancy Hughson, Ruta Graff, and Anne Smith.

Thanks are also due to Rolph Anderson, chairman of the marketing department at Drexel University, for his encouragement and assistance provided during the revision process and to the students in my marketing channels classes at Drexel who were subjected to various drafts of this revision.

Finally, as with the first edition, my deepest thanks goes to my wife, Pearl, for her unfailing support and assistance during every phase of the revision process.

Bert Rosenbloom
Philadelphia, Pennsylvania

Lists of Figures and Tables

Part One
Marketing Channel Systems

In this first part of the text we discuss the basic foundations of marketing channel systems.

Chapter 1 begins with a managerial definition of the marketing channel and then moves on to a discussion of how marketing channel strategy relates to strategic marketing management. Then basic concepts such as channel flows, channel structure, and the rationale for the existence of marketing channels are discussed.

Chapter 2 discusses the role played by channel participants at the manufacturer, wholesaler, and retailer levels.

Chapter 3 presents an analysis of the impact of external uncontrollable environmental factors on marketing channels.

Chapter 4, the last chapter in Part I, discusses behavioral processes in the marketing channel.

Chapter 1
Marketing Channel Concepts

When consumers enter the typical supermarket they are exposed to thousands of products from all over the world—tea from China, coffee from Brazil, cheese from Wisconsin, beef from Texas, fresh fruits from California and many, many others. They need only reach for the products desired as they stroll the aisles, place the items in their shopping carts, and pay for them at the checkout counter to have these products available for immediate consumption.

How ordinary this event, but how extraordinary it is that it can appear to be so ordinary. For behind this commonplace activity of shopping at the supermarket—or most any other type of store for that matter—lies a host of rather complex activities that have made the act of shopping so ordinary and simple. Thousands of people in perhaps hundreds of different organizations have been involved "behind the scenes." These organizations and the people working in them make up the marketing channels that have performed all of the tasks and activities necessary to make those products in the store so conveniently available to the consumer.

This text is all about marketing channels—what they are, how they are developed, how they operate, problems that occur in marketing channels, the administration of marketing channels, and many other aspects.

The Marketing Channel Defined

Unfortunately, there is much confusion about the definition of the marketing channel. Sometimes it is thought of as the route taken by products as they move from producer to the consumer or other ultimate user. Some define it as the path taken by the title to goods as it moves through various agencies. Still others describe the marketing channel in terms of a loose coalition of business firms who have banded together for purposes of trade. Many other definitions also exist.[1]

Much of the confusion probably stems from the differing perspectives or viewpoints used. The manufacturer, for example, may focus on the different middlemen needed to go through to get the products to the ultimate consumer. So, the manufacturer might define the marketing channel in terms of the movement of the products through these various intermediaries. Middlemen such as wholesalers or retailers who are expected to carry substantial inventories from various manufacturers and bear the risks associated with this function may view the flow of the title to the goods as the proper delineator of the marketing channel. Consumers may view the marketing channel as simply "a lot of middlemen" standing between them and the producer of the product. Finally, the researcher observing the marketing channel as it operates in the economic system may describe it in terms of its structural dimensions and efficiency of operation.

Given these differing perspectives, it is not possible to have one definition of the marketing channel which can satisfy all positions. So, before attempting to define the marketing channel, the viewpoint to be used must be clearly specified.

In this text, we take a *managerial decision-making viewpoint* of the marketing channel as seen *through the eyes of marketing management in producing and manufacturing firms*. Thus, the marketing channel is viewed as one of the key marketing decision areas that marketing management must address. In this context, the marketing channel may be defined as:

The external contactual organization which management operates to achieve its distribution objectives.

There are four key terms in this definition which should be especially noted. These are: (1) external, (2) contactual organization, (3) operates, and (4) distribution objectives. These are discussed in some detail below.

---

[1] For an excellent discussion of various definitions of the marketing channel see: Bert C. McCammon and Robert W. Little, "Marketing Channels: Analytical Systems and Approaches," in *Science in Marketing*, ed. George Schwartz (New York: John Wiley, 1965), pp. 324–327.

The term *external* means that the marketing channel exists outside of the firm. In other words, it is not part of a firm's internal organization structure. Management of the marketing channel therefore often involves the use of *interorganizational management* (managing more than one firm) rather than *intraorganizational management* (managing one firm).[2] It is very important to keep this point clearly in mind, because many of the special problems and peculiarities of managing the marketing channel discussed later in the text stem from this external or interorganizational structure.

Contactual organization refers to those firms or parties who are involved in negotiatory functions as a product or service moves from the producer to its ultimate user. Negotiatory functions consist of buying, selling, and transferring title to products or services. Consequently, only those firms or parties who engage in these functions are members of the marketing channel.[3] Other firms usually referred to as facilitating agencies such as transportation companies, public warehouses, banks, insurance companies, advertising agencies, and the like, which perform functions other than negotiatory, are excluded. This distinction is by no means a matter of academic hairsplitting. The channel management problems involved when dealing with firms or parties performing negotiatory functions are often fundamentally different from those encountered when dealing with agencies which do not perform these functions. This will be apparent at many points as we proceed through the text.

The third term in the definition, *operates*, is meant to suggest involvement by management in the affairs of the channel. This involvement may range from the initial development of channel structure all the way to some of the details of the day to day management of the channel. When management operates the external contactual organization it has made a conscious decision not to let this organization simply run by itself. This does *not* mean that management can have total control of the channel. In many cases, as we shall see in subsequent chapters, this is not possible. On the other hand, by operating the channel, management is acting to avoid undue control of its actions *by* the channel.

Finally, *distribution objectives*, the fourth key term in the definition, means that management has certain distribution goals in mind. The marketing channel exists as a means for reaching these goals. The structure and management of the marketing channel are thus in part a function of a firm's distribution objectives. As these objectives change, variations in the external contactual organization and the way management attempts to operate it can also be expected to change.

[2] An in-depth discussion of the interorganizational point of view can be found in: William Evan, "Toward A Theory of Inter-Organizational Relations," in *Distribution Channels: Behavioral Dimensions*, ed. Louis W. Stern (New York: Houghton Mifflin, 1969), pp. 73–89. See also: R. L. Warren, "The Interorganizational Field as a Focus for Investigation," *Administrative Science Quarterly*, 12 (1967): 396–419.

[3] This view is similar to that taken by Louis P. Bucklin, *Competition and Evolution in the Distributive Trades* (Englewood Cliffs, New Jersey: Prentice-Hall, 1972), p. 9.

The Marketing Channel and the Marketing Mix

The well-known marketing mix strategy model provides the basic framework for viewing the marketing channel from a marketing management perspective.[4] Recall that the marketing mix model portrays the marketing management process as a strategic blending of four basic controllable marketing variables (the marketing mix) to meet the demands of market segments to which the firm wishes to appeal (the target markets) in light of internal and external uncontrollable variables. The basic marketing mix variables, often referred to as the four P's, are product, price, promotion, and distribution (place). The external uncontrollable variables are such major environmental forces as the economy, socio-cultural patterns of buyer behavior, competition, government and technology; the non-marketing functions of the firm constitute internal uncontrollable variables. Figure 1.1 shows a typical portrayal of the marketing mix strategy model. The major tasks of marketing management are to seek out potential target markets and to develop appropriate and coordinated product, price, promotion, and distribution strategies to serve those markets in a competitive and dynamic environment.

Marketing channel management, as one of the major strategic areas of marketing management, fits under the distribution variable in the marketing mix.[5] Management must develop and operate the external contactual organization (the marketing channel) in such a way as to support and enhance the other strategic variables of the marketing mix in order to meet the demands of the firm's target markets. The case of Perrier, the highly successful bottled water introduced into the United States on a large scale in the late 1970s, helps to illustrate the relationship of channel management to the other strategic variables of the marketing mix:[6]

Before 1977 Perrier water was available in the United States only in a relatively small number of gourmet food shops. Total U.S. sales had never been more than one million dollars. Spotting a growing target market in the United States of people who had an interest in natural food products, weight control and physical fitness, Source Perrier of France, the producer of Perrier water, decided to exploit this growing U.S. market on a larger scale.

Perrier's product strategy was developed to position Perrier water as an alternative to liquor and soft drinks rather than as a bottled water.

---

[4]For a review of the basic marketing mix strategy model see: E. Jerome McCarthy, *Basic Marketing: A Managerial Approach*, 6th ed. (Homewood, Illinois: Richard D. Irwin, 1978), Chapter 2, or any other basic marketing text having a managerial orientation.

[5]William R. Davidson, "Channels of Distribution—One Aspect of Marketing Strategy," *Business Horizons*, Special Issue, (February 1961): 84–90.

[6]The example is based on information contained in: Bernice Finkleman, "Perrier Pours into U.S. Market, Spurs Water Bottle Battle," *Marketing News*, (September 7, 1979): 1, 9. Reprinted from *Marketing News*, published by the American Marketing Association.

Figure 1.1
Marketing Mix Strategy Model

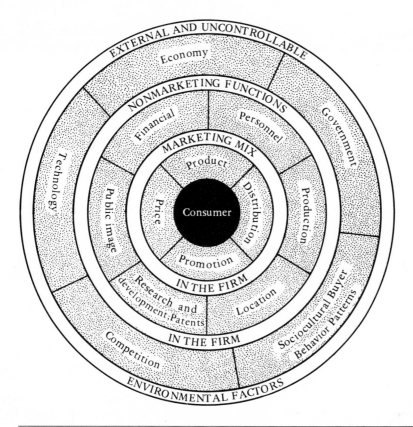

Source: Bert Rosenbloom, *Retail Marketing*. New York: Random House, 1981, p. 14.

This ingenious product strategy put Perrier into a position to compete in the vast multibillion dollar soft drink and liquor market instead of the relatively tiny (240 million dollar) bottled water market.

Pricing strategy was set to allow Perrier to attract the mass market while still keeping somewhat of its "snob" appeal. The 23 oz. bottle which had previously sold in gourmet shops for almost $1.00 was reduced to 69¢.

Promotional strategy emphasized massive national advertising in television and print media. The television ads featured Orson Wells explaining the natural qualities of the product, while the print ads, mainly in women's magazines, stressed the health and fitness theme.

But these formidable product, pricing and promotional strategies would have gone for naught if Perrier could not get the product into the distribution channels that would enable it to sell to the mass target market it was aiming at. Hence, *distribution strategy* was the link pin to the success of Perrier's entire U.S. marketing strategy. In other words, Perrier had to build an external contactual organization (a marketing channel) in the U.S. that could achieve Perrier's distribution objective of making Perrier conveniently available to millions of consumers throughout the U.S.

Perrier was able to accomplish this through a distribution channel strategy that depended on the capability of existing independent soft drink bottlers and beer distributors to get Perrier into supermarkets, set up displays, and continually restock the supermarkets rapidly as the product moved off of the shelves.

This distribution strategy worked superbly for Perrier. By 1978, just one year after introduction, U.S. sales of Perrier were $30 million and reached $120 million in 1981.

Channel Management vs. Physical Distribution Management

As pointed out above, channel management fits under the distribution variable of the marketing mix. Physical distribution management also fits under the distribution strategy variable of the marketing mix. The two components, channel management and physical distribution management, together comprise the distribution variable of the marketing mix. This is illustrated in Figure 1.2.

Channel management and physical distribution management, though closely related, are actually quite different. Unfortunately, there is often considerable confusion regarding the distinction between these two areas. Actually, channel management is a much broader and more basic component of the distribution strategy variable of the marketing mix than is physical distribution management. Channel management is concerned with the *entire process* of setting up and operating the contactual organization that is responsible for meeting the firm's distribution objectives.[7] Physical distribution management, on the other hand, is more narrowly focused on providing product availability at the appropriate times and places in the marketing channel. Quite often, channel management must be well underway *before* physical distribution strategy can even be considered. An example which continues with the case of Perrier, discussed earlier, will help to clarify this point:

Recall that in order to market Perrier on a large scale in the United States, the French producer of Perrier had to get its products into thousands of supermarkets throughout the U.S. To do so, Source Perrier had

---

[7] For a related discussion see: Ralph F. Breyer, "Some Observations on Structural Formation and Growth of Marketing Channels," in *Theory in Marketing*, eds. Reavis Cox, Wroe Alderson, and Stanley J. Shapiro (Homewood, Illinois: Richard D. Irwin, 1964), pp. 163–164.

Figure 1.2
Marketing Mix Strategic Variables with Distribution Variable Divided into Channel and Physical Distribution Components

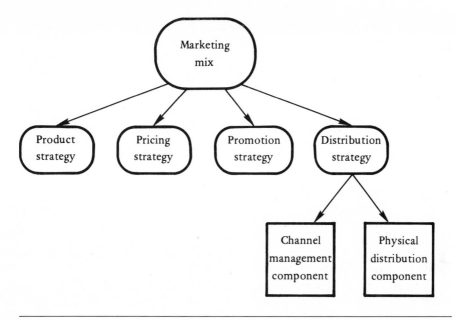

to plan a comprehensive distribution strategy, identify and select high quality bottlers and beer distributors, convince them to carry the product, negotiate various terms of the relationship such as credit, payment procedures, and inventory levels, provide promotional support, and oversee the job done by the bottlers and beer distributors. Further, continued contact between Source Perrier and the bottlers and beer distributors would be needed to make sure that the distribution strategy was actually being carried out and to resolve the inevitable problems that would arise in the course of distributing Perrier.

Only after *channel* management strategies had been developed and implemented to accomplish these objectives would physical distribution management enter the picture. For clearly, if the soft drink bottlers and beer distributors could not be convinced to carry and aggressively sell Perrier, there would be little need for physical distribution management that provided for delivery of the right quantities of Perrier at the right times. It is only *after* a successful channel strategy had been developed that the need for physical distribution management arose.

This is not to argue that physical distribution is not an important part of distribution strategy. On the contrary, effective physical distribution management is often vital to the success of the firm's overall distribution strategy. Perrier could hardly have been successful if the

**product was not in the supermarkets when consumers came to buy it.
But it does suggest that physical distribution management is subsidiary
to the more basic and broader area of channel management.**

Flows in Marketing Channels

Once a channel of distribution has been developed, a series of flows
emerges. These flows provide the links that tie channel members and
other agencies together in the distribution of goods and services.[8] From a
channel management standpoint, the most important of these flows are:

1. Product flow
2. Negotiation flow
3. Ownership flow
4. Information flow
5. Promotion flow

These flows are illustrated for Perrier water in Figure 1.3.

The *product flow* refers to the actual physical movement of the product from the manufacturer (Source Perrier) through all of the parties who
take physical possession of the product, from its point of production to
final consumers. In the case of Perrier, the product is produced in France
and shipped over the Atlantic Ocean via a common carrier (transportation
company). It is then stored in Perrier's own storage facilities in the U.S. or
in public warehouses, from which it is shipped again via common carriers
to the various bottlers and beer distributors throughout the U.S. These
bottlers and beer distributors in turn distribute Perrier to supermarkets,
where it is finally purchased by consumers.

The *negotiation flow* represents the interplay of buying and selling
functions associated with the transfer of title to Perrier. Notice that the
transportation and warehousing firms are not included in this flow because they do not participate in negotiatory functions. Notice also that
the arrows flow in *both* directions indicating that negotiations involve a
mutual exchange between buyers and sellers at all levels of the channel.

The *ownership flow* shows the movement of the title to the product as
it moves from manufacturer to final consumer. Here again, the transportation and warehousing firms are not included in this flow because they
do not take title to the product nor are they actively involved in facilitating its transfer. They are involved only in the transportation or storage of
the *physical product* itself.

Turning now to the *information flow*, we see that the transportation

---

[8] The origin of the concept of flows in marketing channels is generally attributed to: Roland S. Vaile, E. T.
Grether, and Reavis Cox, *Marketing in the American Economy* (New York: Ronald Press, 1952),
pp. 113–129.

Figure 1.3
Five Flows in the Marketing Channel for Perrier Water

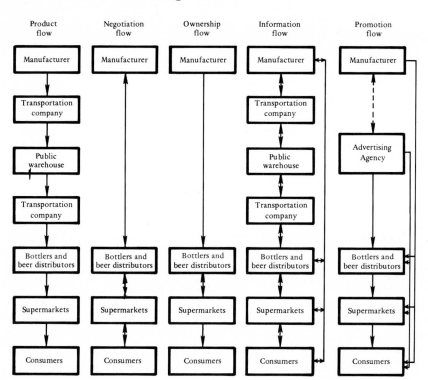

and warehousing firms have reappeared in this flow and all of the arrows in the centers of the rectangles showing the flow of information from manufacturer to consumers are two directional. This indicates that all of these parties participate in the flow of information and the information can flow in either an up or down direction. For example, the manufacturer, Source Perrier, may obtain information from the transportation company about its overseas shipping schedule and rates, and the transportation company may in turn seek information from Source Perrier about when and in what quantities it plans to ship Perrier water to the U.S. The arrow leading from the right hand side of the manufacturer going directly to the bottlers and beer distributors, supermarkets and consumers shows that the flow of information sometimes bypasses the transportation and warehousing firms. This route of information flow would occur for information that is not of concern to the transportation and warehousing firms. Most information associated with the buying, selling, and promotion of Perrier would be in this category. For example, if the manufacturer makes available a special reduced price on Perrier for bottlers and beer distributors, this information would be passed directly to the bottlers and beer distributors but would be of no concern to the transportation and warehousing firms.

Finally, the *promotion flow* refers to the flow of persuasive communication in the form of advertising, personal selling, sales promotion, and publicity. Here, a new type of firm, an advertising agency, is included in the flow because the advertising agency is actively involved in providing and maintaining the promotion flow, especially the advertising element of promotion. The two-directional arrow connected by a broken line between the manufacturer and the advertising agency is meant to show that the manufacturer and advertising agency work together closely to develop promotional strategies. All other arrows are one-directional from the advertising agency or directly from the manufacturer to the other parties in the marketing channel.

Significance of the Channel Flows Concept

The channel flows concept is useful from both theoretical and managerial standpoints.

From the theoretical standpoint, the flow concept provides another basis for distinguishing between physical distribution management and channel management. Earlier in this chapter we pointed out that channel management is a much broader and more comprehensive component of distribution than is physical distribution management. In the context of the channel flows concept, this follows because channel management involves management of *all* of the flows while physical distribution is concerned almost entirely with the management of the product flow.

Also at the theoretical level, the concept of channel flows provides a good basis for separating channel members from non-channel members. Recall that in our definition of the marketing channel, only those parties who were engaged in the negotiatory functions of buying, selling, and transferring title were considered to be members of the contactual organization (the marketing channel). From the standpoint of channel flows then, only those parties who participate in the negotiation or ownership flows would be members of the marketing channel.

From a management standpoint, the concept of channel flows provides a very useful framework for understanding the scope and complexity of channel management. By thinking in terms of the five flows, it becomes obvious that channel management involves much more than merely managing the physical product flow through the channel. The other flows of negotiation, ownership, information, and promotion must also be effectively managed and coordinated to achieve the firm's distribution objectives.[9] Indeed much of the material in this text is concerned

[9] For a related discussion dealing with new types of intraorganizational management structures for providing better management and coordination of marketing channel flows see: Donald W. Jackson and Bruce J. Walker, "The Channels Manager: Marketing's Newest Aide?" *Business Horizons*, (Winter, 1980): 52–58.

with channel management activities that involve these channel flows. Developing channel strategy to cope with environmental changes and dealing with the behavioral dimensions of channels, topics treated in Chapters 3 and 4, certainly involve the information flow. Designing the channel and selecting the channel members, the topics of Chapters 5 and 6, are very much concerned with the negotiation, ownership, and information flows as well as the product flow. Motivating channel members, which is discussed in Chapter 8, is highly dependent upon effective management of the information and promotion flows. Chapters 9, 10, 11, and 12 deal with the interfaces between channel management and management of the other variables in the marketing mix which require management and coordination of all of the flows. Finally, the evaluation of channel member performance, discussed in Chapter 13, is dependent almost entirely on effective management of the information flow.

Also from the perspective of channel management, the concept of flows in marketing channels helps to convey the dynamic nature of marketing channels. The word *flow* suggests movement or a fluid state and indeed this is the nature of channels of distribution. Changes, both obvious and subtle, always seem to be occurring. New forms of distribution emerge, different types of middlemen appear in the channel while others drop out, unusual competitive structures close off some avenues of distribution and open up others. Changing patterns of buyer behavior and new forms of technology add yet another dimension of change to channels of distribution. Channel flows must be adapted and adjusted to meet these changes. Innovative channel strategies and effective channel management are needed to make this happen.

Distribution through Intermediaries

A question that has been asked since the time of ancient Greece is: why do middlemen so often stand between producers and the ultimate users of products?[10] Even today, this question is still being posed by consumer groups, government officials, business people, and others. Unfortunately, the question has usually been tied so closely to emotional issues and political controversies that even the most cogent answers to it have often been misunderstood or ignored. It is not our purpose here to attempt to answer this question to the satisfaction of all parties. Since our viewpoint is a managerial one, we will approach the question with this in mind. Specifically we will discuss two basic concepts which management in producing or manufacturing firms can use for deciding whether or not intermediaries should be used. These are (1) specialization and division of labor, and (2) contactual efficiency.

---

[10] For an interesting historical discussion of this question see: Ronald R. Gist, *Retailing: Concepts and Decisions* (New York: John Wiley, 1968), pp. 7–17.

Specialization and Division of Labor

The principle of specialization and division of labor is well known to anyone who has had a brush with the basic college economics or production management course. The first clear exposition of the principle is generally attributed to Adam Smith's classic book *The Wealth of Nations*, published in 1776. In this work Smith cited an example from a pin factory. He noted that when the production operations necessary in the manufacture of pins were allocated among a group of workers so that each worker specialized in performing only one operation, a vast increase in the output of pins resulted over what was possible when this same number of workers each performed all of the operations.

The logic of this principle has been well understood as it applies to a production setting. Unfortunately, this understanding is often lacking when specialization and division of labor is applied to a distribution situation, particularly when more than one firm is involved. Yet, whether applied to a production or distribution situation, or within one firm or among several, the concept is fundamentally the same.[11] By breaking down a complex task into smaller, less complex ones, and allocating them to parties who are specialists at performing them, much greater efficiency results. Figure 1.4 helps to illustrate this by comparing specialization and division of labor as applied to production vs. distribution for a manufacturer of brier pipes.[12] Though somewhat oversimplified, Figure 1.4 shows seven production tasks and a similar number of distribution tasks involved in transforming a chunk of brier into a pipe and getting it into the hands (or mouths) of consumers. The seven production tasks have been allocated to various production stations in the factory where workers specialized in these tasks will perform them. On the right hand side of Figure 1.4, the distribution tasks have been allocated among several firms, including intermediaries (wholesalers and retailers) as well as facilitating agencies (advertising agency and a transportation company). Note that some of the firms perform similar tasks. This does not indicate redundancy of the tasks. It simply shows that firms often share in the performance of distribution tasks.

The only difference in the application of the specialization and division of labor concept, as applied to production vs. distribution depicted in Figure 1.4, is that the production tasks have been allocated intraorganizationally while the distribution tasks have been allocated interorganizationally. Hence, just as the manufacturer's production manager should allocate production tasks on the basis of specialization and division of labor, so should the channel manager. Ideally he should allocate the distribution tasks to those firms which can perform them most efficiently. His

---

[11] The theoretical basis for this argument can be found in: George J. Stigler, "The Division of Labor Is Limited by the Extent of the Market," *Journal of Political Economy* (June, 1951): 185–193.

[12] Carl Weber, *Weber's Guide to Pipes and Pipe Smoking* (New York: Cornerstone Library Publications, 1962), pp. 93–100.

Figure 1.4
Specialization and Division of Labor Production vs. Distribution for a Pipe Manufacturer

Production tasks

1. cutting the brier
2. curing the brier
3. shaping the bowl
4. shaping the pipe
5. boring the shank
6. attaching the stem
7. applying the finish

Distribution tasks

1. buying
2. selling
3. transferring the title
4. transportation
5. storage
6. order processing
7. providing information

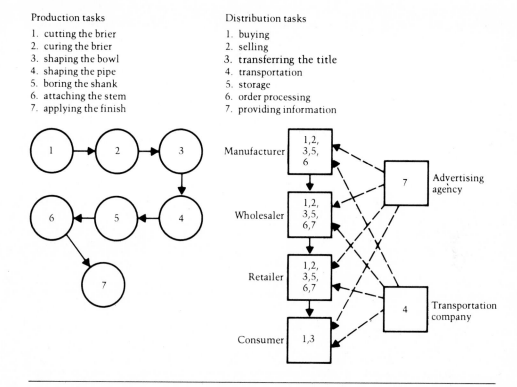

contactual organization and attendant facilitating agencies would then reflect an optimal allocation of the distribution tasks. In reality, of course, this is not always possible. Nevertheless, by thinking in terms of the specialization and division of labor principle as applied to distribution, the channel manager will be better equipped to at least approach an optimal allocation of distribution tasks. In Chapter 5 (Designing the Marketing Channel) we will deal with this area in much greater detail.

Contactual Efficiency

The second concept on which the framework for deciding whether to use middlemen rests, is contactual efficiency.[13] From the channel manager's viewpoint, contactual efficiency is the level of negotiation effort between

[13] The theoretical basis for contactual efficiency can be found in: Wroe Alderson, "Factors Governing the Development of Marketing Channels," in *Marketing Channels for Manufactured Products*, ed. Richard M. Clewett (Homewood, Illinois: Richard D. Irwin, 1954), pp. 5–22.

Table 1.1
An Example of Contactual Efficiency for the Samson Pipe Company Negotiating Directly with Retailers

Negotiation Effort (input)	Estimated Dollar Cost of Inputs	Distribution Objective (output)	Contactual Efficiency
2500 sales visits	e$20. = 50,000	Get 1000 pipe stores to carry new pipe line	negotiation effort in $ terms relative to achieving the objective = $56,000
500 phone calls	e2.00 = 1,000		
10 magazine ads	e500 = 5,000		
	Total $56,000		

Table 1.2
An Example of Contactual Efficiency for the Samson Pipe Company Negotiating with Wholesalers

Negotiation Effort (input)	Estimated Dollar Costs of Inputs	Distribution Objective (output)	Contactual Efficiency
200 sales visits	e$20. = 4,000	Get 1000 pipe stores to carry new pipe line	negotiation effort in $ terms relative to achieving the objective = $14,000
20 magazine ads	e500 = 10,000		
	Total $14,000		

sellers and buyers relative to achieving a distribution objective. Thus, it is a relationship between an input (negotiation effort) and an output (the distribution objective). To illustrate this concept, consider the pipe manufacturer mentioned in the last section, hereafter referred to as the Samson Pipe Company. Suppose the Samson Company sets a distribution objective of getting 1000 pipe stores to carry a new line of its pipes. Assuming the firm were to deal directly with the retailers, the input would be the level of negotiation effort it expends in achieving the output—getting 1000 pipe stores to carry the new line. To achieve this objective Samson estimates it would need to have its sales force contact 3000 stores, with many of these contacts requiring personal sales visits. Further, Samson believes it must use trade paper advertising to support the efforts of its salespeople. Management estimates it will take 2500 sales calls, 500 telephone calls, and 10 trade magazine ads to finally achieve the objective. These figures are summarized in Table 1.1 along with some hypothetical estimates of dollar costs.

Based on the figures shown in Table 1.1, Samson estimated it will cost $56,000 to achieve this particular distribution objective.

Suppose Samson goes on to consider adding wholesale intermediaries to its contactual organization. Samson believes that 50 wholesalers carrying the new line would be sufficient to get it accepted by the 1000 retailers. Samson further estimates that it will take 200 personal sales calls on wholesalers to secure acceptance by 50. However, Samson forecasts that double the advertising will be needed to support the salesmen (i.e., twenty magazine ads). These estimates are summarized in Table 1.2, which shows that the use of wholesalers provides a much higher level of contactual efficiency than if retailers alone were used. The reason for this is that the use of wholesalers has eliminated the need for direct contact with retailers, thereby greatly reducing the number of contacts needed.

This example points to an important relationship between contactual efficiency and the use of intermediaries: *The use of additional intermediaries will often increase the level of contactual efficiency.* This principle is further illustrated in Figure 1.5.

This does not mean that considerations of contactual efficiency and specialization, and division of labor are all that is needed to make a decision on intermediary usage. Many other variables to be discussed in Part II of the text must also be evaluated. But contactual efficiency along with the concept of specialization and division of labor do provide the channel

Figure 1.5
How the Introduction of an Additional Intermediary Reduces the Number of Contacts

Four manufacturers contact
four retailers *directly*

Four manufacturers contact
four retailers *indirectly*
through a wholesale intermediary

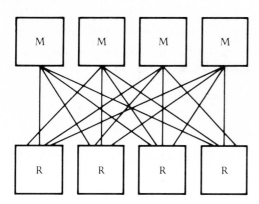

Number of contacts needed for all manufacturers to contact all retailers = (number of manufacturers) x (number of retailers) = (4) x (4) = 16 contacts.

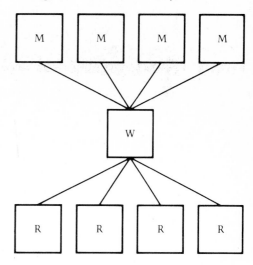

Number of contacts needed for all manufacturers to contact all retailers = (number of manufacturers) + (number of retailers) = (4) + (4) = 8 contacts.

Figure 1.6
A Typical Portrayal of Channel Structure for Consumer Goods

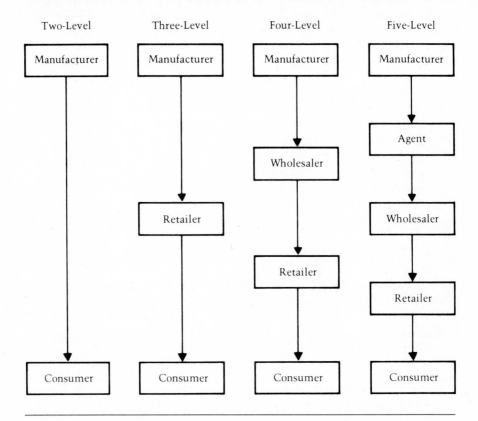

manager with a basic framework for incorporating these other variables into his decisions on the use of intermediaries.

Channel Structure

The concept of channel structure is one that is often vaguely defined in the marketing literature. Authors tend to emphasize a particular dimension of channel structure and then proceed to a detailed discussion without explicitly defining what they mean by channel structure itself. Perhaps the most typically discussed dimension is the number of levels of intermediaries in the channel.[14] When channel structure is discussed we frequently see diagrams showing illustrations such as that shown in Figure 1.6. Or sometimes symbolic notations such as the following are used:

[14]See for example: William J. Stanton, *Fundamentals of Marketing* (New York: McGraw-Hill, 1975), pp. 408–409.

M→C   (two level)
M→R→C   (three level)
M→W→R→C   (four level)
M→A→W→R→C   (five level)

where: A = Agent
        C = Consumer
        M = Manufacturer
        R = Retailer
        W = Wholesaler

While these approaches do convey a general idea of the kinds of participants in the marketing channel and the levels at which they appear, they
do not explicitly define channel structure. Moreover, they fail to suggest
the relationship between channel structure and channel management.

Channel Structure Defined

Our definition of channel structure takes a definite managerial perspective by viewing channel structure as:

**The group of channel members to which a set of distribution tasks has
been allocated.**

This definition suggests that in the development of channel structure, the
channel manager is faced with an *allocation decision*. That is, given a set
of distribution tasks which must be performed to accomplish a firm's distribution objectives, the manager must decide how to allocate or structure the tasks. Thus, the structure of the channel will reflect the manner
in which he or she has allocated these tasks among the members of the
channel. For example, if after making the allocation decision the channel
structure appears as M→W→R→C, this means that the channel manager
has chosen to allocate the tasks to his or her own firm as well as to wholesalers, retailers, and consumers. The diagrams or symbolic notations of
channel structure are really nothing more than a "blueprint" showing the
locus of the distribution tasks. Figures 1.7 through 1.11, for example,
illustrate channel structures for a variety of products and services.

As pointed out earlier in the chapter, the basis for making such allocation decisions is specialization and division of labor. Ideally the channel
manager would like to have total control over the allocation of distribution tasks so that he or she could assign these tasks to the particular
firms or parties who are best suited to perform them. However, since the
channel includes members which are independent firms, and because the
channel is subject to environmental constraints, in reality the channel
manager does not often have total control of the allocation of distribution
tasks.

In Part Two of the text (Developing the Channel), we will discuss the

Figure 1.7
Marketing Channels for Automobiles

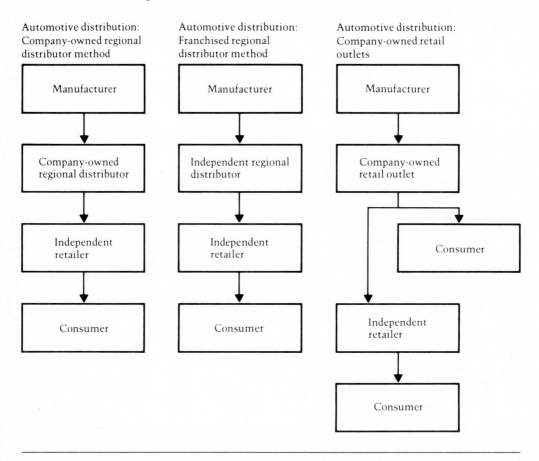

Source: E. Patrick McGuire, *Franchised Distribution* (New York: The Conference Board, Report No. 523, 1971), p. 11.

problems and constraints faced by the channel manager in attempting to develop an optimal channel structure.

Ancillary Structure

Since we have defined the marketing channel as including only those participants who perform the negotiatory functions of buying, selling, and transferring title, those who do not perform these functions are not part of the channel structure. We will consider these non-member participants (facilitating agencies) as belonging to the ancillary structure of the marketing channel. More specifically we will define ancillary structure as:

Figure 1.8
Marketing Channels for Magazines and Paperback Books

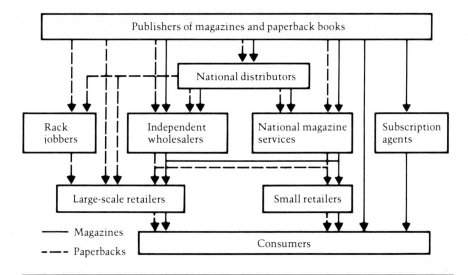

Source: Edwin H. Lewis, "Description and Comparison of Channels of Distribution," in *Handbook of Modern Marketing*, ed. Victor P. Buell (New York: McGraw-Hill Book Company, 1970), p. 4–6.

Figure 1.9
Marketing Channels for Phonograph Records

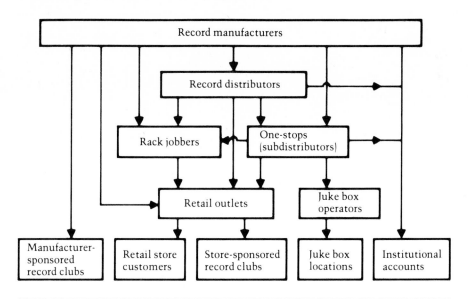

Source: Edwin H. Lewis, "Description and Comparison of Channels of Distribution," in *Handbook of Modern Marketing*, ed. Victor P. Buell (New York: McGraw-Hill Book Company, 1970), p. 4–7.

Figure 1.10
Marketing Channels of a Manufacturer of Electrical Wire and Cable

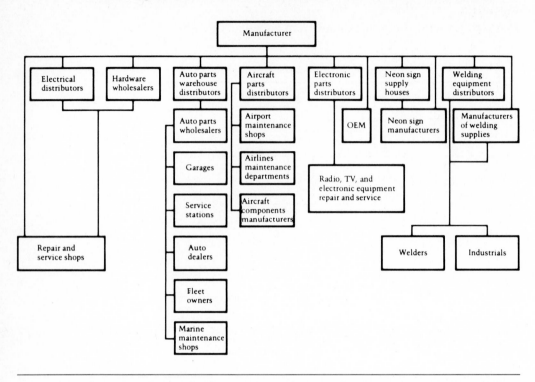

Source: From *Marketing Electrical Apparatus and Supplies* by Edwin H. Lewis, p. 215. © 1961 by McGraw-Hill, Inc. Used with permission of McGraw-Hill Book Company.

Figure 1.11
Dominant Channel Configurations in the Service Sector

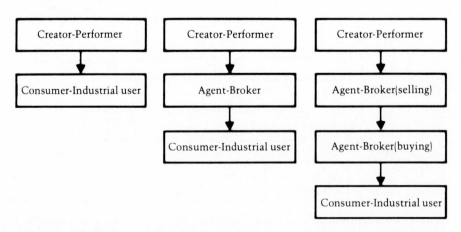

Source: From John M. Rathmell, *Marketing in the Service Sector*, p. 110. © 1974 Winthrop Publishers, Inc. Reprinted by permission.

Table 1.3
Illustrations of Channel Systems and Facilitating Agencies

(1) Company	(2) Product/Service	(3) End-User Market Served	(4) Participating Firms	(5) Facilitating Firms
Burrough's Corp. (manufacturer)	Computer systems, business machines, and supplies	Business firms, government, and other institutions	Markets direct to end-users using company sales force (no participating firms are involved)	Burroughs Finance Corp., advertising agency; transportation firms
Garcia Corp. (distributor)	Recreational equipment for fishing, hunting, camping, tennis, and skiing	Primarily ultimate consumers	Wholesalers, retailers, and manufacturers of equipment (both corporate owned and independent firms)	Advertising, transportation, financial institutions
Holiday Inns of America, Inc. (motel and hotel chain)	Motel and hotel facilities; motel equipment and services; bus and water transportation	Business and pleasure consumers of hotel and transportation services	Franchised motel operations (some owned by Holiday Inns); suppliers of services and equipment for motels (some corporate owned)	Insurance, finance, and construction firms (some corporate owned); advertising services
Royal Crown Cola Company (producer)	Carbonated beverages	Consumers	Independent and owned bottlers, brokers, food and beverage retailers	Advertising services; transportation firms
Scrivner Inc. (wholesaler)	Foods (also handles line of general merchandise)	Consumers and institutional end-users (e.g., hospitals)	Suppliers of food products (including company owned bakery, ice-cream suppliers); brokers; retailers (independent, franchised, and corporate owned); institutional customers	Banks; transportation firms; insurance firms

Source: Adapted with permission from D. W. Cravens, G. E. Hills, and R. B. Woodruff, *Marketing Decision Making: Concepts and Strategy* (Homewood, Illinois: Richard D. Irwin, © 1976), p. 523.

The group of institutions and parties that assists channel members in performing distribution tasks.

The basic decision facing the channel manager in attempting to develop ancillary structure is the same as for developing channel structure. That is, he or she must attempt to allocate distribution tasks to those parties best suited to performing them. Because the channel manager is dealing with nonmember channel participants, however, the problems faced in developing and managing the ancillary structure are likely to be simpler than those encountered in developing (and managing) channel structures. This is because the facilitating firms do not play a part in the channel decisions that ultimately control the distribution of goods and services to their target market. The role of facilitating agencies is rather one of providing services to the channel members once the basic channel decisions have been made. As an example of this distinction, consider the breakdown shown in Table 1.3.

Those firms comprising the channel structure are listed in column 4 (participating firms), while those firms making up the ancillary structure are shown in column 5 (facilitating firms). The companies listed in column 1 (with the exception of the Burrough's Corp.) must establish relationships, negotiate, and work with the *independent* intermediaries in column 4. The decisions which the channel members make and how well they are able to work together over time will ultimately determine how successful they are in making products and services available to their markets (column 3). Thus, the channel members who comprise the actual channel structure have an important and often long-term commitment to the success of the channel. Consequently in developing channel structures, the channel manager is faced with such difficult issues as the proper choice of channel members, how much of a role each will play in decision making, how control will be exercised, how performance will be evaluated, and many others to be discussed throughout this text.

On the other hand, in developing ancillary structure, the channel manager is dealing with facilitating agencies who are outside of the channel decision-making process and who generally do not have as great a stake in the channel as the channel members. Hence, the channel manager does not have to negotiate or deal with them on the same basis as channel members. For example, it is a much more formidable task for the Garcia Corp. (see Table 1.3) to convince independent retailers (channel members) to stock and enthusiastically promote its products against the competition of other manufacturers than it is to get a trucking company (facilitating agency) to ship a load of sporting goods to those retailers.

Summary

Marketing channels enable both consumers and industrial users to have a vast array of products and services conveniently available. This major feat performed by marketing channels is given relatively little attention, however, because so much of the work of marketing channels is performed "behind the scenes."

While there are a number of ways to view marketing channels, a managerial viewpoint from the perspective of producing and manufacturing firms is used in this text. In this context, the marketing channel is defined as the external contactual organization which management operates to achieve its distribution objectives. Only parties who perform the negotiatory functions of buying, selling, and transferring title are considered to be members of the marketing channel.

The basic marketing mix strategy model provides the framework for examining the marketing channel from a marketing management perspective. In this framework, marketing channel management fits under the distribution variable of the four basic strategic variables of the marketing mix (product, price, promotion, and distribution). The channel manager must develop and operate the external contactual organization (the marketing channel) in such a way as to support and enhance the other strategic variables of the marketing mix in order to meet the demands of the firm's target markets.

Though closely related, channel management and physical distribution management are quite different. Channel management is a much more basic and comprehensive component of distribution strategy than is physical distribution. Channel management is concerned with the *entire process* of setting up and operating the contactual organization that is responsible for meeting the firm's distribution objectives, while physical distribution management is more narrowly focused on providing product availability at the appropriate times and place in the marketing channel.

The links that tie channel members and other agencies together in the distribution of goods and services are referred to as channel flows. From a channel management standpoint, the most important of these flows are: (1) product flow, (2) negotiation flow, (3) ownership flow, (4) information flow, and (5) promotion flow. The channel manager must effectively manage and coordinate *all* of these flows to achieve the firm's distribution objectives.

A basic decision facing the channel manager in the development of the marketing channel is whether to use intermediaries such as wholesalers and retailers in the contactual organization and whether facilitating agencies should also be used. The basis for making this decision rests on the two fundamental concepts of specialization and division of labor and contactual efficiency.

Channel structure refers to the group of channel members to which a set of distribution tasks has been allocated. Ancillary structure is the group of institutions and parties that assists channel members in performing distribution tasks. The channel manager would like to develop optimum channel and ancillary structures based on specialization and division of labor. The ability to do so is limited, however, because the interorganizational setting in which the channel manager must operate, limits control over independent channel members.

Discussion Questions

1. Much of the work of marketing channels occurs "behind the scenes." What is meant by this statement?
2. How does a management perspective of the marketing channel differ from some other views of the channel?
3. What is the distinction between interorganizational management and intraorganizational management?
4. Is management of the marketing channel the only instance of interorganizational management for a producing or manufacturing firm?
5. Operating the channel does not imply total control of the channel. Can you think of an example where the channel manager does not have total control of the channel but is still able to operate it?
6. Discuss the relationship between channel management and the marketing mix.
7. What is the difference between channel management and physical distribution management?
8. Identify the various flows in marketing channels, and the direction of the flows. Why is the concept of channel flows useful for a better understanding of channel management?
9. Could the product flow operate independently of the other channel flows?
10. Suppose you had recently developed a new product for a specific target market and were in the process of developing your channel strategy for the product. At that point do marketing channels for that product already exist? Explain.
11. Discuss the concept of specialization and division of labor as it applies to marketing channels.
12. Since specialization and division of labor is the fundamental basis for allocating distribution tasks, can the channel manager make decisions on using intermediaries and facilitating agencies solely on that basis?
13. What is contactual efficiency? Can you think of some other examples of contactual efficiency that are not in a marketing channels context?
14. Discuss the distinction between channel structure and ancillary structure.
15. Why is it so difficult for the channel manager to develop a truly optimal channel structure?

Chapter 2
The Channel Participants

The last sections of Chapter 1 discussed the role of intermediaries and facilitating agencies in the marketing channel. We pointed out that management should consider using intermediaries (and facilitating agencies) if they appear to offer a higher level of efficiency through specialization and division of labor and/or greater contactual efficiency.

In the present chapter we build on this by discussing various types of channel participants and the distribution tasks for which they are especially well suited. By knowing something about the capabilities of particular institutions for performing distribution tasks, the channel manager can make better decisions about who should participate in the channel.

An Overview of the Channel Participants

Figure 2.1 illustrates our basic dichotomy between channel membership based on performance or nonperformance of the negotiatory functions (buying, selling, and transferring title). Participants who engage in these functions are linked together by the flows of negotiation or ownership (see Figure 1.3 in Chapter 1) and are therefore members of the contactual organization (the marketing channel).

The three basic divisions of the marketing channel depicted in Figure

Figure 2.1
Classification of Channel Participants

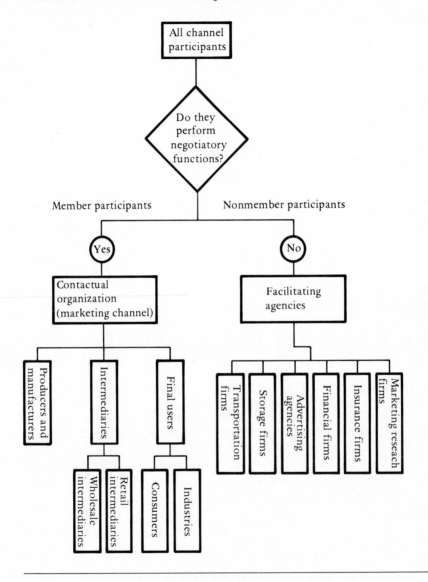

2.1 are: (1) producers and manufacturers, (2) intermediaries, and (3) final users. The latter two are broken down further into wholesale and retail level intermediaries, and consumer and industrial users respectively. The final users, though members of the marketing channel because they are involved in negotiatory functions, will, from this point on, *not* be viewed as channel members in this text. In the context of the management perspective we are using, it is more appropriate to view final users as target markets which are served by the *commercial subsystem* of the channel.

The *commercial channel* by definition excludes final users. Thus, whenever the term marketing channel is mentioned in the remainder of the text it is understood that we are referring to the commercial channel. Final users viewed as target markets are the subject of Chapter 7 (Target Markets and Channel Design Strategy).

Since facilitating agencies do not perform negotiatory functions, they are not members of the channel. They *do*, however, participate in the operation of the channel by performing other functions. Six of the more common types of facilitating agencies are shown in Figure 2.1

The structure of this chapter is derived from the diagram shown in Figure 2.1. We begin by discussing the commercial channel: producers/manufacturers and intermediaries. We then move to a brief discussion of the facilitating agencies.

Producers and Manufacturers

For the purpose of this text, producers and manufacturers consist of firms that are involved in extracting, growing, or making products. This includes, then, those firms that the U.S. Bureau of the Census classifies under agriculture, forestry and fishing, mining, construction, manufacturing, and some service industries.

The range of producing and manufacturing firms is enormous both in terms of the diversity of goods and services produced and the size of the firms. It includes firms that make everything from straight pins to jet planes and that vary in size from a "one man operation" to giant multinational corporations with many thousands of employees and multibillion dollar sales volumes. But even with all this diversity, a thread of commonality runs through all producing and manufacturing firms. All of them exist to offer products that satisfy the needs of markets. For the needs of those markets to be satisfied the products of producing and manufacturing firms must be made available to those markets. Thus, producing and manufacturing firms must somehow see that *their products are distributed to their intended markets*. Most producing and manufacturing firms, both large and small, however, are not in a favorable position to distribute their products directly to their final user markets.[1] Quite often, they lack both the requisite expertise and economies of scale to perform all of the distribution tasks necessary to distribute their products effectively and efficiently to their final users.

With respect to expertise, many producers and manufacturers do not have nearly the level of expertise in distribution that they have attained in production or manufacturing. An electronics manufacturer may be operating at the leading edge of electronics technology and yet know very little about the best way to distribute its sophisticated products to its

---

[1]George J. Stigler, "The Division of Labor Is Limited by the Extent of the Market," *Journal of Political Economy* (June, 1951): 185–193.

markets.[2] A drill bit manufacturer may make the finest products that use the most advanced alloys and yet be quite naive when it comes to performing the tasks necessary to distribute those products. A west coast farm that grows the finest produce based on the latest developments in agricultural technology may know very little about how to make that produce available in good condition and at low cost to consumers on the east coast. In short, expertise in production or manufacturing processes does not automatically translate into expertise in distribution.

But even for those producing and manufacturing firms who do have, or are capable of developing expertise in distribution, the economies of scale that are necessary for efficient production do not necessarily make for efficient distribution. To illustrate this point, consider a company such as Binney & Smith, the manufacturer of the famous Crayola Crayons.[3] Binney & Smith is a relatively small manufacturer located in Easton, Pennsylvania, but it is the world's foremost manufacturer of crayons. From a manufacturing standpoint, Binney & Smith (B&S) is generally recognized as a very efficient manufacturer of crayons. With approximately 80% of the fifty-five million dollar U.S. crayon market, Binney & Smith is able to manufacture crayons in huge quantities and has thus achieved considerable economies of scale in production. If one were to visualize the average cost curve for the production of crayons by B&S, it might appear as in Figure 2.2. Figure 2.2 shows that B&S by producing at the output level of Q_1, is incurring a cost of C_1 per box of crayons produced. This is just about at the optimum point on the average cost curve. In other words, B&S is able to achieve economies of scale in production by spreading the firm's fixed costs over a great many crayons.

When it comes to the performance of distribution tasks, however, such economies of scale may not be attainable. Suppose B&S were to attempt to distribute its crayons *directly* to the millions of consumers who use crayons. To provide adequate purchase convenience for these consumers, B&S would probably need a huge order processing facility to handle the volume of small individual orders received. Moreover, B&S would need to maintain a huge inventory to meet demand, would probably need at least several separate warehouse locations at different parts of the country and would have to provide for transportation of the product to consumers.

The cost of setting up such an organization to perform these distribution tasks would be monumental. Indeed, it would be extremely unlikely that B&S could ever sell enough crayons to absorb these costs. If one were to visualize the average cost curve for the distribution of crayons directly to consumers by B&S, it might appear as in Figure 2.3.

Looking at Figure 2.3, we can see that at the Q_1 level of boxes of crayons distributed, the cost of distribution per box of crayons is C_2. This

[2]See for example: "Computer Stores: Tantalizing Opportunity Selling Computers to Consumers," *Business Week*, (September 28, 1981): 76–82.
[3]This example is based on the article "Redrawing the Crayola Image," *Business Week*, (August 31, 1981): 83.

Figure 2.2
Hypothetical Average Cost Curve for the Production of Crayons

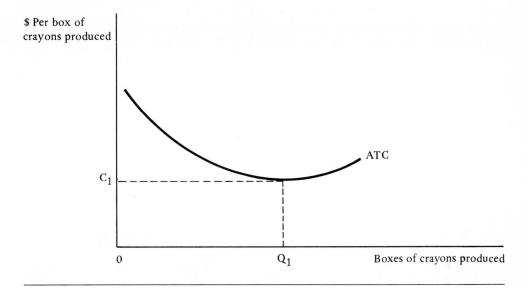

Figure 2.3
Hypothetical Average Cost Curve for the Distribution of Crayons

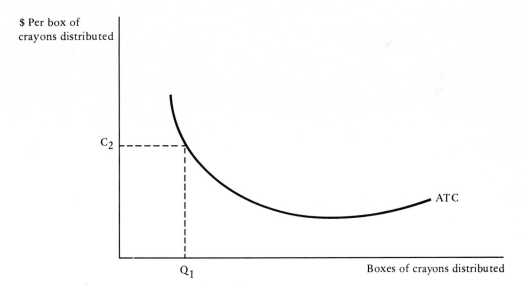

is not even close to the optimum point on the average cost curve for the distribution of crayons. Thus, even though the Q_1 level was close to the optimum point on the average cost curve for the production of crayons (see Figure 2.2), it does not even approach the optimum point on the average cost curve for distribution. In short, B&S would probably never be able to sell enough crayons to absorb the enormous fixed costs associated with the performance of the distribution tasks. By shifting the distribution tasks to other channel participants, however, such as wholesalers and/or retailers, B&S could achieve substantial savings. The reason being that these intermediaries distribute the products of many other manufacturers and are therefore able to spread the high fixed costs of performing the distribution tasks over large quantities of diverse products. This allows them to operate closer to the optimum points on their average cost curves, which are often well below the corresponding points on manufacturers' average cost curves for distribution tasks.[4]

The example presented above suggests the following generalization: *Producing and manufacturing firms often face high average costs for distribution tasks when they attempt to perform them by themselves.* This applies not only to small producers and manufacturers, but to many very large ones as well. The scale economies that enable producers and manufacturers to operate at a low average cost for production processes are often absent in the performance of distribution tasks. Consequently, producing or manufacturing firms must frequently search for channel members to whom they can shift to share the distribution tasks. Intermediaries at the wholesale and retail levels are the two basic types of institutions they can call upon to participate.

Intermediaries

Intermediaries or middlemen are independent businesses that assist producers and manufacturers (and final users) in the performance of negotiatory functions and other distribution tasks. Intermediaries thus participate in the negotiation and/or ownership flows (see Chapter 1, pp. 10–13). They operate basically at two levels, wholesale and retail.

Wholesale Intermediaries

Wholesalers consist of businesses that are engaged in selling goods for resale or business use to retail, industrial, commercial, institutional, professional, or agricultural firms, as well as to other wholesalers. Also included are firms acting as agents or brokers in either buying goods for, or selling them to such customers.

---

[4]For a related discussion see: Bruce Mallen, "Functional Spin-Off: A Key to Anticipating Change in Distribution Structure," *Journal of Marketing* (July, 1973): 18–25.

Types and Kinds of Wholesalers.   The most comprehensive and commonly used classification of wholesalers is that used by the *Census of Wholesale Trade*, which breaks them down into three major types:

1.   Merchant wholesalers
2.   Agents, brokers, and commission merchants
3.   Manufacturers' sales branches and offices

Merchant wholesalers are firms engaged primarily in buying, taking title to, usually storing and physically handling products in relatively large quantities and reselling the products in smaller quantities to retailers, industrial, commercial, or institutional concerns, and to other wholesalers. They go under many different names, such as wholesaler, jobber, distributor, industrial distributor, supply house, assembler, importer, exporter and many others.

Agents, brokers, and commission merchants are also independent middlemen who do not, for all or most of their business, take title to the goods in which they deal, but they are actively involved in negotiatory functions of buying and selling while acting on behalf of their clients. They are usually compensated in the form of commissions on sales or purchases. Some of the more common types go under the names of manufacturers' agents, commission merchants, brokers, selling agents and import and export agents.

Manufacturers' sales branches and offices are owned and operated by manufacturers but are physically separated from manufacturing plants. They are used primarily for the purpose of distributing the manufacturer's own products at wholesale. Some have warehousing facilities where inventories are maintained, while others are merely sales offices. Some of them also wholesale allied and supplementary products purchased from other manufacturers.[5] Because these wholesalers are owned and operated by the manufacturer, they are *not* considered to be intermediaries for our purposes.

Figure 2.4 provides a schematic diagram of these three types of wholesalers.

The *Census of Wholesale Trade* also classifies wholesalers by kind-of-business, of which there are eighteen different categories. These kind-of-business groupings are shown in Figure 2.5.

For data gathering and reporting purposes, the *Census of Wholesale Trade* cross-classifies these kind-of-business groupings with the three major types of wholesalers. Hence data are available for the three types of wholesalers by various kind-of-business classifications for the United States as a whole and for many smaller geographical areas (see Figure 2.6).

[5]For a more complete discussion of all wholesale intermediaries see any of the following sources: Theodore N. Beckman, Nathanael H. Engle, and Robert D. Buzzel, *Wholesaling*, 3rd ed. (New York: Ronald Press, 1959), Chapters 1–3; David A. Revzan, *Wholesaling in Marketing Organization* (New York: John Wiley and Sons, 1961), Chapters 2 and 3; Richard M. Hill, *Wholesaling Management Text and Cases* (Homewood, Illinois: Richard D. Irwin, 1963), Chapter 2.

Figure 2.4
Schematic Overview of the Three Major Types of Wholesalers

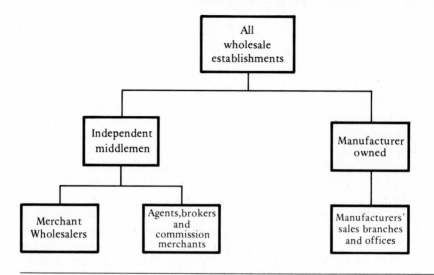

Figure 2.5
Kind-of-Business Groupings for Wholesalers

Kind of Business Group

1. Motor vehicles and automotive parts and supplies
2. Furniture and home furnishings
3. Lumber and other construction materials
4. Sporting, recreational, toys, hobby goods and supplies
5. Metals and minerals
6. Electrical goods
7. Hardware, plumbing, heating equipment and supplies
8. Machinery equipment and supplies
9. Miscellaneous durable goods wholesalers
10. Paper and paper products
11. Drugs, drug proprietaries and druggists' sundries
12. Apparel, piece goods, notions
13. Groceries and related products
14. Farm product—raw materials
15. Chemicals and allied products
16. Petroleum and petroleum products
17. Beer, wine and distilled alcoholic beverages
18. Miscellaneous nondurable goods wholesalers

Figure 2.6
Sample Table from Census of Wholesale Trade

SIC code	SMSA and kind of business	Total — Establishments (number)	Total — Sales ($1,000)	Total — Payroll entire year ($1,000)	Total — Paid employees for week, including March 12 (number)	Merchant wholesalers — Establishments (number)	Merchant wholesalers — Sales ($1,000)	Manufacturers' sales branches and sale offices — Establishments (number)	Manufacturers' sales branches and sale offices — Sales ($1,000)	Agents, brokers, and commission merchants — Establishments (number)	Agents, brokers, and commission merchants — Sales ($1,000)
	ANN ARBOR SMSA										
	Wholesale trade, total	228	199 072	13 753	15 684	192	130 645	36	68 427	36	68 427
	Durable Goods										
50	Total	132	96 374	9 702	1 102	118	69 171	14	27 203	15	10,569
501	Motor vehicles and automotive parts and supplies	26	15 272	2 085	264	24	2	(D)	(D)	(D)	(D)
502	Furniture and home furnishings	5	(D)	(D)	(D)	5	(D)	(D)	(D)	—	—
503	Lumber and other construction materials	9	19 692	1 005	96	8	(D)	1	(D)	(D)	(D)
504	Sporting, recreational, photographic, and hobby goods, toys, and supplies	10	7 730	978	120	9	(D)	1	(D)	2	(D)
505	Metals and minerals, except petroleum	2	(D)	(D)	(D)	2	(D)	1	(D)	—	—
506	Electrical goods	14	9 100	1 158	(D)	2	(D)	3	(D)	5	964
507	Hardware, plumbing, heating equipment, supplies	8	7 017	905	83	8	7 954	—	—	—	—
508	Machinery, equipment, and supplies	51	27 361	2 933	365	44	23 126	7	4 235	6	2 691
509	Miscellaneous durable goods	7	2 528	217	35	7	2 528	—	—	—	—
	Nondurable goods										
51	Total	96	102 698	5 982	628	74	61 474	22	41 224	25	36 789
511	Paper and paper products	9	6 998	538	145	55	7	2	(D)	4	(D)
512	Drugs, drug proprietaries, druggists' sundries	1	(D)	(D)	(D)	1	(D)	—	—	—	—
513	Apparel, piece goods, and notions	15	863	214	106	13	(D)	2	(D)	6	(D)
514	Groceries and related products	4	(D)	(D)	(D)	3	2 999	1	(D)	3	(D)
515	Farm-product raw materials	6	(D)	(D)	(D)	5	(D)	1	(D)	4	(D)
516	Chemicals and allied products	26	21 851	1 417	154	11	8 569	15	13 282	16	10 346
517	Petroleum and petroleum products	11	21 513	1 501	106	11	21 513	—	—	—	—
518	Beer, wine, and distilled alcoholic beverages	24	17 514	1 220	167	23	(D)	1	(D)	2	(D)
519	Miscellaneous nondurable goods	24	17 514	1 220	167	23	(D)	1	(D)	2	(D)

Figure 2.7
Wholesale Sales by Type of Wholesaler: 1972 and 1977

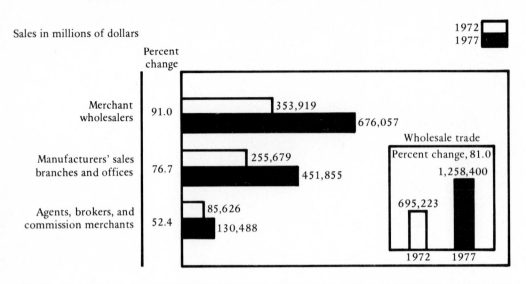

Sales in millions of dollars

1972
1977

Percent change

Merchant wholesalers — 91.0 — 353,919 / 676,057

Manufacturers' sales branches and offices — 76.7 — 255,679 / 451,855

Agents, brokers, and commission merchants — 52.4 — 85,626 / 130,488

Wholesale trade
Percent change, 81.0
1,258,400
695,223
1972   1977

Structure and Trends in Wholesaling. As of 1977 there were 382,837 wholesale establishments in the United States with sales totaling 1.3 trillion dollars, an increase of 81.0% over wholesale sales of 1972, when the last census was taken. Figure 2.7 compares total sales of wholesalers broken down by the three major types of wholesalers for the two census years 1972 and 1977, while Figure 2.8 shows the percentage of total sales for each of the three types of wholesalers for those two census years.

As shown in Figure 2.7, absolute sales of all three types of wholesalers have increased substantially over this period, but the percentages of increases have varied significantly. The largest increase of 91% was for merchant wholesalers, and the smallest increase of 52.4% for agents, brokers, and commission merchants. The 76.7% increase for manufacturers' sales branches and offices was in the middle. The result, as Figure 2.8 indicates, is that the percentage of total sales of merchant wholesalers had increased from 50.9% in 1972 to 53.7% in 1977, while the percentage of total sales for both agents, brokers, and commission merchants, and manufacturers' sales branches and offices had decreased from 12.3% to 10.4% and from 36.8% to 35.9%, respectively. For merchant wholesalers and agents, brokers, and commission merchants this pattern continues a very long-term trend dating back to 1948. But for the manufacturers' sales branches and offices, the change from 1972 to 1977 reflects a significant change in trend. This is shown in Table 2.1.

As shown in the table, between 1948 and 1977 merchant wholesalers' percentage of total sales has continually increased while sales for agents, brokers, and commission merchants have steadily decreased. But the percentage of total sales for manufacturers' sales branches and offices, which

Figure 2.8
Percent of Wholesale Sales by Type of Wholesaler: 1972 and 1977

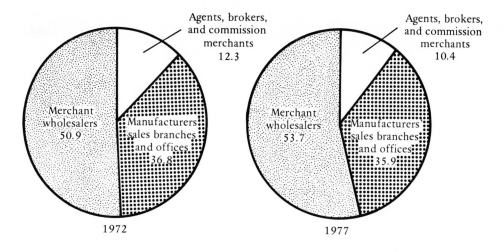

1972   1977

Table 2.1
Percentage Breakdown of Wholesaler Sales by Type of Operation:
1948–1977

Type of Wholesaler	Percentage of Total Sales					
	1948	1958	1963	1967	1972	1977
Merchant Wholesalers	42.4	42.8	43.9	44.9	50.9	53.7
Agents, Brokers, and Commission Merchants	18.2	16.3	14.9	13.3	12.3	10.4
Manufacturers' Sales Branches and Offices	28.1	30.9	32.5	34.2	36.8	35.9

had been continually increasing from 1948 to 1972, showed a decline between 1972 and 1977. This decline in the percentage of total wholesaler
sales by manufacturers' sales branches and offices and the continued increasing percentage enjoyed by merchant wholesalers reflects the continued shifting of more of the distribution tasks from manufacturers to
independent merchant wholesalers.

These aggregate trends, however, vary significantly across different
kinds of wholesale businesses. For example, Moore and Adams argue that
much of the decline in the sales percentage for agents and brokers is
attributable to manufacturers of lumber, construction materials, piece
goods, notions and apparel shifting from agents and brokers to their own
sales branches. Other changing patterns which these authors noted are as
follows:[6]

[6]James R. Moore and Kendall A. Adams, "Functional Wholesaler Sales: Trends and Analysis," in *Combined Proceedings of the American Marketing Association 1975*, ed. Edward M. Mazze (Chicago: American Marketing Association, 1976), pp. 403–405.

Figure 2.9
Wholesale Sales by Kind of Business: 1972 and 1977

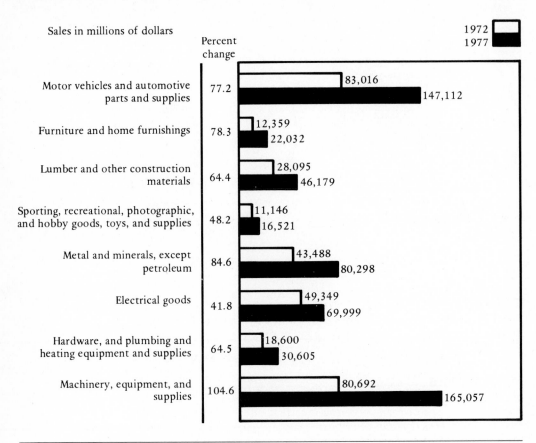

1. Sales of automobiles, drugs, paper, and paint have shown a shift from merchant wholesalers to company owned sales branches.
2. A shift from sales branches to merchant wholesalers has taken place in the electrical appliance, meat, metal, service equipment, transportation equipment, and tobacco industries.
3. A shift from sales branches and offices to agent wholesalers was found in the electrical equipment, plumbing, and tobacco industries.
4. In the confectionary industry, there has been some shifting from merchant wholesalers to agents.

Other changes in combined sales for the three types of wholesalers by kind of business between 1972 and 1977 are shown in Figure 2.9.

Size and Concentration in Wholesaling.   While it may be said that wholesalers come in all shapes and sizes, from small one person operators to

Figure 2.9 (continued)

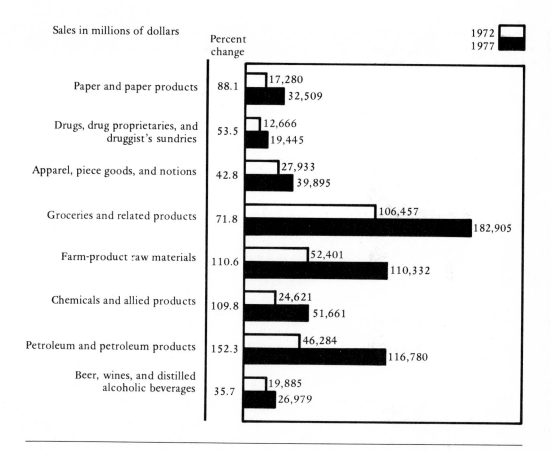

Sales in millions of dollars

Percent change

1972
1977

	Percent change	1972	1977
Paper and paper products	88.1	17,280	32,509
Drugs, drug proprietaries, and druggist's sundries	53.5	12,666	19,445
Apparel, piece goods, and notions	42.8	27,933	39,895
Groceries and related products	71.8	106,457	182,905
Farm-product raw materials	110.6	52,401	110,332
Chemicals and allied products	109.8	24,621	51,661
Petroleum and petroleum products	152.3	46,284	116,780
Beer, wines, and distilled alcoholic beverages	35.7	19,885	26,979

large scale organizations with hundreds or even thousands of employees, in general, wholesaling is characterized by relatively small businesses. Many merchant wholesalers and agents and brokers are still privately held, family run businesses with a small number of employees. In the majority of cases, their scope of operations is generally local, or at most regional; it is the rare wholesaler who operates at a national level. Indeed, as Figure 2.10 shows, as of 1977 almost 43% of all wholesale establishments had less than five employees, and only 3.5% had more than fifty employees. Moreover, less than 1% of all wholesale establishments had over 100 employees, and only twenty-one had over 1,000 employees.

Economic concentration in terms of the percentage of total wholesale sales enjoyed by the largest firms is relatively low for merchant wholesalers as well as agents, brokers, and commission merchants but significantly larger for manufacturers' sales branches and offices. As shown in Figure 2.11, the fifty largest merchant wholesalers and the fifty largest agents, brokers, and commission merchants accounted for only 14.9%

and 11.9% of total sales for these two types, respectively, while the fifty
largest manufacturers' sales branches and offices accounted for 52.4% of
total sales for this type of wholesaler. There are, however, exceptions to
these patterns in some lines of wholesale trade. For example, in electrical
supplies, hospital supplies, and metals, a small number of merchant
wholesalers has captured large portions of the markets for these products,

Figure 2.10
Percent Distribution of Wholesale Establishments and Sales
by Employment Size: 1977

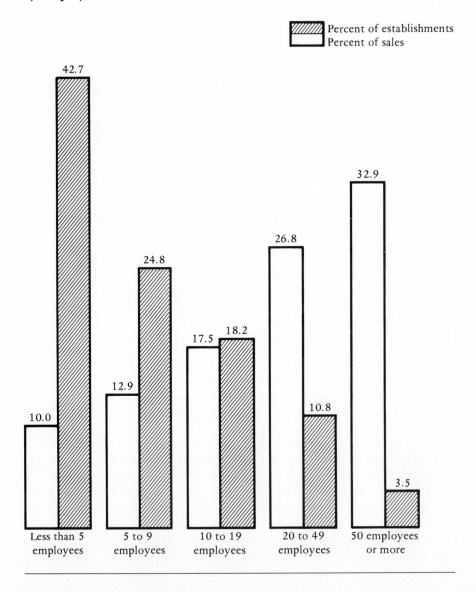

Figure 2.11
Concentration of Wholesale Sales by Type of Wholesalers of Various Sizes: 1977

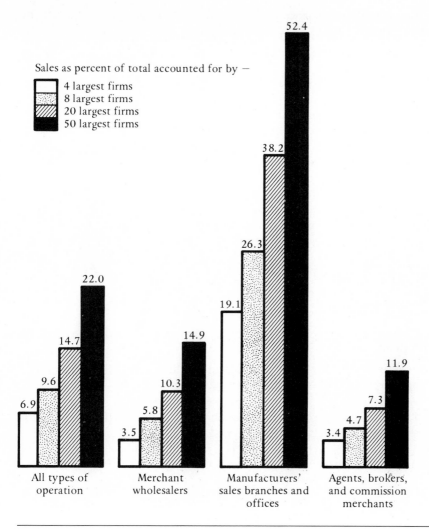

Sales as percent of total accounted for by —

☐ 4 largest firms
▦ 8 largest firms
▨ 20 largest firms
■ 50 largest firms

causing a relatively high level of concentration.[7] Moreover, at a local level many merchant wholesalers may dominate or even enjoy near monopoly positions in their markets. Thus, an accurate picture of the competitive situation for wholesalers can best be gained by examining the line of trade (kind of business) they are in and the particular geographical markets in which they operate.

[7] Louis W. Stern and Adel I. El-Ansary, *Marketing Channels* (Englewood Cliffs, N.J.: Prentice-Hall, 1977), p. 10.

From the standpoint of the producer or manufacturer considering the use of wholesalers in the channel of distribution, the levels of competition facing wholesalers can be an important factor in selecting them. Often, the wholesaler who dominates a market will be very independent and more difficult for the manufacturer to influence than the wholesaler who is faced with strong competition. This issue will be addressed more fully in Chapter 6 (Selecting the Channel Members).

Distribution Tasks Performed by Wholesalers. Merchant wholesalers and agents, brokers, and commission merchants as intermediaries between their suppliers (producers and manufacturers) and their customers (retailers, industrial, commercial, institutional, professional and agricultural) have survived in the marketing channel because, as specialists in the performance of distribution tasks, they can operate at higher levels of effectiveness and efficiency. Often the average cost curves for distribution tasks are lower for wholesalers, or they are able to operate closer to the optimum points on the curves than their suppliers.[8] This is particularly true for merchant wholesalers who are especially well suited for performing the following types of distribution tasks for their suppliers:[9]

1. Planning local distribution
2. Providing low cost sales contact over a wide geographical area
3. Providing low cost warehousing and delivery
4. Offering credit and capital to finance inventories and for extending credit
5. Accepting relatively large shipments, thus achieving substantial transportation and order processing savings

For their customers, merchant wholesalers are equally well suited for efficiently performing such distribution tasks as:

1. Anticipating customers' requirements and maintaining inventories tailored to meet these requirements
2. Assembling locally the varied products of many suppliers and holding them available for delivery on short notice
3. Buying in large quantities and breaking bulk to suit customers while passing on some of the savings effected from buying in larger lots
4. Providing rapid delivery
5. Extending credit
6. Providing guarantees, making adjustments, and handling returns and allowances

---

[8] Stigler, pp. 187–89.
[9] For two excellent discussions of the wholesaler's role in the marketing channel see: Paul L. Courtney, "The Wholesaler as a Link in the Distribution Channel," *Business Horizons* (February, 1961): 90–95; Richard M. Hill, "Profit by Your Wholesalers' Services," (Washington, D.C.: U.S. Small Business Administration, Small Marketers AID No. 140), pp. 2–6.

Table 2.2
Distribution Tasks of Agents, Brokers, and Commission Merchants

Functions	Auction companies	Brokers	Commission merchants	Manufacturers agents	Selling agents
Functions for customers:					
Anticipates needs		Some		Sometimes	
"Regroups" goods (one or more of four stages)	X		X	Some	
Carries stocks	Sometimes		X	Sometimes	
Delivers goods			X	Sometimes	
Grants credit	Some		Sometimes		X
Provides information and advisory services		X	X	X	X
Provides buying function	X	Some	X	X	X
Owns and transfers title to goods	Transfers only		Transfers only		
For producers and manufacturers:					
Provides selling function	X	Some	X	X	X
Stores inventory	X		X	Sometimes	
Helps finance by owning stocks					
Reduces credit risk	Some				X
Provides market information		X	X	X	X

Source: E. Jerome McCarthy, *Basic Marketing*, 5th ed. (Homewood, Illinois: Richard D. Irwin, Inc., © 1975), p. 355.

Agents, brokers, and commission merchants are important in performing such distribution tasks as those shown in Table 2.2.

As an example of the wholesaler's role in performing distribution tasks, consider the case of Thruway Fasteners, a New York State based industrial distributor of many types of fasteners:

Thruway Fasteners would generally be classed as a medium size wholesaler with sales volume of fourteen million dollars, and 122 employees, including fourteen outside salesmen. The company is headquartered in Syracuse, and has three branches in Binghamton, Buffalo, and Rochester. Thruway, as a merchant wholesaler of industrial fasteners, provides a vital link between manufacturers of all different kinds of fasteners and the diverse needs of the users of those fasteners, mostly small manufacturers. It is Thruway's job to search out its customers' needs and carry the products to meet those needs quickly and conveniently. A comment by Paul Lemke, the president of Thruway, captures the essence of this role perfectly: "I have an obligation to my customers. I can't tell him I have no product for him. . . . I have to be good enough so that I have the product he needs under any condition. . . ."[10] Thruway thus pays very

[10] "Up-Front, No-Frills Management," *Industrial Distribution*, (March 1981): 66.

careful attention to *anticipating* the needs of its customers and it has tailored the inventory at each of its branches to fit the needs and demands of the local area. The Rochester branch stocks small set screws and fasteners for the electronics industry. Syracuse has heavy industry parts, Buffalo carries large bolts, and Binghamton heavy bolts and nuts. To provide this kind of service, Lemke still goes out on the road twice a week to keep in touch with the market and has developed a very close and strong relationship with fastener manufacturers. This knowledge of market needs and strong relationships with manufacturers, coupled with the efficiency of its operations, enables Thruway to provide a level of service and cost effectiveness in the performance of distribution tasks that virtually assures its viability in the marketing channel for fasteners.

Retail Intermediaries

Retailers consist of business firms engaged primarily in selling merchandise for personal or household consumption and rendering services incidental to the sale of the goods.

Kinds of Retailers. The 1,855,068 retail establishments in the United States form an extremely complex and diverse conglomeration. They range in size from the small so-called "mom and pop" stores to the gigantic Sears and Roebuck with sales over eighteen billion dollars and over 400,000 employees. Methods of operation run from minimum service, spartan discount stores to the vast array of services offered by a retailer such as Marshall Field. Further, there are store retailers and nonstore retailers, discount retailers and high price retailers, fashion oriented retailers and staple goods retailers, single unit retailers and chain store retailers, and the list can go on and on. Over the years, a variety of classification schemes has been developed to help lend some order to this almost bewildering complexity. Figure 2.12, for example, outlines some of these.

The most comprehensive and widely used approach to classifying retailers is that used by the *Census of Retail Trade* which places all retailers into 100 kind-of-business classifications within the ten major groups listed below. Figure 2.13 compares 1972 and 1977 sales for each of these groups.

1. Building materials, hardware, garden supply, and mobile home dealers
2. General merchandise group stores
3. Food stores
4. Automotive dealers
5. Gasoline service stations

Figure 2.12
Alternative Bases for Classifying Retailers

A. By Ownership of Establishment:
1. Single-unit independent stores
2. Multiunit retail organizations:
    a. chain stores
    b. branch stores
3. Manufacturer-owned retail outlets
4. Consumers' cooperative stores
5. Farmer-owned establishments
6. Company-owned stores (industrial stores) or commissaries
7. Government operated stores (post exchanges, state liquor stores)
8. Public utility company stores (for sale of major appliances)

B. By Kind of Business (Merchandise Handled)
1. General merchandise group:
    a. department stores
    b. dry goods, general merchandise stores
    c. general stores
    d. variety stores
2. Single-line stores (e.g., grocery, apparel, furniture)
3. Specialty stores (e.g., meat markets, lingerie shops, floor coverings stores)

C. By Size of Establishment:
1. By number of employees
2. By annual sales volume

D. By Degree of Vertical Integration:
1. Nonintegrated (retailing functions only)
2. Integrated with wholesaling functions
3. Integrated with manufacturing or other form-utility creation

E. By Type of Relationship with Other Business Organizations:
1. Unaffiliated
2. Voluntarily affiliated with other retailers:
    a. through wholesaler-sponsored voluntary chains
    b. through retailer cooperation

3. Affiliated with manufacturers by dealer franchises

F. By Method of Consumer Contact:
1. Regular store:
    a. leased department
2. Mail order:
    a. by catalog selling
    b. by advertising in regular media
    c. by membership club plans
3. Household contacts:
    a. by house-to-house canvassing
    b. by regular delivery route service
    c. by party plan selling

G. By type of Location:
1. Urban:
    a. central business district
    b. secondary business district
    c. string street location
    d. neighborhood location
    e. controlled (planned) shopping center
    f. public market stalls
2. Small city:
    a. downtown
    b. neighborhood
3. Rural stores
4. Roadside stands

H. By Type of Service Rendered:
1. Full service
2. Limited service (cash-and-carry)
3. Self-service

I. By Legal Form of Organization:
1. Proprietorship
2. Partnership
3. Corporation
4. Special types

J. By Management Organization or Operational Technique:
1. Undifferentiated
2. Departmentalized

Source: Theodore N. Beckman, William R. Davidson, and W. Wayne Talarzyk, *Marketing*, 9th ed. © 1973, The Ronald Press Company, New York, p. 239.

6. Apparel and accessory stores

7. Furniture, home furnishings, and equipment stores

8. Eating and drinking places

9. Drug and proprietary stores

10. Miscellaneous retail stores

Data are reported in the *Census of Retail Trade* for each group and for each kind of business classification contained within each group for the United States as a whole and for many smaller geographical areas (see Figure 2.14).

Figure 2.13
Sales of Ten Major Kind-of-Retail-Business Groups: 1972 and 1977

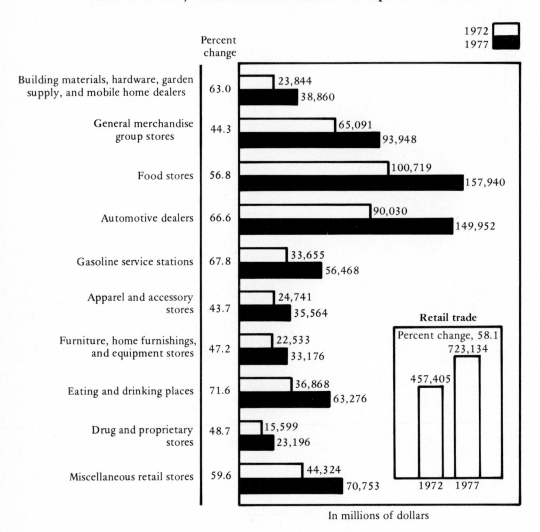

Percent
change

1972
1977

Building materials, hardware, garden supply, and mobile home dealers — 63.0 — 23,844 / 38,860

General merchandise group stores — 44.3 — 65,091 / 93,948

Food stores — 56.8 — 100,719 / 157,940

Automotive dealers — 66.6 — 90,030 / 149,952

Gasoline service stations — 67.8 — 33,655 / 56,468

Apparel and accessory stores — 43.7 — 24,741 / 35,564

Furniture, home furnishings, and equipment stores — 47.2 — 22,533 / 33,176

Eating and drinking places — 71.6 — 36,868 / 63,276

Drug and proprietary stores — 48.7 — 15,599 / 23,196

Miscellaneous retail stores — 59.6 — 44,324 / 70,753

Retail trade
Percent change, 58.1
723,134
457,405
1972   1977

In millions of dollars

Structure and Trends in Retailing.   Retailing in the United States is, to an increasing extent, being characterized by large scale operations and growing economic concentration.[11] Average sales per retail establishment, one of the most basic measures of retailer size, has been increasing steadily over the past three decades. Table 2.3 shows this pattern.

From the standpoint of economic concentration, retailing is also increasingly being dominated by large retailers. In 1977, for example, large retailers (those with sales of $1 million or more), though accounting for

[11]Bert Rosenbloom, *Retail Marketing* (New York: Random House, 1981), pp. 376–379.

Figure 2.14
Sample Table from Census of Retail Trade

SIC code	Kind of business	All establishments Number	All establishments Sales ($1,000)	Unincorporated Sole proprietorships (number)	Unincorporated Partnerships (number)	Establishments with payroll Number	Establishments with payroll Sales ($1,000)	Payroll entire year ($1,000)	Payroll first quarter ($1,000)	Paid employees for week including March 12 (number)
52	Retail trade	71 795	20 630 308	40 394	6 919	49 111	19 993 249	2 383 330	553 230	461 845
52	Building materials, hardware, garden supply, and mobile home dealers	3 577	1 144 174	1 526	445	2 720	1 109 604	127 841	28 716	17 495
521,3	Building materials and supply stores	1 557	717 071	501	163	1 287	707 030	84 757	19 323	9 953
521	Lumber and other building materials dealers	1 148	664 725	371	121	948	655 499	76 327	17 200	8 664
523	Paint, glass, and wallpaper stores	409	52 346	130	42	339	51 531	8 430	2 123	1 289
525	Hardware stores	1 327	226 491	718	232	979	212 164	25 884	5 812	4 918
526	Retail nurseries, lawn and garden supply stores	252	60 183	147	21	147	57 434	7 121	1 352	1 152
527	Mobile home dealers	441	140 429	160	29	307	132 976	10 079	2 229	1 472
53	General merchandise group stores	1 617	2 929 434	508	118	1 366	2 921 360	383 413	86 107	73 634
531	Department stores	346	2 494 147	—	2	346	2 494 147	324 757	73 067	60 042
533	Variety stores	712	272 666	244	46	626	270 265	40 300	8 962	9 634
539	Miscellaneous general merchandise stores	559	162 621	264	70	394	156 948	18 356	4 078	3 958
54	Food stores	9 817	4 710 000	5 471	995	6 986	4 570 327	398 183	93 408	72 111
541	Grocery stores	6 634	4 393 783	3 662	705	4 890	4 289 122	355 968	83 688	60 809
542	Meat, fish (seafood) markets, incl. freezer prov.	490	106 974	258	86	359	101 051	10 409	2 429	2 003
5422	Freezer and locker meat provisioners	**	**	**	**	35	12 946	1 655	412	326
5423 pt.	Meat markets	**	**	**	**	287	83 337	8 351	1 922	1 568
5423 pt.	Fish (seafood) markets	**	**	**	**	37	4 768	403	95	109
543	Fruit stores and vegetable markets	411	41 834	298	47	205	36 888	3 164	533	641
544	Candy, nut, and confectionery stores	540	33 160	282	28	299	28 454	5 605	1 337	1 616
546	Retail bakeries	1 048	82 806	490	91	902	78 371	18 866	4 500	5 672
5462	Retail bakeries—baking and selling	**	**	**	**	596	53 220	15 461	3 614	4 711
5463	Retail bakeries—selling only	**	**	**	**	306	25 151	3 405	886	961

only 7.5 percent of all retail establishments, accounted for almost 62 percent of total retail sales. On the other hand, small retailers (those with sales of under $100,000) constituted over 45 percent of the total number of retail establishments yet accounted for a mere 4.1 percent of total retail sales. Figure 2.15 portrays these figures graphically.

Table 2.3
Total Retail Sales, Number of Establishments and Average Sales per Establishment: 1948–1977

Years	Total Sales (Billions)	Number of Stores (Millions)	Average Sales per Store
1977	723.1	1.86	388,000
1972	470.8	1.91	246,000
1967	310.2	1.76	176,000
1963	244.2	1.71	143,000
1958	199.6	1.78	112,000
1948	130.5	1.77	74,000

Figure 2.15
Percentage Distribution of Retail Establishments and Sales by Size of Establishment: 1977

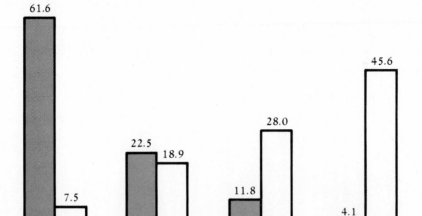

Source: *1977 Census of Retail Trade*, pp. 1–3.

Figure 2.16
Concentration of Sales among the Fifty Largest Retail Firms—for All of Retail Trade, Department Stores, and Food Stores: 1977

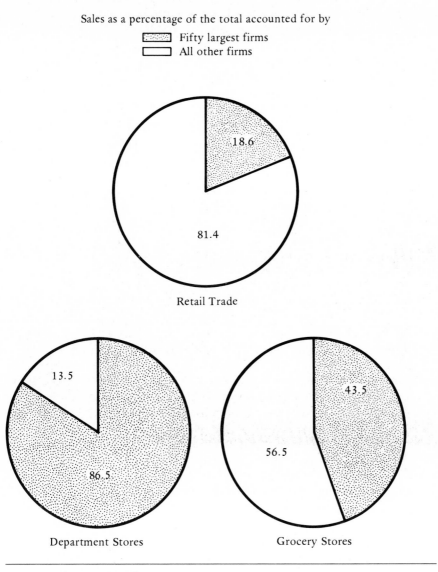

Sales as a percentage of the total accounted for by

▨ Fifty largest firms
☐ All other firms

18.6

81.4

Retail Trade

13.5

86.5

Department Stores

43.5

56.5

Grocery Stores

Source: *1977 Census of Retail Trade*, pp. 1–6.

The domination of retailing by large retailers in the United States is also evident in Figure 2.16 which shows that in 1977, in retail trade as a whole, the fifty largest firms accounted for 18.6 percent of total retail sales. When one looks specifically at department stores and food retailers, the domination of the giants is even more striking: the fifty largest accounted for 86.5 percent and 43.5 percent of department store and food store sales, respectively.

But these data only begin to convey the size and concentration of retailing. A more vivid picture emerges when the absolute size of the nation's largest retailers is considered. Table 2.4 lists retailers with sales of $1 billion or more in 1980. Some fifty-two retailers are in this category. Moreover the top four retailers each had sales of over $10 billion, and the nation's largest retailer, Sears, had sales approaching $18 billion. If the sales of the top ten retailers are added together, these ten alone account for almost 5 percent of *all* retail sales in the United States.

Finally, a study by *Chain Store Age Executive* found that over 300 retail chains each had sales in excess of $100 million as of 1980. Combined, these retailers produced sales in excess of $300 billion, making chain retailing the second largest business sector in the United States, surpassed only by the manufacture and sale of durable goods.

There is little question, then, that many retailers are big, even huge, businesses. Furthermore, they are likely to grow even larger in the future and account for an increasing proportion of the sales in their respective lines of trade.

Since size often translates into power, as retailers become larger their capacity to influence the actions of other channel members (wholesalers and manufacturers) also generally becomes greater. Most of the manufacturers who supply Sears, for example, are considerably smaller than Sears and are hardly in a position to exert a significant influence on Sears' operating policies. On the contrary, because of Sears' huge size and buying power, it is in a position to exert considerable influence on its suppliers. Indeed, in many cases Sears can literally dictate to manufacturers what kinds of products they should make if they expect to sell their products through Sears, and it can exert tremendous influence over the terms of sale. In short, Sears and the other giant retailers, which are bigger than many of the manufacturers that supply them, have the capacity to assume a dominant role in the marketing channel.

Distribution Tasks Performed by Retailers.   The role of retailers in performing distribution tasks is summarized very succinctly by Lazarus:

"The role of the retailer in the distribution channel, regardless of his size or type, is to interpret the demands of his customers and to find and stock the goods these customers want, when they want them, and in the way they want them. This adds up to having the right assortments at the time customers are ready to buy." [12]

Elaborating on Lazarus's list we may specify the distribution tasks for which retailers are especially well suited as follows:

---

[12] Charles Y. Lazarus, "The Retailer as a Link in the Distribution Channel," *Business Horizons*, (February 1961): 95–98.

Table 2.4
U.S. Retailers with Sales of One Billion Dollars or More as of 1980

		Sales	
		Most Recently Completed Fiscal Year (000)	Previous Fiscal Year (000)
1.	Sears	17,514,212	17,946,336
2.	Safeway Stores	13,717,900	12,550,569
3.	K-Mart	12,731,145	11,695,539
4.	J. C. Penney	11,274,000	10,845,000
5.	Kroger	9,029,300	7,828,000
6.	F. W. Woolworth	6,785,000	6,103,000
7.	A&P	6,684,179	7,469,659
8.	American Stores	6,120,963	5,138,404
9.	Fed. Dept. Stores	5,806,442	5,405,000
10.	Lucky Stores	5,735,666	4,592,000
11.	Montgomery Ward	5,251,085	5,014,000
12.	Winn-Dixie	4,930,000	4,444,255
13.	Southland Corp.	3,876,049	3,090,094
14.	Jewel Companies	3,764,300	3,516,352
15.	Dayton Hudson	3,359,849	2,961,884
16.	City Products	3,198,162	2,666,000
17.	Cavenham	3,137,612	2,398,944
18.	May Dept. Stores	2,747,898	2,567,000
19.	Albertson's	2,673,848	2,268,970
20.	Carter Hawley Hale	2,408,000	2,116,600
21.	Supermarkets Gen.	2,372,300	2,062,400
22.	Macy's	2,058,550	1,834,200
23.	Allied Stores	2,210,301	2,082,686
24.	Melville	2,022,770	1,747,372
25.	Publix	1,942,562	1,679,112
26.	Stop & Shop	1,878,864	1,762,144
27.	Dillon	1,792,213	1,465,277
28.	Brown & Williamson (BWI)	1,789,007	1,600,000
29.	Assoc. Dry Goods	1,783,200	1,605,600
30.	Gamble-Skogmo	1,751,995	1,140,880
31.	Rapid American	1,625,000	1,543,000
32.	Chromalloy Corp.	1,500,000	1,400,000
33.	Zayre	1,549,729	1,394,109
34.	Food Fair	1,461,000	2,800,000
35.	Tandy Corp.	1,384,600	1,215,483
36.	First National	1,364,797	1,111,691
37.	Walgreen's	1,344,542	1,192,855
38.	J. Eckerd	1,325,140	1,131,445
39.	Fisher Foods	1,336,293	1,451,676
40.	Wickes	1,308,736	1,189,106
41.	PET Inc.	1,259,000	N/A
42.	Wal-Mart	1,248,176	900,298
43.	Giant Food	1,242,620	1,080,842
44.	Interco	1,205,900	1,120,200
45.	Brown Group Inc.	1,144,922	983,980
46.	Belk Stores	1,125,000	892,700
47.	Waldbaum's	1,103,443	941,749
48.	Revco	1,090,000	927,533
49.	Gibson Products	1,068,000	1,311,000
50.	Mercantile Stores	1,067,937	922,141
51.	National Tea	1,045,696	918,365
52.	Zale	1,040,000	904,464

Source: "The 100 Million Club," *Chain Store Age Executive*, August 1980, pp. 25–26. Reprinted by permission from *Chain Store Age Executive* © August 1980. Copyright Lebhar-Friedman, Inc., 425 Park Avenue, New York, N.Y. 10022.

1. Offering manpower and physical facilities which enable producers/manufacturers and wholesalers to have many points of contact with consumers close to their places of residence

2. Providing personal selling, advertising and display to aid in selling his suppliers' products

3. Interpreting consumer demand and relaying this information back through the channel

4. Dividing large quantities into consumer sized lots, thereby providing economies for his suppliers (by accepting relatively large shipments) and convenience for consumers

5. Offering storage so that suppliers can have widely dispersed inventories of their products at low cost and enabling consumers to have close access to the products of producers/manufacturers and wholesalers

6. Removing substantial risk from the producer/manufacturer (or wholesaler) by ordering and accepting delivery in advance of the season

The growing size of retailers discussed earlier in the chapter has affected the allocation of distribution tasks among the channel members. Specifically, distribution tasks which were formerly the province of the wholesaler or manufacturer have increasingly been taken over by the large-scale retailer. For example, most large chain store organizations and department stores have their own modern warehousing facilities enabling them to perform storage and order processing tasks very efficiently.[13] This in turn has reduced their use of merchant wholesaler intermediaries to a very marginal level. Voluntary associations of retailers, such as retailer cooperatives, wholesaler initiated voluntary chains, and franchise systems, have also grown enabling many of these organizations to rival the scale economies of the corporate chains (see Chapter 14). Even single unit independent retail stores have, on the average, grown larger, have utilized more modern facilities and equipment, and perform distribution tasks more efficiently.

This poses somewhat of a dilemma for the producer or manufacturer. On the one hand, the potential of retail intermediaries to perform distribution tasks effectively and efficiently has increased. But on the other hand, the larger scale of retailers has increased their power and independence; hence, they are less easily influenced by the producer or manufacturer. So, the channel manager in the producing or manufacturing firm will face both increased opportunities as well as difficulties in the course of using retailers in the channel of distribution.[14] This will place an especially high premium on effective channel management.

---

[13] See for example: Susan B. Miller, "Furniture Warehouses That Sell to Public Spring Up and Do Well Across the Land," *Wall Street Journal*, 30 May 1972, p. 26.

[14] For a related discussion see: Arthur I. Cohen and Ana L. Jones, "Brand Marketing in the New Retail Environment," *Harvard Business Review*, (September–October 1978): 141–148.

The Retailer's Changing Role in the Marketing Channel.   Another phenomenon occurring in retailing that will provide a further challenge to channel management by producers and manufacturers is the changing role of retailers in the marketing channel. In a sense, the retailer plays a dual role in the marketing channel.[15] On the one hand, the retailers' suppliers—whether at the manufacturer or wholesaler level—expect the retailer to serve as their selling agent. That is, suppliers expect retailers to stock and aggressively promote their merchandise regardless of the extent to which that merchandise fits the needs of the individual retailer's customers when compared with the merchandise available from other suppliers. On the other hand, retailers also serve as the buying agents for their customers. In this role, retailers attempt to understand the needs of their customers and then seek out and buy only from those suppliers who have the types of merchandise that will best satisfy their customers' needs.

Virtually all retailers fill both of these roles. But the relative emphasis given to each role appears to be changing.

As increasing numbers of retailers embrace the marketing concept, which stresses a *customer orientation* to marketing, the primary cues as to what merchandise to stock and how to sell it will increasingly come not from suppliers but from the retailer's *own analysis* of target markets (customers).[16] Further, because of the growing size of retailers, the capacity of retailers to assume a heavily customer-oriented role will also increase. Many retailers will be large enough to resist the pressure put on them by producers and manufacturers to sell their merchandise whether it offers the best fit with the needs of the retailer's customers or not. Only those producers and manufacturers who enjoy extremely high levels of customer demand for their products through entrenched brand acceptance will be in a position to "dictate" to retailers the kinds of merchandise they should stock and the terms under which it may be sold.

Facilitating Agencies

Facilitating agencies are business firms that assist in the performance of distribution tasks other than buying, selling and transferring title. From the standpoint of the channel manager, they may be viewed as subcontractors to whom various distribution tasks can be "farmed out" based again on the principle of specialization and division of labor. By properly allocating distribution tasks to facilitating agencies, the channel manager will have an ancillary structure that is an efficient mechanism for carry-

[15] Philip McVey, "Are Channels of Distribution What the Textbooks Say?" *Journal of Marketing*, (January 1960): 61–65.
[16] Bert Rosenbloom, "The Retailer's Changing Role in the Marketing Channel," in *1979 Marketing Educators Conference Proceedings*, eds. Neil Beckwith, et al. (Chicago: American Marketing Association 1979), p. 393.

ing out the firm's distribution objectives. Below we discuss briefly some of the more common types of facilitating agencies.

Transportation agencies—include all firms offering transportation service on a public basis. The major modes of transport, of course, are rail, truck, water, air, and pipe lines. Each of these modes has its particular advantages and disadvantages. For example, air freight is the fastest but also the most costly. Water on the other hand usually has the lowest cost per ton/mile but is the slowest.[17]

Storage agencies—consist mainly of public warehouses that specialize in the storage of goods on a fee basis. Many of these firms provide great flexibility in performing the storage tasks. For example, in some instances the goods of a channel member (producers/manufacturers, wholesalers, or retailers) are not physically stored in the warehousing firm's facilities but rather in the channel member's own facilities. Under this so-called field warehousing arrangement, the warehousing agency looks up the goods and issues a receipt which often serves as collateral on a loan taken by the channel member.

Advertising agencies—offer the channel member expertise in developing his promotion strategy. This can range from complete design and execution of the advertising campaign to providing a small amount of assistance in writing an ad.

Financial agencies—consist of firms such as banks, savings and loan associations, finance companies, and factors who specialize in discounting accounts receivable. Common to all of these firms is that they possess the financial resources and expertise that the channel manager often lacks.

Insurance companies—provide the channel manager with a means for shifting some of the risks inherent in any business venture such as fire and theft losses, damage in transit of goods, and in some cases even inclement weather.

Marketing research firms—this category of facilitating agency has grown substantially in the past twenty years. Most large cities now have a number of marketing research firms offering a wide range of marketing research skills. The channel manager can call on these firms to provide information when his own firm lacks the necessary skills to obtain marketing information relevant to distribution.

Summary

Many different types of parties participate in the marketing channel. Some are considered to be members while other participants are non-

---

[17] For a more complete discussion on modes of transport see: Edward W. Smykay, *Physical Distribution Management*, 3rd ed. (New York: Macmillan Publishing Co., 1973), Chapters 6 and 7.

members. The former perform negotiatory functions and participate in the flows of negotiation and/or ownership while the latter participants do not. Though final users (target markets) are members of the marketing channel, they are excluded from the *commercial channel*, which by definition excludes final users.

Producers and manufacturers consist of firms that are involved in extracting, growing, or making products. Though the range of types and sizes of producing and manufacturing firms is enormous, all are faced with the common task of distributing their products to their intended users. Many producers and manufacturers, however, lack the expertise and economies of scale to distribute their products directly to their final users. Hence, in most cases it is difficult and inefficient for manufacturers to distribute their products directly to final users. So they must often call on intermediaries at the wholesale and/or retail levels as well as facilitating agencies to share in the performance of the distribution tasks.

Wholesalers consist of businesses that are engaged in selling goods for resale or business use to retail, industrial, commercial, institutional, professional or agricultural firms or organizations, as well as to other wholesalers. Wholesalers are classified into three basic types: (1) merchant wholesalers, (2) agents, brokers, and commission merchants, and (3) manufacturers' sales branches and offices. The first two are independent middlemen while the third is owned by the manufacturer. Over the last three decades, the percentage of total wholesale sales enjoyed by merchant wholesalers has been increasing while it has been decreasing for agents, brokers, and commission merchants.

The sales percentage held by manufacturers' sales branches and offices had increased between 1948 and 1972 but registered a significant decline between 1972 and 1977. Most wholesalers are relatively small businesses and the level of economic concentration in wholesaling is generally quite low. Wholesalers are especially well suited for performing distribution tasks such as:

1. Planning local distribution
2. Providing low cost sales contacts
3. Providing low cost warehousing
4. Offering credit and financing inventories
5. Accepting large shipments and breaking them down into smaller ones
6. Anticipating customer requirements and maintaining warehouses
7. Assembling products from many suppliers
8. Providing rapid delivery
9. Providing guarantees, making adjustments, and handling returns and allowances

Retailers consist of business firms engaged primarily in selling merchandise for personal or household consumption and rendering services incidental to the sale of the goods. Retailers comprise an extremely diverse group in both type and size. The *Census of Retail Trade* classifies retailers into one hundred different kinds of business categories to provide some degree of order to this great diversity. Retail firms have been steadily growing larger over the last three decades and the level of economic concentration has become relatively high. In some lines of trade the fifty largest firms account for over 80% of total sales. Retailers are particularly well suited for performing such distribution tasks as:

1. Offering manpower and physical facilities that enable producers, manufacturers and wholesalers to have many points of contact with consumers
2. Providing personal selling, advertising and display to sell suppliers' products
3. Interpreting consumer demand and relaying it through the channel
4. Dividing large quantities of products into consumer sized lots
5. Offering storage close to points of consumer contact
6. Reducing risks of producers, manufacturers and wholesalers by accepting delivery of merchandise in advance of the selling season

As retailers continue to grow larger and as more of them embrace the marketing concept, their role in the marketing channel will become a more independent and dominant one. This will pose an increasing challenge to channel management in producing and manufacturing firms.

Facilitating agencies such as transportation companies, storage firms, advertising agencies, financial institutions, insurers, and marketing researchers, while not members of the marketing channel, are still called upon frequently by any or all of the channel members to help perform many different distribution tasks.

Discussion Questions

1. Explain the classification scheme of the channel participants shown in Figure 2.1.
2. Expertise and economies of scale in production do not automatically translate into expertise and economies of scale in distribution. Discuss this statement.
3. Why do you suppose the average costs of performing many distribution tasks are lower for intermediaries and facilitating agencies than for producers and manufacturers?
4. How does the *Census of Business* classify wholesale intermediaries?
5. In this text we do not consider manufacturers' sales branches to be intermediaries. Is this justified? Hint: Go back to Chapter 1 and re-examine our definition of the marketing channel.

6. Contrary to some prophecies, wholesalers have not died out. What has happened to wholesalers in recent years?

7. Discuss the basic trends with regard to total wholesale sales for merchant wholesalers, manufacturers' sales branches and offices, and agents, brokers, and commission merchants over the last thirty years.

8. Describe the distribution tasks which wholesalers and retailers are especially well suited for performing.

9. The average size of retail units (as measured by sales volume) has been increasing. What are some of the implications of this trend for channel management in producing and manufacturing firms?

10. Discuss the retailer's changing role in the marketing channel in terms of the possible implications for channel management.

Chapter 3
The Environment of
Marketing Channels

Marketing channels do not exist in a vacuum. Rather, they develop and are operated in a complex environment that is continually changing. These environmental changes and their underlying forces can have profound effects on marketing channels in the short as well as the long run. The channel manager must therefore be sensitive to the environment and environmental changes in order to *plan* effective marketing channel strategies for meeting these changes successfully. To do so, the channel manager must have a good understanding of the environment and how it influences channel management.

In this chapter we examine the environment of marketing channels in the context of how it interfaces with the management of the marketing channel.

The Marketing Channel and Environment

In the broadest sense, the environment consists of all external uncontrollable factors within which the marketing channel exists. This means that there are a myriad of variables affecting the channel. In order to give some semblance of order to this huge array of external uncontrollable variables, we will categorize them in this chapter under the following five general categories:

1.   Economic environment
2.   Competitive environment
3.   Socio-cultural environment
4.   Technological environment
5.   Legal environment

Obviously this is not the only way, or necessarily the best way to categorize environmental variables. Numerous other category systems (taxonomies) exist. We have used this taxonomy simply because it provides a convenient and workable basis for discussing the environment of marketing channels. It should also be noted that the order in which the categories are listed and discussed does not imply any order of importance. The relative importance of legal vs. competitive vs. technological factors etc., to the external contactual organizations of different firms varies. Moreover, for any given channel, the importance of particular environmental factors will vary over time. As we proceed through this chapter, numerous examples of the diverse effects of environmental factors on different channels and at different times will be presented.

Before discussing each of these environmental categories and their influence on the marketing channel, a peculiarity of the influence of environment in a marketing channels context should be noted.

Because the marketing channel includes other member firms such as retailers and wholesalers, the channel manager must also be concerned with the impact of the environment on these channel members. Further, since the effectiveness of the channel is also influenced by the performance of nonmember participants, such as facilitating agencies, he must also take into account how the environment affects these nonmember participants as well. Thus, the channel manager must analyze the impact of environment not only on his own firm and his ultimate target markets, but also on *all* of the participants in the marketing channel. Figure 3.1 illustrates this by showing the environment impacting on all channel participants and the target markets. The locus of channel management (not necessarily control) may be in producing and manufacturing firms, or intermediary firms, such as large wholesale or retailing organizations who are capable of administering the channel (see Chapter 14, especially the discussion on channel management by intermediaries). This is shown in the rectangle at the lower left hand corner of Figure 3.1. Finally, the circle at the lower right hand corner has four arrows pointing to each of the channel participants and target markets. This indicates that management's analysis of environmental effects must consider all of these parties.

This view of the impact of environment in a marketing channels context represents a key distinction between channel management and man-

Figure 3.1
The Impact of Environment in a Marketing Channel Context

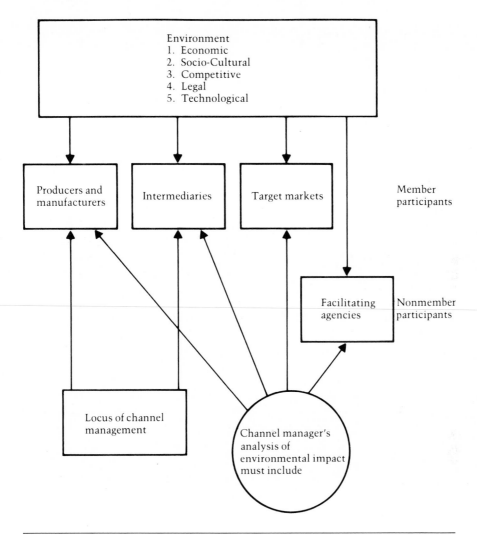

agement of the other major variables in a firm's marketing mix (product, price and promotion). In short, when the channel manager considers environmental influences on channel strategy he or she has a lot more to think about. An example will help to clarify this more fully.

The economic impact of inflation has resulted in high construction costs, rents, taxes, wages, and other costs. This is causing many retailers in the specialty goods lines, particularly men's clothing and furnishings, to "think small." That is, currently and for the foreseeable future these retailers are planning smaller stores—on the average about one-half to two-thirds the size of current units.[1] This reduction in unit size for these stores has important implications for channel management in the supplier firms—manufacturers and wholesalers. For example, the amount of storage space offered by these retailers will be substantially reduced. This means in turn that the levels of inventory carried by the stores will be lower. Consequently, supplier firms, particularly manufacturers who fail to take this into account in planning channel strategy, are likely to be caught with too much inventory for the smaller sized retailers to carry. By being aware of this economic impact on retailers, however, management can plan its channel strategy more appropriately. A perceptive channel manager would realize that this reduced inventory capacity on the part of retailers will result in a shifting of more of the storage function to supplier firms thus increasing their costs. Hence the channel manager in the supplier firm may want to reevaluate the trade discount structure to see if it might have to be changed. Or an examination of the existing channel structure may be needed to see if the increased demand for inventory storage by the firm will require a *planned* restructuring of this function among the channel members. Failure to do this will result in the channel manager simply allowing this restructuring to take place insidiously. Ultimately, the manufacturer may end up performing the major portion of the storage function de facto.

This extended view of environmental analysis to include all channel participants should be kept in mind throughout this chapter—and for that matter for the remainder of the text.

We now turn to a discussion of each of the major environmental categories. The discussion will focus on some of the key issues for each category and how they influence the marketing channel.

The Economic Environment

The economy is probably the most obvious and pervasive category of environmental variables affecting all members of the marketing channel. Hardly a day goes by without the state of the economy drawing the notice of consumers and executives in manufacturing, wholesaling and retailing firms. All of these parties must pay careful attention to what is happening in the economy. From raising capital for a long-term investment by a manufacturer to buying a pound of coffee in the supermarket by the consumer, are all affected by economic variables.

In a channel management context, economic factors are a critical determinant of channel member behavior and performance. The channel manager must therefore be aware of the influence of economic variables on the participants in the channels of distribution. In this section we discuss several major economic phenomena in terms of their effects on vari-

[1] Robert Stone, "Specialty Chains: If the Store Fits, Take It," *Chain Store Age Executive*, (September, 1975): 96.

Table 3.1
Inflation Rates in The United States as Measured
by the Consumer Price Index: 1974–1981

Year	Annual Consumer Price Index Increases
1974	11.0
1975	9.1
1976	5.8
1977	6.5
1978	11.3
1979	14.4
1980	12.4
1981	8.9

ous parties in the marketing channel and their implications for channel management.

Inflation

Since the mid-1970s, high inflation became a common pattern in the U.S. economy. Table 3.1 shows the rate of inflation as measured by the Consumer Price Index for the eight years beginning with 1974.

The reactions of channel members at the wholesale and retail levels to high rates of inflation are in large measure determined by the reactions of consumers or other final users. Unfortunately, reactions of consumers (or other final users) during inflationary periods are not easy to predict. High spending may continue even in the face of growing inflation as consumers and other users follow a "buy now before the price goes higher" psychology, as was the case during much of the 1970s. This, of course, further fuels the inflationary spiral. On the other hand, this psychology can be suddenly replaced by a "hold on to your money" psychology if consumers and other final users see a recession just around the corner. Ironically, such precipitate dropoffs in spending can help to bring on and aggravate the very recession that they had feared.

In addition to the dangers of dramatic shifting in consumer spending that can occur during inflationary periods, many other more subtle changes in consumer buying patterns may occur. For example, a study by the Food Marketing Institute (FMI), a trade association in the supermarket industry, found that during the inflationary period of the late 1970s, consumer buying patterns increasingly reflected such tactics as:[2]

going to the supermarket without bringing along extra money

putting items back at the end of the shopping trip

---

[2]"Inflation Changes Supermarket Shopping Habits," *Marketing News*, (August 10, 1979): 1, 16.

buying just the amount needed

buying less meat

stocking up on bargains

buying lower quality brands

buying unplanned items only if they are on special sales

The FMI study argued that these patterns of consumer shopping behavior reflected an attempt by consumers to cope with inflation. As the study stated:

The full impact of inflation has finally begun to catch up with the American consumer. Their attitudes and shopping behavior are now beginning to reflect in day to day life the "finding it hard to cope mood" of the public.[3]

From the perspective of the channel manager in the producing or manufacturing firm, such changes in consumer buying behavior should be viewed in the context of how they might affect channel member behavior and what the implications might be for channel strategy. For example, in the face of slower and more prudent consumer spending, supermarkets (and most other retailers) become increasingly cautious about what products they will handle. Moreover, because of higher interest rates they generally try to reduce their inventory levels to the minimum. Finally, they will seek more special price deals from manufacturers and a higher level of promotional support. In the face of such increased channel member demands, an effective channel strategy must be developed to satisfy the channel members. Such a strategy might stress a change in emphasis on the manufacturer's product mix from higher price to lower price products. The Scott Paper Company, for example, recently began to offer a lower priced line of paper products to supermarkets so as not to lose shelf space in the face of strong price competition from competitors' products. Reducing the inventory burden on channel members through a streamlined product line, faster order processing and delivery, and higher inventory turnover through stronger promotional support may also have to be incorporated into a channel strategy for meeting the demands of channel members who are attempting to operate profitably under the intense cost pressures imposed by high inflation.

Recession

As a recessionary period unfolds, consumer spending, especially for such durable goods as automobiles and major appliances that consumers can postpone purchasing, slows down, sometimes drastically. All members of

[3]Ibid., p. 1.

the marketing channel may feel the effects of recession in the form of substantial reductions in sales volume and profitability. Firms caught with heavy inventories which they cannot sell may be more drastically affected, even to the point of bankruptcy. Consider, for example, the case of automobile dealers:[4]

For automobile dealers, 1980 was a nightmare. The sales crunch that began during the recession of 1979 wiped out more than 1,600 domestic dealerships. Of the 26,600 survivors, less than 50 percent were able to eke out a profit. Low sales and the high costs of carrying inventory made it extremely difficult for automobile dealers to survive, let alone be profitable in the face of a slow economy.

Confronted with these drastic problems, the auto dealers turned to the auto manufacturers for help. Yet according to many of the dealers, the help offered was too limited and not directed at the dealers' main concern of financing high inventory costs. Indeed, many dealers felt that the manufacturers were indifferent to this problem. No significant program was offered to ease the dealers' financial burden of carrying huge inventories during the economic slowdown. As Wendell H. Miller, president of the National Automobile Dealers Association, commented: "If Detroit needs us to carry large inventories to maintain production, it follows that it should be a shared responsibility." Needless to say, many auto dealers were extremely disappointed and angry over the auto manufacturers' failure to do more to help them solve their inventory financing problem.

This case points up the major channel management challenge faced by manufacturers during recessionary periods—*how to help channel members weather the economic slowdown.* Apparently the domestic auto manufacturers did not meet this challenge successfully. What might Detroit have done differently? Unfortunately, there are no "cookbook recipes" for channel management strategies in recessionary periods. Strategies will vary depending on the type of industry involved and the particular set of circumstances. What is possible, however, is for manufacturers to develop *special or contingency channel management strategies* for helping channel members during recessionary periods. Such strategies should be developed *before* a recession takes hold so that they can be quickly implemented if and when a recession develops. For example, the auto manufacturers in cooperation with their dealers might have set up a contingency fund built up during better economic periods when sales were good. A very small percentage taken from each auto sale made during these periods could provide a substantial fund to offset high inventory financing costs during slow economic periods. Whether this particular approach is feasible would, of course, have to be carefully examined by the auto manufacturers and dealers. But regardless of the specific approach

---

[4]"Auto Dealers Try to Hang On," *Business Week,* (May 4, 1981): 128–29.

used, *advanced planning* of channel management strategies for assisting channel members operating in recessionary periods should be a fundamental part of the manufacturer's overall strategic planning effort.

Shortages

For much of the 1970s, shortages, especially of petroleum and petroleum-based products, became an everyday reality in the U.S. economy. Sudden shortages of such products as sugar, coffee, home insulation, and even peanut butter also became fairly common occurrences. Unfortunately, such shortages are not, according to most experts, simply unusual quirks or one-time occurrences, nor are they unique to the decade of the 1970s. Most authorities believe that periodic shortages of a variety of products are highly probable during the remainder of this century and are virtually certain to occur in the case of energy and energy related products.

Shortages can adversely affect all of the channel members. Retailers face hostility from consumers who may hold the retailers directly responsible for the shortages. As Hollander points out:

Retailers are particularly susceptible to public ill will in times of shortages. . . . Stores are the points of contact between consumers and production—marketing channels. Breakdowns in supply become manifest through the disappearance of familiar items from the store assortments. Consequently, consumers are likely to feel the merchants are at fault, possibly through some nefarious plot to manipulate quantities and prices, if the normal varieties of goods are not available at what the public considers normal prices.[5]

Channel members at the wholesale level also feel the effects of shortages by not being able to supply their customers with adequate quantities of those products in short supply. The problem is compounded when wholesalers attempt to allocate the scarce products in question among their customers. Such allocations can never be perfectly fair and some customers are bound to feel short-changed.

Finally, manufacturers of products in short supply face hostility from all members of the marketing channel, including the final consumer or user.

The major issue facing the channel manager with regard to shortages is how to deal with shortages in ways that minimize adverse channel member reactions, which in the long run can have serious negative consequences. While there are no clear-cut or simple solutions, several gen-

---

[5]Stanley C. Hollander, "Merchandise Shortages and Retail Policies," *MSU Business Topics*, (Summer 1978): 28.

eral strategies involving each component of the marketing mix can be suggested.[6]

Product strategy might be used during shortage periods to help mitigate channel member dissatisfaction by emphasizing possible substitute products. Such a strategy is, of course, dependent upon the manufacturer's capacity to offer a realistic substitute and upon the manufacturer's ability to convince the channel members of the acceptability of the substitute.

With respect to pricing strategy, manufacturers do face strong pressures to increase prices during periods of shortage. Some price increases are virtually unavoidable in the face of increasing costs. But additional price increases may reflect the manufacturer's attempt to take advantage of the shortage situation. Such an approach to pricing strategy may increase short-term profits but from a long-term standpoint it may weaken channel member support when the shortage situation is over. Channel members, especially those who were not able to pass on all of the higher prices to *their* customers, may feel that the manufacturer had taken advantage of them during the shortage situation. Consequently, as soon as they are able, they may emphasize the products of competitive manufacturers, particularly those whom they believe will give them a "fair shake" during a shortage situation. Hence, an attempt to hold the line on price increases can be very prudent channel management strategy during periods of shortage.

Turning now to promotional strategy. During periods of shortage, it is very tempting for the manufacturer to cut back sharply on promotion, especially on the product or products that are in short supply. Conventional wisdom argues that promoting such products will only stimulate demand further and thus worsen the shortage. There is, of course, a good deal of merit to this argument if the same type of promotion that was used for the product before a scarcity situation arose is followed by rote even as a shortage of the product develops. But, if promotional strategy is used to help mitigate the adverse effects of the shortage on the channel members, it can serve a very useful purpose. In this case, promotion could be used to inform the channel members about possible substitute products offered by the manufacturer (see above), to explain why prices of the scarce product are rising, as well as what the manufacturer is attempting to do to control prices and increase the availability of the product.

Finally, with regard to physical distribution strategy, if the manufacturer can expedite shipments of scarce products to his channel members, an important benefit will be provided. Special efforts taken by the manufacturer to speed shipments, such as changing to a faster mode of transport, cutting down on the paperwork involved in shipping the scarce products, or, if feasible, bypassing the channel member's warehouse and

---

[6]For a related discussion see: Philip Kotler, "Marketing During Periods of Shortage," *Journal of Marketing*, (July 1974): 25–26.

Figure 3.2
Types of Competition

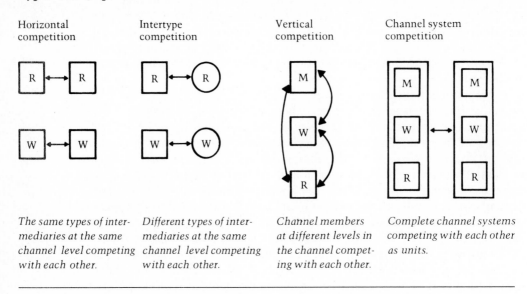

Horizontal competition	Intertype competition	Vertical competition	Channel system competition

The same types of inter-mediaries at the same channel level competing with each other.

Different types of inter-mediaries at the same channel level competing with each other.

Channel members at different levels in the channel compet-ing with each other.

Complete channel systems competing with each other as units.

shipping directly to the store or manufacturing plant, can all help to make scarce products more quickly available to channel members.

The Competitive Environment

There are four types of competition for the channel manager to consider:[7]

1. Horizontal competition
2. Intertype competition
3. Vertical competition
4. Channel system competition[8]

These are depicted in Figure 3.2.

Horizontal competition is competition between intermediaries of the same type. For example, merchant wholesalers vs. other merchant whole-salers, or full service department stores vs. other full service department stores, etc. This is the most visible and frequently discussed form of com-petition. In economic theory much of the treatment of competition deals

[7] These classifications of competition are based on the work of Joseph C. Palamountain, *The Politics of Distribution* (Cambridge, Mass.: Harvard University Press, 1955).

[8] This mode of competition is derived from the work of Bert C. McCammon, "The Emergence and Growth of Contractually Integrated Channels in the American Economy," in *Marketing and Economic Development*, ed. P. D. Bennett (Chicago: American Marketing Association, 1965), pp. 496–515.

with this horizontal type, although it is usually referred to simply as competition, and often the firms involved are producers or manufacturers rather than intermediaries.

Intertype competition is that competition between different types of intermediaries at the same channel level, for example, the discount store vs. the department store, or merchant wholesaler vs. agents and brokers.

Vertical competition refers to competition between channel members at different levels in the channel, such as retailer vs. wholesaler, wholesaler vs. manufacturer, or manufacturer vs. retailer. Under some conditions, vertical competition becomes vertical conflict whereby one channel member acts so as to impede another channel member's attempts to achieve his objectives. This conflict aspect will be discussed in detail in Chapter 5.

Finally, *channel system competition* refers to complete channels competing with other complete channels. In order for channels to compete as complete units, they must be highly organized and cohesive organizations. Such channels have been referred to as *vertical marketing systems* and are classified into three types: (1) corporate, (2) contractual, and (3) administered.[9] In corporate channels, production and marketing facilities are owned by the same company. Firestone Tire and Rubber Company and Sherwin Williams Paints are examples. In the contractual channel, independent channel members—producers or manufacturers, wholesalers and retailers—are linked together by a formal contractual agreement. Wholesaler sponsored voluntary chains, retailer cooperatives, and franchise systems are the three major forms of contractual marketing systems. Administered channel systems result from strong domination by one of the channel members (usually a manufacturer) over the other members. This dominant position is a function of the leverage that the dominant channel member can achieve over the others based on a monopoly of supply, special expertise strong consumer acceptance of its products, or other factors. Companies such as Scott (lawn products), Magnavox (home entertainment), Samsonite (luggage) and Coors beer are examples of firms which operate administered marketing channels.

Although little precise data exist, it is generally recognized that vertical marketing systems have grown dramatically during the last decade, with the most spectacular growth occurring for contractual systems, particularly franchises. As these vertical marketing systems take a larger and larger share of the total distribution system, the extent of channel system competition is also expected to grow.

In Chapter 14, where emerging channel trends are discussed, we will return to some of the developments in vertical marketing systems and discuss them in more depth.

From the preceding discussion we can see that the channel manager faces a competitive environment which is rather complex. Should he worry about horizontal, intertype, vertical, or channel system competi-

---

[9]McCammon, "Emergence and Growth," pp. 498–504.

tion, or perhaps all of these? Fortunately, it is unlikely that he will face all of these types of competition simultaneously. Nevertheless, he should be sufficiently familiar with these four different types of competition so that he can recognize and distinguish among them. In practice, some of these competitive forms are subtle and develop insidiously. This is particularly the case for channel system competition. For example: In early 1976 United Airlines made available to independent travel agents its own automated reservation and ticketing equipment which links the agents to United's central computerized reservation system. United believed this would give it a strong competitive edge over the other airlines in attracting a larger share of passengers from independent travel agents. In the context of the four categories of competition previously discussed, United's move belongs in the realm of channel system competition. It was an attempt to bring its marketing channel closer to the state of an administered system. This would presumably give United a strong competitive edge over the other airlines whose existing channels were more loosely aligned. This is the view apparently taken by two other airlines—American and T.W.A.—which shortly after hearing about United's action, decided to follow suit by offering travel agents their own automated systems in an attempt to neutralize United's competitive edge in channel domination.[10]

Thus, this seemingly minor strategy of supplying agents with reservation terminals, initiated by United, has touched off a competitive struggle to gain increased control over independent travel agents. As this competitive struggle continues, each strategy and counter strategy introduced by the airlines will be an attempt to further increase their control over the agents. Ultimately the airlines may compete as totally administered marketing systems.

The foregoing discussion suggests that an understanding of the various types of competition affecting the channel provides the channel manager with a sharper focus to discern what is happening in the competitive environment. As we proceed through the text we will deal with many types of decisions which the channel manager must face. Many of these decisions will require a consideration of the competitive environment faced by a firm or complete channel. A facility for recognizing and distinguishing among horizontal, intertype, vertical, and channel system competition is crucial for developing an analysis and strategy that is on target.

The Socio-Cultural Environment

The structure of the marketing channel is significantly affected by the socio-cultural environment within which it exists. Indeed, some channel

---

[10]"American Air, TWA To Offer Travel Agents Automated Systems," *Wall Street Journal*, (2 February 1976): 2.

analysts argue that this is the major force affecting channel structure.[11] A number of studies of channel structure in different parts of the world lend support to this view. For example, Wadinambiaratchi studied channels for consumer goods in several developing countries, as well as in Japan, and found wide variations in channel structures, which he attributed to their different "social, psychological, cultural, and anthropological climates."[12] Figure 3.3 shows these variations in channel structure. A major study by Hall et al., of distribution channels in Great Britain and North America,[13] others by Guirdham in Western Europe,[14] Galbraith and Holten in Puerto Rico,[15] Baker in tropical Africa[16] and several others[17] also lend support to this proposition. Take, for example, the case of tropical Africa. In some of the countries it is not unusual to find as many as ten levels of channel structure for imported consumer goods.[18] Most of the very small retail intermediaries, often referred to as "mammy traders," deal in tiny quantities of products, such as a handful of salt, half a bar of soap, or two or three cigarettes. Western observers, as well as some government officials in tropical African countries, are often appalled at this, believing it to be a highly irrational and inefficient channel structure. These observers, however, make the mistake of failing to consider the socio-cultural context within which this channel structure exists. That is, the seemingly archaic channels with layers upon layers of tiny middlemen are quite rational and efficient when due allowance is made for the socio-cultural factors involved. In terms of tropical Africa these include a wide geographic dispersion of the population, extremely limited consumer mobility, and a necessary tradition of hand to mouth buying. Given these conditions, a modern Western style supermarket would actually be highly irrational and inefficient.

Clearly then, the channel manager must be sensitive to the socio-cultural environment of the marketing channel when the channel extends into foreign cultures. But the channel manager does not have to extend the marketing channel overseas or into developing countries to find "strange" environments. Change, and the accelerating pace of change of socio-cultural variables right here at home can make what once seemed a tried and true domestic environment appear almost equally as strange as a foreign one.

[11] See for example: Jac L. Goldstucker, "The Influence of Culture on Channels of Distribution," in *Marketing and the New Science Planning*, ed. Robert L. King (Chicago: American Marketing Association, 1968), pp. 468–73.

[12] George Wadinambiaratchi, "Channels of Distribution in Developing Economies," *Business Quarterly*, (Winter 1965): 74–82.

[13] Margaret L. Hall, John Knapp, and Christopher Winsten, *Distribution in Great Britain and North America* (London: Oxford University Press, 1961).

[14] Maureen Guirdham, *Marketing: The Management of Distribution Channels* (Oxford: Pergamon Press, 1972), pp. 91–99.

[15] J. K. Galbraith and Richard H. Holton, *Marketing Efficiency in Puerto Rico* (Cambridge, Mass.: Harvard University Press, 1955).

[16] Raymond W. Baker, "Marketing in Nigeria," *Journal of Marketing*, 29 (July 1965): 40–48.

[17] See for example the selections in: Reed Moyer and Stanley C. Hollander, eds., *Markets and Marketing in Developing Economies* (Chicago: American Marketing Association), 1968.

[18] Baker, "Marketing in Nigeria," pp. 40–45.

Figure 3.3
Marketing Channel Structures in Developing Countries and Japan

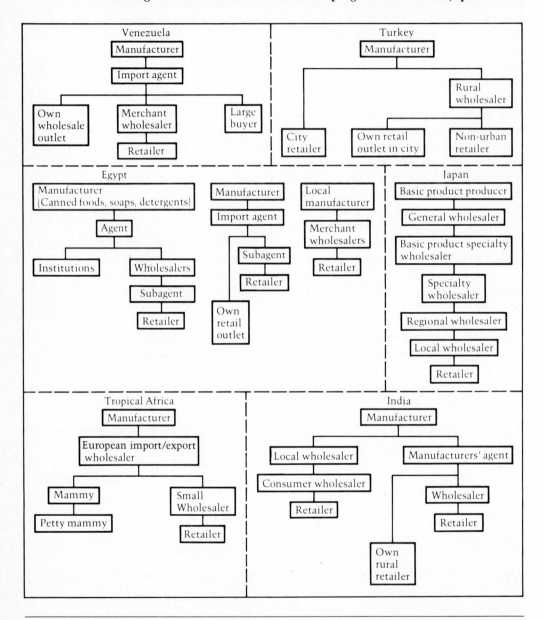

An in-depth discussion of these changing socio-cultural patterns is far beyond the scope of this chapter. Our discussion, therefore, will be limited to some of the more fundamental socio-cultural developments occurring in the United States and their possible implications for channel strategy.

Growth of Higher Education

As of 1979, almost ten million students were enrolled in institutions of higher learning in the United States. This large student population includes an increasingly higher proportion of older students who have returned to school to prepare for or further their careers, as well as those who attend for the sense of personal growth and enrichment provided by a college education.

The large numbers of people of all ages exposed to higher education raises the level of sophistication and broadens the range of tastes of the U.S. population. In their role as consumers, people will be sharper and more demanding of those who make and sell the products they buy. Specifically, consumers will demand more information and more services from all of the channel members. They will, for example, want to know more about the quality of products, the ingredients or components used in them, how they can be used for maximum benefit and what kinds of warranties are being offered. They will want the products to be easily and quickly available, attractively displayed, and sold through channel members who stand behind and service the products. In short, to meet the demands of an increasingly educated and sophisticated consumer market, all of the channel members will have to become more effective and efficient in performing distribution tasks.[19]

Changing Role of Women

One of the most fundamental and widely discussed socio-cultural changes of the last several decades has been the changing role of women. The 1970s probably represented the period of most rapid change, but changes will continue to occur for the remainder of this century. Women now have far more choices available to them than the traditional role of housewife. New opportunities have emerged in recent years for women to become well educated, to obtain employment outside the home, to limit the size of the family, and to end an unsatisfactory marriage.

This new range of options or freedoms, which are encompassed by the term "women's liberation," has already had, and will continue to have,

[19] See for example: Bert Rosenbloom, "The Department Store and Mass Merchandiser: Marketing Challenges and Strategic Responses," in *Competitive Structures in Retail Markets: The Department Store Perspective*, eds. Ronald W. Stamphl and Elizabeth Hirschman (Chicago: American Marketing Association, 1980), pp. 168–177.

very important implications for distribution. In particular the growth of women's liberation and career oriented women may lessen the role of women as the main buyers for the family unit, or at least reduce the time available for shopping.[20] Hence, retailers will be called on to make it much easier and quicker for women to shop. In-home shopping may enjoy a much larger role in retailing than at present. Channel managers may want to rethink their channel strategies for reaching the career and working women market segments by emphasizing retail participants or methods of retailing which are particularly well suited to serving the needs of this market.

The Emergence of Minority Groups

The emergence of minority groups, especially Black and Hispanic Americans during the last decade, has been reflected in more economic and political power for both minority consumers and entrepreneurs.

Minority businesses, especially in the retail trades, are expected to grow during the 1980s and beyond. Many of these minority owned businesses will specialize in serving minority markets. The manufacturer that wants to reach minority group target markets is therefore likely to find that an increasing number of the channel members needed to distribute products to these markets will also be from minority groups. Thus, to an increasing extent a manufacturer's ability to sell products in minority markets will be dependent upon developing a strong relationship with minority group channel members. Old patterns of prejudice and discrimination which may still be practiced by some firms, even if inadvertently, will make less sense than ever. Astute manufacturers will realize that minority channel members provide a unique and valuable resource for understanding the needs of minority consumers and for developing marketing strategies that meet those needs. In short, minority channel members increasingly will hold the key to securing strong distribution in minority markets.

Changing Family Life Cycle Patterns

The American family has undergone some significant changes in recent years which have changed the lifestyles of many people. Among the most important of these are the following:[21]

1. Families have become smaller with the average couple now having only two children.

---

[20] For a study that reports contrary findings on the shopping behavior of working women see: Myra H. Strober and Charles B. Weinberg, "Strategies Used by Working and Nonworking Wives to Reduce Time Pressures," *Journal of Consumer Research*, (March 1980): 338–348.

[21] Paul C. Glick, "The Future of the American Family," *Current Population Reports* Special Studies Series P-23, No. 78 (Washington, D.C.: U.S. Department of Commerce, 1979), pp. 1–3.

2. The period of child rearing has been shortened by about three years, and the period after the last child leaves home has increased on the average by about eleven years. A married couple can thus expect to live as a child-free two some for about fourteen more years than couples of a generation ago.

3. Seven percent of the U.S. population now lives alone as one-person households.

4. The number of unmarried couples (of opposite sexes) living together is growing rapidly. In 1977 nearly two million people were in this category, an eight percent increase over 1970.

These changing patterns in the life cycle of American families will significantly influence patterns of consumer shopping behavior which, in turn, will have implications for channel management strategy. For example, the growth of smaller families, childless couples, single people, and single people living together means higher levels of discretionary income and more freedom for people to purchase and use sophisticated and expensive consumer goods. Such products as the home computer, sophisticated electronic games, video disc recorders, and large projection television sets are already making a strong impact on consumers who have the discretionary income to afford such products as well as the time and lifestyles to make use of them. While most of these products are still distributed through traditional channels, new types of specialized distributors and retailers may be needed to market such products successfully in the future. Specialized stores that appeal to more sophisticated consumers are already appearing in the form of computer stores featuring home computers[22] and video stores that offer a wide array of sophisticated and expensive video equipment. Manufacturers will thus need to pay careful attention to changing consumer lifestyle patterns in order to make sure that their products are made available in marketing channels that appeal to a "new breed" of consumer.

Technological Environment

Technology is perhaps the most continually and rapidly changing aspect of the environment, particularly in industrialized societies. Everyone could probably recite long lists of technological advances occurring in their lifetimes or for that matter during the last decade. The widespread use of computers, supersonic air travel, radial tires, polyester fabrics, video tape, freeze dried coffee, and the ubiquitous electronic calculator are some of the more obvious examples.

In the face of this rapidly changing and accelerating technology, the

---

[22] See for example: "Computer Stores Tantalizing Opportunity Selling Computers to Consumers," *Business Week*, (September 28, 1981): 76–82.

channel manager is faced with the tasks of sorting out those developments that are relevant to his or her own firm and the participants in the marketing channel, and determining how these changes are likely to affect the channel participants. Obviously, this is not an easy task, or one that can be precisely programmed. Technological changes though continual, do not occur evenly or predictably over time.

While it is not possible to present a comprehensive list of technological developments impinging on the marketing channel, several presented below are indicative of the kinds of technological developments that should be watched carefully.

Teleshopping

Teleshopping (TS) refers to the purchase of goods by the consumer using a remote electronic device placed in the home. The device may be built into the television set, or it may be a separate attachment used in conjunction with the TV. The teleshopping device enables consumers to shop for products by simply tuning in to a shopping station which displays and even demonstrates many different kinds of products. Actual ordering of the product then takes place by telephone using a toll-free number or, in the case of more advanced systems, directly through an interactive cable linked with the shopping station. In the latter case the consumer simply presses a button on the teleshopping device and punches in his or her credit card number to order the item.

The technology for teleshopping already exists, and shopping stations have also emerged. The "Home Shopping Show," for example, a program offered by Modern Satellite Network, a cable-TV program service based in New York, transmits this show to some 3.5 million households.[23] The Monday-through-Friday program charges manufacturers $6,000 for a ten-minute product demonstration that is repeated five times in 35 days. Maytag washing machines, Encyclopedia Britannica and Walt Disney books are among the products that have been featured on the show.

A widespread acceptance of teleshopping, which some observers have predicted as a distinct possibility by the end of this decade, could have profound implications for marketing channel strategy.[24] If consumers are willing to buy a wide range of products at home by shopping from their TV sets, the need for traditional retail stores and their wholesale suppliers to store, display, promote, sell, and accept payment could be significantly reduced. Moreover, in addition to producers and manufacturers, new types of nonstore retailers specializing in retailing through teleshopping may appear in significant numbers to challenge traditional retail stores. Such a scenario is not at all far-fetched, especially when considered in

[23] John E. Cooney, "With Video Shopping Services, Goods You See on the Screen Can be Delivered to Your Door," *Wall Street Journal*, (July 14, 1981): 1.

[24] Larry J. Rosenberg and Elizabeth C. Hirschman, "Retailing Without Stores," *Harvard Business Review*, (July–August, 1980): 103–112.

light of such factors as the energy crisis (which has reduced consumer mobility), inflation (with its consequent increases in labor and operating costs for traditional retailers and wholesalers), and the reduced time available to the working women for shopping. All of these developments tend to favor the growth of teleshopping.

Thus, the channel manager should pay careful attention to the developments taking place in teleshopping. Large markets anxious to be served by teleshopping may be growing rapidly. Producers and manufacturers who are able to serve these markets via teleshopping on an effective and cost-efficient basis may gain a viable and profitable differential advantage in distribution strategy.

Electronic Scanners

Electronic scanners (ES) are laser devices that "read" prices and other information from product labels and record them at a rate of speed and accuracy far beyond the capacity of humans to do so manually. When coupled with the Universal Product Code (UPC) now widely appearing on many packaged goods, especially grocery products, the speed and efficiency of electronic scanners in processing consumer transactions is formidable. Rather than having the check-out clerk manually punch the price and inventory code of each item into a cash register or terminal one by one, the scanner allows the clerk to simply pass the products by the scanner to have all the necessary information recorded instantaneously. Moreover, the UPC coding eliminates the costly and time-consuming process of manually stamping prices on each item.

But electronic scanners are now going well beyond simple reading of product labels. When coupled with modern computerized inventory control systems, scanners can be used to replenish inventory electronically without having to rely on manually produced purchase orders. Using the check-out sales data from scanners, the computer can tally items sold and then automatically subtract items from those in inventory records. A computer generated order list of items falling below minimum inventory levels can then be transmitted to wholesalers and manufacturers. International Business Machines Corp. (IBM) is pushing out the frontiers of electronic scanner applications still further by developing computer software for what it has identified as 46 key scanning applications, including sales reporting to headquarters and calculating customer flow to better schedule employee hours. Finally, a scanner system built by National Semiconductor Corp. actually "talks" by calling out the prices of items as they pass the scanner.[25]

Electronic scanners coupled with modern inventory management systems are thus enabling retailers, especially supermarkets, drug chains, and mass merchandisers, to improve their productivity by making it pos-

[25] "Supermarket Scanners Get Smarter," *Business Week*, (August 17, 1981): 88–92.

sible for them to process larger volumes of transactions with less labor input.

From the manufacturer's point of view, this development presents both an opportunity and a challenge. Improved productivity on the part of retail channel members offers the manufacturer the opportunity to sell more of his products through retail outlets. On the other hand, the speed and efficiency of order processing made possible by scanning systems presents manufacturers (and wholesalers) with a challenge to be equally speedy and efficient in responding. In short, channel managers in supplier firms will have to give increased attention to improving *their* performance to match the expectations of their retail channel members.

Computerized Inventory Systems and Point of Sale

Closely related to electronic scanning devices is the use of point of sale (POS) terminals and computerized inventory management and control systems. Computerized inventory systems based on data received from point of sale terminals have created a revolution in inventory management and control at the retail level and, to a growing extent, at the wholesale level as well. While much of the growth in the use of these systems has been associated with large scale retailing organizations and a relatively small number of wholesaling firms, rapid advances in computer technology and substantial decreases in the cost of computer hardware have made computer based inventory management systems widely available to small retailers and wholesalers. In fact, most of the major computer manufacturers believe that great potential exists for rapid growth in the use of computer based inventory management systems by small business, especially among retailers and wholesalers.

Computerized inventory control systems have thus created a new world in retailing and wholesaling by not only drastically reducing the amount of labor and paperwork involved in inventory management, but by making available to managers a vast array of timely and valuable information for making better merchandising decisions. Information which might have taken weeks to obtain with a manual inventory system can now be obtained in minutes or seconds. Retailers and wholesalers of all sizes are now able to monitor the success or failure of products they handle much more closely than was possible just a few short years ago. If a newly introduced product is not catching on they know about it—and very quickly. When the rate of sales growth of a successful product begins to slow down they are able to spot this pattern at a very early stage. And products whose sales are stagnant are hardly likely to go unnoticed. On the other hand, hot selling products can also be spotted more quickly by retailers and wholesalers and re-ordering can be equally rapid.

Thus, superior inventory management and control made possible through sophisticated computer-based inventory management systems in growing use by retailers and wholesalers is a two edged sword for manufacturers.[26] On one edge, quicker responses by these channel members to fast-selling products can allow the manufacturer more time to plan ahead to increase production. But on the other edge, faster responses by retailers and wholesalers to slow sellers can mean a sudden halt in orders as these channel members use their up-to-the-minute, computer-generated inventory data to reduce their risk and protect their profit positions.

Legal Environment

Perhaps the most complicated, or at least the most technical, environmental category is the legal environment. The varied and continually proliferating court interpretations of laws impinging on channel management may appear to the channel manager as a morass of legal hodgepodge. Fortunately, the marketing channel manager need not be an expert on the legal aspects of marketing channels. Nor, given the technical nature of the subject, should he or she aspire to such a position as this would be a full time job in itself. Only trained legal experts are in a position to deal competently with the legal complexities relevant to the marketing channel. Nevertheless, the channel manager still needs a general knowledge of some legislation pertaining to the channel and familiarity with some of the basic legal issues relevant to channel management. This general background and awareness of the legal side of channel management will help the manager to communicate better with legal experts and perhaps help avoid potentially serious and costly legal problems that can arise in the management of marketing channels.

Legislation Affecting Marketing Channels

While there are many federal, state, local, and even international laws that can affect marketing channels, the following five pieces of federal legislation underlie most of the major channel management legal issues which we will discuss later in this chapter. These are:

1. The Sherman Antitrust Act (1890)
2. The Clayton Act (1914)
3. The Federal Trade Commission Act (1914)
4. The Robinson-Patman Act (1936)
5. The Celler-Kefauver Act (1950)

[26]Bert Rosenbloom, "The Retailer's Changing Role in the Marketing Channel," in *Marketing Educators Conference Proceedings*, ed. Neil Beckwith, et al. (Chicago: American Marketing Association, 1979) pp. 390–393.

Sherman Antitrust Act.   The Sherman Antitrust Act passed in 1890 is the fundamental antimonopoly law of the United States. The philosophy underlying this piece of legislation is that public welfare is served best through competition. Thus, the act was aimed at prohibiting practices which would restrain competition in the marketplace. Section 1 of the Sherman Act forbids contracts or combinations that restrain interstate or foreign commerce. The act provides federal courts with the power to break up or dissolve monopolies and also provides for criminal penalties against individuals involved in the creation of illegal monopolies.

Clayton Act.   The Clayton Act of 1914 was passed in an attempt to strengthen the Sherman Antitrust Act. The Clayton Act supplements the Sherman Act by specifically prohibiting such practices as price discrimination, tying clauses, exclusive dealing, intercorporate stockholding, and interlocking corporate directorates among competitive firms if these practices tend to substantially lessen competition or tend to create monopolies in any line of trade.

Federal Trade Commission Act.   This act, also passed in 1914, established the Federal Trade Commission (FTC). The FTC, as a federal agency, was granted the power to investigate and enforce, through the use of injunctions, unfair methods of competition in interstate commerce. Such "unfair methods of competition" include not only those specifically stipulated in the Sherman and Clayton Acts, but any other practices which might be injurious to competition. Thus, the Federal Trade Commission Act significantly expanded the scope of the federal government in the regulation of interstate commerce.

The Robinson-Patman Act.   This act was passed in 1936 as an amendment to the Clayton Act. The Robinson-Patman Act was aimed at prohibiting a variety of forms of price discrimination that tended to lessen competition but which were inadequately covered by the Clayton Act.

Sections 2a and 2b of the act prohibit persons engaged in interstate commerce from discriminating in price or terms of sale for goods of like grade and quality if the effects of such discrimination are to substantially lessen competition or foster monopolies in any line of commerce, or to injure, destroy, or prevent competition with any person who either grants or knowingly receives the benefit of such discriminations, or with customers of either of them. The act does, however, allow for price differentials to different customers, under the following circumstances:

1. When the differentials in prices charged to different customers do not exceed the differences in the cost of manufacture, sale, or delivery resulting from the differing methods or quantities in which such goods are sold or delivered to purchasers.
2. Price changes which result in price differentials to meet changing market conditions, avoid obsolescence of seasonal merchandise, to

dispose of perishables, or in the case of conducting legitimate close out sales or court imposed distress sales.

3. When the price differentials quoted to selected customers are offered in good faith to meet competitors' prices and are not intended to injure competition.

Section 2c of the act covers another form of price discrimination—unearned brokerage fees. Unearned brokerage fees are a device used by buyers to gain a lower price from the seller. Under this arrangement a buyer would set up a phony brokerage firm which was actually part of its own organization and bill the seller for the "cost" of the brokerage fee. The result of this, of course, is to reduce the effective price paid by the buyer to the seller. Those buyers who did not set up such brokerage schemes would thus pay a higher price. Since typically those buyers who were able to set up such phony brokerage schemes were large scale businesses, smaller businesses were at a significant disadvantage. Such practices were common before passage of the Robinson-Patman Act.

Sections 2d and 2e of the act cover what is perhaps the most nebulous area of price discrimination in marketing channels—that of promotional allowances and services. Promotional allowances and services refer to various forms of assistance from the seller to the buyer. This is often in the form of cooperative advertising allowances, payments for displaying of the suppliers' products, point of purchase materials, catalogs, display equipment, training programs, management assistance, and a variety of others (see Chapter 11).

In order to legally offer such promotional allowances and services to customers, sellers must do so on a proportionally equal basis to all other customers distributing the sellers' products.

Celler-Kefauver Act.   This act, passed in 1950, was an amendment to Section 7 of the Clayton Antitrust Act which prohibited acquisitions or mergers that tended to lessen competition or create monopolies. The Celler-Kefauver Act broadened the scope of the Clayton Act so that the prohibitions against acquisitions and mergers that tended to lessen competition and foster monopolies as a result of horizontal mergers between firms would also apply to vertical mergers and acquisitions as well. Thus, the act is particularly relevant to situations involving vertical integration through acquisitions and mergers. In essence, such vertical integration is prohibited if it tends to substantially lessen competition or foster monopolies.

Legal Issues in Channel Management

Having discussed some of the basic federal legislation underlying the legal environment of marketing channels, we now turn our attention to some of the major legal issues in channel management which are affected by this legislation.

Dual Distribution. Dual distribution refers to the practice whereby a producer or manufacturer uses two or more different channel structures for distributing the same product to his target market. The selling of the same or similar products under different brand names for distribution through two or more channels is also a form of dual distribution.

Dual distribution, which is a common practice, is not illegal per se under federal antitrust laws. Antitrust controversies have emerged, however, in such cases when a firm distributes through its own vertically integrated channel in competition with independent channel members at the wholesale or retail levels,[27] a quite common distribution arrangement in the marketing of petroleum products, automotive tires, shoes, paint and drugs. Under such an arrangement, the manufacturer may gain an unfair competitive advantage by using his company-owned outlets to undercut the prices charged by the independents. This makes it very difficult for the independent distributors or dealers to compete and indeed may threaten their very existence. If such undercutting is carried to an extreme by a dominant manufacturer, the manufacturer could gain a monopoly position by driving independent distributors or dealers out of business. In recent years, therefore, the courts have taken the position of requiring a manufacturer with a dominant role in a particular product line to seek to preserve the independent distributors or dealers of that product if such independent distributors or dealers exist. Dual distribution arrangements that work to eliminate the independent distributor (or dealer) are inconsistent with this position.[28] Consequently, they may be viewed by the courts as tending to lessen competition and as such may be in violation of the antitrust provisions of the Sherman and Clayton Acts.

Exclusive Dealing. Exclusive dealing occurs when a supplier requires its channel members to sell only its products or to refrain from selling products from other suppliers which are directly competitive.

With an exclusive dealing arrangement the supplier gains a substantial degree of market protection from competitive products in the market areas covered by his channel members. If a channel member refuses to abide by the exclusive dealing arrangement, the supplier can cut him off from selling his products.

Such exclusive dealing arrangements are in violation of the antitrust provisions of the Clayton Act if their effect is to substantially lessen competition or foster monopolies. The substantiality test has usually been

---

[27] For further discussion of this issue see: Lee E. Preston and Arthur E. Schramm Jr., "Dual Distribution and Its Impact on Marketing Organizations," *California Management Review*, (Winter 1965): 59–69. William L. Shanklin, "Dual Distribution as a Source of Channel Conflict," *Proceedings of the Southern Marketing Association*, 1973, pp. 357–367.

[28] See for example: "Copy-Data Systems, Inc., et al. vs. Toshiba America, Inc." *Journal of Marketing*, (Winter 1980): 85.

based on three conditions:[29] (1) whether the exclusive arrangement excludes competitive products from a substantial share of the market, (2) whether the dollar amount involved is substantial, and (3) whether it is between large suppliers and a smaller distributor or dealer where the supplier's disparate economic power can be inherently coercive. If any or all of these conditions exists, the exclusive dealing arrangement may be open to attack as anticompetitive under both the Sherman Act and the Federal Trade Commission Act.[30] For example:

An exclusive dealing arrangement between Pillsbury Co. and Kraft has recently come under FTC attack based on the share of market and dollar volume provisions related to exclusive dealing.[31] Pillsbury is the nation's largest manufacturer of refrigerated dough bakery products with sales in excess of 200 million dollars, and fifty-five percent of the market. The Kraft Company served as distributor of these products to retail stores. Under the exclusive dealing agreement, Kraft was not permitted to distribute refrigerated dough products of other manufacturers. The FTC charged that the large volume and high market share enjoyed by Pillsbury Co. in the sale of refrigerated dough products and protected by the exclusive dealing arrangement with Kraft tended to lessen competition in the sale of such products. In response to the FTC's charge, Pillsbury and Kraft consented to change their exclusive dealing arrangement to allow other manufacturers of competitive products to distribute through Kraft.

Full-Line Forcing.   This practice exists when a supplier requires channel members to carry a broad group of its products (full-line) in order to sell any particular products in the supplier's line.

Full-line forcing is practiced to varying degrees in a wide range of industries. It represents, up to a point, a legitimate effort by the manufacturer to see that a broad range of products is carried by the channel members and to discourage "cherry picking" by channel members of only the "hottest" items in the manufacturer's product line.

The antitrust issue emerges when the full-line forcing occurs to such an extent that it prevents other suppliers from selling competitive lines through channel members who are loaded up with the products of the supplier practicing full-line forcing.

One illegal use of a type of full-line forcing, known in the movie industry as "block booking," was practiced by Twentieth Century–Fox in the distribution of the spectacularly successful film *Star Wars*:[32] Twen-

---

[29] William L. Trombetta and Albert L. Page, "The Channel Control Issue Under Scrutiny," *Journal of Retailing*, (Summer 1978): 55.

[30] In some industries, exceptions to these provisions are often made. See: Marianne M. Jennings, "Exclusive Distributorships In Soda Pop Industry Exempted from Antitrust Laws," *Marketing News*, (January 23, 1981): 12.

[31] "Kraft and Pillsbury Agree They'll Relax Distribution Accord," *Wall Street Journal*, (February 17, 1981): 41.

[32] "Fox Film Is Fined $25,000 on a Charge of Forcing Block-Booking on Theaters," *Wall Street Journal*, (September 12, 1978): 8.

tieth Century–Fox Film Corporation was fined $25,000 by the Justice Department in the fall of 1978 after pleading no contest to a charge that the film corporation forced theaters that wanted to show the hit *Star Wars* to also show the *much* less popular film *The Other Side of Midnight* for a specified number of weeks. This effectively prevented the theaters from showing competitive films which might have had much better attendance. Thus, full-line forcing, if it is used, must not be practiced to such an extent that it restrains competitive products from getting into the channel of distribution.

Price Discrimination.   Price discrimination, which is covered specifically under the Robinson-Patman Act, refers to the practice whereby a supplier, either directly or indirectly, sells at different prices to the same class of channel members to the extent that such price differentials tend to lessen competition.

Discriminatory price differentials can take a variety of forms, some of which can be quite subtle. The classic case of the Simplicity Pattern Company illustrates just how subtle such price discrimination can be:

In 1959 the Federal Trade Commission charged the Simplicity Pattern Company with violating section 2e (see earlier discussion in this chapter) of the Robinson-Patman Act. The FTC argued that Simplicity, a manufacturer of dress patterns, had practiced discrimination in offering promotional services to retailers. Specifically, Simplicity offered a large chain of retail variety stores free catalogs and display cases but did not offer them to small, independent fabric stores. The FTC found Simplicity guilty of violating section 2e of the Robinson-Patman Act. Simplicity appealed to the circuit court which reversed the FTC's decision. On appeal by the FTC, the Supreme Court upheld the original FTC decision. In finding for the FTC, the court argued that since the variety stores and independent fabric stores were in competition, the granting of the free catalogs and display cases was a discriminatory promotional allowance favoring the variety stores, resulting in a competitive disadvantage to the independents. Simplicity argued that the variety stores and independent fabric stores were not actually in competition because their motives for selling patterns were different. In the case of the variety stores, the patterns were sold on a volume basis as an important merchandise item on which the stores intended to make a profit. For the fabric stores, however, Simplicity argued that patterns were sold on a limited basis as an accommodation to customers and were not a significant merchandise category on which the stores intended to make a profit. Hence Simplicity argued, if the stores were not actually in competition then the actions of Simplicity with respect to promotional allowances could not be viewed as impeding competition *because such competition had never existed.*

This case actually hinged on the competitive structure issue of whether the two types of stores actually were in competition with each

other in the sale of dress patterns. Subsequent observers of this case believe that had Simplicity had a better documented case for its argument of no competition between the variety and fabric stores, it might have won the case.[33]

It is, of course, debatable as to whether the outcome would have been different if the competitive structure issue had been better articulated. But the case does point up the kinds of subtle issues and interpretive difficulties that often emerge when dealing with the issues of price discrimination in channels of distribution as governed by the Robinson-Patman Act. It is no wonder then that confusion and inconsistencies have been common in court interpretations involving the Robinson-Patman Act throughout its history. Consequently, accurate generalizations about whether specific channel pricing policies and practices constitute price discrimination are extremely difficult to make.

Price Maintenance.   Price maintenance refers to a supplier's attempt to control the prices charged by its channel members for the supplier's products. The supplier, in effect, "dictates" the prices charged by channel members to their customers. Thus, prices at which products are sold by channel members are not based on the discretion of the channel members in response to market forces, but rather on the "orders" of the supplier.

Strangely enough, such anticompetitive price fixing (which is really what such practices amount to) was exempted from federal antitrust legislation through passage of the Miller-Tydings Act in 1937 and the McGuire Act in 1952. These acts exempted retail price fixing by manufacturers in states that permitted vertical pricing arrangements between manufacturers and retailers. Such vertical price fixing agreements were typically referred to euphemistically as *fair trade laws* and most states enacted various forms of these laws.

With the passage of the Consumer Goods Pricing Act in 1975, which repealed the Miller-Tydings and McGuire Acts, the legal basis for exempting state fair trade laws from federal antitrust legislation no longer existed. Consequently, most state fair trade laws were no longer legal.

Although the demise of fair trade laws removed the legal underpinnings for the practice of price maintenance in the marketing channel, the practice has by no means disappeared. Many manufacturers still try to influence the prices charged by their channel members. While direct attempts by the supplier to dictate through coercion the prices that existing channel members can charge their customers are clearly illegal, recent court decisions suggest that certain forms of persuasion by the manufacturer to get channel members to adopt the desired prices may be permissible. Specifically, if the manufacturer's attempts to influence the pricing decisions of channel members do not involve "coercion, conspiracy, threats, or warnings," the acquiescence of the channel members to the

---

[33] See for example: Lawrence X. Tarpey, "Who Is A Competing Customer?" *Journal of Retailing*, (Spring, 1969): 46–58.

manufacturer's pricing suggestions can be construed as having been based on the free will of the channel members.[34] That is, the channel members presumably have decided for themselves to price in accordance with the manufacturers' pricing objectives. Consequently, in order to stay within the law, the manufacturers' attempts at price maintenance must be handled very carefully so as to avoid any indication of an attempt to force their will on channel members. Manufacturers, in other words, can suggest, recommend, and attempt to persuade channel members to see things their way, but cannot go beyond these limits.

Refusal to Deal.   In general, suppliers may select whomever they want as channel members and refuse to deal with whomever they want. This right is based on the precedent established in a classic Supreme Court case of 1919 (U.S. v. Colgate and Co.) and is often referred to as the "Colgate Doctrine." The Court argued as follows:

"The Sherman Act does not restrict the long recognized right of a trader or manufacturer engaged in an entirely private business, freely to exercise his own independent discretion as to the parties with whom he will deal. And, of course, he may announce in advance the circumstances under which he will refuse to deal."

Thus, there are no legal barriers to sellers using their own criteria and judgement in the selection of channel members and announcing in advance the conditions under which they will refuse to deal.

In the case of existing channel members, however, there are legal restrictions on the seller's use of refusal to deal. Specifically, refusal to deal cannot be used coercively to cut off channel members who will not conform to policies stipulated by the seller which may be illegal or in restraint of trade. Further, the seller's refusal to deal must not be part of a joint action or conspiracy involving other channel members. A case involving Coors Beer illustrates such violations: [35]

During the early 1970s, price cutting retailers were put on notice by Coors that they would be refused sales if they did not adhere to the prices suggested by Coors. In the course of implementing this policy, the following events took place: (1) an area representative of Coors threatened to refuse sales to an offending retailer unless he would adhere to Coors' suggested prices; (2) Coors used its distributors to secure retailers' adherence to suggested minimum prices; (3) an area representative reported that a distributor planned to take appropriate action against a retailer who refused to sell at suggested prices; (4) a distributor reported that beer was not delivered to a retailer who cut prices; (5) a Coors area representative reported that action would be taken against a retailer who refused to raise his prices to a predetermined profit level.

[34] Trombetta and Page, p. 46.
[35] Trombetta and Page, p. 45.

Based on these events, the court ruled that Coors had clearly engaged in conspiracies with the distributors to get retailers to conform to Coors' policies that were in restraint of trade and had used refusal to deal in a coercive fashion to enforce anticompetitive pricing policies stipulated by Coors.

Thus, a supplier who uses refusal to deal as a means of enforcing what might be viewed as anticompetitive policies and/or uses other channel members as assistants in enforcing these policies is open to charges of anticompetitive behavior that may be in violation of federal antitrust legislation.[36]

Resale Restrictions.   Resale restrictions refer to a manufacturer's attempt to stipulate to whom channel members may resell the manufacturer's products and in what specific geographical market areas (territories) they may be sold.

Such restrictions can be very advantageous to both the manufacturer and the channel members. From the manufacturer's standpoint, the capacity to stipulate to whom products may be resold enables the manufacturer to retain and reserve certain accounts as "house accounts" (customers to whom the manufacturer sells directly) by prohibiting channel members from selling to those customers. Further, by delineating the particular territories in which channel members are allowed to resell the manufacturer's products, the manufacturer can maintain a high degree of control over the distribution of products. From the channel members' standpoint, the territorial restrictions minimize intrabrand competition because each channel member is in effect given a "protected" geographical market area in which to sell the manufacturer's products. Other channel members selling the same products are then prohibited from selling in a geographical market area other than their own.

In deciding whether such restrictions constitute an illegal restraint of trade, the courts had, for decades, used the so-called "rule of reason." Under this rule, the courts weighed the intentions of the supplier and the effects of the supplier's resale restrictions on the market. If the restrictions were not intended and did not appear to result in a restraint of trade they were generally allowed to stand.

In 1967, however, the landmark Supreme Court case of U.S. v. Arnold Schwinn and Co. radically changed this rule of reason approach.[37] The Supreme Court ruled that under the Sherman Act resale restrictions imposed by suppliers on their channel members are illegal per se. The court argued as follows:

"Under the Sherman Act, it is unreasonable . . . for a manufacturer to seek to restrict and confine areas or persons within which an article may

---

[36] For a related discussion see: "Continental Distributing Co., Inc., et al. v. Somerset Importers, Ltd.," *Journal of Marketing*, (Spring, 1979): 109.

[37] U.S. v. Arnold Schwinn and Co., 388 U.S. 365 (1967).

be traded after the manufacturer has parted with dominion over it. . . .
Once the manufacturer has parted with title and risk, he has parted with
dominion over the product, and his effort thereafter to restrict territory
or persons to whom the product may be transferred, whether by explicit
agreement or by silent confirmation or understanding with the vendee, is
per se a violation of Section I of the Sherman Act."

The effect of this ruling was to severely limit the legality of resale restrictions. Restrictive distribution policies which had for so many years been
practiced routinely by many firms were now open to attack as violations
of the Sherman Act.[38] Yet some ten years later, in 1977, another landmark
Supreme Court case (Continental T.V. Inc., et al. v. GTE Sylvania, Inc.)
overturned the Schwinn Case per se doctrine and essentially restored the
"rule of reason" doctrine to govern the use of resale restrictions. The
Court ruled that resale restrictions are not necessarily anticompetitive if
competition is viewed in a broader perspective. The Court argued that resale restrictions can have "redeeming virtues" by promoting interbrand
competition, including fostering new companies and new products. Further, by inducing competent and aggressive retailers to undertake new
efforts and offer special services and promotions, marketing efficiency can
be improved and smaller firms can be aided in competing with larger
ones. In essence, the Court's position was that while resale restrictions
might limit intrabrand competition (competition between middlemen
over the product of a particular manufacturer), they could foster interbrand competition (competition between different brands of the product).
    Even with the ruling in the GTE Sylvania Case, however, the legality
of resale restrictions is still up in the air.[39] The Court left the door open
for antitrust action against resale restrictions if such resale restrictions
have a "demonstrable economic effect." Hopefully, future cases and precedents will clarify the issue of resale restrictions once and for all—but
most authorities on this issue would not be likely to bet on this.

Tying Agreements.   Agreements whereby a supplier sells a product to a
channel member on condition that the channel member also purchase another product as well, or at least agrees to not purchase that product from
any other supplier, are known as tying agreements.
    Tying agreements put the supplier in a very advantageous position
with respect to the channel members with whom the tying arrangement
has been made. Since the channel member must accept tied products in
order to obtain other products from the supplier and since the channel
member is not free to purchase the tied products on the open market, the
supplier has a great deal of pricing leverage over the channel member. In
effect, the supplier is in a position to virtually dictate the terms of sale to

---

[38] For an excellent discussion and analysis of this case see: S. Powell Bridges, "The Schwinn Case: A Landmark Decision," *Business Horizons,* (August, 1968): 77–85. 20. 360 U.S. 55 (1959).
[39] For an excellent analysis of this case see: "Continental T.V., Inc., et al. v. GTE Sylvania, Inc." *Journal of
Marketing,* (January, 1978): 106–107.

channel members. Such tying agreements were for many years quite common in franchised marketing channels (see Chapter 14). The rationale for tying agreements used by suppliers, particularly those operating franchised channels, is that such agreements are necessary to assure the quality of the products sold by channel members and to protect the reputation of the supplier.

In recent years, the courts and the FTC have become increasingly concerned with the antitrust implications of tying agreements.[40] In 1971, a major case dealing with tying agreements in the well-known Chicken Delight fast food franchise established a precedent that significantly limited the use of tying agreements.[41] Based on the rulings emerging from this case, tying agreements that require channel members to purchase most or all of the products used in their businesses from the tied supplier are likely to be considered violations of the Sherman Act if the same products could be purchased from other suppliers. Only in cases where no other suppliers can provide the desired products to the specifications or quality standards of the supplier using the tying agreement is the tying agreement likely to be considered legal.

Vertical Integration.   Vertical integration occurs when a firm owns and operates organizations at other levels of the distribution channel (e.g. a manufacturer owning and operating its own wholesaling facilities and retail stores). Vertical integration is practiced by a number of manufacturers in a variety of industries, such as Goodyear and Firestone in tires, Sherwin Williams in paints, Singer in sewing machines, and Melville in shoes.

Vertical integration can occur as a result of growth and evolution of the firm whereby the firm decides to expand its organization to include wholesale and retail facilities as part of its organization. The reasons for doing so are often based on the firm's desire to gain scale economies and a high degree of control which it believes vertical integration can offer.

Vertical integration can also occur, however, through acquisition of and mergers with other firms at different levels of the channel. A manufacturer, for example, may acquire or merge with a wholesale or retailing organization.

Under the Celler-Kefauver Amendment to the Sherman Act (see earlier discussion), such vertical integration by acquisition and merger is subject to antitrust actions if the acquisitions or mergers tend to substantially lessen competition or foster monopoly. This can happen when the vertical integration occurs in a highly concentrated industry, thus eliminating an important source of supply to independent firms or significantly reduces the opportunity for competitive firms to reach the market. For example, a merger between Brown Shoe Company, a major shoe manufacturer, and G.L. Kinney Company, the largest independent chain of retail shoe stores in the U.S., was ruled illegal by the Supreme Court

---

[40] See for example: Shelby D. Hunt and John R. Nevin, "Tying Agreements in Franchising," *Journal of Marketing*, (July, 1975): 20–26.

[41] H. Siegal, et al. v. Chicken Delight, et al. 448 F. 2d 43 (1971).

because the merger might have prevented other shoe manufacturers from selling through Kinney.[42]

The Marketing Channel as an Open System

To gain a summary overview of the marketing channel in relation to its environment, it is useful for the channel manager to view the channel and its attendant facilitating agencies as an open system. An *open system* is one that adapts to its environment by changing the structures and processes of its components. This open system viewpoint has been implicit in much of the discussion of this chapter. That is, we have stressed the theme of environmental change and the need for channel management to adjust to these changes. In systems theory jargon, such adjustments are made to avoid *entropy* of the system (a disorganization or randomization which reduces the effectiveness of the system or can lead to its ultimate destruction). *Closed systems*, which by definition are self-contained and therefore do not interact with their environment, have an inherent tendency to move toward entropy. A closed systems viewpoint is inappropriate for systems which are in a dynamic relationship with their environments.

This is not the place to go into a detailed discussion of the fine points of systems theory and the nuances of open vs. closed systems. Our purpose in mentioning systems theory at the close of this chapter is simply to suggest in a more formal way the point which we have made repeatedly throughout this chapter: *Those responsible for managing the channel must be aware of the impacts of environment on the channel and make the appropriate strategic changes to adjust to them.*

Summary

Marketing channels develop and operate in a complex environment that is continually changing. These changes can have major effects on marketing channels. The channel manager must therefore be sensitive to environmental changes in order to *plan* effective marketing channel strategies for meeting these changes successfully. To do so, he or she must have a good understanding of the environment and how it can influence channel management.

While there are many ways to categorize the myriad of environmental variables, the following five-category taxonomy was used in this chapter: (1) economic environment, (2) competitive environment, (3) socio-cultural environment, (4) technological environment, and (5) legal environment.

When dealing with any or all of these environmental categories, the

---

[42]Louis W. Stern and Adel I. El-Ansary, *Marketing Channels* (Englewood Cliffs, New Jersey: Prentice-Hall, 1977), p. 344.

channel manager needs to consider the effects of environmental variables not only on his or her own firm and on the firm's target markets, but also on *all* of the channel members and participants.

The economic environment is probably the most obvious and pervasive category of environmental variables affecting all members and participants in the channel. Especially important are the effects of inflation, recession, and shortages. The fundamental challenge confronting the channel manager in the face of these economic developments is to help channel members weather these difficult economic conditions. *Advanced planning* to develop channel strategies for dealing with economic changes is the basis for successfully meeting this challenge.

The competitive environment facing the channel manager consists of (1) horizontal competition where similar firms at the same level of the channel compete with each other, (2) intertype competition where different types of firms at the same level of the channel compete, (3) vertical competition where firms at different levels in the same channel compete with one another, and (4) channel system competition where entire channels compete with each other. All of these types of competition must be carefully watched by the channel manager in order to determine how the competitive structure in which his or her channels operate is changing and what implications these changes may have for channel management strategy.

The socio-cultural environment has a significant impact on marketing channels because the structure of marketing channels reflects the socio-cultural environment within which they exist. So, the channel manager must carefully observe changing socio-cultural patterns in order to discern what implications these pattern changes will have for marketing channel strategy. Because of their profound influence in recent years, certain developments should be especially noted by the channel manager. These include the growing sophistication of more highly educated consumers, the changing role of women and its influence on patterns of shopping behaviors, the emergence of minority groups with their growing potential for playing a larger role as channel members, and changing family life cycles with their consequent influences on consumer life styles and buying behaviors.

The technological environment must be watched carefully to evaluate the effects of technological changes on marketing channels. Such developments as teleshopping, electronic scanners, and computerized inventory management systems already have had, and will continue to have, profound effects on marketing channel strategy.

Finally, the legal environment with its complex laws and continually changing precedents cannot be ignored by the channel manager. While the channel manager can not be expected to be an expert in the technicalities and nuances involved in the complex and changing legal environment affecting channel management, a general knowledge and awareness of some of the basic laws and legal issues is needed. In particular, the channel manager should be familiar with the basic provisions of the Sherman Act, Clayton Act, Federal Trade Commission Act, Robinson-Patman Act, and the Celler-Kefauver Act and how the provisions of this legislation affect such legal issues in channel management as (1) dual distribution, (2) exclusive dealing, (3) full-line forcing, (4) price discrimination, (5) price maintenance, (6) refusal to deal, (7) resale restrictions, (8) tying agreements, and (9) vertical integration through acquisitions and mergers.

By viewing the marketing channel as an open system, the channel manager is better able to view strategic adjustments to the environment as a means of avoiding entropy of the channel system.

Discussion Questions

1. How does the impact of the environment on channel strategy differ from the other major strategy areas of the marketing mix?
2. In dealing with the effects of environment on channel strategy, the channel manager has a lot more to think about. Discuss this statement.
3. Discuss the fundamental channel management issues associated with inflationary and recessionary periods in the economy.
4. How may shortages affect the various members of the marketing channel? What are some marketing mix strategies for dealing with shortages?
5. Explain the four types of competition discussed in the chapter. Why is it important to recognize these different forms of competition?
6. Marketing channels reflect the socio-cultural environments within which they exist. Explain this statement.
7. Discuss several major socio-cultural developments that have occurred in the United States during the past several decades. How have these developments affected marketing channel strategy and how might they affect it in the future?
8. Technological changes, though continual, do not occur evenly or predictably over time. Discuss the implications of this statement for channel management strategy.
9. How might teleshopping change the basic "distribution landscape" in the future?
10. Discuss the channel management implications of such technological developments as electronic scanners, point of sale systems, and computerized inventory management systems.
11. What is the underlying philosophy of the Sherman Act with respect to the role of competition vs. monopoly in promoting public welfare? Discuss.
12. Discuss the basic provisions of (1) the Sherman Antitrust Act, (2) the Clayton Act, (3) the Federal Trade Commission Act, (4) the Robinson-Patman Act, and (5) the Celler-Kefauver Act.
13. Exclusive dealing, full-line forcing, and tying agreements all have something in common. What is it? Discuss the antitrust implications of this common element.

14. Price maintenance, refusal to deal, and resale restrictions all represent attempts by the supplier to exercise control over his channel members. What are the legal limits on the degree of control the supplier can exercise through these three approaches?
15. Discuss the basic legal implications associated with the policies of dual distribution, price discrimination, and vertical integration through acquisitions and mergers.

Chapter 4
Behavioral Processes in Marketing Channels

In Chapter 1 we discussed the need for management to operate the marketing channel. By this we meant that the channel manager must play a major role in the development (design) and management of the channel. This is necessary if a channel structure which simply evolves in a haphazard fashion is to be avoided. Such channel structures are often less efficient than they should be and present needlessly difficult management problems. In Chapters 2 and 3 of the text we went on to discuss some of the basic background knowledge needed by the channel manager. Such fundamentals as the economic basis for the emergence of various channel participants, the characteristics of the participants, and the environmental constraints within which all of the channel participants operate were discussed.

In this chapter we turn to another kind of knowledge needed by the channel manager in order to operate the channel effectively—a knowledge of the behavioral dimensions of the channel. An understanding of the behavioral dimensions of marketing channels is necessary because the marketing channel is not simply a rationally ordered economic system devoid of social interactions and processes. On the contrary, the marketing channel is very much a *social system* subject to the same behavioral processes characteristic of all social systems.[1] Consequently the

[1]For a seminal discussion of the marketing channel as a social system see: Louis W. Stern and Jay W.

need for the channel manager to have knowledge of the behavioral processes occurring in marketing channels and an ability to apply this knowledge in the development and management of the marketing channel is an important part of the job.

The Marketing Channel as a Social System

Parsons and Smelser define a social system as:

". . . the system generated by any process of interaction on the sociocultural level, between two or more actors. The actor is either a concrete human individual (a person) or a collectivity . . ."[2]

Most actors in the marketing channel are collectivities (firms rather than individual persons). There are occasional exceptions in that some channel members are indeed comprised of one person—a one man retailer or broker for example. For the most part, however, the members of the marketing channel fit the latter part of Parsons' and Smelser's definition.

When these collectivities (firms or agencies) or individuals interact as members of the marketing channel, an interorganizational social system exists. So, the channel may no longer be viewed as simply an economic system affected solely by economic variables. Rather, the fundamental behavioral dimensions present in all social systems such as *conflict*, *power*, *role*, and *communication processes* come into play. A brief example involving the interaction of two channel members provides an initial overview of the operation of behavioral processes in the channel: A manufacturer of pipes produced two lines. A high quality first line with strong consumer brand preference and a lower quality second line with significantly less consumer brand preference. The manufacturer had been using a wholesaler to distribute both lines to retail pipe shops in a major East Coast metropolitan area. In light of the growing demand for his first line of pipes, the manufacturer decided to bypass the wholesaler and sell the line directly to the retail pipe stores. The wholesaler was expected to continue distributing only the second line. This intended behavior by the manufacturer (bypassing the wholesaler with the first line), however, quickly elicited a retaliatory response behavior by the wholesaler. The wholesaler informed the manufacturer that he would drop the second line

Brown, "Distribution Channels: A Social Systems Approach," in *Distribution Channels: Behavioral Dimensions*, ed. Louis W. Stern (New York: Houghton Mifflin Co., 1969), pp. 6–19. See also: Michael F. Foran and Anthony F. McGann, "A Scheme for Examining Marketing Channels as Social Systems," *Business Ideas and Facts*, (Fall 1974): 51–54; Louis W. Stern and Torger Reve, "Distribution Channels as Political Economies: A Framework for Comparative Analysis," *Journal of Marketing*, (Summer, 1980): 52–64; James R. Brown and Sherman A. Timmins, "Substructural Dimensions of Interorganizational Relations in Marketing Channels," *Journal of the Academy of Marketing Science*, (Summer, 1981): 163–173.

[2] Talcott Parsons and Neil J. Smelser, *Economy and Society: A Study in the Integration of Economic and Social Theory* (New York: The Free Press, 1956), p. 8.

of pipes if the manufacturer went through with his plan to bypass the wholesaler with the first line. Since the manufacturer still needed the wholesaler to distribute the second line, he decided not to go through with his original plan to drop the wholesaler.

It is apparent from this example that the actors in this channel (a manufacturer and a wholesaler) were interacting with each other in both economic and behavioral contexts. The behavior by the manufacturer and the wholesaler's response behavior may be viewed as a kind of bargaining process whereby each of the two jockeyed for a desired outcome. The outcome desired by the manufacturer was to sell the first line of pipes directly to the retailers in the East Coast market, and have the wholesaler continue to do a diligent job with the second line. The wholesaler, however, wanted to maintain the status quo.

Two of the underlying behavioral dimensions present in this example are *conflict* and *power*. Conflict arose in this case when each of the participants perceived the behavior of the other to be impeding the attainment of his desired outcome. Power was used in the bargaining process to resolve the conflict, with the wholesaler emerging as the "winner" because he achieved his desired outcome—maintenance of the status quo.

Two additional behavioral dimensions, *role* and *communication* were also present in the example, though their presence is more subtle than that of conflict and power. Role was involved because the differing roles of the manufacturer and wholesaler influenced their behaviors. Communication was used by the participants to send and receive "signals" about each other's behavior.

In the remainder of this chapter we discuss these basic behavioral processes of conflict, power, role, and communication in a marketing channels context. The emphasis will be on showing how these behavioral processes operate in the channel, and on their importance to the channel manager in the development and management of the channel.

Conflict in the Marketing Channel

Conflict is an inherent behavioral dimension in all social systems including the marketing channel. As Stern and Gorman state:

"In any social system, when a component perceives the behavior of another component to be impeding the attainment of its goals or the effective performance of its instrumental behavior patterns, an atmosphere of frustration prevails. A state of conflict may, therefore, exist when two or more components of any given system of action, e.g., a channel of distribution, become objects of each other's frustration."[3]

[3] Louis W. Stern and Ronald H. Gorman, "Conflict in Distribution Channels: An Exploration," in *Distribution Channels: Behavioral Dimensions*, ed. Louis W. Stern (New York: Houghton Mifflin Co., 1969), p. 156.

As an example of the emergence of conflict in the marketing channel, consider a manufacturer and a group of retailers linked together to form a marketing channel (and therefore a social system). An action by the manufacturer such as reducing the trade discount available to the retailers on some of his more popular products can foster a state of conflict. This is likely to happen if the retailers perceive the manufacturer's behavior to be impeding their opportunity to achieve certain goals that are dependent upon the manufacturer's existing trade discount structure. These goals could be in terms of sales volume, profits, share of market, or others. Hence, the manufacturer might become the object of the retailers' frustration, which in turn manifests itself in retaliatory behavior by the retailers. For example they might "football" (disparage) the manufacturer's products in the eyes of consumers.

Conflict vs. Competition

Conflict in the marketing channel should not be confused with competition which also occurs in the channel. Competition is behavior which is object centered, indirect, and impersonal. Conflict, on the other hand, as shown in the above discussion is direct, personal, and opponent centered behavior. Consequently in a conflict situation it is not the forces of the impersonal market that firms attempt to overcome, but other firms in the system with whom they are in conflict. Schmidt and Kochan make this distinction quite well:

". . . in the process of both competition and conflict the goals (of the various units) are perceived to be incompatible, and the units are striving respectively to attain these goals. In this context, competition occurs where, given incompatible goals, there is no interference with one another's attainment. The essential difference between competition and conflict is in the realm of interference or blocking activities."[4]

A concrete illustration of this distinction between competition and conflict can be seen in food marketing. An example of competition between supermarket retailers and manufacturers is the so-called "battle" of private vs. national brands. To call this a battle, struggle, or conflict is, in a stricter sense, a misnomer because what is actually taking place is competition. The attempts by manufacturers and supermarket retailers to gain wider acceptance of their respective brands is usually impersonal and market centered. That is, the parties are not engaged in direct blocking activities aimed at impeding each other's goals of increased consumer acceptance of their brands. Rather, for the most part, the parties com-

[4]Stuart M. Schmidt and Thomas A. Kochan, "Conflict: Toward Conceptual Clarity," *Administrative Science Quarterly*, 17 (September, 1972): 361. For further discussion on the distinction see: Louis W. Stern, Brian Sternthal, and C. Samuel Craig, "Managing Conflict in Distribution Channels: A Laboratory Study," *Journal of Marketing Research* (May, 1973): 169–70.

pete in the consumer market. The level of consumer acceptance for the manufacturer's vs. retailer's brand thus becomes a function of consumer preference.

On the other hand, some of the behavior of manufacturers and super-markets relating to grocery coupons belongs very much in the realm of conflict. The situation which has led to conflict between manufacturers and supermarkets is the practice of supermarkets' encouraging misre-demption by consumers. In one extreme case, several food chains were involved in a four-day "coupon war." Some of the stores were accepting any amount of coupons regardless of what products were purchased. One supermarket executive remarked that "Lines were way out into the park-ing lots, and the people were waiting two and three hours to get into the stores." Some people cashed in coupons worth several hundred dollars, and according to some estimates, the four-day total redemptions exceeded $300,000. Some of the manufacturers viewed this behavior by the super-markets as an attempt to make a mockery of their intended objectives in the use of coupons. Consequently heated conflicts between the manufac-turers and supermarkets resulted over how many coupons the manufac-turers would redeem.[5]

Causes of Conflict

A number of causes of conflict have been advanced by channel analysts. Little points to such causes as misunderstood communications, divergent functional specializations and goals of the channel members, and failings in joint decision making processes.[6] Assael suggests differing economic objectives, and ideological differences among channel members as causes of conflict.[7]

The most comprehensive list of conflict causes in the marketing chan-nel is that presented by Stern and Gorman. They identify the following seven as the fundamental underlying causes of channel conflict:[8]

1. Role incongruities
2. Resource scarcities
3. Perceptual differences
4. Expectational differences
5. Decision domain disagreements
6. Goal incompatibilities
7. Communication difficulties

[5] Roger M. May, "Grocery Coupons Are Seen Threatened by Growth of Fraudulent Redemptions," *Wall Street Journal*, (12 April 1976), p. 30.

[6] Robert W. Little, "Power and Leadership in Marketing Channels," *Proceedings of the American Market-ing Association*, (August, 1968): 6–7.

[7] Henry Assael, ed., *The Politics of Distributive Trade Associations: A Study in Conflict Resolution* (Hemstead, New York: Hofstra University Press, 1967), p. 413.

[8] Stern and Gorman, "Conflict in Distribution," pp. 157–61.

Role Incongruities.   A role is a set of prescriptions defining what the be-havior of position members should be. When applied to the marketing channel any given member of the channel has a series of roles which he or she is expected to fulfill. For example, a franchisor is expected to provide extensive management assistance and promotional support for his fran-chisees. In return the franchisees are expected to operate in strict accor-dance with the franchisor's standard operating procedures. If either the franchisor or franchisee deviates from the given role (e.g., the franchisee decides to institute some of his or her own policies) a conflict situation may result. We will discuss the concept of the role as it applies to the mar-keting channel in greater depth in a later section of this chapter.

Resource Scarcities.   This refers to conflict stemming from a disagree-ment between channel members over the allocation of some valuable re-sources needed to achieve their respective goals. A common example of this is the allocation of retailers between a manufacturer and the whole-salers. In this case the retailers are viewed by both the manufacturer and the wholesaler as a valuable resource necessary to achieve their distri-bution objectives. Frequently the manufacturer will decide to keep some of the higher volume retailers as *house accounts*. This leads to objections by the wholesaler over what is considered to be an unfavorable allocation of this resource (the retailers). This kind of dispute often leads to conflict.

Perceptual Differences.   Perception refers to the way an individual se-lects and interprets environmental stimuli. The way such stimuli are per-ceived, however, is often quite different from objective reality. In a mar-keting channel context, the various channel members may perceive the same stimuli but attach quite different interpretations to them. A com-mon example of this in the marketing channel is in the use of point of purchase displays. The manufacturer who provides these usually per-ceives POP as a valuable promotional tool needed to move products off the retailer's shelves. The retailer, on the other hand, often perceives this point of purchase material as useless junk which serves only to take up valuable floor space.

Expectational Differences.   Various channel members have expectations about the behavior of other channel members. In practice, these expecta-tions are predictions or forecasts concerning the future behaviors of other channel members. Sometimes these forecasts turn out to be inaccurate, but the channel member who makes the forecast will take action based on the predicted outcomes. By doing so, a response behavior can be elic-ited from another channel member which might not have occurred in the absence of the original action. In effect, a self-fulfilling prophecy is cre-ated. The case of W. T. Grant, the large variety store chain which went bankrupt, offers a good example of this phenomenon. Many suppliers who were aware of Grant's financial difficulties expected that Grant would not be able to pay its bills, even though Grant had been paying its bills promptly. Nevertheless, based on their expectations, the suppliers reduced or eliminated their credit shipments to Grant, creating bitter conflicts which contributed to Grant's failure and, of course, its inability to pay its bills.

Decision Domain Disagreements.   Channel members explicitly or implicitly carve out for themselves an area of decision making which they feel is exclusively theirs. In contractual channel systems, such as a franchise, these decision domains are quite explicit and usually meticulously spelled out in the franchise contract. McDonalds, for example, has a detailed manual specifying the allocation of decision-making responsibilities between the franchisor and the franchisee. But in the more traditional loosely aligned channels, made up of independent firms, the decision domains are sometimes "up for grabs." Hence, conflicts can arise over which member has the right to make what decisions.

A traditional and pervasive example of this has been in the area of pricing decisions. Many retailers feel that pricing decisions are in their decision-making domain. Some of the manufacturers supplying these retailers, however, believe that they should have a say in price-making decisions. Fair trade laws, which were made illegal in 1975, were in some cases supported by manufacturers because the force of law helped them to extend their domain into pricing decisions at the retail level. Even with the demise of formal fair trade laws, however, a substantial amount of de facto fair trading still occurs. Under this approach, the manufacturer subtly (and sometimes not so subtly) makes it known to the retailer that if he does not abide by the manufacturer's pricing "recommendations" he will lose the product line. Retailers who need price flexibility in highly competitive markets often feel that by attempting to dictate pricing, the manufacturer is encroaching on the retailer's domain. The result is sometimes long and bitter conflicts.[9]

Goal Incompatibilities.   Each member of the marketing channel has his or her own goals. When the goals of two or more of the members are incompatible, conflict can result. Incompatible goals often arise between channel members. Take for example a men's shirt department in a department store selling three brands of shirts, Arrow, Van Heusen, and Gant. The goals of the shirt department are set in terms of sales volume, gross margin, and contribution to the store's overhead and profits. It makes little difference to the department manager and store executives which particular brand of shirts it sells so long as the department meets or exceeds its goals. The shirt manufacturers, on the other hand, "sink or swim" on goals set in terms of sales volume and market share for their particular brands. To them it makes a world of difference which brands are selling at the retail level. If one of these shirt manufacturers feels that some

[9] For a related discussion dealing with the domain of warranties in the marketing channel see: Laurence P. Feldman, "New Legislation and the Prospect for Real Warranty Reform," *Journal of Marketing*, (July, 1976): 43.

retailers are doing a particularly poor job with the brand he may view the actions of these retailers as impeding the attainment of his or her goals. In so doing he has planted the seeds for a conflict over divergent goals.

Communication Difficulties. Communication is the vehicle for all interactions among the channel members whether such interactions are cooperative or conflicting. A foul up or breakdown in communications can quickly turn a cooperative relationship into a conflicting one. For example, manufacturers often make changes in product designs, prices, and promotional strategies. Resellers generally feel that they are entitled to ample advance notice of such changes so that they can make appropriate strategy adjustments if necessary. If adequate communication is not provided, and this failing results in negative consequences for a channel member, a serious conflict can result. One such case occurred when a manufacturer of stereo equipment changed the warranty provisions on speakers from one year to ninety days but neglected to communicate this change to his retailers. It was not until some customers with speaker problems had returned them to the dealers after ninety days for warranty service that this change became apparent to most of the retailers. This placed the retailers in the unenviable position of having to tell these customers that they would have to pay for the repairs. Many of the dealers were resentful of the manufacturer's failure to communicate the changed warranty policy. Some even dropped the line outright.

Effects of Conflict

A number of relationships on the effects of conflict on marketing channels have been postulated by channel analysts. Alderson, in one of the earliest works on the subject, argued that the effects of conflict on channel performance are generally negative.[10] Stern has also taken a similar position though he points to possible positive effects as well.[11] Dixon and Layton suggest that conflict can result in a threat to the survival of the channel,[12] while Assael has emphasized the possible positive effects of conflict on various aspects of the channel.[13]

The key question about the effects of conflict from the channel manager's point of view is how conflict affects channel efficiency. Does conflict reduce the efficiency with which distribution objectives are achieved? Can

[10]Wroe Alderson, *Dynamic Marketing Behavior* (Homewood, Illinois: Richard D. Irwin, 1965), pp. 239–258.

[11]Louis W. Stern, "The Interorganizational Management of Distribution Channels: Prerequisites and Prescriptions," in *New Essays in Marketing Theory*, ed. George Fisk (Boston: Allyn and Bacon, 1971), pp. 301–314.

[12]Donald F. Dixon and Roger A. Layton, "Initiating Change in Channel Systems," in *New Essays in Marketing Theory*, ed. George Fisk (Boston: Allyn and Bacon, 1971), p. 315.

[13]Henry Assael, "The Constructive Role of Interorganizational Conflict," *Administrative Science Quarterly* (December, 1969): 573–575.

it increase efficiency? Might it not have any effect at all? Unfortunately little empirical data on these questions are available.[14] Nevertheless, some useful conceptual models have been presented on how conflict can affect channel efficiency.[15] Before discussing these relationships, however, it is necessary to define more precisely what we mean by channel efficiency. *Channel efficiency* may be defined as:

The degree to which the total investment in the various inputs necessary to achieve a given distribution objective can be optimized in terms of outputs.[16]

The greater the degree of optimization of inputs in carrying out a distribution objective, the higher the efficiency and vice versa. These inputs can include anything necessary to achieve the distribution objective. For example, a manufacturer may set a distribution objective of getting 80 percent of his or her wholesalers to carry a new product line. Suppose that in an attempt to achieve this objective, the manufacturer encounters strong resistance from wholesalers, most of whom feel that they are already carrying too much inventory from this manufacturer. The resulting conflict could cause the manufacturer to direct the sales force to spend an extraordinary amount of time and effort to convince the reluctant wholesalers to carry the new line. In this example, extra input would be needed (time and effort of salespeople) to achieve the distribution objective and this extra input could be measured in added dollar costs. Had the manufacturer been able to gain the acceptance of the new line with less sales effort (and without increasing other inputs) he or she could have achieved the distribution objective with less total input; and a higher degree of channel efficiency would have resulted.

This concept of channel efficiency provides the channel manager with a criterion against which to appraise the effects of conflict. Thus, conflict can be seen as a behavioral dimension that can influence how efficiently distribution objectives are achieved. Some conceptual models are presented below which illustrate possible effects of conflict on this concept of channel efficiency.

Negative Effect–Reduced Efficiency. Figure 4.1 illustrates the most commonly held belief about the effect of conflict on channel efficiency. Figure 4.1 shows a negative relationship indicating that as the level of conflict increases, channel efficiency declines.

An example of this relationship can be seen in situations such as the following: A large wholesaler (W) carries similar products from two manufacturers (M_1) and (M_2). At some point M_1 notices that the wholesaler has

---

[14] The existing work that does appear in the literature will be discussed in a later section of this chapter.

[15] This section is based heavily on the author's article: "Conflict and Channel Efficiency: Some Conceptual Models for the Decision Maker," *Journal of Marketing* (July, 1973): 26–30.

[16] Ibid., p. 27.

greatly reduced purchases from him. M_1 is concerned about the reduction and makes a decision to attempt to regain the previous volume level from this wholesaler. A distribution objective has now been set by M_1 to regain the previous volume from W. The level of input that M_1 uses to achieve this objective will determine the level of channel efficiency achieved. Suppose M_1 after talking to W learns that the latter is doing quite well with the products from M_2 and feels that he cannot carry more products from M_1. M_1 becomes angry and makes a threat to W to cut off other product lines which W still buys and finds very profitable. Yet suppose as a reaction to the threats from M_1, W simply further reduces purchases from M_1. A conflict situation has now been created whose level continues to increase with each subsequent action of the two channel members. M_1 not only finds it necessary to devote more and more sales effort to get W to give in, but also increases advertising expenditures to create more consumer pull for added leverage on W to carry the new product line. It has now become increasingly difficult for M_1 to move products through the channel. That is, M_1 has to use higher levels of inputs (personal selling and advertising) to do so. Thus, the level of channel efficiency from M_1's standpoint declines; and as the conflict becomes more intense (movement along the horizontal axis in Figure 4.1), M_1's efficiency level continues to decline.

Figure 4.1
Conflict and Channel Efficiency–Negative Effect

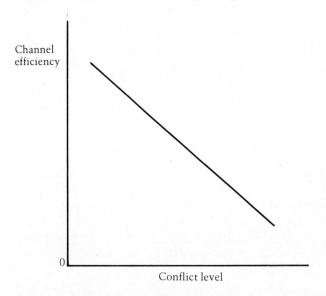

Source: Bert Rosenbloom, "Conflict and Channel Efficiency: Some Conceptual Models for the Decision Maker," *Journal of Marketing* 37 (July 1973): 28. Reprinted with permission from the *Journal of Marketing*, published by the American Marketing Association.

Figure 4.2
Conflict and Channel Efficiency–No Effect

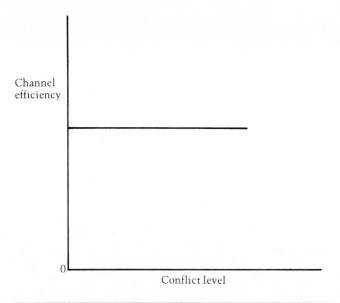

Channel
efficiency

0

Conflict level

Source: Bert Rosenbloom, "Conflict and Channel Efficiency: Some Conceptual Models for the Decision Maker," *Journal of Marketing* 37 (July 1973): 28. Reprinted with permission from *Journal of Marketing*, published by the American Marketing Association.

No Effect–Efficiency Remains Constant.   Another possible relationship between conflict and channel efficiency is shown in Figure 4.2. In this relationship, the existence of conflict has caused no change in channel efficiency. Hence, the effect of conflict on input levels necessary to achieve distribution objectives is insignificant.

This type of relationship is thought to exist in channels that are characterized by a high level of dependency and commitment among the channel members. That is, the parties to the conflict, consciously or unconsciously, are aware of the necessary nature of their relationship to one another. They feel that their need for each other to achieve their respective distribution objectives is so great that the conflict can have no more than a superficial effect on their efficiency in operating the channel to achieve these objectives. In effect, the channel members learn to live with the conflict so that even in the face of hostilities and acrimony, channel efficiency is not affected.

Positive Effect–Efficiency Increased.   Figure 4.3 shows a third possible effect of conflict on channel efficiency. Here conflict is shown to cause an increase in channel efficiency. An example will help to illustrate this possibility. A wholesaler finds that a manufacturer with whom a very profitable relationship had been enjoyed has decided to bypass the wholesaler

Figure 4.3
Conflict and Channel Efficiency–Positive Effect

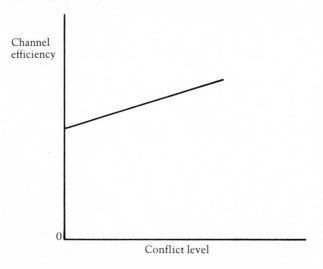

Source: Bert Rosenbloom, "Conflict and Channel Efficiency: Some Conceptual Models for the Decision Maker," *Journal of Marketing* 37 (July 1973): 29. Reprinted with permission from *Journal of Marketing*, published by the American Marketing Association.

with certain products and sell these directly to retailers. The wholesaler at first reacts angrily towards the manufacturer's behavior. The seeds of conflict might develop further and ultimately lead to a conflict situation which could negatively affect channel efficiency for one or both of the parties to the conflict (see "Negative Effect" above and Figure 4.1). The conflict might, however, serve as an impetus for either or both of the channel members to reappraise their respective policies. For example, the wholesaler might overcome his or her anger and focus on his or her own performance and find it lacking. The wholesaler might find that the previous level of selling effort on behalf of some of the manufacturer's products was not as high as it could have been. Thus, he or she might view the manufacturer's behavior as justified under the circumstance and attempt to make some changes to do a more effective selling job.

The manufacturer might also reexamine policies and find efforts in support of the wholesaler to be lacking. The manufacturer may decide that more special efforts and inducements are necessary to maintain the support of the wholesaler.

The result of this two-party reappraisal could be a reallocation of inputs based on the comparative advantages of each channel member for performing the distribution tasks necessary to achieve their respective distribution objectives. The reallocation of inputs between the two channel members stemming from the reappraisal could represent a better division of labor resulting in increased channel efficiency for one or possibly both channel members.

Conflict and Channel Efficiency–General Curve. By combining the above models, a general curve showing the possible effects of conflict on channel efficiency results. This is shown in Figure 4.4.

In Figure 4.4 the level of conflict represented by OC_1 suggests a tolerance range over which the conflict has no effect on channel efficiency. Over the range C_1C_2, the effect of conflict is positive, while beyond C_2, the effect is negative. The level C_2 in Figure 4.4 represents a threshold effect of conflict. Once the tolerance range is passed, the higher the level of conflict between C_1C_2, the greater the level of channel efficiency. Beyond C_2 (the threshold level) the greater the conflict level, the lower will be the level of channel efficiency.

Managing Channel Conflict

Our previous discussion on conflict in the marketing channel points to the following four generalizations:

1. Conflict is an inherent behavioral dimension in the marketing channel.
2. Given the numerous causes from which conflict may stem, it is a pervasive phenomenon in marketing channels.
3. Conflict can affect channel efficiency.

Figure 4.4
Conflict and Channel Efficiency–General Curve

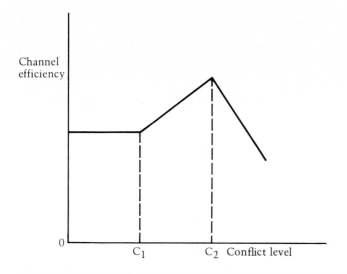

Source: Bert Rosenbloom: "Conflict and Channel Efficiency: Some Conceptual Models for the Decision Maker," *Journal of Marketing* 37 (July 1973): 29. Reprinted with permission from *Journal of Marketing*, published by the American Marketing Association.

4. Various levels of conflict may have both negative and positive effects on channel efficiency, or possibly no effect.

Thus, the literature on the nature, causes, and effects of conflict in the marketing channel, though by no means definitive, does make a case for the significance of conflict in the channel. Unfortunately the state of the art is such that the channel manager does not have a set of precise principles or guidelines or a large body of empirical evidence which can be referred to in attempting to manage conflict in the marketing channel. Nevertheless, some approaches for managing conflict have been discussed in the literature. These are discussed below under the following three headings: (1) approaches aimed at helping the manager to detect conflict or potential conflict; (2) approaches designed to assist the channel manager in appraising the possible effects of conflict; and (3) approaches for resolving channel conflict.

Detecting Channel Conflict.   In practice, conflict is usually spotted after it is well developed and obvious. This "after the fact" approach to the detection of channel conflict is often unsatisfactory because the potentially negative effects of the conflict may have gotten a head start and may already be festering. Therefore it is generally better if the channel manager has some kind of "early warning system." Foster and Shuptrine suggest that a channel member can help spot potential conflict areas by surveying other channel members' perceptions of his or her performance.[17] The study on which their suggestion is based measured retailers' perceptions of wholesalers' and manufacturers' performances in five distribution related tasks. Though their findings were basically preliminary and tentative, this approach does appear to offer promise as a basis for obtaining an early warning of conflict. In order to be of real value, however, these perceptual measurements would have to be done on a regular and continuing basis.

The marketing channel audit, a term used by Cox and Schutte, offers another possible approach for uncovering potential conflict between channel members.[18] While the authors do not spell out the precise procedures for conducting a marketing channel audit aimed specifically at detecting conflict, their approach suggests a periodic and regular evaluation of key areas of the relationship of a given channel member with other members. In the process of appraising various areas of the relationship, potential conflicts are more likely to be detected. For example, the authors discuss a case involving a large tire manufacturer who performed a marketing channel audit. One of the key areas evaluated was the manufacturer's promotional support for the retailers. A surprising finding in this area, and one that had the potential for generating conflict, involved

[17] Robert J. Foster and Kelly F. Shuptrine, "Using Retailers' Perception of Channel Performance to Detect Potential Conflict," *Proceedings of the American Marketing Association*, (August, 1973), pp. 110–123.
[18] Revis Cox and Thomas F. Schutte, "A Look at Channel Management," *Proceedings of the American Marketing Association*, (August, 1969), pp. 99–105.

the manufacturer's use of point of purchase promotional material. It turned out that the manufacturer's and the retailers' perceptions of the value of the POP material were very much at odds. The manufacturer perceived the material as an important and valuable dealer aid for helping the retailers sell to customers who had come into their stores. The retailers, on the other hand, perceived it as superfluous junk which did not help them solve their main promotional problem, which was how to get customers into the stores in the first place! Thus, they felt that the manufacturer was letting them down in providing promotional support where they really needed it. This perceptual difference (see our earlier discussion on perceptual differences as a cause of conflict) over promotional strategy had planted the seeds for a potentially serious conflict situation. The advanced warning provided by the channel audit, however, enabled the manufacturer to make appropriate changes and thus avoid the conflict.

Distributors' advisory councils or channel members' committees offer another approach to early detection of channel conflict.[19] Distributors' advisory councils or channel members' committees consist of top management representatives of the manufacturer and key executives from a select group of distributors and/or dealers. The group meets on a regular basis to discuss a wide range of channel issues and strategies. Though not concerned primarily with channel conflict issues, such councils or committees provide a forum for bringing out potential areas of conflict between channel members which might otherwise go unnoticed. The role of distributors' advisory councils or channel members' committees will be discussed in more detail in Chapter 8 (Motivating the Channel Members).

All of these approaches to spotting conflict in the marketing channel share a common theme: *Channel managers must make a conscious effort to detect conflict or its potential if they expect to deal with it before it becomes highly developed or extensive.*

Some of those responsible for channel management may believe that it is impractical to develop formal methods and procedures (such as a questionnaire for measuring channel members' perceptions, or using a marketing channel audit) for spotting channel conflict. They may believe, and perhaps rightly so, that such approaches are not justified on a cost benefit basis. Even if this is the case, however, the channel manager who at least gives some regular thought and attention to the possibility of conflict developing in the channel relationships is likely to be more tuned in and sensitive to potential conflict areas. So, with or without formal approaches for spotting channel conflict, there is still a need for the channel manager to devote some effort to detecting conflict in the channel.

Appraising the Effects of Conflict.   In recent years a growing body of literature has been emerging to assist the channel manager in developing formal methods for measuring conflict and its effects on channel effi-

---

[19] Gene L. Bego, "Joint Benefits of a Distributor Council," in *Building a Sound Distributor Organization* (New York: The National Industrial Conference Board, 1964), pp. 44–49.

ciency. For example, Pruden, in one of the earliest attempts to measure conflict in a marketing channel setting, developed a scale for measuring the intensity of conflict between producers and distributors of building products.[20] Shortly thereafter, Rosenberg and Stern investigated a channel for household durable goods and developed a scale for measuring the intensity of channel conflict associated with four different causes.[21] Pearson measured the intensity of conflict in a channel of distribution for grocery products and then attempted to relate this conflict measure to the performance of the channel.[22] Taking a somewhat different approach, Lusch measured channel conflict in terms of the frequency of disagreements between manufacturers and dealers in the automobile industry and related this conflict measure to dealer performance.[23] Using a conjoint measurement technique, Brown developed an approach for measuring the relative importance of conflict issues to the overall levels of conflict in a hypothetical channel conflict situation,[24] and Brown and Day developed a method for measuring both the intensity and frequency of conflict in a channel for automobiles.[25] Several other studies dealing with conflict measurement in marketing channels also appear in the literature.[26]

The significance of this work is that it demonstrates that methods *can* be developed for measuring conflict in real world marketing channels. While this work is still very much on the frontiers of marketing thought, it should not be dismissed by the channel manager as little more than so much esoterica suitable only for the academic. As more of this kind of research is done, the methods involved are likely to become more refined and applicable to a wider range of channels. Conceivably, in the not too distant future, such work may prove to be of real practical value to those responsible for channel management. For the present, most attempts to measure conflict and appraise its effects on channel efficiency will still be made at a conceptual level that relies on the manager's subjective judgement.

[20] Henry O. Pruden, "Interorganizational Conflict, Linkage, and Exchange: A Study of Industrial Salesmen," *Academy of Management Journal*, (September, 1969): 339–350.

[21] Larry J. Rosenberg and Louis W. Stern, "Conflict Measurement in the Distribution Channel," *Journal of Marketing Research* (November, 1971): 437–442.

[22] Michael M. Pearson, "The Conflict-Performance Assumption," *Journal of Purchasing*, (February, 1973): 57–69.

[23] Robert F. Lusch, "Channel Conflict: Its Impact on Retailer Operating Performance," *Journal of Retailing*, (Summer, 1976): 3–12.

[24] James R. Brown, "Toward Improved Measures of Distribution Channel Conflict," *Proceedings, Educators Conference of the American Marketing Association* (Chicago: American Marketing Association, 1977), pp. 385–89.

[25] James R. Brown and Ralph L. Day, "Measures of Manifest Conflict in Distribution Channels," *Journal of Marketing Research*, (August, 1981): 263–74.

[26] See for example: Louis W. Stern, Brian Sternthal and C. Samuel Craig, "Managing Conflict in Distribution Channels: A Laboratory Study," *Journal of Marketing Research*, (May, 1973): 169–79; Michael M. Pearson and John F. Monoky, "The Role of Conflict and Cooperation in Channel Performance," in *Proceedings of the Educators Conference of the American Marketing Association* (1976), pp. 240–44; J. Stephen Kelly and J. Irwin Peters, "Vertical Conflict: A Comparative Analysis of Franchisees and Distributors," in *Proceedings, Educators Conference of the American Marketing Association* (Chicago: American Marketing Association, 1977), pp. 380–84; James R. Brown and Gary L. Frazier, "The Application of Channel Power: Effects and Connotations," in *Proceedings of the Educators Conference of the American Marketing Association* (Chicago: American Marketing Association, 1978), pp. 266–70; Michael Etgar, "Sources and Types of Intrachannel Conflict," *Journal of Retailing*, (Spring, 1979): 61–78.

Resolving Conflict.   If conflict exists in the channel, the channel manager should take action to resolve the conflict if it appears to be adversely affecting channel efficiency. Here again, unfortunately, there is only a limited body of empirical work to guide the channel manager in attempting to resolve channel conflict. There are, however, some approaches and recommendations which can be derived from the limited literature that does exist on the subject. Rosenberg, for example, makes several suggestions for dealing with channel conflict.[27] These include the following:

1.   A *channel-wide committee* might be established for periodic evaluations of emerging problems related to conflict. Such a committee could function in a crisis management capacity by providing a forum for the diverse points of view of the various channel members. Rosenberg suggests that some committee members could be appointed as representatives by the manufacturer, while distributors and retailers could elect their own representatives to the committee.

2.   *Joint goal setting* by the committee (or some other vehicle) which takes into account the goals and special capacities of the various channel members, the needs of consumers, and environmental constraints would help to mitigate the effects of conflict. Even if it is not possible to develop joint goals which are in perfect harmony, the dialog attendant to the attempt would in itself be beneficial in reducing conflict.

3.   A *distribution executive* position might be created for each major firm in the channel. The individual(s) filling this position would be responsible for exploring the firm's distribution related problems. Further, this individual could try to make other executives in the firm more aware of the potential impact of conflict on the firm's efficiency. Finally, he or she could seek to identify the current shape of conflict issues in the channel.

Another approach suggested by Weigand and Wasson for resolving channel conflict is to have the parties involved submit to arbitration.[28] The authors state:

"A . . . highly pragmatic approach [for resolving marketing channel conflict] apparently growing in importance, is to provide for a third party to enter and resolve a dispute before it becomes too difficult to settle in a reasonably friendly fashion."[29]

Weigand and Wasson point to the following five advantages of arbitration for resolving channel conflicts:

---

[27] Larry J. Rosenberg, "A New Approach to Distribution Conflict Management," *Business Horizons,* (October, 1974): 67–74.

[28] Robert E. Weigand and Hilda C. Wasson, "Arbitration in the Marketing Channel," *Business Horizons,* (October, 1974): 39–47.

[29] Ibid., p. 39.

1. *Arbitration is fast.* The parties to a dispute can be quickly informed that a quarrel exists and told the time of a hearing; the evidence heard by a panel, and the decision rendered—all within a few weeks.

2. *Arbitration preserves secrecy.* Outside parties can be barred from the hearings. Decisions which are not matters of public record can be kept secret.

3. *Arbitration is less expensive than litigation.* There is an element of "corner-cutting" that takes place which reduces the cost of a tolerable decision.

4. *Arbitration confronts problems in their incipient stage when they are easier to solve.* The attitude can become: "We have a potential problem here; let us solve it before positions and options get too fixed."

5. *Arbitration often takes place before industry experts.* In many instances, the arbitrator or the arbitration panel is composed of those who know an industry and its practices. Some argue that this produces a fairer decision.

Another approach suggested by Stern and Heskett is for the channel to set up a special organization for planned information gathering.[30] Such an organization would be charged with providing all of the channel members with information relevant to all aspects of the channel. The authors argue that this regular flow of information disseminated to the channel members by the organization would aid in channel member goal setting, help clarify their domain responsibilities, and reduce discrepancies in perceptions among the members.

Still another approach offered by Zikmund and Catalanello is to apply organizational development (OD) concepts and methods to the resolution of conflict in the marketing channel.[31] Basically, this involves using behavioral scientists as consultants to develop educational strategies for helping channel members to cope with changes that may foster conflict.

Finally, based on behavioral laboratory research which simulated a channel environment, Dwyer and Walker argue that specialized bargaining and negotiation procedures might be fruitfully applied to the resolution of channel conflict.[32]

The feasibility and applicability of any of these approaches for resolving conflict will vary for different kinds of channels and under differing sets of circumstances. For example, a relatively small manufacturing firm distributing through several relatively small wholesalers may find it somewhat impractical to set up a channel-wide committee or establish

---

[30] Louis W. Stern and J. L. Heskett, "Conflict Management in Interorganizational Relations: A Conceptual Framework," in *Distribution Channels: Behavioral Dimensions*, ed. Louis W. Stern (New York: Houghton Mifflin, 1969), p. 297.

[31] William G. Zikmund and Ralph F. Catalanello, "Managing Channel Conflict Through Channel Development," *Journal of the Academy of Marketing Science*, (Fall, 1976): 801–813.

[32] Robert F. Dwyer and Orville C. Walker Jr., "Bargaining in an Asymmetrical Power Structure," *Journal of Marketing*, (Winter, 1981): 104–115.

the position of distribution executive as suggested by Rosenberg. A group of franchisees in conflict with their franchisor may feel that a resort to litigation in the courts would offer them a more powerful weapon than arbitration for resolving the conflict. An autonomous information gathering unit in the channel as suggested by Stern and Heskett may be cumbersome and too costly for long channels with many members.

What is more important than the specifics of any of these particular approaches, however, is the underlying principle common in all of them. It may be stated as follows: *Creative action on the part of some party to the conflict is needed if the conflict is to be successfully resolved. Conversely, if conflict is simply "left alone" it is not likely to be successfully resolved and may get worse.* In short, channel conflict is not likely to go away by simply ignoring it. Rather, channel members must make an effort to resolve it. Regardless of the specific approaches used in making that effort, as long as they promote candid dialog among the channel members and help to bring differences out into the open, they are likely to be beneficial for resolving conflict. As in so many instances of conflict in other realms besides the marketing channel, solutions generally will involve some measure of compromise. But such compromises are not possible without substantial dialog between the parties to the conflict. Thus, it is up to the channel manager to develop approaches for doing this, whether it be through arbitration, a channel-wide committee, organizational development, bargaining processes, or whatever approach deemed appropriate. Indeed, taking one's adversary out to lunch to discuss the problem may be all that is necessary in some cases.

Power in the Marketing Channel

The concept of power is at best a nebulous one. As Bierstedt points out:

"We may say about it (power) only what St. Augustine said about time, that we all know perfectly what it is—until someone asks us."[33]

Bierstedt goes on in an attempt to distinguish power from other terms which are often used interchangeably such as prestige, influence, dominance, force, and authority. He argues that power is not the same as any of these terms although it is intimately related to force and authority and can be defined in terms of these words. Force he defines as the application of sanctions while power is the predisposition to use force. Hence, he states that power is the ability to employ force, not its actual employment, the ability to apply sanctions, not their actual applications. Power symbolizes the force which may be applied in a social situation and supports the authority which is applied.

[33] Robert Bierstedt, "An Analysis of Social Power," *American Sociological Review*, 15 (December, 1950): 730.

Numerous other concepts of power exist in the literature. Dahl, for example, argues that "A has power over B to the extent that he can get B to do something that B would not otherwise do."[34] Miller and Butler argue simply that power refers to a person's ability to control the behavior of others.[35] Etzioni views power as the capacity to overcome part or all of the resistance to change in the face of opposition.[36] Price suggests that the essence of power is the capacity to influence the behavior of others.[37]

As we can see from the above discussion, there are many views on the concept of power. Yet we may also observe that there is a common theme running through all of them. This is that power has to do with the capacity of one party to control or influence the behavior of another party or parties. Thus, when we use the term *power* in a marketing channel context we are referring to *the capacity of a particular channel member to control or influence the behavior of another channel member(s).* For example, a retailer, in an attempt to reduce inventory costs, may try to limit the selection of products carried from a particular manufacturer. The manufacturer, however, may want the retailer to carry the full product line. Both channel members may attempt to exercise power to influence the other's behavior. The ability of either of the parties to achieve the desired outcomes will depend upon the amount of power that each can bring to bear. Although it is frequently implied in marketing literature that manufacturers have far more power than retailers and hence the manufacturer would be the most likely winner in the kind of power struggle described above, such is often *not* the case.[38] Quite often retailers (as well as other channel members) can exert considerable power over manufacturers. The key to determining which channel members are likely to have the most power in any given situation lies in an understanding of the sources or bases of power available to the channel members. These are discussed in the following section.

Bases of Power for Channel Control

French and Raven define a power base as the source or root of the power that one party exercises over another. They delineate five such power bases:[39]

[34] Robert A. Dahl, "The Concept of Power," *Behavioral Science*, 2 (July, 1957): 203–204.

[35] Norman Miller and Donald C. Butler, "Social Power and Communication in Smaller Groups," *Behavioral Science*, 14 (January, 1969): 11.

[36] Amitai W. Etzioni, *The Active Society* (New York: The Free Press, 1968), p. 314.

[37] James L. Price, *Organizational Effectiveness: An Inventory of Propositions* (Homewood, Illinois: Richard D. Irwin, 1969), p. 48.

[38] See for example the classic article by Phillip McVey, "Are Channels of Distribution What the Textbooks Say?" *Journal of Marketing*, 24 (January, 1960): 61–65; see also Wilke English, Dale M. Lewison and M. Wayne Delozier, "Evolution in Channel Domination: Who Will Be Next?" *Proceedings Southwestern Marketing Association Conference* (1981), pp. 78–81.

[39] John R. P. French and Bertram Raven, "The Bases of Social Power," in *Studies in Social Power*, ed. Dorwin Cartwright (Ann Arbor, Michigan: University of Michigan, 1959), pp. 612–613.

1.   Reward power
2.   Coercive power
3.   Legitimate power
4.   Referent power
5.   Expert power

Definitions and examples of each of these power bases in a marketing channels context are discussed below:

Reward Power.   This refers to the capacity of one channel member to reward another if the latter conforms to the influence of the former. This power base is present in virtually all channel systems. The rewards are usually manifest in the perceived or actual financial gains which channel members experience as a result of conforming to the wishes of another channel member. Channel members whether at the producer, wholesale, or retail levels will in the longer run remain viable members only if they can realize financial benefits from their channel membership. There are exceptions to this general proposition when the channel relationship is based on contractual agreements which constrain the abilities of channel members to cease membership in an unprofitable channel. But even in this case, when the contract expires, the channel member who believes that the financial rewards from the channel have not been sufficient is likely to leave the channel.

Figure 4.5, an advertisement from the *Wall Street Journal*, is an example of a manufacturer of industrial plastic products attempting to solicit channel members on the basis of reward power. Notice that this manufacturer is in effect holding out a "carrot" (profitable sales territories) to attract distributors and manufacturer's representatives to participate in the channel. The manufacturer's success in getting these middlemen to become channel members and to keep them as members will depend heavily upon the power to reward members for their services. If the manufacturer fails to convince the prospective channel members that he or she is able to offer them sufficient rewards, the manufacturer's influence attempts in terms of getting these prospective channel members to become actual members is unlikely to meet with much success.

Clearly then the fundamental basis which must be available to the channel manager attempting to influence middlemen to become members of the channel, and to influence their behavior thereafter, is a capacity to offer them rewards. The channel manager must therefore be capable of communicating the specific benefits that can be offered to channel members in return for their cooperation.

Coercive Power.   This is essentially the opposite of reward power. In this case a channel member's power over another is based on the expectation that the former will be able to punish the latter upon failure to conform to the former's influence attempts. Coercive power is frequently present

Figure 4.5
An Advertisement Soliciting Channel Participants

Distributors and
Manufacturer's Representatives

We are seeking distributors and manufacturers representatives who service architectural and engineering specifiers involved in the heavy construction and commercial building markets. Profitable territories still open in Greater New York City, Southeastern New York State, Upper New Jersey and Southern Connecticut as well as other New England States.

Acme manufactures a complete line of Neoprene compression expansion joint seals and other allied products for expansion and contraction; building, structural and paving joints.

Acme is a 40 year old company, originators of the field proven compression seal concept used in their expansion joint sealing system. These high volume products are used in parking decks, stadiums, warehouses, bridges and other commercial and industrial buildings. The product is normally purchased by building, paving and waterproofing contractors. See SWEETS CATALOG section 5.18/AC.

Contact: **V.P. Marketing, Acme Highway Products, 33 Chandler St., Buffalo, N.Y. 14207, 716/876-0123.**

Source: *Wall Street Journal* (12 April 1976), p. 17.

in channel relationships. Some excerpts taken from a recent FTC ruling involving the Gallo Wine Company offer a good example of coercive power in the marketing channel:

Gallo, the nation's largest wine seller, has been ordered [by the FTC] not to coerce its dealers into selling the more than forty different brands of wine it produces.

The agency [FTC] announced the settlement of a complaint against Gallo that alleged the company pressured more than 300 independent wholesalers in selling its products.

The FTC said the company used its dominant position, size and power to restrain competition and to establish and maintain exclusionary marketing policies through coercion of distributors.

Under the consent order, Gallo will be prohibited from telling wholesalers they cannot sell wine outside of designated territories or deal in wine from other companies.

The company [Gallo] will also be forbidden from telling dealers they must carry certain Gallo products to be allowed to sell others.[40]

[40] "FTC Curbs Wine Maker Over Sales," *New York Times* (20 May 1976), p. 21.

In the above example, Gallo's capacity to use coercive power stemmed from its great size and dominant position in the industry. It was thus able to exert very substantial pressure on its wholesalers to conform to its wishes. If they did not choose to behave as Gallo wanted them to, Gallo could cut them off with no significant loss to itself. This is typical of the operation of coercive power in the marketing channel. That is, those firms who are able to use it are either large or in a very advantageous position—one resulting from a near monopoly or a formal contractual status such as that enjoyed by many franchisors. In the absence of external constraints (such as governmental action if a law is violated as in the case of Gallo) powerful channel members are in a position, at least in the short run, to dominate the weaker channel members even to the extent of using threats and coercion. We should point out that such firms are not limited to producers or manufacturers. Wholesalers and retailers in a dominant position by virtue of their size or monopoly positions in particular trade areas may also resort to the use of coercive power. For example, Sears has for many years enjoyed a reputation of being very "tough" with many of its suppliers. Even modest sized independent retailers with strong reputations in their particular communities are also, at times, able to use coercive power to win concessions from suppliers.

Legitimate Power.   This power base stems from internalized norms in one channel member which dictate that another channel member has a legitimate right to influence the first, and that an obligation exists to accept that influence.

In an intraorganizational system, as typified by a large business firm, legitimate power is pervasive and routinely accepted. Indeed it would be extremely difficult for the organization to operate without it. At each level in the chain of command, the subordinate recognizes that his or her superior has a legitimate right to influence behavior and that the obligation exists to accept such influence. Thus, a sales person reporting to a sales manager expects to take orders from the sales manager who in turn takes orders from the vice-president of marketing, etc.

In an interorganizational system such as the marketing channel, legitimate power does not operate in the same fashion and is by no means a pervasive or well accepted phenomenon. Given that many channels are comprised of independent business firms, there is no definite superior-subordinate relationship, and there are no clear-cut lines of authority or chains of command. It is only in contractually linked channels that anything approaching an organization structure based on legitimate power exists. Consequently, for more loosely aligned marketing channels, legitimate power is a virtually nonexistent power base. A manufacturer selling through independent wholesalers, for example, cannot order the wholesaler to do something based on any legitimate power vested in the manufacturer which the wholesaler is obliged to accept. The manufacturer can, of course, offer inducements or use coercion (e.g., threaten to drop the wholesaler) if the wholesaler refuses to comply with the manufacturer's influence attempt. But in these cases, the power bases involved would be reward and coercion respectively rather than a legitimate base.

In general then, the channel manager operating a loosely aligned channel cannot rely on a legitimate power base to influence channel members. He or she must instead resort either to other power bases or attempt to restructure the channel into a more formal system such as a contractually linked vertical system (see Chapter 14) in an attempt to increase a legitimate power base.

Some of the strongest legitimate power bases are held by franchisors because legitimacy accrues to the franchisor through the franchise contract agreement with his franchisees. These contracts almost always spell out the specific rights and obligations of the parties. With few exceptions, the bulk of the legitimate power base is held by the franchisor rather than by the franchisees (see the appendix to Chapter 14).

In summary, legitimate power is virtually nonexistent in conventional loosely aligned channels of independent business firms. It does, however, exist in formal contractually linked channel systems. Since this latter type of channel is becoming increasingly common, the usefulness of legitimacy as a basis for exercising power in the marketing channel is also likely to increase.

Referent Power.   When one channel member perceives his or her goals to be closely allied to, or congruent with, those of another member, a referent power base is likely to exist. That is, they may see each other as both "being in the same boat." Hence, when this situation prevails, an attempt by one of the channel members to influence the behavior of the other is more likely to be seen by the latter as beneficial to the achievement of his or her own goals. An example will help to illustrate this kind of situation.

A local wholesaler of musical instruments and accessories asked one of his retailers to speed up the payment of his account. This retailer usually took about three months to pay his bills. The retailer balked, arguing that "things were tough" and that "this was the best he could do." Rather than threaten to stop shipping to the retailer (coercive power) the owner of the wholesale company asked to have lunch with the owner of the retail establishment. During the luncheon they discussed some of their problems. One such problem was shared by both parties—slow paying accounts. The retailer explained that his slow payments to the wholesaler were largely accounted for by the retailer's own slow paying customer accounts who used the retailer's traditional store charge account system. The wholesaler replied that this "slow pay" customer problem shared by both channel members was doing neither of them any good. If the problem continued, he argued, it would no doubt lead to serious consequences for both businesses. The wholesaler then suggested that the retailer discontinue his use of his store charge system and instead change over to one of the bank credit cards such as Visa or

Master Charge. The retailer was very receptive to the wholesaler's suggestion. Within several weeks he went ahead and made the change. This did in fact improve the retailer's cash flow position and enabled him to speed up his payments to the wholesaler.

The kind of situation described above, where one member of the channel is able to influence another member's behavior through a reliance on referent power, is not common in the marketing channel. In order for the referent power base to be effective, a good deal of empathy between channel members is necessary. In the case above, such empathy was established through a face to face meeting during which a candid discussion of mutual problems took place. Obviously, for large manufacturers and wholesalers serving hundreds or thousands of accounts, such direct meetings are much more difficult, if not impossible, to achieve. Yet the principle of finding and sharing mutual problems through empathy among channel members could be operationalized by larger channel members using other means such as periodic surveys, channel-wide committees, or channel audits referred to previously in this chapter. The result would be increased understanding among channel members of each other's circumstances and problems leading to a higher awareness of issues of common concern among the members. This in turn is likely to foster greater use of referent power as a basis for influencing channel members.

Expert Power.   This base of power is derived from knowledge (or perception of knowledge) which one channel member attributes to another in some given area. In other words, one channel member's attempts to influence the other's behavior is based on superior expertise.

Expert power is quite common in the marketing channel. Many manufacturers and wholesalers, for example, have traditionally supplied retailers with management assistance relevant to various phases of the retailer's operations. Retailers will often make changes based on the advice received out of respect for the expertise of the manufacturer or wholesaler who offers it. Expert advice also flows up the channel as well, from retailer to wholesaler or manufacturer. Retailers are often in an excellent position to "feel the pulse" of the consumer market and send this information up through the channel.[41] The influence that such information has on the wholesaler's or manufacturer's behavior will depend upon their perceptions of the retailer's expertise.

In franchised channels, expertise is a very important power base for the franchisor to influence his or her franchisees. Though obviously the franchisor may also use other power bases, particularly legitimacy, the use of expert power is extremely important in gaining cooperative compliance from franchisees. The franchisees expect the franchisor to offer expertise on a regular and continuing basis. Indeed, one of the principal

---

[41]Bruce Mallen, "A Theory of Retailer-Supplier Conflict, Control and Cooperation," *Journal of Retailing*, (Summer, 1963): 31.

values of the franchise to the franchisee is the expertise of the franchisor in the particular line of business.[42]

Using Power in the Marketing Channel

From the standpoint of the channel manager in the producing or manufacturing firm, power must be used to influence the behavior of the channel members towards helping the firm to achieve its distribution objectives. Thus, the channel manager must use the power bases available, in order to exercise power in the marketing channel. This raises two basic channel management issues: (1) which power bases are available, and (2) which base or bases should be used.

Availability of Power Bases.   In most cases, dealing with this issue is straightforward because the power bases available to the channel manager at any given time can usually be readily identified. Generally, they are a function of the size of the producer or manufacturer relative to channel members, the organization of the channel, or a particular set of circumstances surrounding the channel relationship.[43]

With respect to size, typically a large producer or manufacturer dealing with relatively small channel members at the wholesale or retail levels has high reward and coercive power bases available and vice versa. The sheer size of the Gallo Wine Company discussed earlier, for example, provided Gallo with strong power bases for punishing or rewarding channel members.

In terms of channel organization, channels which are contractually linked, such as in a franchised system, provide the franchisor with a strong legal power base which derives from the contract. Conversely, conventional loosely aligned channels offer the producer or manufacturer virtually no legal power base.

Finally, at any given time in the channel relationship, circumstances may develop which may have fairly obvious associations with particular power bases. For example, the expert power base may be available to the manufacturer in the early stages of the introduction of a new product because the manufacturer may be the only channel member who knows how to promote the product effectively. Consequently, retailers may conform closely to the manufacturer's promotional "recommendations" because the manufacturer has the necessary expertise. The referent power base may become available to the manufacturer during a shortage situation if the shortage is having similar adverse effects on all of the channel members. The manufacturer's power to allocate the scarce products among the various channel members would, in this case, be based largely

---

[42]Bert Rosenbloom, "The Pros and Cons of Franchising," *Audio Video International*, 4 (March, 1976): 18–20.

[43]Michael Etgar, "Channel Environment and Channel Leadership," *Journal of Marketing Research*, (February, 1977): 69–76.

on the channel members' belief that the manufacturer is acting in the best interests of all of the members of the channel.

While there may be some cases where the availability of power bases may be difficult to identify, in most cases a careful appraisal of the basic channel relationship with respect to size and organizational structure of the channel, and any changing circumstances relevant to the channel relationship will reveal the bases of power available.

Which Bases Should Be Used.   Which bases should be used to exercise power in the marketing channel is a more difficult and complex issue for the channel manager to deal with than the previous issue of identifying the power bases available. In order to select and use the right power bases, the channel manager needs to know how effective the various power bases are for influencing the channel members to carry out the firm's distribution objectives, what possible reactions the channel members might have to the use of different power bases, and how the use of various power bases will affect the overall channel relationship. While there is as yet no definitive set of principles or guidelines for dealing with this issue of power base usage in the marketing channel, a growing body of analysis and empirical research has emerged in recent years which provides some useful insights into this issue.

With regard to the effectiveness of various power bases for influencing the behavior of channel members, two studies conducted by Etgar are particularly relevant.

In the first of these studies,[44] Etgar examined the use of power in a conventional channel in the property and casualty insurance industry that involved power relationships between insurers and independent insurance agents. One of the principal findings of the study was that in conventional channels where channel members have a degree of countervailing power, nonpecuniary power bases such as expert and referent power may be more effective than direct monetary incentives (reward power base) or threats (coercive power base) in inducing channel members to accept controls. In such channels where dealers are free to enter and leave the channel, and where they have the countervailing power to resist the manufacturer, they may be induced to accept controls as a result of an exchange process in return for services provided to them by suppliers.

Another study by Etgar[45] examined power usage by manufacturers in a cross section of channels involving the distribution of beer, liquor, gasoline, boats, cars, motorcycles, musical organs, and swimming pools which were sold through relatively small local dealers in a large north-

[44] Michael Etgar, "Channel Domination and Countervailing Power in Distribution Channels," *Journal of Marketing Research*, (August, 1976): 254–262; for a critique of the methodology and findings from this study see: Claes Fornell, "Problems in the Interpretation of Canonical Analysis: The Case of Power in Distributive Channels," *Journal of Marketing Research*, (August, 1978): 489–91; see also the reply by Etgar, "Power in Distributive Channels: A Reply," *Journal of Marketing Research*, (August, 1978): 429–494.

[45] Michael Etgar, "Selection of an Effective Channel Control Mix," *Journal of Marketing*, (July, 1978): 53–58.

eastern metropolitan area. The study found that power employed by the manufacturers based on economic rewards or coercion provided a higher degree of control over the channel members than power based on legitimacy, expertise, or reference.

Turning now to the question of channel member reactions to the use of various power bases by the manufacturer and the effects that such usage may have on the overall channel relationship, a number of studies are relevant.

Bier and Stern[46] argue that noncoercive power bases are likely to lead to a higher level of satisfaction for the "weaker" channel members. Hunt and Nevin, in an empirical study, tested this hypothesis in franchised channels for fast foods.[47] Their findings do provide empirical support for the hypothesis. Based on these findings, Hunt and Nevin argue that, at least in a franchise channel, the avoidance of the use of coercive power by the franchisor is likely to yield the following results for the franchisees.[48] They are:

1. likely to have higher morale
2. more likely to cooperate with the franchisor
3. less likely to terminate their contracts
4. less likely to file individual suits against the franchisor
5. less likely to file class action suits
6. less likely to seek protective legislation such as the "Franchise Full Disclosure Act" (1970)

A subsequent study by Lusch[49] in franchised channels of distribution for automobiles reinforced Hunt and Nevin's findings. The study found that the use of particular power bases by the manufacturers can have an impact on channel conflict. Specifically, it was found that the use of noncoercive bases of power (reward, legitimate, referent, and expert) tend to reduce channel conflict, whereas coercive power tends to increase conflict.

Similar findings were also reported in a study of marketing channels for automobiles conducted by Brown.[50]

In one of the most recently reported studies of power use in the marketing channel, Wilkinson[51] investigated a channel of distribution for a

[46] Frederick J. Beier and Louis W. Stern, "Power in the Channel of Distribution," in *Distribution Channels: Behavioral Dimensions*, ed. Louis W. Stern (New York: Houghton Mifflin, 1969), pp. 92–93.

[47] Shelby D. Hunt and John R. Nevin, "Power in a Channel of Distribution: Sources and Consequences," *Journal of Marketing Research*, 11 (May, 1974): 186–193.

[48] Ibid., p. 187.

[49] Robert F. Lusch, "Sources of Power: Their Impact on Intrachannel Conflict," *Journal of Marketing Research*, (November, 1976): 382–90. For a critique of the methodology and findings of this study see: Michael Etgar, "Intrachannel Conflict and the Use of Power," *Journal of Marketing Research*, (May, 1978): 273–4. For Lusch's reply to this critique see: Robert F. Lusch, "Intrachannel Conflict and Use of Power: A Reply," *Journal of Marketing Research*, (May, 1978): 275–6.

[50] James R. Brown and Gary L. Frazier, "The Application of Channel Power: Its Effects and Connotations," *Proceedings Educators' Conference of the American Marketing Association*, (1978), pp. 266–70.

[51] Ian F. Wilkinson, "Power and Satisfaction in Distribution Channels," *Journal of Retailing*, (Summer, 1979): 79–94.

major household durable product in Australia. The study found a direct relationship (though a weak one) between noncoercive bases of power and the degree of satisfaction of channel members with the channel relationship.

Finally, based on a simulated marketing channel comprised of graduate and undergraduate students, Dwyer[52] found that reward, referent, legitimate, and expert power bases tend to promote a more cooperative channel relationship.

Although no clear-cut or precise channel management implications on the use of power in the marketing channel can be gleaned from this research, several general inferences can be derived:

1. Some form of power must be exercised in order to influence channel member behavior.
2. The effectiveness of the various power bases in influencing channel member behavior is probably situation specific. That is, depending upon the particular structure of the channel involved, the nature of the channel members, and the environmental context in which power is exercised, the effectiveness of the various power bases will vary.[53]
3. The use of power can affect the degree of cooperation and conflict in the channel and can affect the levels of channel member satisfaction with the channel relationship.
4. The use of coercive power appears to foster conflict and promote dissatisfaction to a greater degree than the other power bases.
5. The use of coercive power, especially in contractually linked channels, can reduce the stability and viability of the channel and is likely to increase the probability that the coerced channel members will seek outside assistance (such as government action) to reduce the coercion.

While these generalizations should not be considered definitive or "carved in stone," they do offer the channel manager at least some degree of research-based guidance on the use of power in the marketing channel. When coupled with sound managerial judgement, they may prove to be of real value in the development and management of the marketing channel.

Role in the Marketing Channel

As with so many terms springing from the behavioral sciences, there is a good deal of disagreement on the definition of role. The concept of role

---

[52] Robert F. Dwyer, "Channel-Member Satisfaction: Laboratory Insights," *Journal of Retailing*, (Summer, 1980): 45–65.

[53] For additional perspectives on this point see: Michael Etgar, "Differences in the Use of Manufacturer Power in Conventional and Contractual Channels," *Journal of Retailing*, (Winter, 1978): 49–62.

has been used to denote prescription, description, evaluation and action. An acceptable definition of *role* for our purposes is:

A set of prescriptions defining what the behavior of a position member should be.[54]

In applying this definition of role to the marketing channel, Gill and Stern argue that the channel, when viewed as a social system, is comprised of a series of recognizable positions with each organization (e.g., manufacturers, wholesalers, retailers) occupying these positions in the channel. Each position has a set of socially defined prescriptions (roles) delineating what constitutes acceptable behavior for the occupants of these roles.[55] For example, a basic role prescription of the manufacturer's position may be to maximize the sales of his or her particular brand of product. The manufacturer is expected to compete by "social peers" (other manufacturers who are competitors) for market share. This role also prescribes aggressively promoting his or her brand to compete effectively. The role prescriptions of independent wholesalers, however, are likely to be quite different because the position occupied by the wholesaler will have a different set of prescriptions associated with it. For example, to the wholesaler the product brand of this particular manufacturer may be just one of the many brands sold. The wholesaler's role prescriptions are thus defined by his or her position as a wholesaler in competition with other wholesalers. This role may prescribe building sales with whatever brands are most heavily demanded by retailers. If the manufacturer or wholesaler steps too far out of the prescribed role, conflict can result which may adversely affect performance or even their survival. For example, if the wholesaler continues to carry a large stock of the manufacturer's brand even though similar products from several other manufacturers are more in demand at a given time, the wholesaler risks loss of sales volume and the loss of some retail accounts. On the other hand, the manufacturer could not "go along" with the wholesaler for an extended period of time if the latter were to stop buying from him or her and begin buying heavily from the other manufacturers. For clearly, this would serve to reduce the manufacturer's sales volume and market share.

Using the Concept of Role

From the channel manager's standpoint, the key value of the role concept is that it helps to describe and compare the expected behavior of channel members and provides insight into the constraints under which they op-

---

[54]Bruce J. Biddle and Edwin J. Thomas, *Role Theory Concepts and Research* (New York: John Wiley and Sons, 1966), p. 29.
[55]Lynn E. Gill and Louis W. Stern, "Roles and Role Theory in Distribution Channel Systems," in *Distribution Channels: Behavioral Dimensions*, ed. Louis W. Stern (Boston: Houghton Mifflin, 1969), pp. 22–29.

erate. For example, the channel manager can use the concept of role to formulate such questions as the following:

1. What role do I expect a particular channel member to play in the channel?
2. What role is this member (potential or existing) expected to play by his or her peers (other firms of a similar type)?
3. Do my expectations for this member conflict with those of his or her peers?
4. What role does this member expect me to play?

By asking these kinds of questions about the roles of the various channel members, a clearer understanding of what part each is expected to play is more likely to emerge. This will help to minimize the confused and haphazard relationships which too often exist among channel members, and reduce the possibility of role conflicts among the members.

As an example of how clearly defined roles help foster better understanding among channel members, consider the case of steel service centers. Steel service centers are a type of independent middleman operating in the industrial market. They buy steel in bulk from the major steel producers and often process it into various dimensions and forms. They maintain substantial inventories of these products providing quick availability to their customers, usually manufacturers of such products as computers, small appliances, lighting fixtures, furniture, fire engines, restaurant and hotel equipment, air conditioning systems and many others. The use of these steel middlemen has tripled over the past decade and they now account for about 20 percent of all industrial steel products sold in the United States. These steel service centers generally enjoy excellent relations with steel producers and their customers. One of the principal reasons for this, according to industry sources, is the clear understanding among the channel members of their respective roles.[56] For example, the role of steel producers as a direct supplier to smaller users has been decreasing because of rather high minimum order requirements (20–50 tons for some types of steel products). The steel producers saw in the emerging steel service centers, channel members who were ideally suited for filling the role of supplier to the smaller customers. The smaller customers in turn expect the steel service centers to provide processing such as cutting and shearing, storage, and the ability to deliver within short periods of time and in quantities smaller than the steel producers will handle. Though the "marriage" is not perfect, most indications are that these channel relationships are characterized by a very high level of understanding among the members of their respective roles.

In summary, a familiarity with the concept of role in the marketing channel fosters more extensive and sharper thinking about what is ex-

---

[56] For additional background on the role of steel service centers in the marketing channel see: Gene Smith, "Steel Service Centers Expanding Role as Middlemen," *New York Times* (2 June 1976), pp. 49, 54.

pected of each of the channel members. This is likely to promote the development of more congruent roles among channel members which in turn should result in more cooperative and efficient channels.

Communication Processes in the Marketing Channel

Communication provides the basis for sending and receiving information among the channel members and between the channel and its environment. Communication activities undertaken by channel members create a flow of information within the channel which is necessary for an efficient flow of products or services through the channel. Indeed it is almost impossible to visualize an efficient product or service flow without an effective information flow.[57] Consequently, the channel manager must work to create and foster an effective flow of information within the channel. The approaches and methods which may be used to do this will be discussed in detail in Chapter 8 (Motivating the Channel Members) where we discuss the role of communication in fostering channel member cooperation. Our purpose in introducing the subject of communication in the present chapter is to provide a backdrop of some of the basic behavioral problems attendant to communication in the marketing channel. A familiarity with the behavioral problems of channel communications is necessary if the channel manager is to avoid the pitfalls which await him or her in attempting to create an effective information flow through the channel.

Behavioral Problems of Channel Communications

The work of Wittreich stands out as a landmark effort in pointing to the behavioral problems affecting communications in the marketing channel.[58] While Wittreich's analysis deals specifically with those problems encountered by large corporate manufacturers attempting to communicate with relatively small independent retailers, his findings also provide insight for understanding behavioral communications problems in other channel structures, so where appropriate, we have pointed to different kinds of channels to which his findings may also apply.

Wittreich delineates two basic behavioral problems which create communication difficulties in the manufacturer–small independent retailer

---

[57] See Chapter 1 for a discussion of flows in marketing channels; see also: Roland S. Vaile, E. T. Grether, and Revis Cox, *Marketing in the American Economy* (New York: Ronald Press, 1952), pp. 113–129.

[58] Warren J. Wittreich, "Misunderstanding the Retailer," *Harvard Business Review*, 40 (May–June, 1962): 147–159.

channel structure. These are: (1) differences in goals between manufacturers and their retailers, and (2) differences in the kinds of language which they use to convey information. Wittreich summarizes these very succinctly:

"The people who manufacture the goods and the people who move the goods into the hands of the ultimate consumer do not share the same business philosophy (goals) and do not talk essentially the same language." [59]

These two behavioral dimensions which can lead to serious breakdowns in channel communications are discussed in some detail below.

Differing Goals. Wittreich argues that corporate management in large manufacturing firms is characterized by a growth psychology. In its marketing strategy this translates into an aggressive effort to build sales volume. Those who participate in its marketing channel are thus expected to join wholeheartedly in this quest. On the other hand, Wittreich argues that this growth goal is not shared by the typical retail dealer. Rather, the small to medium-sized independent retailer is characterized by an essentially static psychology. That is, he or she is often quite satisfied with the existing level of business or, at the most, a modest and gradual expansion.

This difference in goals, according to Wittreich, accounts for a large part of the communication problems in the marketing channel between manufacturers and retailers. To illustrate this, he cites the example of dealer incentives which are widely used by appliance manufacturers. Such incentives usually take the form of financial stimuli to the retailers to increase their sales volume. The volume discount is one such example whereby an increasingly larger percentage discount on purchases is given to the dealer as volume increases. Manufacturers are frequently puzzled by their inability to communicate the benefits of these discounts effectively so that dealers will enthusiastically attempt to take advantage of them. Wittreich explains this communication problem as follows.

"To understand such a puzzling point of view, we should recall one of the two basic points stated at the outset of this article—that while management [of manufacturers] is characterized by the unrelenting surge of expansion, the dealer is often not the least bit interested in going beyond the level of business he has achieved. The latter, enjoying a good living as far as he is concerned, is not only satisfied to stay at his present level, but is annoyed at what he considers a supplier's "prodding" him into moving beyond that level. Furthermore, he not only resents such prodding, but considers it to be "unfair discrimination" in favor of dealers who are bigger than he is." [60]

[59] Ibid., p. 148.
[60] Ibid., p. 151.

Although as mentioned previously, Wittreich cited this goal difference in the context of large manufacturers distributing through relatively small retailers, the same problem may exist in other channel structures where one of the members is large and the others relatively small. Thus, it may hold for channels such as: (1) manufacturer distributing through small wholesalers, (2) large wholesaler and small retailers, (3) a franchisor and comparatively small franchisees, and possibly others. Obviously, without empirical evidence we cannot know this with any degree of certainty, but the extension of Wittreich's findings to other channel structures involving large and smaller members is certainly reasonable—particularly since these goal differences which Wittreich points to are not a function of a particular kind of business such as manufacturer per se but rather appear to be closely related to the size of the firm and the philosophy of its management. A large wholesaler run by professional management, for example, may have high growth goals which are inconsistent with the retailers through whom he or she distributes.

With this in mind, the channel manager working in large firms, whether it be a producer, manufacturer, wholesaler, or service franchisor, should attempt to understand the goals of the smaller channel members to learn whether they are much different from those of his or her own firm.

Language Differences.   According to Wittreich this communication problem between the manufacturer and small retailer stems from the terminology or jargon used by professional corporate management in large manufacturing firms. Wittreich argues that although such language is well understood among professional managers, it is almost totally alien to the small retailer. To elucidate his point, he cites an example from the American brewing industry. Specifically he asserts that the large brewers have a great deal of difficulty in communicating with small retail tavern owners. He states:

"The typical tavern owner is essentially not *a businessman. He is* not *used to thinking in terms that are familiar to the businessman. To him "profit" is a highfalutin esoteric word used by wise guys who think they are better than he is. Being in business to "make money" he is more likely to respond to arguments or appeals which will help him do that than to arguments or appeals which are supposed to lead to "better profits." By the same token, talk about "merchandising," or "promotion" is likely to sail over his head. In order to get him to act, you have to speak to him in terms which are familiar and meaningful to him and which promise concrete rewards that he can grasp and understand."*[61]

Here again, Wittreich's argument may be applicable to other channel structures besides those consisting of a large manufacturer and small in-

---

[61] Ibid., p. 155.

dependent retailers. Thus, it is certainly wise for the channel manager to make an effort to find out whether the language used in channel communications is well understood by all channel members.

Other Behavioral Problems in Channel Communications. Besides the behavioral problems of differing goals and language among channel members, two other behavioral problems which can inhibit effective channel communications are those associated with perceptual differences among channel members and secretive behavior.

In the case of perceptual differences, channel members may perceive the same stimuli in different ways. One such difference was already discussed above which involved differing perception of language. But there are perceptual differences among channel members which may distort communications that are not the result of differing perceptions of language. For example, such issues as "delivery time" may be perceived quite differently by various channel members. One instance of this involved a manufacturer of a small portable hoist and a wholesaler with whom an exclusive franchise for the product had been agreed to:

The manufacturer's first shipment to the wholesaler turned out to have 100 percent product defects. The wholesaler ended up having to take back every hoist sold. The manufacturer allowed the wholesaler to return the hoists and began work on correcting the defect. The manufacturer then became very cautious, wanting to be sure that the hoists were completely free of defects. This slowed up production, resulting in delivery times to the wholesaler of nine to ten months. The wholesaler complained bitterly to the manufacturer that customers were not willing to wait that long. The manufacturer responded: "If you don't like it then let's call off the franchise deal here and now. I'll get some other distributor!"

The wholesaler's response was to sue the manufacturer for lost profits on orders not delivered on time. The manufacturer argued that under the circumstances a delivery time of nine to ten months was reasonable. The wholesaler argued that a period of approximately thirty days was what is meant by a reasonable delivery time. The court found for the wholesaler based on expert testimony that supported the wholesaler's perception of thirty days as a reasonable delivery time.[62]

While the example cited above involved the issue of delivery time, perceptual differences may occur among channel members on a wide variety of other issues. It is therefore important for the channel manager to make sure that the channel members perceive issues such as delivery time, margin and discounts, return privilege, warranty provisions, etc. in essentially the same way he does. He should not make the mistake of simply

---

[62] For additional background on this case see: "Late Deliveries: Must Manufacturers Pay For Making a Distributor Wait Too Long?" *Marketing News*, (4 June 1976), p. 3.

assuming that "everybody knows" what a particular provision means or that "it is standard practice" in the industry. A little more care in this area is likely to make for more effective channel communications and minimize the possibilities of conflict and legal actions.

The tendency of channel members to behave in a secretive fashion can also inhibit effective channel communications. For example, McVey has pointed to the secretive behavior of many manufacturers when it comes to disclosing a forthcoming promotional plan.[63] They are often reluctant to divulge many of the details of the plan to their channel members. By not divulging the plan before it is executed the manufacturer fails to get potentially valuable feedback from middlemen on whether the plan will be appropriate, timely, and amenable to their support. Grabner and Rosenberg suggest that channel members often behave secretly because many of the participants in any given channel are also members of other competing channels.[64] Thus, the possibility of information leaks occurring is high. Even though less effective coordination of efforts may result, the various channel members will often omit or distort information to guard against the transmittal of competitively sensitive information.

We should point out that a certain amount of secrecy is often necessary in the channel. For example, in launching a major promotional campaign a firm frequently needs the element of surprise. By divulging the specifics of the campaign the firm is more likely to lose this competitive advantage.

Unfortunately, there is no clear cut answer as to when secrecy by channel members is a necessary form of behavior and when it works to inhibit effective channel communications. Clearly, an across-the-board high level of secrecy under all circumstances is probably unnecessary. On the other hand, complete openness at all times is probably unwise. The channel manager must therefore decide the issue on a situation by situation basis.

Summary

The marketing channel is characterized not only by economic processes but by behavioral processes as well. The marketing channel may therefore be viewed as a social system affected by such behavioral dimensions as conflict, power, role, and communications processes.

The channel manager needs a general knowledge of these behavioral dimensions as they operate in the marketing channel so that their effects can be incorporated into his or her decision making.

Conflict is an inherent behavioral dimension in marketing channels

[63]McVey, "Channels of Distribution," p. 64.

[64]John R. Grabner and Larry J. Rosenberg, "Communication in Distribution Channels," in *Distribution Channels: Behavioral Dimensions*, ed. Louis W. Stern (Boston: Houghton Mifflin, 1969), p. 240.

and is pervasive because it stems from many causes such as role incongruities, resource scarcities, perceptual differences, expectational differences, decision domain disagreements, goal incompatibilities, and communication difficulties. Conflict may have both negative and positive effects on channel efficiency and in some cases no effect. The management of channel conflict involves three basic tasks: (1) detecting channel conflict, (2) appraising the effects of conflict, and (3) resolving the conflict if it is having negative effects on channel efficiency. A variety of approaches can be used for detecting channel conflict such as surveys of channel members' perceptions, channel audits, and distributors' advisory councils. The measurement of channel conflict has received considerable research attention in recent years and a number of sophisticated methods now exist for measuring conflict and relating its effects to channel efficiency. While most of these methods have not been widely used in practice, they can provide the channel manager with valuable insights for dealing with channel conflict. The resolution of conflict can be facilitated through the use of channel wide committees, joint goal setting, distribution executives, arbitration, special organizations for gathering information, organizational development methods, and bargaining procedures. All of these approaches attempt to promote increased dialog among the channel members in order to mitigate the effects of negative conflict.

Power is used in the marketing channel to influence the behavior of other channel members. Power is derived from five sources or bases: (1) reward, (2) coercion, (3) legitimacy, (4) reference, and (5) expertise. The most fundamental and important issue facing the channel manager in the use of power in the marketing channel is which power base or combination of power bases should be used to attain maximum influence over channel members while at the same time avoiding conflict and promoting channel member satisfaction. This issue has received considerable research attention over the last decade. The findings from this research can provide some guidance for using power in the marketing channel. Among the most important findings are that power effectiveness in the marketing channel appears to be situation specific, the use of power can affect the degree of cooperation and conflict in the channel and levels of channel member satisfaction, and that the use of coercive power appears to foster conflict and promote dissatisfaction to a greater degree than the other power bases.

Role, the set of prescriptions defining what the behavior of a position member should be, provides the channel manager with a basis for delineating what part he or she expects each channel member to play and what role the firm is expected to play in the marketing channel. By developing more congruent roles among the channel members, the channel manager is more likely to achieve a more effective and efficient marketing channel.

Communications flows within the channel are vital to the operation of the channel. However, behavioral problems such as divergent goals among channel members, language difficulties, perceptual differences, and secretive behavior can cause distortions in the communications flow which may reduce channel efficiency. The channel manager should therefore try to detect any behavioral problems that tend to inhibit the effective flow of information through the channel and try to solve those problems before the communications process in the channel becomes seriously distorted.

Discussion Questions

1. A purely economic model of the marketing channel is inadequate. Explain.
2. Why does the channel manager need a familiarity with some of the behavioral processes occurring in the channel?
3. Discuss the distinction between conflict and competition in the marketing channel.
4. What are some of the underlying causes of conflict? Are these causes usually obvious? Are issues over which conflict may develop the same as the underlying causes?
5. Are the effects of conflict necessarily detrimental to channel efficiency? Explain.
6. Discuss some of the approaches the channel manager may use in attempting to manage conflict. Do all of these approaches share a common theme? What ideas do you have for managing channel conflict?
7. Why is it necessary to use power in the development and management of the channel?
8. What are the bases of power in the marketing channel? Is it possible to rank these bases according to their degree of effectiveness in influencing the behavior of another channel member before examining the particular set of circumstances or context of the influence attempt as it takes place in the channel?
9. How can the channel manager use the concept of role to develop a more effective and efficient channel?
10. Discuss some of the behavioral problems which can "foul up" effective communications in the marketing channel. Can you think of others?

Part Two
Developing the Marketing Channel

The three chapters in this part of the text deal with setting up effective and efficient marketing channels.

Chapter 5 presents a comprehensive discussion of channel design.

Chapter 6 analyzes the process of selecting channel members.

Chapter 7 offers an in-depth discussion of how market variables affect channel design strategy.

Chapter 5
Designing the Channel

There is wide variation in the use of the term *design* as it applies to the marketing channel. Some authors use the term as a noun to describe channel structure. Others use it to denote the formation of a new channel from scratch, while still others use it more broadly to include modifications to existing channels. Finally, *design* has also been used synonymously with *selection* with no distinction made between the two terms.

Such variations in usage lead to a good deal of confusion. So, before proceeding further into this chapter we will define more precisely what we mean by *design* as it applies to the marketing channel:

Channel design refers to those decisions involving the development of new marketing channels where none had existed before, or to the modification of existing channels.

The first key point to note in this definition is that channel design is presented as a decision which the marketer faces. In this sense channel design is similar to the other decision areas of the marketing mix, namely product, price, and promotion. That is, when viewed from a management perspective, the marketer must make decisions in each of these areas of the marketing mix.

A second point to note is that channel design is used in the broader sense to include setting up channels from scratch as well as modifying existing channels. In practice, the former is actually a much less frequently encountered problem than the latter.

Thirdly, the term *design* (verb form) implies that the marketer is consciously and actively allocating the distribution tasks in an attempt to develop an efficient channel structure. Design is not used to refer to channel structures which have simply evolved.[1] In short, design means that management has taken an active role in the development of the channel.

Finally, the term *selection*, as we will be using it, refers to only one phase of channel design—the selection of the actual channel members.

Who Engages in Channel Design?

Producers, manufacturers, wholesalers (consumer and industrial) and retailers, all face channel design decisions. For retailers, however, channel design is viewed from the opposite perspective from that of producers and manufacturers. That is they look "up the channel" in an attempt to secure suppliers rather than "down the channel" towards the market as is the case for producers and manufacturers. Wholesale intermediaries face channel design decisions from both perspectives.

In this text we have used the perspective of a firm (mainly producers and manufacturers) looking down the channel towards the market. Hence, we will discuss the topic of channel design from this perspective. This is not to minimize the importance of the other perspective. Indeed this can be a very important problem for retailers (and for wholesalers as well). But an adequate treatment of this perspective is outside the scope of this text.[2]

Differential Advantage and Channel Design

Differential advantage refers to a firm's attempt to gain a competitive advantage in the marketplace. In other words, to find a niche for itself which enables it to use its particular strengths to satisfy customer demands better than its competitors.[3] The whole range of resources available to the

---

[1] For a discussion of some of the problems associated with marketing channels that have been based on evolution rather than planning see: Douglas M. Lambert, *The Distribution Channels Decision* (New York: National Association of Accountants, 1978); Joseph P. Guiltinan, "Planned and Evolutionary Changes in Distribution Channels," *Journal of Retailing*, (Summer, 1974): 79–91.

[2] For a discussion of some of these issues see: John W. Wingate and Joseph S. Friedlander, *The Management of Retail Buying* (Englewood Cliffs, New Jersey: Prentice-Hall, 1963); David A. Revzan, *Wholesaling in Marketing Organization* (New York: John Wiley and Sons, 1961), chap. 12; Ralph S. Alexander, James C. Cross, and Richard M. Hill, *Industrial Marketing*, 3rd ed. (Homewood, Illinois: Richard D. Irwin, 1967), chap. 4; Edwin W. Crooks, "The Case for Concentration of Purchases," *Journal of Retailing*, 42 (Summer, 1966): 14–18.

[3] Wroe Alderson, *Marketing Behavior and Executive Action* (Homewood, Illinois: Richard D. Irwin, 1957), pp. 101–109.

firm and all of its major functional activities contribute to creating differential advantages. The level of capital, the quality of its management and employees, and its overall production, financial, and marketing strategies all play a part.

Channel design strategy, though just one component of this overall attempt to gain differential advantage, is nevertheless an important part. As one of the major controllable variables of the marketing mix, it is no less important for the firm to seek differential advantage in its channel design, as to seek it in its product, pricing, and promotional strategies. In fact, there are times when channel design strategy comprises the principal basis for gaining differential advantage:[4]

Consider, for example, the case of the Caterpillar Tractor Company. Caterpillar is a company whose products and approach to doing business are highly respected throughout the world. Over the last fifty years Caterpillar has also had one of the best financial track records in the heavy equipment industry or, for that matter, among most major U.S. corporations. It has suffered a loss just once in that fifty year period and that was in 1932 during the height of the great depression.

What lies behind Caterpillar's success? While there are several factors that differentiate Caterpillar from competitors, the key ingredient of its success is a well-designed marketing channel system based on a superb dealer organization. The dealer network comprising the channel for most of Caterpillar's products consists of 93 domestic and 137 overseas dealerships, all of which are independently owned and relatively large. The average dealer's sales are 100 million and each has an average net worth approaching four million dollars. This financially strong and high powered group of dealers has enabled Caterpillar to provide a level of product availability and service to its customers that is unrivaled in the industry. But this well-designed channel system that has given Caterpillar such a strong differential advantage is no mere accident. Over the years Caterpillar has placed great emphasis on building and nurturing its marketing channel system in a conscious effort to make it superior to the competition. One feature of the system, for example, is a national computer network linking all dealers to the Morton, Illinois distribution center. This network enables dealers to order any part they need for delivery the next day. Caterpillar also conducts dozens of training programs for dealers both in the U.S. and abroad. Indeed, the company even conducts a course in Peoria, Illinois to encourage dealers' children to remain in the business!

As this example suggests, the quest to gain differential advantage in the market through an effective channel design should be uppermost in the channel manager's thinking while attempting to design marketing channels.

[4]"Caterpillar's Backbone: A Long Dealer Network," *Business Week*, (4 May 1981): 77.

A Paradigm of the Channel Design Decision

The channel design decision may be broken down into seven phases or steps. These are:

1. recognizing that a channel design decision is being faced
2. setting and coordinating distribution objectives
3. specifying the distribution tasks
4. developing possible alternative channel structures
5. evaluating the variables affecting channel structure
6. choosing the "best" channel structure
7. selecting the channel members

These seven phases are shown schematically in Figure 5.1.

   The organization of this chapter and Chapter 6 follows this channel design paradigm. Each major section of the chapter discusses one of the phases, from phase one through six. Phase seven, dealing with selection of channel members, is discussed separately in Chapter 6.

Phase 1: Recognizing the Need for Making Channel Design Decisions

There are many conditions which make it necessary for the firm to face channel design decisions. Among these conditions are the following:

1. when a new product or product line is developed. (If existing channels for other products are not suitable for the new product or product line, a new channel may have to be set up or the existing channels modified in some fashion.)
2. when an existing product is aimed at a new target market. (A common example of this is when a firm which has been selling a product in the industrial market attempts to sell it in the consumer market.)
3. when a major change is made in some other component of the marketing mix. (For example, a new pricing policy emphasizing lower prices may require a shift to lower price dealers such as discount department stores.)
4. when a new firm is established from scratch or as a result of mergers or acquisitions.
5. when existing intermediaries have changed their policies so as to inhibit the attainment of a firm's distribution objectives. (For example, intermediaries begin to emphasize their own private brands.)

Figure 5.1
A Flow Chart of the Channel Design Decision Paradigm

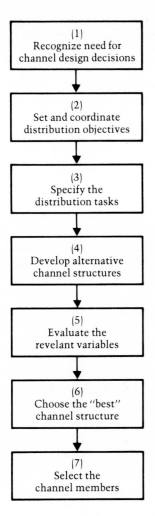

6. when the availability of particular kinds of intermediaries changes. (For example, recall from the previous chapter the case of steel service center middlemen. As these middlemen grew, most of the major steel producers decided to use them in their channels to distribute to smaller accounts.)

7. when new geographical marketing areas (territories) are opened up.

8. when major environmental changes occur. (These may be in the economic, socio-cultural, competitive, technological, or legal spheres. See Chapter 3 for a discussion of the influence of environment on marketing channels.)

9. when conflict or other behavioral problems occur. (For example, in some instances conflict may become so intense that it is not possible to resolve it without modifying the channel. A loss of power by a manufacturer to his distributors may also foster the need to design an entirely new channel. Further, changing roles and communications difficulties may confront the marketer with channel design decisions. See Chapter 4.)

10. when regular periodic reviews and evaluations (see Chapter 13) undertaken by a firm point to the need for changes in the existing channels and possibly the need for new channels.

The above list of conditions, though by no means comprehensive, does offer an overview of some of the more common conditions which may require the channel manager to make channel design decisions.[5] It is important to be familiar with this list because channel design decisions are not necessarily obvious, especially those involving modification rather than the setting up of new channels. A critical part of the decision making process which is too often forgotten is to know *when one is confronted with the need to make decisions.* A development in the lumber industry helps to illustrate this for channel design decisions:[6]

Evans Products Company, a relatively small producer of lumber and plywood had been distributing through independent wholesalers and retailers for many years. In the mid 1960s Evans suspected that channel design changes were needed after observing that the typical retail lumber yard was trying to be all things to all people. As one Evans executive remarked: "They try to sell to contractors and homeowners alike, all across the counter." Evans thus decided to change its channel structure to direct marketing to consumers through its own retail stores.

Evans has been highly successful with its new channel structure, having gone from a relatively obscure lumber producer to second in the country in retail sales of building materials in the span of only five years.

Some of the nation's major lumber producers such as Georgia-Pacific, Weyerhauser, and U.S. Plywood, taking their cue from Evans, have since modified their distribution channels by eliminating some of their independent wholesalers and establishing company owned wholesale yards.

The salient point of this example is, of course, that Evans was quick to realize that it faced a channel design decision after observing the inadequate performance of the typical independent retail lumber yards. The larger companies were slower to realize the problem, and hence Evans beat them to the punch in designing a channel to reach the consumer mar-

---

[5]For some additional conditions see: Maureen Guirdham, *Marketing: The Management of Distribution Channels* (Oxford: Pergamon Press, 1972), pp. 129–130.

[6]"Evans Products Cuts Out the Middleman," *Business Week*, (31 July 1971): 70–71.

kets more successfully. In doing so, Evans gained a significant differential advantage.

Phase 2: Setting and Coordinating Distribution Objectives

Having recognized that he or she faces a channel design decision, the channel manager should try to develop a channel structure, whether from scratch or by modifying existing channels, that will help achieve the firm's distribution objectives efficiently. Yet quite often at this stage of the channel design decision, the firm's distribution objectives are not explicitly formulated, particularly since the changed conditions which created the need for channel design decisions (see previous section) might also have created the need for new or modified distribution objectives. It is important for the channel manager to evaluate carefully the firm's distribution objectives at this point to see if new ones are needed. An examination must also be made of the distribution objectives to see if they are coordinated with objectives and policies in the other areas of the marketing mix (product, price and promotion), and with the overall objectives and policies of the firm.

In order to set distribution objectives which are well coordinated with other marketing and firm objectives and policies, channel managers must perform three tasks:

1. They must familiarize themselves with the objectives and policies in the other marketing mix areas and any other objectives and policies of the firm which are relevant.
2. They must set distribution objectives and state them explicitly.
3. They must check to see if the distribution objectives they have set are congruent with marketing and other general objectives and policies of the firm.

Each of these is discussed below.

Becoming Familiar with Objectives and Policies

Whoever is responsible for setting distribution objectives must also make an effort to learn precisely what objectives and policies exist in the firm which may impinge on the distribution objectives he or she intends to set. In practice, quite often the same individual(s) who sets objectives in the other areas of the marketing mix will also do so for distribution.[7] But

---

[7] For a study of which executives in manufacturing firms are responsible for making channel design decisions see: Joe L. Welch, "An Investigation of Distribution Channel Selection Policies of U.S. Manufacturers," in *Proceedings of the Southeastern AIDS*, 1976, pp. 183–185.

even in this case, it is necessary to "think through" the interrelationships of the various marketing objectives and policies. The case of the Daily Salad Company helps to illustrate this point.[8]

The Daily Salad Company manufactured a variety of salads which were highly perishable. The firm's success in the sale of these salads was highly dependent upon its basic policy of providing absolute freshness to the consumer. Daily's main distribution objective for this product was set with this policy clearly in mind. It called for maximum control over the frequency of delivery of the product to the point of final purchase by the consumer. The Daily Company believed it could achieve this objective best by using a channel structure of direct sales to retail food stores.

Notice that so far in this example, effective coordination between the distribution objective and basic company policy has taken place. That is, the distribution objective was set to reflect the policy of providing absolutely fresh products. Now consider what happened in a subsequent development:

At a later point, the Daily Company introduced two new products— pickles and jelly. Daily did not, however, recognize that the introduction of new products often creates the need to evaluate existing distribution objectives. Since Daily did not make such an evaluation, it simply extended its existing distribution objective for salads to include pickles and jelly as well. Given this distribution objective, Daily continued to use its existing channel structure (selling directly to retailers) for the pickles and jelly.

As sales of these new products increased, Daily's top management decided to expand its territory. They soon found out, however, that the cost of using the direct channel over the larger territories was much too high. At this point Daily Company's expansion objective appeared to be frustrated by a channel design problem.

This part of the Daily Company case points to *poor* coordination between objectives and policies because when the new product was introduced, no evaluation of distribution objectives was made. The outcome from this was a stifling of Daily's expansion objective:

Eventually, Daily's management began to examine its existing distribution objectives in light of the firm's new expansion objective and its basic policy of providing absolute freshness to the consumer. Once the problem was cast in this light, Daily soon realized that the distribution objective for salads did not hold for the new product line. Since pickles and jelly have a much longer shelf life than salads, they do not require

---

[8]This case is adapted from: Richard M. Clewett, "Checking Your Marketing Channels," *Management Aid Series*, U.S. Small Business Administration, 1961.

the same control and speed of delivery specified in the distribution objective for salads. Consequently, Daily Company was able to set a new, less stringent distribution objective for pickles and jellies which led to a less costly channel structure. This new channel design used wholesalers and chain warehouses for these products, enabling Daily to pursue its growth objective for the new product lines while still maintaining its basic policy of absolute freshness for the salads.

As this case points out, distribution objectives cannot be set in a vacuum—those responsible for developing them must be aware of what is going on in the other areas of the firm.

Setting Distribution Objectives

Distribution objectives are essentially statements describing what part distribution is expected to play in achieving the firm's overall marketing objectives. Three examples of distribution objectives are as follows:

1. A manufacturer of children's breakfast cereals might state the following distribution objective: "Our distribution objective for 'Sugardandies' is to ensure that all consumers with children under eight years old have the opportunity to buy these products on every occasion when they shop for groceries."
2. A shoe manufacturer setting a distribution objective for a product line appealing to young women might state this distribution objective: "Our distribution objective for our 'Young Design' shoes is to ensure that at least half the females between the ages of thirteen and nineteen, living on the East Coast, and spending between $20.00 and $30.00 on a pair of shoes have the opportunity to buy our shoes at least once out of every two occasions when they shop for shoes."
3. A manufacturer of high quality pipes might set this objective: "Our distribution objective for 'Sandhill' Pipes is to ensure that at least 50 percent of the quality tobacconist shops who handle pipes in the $35.00–$75.00 price range will carry the minimum assortment (25 pipes covering the complete price range from $35.00–$75.00)."

These distribution objectives are, of course, merely a sample of the many kinds of distribution objectives that may be developed. But they do show that there is nothing elusive or mystical about distribution objectives. They can be stated in a straightforward and explicit fashion.

Checking for Congruency

A congruency check in the context of channel design involves verifying that the distribution objectives do not conflict with objectives in the other

Figure 5.2
Interrelationships and Hierarchy of Objectives and Policies in the Firm

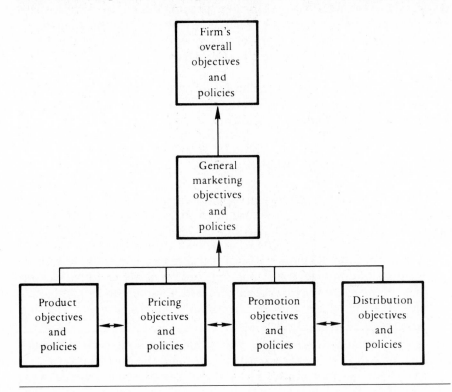

areas of the marketing mix (product, price, and promotion) and with the overall marketing and general objectives and policies of the firm.

In order to make such a check, it is important to examine the interrelationships and hierarchy of objectives and policies in the firm. This is portrayed in Figure 5.2.

In Figure 5.2, objectives and policies in the four basic areas of the marketing mix are connected together via two-way arrows. This is meant to convey the idea that these areas are all interrelated. Hence, objectives and policies pursued in any of these areas must generally be congruent with the other areas. A high quality objective in the product area, for example, would most likely call for a pricing objective that would cover the probable higher costs of the product and enhance its quality image. Promotional objectives would have to focus on communicating the superior quality of the product to the target market. At the same time, distribution objectives would need to be developed in terms of making the product conveniently available to that market in the types of outlets in which customers in that market are likely to shop.

Figure 5.2 also suggests a hierarchy of objectives and policies in the sense that objectives and policies in each area of the marketing mix must also be congruent with higher level marketing objectives and policies. These in turn must be congruent with the even higher set of overall objectives and policies of the firm.

Checking for congruency in this fashion is particularly important when setting distribution objectives because distribution objectives can have a substantial long term impact on the firm, especially if the distribution objective departs significantly from established objectives and policies. Recall, for example, the case of Perrier water discussed in Chapter 1 (see pp. 6–8). Source Perrier, the French producer of Perrier water, set a distribution objective that called for making Perrier water available to millions of American consumers. To meet this objective the product would have to be sold in large quantities through thousands of U.S. supermarkets right along with beer and soft drinks. For a company that had a highly exclusive, almost mystical, image and whose product had been sold only in gourmet shops, such a mass distribution objective would appear to be highly incongruent with company objectives and policies. Yet when Source Perrier's overall company objectives, which called for rapid growth, and its basic marketing objective of repositioning Perrier water as an alternative to liquor and soft drinks rather than as a bottled water are considered, the distribution objectives calling for mass distribution through supermarkets is perfectly congruent with these higher level objectives. Had the overall company and marketing objective not called for such growth and product repositioning, however, the mass marketing distribution objective set for Perrier water would have been highly incongruent with established objectives and policies of the firm. This is not to argue that the product would not have been successful anyway—it might very well have been. But the chances for success are likely to be higher when all of the objectives are working in concert rather than at cross purposes.

Phase 3: Specifying the Distribution Tasks

After the distribution objectives have been set (and coordinated), a number of distribution tasks (functions) must be performed if the distribution objectives are to be met. The channel manager must, therefore, specify explicitly the nature of these tasks.

Over the years marketing scholars have discussed numerous lists of marketing tasks (functions). These lists generally included such activities as buying, selling, communication, transportation, storage, risk-taking, financing, breaking-bulk, and others.[9] Such classifications of marketing functions, while perhaps useful to those seeking to explain the role of marketing in a macro context, are of little direct value to the channel

---

[9] See for example: Franklin W. Ryan, "Functional Elements of Market Distribution," *Harvard Business Review*, 13 (January, 1935): 205–221; Edmund D. McGary, "Some Functions of Marketing Reconsidered," in *Theory in Marketing*, eds. Revis Cox and Wroe Alderson (Homewood, Illinois: Richard D. Irwin, 1950), pp. 263–279; John C. Naver and Ronald Savitt, *The Marketing Economy* (New York: Holt, Rinehart and Winston, 1971), pp. 118–128.

manager operating in the individual firm. The job of the channel manager in specifying distribution functions or tasks is a much more specific and situationally dependent one. That is, the kinds of tasks required to meet specific distribution objectives must be precisely specified. Take, for example, a steel or metal producer whose distribution objectives call for dealing with a target market that contains many small customers. Along with such basic distribution tasks as selling, communication, transportation, storage, risk-taking, and financing, in order to adequately serve the smaller customers, the producer would most likely have to perform many more specialized tasks such as the following: [10]

1. provide readily available inventory (specified in terms of quantity and type)
2. provide rapid delivery (specified in days or hours)
3. offer credit
4. provide emergency service
5. provide semifabrication such as: cutting, shearing, slotting, threading, pattern cutting, pattern rolling, rerolling, stretcher leveling, welding, grinding, forcing, reaming
6. provide packaging and special handling
7. provide technical assistance such as: problem analysis, product selection, application, end use product
8. provide market information
9. offer storage space
10. provide for absorption of size and grade obsolescence
11. provide order processing and billing for many accounts
12. offer return provisions

Though a number of these tasks appear to be production rather than distribution tasks, when viewed in the context of being necessary to meet a particular distribution objective (such as dealing with smaller customers) they are indeed distribution tasks. The performance of these specialized tasks would be necessary because the distribution objective called for dealing with many small customers and in most cases these small customers could not perform these tasks for themselves. Consequently, the specific kinds of distribution tasks required are mainly a function of the distribution objectives that have been set and, of course, the types of firms involved. For example, if the metal producer's distribution objective had called for dealing only with large customers, a number of the above mentioned tasks could be eliminated or significantly reduced, particularly 2, 4, 5, 6, 7, 9.

[10]John M. Brion, *Marketing Through the Wholesaler/Distributor Channel* (Chicago: American Marketing Association, 1965), pp. 6–7.

Phase 4: Developing Possible Alternative Channel Structures

Having specified in detail the particular distribution tasks that must be performed to achieve the distribution objectives, the channel manager must then consider alternative ways of allocating these tasks. The allocation alternatives (possible channel structures) should be in terms of the following three dimensions: (1) number of levels in the channel, (2) intensity at the various levels, and (3) types of intermediaries at each level.

Number of Levels

The number of levels in a channel can range from two levels which is the most direct (manufacturer → user), up to five levels and occasionally even higher. Figure 5.3 shows a variety of channels in both the consumer and industrial markets ranging from two to six levels.

The number of alternatives which the channel manager can realistically consider for this structural dimension is often limited to no more than two or three choices. For example, it might be feasible to consider going direct (two level), using one intermediary (three level) or possibly two intermediaries (four level). These limitations result from a variety of factors such as the particular industry practices, nature and size of the market, availability of middlemen, and other variables which we will discuss more fully in Phase 5. In some instances, this dimension of channel structure is the same for all manufacturers in the industry and may remain virtually fixed for long periods of time. In other industries this dimension of channel structure is more flexible and subject to change in relatively short time periods.

Intensity at the Various Levels

Intensity refers to the number of intermediaries at each level of the marketing channel. Traditionally this dimension has been broken into three categories: (1) *intensive*, (2) *selective*, and (3) *exclusive*. *Intensive* (sometimes termed saturation) means as many outlets as possible are used at each level of the channel. Many consumer convenience goods and industrial operating supplies fit this category. *Selective*, as the name suggests, means that not all possible intermediaries at a particular level are used, but rather that those included in the channel are carefully chosen. Consumer shopping goods are often in this category. *Exclusive* is actually a way of referring to a very highly selective pattern of distribution. In this case only one intermediary in a particular market area is used. Specialty

Figure 5.3
Alternative Channel Levels

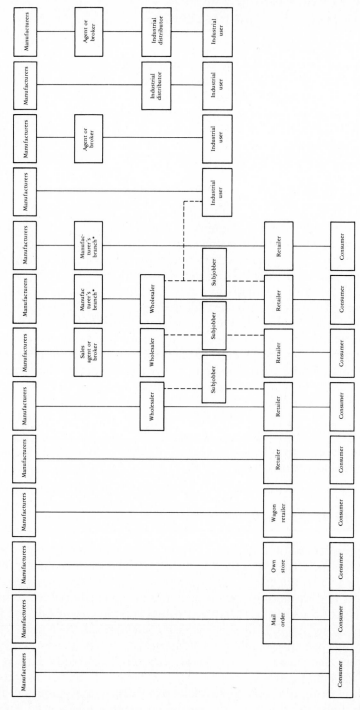

*A manufacturer's branch is owned by the manufacturer.

Source: David T. Kollat, Roger D. Blackwell and James F. Robeson, *Strategic Marketing* (New York: Holt, Rinehart and Winston, 1972), p. 284.

Figure 5.4
Relationship Between the Intensity of Distribution Dimension and Number of Retail Intermediaries Used in a Given Market Area

Intensity dimension

Intensive	Selective	Exclusive

Numbers of intermediaries (retail level)

Many	Few	One

goods often fit this category. Figure 5.4 illustrates the intensity of distribution dimension graphically as it might apply to retail intermediaries. Figure 5.4 shows that for a given market area (territory), a very high degree of selectivity or exclusive distribution corresponds to only one retailer in the territory. A lower degree of selectivity corresponds to a few retailers, while very low selectivity (or stated conversely, an intensive level of distribution) is associated with many retailers in the territory. The actual numbers involved will, of course, vary for different firms.

The intensity of distribution dimension is a very important aspect of channel structure because this dimension is often a key factor in the firm's basic marketing strategy and will also reflect the firm's overall business policies. A marketing strategy that seeks to blanket the market with a product such as that used by Timex watches, for example, requires a channel structure that stresses a very high level of distribution intensity. On the other hand, a marketing strategy that focuses on carefully chosen target markets such as that used by Rolex watches requires that a high degree of selectivity be built into the channel structure. In general, then, if a firm's basic marketing strategy emphasizes mass appeal for its products it will most likely have to develop a channel structure that stresses intensive distribution, while a marketing strategy that stresses more narrow segmented marketing will most probably call for a more selective channel structure.

Beyond this basic relationship with the firm's marketing strategy, the degree of intensity decision is also often reflective of a firm's basic policies for operating its business. Some firms like to choose their channel members very carefully and then work closely with them in the distribution of the firm's products. Other firms believe in selling through "almost anyone" and pay little attention to how the product is sold once it is in the hands of the firm's many channel members. Other firms are somewhere in between these two extremes. Thus, in considering the intensity dimension when designing the channel, the channel manager should carefully consider the firm's established policies for dealing with middlemen and try to stay within these policy guidelines when dealing with the issue of distribution intensity.

Types of Intermediaries

The third dimension of channel structure deals with the particular types of intermediaries to be used (if any) at the various levels of the channel. In Chapter 2 we discussed different types of intermediaries available. Recall that there are many types listed in the *Censuses of Wholesale and Retail Trade*. Unfortunately, there are many different names given to intermediaries, particularly those at the wholesale level, which were derived from the industry or trade long ago but which today convey little meaning about what services these firms offer.

Nevertheless, at this phase of the channel design decision, the channel manager is likely to have a general awareness of the kinds of intermediaries available to serve his or her industry, or have a readily available means for finding out. Trade association data, noncompeting firms in his industry, customers, or independent consultants are also good sources of information[11] (see Chapter 6, pp. 175–182).

The emphasis of the channel manager's analysis at this point should focus on the basic types of distribution tasks which these intermediaries generally perform. For example, metal warehouse distributors, a type of industrial wholesaler, generally have the capability for performing all of the distribution tasks which metals producers discussed earlier need performed to deal with smaller accounts.

Number of Possible Channel Structure Alternatives

Given that the channel manager should consider all three of these structural dimensions of level, intensity, and type of intermediaries in developing alternative channel structures, there are, in theory, a high number of possibilities. Consider the following: three levels, three degrees of intensity, five different types of intermediaries. The number of possible channel structures based on these three dimensions is:

$$3 \times 3 \times 5 = 45 \text{ possible channel structures.}$$

Realistically, this number of alternative channel structures cannot usually be considered except when certain management science approaches are used (see Phase 6). Fortunately, in practice, the number of feasible alternatives for each dimension is often limited so that it is seldom necessary to have more than a dozen alternative channel structures from which to choose. Usually the number is considerably less than that.

[11] For additional sources see: Roger M. Pegram, *Selecting and Evaluating Distributors* (New York: The National Industrial Conference Board, 1965), pp. 11–17.

Phase 5: Evaluating Variables Affecting Channel Structure

Having laid out several possible alternative channel structures, the channel manager must then evaluate a number of variables to determine how they are likely to influence various channel structures. Although there are a myriad of such variables, it is possible to discuss some basic categories of variables which are frequently of relevance in the analysis of alternative channel structures. We have broken these down into six categories as follows:

1. Market variables
2. Product variables
3. Company variables
4. Middlemen variables
5. Environmental variables
6. Behavioral variables

In the course of discussing the variables in these categories we will often cite a number of heuristics (rules of thumb) that relate these variables to channel structure. An example of one such heuristic is as follows:

If a product is technically complex the manufacturer should sell directly to its user instead of through middlemen.

Here a product variable (technical complexity) seemingly yields a simple prescription for channel structure. It would be nice if things were this simple but unfortunately such is *not* the case. It is important to keep in mind that such heuristics which are commonly mentioned in the marketing literature are extremely crude guides to decision making. They should not be viewed as clear cut prescriptions for choosing a particular channel structure. They are useful only to the extent that they offer some rough reflection of what would typically be expected given a particular condition, and thereby provide a point of departure for the analysis of different channel structures.

With this caveat in mind, we turn to a discussion of these six categories of variables and some of the related heuristics relevant to choosing channel structure.

Market Variables

Market variables are of such importance in channel decision making that we have devoted an entire chapter to this topic (Chapter 7). So in this section we will discuss market variables only briefly as they apply to channel design.

There are four basic subcategories of market variables that are particularly important in influencing channel structure. These are (1) market geography, (2) market size, (3) market density, and (4) market behavior.

Market Geography.   Market geography refers to the geographical size of markets and their physical location and distance from the producer or manufacturer.

From a channel design standpoint, the basic tasks that emerge when dealing with market geography are the development of a channel structure that adequately covers the markets in question and providing for an efficient flow of products to those markets.

While we will go into greater detail on these issues in Chapter 7, a general heuristic for relating market geography to channel design can be stated at this point:

The greater the distance between the manufacturer and his markets, the higher the probability that the use of intermediaries will be less expensive than direct distribution.

The case of the Daily Salad Company discussed earlier conformed to this heuristic. Recall that as Daily attempted to distribute directly to more geographically distant markets, its costs increased dramatically, and hence the company had to turn to intermediaries (wholesalers) to reduce its costs.

Market Size.   The number of customers making up a market (consumer or industrial) determines the market size. From a channel design standpoint, the larger the number of individual customers, the larger the market size.

The usual operational measures of market size are the actual number of potential consumers or firms in the consumer and industrial markets, respectively. Dollar volume is typically not a useful measure of market size because of the wide variations in dollar volume; that is, it is possible to have high dollar volumes from a small number of customers and vice versa. Only if dollar volume is highly correlated with the numbers of customers will it serve as a reliable measure of market size.

A very general heuristic about market size relative to channel structure is:

If the market is large the use of middlemen is more likely to be needed. Conversely, if the market is small, a firm is more likely to be able to avoid the use of middlemen.

Market Density.   The number of buying units (consumers or industrial firms) per unit of land area determines the density of the market. A market having one thousand customers in an area of 100 square miles is more dense than one containing the same number of customers in a 500 square mile area.

In general, the less dense the market, the more difficult and expensive is distribution. This is particularly true for the flow of goods to the market, but it also applies to the flow of information. Consequently, a typically cited heuristic for market density and channel structure is:

The less dense the market, the more likely it is that intermediaries will be used. Stated conversely, the greater the density of the market, the higher the likelihood of eliminating middlemen.

For example, a firm selling specialized industrial equipment such as drilling equipment for petroleum producers will have its market concentrated in a relatively small area in several states. On the other hand, a firm selling basic operating supplies such as oils and greases, abrasives, cleaning supplies, detergents, stationery supplies, and the like, will find that its market is dispersed over a vast geographical area because there are so many potential users of these products. The possibility of designing a direct channel to serve such low density markets is usually low because of the high costs involved in providing adequate service.

Buying Behaviors of the Market.   Buying behaviors refer to the following four types of market behavior:

1.   how customers buy
2.   when customers buy
3.   where customers buy
4.   who does the buying

Each of these patterns of buyer behavior may have a significant effect on channel structure. Table 5.1 provides some examples of these. Here again we should keep in mind that the heuristics shown in Table 5.1 are merely rough indicators of what is typical. There are many exceptions to these heuristics under differing sets of circumstances. The material shown in Table 5.1 should be seen as providing illustrative examples only, and not as a source of reference for choosing a channel structure. We will examine these issues in much more detail in Chapter 7.

Product Variables

Product variables are another important category to consider in evaluating alternative channel structures. Some of the most important product variables are the following:

1.   Bulk and weight
2.   Perishability

Table 5.1
Examples of Market Buying Habits and Some Corresponding Heuristics for Channel Structure

Buying Habits	Corresponding Channel Structure Heuristics
How Customers typically buy in very small quantities.	Use long (perhaps several levels of intermediaries) to reach the market.
When Buying is highly seasonal.	Add intermediaries to the channel to perform the storage function thereby reducing peaks and valleys in production.
Where Increasing tendency of consumers to shop at home.	Eliminate wholesale and retail intermediaries and sell direct.
Who Consumer market: husband and wife are generally both involved in the purchase.	Distribute through retailers who successfully cater to both spouses.
Industrial market: multiple influence on purchasing decision	Direct distribution for greater control of sales force to successfully reach all parties responsible for making purchase decisions.

3. Unit value

4. Custom-made vs. standardized

5. Technical vs. nontechnical

6. Newness

Bulk and Weight.   Heavy and bulky products have very high handling and shipping costs relative to their value. The producer of such products should therefore attempt to minimize these costs by shipping them only in large lots to the fewest possible points. Consequently the channel structure for heavy-bulky products should, as a general rule, be as short as possible. This usually means direct from producer to user. The major exception to this occurs when customers buy in small quantities and need quick delivery. In this case it may be necessary to use some form of intermediaries.

Perishability.   Products which are subject to rapid physical deterioration (e.g., fresh foods), and those that experience rapid fashion obsolescence are considered to be highly perishable. The *sine qua non* of channel design in this case is rapid movement of the product from production to its final user to minimize the risks attendant on high perishability. The appropriate heuristic here is:

Channels should be as short as possible.

(See the Daily Salad Company example discussed earlier in this chapter.)

Unit Value.   In general, the lower the unit value of a product, the longer the channels should be. This is because the low unit value leaves a small margin for distribution costs. Such products as convenience goods in the consumer market, and operating supplies in the industrial market typically use one or more intermediaries so that the costs of distribution can be shared by many other products which the intermediaries handle. For example, it would be difficult to imagine the sale of a package of chewing gum directly from the Wrigley Company to the consumer. Only by spreading the costs of distribution over the wide variety of products handled by wholesale or retail intermediaries is it possible to buy a package of chewing gum at retail for twenty-five cents.

Degree of Standardization.   In general, the influence of this product variable on channel structure is characterized by the relationship shown in Figure 5.5.

In Figure 5.5, degree of standardization is shown on the horizontal axis as a continuum ranging from custom made products to those which are identical. Channel length, on the vertical axis, is represented by the number of intermediaries from none to several. Essentially, Figure 5.5 shows that custom made products go directly from the producer to the user, but as products become more standardized, the opportunity to lengthen the channel by including intermediaries increases. For example, totally custom made products, such as industrial machinery, very often are sold directly from the manufacturer to the user. Semicustom products such as

Figure 5.5
Relationship between Degree of Product Standardization
and Channel Length

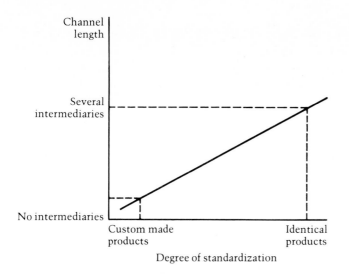

accessory equipment in the industrial market and furniture in the consumer market will often include one intermediary. On the other hand, highly standardized products such as operating supplies in the industrial market and convenience goods in the consumer market will frequently include more than one intermediary.

Technical vs. Nontechnical.   In the industrial market, a highly technical product will generally be distributed through a direct channel. The overriding reason for this is that the manufacturer needs sales and service people who are capable of communicating the product's technical features to potential customers and who can provide continuing liaison, advice and service after the sale is made. Many industrial distributors cannot perform these services effectively.

Newness.   Many new products in both consumer and industrial markets require extensive and aggressive promotion in the introductory stage to build primary demand. Usually, the longer the channel, the more difficult it is to achieve this kind of promotional effort from all of the channel members. Consequently, in the introductory stage a shorter channel is generally viewed as an advantage for gaining product acceptance. Further, the degree of selectivity also tends to be higher for new products because a more carefully selected group of intermediaries is more likely to provide more aggressive promotion.

Company Variables

The most important company variables affecting channel design are: (1) size, (2) financial capacity, (3) managerial expertise, and (4) objectives and policies of the company.

Size.   In general, the range of options for different channel structures is a positive function of a firm's size.

The power bases available to large firms, particularly those of reward, coercion, and expertise, enable them to exercise a substantial amount of power in the channel. This gives large firms a relatively high degree of flexibility for choosing channel structures compared with smaller firms. Consequently, the larger firm's capacity to have channels which at least approach an optimal allocation of distribution tasks is typically much higher than for smaller firms.

Financial Capacity.   Generally, the greater the capital available to a company, the lower is its dependence on intermediaries.

In order to sell directly to the ultimate consumer or industrial user, a firm usually needs its own sales force and support services. Larger firms are better able to bear the high costs of these activities. Only if the small firm deals with an extremely small number of customers is it likely to be able to sell to them directly.

Managerial Expertise.   Some firms lack the managerial skills necessary to perform distribution tasks. When this is the case, channel design must of necessity include the services of intermediaries which may range through full function wholesalers, manufacturers' representatives, selling agents, brokers, or others. Over time, as the firm's management gains experience, it may be feasible to change the structure to reduce the amount of reliance on intermediaries.

Basic Objectives and Policies.   Marketing and general firm policies and objectives such as a desire to exercise a high degree of control over the product and its service may limit the use of middlemen. Further, such policies as an emphasis on aggressive promotion and rapid reaction to changing market conditions will constrain the types of channel structures available to those firms having such policies.

Middlemen Variables

The key middlemen variables related to channel structure are: (1) the availability of middlemen, (2) cost of using middlemen, (3) the service which various middlemen offer.

Availability.   In a number of cases, the availability of adequate intermediaries will influence channel structure. For example, the Melville Shoe Corp. markets directly to the consumer through its own chain of Thom McAn retail stores. This channel structure—in part—reflects Melville's belief that available independent retail shoe stores could not do an adequate job of providing market information needed to offer the right shoe products to consumers.

Cost.   The cost of using intermediaries is always a consideration in choosing a channel structure. If the channel manager determines that the cost of using intermediaries is too high for the services which they perform, the channel structure is likely to minimize the use of intermediaries. Approaches for making this kind of decision will be discussed in Phase 6.

Services.   The third middleman variable, the services offered by particular middlemen, is closely related to the problem of selection which is discussed in detail in the following chapter. At this point we will simply mention the basic approach to the evaluation of middlemen services. Essentially this involves evaluating the services offered by particular middlemen to see which ones can perform them most effectively at the most favorable cost.[12]

---

[12] For a related discussion see: "How Much Service Can You Afford?," *Industrial Distribution*, (June, 1979): 43–48.

Environmental Variables

As we pointed out in Chapter 3, environmental variables may affect all aspects of channel development and management. Economic, sociocultural, competitive, technological, and legal environmental forces can have a significant impact on channel structure. Indeed, as we mentioned in an earlier section of the present chapter, the impact of environmental forces is one of the more common reasons for making channel design decisions. Since Chapter 3 presented numerous examples of how the environment affects the channel, we need not go into detail here.

Behavioral Variables

When choosing a channel structure, the behavioral variables discussed in Chapter 4 should be reviewed. For example, by developing more congruent roles for channel members, a major cause of conflict can be reduced. By giving more attention to the influence of behavioral problems that can distort communications such as those discussed by Wittreich (see Chapter 4), a channel structure with a more effective communications flow is more likely to be chosen. By keeping in mind the power bases available, the channel manager's final choice of a channel structure is more likely to reflect a realistic basis for influencing channel members. For instance, a small, specialized manufacturer who decides to use large chain retailers in the channel structure is unlikely to be able to gain much influence or control if coercive power is used, yet he or she might very well be able to do so if expert power is stressed. A channel manager who needs a very high level of control to achieve his or her distribution objectives may find that the legitimate power base (manifest in a strong franchise contract) should serve as the basis for the channel structure. These and many other implications of behavioral variables may in particular instances be relevant for choosing an appropriate channel structure.

Phase 6: Choosing the "Best" Channel

In theory, the channel manager should choose a channel structure alternative which is optimal. Such a structure would offer the desired level of effectiveness in performing the distribution tasks at the lowest possible cost. If the firm's goal is to maximize its long term profits, an optimal channel structure would be completely consistent with that goal.[13]

In reality, choosing an optimal channel structure, in the strictest sense

---

[13] A theoretical discussion related to this point can be found in: Louis P. Bucklin, *A Theory of Distribution Channel Structure* (Berkeley, Cal.: Institute of Business and Economic Research, University of California, 1966).

of the term, is not possible. To do so would require the channel manager to have considered all possible alternative channel structures, and to be able to calculate the exact payoffs associated with each alternative structure in terms of some criterion (usually profit). The channel manager would then choose the one alternative which offers the highest payoff.[14]

Why is this not possible? First, as we pointed out in discussing Phase 4 (Determining Possible Alternative Channel Structures), management is not capable of knowing all the possible alternatives. The amount of information and time necessary to develop all possible alternative channel structures for achieving a particular distribution objective would be prohibitive. Moreover, even if management were willing to expend this time and effort, it would have no way of knowing when it had actually specified all of the possible alternatives.

Secondly, even if it were possible to specify all possible channel structures, precise methods do not exist for calculating (forecasting) the exact payoffs associated with each of the alternative structures. As we pointed out in the last section and in earlier chapters, the number of·variables affecting the channel is legion and these variables are continually changing. Any method claiming to offer a means for calculating exact payoffs for each of the alternative channel structures would have to offer its user the ability to identify all relevant variables, and tell precisely what effects each variable has on the structure. Moreover, the method would also have to be capable of predicting the level and direction of change in all of the variables. Such a method (some might prefer to call it a model) is not a very realistic possibility, at least in the foreseeable future.

Nevertheless, even though no exact methods for choosing an optimal channel structure exist, some pioneering attempts at developing more exact methods do appear in the literature. We will discuss some of these briefly below because they provide insight for making good (if not optimal) choices of channel structure. Specifically, the approaches and methods discussed below can help to sharpen the channel manager's ability to evaluate variables affecting channel structure. Armed with this knowledge, the channel manager is then better prepared to choose channel structures which at least approach an optimal allocation of distribution tasks.

Aspinwall's Characteristics of Goods and Parallel Systems Approach

Aspinwall's approach places the overwhelming emphasis for choosing a channel structure on product variables.[15]

[14] For a related discussion of the limitations of the decision maker to operate optimally see: Herbert A. Simon, "Theories of Decision-Making in Economic and Behavioral Sciences," *American Economic Review* 49 (June, 1959): 253–283.

[15] Leo Aspinwall, "The Characteristics of Goods and Parallel Systems Theories," in *Managerial Marketing*, eds. Eugene J. Kelley and William Lazer (Homewood, Illinois: Richard D. Irwin, 1958), pp. 434–450.

Table 5.2
Aspinwall's Characteristic of Goods Theory
Color Classification Scheme

	Color Classification		
Characteristics	**Red Goods**	**Orange Goods**	**Yellow Goods**
Replacement Rate	High	Medium	Low
Gross Margin	Low	Medium	High
Adjustment	Low	Medium	High
Time of Consumption	Low	Medium	High
Searching Time	Low	Medium	High

Source: W. Lazer and E. J. Kelly, *Managerial Marketing: Perspectives and Viewpoints*, rev. ed. (Homewood, Illinois: Richard D. Irwin, Inc., © 1962). Reproduced by permission of publisher.

Aspinwall begins by arguing that all products may be described by the following five characteristics:

1. *Replacement rate*—the rate at which a good is purchased and consumed by users in order to provide the satisfaction a consumer expects from the product.
2. *Gross margin*—the money sum which is the difference between the laid-in cost and the final realized sales price. (This includes all gross margins as products move through the channel, i.e., the sum of these).
3. *Adjustment*—services applied to goods in order to meet the exact needs of the consumer.
4. *Time of consumption*—the measured time of consumption during which the product gives up the utility desired.
5. *Searching time*—a measure of average time and distance from the retail store.

Aspinwall continues by presenting a method for classifying all products based on the degree to which they possess each of these characteristics. He does so by using an ingenious analogy to the color spectrum: any product could be represented by its "shade" on this spectrum—which uses only three colors instead of the usual seven. As Table 5.2 shows, products with high replacement rates but low values for the other four characteristics are "red goods." Those products having medium values on all five characteristics are "orange goods," while those with a low replacement rate but that have higher values for the other four characteristics are "yellow goods." By visualizing a blending of these colors from red to yellow with orange in between, an infinite gradation of values for products can be perceived.

Aspinwall argues that the channel structures used in the distribution (as well as promotion) of products are closely related to their "color" (i.e., the degree to which they possess each of the five characteristics). For example, as Table 5.2 shows, red products have a high replacement rate. The high frequency of purchase of red goods allows for a high degree of standardization and specialization in the performance of the distribution tasks. This in turn creates the opportunity for more specialized marketing institutions to participate, resulting in long channels for red goods. Convenience goods in the consumer market and operating supplies in the industrial market fit this pattern.

Looking again at Table 5.2 we can see that yellow products are low in replacement rate but high in the other characteristics. This makes the performance of distribution tasks relatively expensive because of the lower opportunity for standardization and routinization compared with red goods. Custom-made products such as a made to order suit or industrial equipment specifically designed for its user's needs, are illustrative of yellow goods which generally call for short channel structures.

Finally, we notice from Table 5.2 that orange goods rate a medium ranking on all five characteristics. These goods, though produced to standard specifications, will still require some degree of adjustment to adequately meet their user's needs. Automobiles and furniture are examples of orange products. The replacement rate for orange products is high enough to offer moderate opportunity for standardization and specialization. At least one intermediary is likely to enter the channel: for example, an automobile dealer buying from the manufacturer and selling to the consumer or an industrial distributor operating between two manufacturers. Channel structures for orange goods tend to be medium in length, that is, generally containing at least one level of middleman.

Figure 5.6 illustrates this parallel relationship between the characteristics of products and channel length.

Figure 5.6
**Relationship between Product Characteristics
and Length of Marketing Channels**

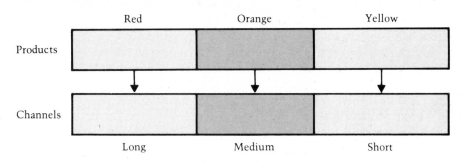

Source: W. Lazer and E. J. Kelly, *Managerial Marketing: Perspectives and Viewpoints*, rev. ed. (Homewood, Illinois: Richard D. Irwin, Inc., © 1962). Reproduced by permission of publisher.

As Figure 5.6 shows, the structure of the channel in terms of its length dimension parallels the characteristics of products.

Using Aspinwall's Approach.   The major value of Aspinwall's approach for the channel manager is that it provides a neat (some would even say elegant) way of describing and relating a number of heuristics about how product characteristics affect channel structure. As a result, it provides the channel manager with a better handle for dealing with the very important class of product variables. Rather than trying to enumerate many different product variables for each product, the channel manager can turn to Aspinwall's framework and describe any product in terms of the five characteristics. Then on the basis of judgement or by assigning numerical weights to each of the characteristics, the product may be classified as red, orange, or yellow.

The major problem with Aspinwall's approach is that it puts too much emphasis on product characteristics as the determinant of channel structure. It becomes tempting to use this approach while giving inadequate consideration to the other categories of variables which may be important determinants of structure. There are also practical problems involved in getting the necessary information for developing appropriate measurements of the product characteristics. For example, searching time is a particularly difficult type of information to obtain.

Nevertheless, if Aspinwall's approach is used as one of the tools which the channel manager uses for choosing channel structures rather than the only tool, it has much to offer as a guide for choosing channel structures.

Financial Approach

Lambert offers another approach which argues that the most important variables for choosing a channel structure are financial. He states:

"Examination of the process of choosing a trade channel leads to the conclusion that the choice is determined primarily by financial rather than what are generally thought of as marketing considerations. This is shown to be the case regardless of whether the firm has adequate or limited financial resources to expand marketing operations. It is equally true whether the firm is contemplating shortening the channel, which requires more capital, or lengthening the channel, which will make funds formerly used in distribution available for other employment."[16]

According to Lambert, choosing an appropriate channel structure is analogous to an investment decision of capital budgeting. Basically this involves comparing estimated earnings on capital resulting from alternative

---

[16]Eugene W. Lambert, "Financial Considerations in Choosing A Marketing Channel," *MSU Business Topics*, (Winter, 1966): 17–26.

channel structures in light of the cost of capital to determine the most profitable channel. Further, the use of capital for distribution must also be compared to the alternative of using the funds in manufacturing operations. Unless the firm can earn more than the cost of capital and the return that can be earned on the use of its funds in manufacturing, it should shift performance of marketing functions to intermediaries.

Using the Financial Approach.   Lambert's financial approach certainly serves as a useful reminder of the importance of financial variables in choosing a channel structure. Moreover the perspective used is very appropriate because channel structure decisions are usually long term ones compared with the other decision areas of the marketing mix. By viewing the channel as a long term investment which must more than cover the cost of the capital invested in it and provide a better return than other alternative uses for capital (opportunity cost), the criteria for choosing a channel structure become more rigorous. The channel manager would then have to justify his or her choice of a channel structure based on these investment criteria.

The major problem with Lambert's approach lies in the difficulty of making it operational in a channel decision-making context. Regardless of the investment methods used such as simple rate of return, or the more sophisticated discounted cash flow methods (which take into account the present value of money), obtaining accurate estimates of future revenues and costs from alternative channel structures is exceedingly difficult. Indeed, forecasting future streams of revenues and costs even for capital goods such as buildings, machinery and equipment for one firm is a tricky business often subject to huge errors. Given the number of variables that can affect channel relationships, especially when independent middlemen are involved, the problem becomes far more difficult. Consequently, the financial investment approach to choosing channel structure, as it now stands, must await better methods for forecasting before it can find widespread use as a practical approach for making such choices.[17]

Management Science Approaches

It would indeed be desirable if the channel manager could take all possible channel structures, along with all the relevant variables, and "plug these into a set of equations" which would then yield the optimal channel structure. As we pointed out earlier in this section, such an approach is possible in theory. In fact some pioneering attempts have been made to use management science methods, such as operations research, simulation, and decision theory, in an effort to design optimal marketing channels.

For example, Balderston and Hoggatt developed a simulation model

[17] For another financial approach to channel choice see: Mary A. Higby, *An Evaluation of Alternative Channels of Distribution.* (East Lansing, Michigan: Graduate School of Business Administration, Michigan State University, 1977).

which was used to study the channel structures of the lumber industry on the West Coast.[18] The typical structure in this region is producer → wholesaler → retailer. The product flow is often drop-shipped in carload lots from the lumber producer to the retailer with the wholesalers mainly performing information, risk taking, and financing tasks. Balderston and Hoggatt were able to incorporate these features into their model, achieving a degree of realism which is sometimes lacking in simulation approaches.

This simulation method developed by Balderston and Hoggatt may in the future hold promise for more widespread applications to choosing channel structure, especially for those decisions which are too complex for handling mathematically (where only a limited number of alternatives and variables can be employed). Moreover the approach has the added advantage of allowing the channel decision maker to "see what happens" as a result of the decisions by running the simulation model before actually executing the decisions in the real world.

Artle and Berglund developed a mathematical model which enables its user to calculate the costs of performing distribution tasks for alternative channel structures and then to select the one which offers the lowest total cost and maximum profits.[19] Though their model dealt only with the personal selling tasks and with only two channel structure alternatives (producer → wholesaler → retailer, and producer → retailer), the method holds promise for applications to other distribution tasks and additional channel structure alternatives.

Alderson and Green show how Bayesian statistics can be applied to channel choice.[20] Their example, though somewhat oversimplified, tackles the decision of whether a firm using sales agents should change to its own sales force. This approach requires the channel manager to identify explicitly the various payoffs associated with different channel structures. The cost of information to help in making a decision is also incorporated into the analysis.

Though the Bayesian approach appears to hold much promise, its application to channel design decisions has been very limited. This may be due to the difficulty of obtaining accurate subjective probability estimates from decision makers which are required in the Bayesian approach.

Finally, Baligh developed a comprehensive operations research model for structuring the problems of optimal channel choice.[21] His model allows for the determination of the combination of inputs that leads to channel control and therefore affects revenues and costs. The model thus provides a basis for incorporating the behavioral variable of power into formal mathematical frameworks.

[18] Fredrick E. Balderston and Austin C. Hoggatt, *Simulation of Market Processes* (Berkeley, Cal.: Institute of Business and Economic Research, University of California, 1962), chap. 1–2.

[19] Roland Artle and Sture Berglund, "A Note on Manufacturers' Choice of Distribution Channels," *Management Science*, (July, 1959), 460–71.

[20] Wroe Alderson and Paul E. Green, "Bayesian Decision Theory in Channel Selection," in their text *Planning and Problem Solving in Marketing* (Homewood, Illinois: Richard D. Irwin, 1964), pp. 311–17.

[21] Helmy H. Baligh, "A Theoretical Framework for Channel Choice," in *Marketing and Economic Development*, ed. Peter D. Bennett (Chicago: American Marketing Association, 1965), pp. 631–654.

Using Management Science Approaches. These management science approaches need much more development before they are likely to find widespread application to channel choice. This is not to disparage such formalized approaches. On the contrary, in the future (under certain constrained conditions), they may be of real practical value. Even today such attempts should be encouraged because in the process of building formal models of channel choice decisions, the relevant variables and the relationships among them are made more explicit. But given the state of the art, channel choice, for the present at least, will continue to be less formal, relying heavily upon managerial judgement. These judgemental approaches are discussed in the next section.

Judgemental-Heuristic Approaches

As the name suggests, these approaches to choosing channel structure rely heavily on managerial judgement and heuristics or rules of thumb. There are, however, variations in the degree of precision of judgemental-heuristic approaches. Some attempt to formalize the decision-making process to some degree, while others attempt to incorporate cost and revenue data. Three approaches are discussed below which illustrate these variations in judgemental-heuristic approaches to choosing a channel.

Straight Qualitative Judgement Approach. The qualitative approach is the crudest but, in practice, probably the most commonly used approach for choosing channel structures. Under this approach, the various alternative channel structures that have been generated are evaluated by management in terms of decision factors which are thought to be important. These may include such factors as short and long run cost and profit considerations, channel control issues, long term growth potentials, and many others. Sometimes, however, these decision factors are not stated explicitly, and their relative importance is also not made clear. Nevertheless, an alternative is chosen which, in terms of management's judgement, best satisfies the various explicit or implicit decision factors. As an example of this approach consider the following:[22]

The Commodity Chemical Company has generated the five channel alternatives shown in Figure 5.7 for the distribution of its new swimming pool germicide product.

If the straight qualitative judgement approach were to be used for choosing the "best" alternative, management would subjectively and qualitatively "weigh" each of the alternatives in Figure 5.7 in terms of the decision factors they believe to be important. After considering the pros and

[22]This example is adapted from Philip Kotler, *Marketing Decision Making: A Model Building Approach* (New York: Holt, Rinehart and Winston, 1971), pp. 291–293.

Figure 5.7
Alternative Channels Proposed by the Commodity Chemical Company for its New Pool Germicide Product

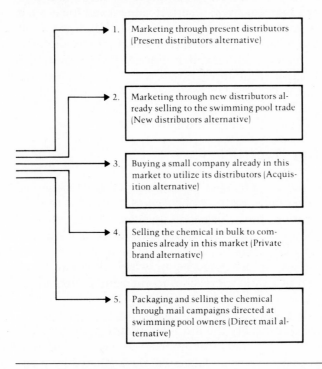

1. Marketing through present distributors (Present distributors alternative)

2. Marketing through new distributors already selling to the swimming pool trade (New distributors alternative)

3. Buying a small company already in this market to utilize its distributors (Acquisition alternative)

4. Selling the chemical in bulk to companies already in this market (Private brand alternative)

5. Packaging and selling the chemical through mail campaigns directed at swimming pool owners (Direct mail alternative)

Source: Philip Kotler, *Marketing Decision Making: A Model Building Approach*, p. 292. © 1971 by Holt, Rinehart and Winston. Reprinted by permission.

cons of the five alternatives, management would then choose the alternative which in its judgement is the best one.

Weighted Factor Score Approach.   A more refined version of the straight qualitative approach to choosing among channel alternatives is the weighted factor approach, suggested by Kotler. This approach forces management to *structure and quantify* its judgements in choosing a channel alternative.[23] The approach consists of four basic steps:

1.   The decision factors on which the channel choice will be based must be stated explicitly.
2.   Weights are then assigned to each of the decision factors in order to reflect their relative importance precisely.
3.   Each channel alternative is rated on each of the decision factors.
4.   The overall weighted factor score (i.e., total score) is computed for each channel alternative.

[23] Ibid., p. 293.

This procedure is illustrated in Table 5.3 for channel alternative number (1) shown in Figure 5.7.

Looking at the left hand column of Table 5.3, we can see that the Commodity Chemical Company has stated five decision factors explicitly (step 1). The factor weights that have been assigned (step 2) are shown in the next column to the right. The checkmarks represent management's ratings of channel alternative number one (see Figure 5.7) on each of the decision factors (step 3). Finally, the factor weights (A) are multiplied by the factor scores (B) for each decision factor and summed to arrive at the total score for channel alternative one (step 4).

This score of .570 is, in effect, a quantitative representation of management's judgement on the merits of this particular channel alternative. By repeating this procedure for each of the four remaining channel alternatives, five total scores will be available. Management would then be able to rank the five channel alternatives shown in Figure 5.7 in terms of their total scores. The one having the highest score would be the one judged as best by management.

Table 5.3
Weighted Factor Score Method Applied to Channel Choice: Channel Alternative One

Factor	(A) Factor weight	(B) Factor score .0	.1	.2	.3	.4	.5	.6	.7	.8	.9	1.0	(A × B) Rating
1. Effectiveness in Reaching Swimming Pool Owners	.15				✓								.045
2. Amount of Profit if This Alternative Works Well	.25						✓						.125
3. Experience Company Will Gain in Consumer Market	.10			✓									.020
4. Amount of Investment Involved (high score for low investment)	.30									✓			.240
5. Ability of Company to Cut Short Its Losses	.20								✓				.140
										Total score			.570

Source: Philip Kotler, *Marketing Decision Making: A Model Building Approach*, p. 292. © 1971 by Holt, Rinehart and Winston. Reprinted by permission.

Distribution Costing Approach.   Under the distribution costing approach, estimates of costs and revenues for different channel alternatives are made, and the figures are compared to see how each alternative stacks up. Brion captures the essential idea of this approach in an example which compares two channel structure alternatives—direct selling (two level structure) vs. the use of distributors (three level structure):[24]

Assume 10,000 potential customers, each one of whom requires 1 call by a salesman every 2 weeks. If salesmen are able to make on the average 8 calls per day, each salesman could then handle 80 customers. Therefore 125 salesmen will be needed.

Assumed Figures

125 salesmen @ $10,000	= $1,250,000
1 field manager per 10 salesmen @ $12,000	= 156,000
5 Branches	
Managers @ $15,000	= 75,000
Warehouses and office help, inventory, interest on inventory and buildings	= 2,000,000
Total selling cost for direct selling	= $3,481,000

30% gross margin on sales would require in sales to cover this cost
$3,481,000/.30 = $11,600,000

Suppose distributors were used with the following different margins allowed on the level of sales:

If 15%, then 11,600,000 × .15 = $1,740,000
If 10%, then 11,600,000 × .10 = 1,160,000
If 5%, then 11,600,000 × .05 =   580,000

Direct vs. Distributors Cost Comparison

	15% Margin Assumption	10% Margin Assumption	5% Margin Assumption
If Direct	$3,481,000	$3,481,000	$3,481,000
Distributor	− 1,740,000	− 1,160,000	− 580,000
Savings	$1,741,000	$2,321,000	$2,901,000

Source: John M. Brion, *Marketing Through the Wholesaler/Distributor Channel*. Marketing for Executives Series, Number II, American Marketing Association, 1965.

This is, of course, a highly simplified example. More elaborate and detailed versions of this kind of approach are discussed in the literature on

[24]Brion, *Marketing Through the Channel*, p. 5.

distribution cost analysis.[25] Regardless of how elaborate or the degree of detail involved, however, the basic theme or tenor of all such approaches stresses managerial judgement and rules of thumb about what the costs and revenues of various channel structure alternatives are likely to be.

Using Judgemental-Heuristic Approaches. Regardless of which of the judgemental-heuristic approaches discussed above is used, large doses of judgement and "guesstimation" are virtually unavoidable. To say otherwise is to imply that a greater degree of precision exists than is actually the case. For even with the weighted factor score or the distribution costing approaches, a large measure of managerial judgement is still needed to come up with the seemingly precise figures. This is not to say that the so-called judgemental-heuristic approaches are totally subjective. On the contrary, in some cases management's ability to make sharp judgements may be quite high and, if this is coupled with good empirical data on costs and revenues, highly satisfactory (though not optimal) channel choice decisions may be made using judgemental-heuristic approaches.

Judgemental-heuristic approaches also enable the channel manager to readily incorporate nonfinancial criteria (decision factors) into channel choice decisions. Nonfinancial criteria such as the degree of control or goodwill available from a particular channel alternative may be of real importance. As Mallen points out:

"These two other elements (channel control and goodwill) must be taken into consideration in arriving at the choice. For example, an analysis may show wholesalers as providing the highest contribution to profit and overhead, but it may very well be that in time these wholesalers, if they gain relative control over the channel, will demand higher and higher margins and provide less and less selling effort. In addition, they may create fierce price competition at the wholesale and retail levels and so engender ill will."[26]

If such criteria as control or goodwill are important considerations, judgemental-heuristic approaches offer the flexibility to include these in the decision. In the case of the straight qualitative judgement approach, this may be done implicitly, while in the weighted factor score approach, control or goodwill criteria can be used as explicit decision factors and weights can be assigned to reflect their relative importance (see Table 5.3). Even with the distribution costing approach, nonfinancial factors such as control and goodwill may be applied after the fact. That is, once the cost and profit potentials for each channel alternative have been calculated, the channel manager may still make judgements about whether that channel alternative producing the highest financial return also meets control and goodwill criteria.

[25] See for example: D. R. Longman and M. Schiff, *Practical Distribution Cost Analysis* (Homewood, Illinois: Richard D. Irwin, 1955); Bruce Mallen and Stephen D. Silver, "Modern Marketing and the Accountant," *Cost and Management*, 38 (February, 1964): 75–85.

[26] Bruce Mallen, "Selecting Channels of Distribution for Consumer Products," in *Handbook of Modern Marketing*, ed. Victor P. Buell (New York: McGraw-Hill, 1970), p. 4–29.

Summary

Channel design refers to those decisions involving the development of new marketing channels where none had existed before, as well as to the modification of existing channels.

Channel design is a very important aspect of the firm's overall marketing strategy because it can be a key factor in helping the firm to gain a differential advantage. Thus, the quest to gain differential advantage should underly the design of marketing channels.

Channel design can be viewed as a seven phase process which was referred to in this chapter as the channel design paradigm. The first six phases were discussed in this chapter.

Phase 1 involves recognizing that a channel design decision is being faced. While there are many situations where the need to make channel design decisions is obvious (such as when a new product is being introduced) often the need is not at all obvious. So, the channel manager must be alert to changing conditions, both internal and external, and determine whether such changes have implications for channel design.

Phase 2 is the setting and coordinating of distribution objectives, explicit statements describing what part distribution is expected to play in reaching the firm's overall marketing objectives. Distribution objectives must be consistent or congruent with the firm's general marketing objectives and policies as well as with its overall objectives and policies. To assure that such congruency will be achieved, the channel manager must carefully examine the firm's other objectives and policies related to the distribution objectives. This check for congruency may even extend to considering the firm's highest level objectives and policies.

Phase 3 is the specification of the distribution tasks that will have to be performed in order to achieve the distribution objectives. Hence, the channel manager should be as specific as possible in delineating precisely what kinds of tasks are involved.

Phase 4 consists of the development of possible alternative channel structures. The channel structures should be specified in terms of three basic dimensions: (1) number of levels, (2) intensities at the various levels, and (3) the types of intermediaries to be used at each level. Levels can range from two to as high as six, and possibly even higher in some cases. Intensity includes the categories intensive (as many intermediaries as possible), selective (fewer intermediaries carefully chosen), and exclusive (only one intermediary per market area). The intensity dimension should be very carefully considered because it often reflects and is a crucial feature of the firm's basic marketing strategy and overall methods of operation. The types of intermediaries dimension should also be carefully considered in light of availability of intermediaries and their capabilities for performing particular distribution tasks.

Phase 5 involves the evaluation of the many variables affecting channel structure. Six major categories of variables need to be considered: (1) market variables, (2) product variables, (3) company variables, (4) middlemen variables, (5) environmental variables, and (6) behavioral variables. In relating these variables to channel structure, various heuristics (rules of thumb) are often used. While such heuristics provide a useful shorthand approach for dealing with complex relationships, they should be considered only as a rough reflection of typical relationships and only as a starting point for a more thorough analysis.

Phase 6 is the choosing of the "best" channel structure for achieving the distribution objectives. It is not possible to choose a truly optimal channel in the strict sense of the term because the kinds of perfect information analysis and forecasting needed to do so are in most cases beyond the range of human capability. Nevertheless, approaches do exist for making good, if not optimal, channel choices. The characteristics of goods and parallel systems approach, the financial analysis approach, and management science methods all help in this regard. Most channel choices, however, are still made on the basis of managerial judgement supplemented by heuristics and whatever data (even if imperfect) are available. Several variations of such judgemental-heuristic approaches to channel choice were discussed in this chapter.

Discussion Questions

1. Discuss the meaning of channel design in relation to such terms as channel structure, selection, evolution of channels, and the allocation of distribution tasks.
2. Discuss the role of channel design in the quest to gain differential advantages.
3. In this chapter we discussed a number of conditions which may foster the need for channel design decisions. Name some others.
4. What is a distribution objective? What does it mean when we say that distribution objectives should be coordinated with other objectives and policies of the firm?
5. Give an example of an incongruent distribution objective.
6. How do distribution tasks viewed from the perspective of the channel manager in a producing or manufacturing firm differ from the traditional lists of marketing functions?
7. Briefly describe the major categories of variables that should be considered when evaluating alternative channel structures.
8. Discuss the three dimensions of channel structure which should be considered in developing alternative channel structures.
9. In discussing the many variables affecting channel choice we cited a number of heuristics about how these variables are likely to influence channel structure. What useful purpose does this serve? What dangers does it hold?

10. Discuss the difficulties involved in attempting to choose an optimal channel structure.

11. Compare and contrast the so-called judgemental-heuristic approach to choosing a channel structure with any of the others discussed in the chapter.

12. Does the "best" channel structure necessarily have to be the one offering the highest monetary payoff? Explain.

Chapter 6
Selecting the Channel Members

Selecting the particular intermediaries who will become members of the marketing channel is the last phase of channel design (Phase 7). We should point out, however, that selection decisions are frequently necessary even when channel structure changes have not been made. That is, selection decisions may or may not be the result of channel design decisions. For example, a common reason for having to make selection decisions independent of channel design decisions is indicated when a firm needs more coverage in existing territories. Thus even though its basic channel structure remains essentially the same in terms of its length, intensity, and types of intermediaries, the firm may still need to add additional outlets to allow for growth. Another common reason for selection, independent of channel design decisions, is to replace intermediaries who have left the channel either voluntarily or otherwise. In fact, this turnover phenomenon is thought to be the most common reason for new intermediary selection.[1]

At any rate, whether the need to make selection decisions comes about as the last phase of channel design decisions (Phase 7) or for other reasons, the basic approach to selecting the channel members is the same.

The approach consists of three basic steps:

---

[1] Roger Pegram, *Selecting and Evaluating Distributors* (New York: National Industrial Conference Board, 1965), pp. 8–9.

1. Finding prospective intermediaries
2. Applying selection criteria to determine the suitability of prospective intermediaries for becoming channel members.
3. Securing the prospective intermediaries as actual channel members.

The organization of this chapter follows this format with each major section discussing one of these steps. Before proceeding to a discussion of this approach for selecting channel members, however, two points about the relationship of channel structure to selection should be mentioned.

First, an obvious point, but one that is sometimes forgotten in the marketing literature, is that those firms who use a direct (manufacturer → user) channel structure do not have to worry about selection decisions. Since their allocation of the distribution tasks did not specify the use of intermediaries, they need not select any. So, for those firms who have chosen a direct channel structure as the best alternative, the channel design decision is a six phase process. Of course, if at a later point a firm decides to change its channel structure to include intermediaries, then selection becomes relevant.

Secondly, and not so obvious, is the relationship between the structural dimension of intensity (see Chapter 5) and selection. As a general rule, *the greater the intensity of distribution, the less the emphasis on selection.* As Pegram points out based on his landmark study of selection practices:

"Such companies (those using intensive distribution) usually place their products in every logical outlet in an attempt to blanket the market and make their products universally available. They seldom exercise much discrimination in the selection of resellers other than ensuring that their credit is satisfactory. Often consumer items are largely "presold" through advertising, so that there is little concern over selection and choice of resellers is, practically speaking, nonexistent."[2]

Conversely, in referring to firms that emphasize more selective distribution, Pegram points to the need for a strong emphasis on the selection of channel members:

"For these manufacturers (those with more selective distribution), distributor selection is critical, representing the juncture at which the manufacturer has greatest control and opportunity in the field for ensuring the marketing success of his products which move through resellers."[3]

In general then, if a channel has been structured to emphasize intensive distribution at the various levels, those intermediaries who are included as channel members usually are "selected" only to the extent that they have a reasonable probability of paying their bills. On the other hand if

[2]Ibid., p. 5.
[3]Ibid., p. 3.

the channel structure stresses more selective distribution, the prospective members should be much more carefully scrutinized and selection decisions become more critical.

Finding Prospective Channel Members

A wide variety of sources is available to help the channel manager find prospective channel members. The most important of these are listed below in order of importance:[4]

1. Field sales organization
2. Trade sources
3. Reseller inquiries
4. Customers
5. Advertising
6. Trade shows
7. Other sources

Field Sales Organization

For those firms who have their own sales force already calling on intermediaries at the wholesale or retail levels, these outside salespeople represent an excellent resource for finding new channel members.

The salesperson is in the best position to know potential channel members in his own territory, usually better than anyone else in the firm. By being on the scene as he makes his calls, he is able to pick up information about which intermediaries are likely to be available in his territory. It is not unusual for a salesperson to be acquainted with the management and sales people of major intermediaries in his territory who are not representing his firm. He may even have prospective channel members virtually lined up if his firm decides that its present channel members in his territory are to be changed or supplemented.

Many firms consider prospecting and the maintenance of cordial relations with potential intermediaries to be major duties of their salespeople. For example, a marketing executive of the Seiberling Tire and Rubber Company comments:

"As part of our formal prospect development program, each territory representative salesman is required to have a minimum of three active prospects working at all times."[5]

---

[4]Ibid., Chapter 3.
[5]Ibid., p. 11.

Clearly then, when channel members are to be changed or added, the channel manager should attempt to make maximum use of the firm's salespeople for finding prospective intermediaries. In fact, the input from the sales force may provide most, if not all, of the information needed to locate prospective intermediaries. A number of companies have found this to be the case.

A potential problem with using the sales force to find prospective channel members is the possibility of the manufacturer not adequately rewarding his salespeople for their efforts in finding potential channel members. If the manufacturer fails to take into account the time and effort expended by his salespeople in seeking out and establishing contacts with potential channel members, but instead rewards salespeople only on sales volume from existing channel members, the sales force is not likely to pay much attention to finding new channel members. Thus, if the sales force is to be an effective resource for finding new channel members, the manufacturer must make it clear that his salespeople will be adequately rewarded for their efforts.

Trade Sources

Trade sources such as trade associations, trade publications, directories, other firms selling related or similar products, trade shows, and the "grapevine" all are valuable sources of information about prospective intermediaries.

Industrial Distribution Magazine publishes a listing of several thousand industrial distributors covering a wide range of industries. This listing shows which geographical territories are covered by the distributors and the lines handled. By using this listing it is possible to find out quickly, for each territory, distributors who are not already handling competitive lines.

The *Verified Directory of Manufacturers' Representatives* presents a geographical listing of over 15,000 manufacturer's representatives serving all industries (except food products). It gives information on the major lines covered and the specific market areas covered.

The *National Association of Wholesale Distributors*, Washington, D.C., has a wealth of information available about wholesalers.

The *National Retail Merchants Association*, New York, offers a great deal of information about retail intermediaries.

The most specific sources of information in a particular industry are the trade associations. Figure 6.1 and 6.2, for example, provide a listing of a number of wholesale and retail trade associations.[6] There are, of course, many others. But these two lists offer a general idea of the extent and scope of trade associations at the wholesale and retail levels.

---

[6] A listing of virtually all trade associations along with their addresses can be found in the *Encyclopedia of Associations*, (Detroit, Michigan: Gale Research, 1977).

Figure 6.1
Sample Listing of Wholesale Trade Associations

American Traffic Services Association
525 School Street, S.W.
Washington, D.C. 20024

Appliance Parts Distributors Association, Inc.
228 East Baltimore
Detroit, Michigan 48202

Associated Equipment Distributors
615 West 22nd Street
Oak Brook, Illinois 60521

Association of Footwear Distributors
c/o McBreen/Bonn Shoe Company
310 Peoria Street South
Chicago, Illinois 60607

Association of Institutional Distributors
1750 Old Meadow Road
McLean, Virginia 22101

Association of Steel Distributors
2680 N. Moreland Boulevard
Cleveland, Ohio 44120

Automotive Service Industry Association
230 North Michigan Avenue
Chicago, Illinois 60601

Bearing Specialists Association
221 North LaSalle
Chicago, Illinois 60601

Beauty and Barber Supply Institute, Inc.
551 Fifth Avenue, Suite 517
New York, New York 10017

Bicycle Wholesale Distributors Association,
   Inc.
c/o Hans Johnsen Company
8901 Chancellor Row
Dallas, Texas 75247

Biscuit and Cracker Distributors Association
111 East Wacker Drive
Chicago, Illinois 60601

Ceramics Distributors of America
410 North Michigan Avenue, Suite 892
Chicago, Illinois 60611

Copper and Brass Warehouse Association,
   Inc.
1900 Arch Street
Philadelphia, Pennsylvania 19103

Council for Periodical Distributors Association
488 Madison Avenue
New York, New York 10022

Farm Equipment Wholesalers Association
1100 Upper Midwest Building
Minneapolis, Minnesota 55101

Federal Wholesale Druggists' Association
393 Seventh Avenue, Room 2018
New York, New York 10001

Food Industries Suppliers' Association
P.O. Box 1213
Sedona, Arizona 86338

Foodservice Equipment Distributors
   Association
332 South Michigan Avenue
Chicago, Illinois 60604

General Merchandise Distributors Council
2530 Crawford Avenue
Evanston, Illinois 60201

Hobby Industry Association of America, Inc.
2000 Fifth Avenue
New York, New York 10010

International Sanitary Supply Association
5330 North Elston Avenue
Chicago, Illinois 60630

Laundry and Cleaners Allied Trades
   Association
543 Valley Road
Upper Montclair, New Jersey 07043

Lawn and Garden Distributors Association
1900 Arch Street
Philadelphia, Pennsylvania 19103

Material Handling Equipment Distributors
   Association
102 Wilmot Road, Suite 210
Deerfield, Illinois 60015

National-American Wholesale Grocers'
   Association
51 Madison Avenue
New York, New York 10010

National Association of Aluminum Distributors
1900 Arch Street
Philadelphia, Pennsylvania, 19103

National Association of Brick Distributors
1750 Old Meadow Road
McLean, Virginia 22101

National Association of Chemical Distributors
1406 Third National Building
Dayton, Ohio 45402

National Association of Container Distributors
c/o M. Jacob and Sons
10101 Lyndon
Detroit, Michigan 48238

National Association of Electrical Distributors
600 Madison Avenue
New York, New York 10022

National Association of Fire Equipment
   Distributors
111 East Wacker Drive
Chicago, Illinois 60601

National Association of Floor Covering
   Distributors
221 North LaSalle Street
Chicago, Illinois 60601

Source: Darlene J. Forte, *Wholesaling* (Washington, D.C.: U.S. Small Business Administration, Small Business Bibliography No. 55), p. 5.

Figure 6.2
Sample Listing of Retail Trade Associations by Kind of Business

Kind of Business	Trade Associations
Building Materials, Hardware and Farm Equipment Dealers	National Retail Hardware Association (NRHA) National Lumber and Building Materials Dealers Association (NLBMDA)
General Merchandise Group	National Retail Merchants Association (NRMA) National Association of Variety Stores (NAVS) Mass Retailing Institute (MRI)
Food Stores	National Association of Retail Grocers of the United States (NARGUS) National Association of Independent Food Retailers (NAIFR) National Association of Food Chains (NAFC) National Association of Convenience Stores (NACS) Supermarket Institute (SMI)
Automotive Group	National Automobile Dealers Association (NADA) National Tire Dealers and Retreaders Association (NTDRA) Recreational Vehicle Dealers Association of North America (RVDA)
Apparel and Accessory Stores	Menswear Retailers of America (MRA) National Shoe Retailers Association (NSRA) Master Furriers Guild of America (MFGA)
Furniture, Home Furnishing, and Equipment Stores	National Home Furnishings Association (NHFA) National Appliance and Radio-TV Dealers Association (NARDA) National Association of Music Merchants (NAMM)
Drug and Proprietary Stores	National Association of Retail Druggists (NARD) National Association of Chain Drug Stores (NACDS)
Miscellaneous Retail Stores	Retail Jewelers of America (RJA) American Booksellers Association (ABA) Florists Transworld Delivery Association (FTDA) National Bicycle Dealers Association (NBDA)

Source: Bert Rosenbloom, "Retail Trade Associations as a Resource for Retailing Education," *Journal of Retailing*, (Fall, 1978), pp. 55–56.

Reseller Inquiries

Many firms learn about potential channel members through direct inquiries from intermediaries expressing an interest in handling their product line. For some manufacturers, this provides the main source of information about potential new channel members.

As would be expected, those firms receiving the highest numbers of inquiries from prospective intermediaries are the more prestigious ones in their respective industries. As one executive in a well-known machine tool manufacturing firm remarked:

"Ninety-five percent of our type of distributor organization would give their right arms to sell our line. We have an enviable reputation and are known also for our cooperative effort. All in all, a distributor can get his foot in the door more quickly with our lines than that of any competitor."[7]

Customers

Some firms look to the customers of prospective intermediaries as a source of information. Manufacturers report that many customers are willing to give frank opinions about the intermediaries who call on them.

The following comments are indicative of the value of using the customers of intermediaries as a source of information.

"We have found information about new potential outlets can best be obtained by conducting an informal survey of the end-users of our products, since they can apprise us firsthand of those distributors that are properly performing their functions."

(Anderson Electric Company)

"Normally we will determine the stronger and more effective merchants by surveying the ultimate buyers and users of paper, and then we try to sell one of the better merchants on the merits of our franchise."[8]

(Kimberly-Clark Corporation)

Advertising

Advertisements in trade publications offer yet another approach to finding potential channel members. Figure 6.3, for example, shows an advertisement placed in *Industrial Distribution* by the 3M Company seeking distributors for its line of coated abrasives. Figure 6.4 shows an advertisement for the Brown Shoe Company that appeared in *Stores* seeking retailers to carry Brown's Life Stride shoe line. This type of trade magazine advertising can generate a large number of inquiries from prospective channel members and thus provides a large pool from which to make selections.

Trade Shows

Trade shows or conventions can be a very fruitful source for finding potential channel members. Many trade associations at both the wholesale

[7] Pegram, *Selecting and Evaluating*, p. 13.
[8] Ibid., p. 13.

Figure 6.3
Trade Magazine Advertisement Seeking Industrial Distributors

Only 3M's coated abrasives give you this special backing.

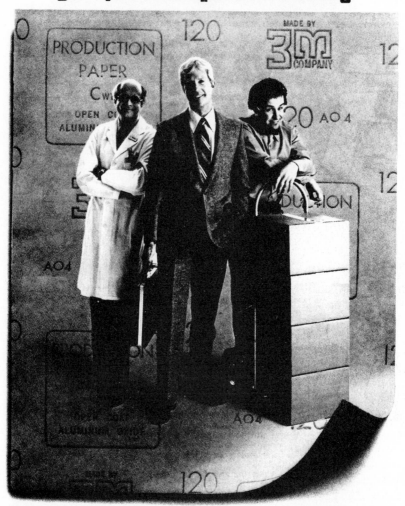

Sure, 3M gives you a broad product line to sell your customers. A broad line of superior quality coated abrasives with a brand name they know and trust. A brand name they've learned to look to for continuing product improvement and cost-saving innovations.

But when you're a 3M distributor, you get a lot more. Because we back our abrasives — and you — with solid service. With convenient branch offices and warehouses to provide prompt delivery. With a knowledgeable 3M methods expert who'll work with you in solving customer problems. And with our Coated Abrasives Methods Center, staffed by abrasive experts to help determine best abrasive usage and to pioneer new applications that open up more selling opportunities for you.

The 3M Industrial Abrasives Division. We back you up all the way.

Source: *Industrial Distribution*, (August, 1978), p. 78.

Figure 6.4
Trade Magazine Advertisement Seeking Retailers

Source: *Stores*, (November, 1981), p. 9.

and retail levels hold annual conventions at which numerous wholesale
or retail organizations in the particular trades are represented. By attend-
ing the relevant conventions, the manufacturer has access to a wide variety of potential channel members brought together at one place and time.
By the same token, many manufacturers attend conventions given by

trade associations in their industries. Representatives from wholesalers and/or retailers also frequently attend these conventions. This provides a good opportunity for manufacturers to find and talk with potential channel members.

Other Sources

Finally, some firms also find the following sources helpful in locating prospective intermediaries:

1. Chambers of commerce, banks, and local real estate dealers
2. Classified telephone directories
3. Direct mail solicitations
4. Contacts from previous applications
5. Independent consultants

Applying Selection Criteria

Having developed a list of prospective channel members, the next step is to appraise these prospects in light of selection criteria to see if the channel members are acceptable.

If a firm has not developed a set of criteria for use in selecting channel members, it must develop one. In practice, many firms do have rather comprehensive lists of criteria and do use them in selecting channel members. Figure 6.5, for example, shows the selection criteria used by the Waste King Corporation.

Unfortunately, no list of criteria, no matter how carefully developed, is adequate for a firm under all conditions. Changing circumstances may at some point require the firm to alter its emphasis. An example of this can be seen in the Parker Pen Company:[9]

During the 1970s, Parker made channel design decisions which resulted in a significant modification to its channel structure. Specifically Parker dropped direct sales to small retailers and decided to use wholesalers to reach them. However, Parker wanted to maintain its larger key retailers. Hence, an overwhelmingly important criterion which Parker used in the selection of wholesalers was that they show an absolute willingness to keep "hands off" Parker's large retail accounts. Regardless of how well prospective wholesalers might have measured up on Parker's other selection criteria, it is very unlikely that Parker would have selected them if they did not meet this hands off criterion.

[9]"Parker Pens: A New Distribution System," *Sales Management*, (24 July 1972): 9.

Figure 6.5
Selection Criteria Used by the Waste King Corporation

WASTE KING CORPORATION
3300 EAST FIFTIETH STREET, LOS ANGELES 58 CALIFORNIA
Philosophy for Selection of a Distributor

1. *Distributor should be financially able to purchase adequate inventories of Waste King/Universal products, carry his accounts, and maintain his financial obligations.*

2. *Distributor should be a well integrated and well organized business with an established sales organization of field personnel as required for proper marketing of Waste King/Universal products among dealers, associate wholesalers, and for new building construction.*

3. *Distributor should provide facilities for adequate warehousing and display which can function as the major source of supply for Waste King/Universal products distributed in the territory.*

4. *Waste King Corporation is desirous of selecting those distributors whose ownership and management,*
   a) *participate in Waste King/Universal sales activities, and*
   b) *provide a motivating force to the distributor sales organization, and*
   c) *are aggressive in their attitude in marketing Waste King/Universal products, and*
   d) *will recognize their responsibility as a key distributor of Waste King/Universal products and the needs of Waste King as a manufacturer.*

5. *Distributor should have attained a history of stability with respect to the products which it distributes and have and maintain a good trade reputation.*

6. *Distributor should have a willingness to invest in territory advertising and promotional activity.*

7. *Distributor should develop acceptance and sales strength for Waste King/Universal products with associate wholesalers, dealers, builders and consumers, and should give specialized sales attention to Waste King/Universal products to accomplish and maintain a fair share of the market for all Distributor products, in a timely way.*

8. *It is preferred that the Distributor will also sell complementing, non-competitive lines of merchandise.*

Source: Roger M. Pegram, *Selecting and Evaluating Distributors* (New York: The Conference Board, Business Policy Study No. 116, 1965), p. 24.

As suggested in the example, particular circumstances require that the firm be flexible in its use of selection criteria to allow for changing conditions.

Generalized Lists of Criteria

Nevertheless, channel analysts have developed several generalized lists of criteria. Brendel, for example, developed a list of some twenty key questions for industrial firms to ask of their prospective channel members.[10] Many of these questions are equally relevant for consumer products firms as well. His list has been widely quoted over the years. The twenty questions are as follows:

1. Does the distributor really want our line or is he after it just because of present-day shortages?
2. How well established is he?
3. What is his reputation among his customers?
4. What is his reputation among manufacturers?
5. Is he aggressive?
6. What other allied lines does the distributor handle?
7. What is his financial position?
8. Has he the ability to discount his bills?
9. What is the size of his plant (facilities)?
10. Will he maintain an adequate inventory for services?
11. What important customers does the distributor sell?
12. Which ones doesn't he sell?
13. Does he maintain stable prices?
14. Does he give yearly sales figures for the last five years?
15. What territory does he actually cover with salesmen?
16. Are the distributor's salesmen trained?
17. How many field men has he?
18. How many inside employees has he?
19. Does he believe in active cooperation, sales training and sales promotion?
20. What are his facilities for these activities?

[10]Louis H. Brendel, "Where to Find and How to Choose Your Industrial Distributors," *Sales Management*, (15 September 1951): pp.128–132. For a somewhat similar but even larger list see: John M. Brion, *Marketing Through the Wholesaler/Distributor Channel* (Chicago: American Marketing Association, 1965), pp. 34–37.

The most definitive list of general selection criteria is that presented by Pegram.[11] The list is empirically based—representing criteria used by a very broad range of firms (over 200 U.S. and Canadian manufacturers).

Pegram divided the criteria into a number of categories. We will discuss ten of these very briefly to offer an overview of the kinds of criteria which many firms find important to consider.

Credit and Finance.   Nearly all of the manufacturers included in the study mentioned the investigation of credit and financial position of prospective intermediaries as vital. This was by far the most frequently used criterion for judging the acceptability of a prospective channel member.

Sales Strength.   Most firms also mentioned the sales capacity of prospective intermediaries as a critically important criterion. Some of the most commonly used measures of sales strength, particularly for wholesale intermediaries, are the quality of salespeople, and even more importantly, the actual number of salespeople employed. Also of growing importance to manufacturers of more technical products is the technical competence of the intermediary's salespeople.

Product Lines.   Manufacturers were generally found to consider four aspects of the intermediary's product line: (1) competitive products, (2) compatible products, (3) complementary products, and (4) quality of lines carried.

As a general rule, manufacturers try to avoid, whenever possible, intermediaries who carry directly competitive product lines. Many of the intermediaries also share this view, particularly those who feel a sense of loyalty to their present suppliers.

Manufacturers do typically prefer intermediaries who handle compatible products. These are any products which by definition are not in direct competition with the manufacturer's line.

Intermediaries who carry complementary products are looked upon favorably because, by carrying such products, they offer a better overall product mix to their customers.

Finally, manufacturers generally seek intermediaries who carry product lines that are equal to or better than its own lines. Manufacturers do not want their products to be associated with inferior, unknown, or "dog" lines if they can help it.

Reputation.   Most manufacturers will flatly eliminate prospective intermediaries who do not enjoy good reputations in their communities. For example, the Goodyear Tire and Rubber Company states the following:

"Although the factors of experience and financial capacity can often be

---

[11] Pegram, *Selecting and Evaluating,* pp. 21–91.

*compromised, the nature of the dealer's character is extremely impor-
tant and is never compromised."*[12]

Market Coverage.   The adequacy of the intermediary in covering the
geographical territory which the manufacturer would like to reach is
known as market coverage. A further consideration is whether the prospective intermediary covers too much territory which could lead to over-
lap of the coverage of existing intermediaries. Generally, manufacturers
will attempt to get the best territorial coverage with a minimum of overlapping. This is an especially important consideration for a manufacturer
using highly selective distribution.

Sales Performance.   The basic consideration here is whether the prospective intermediary has a high probability of capturing the market share
which the manufacturer believes should be the case. Often the manufacturer will seek detailed sales performance data from prospective intermediaries to get a first-hand view of their effectiveness. If such direct
evidence cannot be obtained, other sources include: credit bureaus, competitive and noncompetitive distributors in the area, consumers of the
manufacturers products, customers of the distributor, other supplier
firms, and local trade people. Reports from these sources often give an indication of the intermediary's historical marketing performance. Some
manufacturers report that this is all they require to get a feel for a prospective channel member's sales performance.

Management Succession.   A major consideration here is that many intermediaries are managed by the owner-founder, and most of them, especially at the wholesale level, are independent small businesses. Consequently, if the firm's principal dies, the continuity of management is left
in doubt.

Management Ability.   Many manufacturers feel that a prospective channel member is not even worth considering if the quality of its management is poor. Therefore this is of critical importance to most of them in
choosing a channel member.
    Actually judging the quality of management is difficult because of the
intangibles involved in making an evaluation. One of the key determinants is management's ability to organize, train, and retain salespeople. In
short, a good sales force is often indicative of good management.

Attitudes.   This applies mainly to a prospective intermediary's enthusiasm, initiative, and especially aggressiveness. These qualities are believed
to be closely related to long term success in handling the manufacturer's
product.
    An evaluation of whether the prospective intermediary has the

[12] Ibid., p. 40.

"proper" attitude is generally a matter of managerial judgement because attitudes do not show up in black and white on any financial statements.

Size of Intermediary.   Sometimes a prospective intermediary is judged on his sheer size. The belief is that the larger the organization and sales volume, the larger will be the sales of the manufacturer's products.

Beyond this general belief there are other reasons for considering larger size as an important positive criterion. In general, it is usually a safe assumption that the larger intermediaries in a given market area are more successful, more profitable, better established, and handle better product lines. Further, the larger intermediary usually employs more salespeople, which leads to more exposure for the manufacturer's products and is usually better equipped with offices, personnel, and facilities than smaller ones.

Using Lists of Selection Criteria

While checklists such as those discussed above are not applicable to all firms under all conditions, they are still valuable because they help to point to many of the key areas of consideration for selecting channel members. Even though each firm must develop its own specific set of selection criteria based on its own objectives and policies, such checklists, especially the empirically based criteria represented in Pegram's checklist, provide a good starting point making this task somewhat easier. Moreover, the comprehensiveness of a firm's individualized list of selection criteria is likely to be greater if all of these general criteria are considered during its development. Figure 6.6 provides an overview visualization of the key criteria to consider when selecting channel members.

Securing the Channel Members

It is important to remember that the selection process is often a two-way street. It is not only the producer or manufacturer who does the selecting—intermediaries at both the wholesale and retail levels, particularly those who are large and well established, feel that they too can be selective of whom they will represent. Producers and manufacturers, except for those with truly extraordinary reputations and prestige, cannot expect quality intermediaries to stand in line virtually begging to become channel members. Rather, most producers and manufacturers still need to do an effective selling job to secure the services of good intermediaries.

There are a number of specific inducements which the channel manager in producing and manufacturing firms can use in attempting to secure channel members. All of these, however, should be aimed at conveying to the prospective channel member the firm's commitment to support

Figure 6.6
Key Criteria to Consider When Selecting Channel Members

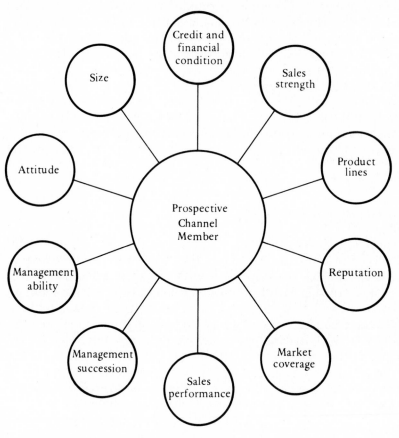

the intermediary so that he or she is more likely to be successful with the line. In other words, the manufacturer or producer should convey to the prospective intermediary that a virtual partnership that will be mutually beneficial is being offered if each of the parties does the job.

Pegram captures this point succinctly in the following:

". . . the keystone of many supplier sales policies is this concept: the supplier produces, the distributor sells, and each is dependent upon the other. Together they form a team, and teamwork is essential if the association is to prove mutually beneficial."[13]

A study by Webster in the industrial market points to the same partnership emphasis:

[13] Ibid., p. 100.

"To summarize greater reliance on distributors of increased size and importance will require that suppliers commit resources to programs for enhancing the distributor's role and improving his effectiveness. The key concept here is that of a partnership where the supplier tries to strengthen his distributors as independent businesses while at the same time supplementing their weakness with a strong "missionary" sales organization."[14]

Figure 6.7 shows one example of this concept in action. It is excerpted from a booklet prepared by the Rust-Oleum Company entitled *We're in Business Together* which is given to its channel members. Note how this policy statement emphasizes the idea of mutuality of commitment by channel members and a willingness of the manufacturer to provide the necessary support to the distributors. We will discuss this topic in much more detail in Chapter 8 (Motivating the Channel Members).

Specific Inducements for Securing Channel Members

Generally, the more specific the manufacturer can be in spelling out what kinds of support and assistance will be offered to channel members the better. Prospective channel members want to know at the outset precisely "what is in it for them" if they decide to join the manufacturer's marketing channel. While there are many possible inducements that the manufacturer might offer, most of them would fit within one of the following four areas.

1.   Good profitable product line
2.   Advertising and promotional support
3.   Management assistance
4.   Fair dealing policies and friendly relationships

Product Line.   At the heart of what the manufacturer has to offer is a good product line with strong sales and profit potential. Indeed, if manufacturers can offer this, they may need to offer little else to secure all of the channel members they want. Obviously those manufacturers that have well-known and highly respected products have a considerable advantage over lesser-known manufacturers. Thus, it is especially important for manufacturers whose products are not as well-known to do a good job of communicating the benefits of handling their products from the *channel member's point of view*. It is all too easy for manufacturers to get caught up in talking about how good their products are rather than stressing how *effective* their products can be in generating *sales and profits* for the channel members.

---

[14] Frederick E. Webster, "The Role of the Industrial Distributor in Marketing Strategy," *Journal of Marketing*, 40 (July, 1976): 16.

Figure 6.7
Statement of Policy towards Intermediaries
of the Rust-Oleum Corporation

RUST-OLEUM STATEMENT

We're in Business Together . . .

Just as you and your organization follow a creed in your business, so we at Rust-Oleum follow ours. We call it doing business by the Golden Rule . . . doing business together with sincerity, honesty, and cooperation.

We Are Mindful . . .

. . . that the Rust-Oleum distributor has played a major role in the successful introduction and growing sales of Rust-Oleum coatings. Down through the years, as we have continued to expand our facilities to meet the demand, we have become increasingly aware of the many and varied contributions made by Rust-Oleum distributors—contributions that are vital to our mutual success.

. . . that the Rust-Oleum distributor has provided local warehousing, invested in the stock necessary for effective service. Distributor salesmen have effectively pioneered Rust-Oleum, introducing it—demonstrating it—to their prized customers. Distributors have supplied the credit necessary to broad coverage selling.

. . . that Rust-Oleum's suggested resale prices have been well observed, to protect the profit structure necessary for effective distributor services, and to provide everyone a fair reward for stock investment and specialized sales effort.

. . . that the Rust-Oleum distributor has lent the prestige and acceptance of his firm name, imprinted on Rust-Oleum advertising and direct mail, sent to thousands of carefully selected accounts. Distributors have presented the Rust-Oleum line in their individually sponsored trade shows, carrying the customer benefits of Rust-Oleum still deeper into their markets.

. . . that these and the many other contributions of our distributors have been of inestimable value in the sound and continuous growth of the Rust-Oleum Corporation.

We Are Resolved . . .

. . . that we shall sell through the distributor, not just to him.

. . . that Rust-Oleum distributors shall be selectively limited to the fewest possible number needed to provide effective coverage of each market.

. . . that constant consideration be given to the distributor's costs of doing business, with profit margins planned accordingly.

. . . that no Rust-Oleum products for industry, farm or home be sold direct, irrespective of the purchaser's size or buying power.

. . . that Rust-Oleum shall provide well-trained and cooperative factory representatives, indoctrinated in this sales philosophy.

. . . that communications between Rust-Oleum management and distributor management be frank, constructive and objective.

. . . that complete stocks of all standard Rust-Oleum products be kept in factory stocks for immediate shipment.

. . . that catalogs, application data, sales help, and direct mail be carefully developed and regularly furnished to distributors.

. . . that Rust-Oleum industrial advertising shall feature the benefits of "buying through your industrial distributor."

. . . that we shall seek to win the distributor's friendship, as well as his effective sales performance.

Source: Roger M. Pegram, *Selecting and Evaluating Distributors* (New York: The Conference Board, Business Policy Study No. 116, 1965), p. 98.

Advertising and Promotion.   Promotional support to the channel member is another key factor which prospective intermediaries look for. In the consumer market, a strong program of national advertising is among the most effective inducements to secure retail intermediaries. The manufacturer who can point to such a program gains almost immediate credibility in the eyes of prospective intermediaries as to the sales potential of the product line. In the industrial market, a strong program of trade paper advertising offers a similar advantage.

Beyond this, in both the consumer and industrial markets, such factors as advertising allowances, cooperative advertising campaigns, point of purchase material, and showroom displays are indicative of strong channel member support and serve as good inducements to prospective intermediaries to join the channel (see Chapter 11).

Management Assistance.   Prospective channel members want to know whether the manufacturer is committed to helping them—not only in the form of providing advertising and promotional support for selling the particular manufacturer's products (see above), but in going beyond this to help them to do a better job of managing their businesses. Management assistance is good evidence of such a commitment. Management assistance can cover a wide range of areas including training programs, financial analysis and planning, market analysis, inventory control procedures, promotional methods and many others. The extent of such management assistance offered by manufacturers varies widely depending upon the type of channel relationship involved. A contractual channel relationship involving a comprehensive franchise agreement between the manufacturer and the channel members would generally be expected to provide for a much more comprehensive management assistance program than a conventional, loosely-aligned channel relationship. But even in the latter situation, some form of management assistance program is still quite possible and desirable. The Wilton Corporation's "Action Line" Program of management assistance offered to wholesale distributors who carry Wilton products provides a good example of a management assistance program that is feasible in a conventional channel relationship. The program offers wholesalers help in market analysis, prospecting, direct mail, promotion, sales training, and advertising. Wilton makes use of this management assistance program to secure new channel members by advertising it regularly in major trade publications such as *Industrial Distribution* magazine (see Figure 6.8).

Fair Dealing and Friendly Relationship.   As we pointed out in Chapter 4 (Behavioral Processes in Marketing Channels), marketing channel relationships are not mechanical or purely economic relationships devoid of the "human element." Rather, a channel relationship is a relationship between organizations of *people* and, as such, is a social system subject to the same behavioral interactions and processes characteristic of all social systems. Channel members may like or dislike, respect or disdain, sus-

Figure 6.8
**Advertisement For A Management Assistance Program
To Attract New Channel Members**

THE WILTON ACTION LINE

The Line that gives you more to sell.

Every distributor wants a product line that really sells. A proven performance line with quality, innovations, and features that spell profitability.

That's the **Wilton Action Line**. A quality line of tools and machinery from a company that backs its distributors in every way. With features and quality construction, plus advertising and support materials to help you close more sales!

Wilton backs its Action Line with in-field assistance for our distributors from the Wilton 26-man company-employed sales force, backed by a comprehensive marketing program. Our factory men will be contacting Wilton distributors to discuss our 1978 Action Line Program.

Big-selling, hard-working tools with a reputation for quality.

VISES Wilton is America's Number One machinist vise manufacturer. Preferred in a nationwide test over every other brand.

CLAMPS Wilton C-Clamps have innovations and features that our distributors find easy to sell. Everything new in C-Clamps in the last decade has been originated by Wilton.

DRILL PRESSES Wilton has the broadest line—15" through 32" models. Wilton engineering has concentrated on more performance features than any other drill line—yet has maintained a competitive price. Delivered completely wired and ready to run.

METAL-CUTTING SAWS Wilton offers a wide variety of popular models and sizes for better distributor turnover.

ACTION LINE PROGRAM ELEMENTS

■ Market identification   ■ Sales training films

■ Industrial prospect list   ■ End user advertising/ In-depth publicity

■ Direct mail program

Wilton Corporation/Tool & Machinery Division
2400 E. Devon Ave., Des Plaines, IL 60018
Telephone: (312) 827-7700

Source: *Industrial Distribution*, (August, 1978), p. 24.

pect or fear each other. They may be cooperative or antagonistic, loyal or disloyal towards each other. In short, a marketing channel relationship is not only a business relationship, but a human relationship as well. Though the relationship may be couched in elaborate or formal agreements or even in legal contracts, the human people-to-people element is never fully removed. This fact should not be forgotten when attempting to secure channel members. Specifically, the manufacturer should convey to prospective channel members that he or she is genuinely interested in establishing a good relationship with them built on the basis of trust and concern for their welfare, not only as business entities but as people as well. In fact, some manufacturers even go so far as to refer to their channel members as their "family" of distributors or dealers. While this may be overstating the case somewhat, it does convey the manufacturer's belief in building a marketing channel that is based on more than simply dollars and cents.

Summary

The selection of channel members is the last (seventh) phase of channel design. Selection decisions can also be made independent of channel design decisions when new channel members are added to the channel or when those who have left are replaced. Only those manufacturers who sell directly to users are not faced with the selection of channel members.

In general, the more selective the intensity of distribution, the more emphasis the firm needs to place on selection and vice versa.

The selection process consists of three basic steps: (1) finding prospective channel members, (2) applying selection criteria to determine whether they are suitable, and (3) actually securing the prospective channel members as actual channel members.

Finding prospective channel members generally poses few problems because there are many sources that can be used for locating them such as: (1) the field sales organization, (2) trade sources, (3) reseller inquiries, (4) customers, (5) advertising, (6) trade shows, and (7) other sources such as chambers of commerce, telephone directories, and independent consultants.

Applying selection criteria is a more difficult problem because there is no simple list of criteria appropriate for all firms to use. Each firm must develop its own list which reflects its particular objectives and policies. Moreover, these criteria must be flexible to allow for changing conditions. Nevertheless, at least ten general criteria are useful as a starting point for most firms to use when developing their own specialized set of selection criteria. These are: (1) credit and financial condition, (2) sales strength, (3) product lines carried, (4) reputation, (5) market coverage provided, (6) sales performance, (7) management succession, (8) management ability, (9) attitude, and (10) size of the channel members.

Finally, actually securing the prospective channel members as actual channel members can be a formidable challenge because, except in unusual cases, prospective channel members do not typically stand in line eagerly awaiting the manufacturer's call. Most manufacturers must therefore do an effective selling job to secure the services of quality channel members. Specific inducements that can be used in the quest to secure channel members are: (1) providing a good profitable product line, (2) offering advertising and promotional support, (3) providing management assistance, and (4) assuring prospective channel members of fair dealing policies and a relationship built on trust and friendship.

Discussion Questions

1.   Are selection decisions always the result of changes in channel structure? Explain.
2.   What is the relationship between intensity of distribution and the amount of emphasis given to selection?
3.   In the case of very intensive distribution where all possible outlets are used in the channel design, has a selection process really occurred? Discuss.
4.   Discuss several sources which the channel manager can use to help locate prospective channel members.
5.   What is a potential problem with the use of the sales force as a means for finding prospective channel members?
6.   Is it possible to develop a truly universal list of selection criteria for appraising prospective channel members? What are some of the problems one might encounter in attempting to develop such a list?
7.   Is Pegram's list of selection criteria a descriptive or normative one? Explain.
8.   Briefly describe each of the ten general criteria for selecting channel members that can be used as a starting point for developing more specialized lists of channel member selection criteria.
9.   What are some of the specific inducements that the manufacturer can use to secure channel members?
10.   In attempting to secure prospective intermediaries as actual channel members the chapter suggested that the offer of a "partnership" by the producer or manufacturer could serve as a strong inducement. What does this mean?

Chapter 7
Target Markets and
Channel Design Strategy

In Chapter 5 we cited the category of market variables as of fundamental importance in channel design. Indeed, from the channel manager's viewpoint, the channel exists to enable channel managers to serve their target markets effectively and efficiently. Consequently, a good deal of their attention must be focused on the markets that their channel(s) serve. More specifically, the channel manager must understand a number of important market dimensions and their implications for channel design.

In this chapter we will examine these market dimensions and discuss their implications on various phases of the channel design decision (see Chapter 5 for a complete discussion of the phases of channel design). Our emphasis, in discussing these implications, will be focused on *channel design strategy*. That is, using channel design to help gain differential advantage in the market.

A Construct for Market Analysis

Markets, whether consumer or industrial, are complex. A myriad of factors may have to be considered in analyzing particular markets. So it is useful to have a basic framework or construct to help provide some order to this complexity.

In this chapter we will use a market construct consisting of four basic dimensions as a framework for discussing markets. These four dimensions are:

1. Market geography
2. Market size
3. Market density
4. Market behavior

This market construct is illustrated in Figure 7.1.

This chapter is structured around these four basic dimensions. Each major section of the chapter discusses one of the dimensions. The emphasis will be on showing how these market dimensions influence channel design strategy. The fourth dimension, market behavior, is by far the most complex. Accordingly, a larger portion of this chapter will be devoted to the market behavior dimension than to any of the other three dimensions.

Market Geography and Channel Design Strategy

Market geography refers to the geographical extent of markets and where they are located. If the channel manager asks the questions: "What do our markets look like geographically?" and "How distant are our markets?" the concern is with the market geography dimension.

There is an old adage which says that "there is nothing so practical as a good theory." While no complete theory of market geography relative to channel design has yet emerged as a basis for guiding channel design strategy, a partial theoretical model developed by Bucklin can be of some practical value to the channel manager.

Bucklin's model attempts to explain the relationship between the distance of a producer from the markets and the use of intermediaries in the channel. Bucklin refers to his construct as the *distance and lot size model*.[1] While Bucklin's model presents a macro view of the total channel system operating in an economy, it nevertheless also provides insight from a micro or managerial perspective. The variables in the model are:

Bd = cost per product-unit mile of moving goods in the lot size purchased by the final user.

Bm = the per product-unit mile cost of moving goods in mass transit lots.

[1] Louis P. Bucklin, *Competition and Evolution in the Distributive Trades* (Englewood Cliffs, New Jersey: Prentice-Hall, 1972), pp. 18–20.

Figure 7.1
A Market Construct for Analyzing Market Dimensions
in Relation to Channel Design

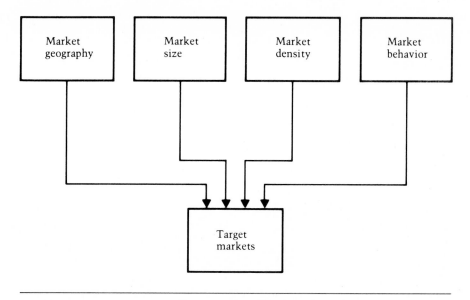

Cd = cost per product-unit mile of moving goods one mile in the final user lot size.

Cm = the cost of the intermediary system per product-unit mile.

I = the per product-unit cost of inventories handled by intermediaries.

Md = the distance between producer and final user (consumer or industrial).

The cost of the direct channel is:

$$Cd = BdMd$$

The cost of the channel using intermediaries is:

$$Cm = BmMd + I$$

Now assuming that $Bm < Bd$ because the costs of moving goods in large lots is cheaper, then the distance and lot size model may be portrayed as in Figure 7.2. This figure shows that because of the expense involved in the holding of inventories, for short distances the channel using intermediaries is more expensive. But, because the marginal cost of transporting goods one additional mile is less via the channel using intermedi-

Figure 7.2
Effect of Distance between Producers and Final Users on the Relative Cost of Direct and Intermediary Channel

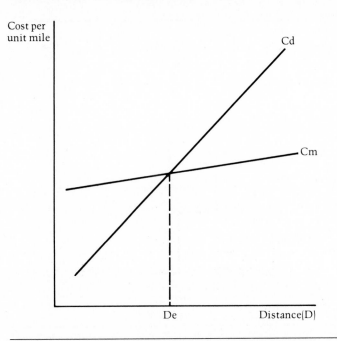

Source: Louis P. Bucklin, *Competition and Evolution in the Distributive Trades*, p. 17. (Reprinted by permission of Prentice-Hall, Inc., Englewood Cliffs, New Jersey © 1972.)

aries, this channel structure is less expensive for reaching more distant markets.

The essence of Bucklin's model is that, other things being equal, *the greater the distance between a producer (manufacturer) and his markets, the higher the probability that a channel structure using intermediaries will be less expensive.*

The channel manager is charged with the task of evaluating market geography relative to channel structure to make sure that the structure is able to serve the markets effectively and efficiently. Changing market locations resulting from the geographical boundaries of existing markets expanding, or the opening up of new more distant markets should signal the channel manager that modifications in channel structure may be needed. Bucklin's model is useful because it can serve as a reminder to the channel manager that changes in market geography may require changes in channel structure. This seemingly obvious point is not at all obvious in actual practice. Recall from Chapter 5 the case of the Daily Salad Company. When this firm's geographical territories expanded, its more distant markets became too expensive to serve via the direct channel which it had been using successfully when its markets were closer. Yet Daily Co. did not anticipate this development; rather it realized what had happened only after it had already occurred. Daily was fortunate in being able to extricate itself by changing its channel structure to include intermediaries. But it would have been better for Daily Co. not to have gotten into this situation in the first place. Indeed, the Daily Salad Company after experiencing its channel design problem, would likely rate any theory that helps bring attention to the relationship between market geography and channel structure as of real practical value.

Locating Markets

As part of the firm's overall marketing strategy, the channel manager may be called on to delineate the geographical locations of target markets. Generally this can be done in terms of one or more commonly accepted geographical units. The Bureau of the Census, for example, lists data for a number of geographical entities such as regions, states, counties, standard metropolitan statistical areas (SMSA's), standard consolidated areas (SCA's), cities, central business districts (CBD's), major retail centers (MRC's), downtown business areas (DBA's), and several other special purpose designations (Figure 7.3 provides definitions for these geographical entities).

Some combination of these geographical entities typically serves as the basis for specifying the location of markets. Table 7.1 lists some useful sources for obtaining additional geographical market data.

Tracking and Forecasting Geographical Changes in Markets

Far more difficult than locating markets is the problem of keeping track of geographical changes in existing markets and forecasting such changes for the future. Given the great mobility of the United States population, the channel manager can hardly expect market geography to remain stable for an extended time period. Among the most fundamental changes in market geography in the United States has been the mass movement of urban residents out of the cities into the suburbs. On the other hand, some reverse movement of population back into the center cities is also taking place. A more recent phenomenon which already has, and is likely to continue to have, an effect on the market geographies of many firms is the exodus of people and industry out of the Northeast and Midwest regions of the U.S. into the so-called "sunbelt" (the South and Southwestern states). Many other changes in market geography are also likely to occur during the remainder of this century.

Fortunately, channel managers do not have to be able to measure, track, and forecast these changes themselves. This is a job for experts in

Figure 7.3
Geographical Areas for which Census Data Are Available

United States—National totals include data from all 50 States and the District of Columbia.

Regions and Divisions—Census regions and divisions are large geographic areas which have been used for many decades for the purpose of providing summary figures at intermediate levels between those for the United States and those for individual States. The nine divisions are groupings of contiguous States, and for Alaska and Hawaii. Each of the four regions is composed of several divisions.

Travel Region—This is a new regional classification for travel statistics which differs from the four census geographic regions and nine census geographic divisions customarily used to present census data and used in previous National Travel Surveys. Since the nine travel regions are also groups of States, a retabulation of data in terms of census geographic regions and divisions is possible if desired. The travel region classification follows an industry standard advanced by Discover America Travel Organization (DATO) and the U.S. Travel Service (USTS) with the exception of Hawaii being placed in the Pacific Region as opposed to an "island grouping" in the DATO scheme. Since "destination" information is important to the tourism/travel industry, the travel regions represent the most natural travel-serving geographic grouping of States within the constraints of the national sample design.

States—Statistics for each State are made available from every census and from many Census Bureau surveys. In almost every case, a report or series of reports with statistics for each of the 50 States will also have separate statistics for the District of Columbia.

Counties—Counties are the primary political and administrative divisions of the States. The only major exceptions are Louisiana, where the divisions are called parishes, and Alaska where 29 census divisions have been created as county equivalents for statistical purposes. There are a number of cities which are independent of any county organization and, because they constitute primary divisions within their States, are accorded the same treatment as counties in the preparation of census tabulations. The District of Columbia and the independent cities within the States of Georgia, Maryland, Missouri, Nevada, and Virginia are all identified as county equivalents. In Puerto Rico, the county equivalent is called a "municipio."

Standard Metropolitan Statistical Areas (SMSA's)—An SMSA always includes a city (cities) of specified population which constitutes the central city and the county (counties) in which it is located. An SMSA also includes contiguous counties when the economic and social relationships between the central and contiguous counties meet specified criteria of metropolitan character and integration. An SMSA may cross State lines. In New England, SMSA's are composed of cities and towns instead of counties.

Each SMSA must include at least: (a) one city with 50,000 or more inhabitants *or* (b) city having a population of at least 25,000 which, with the addition of the population of contiguous places, incorporated or unincorporated, have a population density of at least 1,000 persons per square mile. These together constitute, for general economic and social purposes, a single community with a combined population of at least 50,000, provided that the county or counties in which the city and contiguous places are located has a total population of at least 75,000.

The Office of Statistical Standards in the Office of Management and Budget (OMB), with the advice of representatives of the major Federal statistical agencies, defines SMSA's. As of August 1973, OMB had defined 267 SMSA's in the United States and Puerto Rico.

Standard Consolidated Areas (SCA's)—In view of the special importance of the metropolitan complexes around two of the Nation's largest cities, New York and Chicago, several contiguous SMSA's that do not appear to meet the formal integration criteria but do have strong interrelationships of other kinds, have been combined into (1) the New York-Northeastern New Jersey and (2) the Chicago-Northwestern Indiana Standard Consolidated Areas, respectively.

Places (Cities and Other Incorporated and Unincorporated Places)—The term "place" refers to a concentration of population, regardless of the existence of legally prescribed units, powers, or functions. Places identified in the census are cities, towns, villages, or boroughs, in addition to specially defined unincorporated places and Special Economic Urban Areas (SEUA's).

Incorporated places—Statistics for most cities and some other incorporated places are provided in census reports. The economic censuses provide information for incorporated places of larger than a specified size—2,500 inhabitants in the census of retail trade and selected services, 5,000 in the wholesale trade, and 10,000 in the census of manufacturers. In the census reports, statistics are shown for certain towns and townships which are not usually classified as incorporated places but are defined geographically as Special Economic Urban Areas (SEUA's): Towns in the New England States which have an urban population of 2,500 or more inhabitants (5,000 for the wholesale trade segment) or a total population of 10,000

Figure 7.3 continued

or more; and townships in New Jersey and Pennsylvania which have 10,000 or more inhabitants.

Unincorporated places–An unincorporated place is a closely settled population center without legally defined corporate limits or municipal powers. Data from the 1972 censuses will be published for selected unincorporated places with 25,000 inhabitants or more, as defined in the 1970 population census.

Central Business District (CBD)–CBD, as defined by the Census Bureau, is an area of very high land valuation; high concentration of retail businesses, offices, theaters, hotels, and "service" businesses; and high traffic flow. It is defined in terms of existing census tract lines, i.e., to consist of one or more whole tracts. (Tracts are small relatively permanent areas into which large cities and adjacent areas have been divided for the purpose of showing comparable small-area statistics.) CBD's are all located in cities with 100,000 or more population. (CBD data are shown for the census of retail trade only.)

Major Retail Center (MRC)–MRC is a concentration of retail stores (located inside the standard metropolitan statistical area, but outside the Central Business District) having at least $5 million in retail sales and at least 10 retail establishments during the census year, one of which is classified as a department store. MRC's include the planned suburban shopping centers as well as unplanned centers, such as an older "string street" (continuous businesses along a street or highway with few intersecting cross streets containing any businesses) and neighborhood developments, which meet the above criteria. Where the MRC is a planned center, the boundaries encompass all of the stores in the center and adjacent stores outside of the planned center. Where the MRC is an unplanned center, the boundaries include the block in which the department store is located and all adjacent blocks having at least one general merchandise, apparel, or furniture and appliance store. MRC data are shown for census of retail trade only. For the 1972 data, MRC's will be defined in SMSA's existing as of December 31, 1972.

Downtown Business Area (DBA)–DBA is a specialized type of Major Retail Center which is located in a major city with less than 100,000 population. It is defined in the same manner as Central Business Districts–on the basis of tracts–rather than in the manner of Major Retail Centers which are defined on the basis of field inspection. The level of detail published for DBA's is the same as for Major Retail Centers. In the Major Retail Center reports for cities of less than 100,000 population the DBA can be recognized by the inclusion of tract numbers in the descriptions of the Major Retail Centers.

Other Special-Purpose Districts–Some publications for the economic censuses show statistics for areas defined for special purposes. Detailed descriptions of these areas can be found in the publication showing the statistics for these areas. Examples of such areas follow.

Production areas (27) are used in some of the reports from the census of transportation. They are essentially single SMSA's or clusters of SMSA's selected to represent relatively large but geographically compact concentrations of industrial activity. The 17 oil and gas districts in California, Louisiana, Texas, and New Mexico, made up of counties, are used to present statistics on petroleum and ntural gas industries in the census of mineral industries.

Special-purpose areas defined by other Federal agencies are used in appropriate Census Bureau reports. Statistics for eight petroleum regions (as defined by the Departments of Defense and Interior and by the Executive Office of the President) are given in a report of wholesale trade, *Petroleum Bulk Stations and Terminals*. Statistics for 20 industrial water-use regions (defined by a Federal interagency committee) are given in a subject report from the census of manufacturers, *Water Use in Manufacturing*.

Outlying Areas–The 1972 Censuses of Outlying Areas, conducted by the Bureau of the Census during 1973 as part of the economic censuses, include censuses of The Commonwealth of Puerto Rico, the Virgin Islands of the United States, and Guam.

Source: *Mini-Guide to the 1972 Economic Censuses* (Washington D.C., U.S. Dept. of Commerce, 1973), pp. 7–11.

geography, demography, sociology, and economics and much of the data they generate will be available from secondary sources. What is required of the channel manager, however, is an awareness of and sensitivity to changes in market geography reflected in the data and that an examination be made of its possible implications for channel design decisions.

Table 7.1
Published Sources for Locating Markets in the United States

Source	Description
Commercial Atlas and Marketing Guide (Rand McNally and Company, Chicago)	Contains maps showing counties, cities, SMSA's, a road atlas, and statistical data on manufacturing, retail sales, and population; also contains an international section.
Consumer Trading Area Map of the United States (Hearst Magazine, New York)	Shows 580 principal trading centers as defined by Hearst with area boundaries and county outlines.
Individual State Marketing Maps (Hearst Magazine, New York)	Shows 580 principal trading centers as well as secondary towns within respective area boundary lines.
Sales Management Regional Maps (Sales Management Magazine, New York)	Covers the 50 states and depicts either retail or industrial sales information by county.
Standard Metropolitan Statistical Areas (U.S. Bureau of the Budget: Washington, D.C.)	Maps depicting all officially defined Standard Metropolitan Statistical Areas (SMSA's).
U.S. Geological Survey (Washington, D.C.)	Numerous maps broken down by states, cities and counties.

Figure 7.4
The Effect of Number of Buyers (U) on the Relative Cost of Direct Channel vs. Middleman Channel

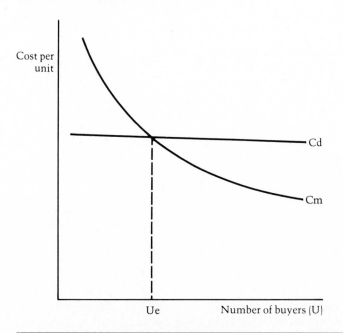

Source: Louis P. Bucklin, *Competition and Evolution in the Distributive Trades* (Reprinted by permission of Prentice-Hall, Inc., Englewood Cliffs, New Jersey, © 1972.)

Market Size and Channel Design Strategy

This second dimension of *market size* refers to the number of buyers or potential buyers (consumer or industrial) in a given market.

Bucklin has also developed a model relating market size to channel structure which provides some insight for using market size data.[2] Bucklin's model is shown in Figure 7.4.

In Figure 7.4 the horizontal axis measures the number of buyers in the market, with each buyer purchasing approximately the same number of units in each transaction. Cd is the cost of the direct channel which is almost constant for each buyer. The slight downward slope is due to the likely existence of external marketplace economies for larger volumes (better marketplace facilities at a lower cost). On the other hand, the channel using intermediaries, Cm, shows high costs for a small market with a sharp decrease for large volume. The high initial costs result from the extra handling and transaction costs necessary for the middleman channel. At a low level of volume, any savings in concentration and dispersion are insufficient to offset these. But as volume increases, and the cost of using intermediaries is spread over a larger number of buyers, costs decrease. When the market size reaches the point Ue in Figure 7.4, the cost of the intermediary structure is equal to the direct structure. As the market becomes even larger (to the right of Ue), the channel structure using intermediaries is lower in cost.

The insight provided by Bucklin's model into the possible relationship between market size and channel structure is of particular use to the channel manager in Phase 1 of the channel design decision (knowing when a channel design decision is being faced). By keeping this theoretical model in mind, the channel manager seeing data on changing market size is likely to be more sensitive to its implications for channel structure. For example, if market forecast data were to indicate a substantial increase in the number of buyers in a particular market, such questions as the following should emerge:

1. Will the increase in the number of buyers increase or decrease the average cost of serving our buyers?
2. If an increase in average costs is likely, can our present channel structure be changed to reduce these costs before the market reaches its forecasted size?
3. If such structural changes could be made, would this yield a differential advantage to our firm?

Certainly it can be argued that the channel manager would, or at any rate should, consider these kinds of questions when analyzing market size data even without being familiar with specific theories such as that pre-

---

[2]Ibid., pp. 17–18.

sented by Bucklin. Nevertheless, a familiarity with at least some theory is likely to increase the odds that the channel manager will pose these important questions.

Unfortunately, the theory does not provide a clear cut basis for answering these questions. A large dose of judgement which takes into account the peculiarities of particular situations and other variables is still needed. Take, for example, the case of the firm attempting to reach additional buyers in new territories. In this situation, a high positive correlation between the market geography and the market size dimensions is very likely because both the geographical size and the number of buyers are increasing together. Given this particular situation, the answer to question 1 above is likely to be that the increasing market size *will* increase the average cost of serving the buyers in the market. On the other hand, if the market size dimension is increasing while the market geography dimension remains constant (that is if additional buyers are attracted within the present geographical territories), the effect on costs may be much less.

Market Density and Channel Design Strategy

Market density refers to the number of buyers or potential buyers per unit of geographical area. This market dimension should also be considered in channel design strategy because of its relationship to channel structure.

A useful concept that helps to illustrate the relationship is that of *efficient congestion*.[3] According to this concept, congested (high density) markets can promote efficiency in the performance of several basic distribution tasks, particularly those of transportation, storage, communication, and negotiation.

With respect to transportation and storage, a high geographical concentration of customers enables goods to be transported in large lots to the concentrated markets and stored in a relatively small number of inventories capable of adequately serving the compact markets. For markets characterized by low levels of density, smaller quantities of goods have to be transported and smaller inventories are needed to serve the sparse buyers within them.[4]

In terms of the communication and negotiation tasks, dense markets facilitate the flows of communication and negotiation.[5] This is especially true when face to face information and negotiation are necessary. For example, if a manufacturer's salesperson must call on 50 accounts, it will take much less sales time and effort to call on these accounts if they are located within an area of 100 square miles instead of 500.

---

[3] Revis Cox, "Consumer Convenience and the Retail Structure of Cities," *Journal of Marketing*, 23 (April, 1959): 359–362.

[4] Louis P. Bucklin, *A Theory of Distribution Channel Structure* (Berkeley, California: University of California Press, 1966), p. 45.

[5] For a discussion of the various flows in marketing channel, see Chapter 1.

The major strategic implication of the above discussion is that the opportunity to achieve a relatively high level of customer service at low cost is higher in dense markets than in more dispersed ones. Thus, the probability of using a shorter channel structure is greater when buyers are highly concentrated.

The real world, however, does not always conform to such neat implications. The old adage, "look before you leap" is particularly relevant here because there are factors that may offset the tendency of dense markets to foster short channels of distribution. A very interesting case in point involves the Japanese market for consumer goods:

Japan appears to have a market which is tailor made for short channel structures. A huge population (about one half as large as the U.S.) concentrated in an area only 4 percent as large as the U.S. Yet channels are anything but short. Direct sales from the manufacturer to consumer are virtually unheard of, and a three level structure (manufacturer→ retailer→ consumer) is almost as rare. Much more common are several levels of wholesalers intervening between the manufacturer and the retailer, resulting in channel structures of four or more levels (see Figure 7.5).

The reasons for such long channel structures even in the face of such dense markets are traceable to two basic phenomena: (1) the market behavior of the Japanese consumer, and (2) the historical background of the Japanese society.

In commenting on the first phenomenon, a market research study of Japanese buyer behavior stated: "The average Japanese housewife shops every day within 500 yards of her home and typically spends 1,000 yen ($3.25) each time. You must have a great number of points of supply for this; it is the logistics of bits and pieces."

The second phenomenon? Historically the long complex channel structures grew from the early development of Japanese villages, which commonly distrusted each other. Many neutral middlemen were needed to sell goods from one village to the next. Then as trading companies began to appear in the late nineteenth century, they became so prominent in buying and selling that many manufacturing companies never bothered to develop sales arms.[6]

Obviously, the main point of this example is that the seemingly straightforward relationship between concentrated markets and short channels must be tempered by careful judgement of how other forces are likely to affect channel structures. The channel manager unfamiliar with the Japanese culture would be in for a rude awakening if he or she eagerly eyed the dense Japanese market as the "perfect opportunity" for direct distribution.

---

[6]William D. Hartley, "Cumbersome Japanese Distribution System Stumps U.S. Concerns," *Wall Street Journal* (2 March 1972), pp. 1, 12.

Figure 7.5
Typical Japanese Channel of Distribution for a Consumer Product

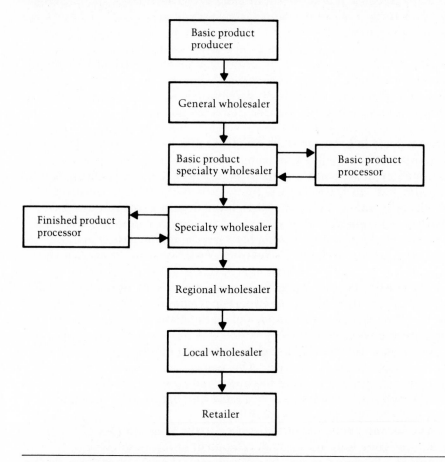

Source: G. A. Elgass and L. P. Dowd, "Wholesaling in Japan," in *Comparative Marketing: Wholesaling in Fifteen Countries*, ed. R. Bartels, p. 162. (Homewood, Illinois: Richard D. Irwin, Inc. 1963) Copyright © 1975, by Richard D. Irwin, Inc.

Market Behavior and Channel Design Strategy

This fourth dimension, *market behavior*, consists of four subdimensions. These are:

1. when the market buys
2. where the market buys
3. how the market does its buying
4. who does the buying

When Customers Buy

Both consumer and industrial markets do not buy products on a precisely predictable time schedule that remains constant per time period. There are frequently seasonal, weekly, and daily variations. For example, far more skis are sold to consumers in the winter than in the summer. Air conditioners, snow tires, antifreeze, eggnog, short sleeve shirts, and garden supplies are other obvious examples of products which customers buy more heavily during different seasons.

Weekly and daily variations in buyer behavior are common at the retail level and vary across different trade areas throughout the country. In some areas, Wednesday may be the big shopping night while in other areas it may be Thursday or Friday. Several shopping trends have followed a fairly similar pattern on a national basis. These include an increasing trend to shop at night and on Sundays.

There are two important implications for the channel manager related to this subdimension of when customers buy.

First, seasonal variations tend to create peaks and valleys in the manufacturer's production scheduling. Sometimes there is hardly enough production capacity to meet the demand while at other times there is an excess capacity. Typically, the manufacturer would like to smooth out these peaks and valleys in production because this will usually lower average production costs. One way of attempting this is to produce in the off-season and maintain the products in inventory for the heavy selling season. But this can be a costly and potentially dangerous strategy if the manufacturer alone maintains the inventory. The costs attendant to carrying the inventory such as those for storage, handling, insurance, financing (opportunity cost), plus the risk of lost, stolen, damaged and/or obsolete goods, can more than offset the production costs savings from producing at a steady level. If, however, the manufacturer can get intermediaries to stock some of this inventory in the off-season, a portion of the costs and risks can be shifted to these channel members. But intermediaries do not like to buy in the off-season unless they are offered special inducements—particularly in the form of price concessions to compensate them for the added costs and risks involved. Only the most powerful manufacturer who enjoys a truly dominant position in the channel can achieve off-season buying without price inducements. For those manufacturers lacking this dominant position, price inducements are necessary. Consequently, manufacturers who experience wide seasonal variations in the purchase of their products should attempt to select channel members who are amenable to price inducements for off-season buying. In other words, a willingness to buy in the off-season (given price inducements) should be used as a criterion for selecting channel members in the selection phase of channel design.

The second implication for when customers buy relative to channel design is also of particular relevance in the selection phase of channel design. This is simply that the channel manager should attempt to select channel members who are in tune with the changing patterns of when people buy. For instance, some retailers continue to remain closed on Sundays, even though this has become the busiest shopping day for suburban consumers for many kinds of products.

Where the Market Buys

The types of outlets from which final buyers choose to make their purchases and the location of those outlets determine where the market buys. This subdimension is closely related to the market geography dimension discussed earlier in this chapter. This is because the types of outlets chosen by customers and their locations, ultimately determine the actual geographical locations of the markets which the channel manager seeks to serve. Our focus in this section will be on briefly examining those underlying behavioral patterns of buyers which affect market locations and, in turn, channel design.

A great deal of research on where consumers buy is based on the assumption that they will behave so as to maximize their convenience in the selection of retail outlets. That is, the consumer is seen as engaged in a balancing of the desirability of near and distant retailers against the cost, time, and energy which must be spent in overcoming distance. If this cost is too high for patronizing a distant store, the customer will seek out one that is closer.[7] Finding a highly convenient location in terms of actual travel distance, driving or walking time, or in some cases, proximity to mass transit points, has been a sine qua non of a good retail location. This has been the case particularly for stores selling convenience goods where intense competition is prevalent and a differential advantage based on nonprice variables is difficult to achieve. Drug store retailers, for example, argue that locational convenience is more important than ever, especially in light of the effect of the energy crunch on the distance that consumers are willing to travel.[8] Supermarket retailers also argue that spatial convenience continues to be a factor of overwhelming importance in supermarket patronage. For retailers handling mainly shopping and specialty goods, a highly convenient location is also of great importance. However, some less prime locations may be offset by retailers who create differential advantages based on unusual merchandise, extraordinary varieties and assortments of merchandise, special services, or other factors. In these cases consumers may be willing to travel somewhat further to gain access to these stores. In doing so they engage in tradeoff behavior, foregoing some convenience for other factors offered by the more distant retailers.[9]

There is also an increasing amount of research coming out of the con-

---

[7] See for example: Douglas J. Dalrymple and Donald L. Thompson, *Retailing: An Economic View* (New York: The Free Press, 1969), pp. 98–104.

[8] Ronald Gargano, "The Changing Drug Store: Escaping From Giganticism," *Chain Store Age Executive,* (September, 1975): p. 39.

[9] Bert Rosenbloom, "The Trade Area Mix and Retailing Mix: A Retail Strategy Matrix," *Journal of Marketing,* 40 (October, 1976): 63–64.

sumer behavior literature which seeks to explain consumer store choice behavior based on factors other than a desire for locational convenience. The self-image of the consumer, his or her social status, attitudes, values and beliefs, as well as the overall image of the retail store have been examined.[10] Some of this work extends beyond consumer behavior related to store choice and considers nonstore alternatives as well, such as mail order, door-to-door, and vending machine retailing.[11] The literature on these topics is far too vast for us to review in this section. This material is covered adequately in texts on consumer behavior.[12]

Less work has been done by researchers in the industrial market on the behavioral processes underlying supplier choice. However, interest in the area is growing, and more research findings are appearing all the time.[13] One of the principal findings of more recent work is that the traditionally held belief portraying industrial buying behavior in supplier choice as a strictly rational process is not so cut and dried. Industrial buyers may not behave in a completely rational manner in choosing suppliers. Nevertheless, such rational criteria as product availability, service, price, and terms of sale still play a major role in determining from whom the industrial buyer will purchase.

In the government sphere of the industrial market, particularly at the federal level, precise and rigid procedures are spelled out for choosing suppliers. These have been developed to carry out the government's basic policy of giving all known suppliers an equal chance to compete for government business.[14] State and local governments follow essentially the same policy, but have their own sets of procedures for choosing suppliers.

The major strategic implication for the channel manager from this discussion of where customers buy may be stated as follows:

It is not enough to know simply the type and locations of outlets from which buyers are currently purchasing. The channel manager must also recognize the dynamic nature of buyer behavior and attempt to anticipate how this will influence the buyer's choice of outlets in the future.

Fortunately, the channel manager does not have to be an expert in consumer or industrial buyer behavior in order to do this. While it helps to have some general background knowledge in these areas to serve as a frame of reference, what is more important is access to information on changing patterns of buyer behavior. As an example of the kind of infor-

---

[10] See for example: Joseph F. Dash, Leon G. Shiffman, and Conrad Berenson, "Risk and Personality-Related Dimensions of Store Choice," *Journal of Marketing*, 40 (January, 1976): 32–39.

[11] See for example: Homer E. Spence, James F. Engel, and Roger D. Blackwell, "Perceived Risk in Mail-Order and Retail Store Buying," *Journal of Marketing Research*, 7 (August, 1970): 364–369.

[12] See for example: James F. Engel, Roger P. Blackwell, and David T. Kollat, *Consumer Behavior*, 3rd ed. (Hinsdale, Illinois: The Dryden Press, 1978).

[13] Theodore Levitt, *Industrial Purchasing Behavior* (Boston: Harvard University Press, 1965); Patrick J. Robinson, Charles W. Faris, and Yoram Wind, *Industrial Buying and Creative Marketing* (Boston: Allyn and Bacon, Inc., 1967); Jagdish N. Sheth, "A Model of Industrial Buyer Behavior," *Journal of Marketing*, 37 (October, 1973): 50–56.

[14] *Selling to the U.S. Government* (U.S. Small Business Administration, 1975).

mation which can be of use to the channel manager, consider the following excerpt from a report issued by Frost and Sullivan, a New York based marketing research firm:

The market for lumber and wood products for home improvements and maintenance will grow 56 percent over the next ten years and the market for hardware, plumbing, paints, and electrical supplies will grow 66 percent. Meanwhile, home improvement supply distribution channels will change. A new high-volume, retail-oriented lumber and building materials dealer—the home center store—is emerging, and old-line distributors of electrical and plumbing supplies are being supplanted by a new breed of wholesalers who merchandise a pre-packaged line of goods distributed directly to consumers. Within the last year or two, for the first time, more than half of all home improvement building materials were bought by homeowners, not contractors.[15]

The channel manager in a lumber and wood products firm should attempt to be the "first on the block" with this kind of information. By having information on where customers are likely to be buying particular products in the future, the channel manager has more time to *plan* changes in channel structure rather than allowing the channel structure to simply evolve to meet these changes. While evolution may do the job satisfactorily it is risky and more likely to result in a haphazard channel structure which is far less efficient than it could be.[16] Recall, for example, the case of Evans Products Co. discussed in Chapter 5. Evans, which coincidentally happened to be a lumber and wood products producer, was able to successfully plan changes in its channel structure based on information about changing buyer behavior in the consumer market. This information helped Evans to correctly anticipate that consumers would increasingly shop at large do-it-yourself type retailers rather than the traditional lumber yards. This enabled Evans to gain a substantial jump on its larger competitors and to secure a strong differential advantage based on a vertically integrated channel structure (see Chapter 5).

How the Market Buys

Customer preferences which are reflected in purchase behavior indicate how the market buys. See Table 7.2 for examples.

Each of the eight behaviors shown in Table 7.2 often varies across different market segments and over time for any given product category. For example, with respect to food purchases, middle income consumers who shop mainly in supermarkets buy in larger quantities than do lower income consumers patronizing smaller neighborhood stores. More affluent

---

[15] "The Market for Lumber and Wood Products," *Marketing News* (13 August 1976): p. 2.
[16] For further discussion of this see: Joseph P. Guiltinan, "Planned and Evolutionary Changes in Distribution Channels," *Journal of Retailing*, 50 (Summer, 1974): 79–91.

Table 7.2
Contrasting Behaviors Related to How Customers Buy
at the Consumer Level

1. large quantities purchased in each transaction vs. small quantities
2. self-service vs. assistance by salespeople
3. one-stop shopping vs. buying from several stores
4. impulse buying vs. extensive decision making prior to purchase
5. using cash vs. credit
6. shopping at home vs. shopping at stores
7. expending substantial effort through comparison shopping vs. little effort
8. demanding extensive service vs. little service

consumers are also likely to demand more assistance by salespeople than less affluent consumers who are amenable to more self-service in many product categories. For almost all market segments, several of these patterns have been changing over time such as the general shift to one-stop shopping, using more credit instead of cash, and an increased use of self-service.

These are, of course, merely some rough generalizations about several of the more obvious aspects of how consumers buy. What is more important from the channel manager's standpoint is an awareness on the part of the channel manager of the many more specific changes that can affect how the market buys. Some of these changes suggest long-term trends in buyer behavior, while others may be more short-lived, reflecting changing conditions in the environment to which customers react by altering their buying behaviors temporarily until conditions return to normal.

Here are several examples for both the consumer and industrial markets which illustrate changes in how customers buy. For several of these, the jury is still out as to whether these developments are long-term ones or temporary:

During the mid-1970s while the energy crisis was burdening many consumers, a study of 500 motorists by the Newspaper Advertising Bureau found that 89 percent were reducing their speed, 61 percent used their cars less, 19 percent were forming car pools, 17 percent were shifting to smaller cars and 14 percent used more public transportation.[17]

Given the great dependence of the consumer on the automobile, any changes in use patterns are bound to affect buying patterns. For example, during this time there was some evidence that consumers were shopping closer to home, making fewer shopping trips, and planning shopping trips more carefully to avoid returning for forgotten items and to minimize distances between retail outlets. Some forecasts were even being made about an accelerated revival of the downtown areas of cities because of the increased use of public transportation.

[17] "The Energy Crunch," *Business Week* (5 October 1974), p. 100.

The inflation-recession has also affected how people buy:

During the height of the inflation-recession (stagflation) of 1981, many consumers turned into "commandos." This refers to shoppers who diligently searched the newspaper advertisements to locate the heavily discounted items, especially loss leaders, and then "raided" the stores buying only the advertised loss leaders and not shopping for anything else. Several major retailers even forecasted that this type of shopping behavior would bring an end to the effectiveness of the loss leader strategy, which relies on the typical shopper purchasing several items in addition to the loss leader.

Some interesting developments are occurring overseas as well:

An insurance supermarket, which allows customers to comparison-shop policies, is grabbing attention in South Africa. David Hersch has opened a shop in Cape Town selling a wide range of policies (life, automobile, home) offered by twenty South African companies and Lloyds of London. Prospects enter the street level mart and browse through policies that have been specially written in a simplified style and select the ones that best serve their needs. Hersch has received inquiries about his mart from several U.S. and overseas insurers, including Midwestern National Life of Ohio; National Liberty Life, in Valley Forge, Pa.; and Armour Hick Parker, of Britain. "I am trying to make purchasing insurance as easy as buying any other commodity," says Hersch.[18]

Finally, here is an example from the industrial market:

Rising costs stemming from inflationary pressures have been a major factor in causing General Electric, American Standard, RCA, and several other highly decentralized companies to begin centralizing their buying. This has caused suppliers to emphasize *national accounts selling*. This means that suppliers will have to consolidate their sales efforts to deal with their customers' total buying needs in certain product areas rather than dealing in a fragmented way with various divisions.

All of these examples underscore the fact that the manner in which buyers make their purchases (i.e. how they buy) is not necessarily stable. Changes *do* occur and they may be rather sudden as in the case of rapidly changing economic conditions.

The potential changing nature of how customers buy means that the channel manager must be closely tuned in to what changes are likely to occur. But the channel manager is also faced with an even more difficult problem—determining whether such changes are temporary or long-term. Because of the generally long-term nature of commitments among

[18]"An Insurance Supermarket," *Business Week* (21 July 1975), p. 73.

the channel members, the channel manager does not want to make substantial changes in the channel structure to respond to changes in buyer behavior which are short-lived. To do so is not only costly, but may also foster serious conflicts, which in turn may have adverse effects on channel performance and viability (see Chapter 4). Yet, if changes in how customers buy do represent fundamental long-term patterns, prompt action in making channel design decisions to meet these changes can result in an important differential advantage to the firm, especially if the channel manager beats competitors to the punch in making the necessary channel design decisions:

One company which has apparently succeeded in doing this is United Electronic Controls Corp., a manufacturer of electronic instruments for the industrial market. United had been distributing its products through thirty-eight large distributors to reach the broad range of industrial firms comprising its market. The growing diversity of this market, which ranges from such firms as food processors to petrochemical companies, resulted in highly specialized buying needs for each of the different market segments. United Electronic decided to meet these diverse market needs by changing its channel structure to include another level of wholesale distributor which it refers to as subdistributors. (Each one of which will serve a particular type of industrial buyer.) This change to an extra level in the channel has enabled United to have a channel structure which is unusually responsive to the particularized buying behaviors of its diverse market segments.[19]

Who Does the Buying

This subdimension of who does the buying is comprised of two aspects: (1) who makes the physical purchase and (2) who takes part in the buying decisions.

Who Makes the Purchases.   From a channel design standpoint, who actually buys the product can affect the type of retailers chosen in the consumer market and may also influence the kinds of intermediaries used to serve industrial markets. For example, traditionally department stores are shopped in far more heavily by women than men. Consequently, products which are known to be purchased mainly by men should not rely on department stores as the primary retail outlet. This point, however, should not be confused with product *usage*. Many products which are used by men (e.g., shirts, ties, underwear, toiletries, jewelry, stationery supplies, radios) are purchased for them by their wives or girlfriends in department stores. Care should therefore be taken to distinguish between who uses the product and who makes the actual purchase. In practice, this is usu-

[19] *Business Week*, (20 July 1974), p. 50.

Table 7.3
Husband and Wife Influences on the Purchase of Various Products and Services

Product or Service	Husband Dominates	Wife Dominates	Share Equally
Automobiles	65%	22%	13%
T.V. Sets	48%	32%	20%
Where to Go on Vacation	36%	34%	30%
Saving Money	40%	40%	20%

Source: Compiled From, "Who Dominates the Family Buying Decision?", *Business Week* (28 Sept. 1974), p. 66.

ally not difficult to do. Finding out who makes the physical purchase at the retail level or in an industrial firm can be determined through observation or surveys at the point of purchase.

Who Takes Part in the Buying Decision. The more difficult aspect to analyze than who actually makes the physical purchase is who *decides* to make the purchase in the first place. Indeed this has been a topic of substantial research in the consumer behavior literature and in industrial marketing as well.

At the consumer level, the question of who takes part in the buying decision is usually in the context of a family unit. Influence on buying decisions revolves around the roles played by the husband, wife, and sometimes children. The results of one study in the consumer market are shown in Table 7.3.

In the industrial market it is not at all unusual to have several people in the buying firm involved in the purchase decision. This phenomenon is sometimes referred to as *multiple influence on the buying decision.* As Kotler points out in referring to a study of industrial buying influences:

"... *a key fact about much industrial purchasing is that often several persons participate in some way in the purchasing decision process. The number of multiple buying influences in a typical purchase has been estimated as anywhere from three to twelve persons. Yet it has also been estimated that the salesman generally contacts only one or two persons in a buying organization. What is more discouraging, he often misconceives who is "important" in the buying organization. Functional responsibilities and job titles are not perfectly matched. Suppliers have significant misconceptions about who in their customers' companies initiates purchases, selects a supplier pool, and actually approves the final supplier."* [20]

[20] Philip Kotler, *Marketing Management, Analysis, Planning and Control*, 3rd ed. (Englewood Cliffs, New Jersey: Prentice-Hall, 1976), p. 105.

So, the task facing both the consumer and industrial marketer is to make a careful evaluation of who is involved in making buying decisions so that he will be better able to target the influential parties. The channel manager's role in this is to determine whether the planned or existing channel structure will inhibit or facilitate the firm's attempts to reach the more influential parties to buying decisions. Unfortunately, there are no clear cut methods for doing this. There are, however, two heuristics which provide some insight for analyzing the relationship of channel structure to reaching the influential parties of buying decisions.

First, as pointed out in earlier chapters (see for example Chapter 5), as the channel becomes longer, the degree of control exercised by the manufacturer is lessened. Consequently, the manufacturer's ability to oversee whether channel members are dealing with the more influential participants in purchasing decisions is also reduced. For example, if a product has gone through a four level channel (M→W→R→C), the manufacturer can exercise little direct control to assure that the retailer's salespeople are focusing on the right family members at the point of purchase. Or, in the industrial market, a manufacturer selling through jobbers and industrial distribution has very limited ability to determine whether these channel members' salespeople are calling on the appropriate parties to buying decisions.

Second, as a corollary to the first heuristic, as the intensity of distribution at each level of the channel becomes greater, the manufacturer's capacity to supervise the selling efforts of channel members becomes lower. Misdirected efforts by channel members as to who influences buying decisions are thus more difficult to detect and change than when more selective distribution exists at each level.

Other than heeding these two general heuristics, the channel manager can help to assure the appropriateness of his channel structure for reaching the influential buying parties through explicit consideration of this issue when selecting channel members (Phase 7 of the channel decision). That is, by putting additional weight on the prospective channel members' management and sales force abilities to understand who influences buying decisions before they become channel members, subsequent problems in this regard can be reduced. While this was not cited explicitly as a specific criterion in Pegram's major study of manufacturers' practices in the selection of intermediaries (see Chapter 6), it is perhaps implicit in the criteria of *Sales Strength* and *Management Ability* (see pp. 185 and 186).

Summary

Market considerations are a key determinant of channel structure. Consequently, market variables are of fundamental importance in channel design decisions. The channel manager should attempt to analyze his or her markets with a view towards gaining differential advantages through channel designs that serve those markets better than the competition.

In order to analyze markets effectively for channel design purposes, a construct consisting of four basic dimensions was used in this chapter. These are: (1) market geography which deals with the physical location of markets and their distance from the producer or manufacturer, (2) market size, the number of buyers in a given market, (3) market density, the number of buyers per unit of geographical area, and (4) market behavior which breaks down into four subdimensions of (1) when the market buys, (2) where the market buys, (3) how the market buys, and (4) who makes the physical purchase as well as who participates in buying dimensions.

The channel manager must attempt to understand how these dimensions and subdimensions operate in various markets and plan channel structures which will enable the firm to serve these markets effectively and efficiently. The channel manager must also be sensitive to changes in these dimensions and, if necessary, be able to make appropriate modifications in the channel structure to adapt to such changes quickly and smoothly.

Discussion Questions

1. The category of market variables was cited in Chapter 5 and the present chapter as one of fundamental importance to channel design. Explain why this is so.
2. Should market variables be examined before other variables when designing the channel? Explain.
3. In this chapter a four dimensional construct was used for analyzing markets in relation to channel design strategy. Define each of these dimensions.
4. In this chapter it was pointed out that market geography is subject to changes. Why should the channel manager be concerned with such changes?
5. If information is available indicating that the market size dimension is increasing, what kinds of questions should this pose for the channel manager?
6. What is efficient congestion? How does this relate to market density? Is this relationship as straightforward as it seems?
7. The market behavior dimension was broken down into four subdimensions in this chapter. Define each of these subdimensions.
8. Discuss the major issues facing the channel manager with respect to where buyers make their purchases.
9. Identify any changing patterns of how consumers (or industrial buyers) purchase goods with which you are familiar. Trace through what effects these changes may have on the channel structure.
10. The subdimension of who participates in buying decisions may be of importance to the channel manager. Under what conditions might this be the case?

Part Three
Managing the Marketing Channel

The administration of existing marketing channels in an interorganizational context is the subject of the five chapters in this part of the text.

Chapter 8 deals with the basic issue of motivating independent channel members to perform their tasks effectively and efficiently.

Chapter 9 examines the relationships between product management and channel management.

Chapter 10 discusses pricing issues in channel management.

Chapter 11 looks at promotion management in marketing channels.

Chapter 12 concludes Part Three with a discussion of the interfaces between channel management and physical distribution management.

Chapter 8
Motivating the Channel Members

Having chosen a channel structure and channel members with the potential for serving the target markets effectively and efficiently, the channel manager must turn his or her efforts to realizing this potential. This requires becoming involved in managing the channel. *Channel management* may be defined as:

The administration of existing channels to secure the cooperation of channel members in achieving the firm's distribution objectives.

Three points should be particularly noted in this definition.

First, channel management deals with *existing* channels. That is, we are assuming that the channel structure has already been designed (or it has evolved) and that all of the members have been selected. Channel design decisions (see Chapters 5, 6, and 7) are viewed as separate from channel management decisions. In practice, this distinction may be obscured at times. This is particularly the case when a channel management decision quickly lapses into a channel design decision. For example, a price incentive used to secure the cooperation of some channel members (channel management decision) may fail to do the job. This may result in management considering the possibility of changing to other types of channel members (channel design decision). Perhaps this distinction can be grasped best by thinking of channel design decisions as concerned with "setting up" the channel, while channel management deals with "running" what has already been set up.

The second point covers the phrase *securing cooperation of channel members*. Implied in this is the notion that channel members do not automatically cooperate merely because they are members of the channel. Rather, administrative actions are necessary to secure their cooperation. If a manufacturer enjoys substantial cooperation from channel members without having to administrate, this is not managing, this is simply luck!

Third, the term *distribution objective*, although discussed in Chapter 5 with respect to channel design decisions, is equally relevant for channel management. Distribution objectives are statements describing what part the distribution component of the marketing mix is expected to play in achieving the firm's overall marketing objectives.[1] In the context of managing the channel, carefully delineated distribution objectives are needed to guide the management of the channel. Clearly, without knowing what the objectives are, it is difficult for the channel manager to know what direction to pursue in managing the channel.

In this chapter we will examine one of the most fundamental and important aspects of channel management—motivating channel members. The discussion is structured around three basic facets involved in *motivation management* in the channel. These are:

1. finding out the needs and problems of channel members
2. offering support to the channel members that is consistent with their needs and problems
3. providing leadership through the effective use of power

Finding Out the Needs and Problems of Channel Members

Before the channel manager can successfully motivate channel members, an attempt must be made to learn what they want from the channel relationship. They may perceive needs and face problems which are quite different from those of the manufacturer. McVey has pointed to these differences with several classic propositions:

"1. The middleman is not a hired link in a chain forged by the manufacturer . . .

---

[1] Maureen Guirdham, *Marketing: The Management of Distribution Channels* (Oxford: Pergamon Press, 1972), p. 134.

2. The middleman acts primarily as a purchasing agent for his customers, and only secondarily as a selling agent for his supplier. . . . He is interested in selling any product which these customers desire to buy from him.

3. The middleman attempts to weld all of his offerings into a family of items which he can sell in combination as a packaged assortment to individual customers. His selling efforts are directed primarily at obtaining orders for the assortment, rather than for individual items.

4. Unless given incentive to do so, middlemen will not maintain separate sales records by brands sold. . . . Information that could be used by the manufacturer in product development, pricing, packaging, or promotion planning is buried in nonstandard records of middlemen, and sometimes purposely secreted from suppliers."[2]

As McVey points out, manufacturers all too often are unaware of the needs and problems of their channel members. Further, the manufacturer frequently fails to make an effort to find out what they are. Two examples, the first taken from the consumer market and the second from the industrial market, provide specific illustrations of typical failures experienced by manufacturers in learning about the needs and problems of their channel members:

A well-known publishing firm secured a manufacturers' representative to perform a part of the firm's distribution tasks—personal selling and promotion. After about eighteen months, the publisher experienced cash flow and sales revenue problems. Upon study, it was found that the manufacturers' representative was not placing the necessary effort behind the line, largely because the publisher had not really understood the needs of the manufacturers' representative. In order to do the job, the manufacturers' representative needed much more information about the marketing plans of the publisher, which the latter had failed to supply. Without being privy to this information, the manufacturers' representative could not possibly develop a coordinated selling effort. The result was serious financial problems for both parties.[3]

Here is the example from the industrial market:

"A well known company making a product of high quality and wide acceptance was pained to find that two of its key distributors had dropped its products and gone over to a competitor. They were not dissatisfied with the product but irritated because what they called the 'turnaround

[2] Phillip McVey, "Are Channels of Distribution What the Textbooks Say?" *Journal of Marketing* 24 (January, 1960): 61–63.

[3] Revis Cox, Thomas F. Schutte, and Kendrik S. Few, "Towards the Analysis of Trade Channel Perception," *Combined Proceedings 1971 Spring and Fall Conference of the American Marketing Association*, ed. Fred C. Allvine (Chicago: American Marketing Association, 1972), pp. 189–93.

order-time' was too long and too variable. They could not count on having a consistent and reasonably short period between placing an order
and receiving the goods. Ironically, at the very time it lost these channel
members, the manufacturer was making an analysis of its procedures for
filling orders. It had in fact interviewed some distributors in an effort to
find out how channel members were reacting to its procedures for handling orders, but the coverage was incomplete. However its existing
channel information flow had failed so badly that it lost two important
channel members before it knew that anything was wrong."[4]

These illustrations point to the need for the channel manager to develop
concrete and practical approaches for finding out what kinds of needs and
problems channel members are facing as they attempt to help move the
firm's products through the channel.

Approaches for Learning about Channel Member Needs and Problems

All marketing channels have a flow of information running through them
as part of the formal and informal communications systems which exist
in the channel. Figure 8.1 provides an overview of most of the major
components that go into making up a typical channel communications
system.

Ideally, such a channel communication system would provide the
manufacturer with all of the information needed on channel member
needs and problems. Given the many sources in the channel communication system from which information can be generated (see Figure 8.1), one
might think it unlikely that any important information would be missed.
In practice, however, this is far from true. Most marketing channel communication systems have not been formally planned and carefully constructed to provide a comprehensive flow of timely information. Rather,
in most cases they have evolved haphazardly over a period of years with
little thought given to correcting imperfections in the systems. And even
those channel communication systems that have been carefully planned
and improved are a long way from being perfect. Consequently, the channel manager should not rely solely on the regular flow of information
coming from the existing channel communication system for accurate
and timely information on channel member needs and problems. Rather,
there is a need to go beyond the regular system and make use of one or all
of the following four additional approaches for learning about channel
member needs and problems: (1) research studies of channel members
conducted by the manufacturer, (2) research studies by outside parties,
(3) marketing channel audits, and (4) distributor advisory councils.

[4]Ibid.

Figure 8.1
Model of a Channel Communication System

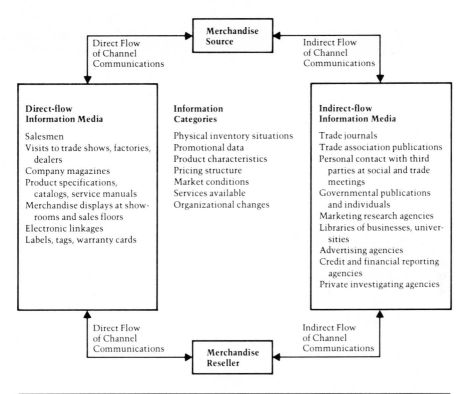

Source: Walter Gross, "Profitable Listening for Manufacturers and Dealers: How to Use A Communication System," *Business Horizons*, 11 (December, 1968): 39. © 1968, by the Foundation for the School of Business at Indiana University. Reprinted by permission.

Research Studies of Channel Members.   While it has become fairly common for manufacturers to conduct research studies dealing with their ultimate customers to learn what kinds of products customers want, what their brand preferences are, the kinds of shopping behaviors they engage in and many other types of information, research studies of channel member needs and problems are much rarer. Indeed, many manufacturers—even large and sophisticated ones—never conduct such research at all. This is unfortunate because sometimes research may be the only way to uncover subtle or hidden channel member needs or problems:

Consider, for example, the case of the Loctite Corporation, a well-known manufacturer of adhesives and sealant products based in Newington, Connecticut. The Loctite Corporation and its distributors were at odds over the sales job the distributors were doing with Loctite products. Loctite felt that the distributors did not care about selling the line

because the distributors' salespeople almost never took along the Loctite product samples when making calls on customers. On the other hand, the distributors believed that Loctite Corporation was insensitive to their sales support needs because the samples, they felt, were not appropriate for use by their salespeople.

Loctite, believing that the samples were an excellent sales aid, was quite befuddled by the distributors' attitude.

Finally, the quandary was solved when Loctite decided to do some research into the distributors' needs and problems in the use of sales aids. The research uncovered a simple explanation for the distributors' failure to use the Loctite samples. As it turned out, the Loctite product samples were designed to be carried in briefcases, but most of Loctite's distributors' salespeople did not carry briefcases! Once this was known, Loctite was quickly able to solve the problem by redesigning the samples, making them small enough to fit into the pockets of the distributors' salespeople.[5]

As suggested by this example, certain types of needs or problems, though simple, may not be at all obvious. In such cases, a manufacturer-initiated research effort can be very useful in zeroing in on the problem.

Research Studies by Outside Parties.   Cox et al. argue that research designed and executed by a *third party* who is *not a member of the channel* is often necessary if complete and accurate data on channel member needs and problems are to be obtained. To support their case they cite the following example:

"The president of a major grocery products manufacturer sought to review the progress of a newly marketed line of dairy products. The chief executive, along with the vice president for marketing and sales, called in all the company's regional sales managers to discuss the marketing performance of the line. The sales managers were instructed to devote the next week to checking with some key grocery trade accounts to learn how the new line was moving. The sales managers conducted their study by talking with acquaintances who headed the buying offices in these key accounts. Except for a few minor technical problems, the president and his vice president for marketing and sales received a very enthusiastic report from the sales managers.

After the final meeting, the president was contacted by the head of a marketing research agency. The marketing researchers convinced the president to do a study on how the grocery trade perceived the marketing program of the manufacturer. The study focused on numerous channel issues such as invoicing, trade margins, sales promotional timing and quality, salesman servicing, case-allowance structure, packing, and

[5]Ellen M. Kleinberg, "Improving Distributor Relations: Communications Solves Most Problems," *Industrial Marketing*, (February, 1981): 72.

many others. The findings were vastly different from the previous 'study'. They were in fact quite negative. In commenting on the results of the study, the president said, 'I held my head between my legs as I could not believe our trade had anything but great things to say about our marketing program. . . . Isn't it amazing that a firm like ours that is successful in sales and profits could score the negatives we did in marketing?'" [6]

As this example suggests, the advantage of using an outside party to conduct research on channel member needs and problems is the much higher assurance of objectivity it provides. Moreover, for manufacturers who do not have marketing research departments or whose capabilities are limited in this area, the use of outside research firms offers them a higher level of expertise than they could provide for themselves.

The Marketing Channel Audit.   As with the periodic accounting audit which virtually all firms have performed, Cox et al. recommend that manufacturers (or possibly other channel members) perform a marketing channel audit periodically.[7] The basic thrust of this approach should be aimed at gathering data on how the channel members perceive the manufacturer's marketing program, its component parts, where the relationships are strong and weak, and what is expected of the manufacturer to make the channel relationship viable and optimal. For example, the manufacturer may want to gather data from channel members on what their needs and problems are in such areas as:

1.   pricing policies, margins, and allowances
2.   extent and nature of the product line
3.   new products and their marketing development through promotion
4.   servicing policies and procedures such as invoicing, order dating, shipping, warehousing, and others
5.   salesforce performance in servicing the accounts

Further, the marketing channel audit should identify and define in detail the issues, problems, strengths, and weaknesses of the manufacturer-wholesaler and/or manufacturer-retailer relationship, all of which should be isolated by kind of channel member, location of the country, sales volume, newness of the account, and any other relevant categories.

Finally, for the marketing channel audit to work effectively it must be done on a *periodic* and *regular* basis so as to capture trends and patterns. Only in this way will it be possible to keep track of those issues which remain constant, those that dissipate, or those that enlarge in scope. New issues which emerge are also more likely to be spotted if the audit is per-

[6]Cox et al., pp. 190–191.
[7]Ibid.

formed on a regular basis. For example, take the issue of physical distribution service levels. Such service levels refer to the quality of service offered by the manufacturer to channel members in processing orders, having the items ordered in stock, providing for rapid delivery and many other aspects of physical distribution service (see Chapter 11).

According to Sabath, such service levels provided by the manufacturer are often way off base in terms of what channel members actually need or want. As Sabath states:

". . . many firms set an in-house or industry standard service level—say 92 percent to 99 percent without even asking their customers (channel members) what level of service they want. . . . Many service levels are usually set arbitrarily, and often much too high—generally, far higher than any customer (channel member) would set them."[8]

Sabath argues that such misdirected attempts to provide uncalled for service levels can be counterproductive, especially if the pressure for high service levels comes from smaller channel members whose poor inventory planning practices and inadequate capital force them to make frequent emergency demands on the manufacturer. Thus, if manufacturers spend most of their time "putting out the fires" of these small channel members, larger channel members are probably being neglected.

A marketing channel audit which reviews the overall relationship of the manufacturer with his channel members could certainly help to bring such problems to light.

Distributor Advisory Councils.   Bego, based on the successful experience of his own firm (B.F. Goodrich Industrial Products Co.), recommends the use of distributor advisory councils as a means for obtaining better knowledge of channel needs.[9] These councils should consist of top management representatives from the manufacturer and representatives of the principals from the channel members. For B.F. Goodrich, the top management members of the council consist of the vice president of marketing, general sales manager, and other top members of sales management. The distributor's representatives number from nine to twelve members. In setting up any distributor advisory council, the normal procedure is to have cochairs, one elected by the members from the distributor group and the other, the top man in sales from the manufacturer.

Bego cites three major advantages of using a distributor advisory council. First, it provides recognition for the channel members. Bego argues that distributors, as do most other people, like to have a voice in planning what affects their own welfare. Channel members are therefore more likely to understand and support a manufacturer's actions if they have

[8]Robert E. Sabath, "How Much Service Do Customers Really Want?," *Business Horizons*, (April, 1978): 26.

[9]Gene L. Bego, "Joint Benefits of a Distributor Council," in *Building a Sound Distributor Organization* (New York: The National Industrial Conference Board, 1964), pp. 44–49.

helped plan them. This gives distributors the feeling of being "in the know," which increases their sense of security, and promotes greater identification with the interests of the manufacturer.

Second, the distributor advisory council provides a vehicle for identifying and discussing mutual needs and problems which are not transmitted through the regular channel information flow. As Bego points out:

"In too many instances, policies and programs inaugurated by a manufacturer are based on the complaints or advice of the 'louder squeaking-wheel' distributor. Sitting down together with the large distributor, the small distributor, the California distributor, and the New York distributor for discussion of common problems will more likely bring out the real source of problems, and not just the superficial causes."[10]

Third, the distributor advisory council results in an overall improvement of channel communications which in turn helps the manufacturer to learn more about the needs and problems of channel members and vice versa. As Bego argues in referring to one of the more common communications problems in the channel:

"How many times have you heard the all-inclusive 'they' used in this manner by the distributor: 'Back in the ivory tower they (the manufacturer) don't know what's going on.' Or, how many times have you heard the ivory tower people referring to the distributor: 'They aren't cooperating' or 'they aren't loyal.' If we can bring all the 'theys' into one room, something has got to happen—hopefully better communications, better cooperation, and better results for all."[11]

Providing Support for Channel Members

Support for channel members refers to the manufacturer's efforts in helping channel members to meet their needs and solve their problems. Such support if properly applied should help to create a more highly motivated group of channel members.

Unfortunately, support for channel members is all too often offered on a disorganized and ad hoc basis. When channel members appear to lack motivation they are "pumped up" with an extra price incentive, advertising allowance, dealer contest, or even a pep talk by the manufacturer. Or if they are having a problem in a particular area, the manufacturer may attempt to "patch it up" and hope that the problem will not come back again—at least for a little while. McCammon, in commenting on the inadequacy of this kind of approach to motivating channel members, states:

[10]Ibid.
[11]Ibid.

". . . many programs (developed by the manufacturer) consist of hastily improvised trade deals, uninspired dealer contests, and unexamined discount structures . . . this traditional attitude toward distributor programming is a luxury that no longer can be easily afforded." [12]

So, as McCammon points out, the attainment of a highly motivated cooperating "team" of channel members in an interorganizational setting increasingly requires carefully planned programs. [13] Such programs for providing channel members support can generally be grouped into one of the following three categories: (1) cooperative, (2) partnership, and (3) distribution programming. While all three of these approaches should emphasize careful planning, the level of sophistication and comprehensiveness of the approaches varies greatly. The cooperative approach represents the least sophisticated and comprehensive approach to channel member support, while distribution programming is the most sophisticated and comprehensive. The partnership approach lies in between. We now turn to a discussion of each of the three approaches.

Cooperative Approach

Cooperative programs arranged between the manufacturer and channel members have traditionally been used as a means of motivating channel members. The range of cooperative activities is quite broad. Table 8.1, for example, lists thirty possibilities. Which of these activities is used and the specific arrangement or features involved vary widely across different industries. Negotiation between channel members usually determines the actual cooperative package available to them subject to legal constraints (see the Robinson-Patman Act discussed in Chapter 3).

The underlying strategy of all such cooperative programs, from the manufacturer's perspective, is to provide incentives for getting extra effort from channel members in the promotion of particular products.

The success realized by manufacturers in securing this extra effort through cooperative programs varies widely. Some have been very successful while others, less so. Here are two examples:

The Palm Beach Company, a manufacturer of men's suits, enjoyed a high degree of success in the use of cooperative advertising (one of the most typical of the cooperative programs between channel members).

---

[12] Bert C. McCammon, Jr., "Perspectives for Distribution Programming," in *Vertical Marketing Systems*, ed. Louis P. Bucklin (Glenview, Illinois: Scott, Foresman and Co., 1970), p. 32.

[13] For related discussions see: Louis W. Stern, "Channel Control and Interorganizational Management" in *Marketing and Economic Development*, ed. Peter D. Bennett (Chicago: American Marketing Association, 1965), pp. 655–665; James R. Moore and Donald W. Eckrich, "Marketing Channels From A Manufacturer's Perspective: Are They Really Managed?" in *Marketing: 1776–1976 and Beyond*, ed. Kenneth L. Bernhardt (Chicago: American Marketing Association, 1976), pp. 248–255. Philip B. Schary and Boris W. Becker, "Distribution As A Decision System," in *Combined Proceedings*, eds. Boris W. Becker and Helmut Becker (Chicago: American Marketing Association, 1973), pp. 310–314.

Table 8.1
Possible Cooperative Activities between Channel Members

1. Cooperative advertising allowances
2. Payments for interior displays including shelf-extender, dump displays, "A" locations, aisle displays, etc.
3. Contests for buyers, salespeople, etc.
4. Allowances for a variety of warehousing functions
5. Payments for window display space, plus installation costs
6. Detail men who check inventory, put up stock, set up complete promotion, etc.
7. Demonstrators
8. Coupon handling allowance
9. Free goods
10. Guaranteed sales
11. In-store and window display material
12. Local research work
13. Mail-in premium offers to consumer
14. Preticketing
15. Automatic reorder systems
16. Delivery costs to individual stores of large retailers
17. Studies of innumerable types, such as studies of merchandise management accounting
18. Liberal return privileges
19. Contributions to favorite charities for store personnel
20. Contributions to special anniversaries
21. Prizes, etc., to store buyers when visiting showrooms—plus entertainment, of course
22. Training retail salespeople
23. Payments for store fixtures
24. Payments for new store cost or improvements
25. An infinite variety of promotion allowances
26. Special payments for exclusive franchises
27. Payments of part of salary of retail salespeople
28. Time spent in actual selling on retail floor by manufacturer's salespeople
29. Inventory price adjustments
30. Store name mention in manufacturer's advertising

Source: Adapted from Edward B. Weiss, "How Much of a Retailer Is the Manufacturer," *Advertising Age*, 29 (21 July 1958): 68. Reprinted with permission from *Advertising Age*. © 1958 by Advertising Publications Inc.

The arrangement provided for Palm Beach to pay 50 percent of the retailer's cost for newspaper, radio, T.V. and outdoor advertising. The retailers could spend up to 4 percent of the net wholesale price of the merchandise shipped to them and would be reimbursed up to a maximum of 2 percent. Palm Beach required that the ads include proper product labels and descriptions and be devoted exclusively to Palm Beach products.

Palm Beach believed the program was highly successful because 65 percent of the available cooperative advertising fund had been used by the retailers.[14]

[14]Neil H. Borden and Martin V. Marshall, *Advertising Management: Text and Cases*, rev. ed. (Homewood, Illinois: Richard D. Irwin, 1959), pp. 261–263.

Here is an example of another kind of cooperative arrangement (promotional allowances) which did not enjoy success:

The Whitehall Company, a manufacturer of proprietary drugs such as *BiSoDol* antacid and *Kolynos* tooth powder attempted to improve retailer support of its products.

A research study had indicated that point-of-sale displays using about 2½ square feet of counter space were highly effective in increasing sales. So Whitehall sought to work out a plan with retailers to get them to use these displays. The key feature of the cooperative arrangement was an allowance to the retailer of 5 percent of the retailer's purchases if the display would be used.

The program failed. First, competitors quickly offered equal or higher allowances. Second, many retailers refused the offer because of their highly limited shelf space. Third, of those who took the allowance, a substantial number did not actually follow through by using the display.[15]

What made the difference between success and failure in these two examples of the use of cooperative programs? While it is difficult to generalize without greatly oversimplifying, there are at least two critical differences in the way these two cooperative programs were designed and executed which may account for a major part of the difference. First, as pointed out in the previous section of this chapter, the support which the manufacturer offers channel members must take into account their particular needs and problems if it is to provide effective motivation. In the case of Palm Beach, the extra advertising dollars made available through the program, though limited to advertising Palm Beach products, still helped to build store patronage through the identification of the particular retailer in the cooperative ads. This is a need that is fundamental to most retailers of shopping goods. Whitehall, on the other hand, simply *assumed* that any retailer would be delighted to get an extra 5 percent promotional allowance. It failed to realize, however, the high opportunity cost that convenience goods retailers have for shelf space. In short, many of the retailers apparently did not need the 5 percent promotional allowance as much as they needed the 2½ feet of shelf space.

The second difference is in the way the cooperative programs were executed. The Palm Beach sales force of fifty was able to spend considerable time with retailers convincing them to tie in their local promotions with the Palm Beach national advertising. They also provided much assistance in developing the ads. In contrast, Whitehall's sales force of one hundred was not able to devote nearly as much time because of the far greater numbers of retailers involved. So they were not able to see to it that the program was actually being carried out as planned.

In summary, three general guidelines for the use of cooperative ar-

---

[15]Harry L. Hansen, *Marketing Text, Techniques and Cases*, 3rd ed. (Homewood, Illinois: Richard D. Irwin, 1967), pp. 615–618.

rangements for motivating channel members can be derived from these examples:

1. The particular types of cooperative arrangement used should be based on an analysis of channel member needs and problems. Only those programs which appear to fill channel members' needs or help solve their problems should be considered.
2. Careful planning is needed to help ensure that the cooperative programs being offered by the manufacturer will be understood by the channel members and have their support.[16]
3. Most cooperative arrangements require careful supervision to see that they are carried out as planned.

"Partnership" Approach

Webster, in a study of marketing channels serving industrial markets, argues strongly for a "partnership" arrangement between the manufacturer and the distributors to increase the latter's level of motivation.[17] This partnership is not one in the legal sense of the term, but rather is meant to suggest a supportive relationship between channel members based on a careful delineation of their mutual roles in the channel. He states:

"The idea of a partnership remains essential; when the manufacturer turns to the distributor for added help, he does not give up his own responsibility for effective marketing, nor can he expect the distributor to respond positively to all suggestions. Rather, he assumes new responsibilities for making the distributor more effective—through programs of product development, careful pricing, promotional support, technical assistance, order servicing, and through training programs for the distributors' salespeople and management."[18]

Webster points to three basic phases in the development of a "partnership" arrangement between channel members. First, if it has not already been done, an explicit statement of policies should be made by the manufacturer in such areas as product availability, technical support, pricing, and any other relevant areas. Figure 8.2, for example, shows such a statement of policy for the Black and Decker Company. This having been done, the roles of the channel members can then be more precisely defined in terms of the tasks they will be expected to perform and the compensation they will receive for doing so.

The second phase is an assessment of all existing distributors as to

---

[16] See for example: George Young, "Owens-Corning Incentive Plan Woos Distributors and Sales," *Industrial Marketing*, (January, 1978): 99–100.

[17] Frederick E. Webster Jr., "The Role of the Industrial Distributor," *Journal of Marketing*, 40 (July, 1976): 10–16.

[18] Ibid.

Figure 8.2
Statement of Policy towards Channel Members of the Black & Decker Corporation

A STATEMENT OF POLICY

INDUSTRIAL DIVISION

It is our firm belief that Black & Decker and its duly Authorized Distributors have fundamental obligations to each other.
We believe that mutually profitable operations depend upon mutual acceptance of those obligations as outlined.

WHAT DISTRIBUTORS CAN EXPECT FROM BLACK & DECKER

1. Selective Distribution:

- Appointed on the basis of power tool potential in each marketing area.
- Adequate to insure penetration of all markets for our products.
- Selected in accordance with the terms of this "Statement of Policy."

2. Specialized Field Sales Assistance Through:

- The largest, best-trained field sales organization in the industry.
- Product and market training for Distributor's sales organization by means of effective sales meetings, power tool clinic sessions and joint sales calls in the field.
- Availability of market potential information to assist Distributor's sales planning.
- Assistance in the maintenance of a well balanced and current power tool and accessory inventory.

3. Healthy Profit Opportunities Through:

- Equitable profit margins on power tools and accessories.
- Assured inventory turnover.
- Maintaining an orderly market.
- Refusal to deal with Distributors who do not feel that the sales policies we suggest are based upon sound business judgment.

4. Aggressive Advertising and Sales Promotion Through:

- The best-known brand name in the industry.
- The largest and best program of national advertising, direct mail assistance and display materials in the power tool field.

5. Leadership in Research and Development Through:

- The broadest, most complete line in the industry.
- Continued leadership in product performance, value, styling and innovation.

6. Leadership in Manufacturing From:

- The largest, most modern plants in the industry.
- Unparalleled quality control standards.
- Thorough testing of all products before shipment.

7. Nation-wide Network of Factory-operated Service Facilities Which:

- Offer prompt, expert repair service at reasonable cost.
- Stock genuine Black & Decker replacement parts.

8. The Famous Black & Decker Guarantee Which:

- Protects the purchaser against defective material or workmanship for the life of the product.

WHAT BLACK & DECKER EXPECTS FROM DISTRIBUTORS

1. Effective Sales Results Through:

- An aggressive sales organization, knowledgeable in the application and selling of Black & Decker products.
- Effective sales management focus on our line.
- Adequate penetration of the potential market for our products in the Distributor's normal trading area.
- Cooperation with Black & Decker's field sales personnel in developing sales programs, meetings and work schedules designed to build sales performance.

2. Vigorous Promotional Activity Through:

- Imaginative advertising, direct mail activity, displays and catalog coverage of the Black & Decker line.

3. Protection of Black & Decker's Brand Name and Reputation By:

- Following the sales policies recommended by the company.
- Restricting sales to the Distributor's normal trading area.
- Discouraging the sale of Black & Decker products through non-authorized sales organizations, so that the customer will receive maximum service after purchase.
- Abstaining from marketing practices that, in any way, damage the reputation of the company or its products.

4. Maintenance of an Adequate Inventory By:

- Stocking tools and accessories of a variety and quantity commensurate with markets served and the highest standards of customer service. ("Adequate Inventory" shall be a matter of agreement between each Distributor and the appropriate Black & Decker sales representative.)

5. Provision of Those Other Services and Functions Which Characterize a Good Distributor, Such As:

- Extending credit to the user.
- Following up customer inquiries.
- Rendering prompt delivery from local stocks.
- Making available prompt technical services to customers.
- Keeping informed on market conditions.

With this STATEMENT OF POLICY, we reaffirm our belief in the economic soundness of the Distributor, our resolve to continually to improve and diversify the products we offer and, through Distributor channels, to cultivate an ever-widening market for Black & Decker products.

THE BLACK & DECKER MANUFACTURING COMPANY

President

Chairman of the Board

Source: Roger M. Pegram, *Selecting and Evaluating Distributors* (New York: The Conference Board, Business Policy Study No. 116, 1965), p. 139.

their capabilities for fulfilling their roles. The approaches suggested for determining channel member needs and problems discussed earlier in this chapter can be applied with equal effectiveness for appraising channel members' strengths and weaknesses. The manufacturer should pay particular attention to helping distributors overcome any weakness by developing specific programs in these areas. For example, if a distributor has an inadequately trained sales force, the manufacturer might develop a training program aimed at improving the distributor's salespeople. If a particular channel member is having problems in controlling inventory, the manufacturer might attempt to offer expertise in this area. In short, the manufacturer's support programs should be clearly and sharply focused on the distributors' areas of greatest need.

Third, the manufacturer should continually appraise the appropriateness of the policies which guide his or her relationship with channel members. In the face of a rapidly changing environment (see Chapter 3) no set of channel policies can remain static for very long.

The Armstrong Cork Company is a good example of a manufacturer that stresses this partnership concept in building a highly motivated team of channel members. In its floor covering division, for example, all of its products are sold through independent wholesale distributors whom Armstrong views as its "partners" in its quest to maintain its strong leadership position in many types of floor coverings. This partnership concept has been a long-standing tradition of Armstrong's channel policy.[19] A major feature of this relationship, which serves as a continuing reminder of the partnership, is the annual conference of Armstrong and its wholesale distributors. For the last sixty years Armstrong has sponsored this annual convention. In recent years, these conventions have developed into meticulously planned programs designed to carefully reiterate the roles that each of the "partners" is expected to play in the marketing success of Armstrong floor products. Figure 8.3, which is the cover page from the program booklet of the 55th Wholesale Distributors Convention, stresses this partnership theme. Much of the three day program consists of a rather unusual "seminar." This seminar is actually a very entertaining play performed by professional Broadway actors and actresses playing the roles of various Armstrong and distributor personnel. The time, places, and setting are, of course, changed to provide entertainment value. Though the play is very entertaining, Armstrong's intent is deadly serious— to show the roles that the channel members are expected to play in the channel partnership. In short, what Armstrong expects from its distributors and what the distributors can expect from Armstrong.

Distribution Programming

The most comprehensive approach for achieving a highly motivated channel team is that of *distribution programming* developed by McCammon.

[19]Bert Rosenbloom, "Motivating Independent Distribution Channel Members," *Industrial Marketing Management*, (August, 1978): 275–281.

Figure 8.3
Cover Page from Program Booklet of the 55th Convention of the
Armstrong Floor Division Wholesale Distributors

**55th Convention
of Armstrong
Floor Division
Wholesale Distributors**

**Hershey, Pennsylvania
Kansas City, Missouri
San Francisco, California**

Welcome to our 55th Convention! 1976 has been an excellent year for our
manufacturer/distributor team, and we expect the years ahead to hold unlimited
opportunities for growth. In fact, the theme of this year's meeting—Opportunity
Seventy-Seven—pinpoints our optimism about our future.

Anticipating these opportunities, we've planned the products and merchandising
programs to keep us firmly entrenched as the best partnership in the flooring industry.
Over the next two days, we'll be detailing a plan to help you take advantage of these
opportunities.

We want to inform you, enthuse you, and entertain you. We're on a tight schedule,
but we've allowed time to meet new friends and greet old ones; because our social
friendship is as important as our professional relationship.

Enjoy yourselves!

Source: From the makers of Armstrong flooring; reproduced by permission.

He defines this as: "A comprehensive set of policies for the promotion of a
product through the channel."[20] The essence of this approach is the development of a planned, professionally managed channel. The program is developed as a joint effort between the manufacturer and the channel mem-

[20] McCammon, "Perspectives," p. 43.

bers to incorporate the needs of both. If done well, the program should offer all channel members the advantages of a vertically integrated channel (see Chapter 14) while at the same time allowing them to maintain their status as independent business firms.

The first step in developing a comprehensive distribution program is an analysis by the manufacturer of marketing objectives and the kinds and levels of support needed from channel members to achieve these objectives. Further, the manufacturer must ascertain the needs and problem areas of channel members (see previous sections of this chapter for methods of doing this). Figure 8.4 outlines some of the major areas that should be included in the analysis for both the manufacturer and the channel members.

Figure 8.4
A Frame of Reference for Distribution Programming

Manufacturer's Marketing Goals

Based on a careful analysis of:
  Corporate capability
  Competition
  Demand
  Cost-volume relationships
  Legal considerations
  Reseller capability

and stated in terms of:

  Sales (dollars and units)
  Market share
  Contribution to overhead
  Rate of return on investment
  Customer attitude, preference and "readiness-to-buy" indices

Manufacturer's Channel Requirements

Reseller support needed to achieve marketing goals (stated in terms of):
  Coverage ratio
  Amount and location of display space
  Level and composition of inventory investment
  Service capability and standards
  Advertising, sales promotion, and personal selling support
  Market development activities

Retailer's Requirements

Compensation expected for required support (stated in terms of):
  Managerial aspirations
  Trade preferences
  Financial goals
    Rate of inventory turnover
    Rate of return on investment
    Gross margin (dollars and percent)
    Contribution to overhead (dollars and percent)
    Gross margin and contribution to overhead per dollar invested in inventory
    Gross margin and contribution to overhead per unit of space
  Nonfinancial goals

Distribution Policies

Price concessions
Financial assistance
Protective provisions

Source: From *Vertical Marketing Systems*, edited by Louis P. Bucklin, p. 33. © 1970 by Scott, Foresman and Company. Reprinted by permission.

After this analysis has been completed, the specific channel policies can be formulated. There are a myriad of possible channel policies which the manufacturer may use depending upon the type of industry involved, the nature of the channel members involved, and past practices in the channel. Nevertheless, McCammon suggests that virtually all of the policy options available can be categorized into three major groups:

1. those offering price concessions to channel members
2. those offering financial assistance
3. those offering some kind of protection for channel members

Figure 8.5 lists a number of the more frequently encountered policy options in each category.

With a comprehensive list of possible channel policy options such as that shown in Figure 8.5, together with the analyses of the manufacturer's goals, and the needs and problems of channel members considered, a programmed merchandising agreement can be developed for the channel members. An outline of such an agreement is shown in Figure 8.6. Finally Figure 8.7 contrasts a conventional channel relationship with one characterized by a distribution programming arrangement.

One example of an especially successful distribution programming arrangement can be seen in the case of the Norwalk Furniture Corporation, one of the few upholstered furniture manufacturers that can guarantee 30-day delivery on all special orders:[21]

In 1977, Norwalk instituted a distribution programming arrangement with its dealers known as the "total-effort-dealer program." The program contained the following key elements:

Dealer Commitment: **Total effort dealers agreed to put their major effort on the Norwalk line by displaying Norwalk furniture in nine out of ten upholstered-furniture room settings. They also agreed to operate only on a "naildown", special-order basis, and they agreed not to sell any floor samples which would jeopardize future sales.**

Norwalk Commitment: **In return for this dealer commitment, Norwalk developed a comprehensive program for supporting the dealers that offered the following features:**

1. **Guaranteed 30-day delivery of custom-ordered furniture**
2. **Customized advertising materials, catalogs, and extra large fabric swatches**
3. **Annual factory authorized sales**
4. **Floor plan financing**

---

[21] Ronald L. Ernst, "Distribution 'Detente' Benefits Suppliers, Retailers, and Consumers," *Marketing News*, (7 March 1980): 19–20.

Figure 8.5
Examples of Channel Policy Options

I. **"Price" Concessions**
  A. Discount Structure:
     trade (functional) discounts
     quantity discounts
     cash discounts
     anticipation allowances
     free goods
     prepaid freight
     new product, display, and advertising allowances (without performance requirements)
     seasonal discounts
     mixed carload privilege
     drop shipping privilege
     trade deals
  B. Discount Substitutes:
     display materials
     premarked merchandise
     inventory control programs
     catalogs and sales promotion literature
     training programs
     shelf-stocking programs
     advertising matrices
     management consulting services
     merchandising programs
     sales "spiffs"
     technical assistance
     payment of sales personnel and demonstrator salaries
     promotional and advertising allowances (with performance requirements)

II. **Financial Assistance**
  A. Conventional Lending Arrangements:
     term loans
     inventory floor plans
     notes payable financing
     accounts payable financing
     installment financing of fixtures and equipment
     lease and note guarantee programs
     accounts receivable financing
  B. Extended Dating:
     E.O.M. dating
     seasonal dating
     R.O.G. dating
     "extra" dating
     post dating

III. **Protective Provisions**
  A. Price Protection:
     premarked merchandise
     fair trade
     "franchise" pricing
     agency agreements
  B. Inventory Protection:
     consignment selling
     memorandum selling
     liberal returns allowances
     rebate programs
     reorder guarantees
     guaranteed support of sales events
     maintenance of "spot" stocks and fast delivery
  C. Territorial Protection:
     selective distribution
     exclusive distribution

Source: From *Vertical Marketing Systems*, edited by Louis P. Bucklin, pp. 36–37. © 1970 by Scott, Foresman and Company. Reprinted by permission.

Figure 8.6
Outline of a Programmed Merchandising Agreement

1. Merchandising Goals
   a. Planned sales
   b. Planned initial markup percentage
   c. Planned reductions, including planned markdowns, shortages, and discounts
   d. Planned gross margin
   e. Planned expense ratio (optional)
   f. Planned profit margin (optional)

2. Inventory Plan
   a. Planned rate of inventory turnover
   b. Planned merchandise assortments, including basic or model stock plans
   c. Formalized "never out" lists
   d. Desired mix of promotional versus regular merchandise

3. Merchandise Presentation Plan
   a. Recommended store fixtures
   b. Space allocation plan
   c. Visual merchandising plan
   d. Needed promotional materials, including point-of-purchase displays, consumer literature, and price signs

4. Personal Selling Plan
   a. Recommended sales presentations
   b. Sales training plan
   c. Special incentive arrangements, including "spiffs," salespeople's contests, and related activities

5. Advertising and Sales Promotion Plan
   a. Advertising and sales promotion budget
   b. Media schedule
   c. Copy themes for major campaigns and promotions
   d. Special sales events

6. Responsibilities and Due Dates
   a. Supplier's responsibilities in connection with the plan
   b. Retailer's responsibilities in connection with the plan

Source: From *Vertical Marketing Systems*, edited by Louis P. Bucklin. © 1970 by Scott, Foresman and Company. Reprinted by permission.

5. Advertising allowances

6. Sales training meetings for floor sales personnel and in-store merchandising assistance

The benefits of this total effort distribution program have been substantial for both the dealers and Norwalk.

From the dealers' standpoint, the program met many of their needs and helped them to solve some significant operating problems faced by furniture retailers. First, and of overwhelming importance, dealer inventories could now be substantially reduced (20–25 percent reduction in total inventory) because all sales would be made on a custom-order basis. So the only inventory dealers would need to carry was floor samples.

Second, since all sales under the total-effort-dealer program would be special orders, the dealers could enjoy higher gross margins as a result of reduced risks of carrying poor selling items as well as being assured of never being "out of stock" of hot selling items, and not having to take as many markdowns.

Third, higher sales productivity would be fostered because the dealers' salespeople could concentrate on one upholstered line and their efforts would be enhanced by well-targeted promotional materials and in-store merchandising help provided by Norwalk.

Finally, the comprehensive financial analysis offered by Norwalk to its total effort dealers as part of the program would help the dealers to become more proficient in using modern financial methods to solve financial problems and manage their businesses more profitably.

The benefits of the distribution program from Norwalk's point of view were also substantial. First, and foremost, Norwalk was able to focus and concentrate its sales efforts through a group of knowledgeable, committed, and highly motivated dealers.

Second, freight expenses were reduced significantly because Norwalk would be shipping larger orders to fewer dealers.

Finally, and perhaps most important from a long-run strategic standpoint, the program enabled Norwalk to develop marketing plans and objectives with the confidence that it now had a team of dealers that was capable and motivated to help Norwalk to realize those plans and objectives.

Distribution programming arrangements, such as the one developed by the Norwalk Furniture Corporation, have become increasingly common in such product categories as garden supplies, major appliances, bedding, sportswear, cosmetics, and housewares. Manufacturing organizations currently engaged in programmed merchandising activities include: General Electric (on major appliances); Baumritter (on its Ethan Allen furniture

---

Figure 8.7
Comparison of Characteristics of Supplier/Retailer Relationships in a Conventional Channel vs. a Programmed System

Characteristics	Conventional Channel	Programmed System
Nature of contacts	Negotiation on an individual order basis	Advanced joint planning for an extended time period
Information considered	Supplier sales presentation data	Retailer's merchandising data
Supplier participants	Supplier's territorial salesperson	Salesperson and major regional or headquarters executive
Retailer participants	Buyer	Various executives, perhaps top management
Retailer's goals	Sales gain and percent markup	Programmed total profitability
Supplier's goal	Big order on each call	Continuing profitable relationship
Nature of performance evaluation	Event centered; primarily related to sales volume and other short-term performance criteria	Specific performance criteria written into the program

Source: Ronald L. Ernst, "Distribution Channel Detente Benefits Suppliers, Retailers, and Consumers," *Marketing News*, (7 March 1981), p. 19. Reprinted from *Marketing News*, published by the American Marketing Association.

line); Sealy (on its Posturepedic line of mattresses); Scott (on its lawn care products); and Villager (on its dress and sportswear lines).

Providing Leadership to Motivate Channel Members

Even if the channel manager has developed an excellent system for learning of channel members' needs and problems, and no matter what approach is used to support these, control must still be exercised through effective leadership on a continuing basis to attain a well-motivated team of channel members.

In the context of the marketing channel, *control* may be defined as:

The ability to predict events or to achieve a desired outcome. Leadership is: the use of power to achieve control.[22]

Seldom is it possible for the channel manager to achieve total control no matter how much power underlies his or her leadership attempts. This state would exist only if the channel manager were able to predict all events related to the channel with perfect accuracy, and achieve the desired outcomes at all times. For the most part, this is a theoretical state not achievable in the reality of an interorganizational system such as the marketing channel. Little explains succinctly the problems of achieving very high levels of control and leadership in this interorganizational setting:

"Because firms are loosely arranged, the advantages of central direction are in large measure missing. The absence of single ownership, or close contractual agreements, means that the benefits of a formal power (superior, subordinate) base are not realized. The reward and penalty system is not as precise and is less easily effected. Similarly, overall planning for the entire system is uncoordinated and the perspective necessary to maximize total system effort is diffused. Less recognition of common goals by various member firms in the channel, as compared to a formally structured organization is also probable."[23]

As Little points out, the interorganizational setting of the marketing channel creates a set of conditions which makes strong leadership more difficult to achieve. This is particularly the case in channels that have evolved as a group of loosely aligned firms. But even in channels which have been designed to foster a higher degree of control, such as those based on contractual commitments or distribution programming, the special circum-

---

[22] Adel I. El-Ansary and Robert A. Robicheaux, "A Theory of Channel Control: Revisited," *Journal of Marketing,* 38 (January, 1974): 2.

[23] Robert W. Little, "The Marketing Channel: Who Should Lead This Extra-Corporate Organization," *Journal of Marketing,* 34 (January, 1970): 32.

stances attendant to interorganizational systems discussed by Little do not completely disappear. Thus, even though the basis for control through strong leadership is significantly greater in formally structured or contractual channels, it does not often equal that achieved in an intraorganizational setting. This is not meant to suggest that the channel manager cannot hope to exercise a high level of leadership in an effort to motivate independent channel members. Rather, we are simply pointing out that in attempting to do so, the channel manager will face a more difficult set of problems.

Using Power Effectively to Motivate Channel Members

The underlying basis of all attempts to provide leadership in the channel is power. Recall from Chapter 4 that power in a channels context was defined as one channel member's capacity to influence the behavior of other channel members. Power bases (also discussed in Chapter 4) refer to the sources from which power springs. Five such bases were identified: (1) reward, (2) coercion, (3) legitimate, (4) referent and (5) expert. Leadership in the channel is actually a manifestation of one or more of these power bases.

In attempting to motivate channel members, the channel manager in a producing or manufacturing firm would like to have as much power as possible to back up his or her leadership thrusts. However, the power bases available to exercise leadership generally are dependent upon the size of the firm relative to other members of the channel, the channel structure, and special or unique conditions, some of which may be temporary.[24] For example, a manufacturer may, for a time, be in command of a scarce product which gives the manufacturer great power for the duration of the scarcity. But barring this or similar developments, there is little the channel manager can do to increase the power available to him or her in the short run. In the long run, power may be increased through channel design decisions which change the channel structure, and through company growth that increases the size of the firm relative to other channel members. For the short run, however, the channel manager must work with what power is presently available in attempting to lead channel members to a higher level of motivation.[25] This requires the use of available power skillfully to maximize its motivational impact on the channel members. The case of Libby-Owens-Ford, discussed in the next section, illustrates how one company handled this task.

Libby-Owens-Ford: Leadership through the Skillful Use of Power.   The discussion in this section revolves around a case involving the Libby-

[24]Michael Etgar, "Channel Domination and Countervailing Power," *Journal of Marketing Research*, 13 (August, 1976): 254–262, and "Channel Environment and Channel Leadership," *Journal of Marketing Research*, 14 (February, 1977): 69–76.

[25]For a related discussion see: Thomas W. Speth and E. A. Bonfield, "The Control Process in Marketing Channels: An Exploratory Investigation," *Journal of Retailing*, (Spring, 1978): 13–26.

Owens-Ford Co. (L.O.F.), one of the largest manufacturers of flat glass in the country.[26] This case not only illustrates the skillful use of power to lead channel members to a more highly motivated effort, but it also includes examples of two other major aspects of motivating channel members discussed earlier in the chapter (learning about channel members' needs and problems, and developing programs to support these). This case provides a good overall vehicle for tying together the major themes discussed in this chapter.

In 1960 L.O.F. found itself faced with a group of lackluster, poorly motivated wholesale distributors (L.O.F. depended on these wholesalers to distribute a major portion of its products to glass, hardware, lumber, and allied retailers, as well as to contractors). After taking a careful look at its wholesalers, L.O.F. described the situation as follows:

". . . a typical L.O.F. distributor found himself confronted with four major problems: (1) engulfment in conditions of rapid change, (2) complacency in the midst of change, (3) poor market penetration, and (4) an ominous decline in profits.

In the face of these compelling problems, many of the wholesalers were doing very little to help themselves. Some were admittedly playing a 'wait-and-see' game, with the idea of getting out while the getting was good. Still others resorted to uneconomical and sometimes questionable business practices. In general, the typical wholesaler was economically and psychologically 'under the rug.' There was a need for strong leadership to generate the knowhow and particularly the 'will to survive.'"

From what has been discussed so far in this case it is clear that L.O.F. has dealt with the first aspect of motivating channel members—it made an effort to learn about their needs and problems.

Further analysis of its wholesalers' plight convinced L.O.F. that what its wholesalers needed most to deal with their problems was a higher level of management knowhow. This need was largely responsible for the wholesalers' poor situation, which in turn led to a poorly motivated group of channel members for L.O.F.

L.O.F. then went on to develop a program for providing support. The approach used by L.O.F. is suggestive of the partnership concept discussed previously in this chapter:

L.O.F. wanted its wholesalers to know that they could look to L.O.F. for support in the form of managerial assistance which they sorely needed. In turn, L.O.F. expected the wholesalers to allow L.O.F. "to exercise a continuing influence on the decisions of the independent distributors."

The overwhelming emphasis and key feature of the program was on

[26] Clinton F. Hegg, "Training Distributor Management," in *Building a Sound Distributor Organization* (New York: National Industrial Conference Board, 1964), pp. 50–64.

the training of the distributors' management through what L.O.F. called the Executive Management Training Program.

Note that what is particularly significant here is that the medicine was right for the "disease"—a major management training program was just what the wholesalers needed. L.O.F. was therefore very much on target with this program for motivating its distributors.

Finally, effective leadership by L.O.F. is evident from the skillful manner in which power was used to motivate the distributors to make use of the program:

Rather than attempt to ram this program "down the distributors' throats" (coercive power), L.O.F. instead emphasized that it had a lot of management knowhow to offer (expert power) and that the program would be mutually beneficial (referent power). But perhaps even more importantly, L.O.F. stressed a high level of participation by the distributors in the development of the program. As Clinton F. Hegg, Vice President of Sales for L.O.F. stated: ". . . we decided to provide leadership in the form of a self-improved or do it yourself program." Given this orientation the final management assistance program relied heavily on the impact of distributors obtained through extensive interviews. Thus in a true sense the program was a joint effort between the manufacturer and distributors. It was highly successful.

Though L.O.F.'s approach to motivating its channel members may not be perfect, it does reflect an understanding of the general tenets for motivating channel members which we have discussed in this chapter. These areas summarized as follows:

1. recognizing the importance of learning about the particular needs and problems of channel members and developing approaches for uncovering these needs
2. developing specific programs for channel members which emphasize the support of those needs
3. recognizing the need for leadership to motivate channel members through the skillful application of power
4. understanding that the skillful application of power in motivating channel members requires an awareness of the interorganizational setting of the channel and the difficulties attendant to this form of organization

Summary

Even though the marketing channel has been carefully designed to reflect a near optimum allocation of the distribution tasks, strong cooperation from the channel members cannot be expected as a matter of course. Rather, channel management—the administration of existing channels to secure the cooperation of channel members in achieving the firm's distribution objectives—is necessary.

A fundamental part of channel management is that of motivating the channel members to perform their tasks effectively and efficiently.

In order to motivate channel members successfully, the channel manager must deal with three major facets of motivation management in the channel: (1) learning about the needs and problems of channel members, (2) developing programs to support their needs and helping them to deal with their particular problem areas, and (3) providing leadership.

Finding out the needs and problems of channel members is not a matter of happenstance. The channel manager cannot rely solely on the existing channel communication systems to yield all of the relevant information concerning channel member needs and problems. Rather, at times the channel manager must look beyond the regular flow of information in the channel to gather the necessary data by using such approaches as: (1) research studies of channel members conducted by the firm, (2) research studies by outside parties to assure objectivity, (3) periodic marketing channel audits, and (4) distributor advisory councils.

Once the channel manager has the necessary information on channel member needs and problems support programs must be developed that will meet channel member needs and help them to solve their problems. Good support programs require careful planning. Ad hoc, piecemeal, or "quick fix" approaches to channel member support are becoming increasingly unacceptable to channel members.

Planned approaches to channel member support can generally be grouped into one of three categories: (1) cooperative, (2) partnership, and (3) distribution programming.

The cooperative approach is the least sophisticated and comprehensive approach to channel member support. Basically, the manufacturer and the channel members agree on a series of cooperative activities such as cooperative advertising, promotional allowances, incentive programs, etc. If the cooperative program offered by the manufacturer is on target in terms of meeting channel member needs and problems, and is carefully planned and supervised, it can be an effective approach for motivating channel members.

The partnership approach represents a more sophisticated and comprehensive approach to channel member motivation. Essentially, the partnership approach is based on a careful delineation of the mutual roles of the manufacturer and the channel members, that is, what kinds of commitments the manufacturer expects from the channel members and what kinds of support the channel members can expect from the manufacturer. The idea underlying such a relationship is mutual support between manufacturer and channel members in order to create a well-organized team effort in the distribution of the manufacturer's products. If well-developed and well-executed, the partnership approach can provide an excellent basis for motivating channel members.

Finally, distribution programming offers the most sophisticated and comprehensive approach to channel member motivation. Distribution programming involves the development of a comprehensive plan for managing the marketing channel. Key areas of the relationship between manufacturer and channel members are studied and a comprehensive channel management plan is developed to cover all of those areas. Typically, such programs are initiated and directed by the manufacturer, but channel members at the wholesale or retail levels can also initiate and direct distribution programming arrangements. Distribution programming, if well done, can provide an outstanding approach for motivating channel members.

Regardless of which approach the channel manager uses to motivate channel members, leadership must still be exercised on a continuing basis if the motivation programs are to operate effectively and viably. In attempting to exercise such leadership, however, the channel manager must remember to deal with several significant challenges characteristic of the interorganizational setting of the marketing channel. Among these are: (1) the looseness of the organization of many channel systems, (2) a proclivity by channel members to avoid central direction, (3) lack of single ownership, and (4) no clear demarcation of a superior-subordinate relationship. This makes it more difficult for the channel manager to exercise strong leadership in the execution of a motivational program. Leadership based on skillful application of power, however, can help to mitigate these interorganizational problems.

Discussion Questions

1. Discuss the distinction between channel management and channel design.
2. Even if a marketing channel has been carefully designed in such a way that its structure reflects a near optimal allocation of distribution tasks, the channel cannot be expected to "run" by itself. Discuss this statement.
3. An effective information flow in the channel is all that is needed to inform the channel manager of the needs and problems of channel members. Do you agree or disagree? Discuss.
4. What are some of the major sources of interaction that exist in the typical channel communication system?
5. Discuss the major features of the four approaches for finding out about channel member needs and problems discussed in this chapter.
6. Compare and contrast the major features of cooperative, partnership,

and distribution programming approaches for motivating channel members.

7. Discuss several characteristics which differ between a conventional channel and a channel based on a distribution programming arrangement.

8. Discuss the concepts of control, leadership, and power as they apply to motivating channel members.

9. What are some of the problems faced by the channel manager in attempting to exercise leadership to motivate channel members in the interorganizational setting of the marketing channel?

10. What particular facets of the Libby-Owens-Ford case indicate effective leadership in motivating the firm's channel members?

Chapter 9
Product Issues in Channel Management

The previous chapter discussed the motivation of channel members as a fundamental element of channel management. But channel management —the administration of existing channels to secure the cooperation of channel members in achieving the firm's distribution objectives—involves more than just motivation management. Even a comprehensive and carefully planned motivation program will not in itself assure the channel manager of a highly cooperative channel team operating at its peak level of effectiveness and efficiency. Rather, the channel manager who aspires to attain this level of channel performance must also be skilled at using the elements of the marketing mix to facilitate the administration of the channel. In other words, the channel manager must use the firm's product, pricing, promotion, and physical distribution variables to their maximum effect in securing cooperation from channel members. In this context, the marketing mix variables may be viewed as *resources*; how these resources are used will affect the performance of the channel members—either facilitating or inhibiting their performance. The channel manager would, of course, like to use the marketing mix so as to achieve the former as often as possible. In order to do this, however, the channel manager needs to understand how the other marketing mix variables interface with the channel variable, and what the implications of these interfaces are for channel management.

In this chapter we discuss some of the interfaces of the product variable with the channel variable and discuss some of the implications for channel management. Chapters 10 and 11 deal with price and promotion as they interface with channel management, while Chapter 12 examines interfaces between physical distribution and channel management.

The Product and Channel Management

There are many potential interfaces between product management and channel management. Though it is not possible to deal with all of these in this chapter, we will discuss a sufficient number of examples to provide an overall idea of some of the more basic relationships and implications. Our purpose in this section is not to present a comprehensive inventory of possible product–channel management interfaces, but rather to develop a sense of awareness on the part of the channel manager to thinking about how product decisions are likely to affect channel management decisions.

The discussion and examples presented below are organized around three major areas of product management:

1.   new product planning and development
2.   the product life cycle
3.   strategic product management

New Product Planning and Channel Management

The development of new products is a challenge faced by virtually all producers and manufacturers serving both consumer and industrial markets. The success achieved by new products in the market is dependent upon many factors such as: the innovativeness and quality of the product itself, its price, the nature of customer demand, competitive factors, timing, and many others.[1] One of these "other" factors is how much support a new product receives from independent channel members. Without a high level of cooperation from the channel members, it is much more difficult to gain market acceptance for a new product. It is, therefore, important for the channel manager to analyze the possible channel implications in the planning and development of new products. The focus of this analysis should be on what can be done in the planning and development stage to promote a higher level of cooperation from the channel members in gaining a successful market for the product. While there are many possible issues which the channel manager may consider depending upon the type

[1] For an excellent discussion of new product planning see: Philip Kotler, *Marketing Management Analysis, Planning and Control*, 4th ed. (Englewood Cliffs, New Jersey: Prentice-Hall, 1980), Chapter 13.

of industry and the particular circumstance involved, the following five are frequently important for a wide range of channels:

1. What input, if any, can be provided by channel members into new product planning?
2. What has been done to assure that the new product will be acceptable to the channel members?
3. Does the new product fit into the present channel members' assortments?
4. Will any special education or training be necessary to prepare the channel members to do an effective selling job for the new product?
5. Will the product cause the channel members any special problems?

Channel Member Input into New Product Planning.   One way of promoting increased enthusiasm and acceptance for new products by channel members is by obtaining some input from them into new product planning. This input may take the form of soliciting ideas for new products during the idea generating stage of new product planning, all the way to getting feedback from selected channel members during the test marketing stage. Kotler makes a strong case for obtaining channel member input into new product planning:

". . . dealers are a particularly good source for product ideas. They have firsthand experience of customers' unsatisfied needs and complaints. They are often the first to learn of competitive developments. An increasing number of companies are developing more systematic procedures to tap their ideas." [2]

Armstrong World Industries, for example, is a firm that puts a great deal of weight on getting input from its wholesale and retail channel members in the development of new products. A case in point involved the development of a highly successful no-wax tile which could be installed by the typical do-it-yourselfer. Prior to the introduction of the tile, no-wax vinyl flooring was available only in large six- or twelve-foot sheets cut from a large roll. Armstrong retailers soon learned that consumers were not buying the product because they were not capable of installing it themselves in this form. Several of the retailers suggested that Armstrong make the product available in 12 × 12-inch tile form for the home do-it-yourselfer. Armstrong took their advice and has enjoyed an extremely successful new product.

Seeking input from channel members into new product planning may, however, require that the manufacturer allow channel members to be privy to new product plans. Many manufacturers are very sensitive about

---

[2] Philip Kotler, *Marketing Management Analysis, Planning and Control*, 3rd ed. (Englewood Cliffs, New Jersey: Prentice-Hall, 1976), chap. 10.

their new product plans for competitive reasons and are reluctant to divulge them to channel members until the last moment before the product is introduced.[3] In some cases this type of secretive behavior may be quite justified. But if competitive considerations do not require such secrecy, the manufacturer has little to lose and much to gain by seeking input from, and sharing new product plans with channel members. The channel members are much more likely to be enthused about supporting new products which they have played a part in developing.

Promoting Channel Member Acceptance of New Products. It is not enough for a new product to be acceptable only to its final user. The product also must be acceptable to the channel members through whom it passes in reaching the final user. There are many criteria which channel members may use to judge the acceptability of new products. These criteria vary for different channel members in particular industries and also vary according to their individual objectives and policies. There is, however, one "bottom line" criterion that is applied by most channel members in judging the acceptability of any new product—its profit potential in terms of meeting established margin structures.

The margins available to channel members at the wholesale and retail levels are largely determined by established practices and customs subject to the legal constraints of the Robinson-Patman Act (see Chapter 3). Often these discounts bear little relationship to the services actually performed by the various channel members.[4] But regardless of how accurately or inaccurately the manufacturer's trade discount reflects a fair payment for channel member services, channel members often become accustomed to the existing level of trade discounts. They, therefore, usually expect that similar trade discount levels will be available on all new products introduced by the manufacturer. If similar trade discounts are not offered on a new product, particularly if the manufacturer attempts to offer a lower discount, the channel members will certainly want to know why the status quo has been upset. And a very good explanation will be needed if the manufacturer has any hope of convincing the channel members that the change was justified. Yet even the most cogent explanation is likely to be received with skepticism, if not outright contempt, on the part of channel members. It is much better practice to give careful thought to the trade discount issue *during* the process of new product planning rather than attempting to change the customary discount after the product has been developed. Specifically, an important criterion to consider in the process of new product planning should be whether the proposed product can be marketed through existing channel members within the established trade discount structure. If it appears that the new product will require that a lower trade discount be offered to the channel members, serious thought should be given as to whether this is a suffi-

[3] Philip McVey, "Are Channels of Distribution What the Textbooks Say?" *Journal of Marketing*, 24 (January, 1966): 64.

[4] William J. Stanton, *Fundamentals of Marketing*, 4th ed. (New York: McGraw-Hill, 1975), p. 288.

ciently important consideration to drop the new product idea or modify it in some fashion to conform to the existing trade discount structure. Only the most powerful manufacturer enjoying a truly dominant position in the channel can afford to disregard this issue. Yet even the most powerful manufacturers in the long run may suffer from less cooperative channel members and reduced channel viability if new products are offered at lower margins. This is not to suggest that trade discount structures should never be tampered with. For, at times, cost and profit considerations make such changes virtually unavoidable. What is being suggested, however, is that *attention be given to the interface between new product planning and established trade discount structures.* Every effort should be made to develop the product so that it can be marketed through the channel members in conformance with the established trade discounts.

Fitting the New Product to Channel Member Assortments. The particular mix of products carried by any given channel member is his *assortment*. All of the products carried by a supermarket, department store, lumber yard, plumbing supply wholesaler, etc. constitute assortments of products which they handle and depend upon to generate sales. Thus, a channel member's assortment is analogous to a manufacturer's *product mix*—all products which the manufacturer produces.

When a manufacturer develops a new product it is adding to its product mix. Presumably, during the development of the new product some consideration has been given to how well the new product fits into the product mix from the standpoints of both production and marketing. In short, the manufacturer has probably evaluated whether the capacity exists to manufacture and market the product efficiently. A key consideration on the marketing side of this evaluation should be whether existing channel members will view the new product as an appropriate one to add to *their* assortments. The fact that the product fits the manufacturer's product mix does not mean that the channel members will necessarily see it the same way for their own assortments. Consider what happened to the Hanes Co. for example:

The Hanes Company is best known as the manufacturer of L'eggs pantyhose which are distributed nationally through drug and food retailers.

In 1976, Hanes was in the process of developing two new products: Feet First (men's socks) and U.S. Male (men's and boys' underwear) which it intended to sell through the same outlets. While these products represent a highly logical extension to Hanes' product mix from a production standpoint, Hanes has learned through its experience with L'eggs that its retailers may be somewhat leery about adding these new products to their assortments. The reason? As a senior executive of Hanes explained in referring to the problem experienced with L'eggs: "The buyer who orders soap just doesn't know how to order women's hosiery." Hanes solved the problem very successfully for L'eggs by stocking the displays using direct company salespeople and by offering

computerized profiles on what the market preferences were for each of their retail outlets. This removed the burden of buying from the drug and supermarket retailers who were unaccustomed to handling these products in their own assortments. Hanes used the same strategy to overcome retailer skittishness in carrying the new socks and underwear products.[5]

As this example suggests, the channel manager should try to learn whether channel members feel competent to handle the new products. If they do have qualms about adding the new product to their existing assortments because they lack experience in handling similar products, steps should be taken to allay these fears before introducing the product.

Educating Channel Members about New Products.   It is not unusual for channel members to need special education or training provided by the manufacturer in order to sell new products successfully. The type and level of special education will, of course, vary depending upon the type of industry involved and the technical complexity of the product. A fairly complex piece of industrial equipment, for example, may require many hours of instruction by the manufacturer to train the channel members in the product's use and the special features to emphasize in sales presentations. On the other hand, a simple consumer package good may require no more than a few minutes of advice on the proper display of the product. Between these two extremes there are many variations in the educational requirements for new products. But it is well worth the effort for channel managers to investigate the possible educational requirements of new products as they are being developed. This will enable them to plan the necessary educational programs which may be needed by the channel members rather than having to throw one together hastily after the product is sitting on the channel members' shelves. Consider for example what happened to the Hoover Company:

After a careful analysis of the growing tendency of consumers to want higher quality, top-of-the-line products, the Hoover Vacuum Cleaner Co. decided to introduce a high quality–high priced canister-type vacuum cleaner retailing for $209.95. But Hoover's chances for gaining market acceptance for this new high quality vacuum cleaner were severely hindered by the resistance of its retailers. The retailers did not believe that consumers wanted such a high end vacuum cleaner and they had little idea of how to sell a canister type vacuum cleaner in this price range.
    The dealer resistance was finally overcome through a training program. As one Hoover executive commented: "We had to institute a kind of educational program to show our dealers that they could sell the more expensive lines."[6]

[5]"Hanes Expands L'eggs to the Entire Family," *Business Week* (14 June 1976), pp. 57, 61.
[6]Philip Revzin, "Affluent Consumers Turn Optimistic, Buy More Expensive Goods," *Wall Street Journal* (23 July 1976), pp. 1, 19.

Hoover was fortunate in being able to develop a successful educational program after the new product was already developed and sitting in its retailers' inventories. But it would have been better to have considered the possible need for such an educational program *before* the situation had developed to this point.

Making Sure New Products Are Trouble Free.   No channel member likes to take on a new product that will cause him trouble. This applies to product problems that may arise while the product is still in the channel members' inventory as well as to those that may appear soon after the product is sold to a customer. Most channel members have enough problems to deal with in running their businesses without taking on new products that add to their problems. Sometimes, however, the product problems that arise and cause headaches for the channel members are not at all obvious until after they occur. For example, Gross relates the following case:

"A manufacturer of bubblegum balls developed a new type of package for the product to make it easier to open. The package consisted of a box with a simple tear-open feature. This new package design resulted from consumer research which concluded that consumers wanted such a feature. But this turned out to be a serious mistake. Retailers did not want a display package that would invite free sampling by children! Moreover, pilferage would not be the only problem; spillage from the opened boxes would mess up the floor."[7]

For another example, consider what happened when the Heublein Corporation developed a new product:

Heublein's new product was a pressurized barbecue sauce called Sizzle-Spray. It seemed like a highly innovative new product idea destined to capture a big share of the market. The only problem was that when the product began flowing through the channel and was exposed to warm temperature areas, it exploded. Fortunately, Heublein had decided to test market the product in Texas and California before going national. As it turned out, this was a wise decision because it revealed the product defect. This not only saved Heublein several million dollars, but spared it from a lot of disgruntled (and possibly injured) channel members and consumers.[8]

As both of these examples suggest, new product problems that turn up after the product is already flowing through the channel may not be so easy to anticipate. While it is not possible to guard against all of these problems, a little extra care in new product planning is likely to reduce

---

[7] Walter Gross, "Profitable Listening for Manufacturers and Dealers: How to Use a Communication System," *Business Horizons* 11 (December, 1968): 35.

[8] Kotler, *Marketing Management*, 3rd edition, p. 217.

Figure 9.1
The Product Life Cycle

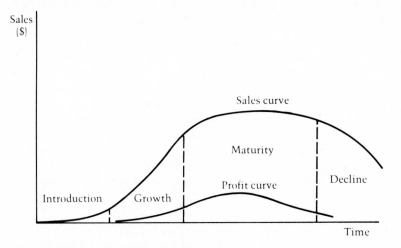

incidences of new products which cause problems for channel members.[9] This extra care in new product planning means putting more weight on studying the interface between new products and what is likely to happen to them as they move through the channel.

The Product Life Cycle and Channel Management

The product life cycle (PLC) is a model for describing the stages through which a new product passes after it has been introduced. The PLC concept has been discussed extensively in the marketing literature and is almost always presented in basic marketing texts.[10] Thus we need not go into detail here in discussing the basic PLC model. We will, however, briefly review the four stages to provide a sharper focus for our forthcoming discussion on the implications of the product life cycle for channel management.

Figure 9.1 is a typical portrayal of the product life cycle model. As Figure 9.1 shows, the sales history of a typical new product follows an S shaped sales curve. The curve is divided into four basic stages usually referred to as, *introduction, growth, maturity,* and *decline.* The introductory stage is one of slow growth as the product begins to gain a foothold in

[9]For a discussion of some of the product liability issues that can emerge from these types of situations see: Karl A. Boedecker and Fred W. Morgan, "The Channel Implications of Product Liability Developments," *Journal of Retailing,* (Winter, 1980): 59–72.

[10]See for example: William E. Cox, "Product Life Cycles as Marketing Models," *Journal of Business,* (October, 1967): 375–84; Theodore Levitt, "Exploit the Product Life Cycle," *Harvard Business Review,* (November–December, 1965): 81–94.

the market. Profits, as shown by the profit curve in Figure 9.1, are non-existent or very low during this stage due to the high costs of introducing the product to the market. The growth stage is marked by rapid market acceptance and relatively high profits as shown by the steeper upward slopes of the sales and profit curves during this stage. Maturity is characterized by a decreasing rate of sales growth (the slope of the curve is less steep) as the market becomes more highly saturated. Profits tend to peak and then decline during the maturity stage because of the heavy selling costs necessary for the product to hold its own against competition. Finally, decline occurs when sales decline absolutely and profits plummet quickly to the zero point.

Not all products pass through this life cycle; there are many exceptions and variations. Moreover, the stages may not be nearly as distinct as those shown in Figure 9.1, and the time during which the product completes its cycle may vary greatly from under one year in some cases to several decades in others.

In spite of such variations, the PLC is still useful as a framework for developing marketing strategies during the different stages. Since this text is concerned with the channel variable, our focus in discussing the product life cycle will be on the strategic implications of each of the stages of the PLC for channel management. Figure 9.2 shows the major channel management implications of the four stages of the product life cycle. These are discussed in more detail below.

The Introduction Stage and Channel Management. During the introductory stage, strong promotional efforts are needed to launch the product. This often entails heavy expenses for advertising and other forms of promotion. All this is for naught, however, if the product is not readily available at the final point of purchase. Thus, during the introductory stage, it is imperative for the channel manager to assure that channel members can provide adequate market coverage for the product.[11] This is by no means a simple task—a good deal of planning and coordination is necessary to provide adequate market coverage at the final point of sale. Breakdowns in planning and coordination such as the following are common:

A manufacturer of consumer leather products introduced a new type of men's wallet to go along with the changes in men's fashions. The wallet was extra thin and light so as not to cause a bulge in the more form fitting men's clothing. The product was nationally advertised in a popular men's magazine that offered its readers a special computerized service listing the retailers from whom the product could be purchased. The response to the new product was excellent as evidenced by the large number of inquiries received by the magazine asking for the names of

---

[11] See for example: Chester R. Wasson, *Product Management: Product Life Cycles and Competitive Marketing Strategy* (St. Charles, Illinois: Challenge Books, 1971), pp. 195–196.

Figure 9.2
Stages of the Product Life Cycle and Their Implications for Channel Management

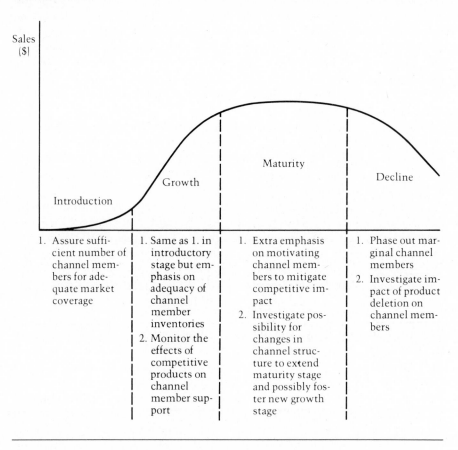

the retailers who carried the product. This favorable response soon turned sour, however, as quite a few disgruntled potential customers found that not only did many of the retailers not have the product in stock when the customers asked for it, but they had not even heard of it! As it turned out, the manufacturer had supplied the magazine with a list of retailers who carried its products, but many of these retailers had not ordered the newly introduced product or even taken note of its existence.

Such problems as these can be avoided by giving more attention to planning and coordinating the availability of newly introduced products. The channel manager should check to see if channel members who are listed as having the product in stock actually do. In many cases this may require little more than a phone call to spot check. Care should be taken, however, to find out whether the product is not only in stock but whether it is on display as well. It is not at all unusual for retailers to have the product in the warehouse or storeroom rather than out on the sales floor even as customers are asking for it.

Growth Stage and Channel Management.   As the product enters the growth stage, rapid market growth begins. In order to help sustain this growth, the channel manager must deal with two important challenges in channel management:

1.   The channel manager must continue to see that product availability provided to the market by channel members is adequate so as not to inhibit market growth.
2.   The channel manager must carefully monitor channel member actions with respect to competitive products already handled by them and keep an eye out for potential competitors who are attempting to "break into" the channel.

The problem of making sure that the product is available to the market, discussed in the previous section, becomes a more difficult one to deal with as the product shifts out of the introductory stage into the stage of rapid growth. This is particularly true for consumer products sold to mass markets through numerous wholesale and retail channel members. Yet dealing with this problem effectively can make the difference between success or failure in sustaining market acceptance for the product. As Luck points out:

"Wholesalers and retailers play major roles in the market success of products which they distribute. Relatively small shifts in shelf facings, out-of-stocks, displays, and other dealer support, may produce favorable or dangerous trends."[12]

The basic approach for dealing with this problem, according to Luck, is through *monitoring* the product flow as it moves through the channel. Formal and systematic reporting procedures are necessary, however, for effective monitoring. While some manufacturers may be able to develop their own reporting systems, relying on sales analysis data, reports from their field sales force, and estimates made by their own research departments, a growing number are turning to specialized independent marketing research firms to provide this kind of information. Such firms as A. C. Nielsen and National Retail Tracking Index, Inc. (NRTI) can provide manufacturers with many types of data on the product as it moves through the channel, such as the level of product inventory in particular retail and wholesale outlets, sales rates, the amount of shelf space given to the product, and many others. Figure 9.3, for example, taken from an

[12]David J. Luck, "Interfaces of a Product Manager," *Journal of Marketing*, 33 (October, 1969): 33.

Figure 9.3
An Advertisement for a Product Monitoring Service

DISTRIBUTION DATA? <u>RETAIL?</u>

LOOK AGAIN

If your retail distribution data doesn't *originate* in the store, get yourself a fortune cookie. It won't tell you less — and *can* be more nourishing. Consider! Warehousing speaks one language, retailing another. *Neither takes the place of the other.*

Warehouse withdrawal data *can* be good. Even informative. But no matter how reshuffled, recycled, re-presented, it remains warehouse withdrawal data.

Missing from warehouse withdrawal figures are data from non-cooperating warehouses; data on private labels, rack jobber deliveries, drop shipments, inter-store transfers.

All this, only in-store observation can report.

NRTI goes *into* the store, reports *real* distribution from *every* source; shelf facings and location; shelf inventory; actual retail prices; displays; promotions. And much more! Projectable, instantly actionable. Full panel store check every four weeks, flash reports in 72 hours. Get it *all* — from NRTI.

We report what the <u>shopper</u> sees — in the store

FOOD • DRUG • MASS MERCHANDISERS . . . and any other retail stores, anywhere, U.S.A.

NATIONAL RETAIL TRACKING INDEX, INC.
a division of EHRHART-BABIC ASSOCIATES, INC.

Executive Offices: Metropolitan City, 120 Route 9W, Englewood Cliffs, N.J. 07632 ☎ (201) 461-6700

Source: Courtesy of Ehrhart-Babic Associates, Inc.

NRTI promotional brochure, describes some of their services more fully. The growth of NRTI and similar research firms in this specialized area of marketing research attests to the growing demand for information that will help enable the manufacturer to monitor what is happening to the products in the channel.

The second problem of monitoring the channel members' actions with respect to competitive products is of equal importance to monitoring one's own products. The high sales enjoyed by a product during the growth stage are bound to attract competitors who are eager to grab a "piece of the action." In a number of cases, some of these competitors' products will find a place on the shelves of a manufacturer's channel members. Consequently a manufacturer must compete against competitors for the channel members' support to sustain the growth of the firm's product. Levitt argues that the key to dealing with this kind of competition in the growth stage lies in the anticipation of competitive actions and the preplanning of appropriate strategy during the previous stage of the product life cycle. He states:

"... At each stage in a product's life cycle, each management decision must consider the competitive requirements of the next stage. Thus a decision to establish a strong branding policy during the market growth stage might help to insulate the brand against strong price competition later; a decision to establish a policy of 'protected' dealers in the market development (introductory) stage might facilitate point-of-sale promotions during the market growth stage, and so on."[13]

While it may not be possible to anticipate all possible competitive actions impinging on the channel and to preplan channel strategies for each stage of the PLC, some effort in this direction is certainly possible. For example, the various programs for supporting channel members' needs such as the cooperative, "partnership" and distribution programming, discussed in the previous chapter, all involve considerations of possible competitive actions and preplanned programs to mitigate the effects of competition in the channel. Thus, when the product enters the growth stage of the PLC, the manufacturer who has developed carefully planned programs for supporting channel members has the edge over the competitor who seeks the support of the same channel member but lacks previously planned programs to support them.

Maturity Stage and Channel Management.   The slow growth or saturation characteristic of the maturity stage suggests two strategic emphases for channel management:

1. Extra emphasis must be put on making sure the product is more desirable for channel members.

---

[13]Levitt, "Product Life Cycle," p. 91.

2. At the same time, possible changes in channel structure, particularly the selection of different types of intermediaries, should be investigated to forestall the decline stage and possibily create a new growth stage.

In the face of slower growth or near saturation, the sales and turnover rate for the product will decline for many of the channel members. In response to this, they may reduce or totally stop ordering the product. Some will have special sales or close outs to get rid of the product as quickly as possible, fearing the possibility of being stuck with a product that nobody wants. In order to lessen the severity of this pattern of channel member behavior, the channel manager must take steps to make the product more attractive to channel members. The most direct tactics for doing this are those that will increase the profit potential of the product and reduce the risks associated with handling it.[14] Such tactics as extra trade discounts, advertising allowances, special package deal discounts, and more liberal return policies are appropriate. Consideration must be given, of course, to whether such stop gap measures are profitable and in the manufacturer's long run interest.

A more comprehensive and long-term channel strategy which may be followed during the maturity stage is to change the channel structure through which the product is distributed. In some cases this may lead to a renewed growth stage for the product. Adler argues that this strategic option is too often overlooked by manufacturers:

"Almost as limiting in its effect on the vision of a business, is being wedded to a given distribution system. It is also almost as frequent a manifestation of marketing backwardness because the forces of inertia, tradition, and myopia all exert their pulls in the same direction."[15]

While the manufacturer should not attempt to change channels for the product as a matter of course in the maturity stage, an investigation of this possibility is probably well worth the effort. Kotler cites such cases as Timex, which got its watches into unconventional outlets such as drug stores and discount stores, and Avon Products, which moved into door-to-door selling of cosmetics, as examples of highly successful channel changes for products in the maturity stage.[16] In general, the wide consumer acceptance of scrambled merchandising during the past twenty years suggests that channel structure changes that place mature products into unconventional outlets are far more feasible today than ever before. Of course, the careful planning and analysis involved in making such channel design decisions are needed to do this successfully (see Chapters 5, 6, and 7).

---

[14] For a related discussion see: Ben M. Enis, Raymond La Grace and Arthur E. Prell, "Extending the Product Life Cycle," *Business Horizons*, (June, 1977): 46–56.

[15] Lee Adler, "A New Orientation for Plotting Marketing Strategy," *Business Horizons*, (Winter, 1964): 46.

[16] Kotler, *Marketing Management*, 3rd ed., pp. 239–242.

The Decline Stage and Channel Management.   Barring a dramatic turn-around, which occasionally does occur, total demise is usually imminent when a product is in the decline stage. Given this situation, the channel manager should focus attention on two final channel implications:

1. Can marginal outlets be phased out quickly to avoid further profit erosion?
2. Will dropping the product cause adverse reaction on the part of existing channel members?

Even when a product has reached the decline stage, a substantial number of channel members may still be carrying the product. Many of them will be low volume, however, often ordering the product in very small quantities. The high volume channel members will, for the most part, already have dropped the product. This leaves the channel manager with a high cost, low volume channel for the product which further erodes an already deteriorating profit picture. Thus, the channel manager must consider whether the very low volume outlets should be phased out. Basically this requires an analysis of the revenues produced by each outlet weighed against the cost of servicing each of them. This procedure will be discussed in more detail in Chapter 13 (Evaluating Channel Member Performance).

The second issue of possible adverse reactions by channel members when a manufacturer drops a declining product has been alluded to by Alexander:

"Products are often associated in the marketing process. The sale of one is helped by the presence of another in the product mix. When elimination of a product forces a customer who buys all or a large part of his requirements of a group of profitable items from the firm to turn to another supplier for his needs of the dropped product, he might shift some or all of his other patronage as well. Accordingly, it is sometimes wise for management to retain in its mix a no-profit item, in order to hold sales volume of highly profitable products. But this should not be done blindly without analysis."[17]

Unfortunately, the procedure for making this kind of analysis is not clear-cut. Nevertheless, Alexander does sketch out the basic guidelines that should be used in such an analysis:

"When this marketing interdependence exists in a deletion problem, the decision-maker should seek to discover the customers who buy the sick (product in the decline stage) product; what other items in the mix they buy; in what quantities; and how much profit they contribute.
. . . marketing research may be conducted to discover the extent to

[17] R. S. Alexander, "The Death and Burial of 'Sick' Products," *Journal of Marketing*, 28 (April, 1960): 5. See also: Joseph P. Guiltinan, "Risk-Aversive Pricing Policies: Problems and Alternatives," *Journal of Marketing* 40 (January, 1976): 11.

*which the customer purchases of profitable items actually are associated
with that of the sick product. Although the results may not be precise,
they may supply an order-of-magnitude idea of the interlocking patronage situation.*"[18]

Strategic Product Management and Channel Management

Strategic management of the product line is a challenge faced by virtually
all manufacturers. No product line can be simply left alone to remain
fixed in time—certainly not if it is to remain a viable and profitable product line.

Successful product strategies depend upon a variety of factors such as
the quality, innovativeness, or technological sophistication of the products themselves, the capabilities of the managers charged with managing the product line, the financial capacity and willingness of the firm to
provide the promotional support often necessary to implement product
strategies, and several other factors. One of these "other" factors, and a
frequently overlooked one, is the role played by channel members in implementing product strategies. Since most manufacturers do not market
their products directly to their final users, they will at some point have to
call on their channel members to implement the product strategies formulated by manufacturers. Thus, the success of the manufacturer's product strategies is, at least to some extent, and sometimes to a very great
extent, dependent upon the effectiveness of the channel members in carrying out the manufacturer's product strategies.

In the sections below we discuss this interface between product strategy and channel management for several different product strategies.

Product Differentiation Strategy.   One of the most basic and important
product strategies pursued by many manufacturers is product differentiation. In essence, product differentiation represents the manufacturer's attempt to portray a product(s) as being different from competitive products
and therefore more desirable to purchase even though the price may be
higher.

Product differentiation is not necessarily based on differences in the
physical characteristics of the product. Product differentiation can also
be created by putting different names on products, packaging them differently, using certain advertising appeals, selling them through different
stores, or some combination of these factors. The real key to creating a
differentiated product is to get the *customer* to *perceive* a significant difference in the product. As long as the customer perceives a significant difference in the product, it makes little difference whether or not the product is physically identical to another product. Conversely, if the customer
does not perceive such a difference, the fact that the product is quite dif-

[18]Alexander, "Death and Burial," pp. 5–6.

ferent physically is inconsequential. So, product differentiation is not so much a matter of making a product that is physically different as it is getting a *customer* to *see* a difference.

The task of conveying this difference is not always the sole province of the manufacturer. Channel members may also need to be called upon to help create the aura of a differentiated product. The kinds of stores the product is sold in, the way it is displayed and sold, as well as the services provided, can be critical in creating a differentiated product. Consider the following case:

Lady Godiva Chocolates, owned by the Campbell Soup Co., enjoys a reputation of being among the finest chocolates available; they sell for over sixteen dollars per pound. While Lady Godiva Chocolates do physically differ somewhat from other chocolate candies, the fact that they are sold only in fine department and candy stores, that they are magnificently displayed and packaged, and that they are sold with the same care one would expect when buying fine diamonds, probably equally contributes to differentiating Lady Godiva Chocolates from other brands. Without this type of retailer support, it is doubtful that Lady Godiva would be able to carry off this quality image no matter how well the chocolates themselves were made.

The Maytag Co. discovered this need for retailer support when it failed to get adequate retailer support for the product differentiation strategy it used to expand its market share for dishwashers:[19]

Maytag, which enjoyed a superior quality image for its washing machines, attempted to differentiate its dishwashers on the same basis— better quality than competitive products. According to objective tests conducted by *Consumer Reports* magazine, Maytag's dishwashers *were* better than competitive brands. The Maytag dishwashers' unique washing mechanism, designed and patented by the company, resulted in a top-rating by *Consumer Reports*. The outward appearance of the Maytag dishwashers, however, was not much different from competitive dishwashers costing considerably less than Maytag. Indeed, the Maytag dishwashers looked more like the low end of the competitive lines. As one retail department store appliance buyer commented, "Maytag always looked too simple to cost a lot." Thus, for Maytag's product differentiation strategy to work, retailers would have to stress the "inside story" of Maytag's superior quality through strong personal selling at the point of sale. Unfortunately, Maytag did not make adequate provisions for this requirement when it developed its product differentiation strategy. It simply assumed that the superior quality of the Maytag dishwasher would be recognized by consumers and hence the dishwashers would "sell themselves." But this did not happen.

[19]"A Duel of Giants in the Dishwasher Market," *Business Week*, (9 October 1978): 137–138.

So, as these examples suggest, when the implementation of a product differentiation strategy depends on both the product itself and channel member support, adequate plans should be made for securing channel member support *at the time the strategy is being formulated.*

Product Positioning Strategy.   Product positioning is another important product strategy practiced by manufacturers. Basically, product positioning refers to a manufacturer's attempt to have its product perceived by consumers in a particular way relative to competitive products. If this is accomplished, the product is then "positioned" in the consumer's mind as an alternative to other products that the consumer currently uses. For example, recall from Chapter 1 that Source Perrier, the manufacturer of Perrier Water, was able to position the product in the U.S. market as being an alternative to liquor and soft drinks. Thus, many consumers began considering drinking Perrier water instead of these other products. Orange juice producers have been engaged in a major promotional campaign to position orange juice as an alternative to soft drinks rather than only a breakfast drink. The dairy industry has a similar campaign aimed at positioning milk as an alternative to many other soft drinks, while 7-Up has tried to position its product as an alternative to cola drinks. Such product positioning strategy is not limited to beverages; the strategy is also employed in a wide range of other product categories from chewing tobacco (as an alternative to cigarettes) to mobile homes (as an alternative to regular homes).

While successful product positioning strategy is dependent upon many factors, the types of stores selling the product and how they display and promote the product can be very important. For Perrier to be positioned as an alternative to soft drinks, it was necessary to have the product sold in supermarkets and displayed in mass in the same aisle as the soft drinks.

Another case in point involved the product positioning strategy used by Black & Decker for its Dustbuster, a small cordless vacuum cleaner introduced in early 1979:

Small hand-held vacuum cleaners had been around for years but consumers had perceived them as a product useful mainly for automotive clean-up jobs such as vacuuming the interior of the car and cleaning out the ash trays. Hence, these products were typically sold in automotive stores or in the automotive departments of hardware, discount, and homecenter stores.

Black & Decker sought to position its Dustbuster in a much broader field. It wanted the Dustbuster to be seen as an indispensable household appliance for quick and easy handling of small household clean-up jobs. If this positioning could be achieved, a vastly larger market would be available since this vacuum cleaner would then be seen by consumers as a basic household appliance rather than merely as an infrequently used auto cleaning device.

For this strategy to work, however, Black & Decker would have to

get the Dustbuster into department stores, discount department stores, mass merchandisers, appliance stores, and most other stores selling appliances. But even more importantly, Black & Decker would have to convince these retailers to display the product in the *appliance or housewares departments* rather than in the automotive or hardware departments. This was no easy task because not only were hand-held vacuum cleaners considered to be an automotive product, but Black & Decker was also viewed by retailers as a manufacturer of power tools—not household appliances.

Fortunately, Black & Decker recognized these obstacles while developing the product positioning strategy for the Dustbuster and thus planned to devote a substantial amount of sales effort and promotion to gain retailer support for the Dustbuster positioning strategy.

So, if product positioning strategy requires channel member support and follow-through to work effectively, this fact needs to be recognized and planned for when the product positioning strategy is being developed. The difference between a successful and unsuccessful product positioning strategy may sometimes depend on the "minor detail" of where retailers decide to position the product on the selling floor.

Product Line Expansion and Contraction Strategies.   At one time or another, most manufacturers will find it necessary to expand or contract particular product lines. They may even engage in both processes simultaneously by adding products even as they drop others that are at the end of their life cycles (see earlier discussion) or that are selling too poorly to continue offering.

Such product line expansion and pruning strategies can often create problems in dealing with channel members because it is very difficult, if not impossible, to find a "perfect" blend of products in the line that will satisfy all channel members. When the product line is expanded, some of the channel members may complain about product proliferation which increases their inventory costs and complicates their selling job; when products are dropped from the line, other channel members or even the same ones who complained about the proliferation of products may carp about losing products for which they still have plenty of customers. During the 1970s, for example, the Scripto Pen Co. wound up with many disenchanted channel members at both the wholesale and retail levels because of what they perceived as a faulty product line expansion strategy being practiced by Scripto.[20] Scripto seemed to be adding more and more products that were not very different from existing products in the line and which were viewed as "me-too" products that did little to enhance the competitiveness of the Scripto line. In fact, many of the channel members felt that the proliferation of products coming from Scripto (e.g., in ball point pens alone, Scripto offered about a dozen models) created confusion

---

[20]Rayna Skolnik, "Scripto's Missing the Point," *Sales and Marketing Management*, (May, 1978): 37–40.

and made the line more difficult and costly to sell. As a result, substantial numbers of wholesalers and retailers deemphasized the Scripto line.

On the other hand, in the early 1980s when Texas Instruments (TI) decided to prune its consumer product line by eliminating its digital watches, a lot of retailers were very unhappy about the decision.[21] The decision announced by TI in the fall of 1981 to be effective by the end of the year left many retailers in a lurch because they had already laid in the TI watch line and other TI products, especially calculators. Many of these retailers were justifiably concerned about the effects of this move by TI on consumer confidence not only as it might affect sales of TI watches but sales of TI calculators as well. As one industry observer noted: "All of TI's major customers will be asking themselves, 'Am I going to go to bed with them in calculators and have the rug pulled out from under me again next year?'"[22]

So, from a channel management standpoint, product line expansion and pruning strategies present the manufacturer with a delicate balancing act of trying to find a happy medium of channel member satisfaction and support for reshaped product lines.

While there are no simple clear-cut approaches for performing this balancing act, several points are worth considering when dealing with the interface between product line expansion and contraction strategies and channel management. First, although a manufacturer must be the master of its own product line and be free to change it in what is believed to be the best interests of the firm, it makes good sense to incorporate channel member views whenever possible. Second, the manufacturer should attempt to explain to channel members the rationale underlying product line expansion or deletion strategies. This can go a long way towards removing the confusion and mystery that sometimes surround such strategies. Finally, the manufacturer should take care to provide adequate advanced notice to channel members of significant product line changes and try to avoid adverse timing (see the Texas Instruments example above) in implementing those strategies.

Trading Up and Trading Down Strategies.   Closely related to product line expansion and contraction strategy is the strategy of trading up or trading down. Trading up refers to adding products to the line which are substantially more expensive than other products in the line, while trading down is essentially the opposite—adding lower priced products to the line than is typical. Trading up represents the manufacturer's attempt to use product strategy to appeal to the higher end of the market, while trading down aims products for appeal to the lower end of the market.

Trading up and trading down can be very high risk strategies because they reflect profound departures from the firm's normal base of operations. The manufacturer must now face: (1) new markets about which he

---

[21] "When Marketing Failed at Texas Instruments," *Business Week*, (22 June 1981): 91–94.
[22] Ibid., p. 92.

may know very little, (2) new competitors that he has not faced before, and (3) quite possibly new channel members and/or new problems with existing channel members.

Since our focus in this section is on the channel management interface with product strategy, we will discuss the third issue—the channel management problems associated with trading up and trading down strategies. Basically there are two problems to consider.

The first and most basic channel problem faced by a manufacturer pursuing either trading up or trading down strategy is whether existing channel members provide adequate coverage of the high end or low end market segments to which the trade up or trade down product is aimed. If they do not, new channel members will have to be added and/or the basic design of the channel may have to be changed. When Creative Playthings, a toy manufacturer which had traditionally specialized in relatively high priced infant toys, introduced a lower priced line in the late 1970s, it suddenly realized that its existing channel members, mainly department stores and small independent toy stores, could not provide adequate access to the lower end of the market at which the lower priced toys were aimed. The company, therefore, had to hastily explore the feasibility of distributing the new line through mass merchandisers, supermarkets, and drugstores. On reflection, Creative Playthings realized that it should have given more thought to this issue much earlier in the process of product strategy planning.

The second channel management problem faced by the manufacturer when trading up or trading down is a more subtle and perhaps more difficult one than the first. It may be stated as follows: Will the channel members have confidence in the manufacturer's ability to successfully market the traded up or traded down product? Channel members, whether at the wholesale or retail levels, develop certain perceptions about the kinds of products that particular manufacturers are associated with. When a manufacturer that has been perceived as a supplier of "good, solid, mid-priced products" suddenly introduces a much more expensive or a much cheaper product, doubts are likely to arise among the channel members about whether the manufacturer is "out of its depth" or really "knows what it is doing" with its trade up or trade down strategy. Some major retailers, for example, reflected this view when hearing about Mattel, Inc.'s plans to introduce a small home computer in 1982.[23] Mattel, Inc. is the nation's largest toy maker and is best known in the retail trade for such products as Barbie dolls and Hot Wheels. The home computer idea, a radical trade up from anything Mattel had previously offered in its product line, left these retailers wondering whether Mattel was really up to the job of successfully producing and marketing such an item. Mattel's dramatic success with its Intelevision video game, which also represented a trade up for Mattel—though not nearly to the extent of the home computer—will

[23]"Mattel: Parlaying an Adults' Toy into a Role in Cable Television," *Business Week,* (June 22, 1981): 102–106.

perhaps help to put these retailers' fears to rest. In any case, if a manufacturer suspects that channel members lack confidence in its ability to carry off a trade up or trade down strategy, a substantial effort should be made to build up channel member confidence well *before* the product is introduced into the channel.

Product Brand Strategy.   Most manufacturers have several options available when considering product brand strategies. A manufacturer might sell all its products: (1) under one national brand, (2) under several national brands (a "family" of brands), (3) under private brands, or (4) under both national and private brands.

Any of these options may at certain times pose channel management problems.[24] But it is the fourth option, selling under both national and private brands, that presents the most difficult channel management problem because when the manufacturer sells under both national and private brands, direct competition with channel members will result. That is, the final users of the product have the choice of buying the manufacturer's brand (national brand) or the channel member's brand (private brand) which are both produced by the same manufacturer. Whirlpool, for example, sells under its own Whirlpool national brand through distributors and dealers and also is a major supplier for Sears' private brand, Kenmore. Stanley tools sells under the national brand name, Stanley, through hardware stores, homecenters, mass merchandisers and other outlets, but also makes many of the hand tools for J.C. Penney's private brand of tools. Borden, the second largest maker of national brand coffee creamers (Cremora), Scott Paper, with the second largest national brand paper towel (Viva) and Union Carbide, with its leading national brand Glad Bags are all manufacturing other versions of these products for private or so-called noname generic brand sales.[25] A host of other manufacturers across a wide spectrum of industries is also engaged in similar brand strategies. Indeed such dual distribution or multimarketing strategies are becoming increasingly common as national brand manufacturers seek to make use of excess production capacity and compete against private brand products made for large chain retailers by nonnational brand manufacturers.

But such competition between manufacturers and channel members fostered by this dual national/private brand product strategy can create serious competitive problems between the manufacturer and his channel members if the competition becomes too direct:

Consider, for example, the case of a well known liquor manufacturer that sold its liquor products both under its own national brand and under many private brands. One of its major channel members, a large chain of liquor stores in New York, sold this manufacturer's products

[24] See for example: Arthur I. Cohen and Ana Laud Jones, "Brand Marketing in the New Retail Environment," *Harvard Business Review*, (September–October, 1978): 141–148.
[25] "No-Frills Food New Power for the Supermarkets," *Business Week*, (23 March 1981): 70–80.

under both the national brand and its own label private brand. Even though the national and private brands might have come from the very same barrel, the private brand liquor sold for considerably less than the national brand. As more and more of the store's customers realized the products were the same, they bought more of the private brand and less of the national brand. Indeed, it was only around the Christmas season when customers were buying liquor as gifts that sales of the national brand picked up. The manufacturer was now in the unenviable position of having created a "monster" in the form of a widely accepted private brand liquor that could have serious negative consequences for the long-term viability of its own national brand products.[26]

Unfortunately, there are no sure and easy solutions for dealing with this type of competitive problem. When a manufacturer pursues a brand strategy that is based on both national and private brands, he has to expect that somewhere down the road he may very well run into the difficult competitive problem of too much direct competition between the national and private brand versions of his products.

The problem can be minimized, however, by following such policies as: (1) not selling both the national and private brand versions of the product to the same channel members, (2) selling the national and private brand versions of the product in different geographical territories so they are less likely to compete in the same market areas, or (3) making the products physically different enough so that even if the first two policies are not feasible, the direct competition between the national and private brand versions of the product will be minimized.

Product Service Strategy.   Many products, both in the consumer and industrial spheres, require service after the sale. Thus, manufacturers of these products must make some provisions for after-sale service either by offering it directly at the factory, through their own network of service centers, channel members, authorized independent service centers, or by some combination of these organizations.

Unfortunately, the provision for product service has too often been overlooked by manufacturers as a strategic issue in product management,[27] especially among consumer goods manufacturers. Service has been relegated to a secondary position in product strategy planning or, even worse, has been considered almost as an afterthought or minor detail in product management. It is no wonder, then, that consumers often express great dissatisfaction with the availability and quality of the after-sale service available on a wide range of consumer products from automobiles to automatic coffee makers.

Such poor product service reflects not only a shortcoming in product

[26]Robert E. Weigand, "Fit Products and Channels to Your Markets," *Harvard Business Review*, (January–February, 1977): 104.
[27]For a related discussion see: Richard M. Hill, "Suppliers Need to Supply Reliability, in Volume, with Value Engineering Analysis, Market Data," *Marketing News*, (4 April 1980): 7.

management but a shortcoming in channel management as well; because it is the job of the marketing channel not only to make the product available to the final user but to make the necessary service available as well. A marketing channel that provides for effective and efficient delivery of the product is still not very effective or efficient if it does not provide for effective and efficient service for the product.

If good product service is to be provided by the channel, however, the manufacturer must view the issue of product service as a basic strategic issue in product management *and* channel management. Indeed the appeal of the product can be significantly enhanced through a strong service image if the manufacturer has developed a strong service capability in the channel. Black and Decker, for example, has a policy whereby the consumer who experiences any problems with a Black and Decker power tool within one year of purchase can simply go to any retailer selling Black and Decker power tools for an instant replacement. Black and Decker also has an extensive national network of service centers to repair their products. This service image, backed up by an organization that can deliver on that image, has created a substantial differential advantage for Black and Decker products.

The General Electric Company has recently introduced an innovative approach to major appliance service with a do-it-yourself program that provides easy-to-follow manuals and repair parts at G.E. dealers. The program is designed to enable most consumers with a modicum of mechanical skills to repair their own appliances at a substantial savings in cost over calling in a professional repairer. G.E. is using this program as a major product management strategy to differentiate G.E. appliances from competitive products.

Product service strategies such as those mentioned above, or any good service strategies, require channel member support if they are to work well. Black and Decker's instant replacement policy would be meaningless without dealers who will follow through on the offer. G.E.'s program depends on dealers carrying and prominently displaying the do-it-yourself manuals and stocking adequate inventories of replacement parts.

Attaining such channel member support is not a matter of good luck, however. The manufacturer that expects strong cooperation from channel members in providing service must make it clear to channel members that service is an important part of the overall product strategy and incentives must be provided for the channel members to cooperate in the service program. Dealer participation in the G.E. service program, for example, provides a drawing card for added patronage while sales of the do-it-yourself repair manuals and replacement parts add to dealer profits. Similarly, Black and Decker's instant replacement policy helps to build consumer confidence, not only in Black and Decker products, but in the dealer who will make the replacement as well.

Summary

Effective channel management requires that the channel manager be aware of how channel management interfaces with the other variables of the marketing mix: product, price, promotion, and physical distribution. The channel manager should view the firm's strategies in each of these marketing mix areas as resources that can be employed for improving the firm's channel management strategies.

In this chapter, the first of these strategic interfaces—product management and channel management—was discussed. Three basic areas of product management as it interfaces with channel management were considered: (1) new product planning and development, (2) the product life cycle, and (3) strategic product management.

With respect to new product planning and development the channel manager should be concerned with such basic product channel management issues as (1) obtaining channel member input into new product planning, (2) promoting channel member acceptance of new products, (3) fitting new products to channel member assortments, (4) educating channel members about new products, and (5) making sure new products are as trouble-free as possible. Care and attention given to these issues can go a long way towards improving the probability of success for new products.

The product life cycle implications for channel management must also be understood by the channel manager if channel management is to be used effectively to enhance the life cycle of a product. During the introduction stage of the life cycle, the channel manager must assure that a sufficient number of channel members is available for adequate market coverage. As the product moves into the growth stage, the adequacy of channel member coverage must be reinforced and the effects of competitive products on channel member support should be carefully monitored. When the product moves into the growth stage, extra emphasis should be placed on motivating the channel members to help mitigate the impact of competitive products, and the possibility of changing the channel structure to extend the maturity stage or to help create a new growth stage should be investigated. Finally, as the product enters the decline stage, marginal channel members should be phased out, and the impact of the deletion of the product from the manufacturer's product line should be investigated.

Strategic management of the product line is a task faced by virtually all manufacturers if the product line is to remain viable and profitable. A number of basic strategies can be pursued in the strategic management of the product. Among the most important of these for a wide variety of manufacturers are: (1) product differentiation strategy, (2) product positioning strategy, (3) product line expansion and contraction strategies, (4) trading up and trading down strategies, (5) product brand strategies, and (6) product service strategy. The channel manager must understand the interrelationships of these product strategies with channel management strategies and attempt to use channel management to support the successful implementation of these product strategies.

Discussion Questions

1. The product, price, promotion, and physical distribution variables may be viewed by the channel manager as resources in helping secure a higher level of channel member cooperation. Discuss this statement.
2. Discuss the importance of gaining channel member support in building market acceptance for a new product.
3. Is it practical to elicit channel member input into the manufacturer's product planning and development process? What problems might this create?
4. Fitting new products to the channel members' assortments may sometimes be a problem. When might this be the case?
5. Discuss the product life cycle stages and the basic implications of each stage for channel management.
6. Under what conditions might a seemingly simple product deletion decision create possible adverse reactions on the part of channel members?
7. Discuss the relationship between strategic product management and channel management. Is one of these areas more important than the other? Explain.
8. Explain the role played by channel management in the implementation of product differentiation and product positioning strategies.
9. What are some of the channel management problems that can arise when pursuing product line expansion and contraction strategies, trading up and trading down strategies and a product brand strategy that uses both national and private brands?
10. Discuss the role of the marketing channel in providing after-sale service.

Chapter 10
Pricing Issues in Channel Management

Pricing decisions are among the most important in the marketing mix. While much has been written about pricing decisions as they relate to the firm's ultimate target markets, relatively little attention has been focused on the implications of pricing decisions on the channel.[1] Yet there are many potential interfaces between pricing and channel decisions. Dean, for example, points to several of these:

"Choice of channels of distribution should be consistent with strategy for initial pricing and for promotional outlays. Penetration pricing (for example) calls for distribution channels that make the product broadly available. . . . Distribution policy also concerns the role the leader is to play in pushing a given product and the margins he must be paid to induce this action. . . .

Estimation of the costs of moving the product through the channels of distribution to the final consumer must enter into the pricing proce-

---

[1] For an example of an early exception to this see: E. R. Hawkins, "Vertical Price Relationships," in *Theory in Marketing*, eds. Revis Cox and Wroe Alderson (Homewood, Illinois: Richard D. Irwin, 1950), chap. 11; for a more recent discussion see: Bruce H. Allen, Ronald L. Tatham, and David R. Lambert, "Flexible Pricing Systems for High Inflationary Periods," *Industrial Marketing Management*, (August–September, 1976): 1–6.

dure. . . . *Margins must at least cover the distributors' costs of warehousing, handling and order taking.*"[2]

Warshaw in referring to wholesale channel members also alludes to the pricing and channel management interface:

"The area of pricing is of special importance in the appraisal by a manufacturer of his marketing program. The policies formulated determine not only the prices which wholesalers pay for a given product, but also exercise a powerful influence over the prices at which these products can be resold. . . . Manufacturer pricing policy, therefore, not only has an effect on the wholesaler's ability to perform the selling function but also influences the wholesaler's willingness to allocate selling effort on a selective basis."[3]

Both Dean's and Warshaw's comments contain an implied but highly important caveat which the manufacturer must observe in his pricing decisions. We may state it explicitly as follows: *It is not enough to base pricing decisions soley on the market, internal cost considerations, and competitive factors. Rather, for those firms using independent channel members, explicit consideration of how pricing decisions affect channel member behavior is an important part of pricing strategy.* In short, pricing decisions can have a substantial impact on channel member performance. Specifically, if channel members perceive the manufacturer's pricing strategy as congruent with their own interests, they are more likely to provide a higher level of cooperation. If, on the other hand, the manufacturer's pricing decisions reflect a lack of awareness of channel member needs, or appear to work against them, a much lower level of cooperation or even conflict is the more likely result.[4] Thus, the major challenge facing the channel manager in the area of pricing is to help foster pricing strategies that promote channel member cooperation and minimize conflict. Those responsible for managing the channel must play a role in the manufacturer's pricing decisions by focusing on the channel considerations attendant to pricing decisions.

Figure 10.1 helps to illustrate this role more clearly. As Figure 10.1 shows, the channel manager's attention should be on the channel considerations involved in making pricing decisions. In other words, the channel manager must analyze and think through the channel implications of pricing decisions. Take for example a manufacturer's decision to cut the price on a product. The channel members may have many possible reactions to this decision—some of which may be positive while others seem

---

[2]Joel Dean, "Techniques for Pricing New Products and Services," in *Handbook for Modern Marketing*, ed. Victor Buell (New York: McGraw-Hill, 1970), p. 60.

[3]Martin R. Warshaw, "Pricing to Gain Wholesalers' Selling Support," *Journal of Marketing* 26 (July, 1962): 50–51.

[4]See for example: Joseph P. Guiltinan, "Risk Aversive Pricing Policies: Problems and Alternatives," *Journal of Marketing*, (January, 1976): 11–12.

Figure 10.1
The Channel Manager's Role in the Manufacturer's Pricing Decisions

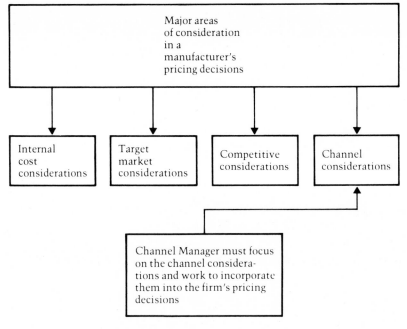

adverse from the manufacturer's point of view. Table 10.1 lists some of the more common possible reactions of channel members to a manufacturer's decision to reduce prices to the ultimate buyer.

As the table indicates, there are many possible reactions which channel members may have to a manufacturer's decision to reduce prices. There are also, of course, many possible channel member reactions to other pricing decisions, some which will enhance the level of cooperation given to the manufacturer and some which may lessen cooperation materially. Further, the reaction of the various channel members may vary. Some may view the manufacturer's pricing action quite favorably and others negatively.

It is the channel manager's job to find out about these reactions, and to appraise their effects on channel member performance. In practice, this kind of evaluation would not usually be conducted as a distinct and separate project. That is, an evaluation of how the manufacturer's existing or proposed pricing strategies influence channel member behavior would normally be included as part of the general evaluation of channel member needs and problems discussed in Chapter 8 (see pp. 220–227). Pricing strategies which are at odds with channel member needs may be brought

Table 10.1
Possible Reactions of Channel Members to a Manufacturer Initiated Price Cut

1. They may expect the price cut to increase their sales volume and profitability.
2. They may become reluctant to deal with the product because of the possible effect of the price cut on the product's quality image.
3. They may be concerned about the price cut on the images of their own firms—because their customers may associate them with handling low-priced mediocre merchandise.
4. They may resent the reduction in their margins which may result from the price cut.
5. They may be concerned about the loss in value of their existing inventories of the product after the price cut.
6. They may feel threatened by the possible proliferation of price cutting on the product by their competitors.
7. They may resent the loss of stability engendered by the price cut.
8. They may be leery of what this price cut portends for the future pricing policies of the manufacturer.

Source: Alfred R. Oxenfeldt, *Pricing Strategies* (New York: AMACOM, A Division of American Management Associations, 1975), p. 227.

up at Distributor Advisory Council meetings, emerge as part of the findings from a survey of channel members, a marketing channel audit, or possibly be conveyed as feedback in the regular flow of channel communications. But because of the importance of pricing strategy in influencing channel member cooperation, the channel manager should be extra sensitive and pay particular attention to channel member views of his or her pricing strategy. Whenever possible, the channel manager should attempt to have channel members' viewpoints on pricing issues included as an integral part of the manufacturer's price making process.[5] If this is done successfully, many of the problems which may arise after pricing decisions have taken effect can be anticipated and hopefully avoided.

Guidelines for Developing Effective Channel Pricing Strategies

Oxenfeldt offers a set of eight basic guidelines for developing pricing strategies that incorporate channel considerations.[6] These guidelines help those involved in pricing decisions to focus more clearly on the channel implications of their pricing decisions. The guidelines also offer some general prescriptions on how to formulate pricing strategies that will help to promote channel member cooperation and minimize conflict. Ob-

[5] For another approach in which the salesforce might be utilized for this purpose see: P. Ronald Stephenson, William L. Cron, and Gary L. Frazier, "Delegating Pricing Authority to the Sales Force: The Effects on Sales and Profit Performance," *Journal of Marketing*, (Spring, 1979): 21–28.
[6] Alfred R. Oxenfeldt, *Pricing Strategies* (New York: AMACOM, A Division of American Management Associations, 1975), p. 140.

viously, there is no guarantee that even scrupulous adherence to these guidelines will ensure this result. In fact, there are sure to be many particular circumstances and situations where some of these guidelines will not apply or will be irrelevant. Nevertheless, these guidelines are worthy of careful study because they do provide a basic framework and benchmark for pricing decisions that incorporate channel considerations. The guidelines are as follows:

1. Each efficient reseller must obtain unit profit margins in excess of unit operating costs.
2. Each class of reseller margins should vary in rough proportion to the cost of the functions the reseller performs.
3. At all points in the vertical chain (channel levels) prices charged must be in line with those charged for comparable rival brands.
4. Special distribution arrangements—variations in functions performed or departures from the usual flow of merchandise—should be accompanied by corresponding variations in financial arrangements.
5. Margins allowed to any type of reseller must conform to the conventional percentage norms unless a very strong case can be made for departing from the norms.
6. Variations in margins on individual models and styles of a line are permissible and expected. They must, however, vary around the conventional margin for the trade.
7. A price structure should contain offerings at the chief price points where such price points exist.
8. A manufacturer's price structure must reflect variations in the attractiveness of his individual product offerings.

Each of these guidelines is discussed in some detail below:

Profit Margins

Clearly, channel members need margins that are more than adequate to cover the costs associated with handling a particular product. (See Tables 10.2 and 10.3 for examples of retailer and wholesaler margins and other operating data.) While this guideline may be relaxed at times as in the case of products which are needed to fill out assortments, or that are to be used for special promotions, these are the exceptional cases rather than the rule. Channel members generally will not carry, let alone enthusiastically support, products whose margins are inadequate to cover their costs and provide room for profit. This applies particularly in a long run sense. In fact, even those manufacturers with an exceptionally strong consumer franchise who can virtually dictate to their channel members will eventually lose their support. Over time, those channel members

Table 10.2
Margins and Other Operating Data of Selected Retailers

Type of Retailer	Gross Margin	Cost of Goods Sold	Operating Expenses	Profit Before Taxes
Department Stores	29.7	70.3	26.8	2.8
Drugs	28.7	71.3	25.6	3.1
Restaurants	44.3	55.7	38.0	6.3
Household Appliances	29.1	70.9	27.4	1.7
Liquor	20.7	79.3	18.3	2.4
Automobiles	15.4	89.6	13.8	1.5
Gasoline Service Stations	12.9	87.1	10.4	2.5
Furs	42.5	57.5	38.5	4.0
Groceries & Meats	20.4	79.6	18.8	1.6
Dairy Products	23.9	76.1	21.7	2.2
Fuel Oil	17.1	82.9	13.5	3.6
Mobile Homes	18.2	81.8	16.8	1.5
Vending Machines	31.4	68.6	29.3	2.1
Furniture	36.1	63.9	32.5	3.6
Sporting Goods	36.0	64.0	31.6	4.5

Source: Compiled from *Annual Statement Studies*, 1976 ed. (Robert Morris Associates, 1976).

Table 10.3
Margins and Other Operating Data of Selected Wholesalers

Type of Wholesaler	Gross Margin	Cost of Goods Sold	Operating Expenses	Profit Before Taxes
Automotive Equip.	28.5	71.5	23.8	4.7
Drugs	18.9	81.1	15.8	3.1
Dairy Products and Poultry	12.4	87.6	10.6	1.8
Groceries	10.3	89.7	9.0	1.3
Wine, Liquor & Beer	17.0	83.0	14.3	2.7
General Merchandise	27.0	73.0	23.0	4.0
Jewelry	25.2	74.8	21.3	3.9
Petroleum Products	10.2	89.8	6.9	3.3
Coffee, Tea & Spices	13.5	86.5	9.5	4.0
Grain	5.9	94.1	4.2	1.8
Chemicals	19.1	80.9	14.5	4.6
Frozen Foods	14.1	85.1	12.4	2.3
Tobacco & Tobacco Products	8.8	91.2	7.4	1.4
Furniture	31.7	68.3	29.8	1.9
Sporting Goods and Toys	25.1	74.9	20.7	4.4

Source: Compiled from *Annual Statement Studies*, 1976 ed. (Robert Morris Associates, 1976).

who feel that the manufacturer is not allowing them sufficient margins are likely to seek out other suppliers or establish and promote their own private brands.

Warshaw underscores this proposition by arguing that manufacturers are in reality buying distribution services through the margins they offer. If these margins are not equal to the prices sought by intermediaries, in the long run the manufacturer will not be able to buy their services in a competitive environment. Warshaw states this viewpoint as follows:

"Viewing the problem as one of buying distribution can be useful in developing effective pricing policies. . . . The concept of buying distribution emphasizes the fact that the price paid to gain channel support must reflect not only the marketing job performed by the channel, but also the competitive environment in which the channel operates."[7]

Thus, the channel manager must be involved in a continuous review of the firm's margin structures to determine if they are adequate. Particular attention should also be paid to changes in the competitive environment in terms of how these changes are likely to influence channel member perceptions of the existing margin structures.

Different Classes of Resellers

Ideally, the channel manager would like to set margins so that they would vary in direct proportion to functions performed by different classes of channel members. In reality, however, few manufacturers have the power or cost accounting data to set margins in strict accordance with this guideline. Margins at the wholesale and retail levels, and for various types of agent middlemen are typically governed by strong traditions which permeate the industry. Precipitate downward deviations from these norms are feasible only for the most powerful manufacturers. Nevertheless, periodic reviews of the margin structures available to different classes of channel members should be made with a view toward making gradual changes if warranted. Oxenfeldt suggests that such questions as the following be posed in this review:

1. Do channel members hold inventories?
2. Do they make purchases in large or small quantities?
3. Do they provide repair services?
4. Do they extend credit to customers?
5. Do they deliver?
6. Do they help train the customers' sales force?[8]

Of course, many other questions might also be posed. But the main point of periodically reviewing channel member services in relation to the margins granted them is to find out whether there are any major inequities that are creating dissension in the ranks of particular classes of channel members. For example, some large retailers who are buying in larger quantities than many wholesalers, and who are providing storage in their own warehouses, may feel that they should be entitled to the wholesale discount. Indeed, they may be quite unhappy about their present discount to the extent that they may already have deemphasized the line and may

---

[7] Warshaw, "Pricing," p. 241.
[8] Oxenfeldt, *Pricing Strategies*, p. 142.

even have plans for dropping it altogether. A periodic review of margins will offer the channel manager an early warning of such developments and provide time to plan for possible changes in existing margin structures to correct such inequities.

Rival Brands

Differentials in the margins available to channel members carrying competitive brands must be kept within tolerable limits. If a particular manufacturer's brand is at a clear disadvantage compared to the margin a channel member can obtain from it relative to another brand (and this cannot be offset by higher volumes) the channel member will not devote much effort to promoting it.

The practical question facing the channel manager attempting to apply this guideline is: *what levels of margin differentials are within tolerable limits?* Unfortunately there is no straight-forward answer to this question. Significant variations in margins may be quite tolerable in some cases but not in others. A manufacturer such as RCA that is well entrenched in many consumer electronics products can depend on its mass advertising and sales promotion to establish strong consumer preference to pull its products through the channel. At the retail level, promotion by the retailer in the form of local advertising and strong personal selling are relatively minor factors in achieving high sales of RCA products. Accordingly, relatively low margins granted to the retailer are feasible. On the other hand, a smaller, specialized manufacturer such as Magnavox has to concentrate its distribution through fewer, more carefully selected and aggressive retailers who can draw customers to themselves with strong local advertising and personal selling. A manufacturer in this position will have to grant larger margins to its retailers to cover the higher costs associated with the more aggressive selling effort expected.[9] So channel managers must attempt to weigh any margin differentials between their own and competitive brands in terms of what kind of support their firms offer and what level of support they expect from channel members. If this relationship is found to differ significantly from the competition, differentials in margins must be examined in terms of these differences.

Special Arrangements

If the usual allocation of distribution tasks between the manufacturer and channel members changes, the margin structure should reflect this. For example the Hanes Corporation, the manufacturer of L'eggs pantyhose (which we cited earlier in Chapter 9 in another context), made such a change. Specifically, Hanes took on all of the risk and service functions

[9]Chester R. Wasson, *Product Management: Product Life Cycles and Competitive Marketing Strategy* (St. Charles, Illinois: Challenge Books, 1971), p. 227.

itself in the marketing of L'eggs rather than allocating them to its retailers (supermarkets and drugstores). As one Hanes executive commented:

"The key word . . . that sold retailers was consignment. Typically retailers buy inventory, but L'eggs is completely paid for by the manufacturer. The retailer makes no financial investment at all . . . and he has no service costs since route girls do all the restocking and cleaning."[10]

As a result of this extraordinary assumption of marketing functions by the manufacturer, most supermarket and drugstore retailers were willing to accept smaller margins than they had become accustomed to in the sale of other brands, such as the 40 percent for Lady Brevoni (the first manufacturer to gain significant supermarket distribution of pantyhose) or from the sale of their own label pantyhose.

Conventional Norms in Margins

Oxenfeldt points succinctly to the almost universal tendency of channel members to expect margins to meet generally accepted norms:

"In most trades, resellers have come to regard some particular percentage margin as normal, fair, and proper. They may not obtain that margin on most of the items they sell; even when it is indeed a typical margin, they may not receive it all of the time. . . . But although the conventional margin may not be an economic reality in the marketplace, it may nevertheless strongly influence the reaction of resellers to the lines they are offered. Failure of a reseller to be 'allowed' the conventional margin may create major resentment that results in resellers giving limited sales support to a brand."[11]

This strong commitment among channel members to what they consider to be the normal, fair, or proper margin makes it very difficult for the manufacturer to deviate from the conventional margin structures. This does not suggest, however, that the manufacturer must slavishly adhere to the norms. As pointed out in previous sections, exceptions are possible if they can be justified in the eyes of the channel members. What may be viewed as quite reasonable by the manufacturer, however, may be seen quite differently by the channel members. It is thus the job of the channel manager to attempt to explain to the channel members any margin changes that deviate downward from the norm. While this will not, of course, guarantee that the channel members will support the change, it will at least convey to them the manufacturer's reasons for taking the action. This type of openness may at least lessen the severity of the almost inevitable adverse reaction of the channel members. In a later section of

[10] "Our L'eggs Fit Your Leggs," *Business Week*, (25 March 1972): 99.
[11] Oxenfeldt, *Pricing Strategies*, p. 144.

this chapter we will have more to say about major changes in margins to channel members.

Margin Variation on Models

Variations in margins on individual models and styles in a product line are common. Manufacturers frequently include in the product line items whose main purpose is to build traffic in the retailers' stores. These products (often referred to as *promotional products*) are usually the lowest price in the line and yield relatively low margins for both the manufacturer and channel members. Fortunately, channel members are often amenable to accepting the lower margins associated with these products so long as they are convinced of the promotional value of the product in building store traffic. For example, automobile manufacturers frequently advertise stripped down versions of various models at low prices. The strategy behind this is to build traffic in the dealer showroom. With this increased traffic, the dealers have the opportunity to trade up the prospective buyer to a higher priced model or to sell him or her on optional equipment for the stripped down promotional model. The margins on the higher priced models or on the options added to the stripped down promotional car are significantly higher.

Margins on products in the line that are significantly below the norm and which are not intended as promotional products are much more difficult to justify in the eyes of the channel members. Channel members are therefore far less likely to promote these products with enthusiasm. Indeed, among the so called "deadwood" items in a product line, a high proportion are likely to be those which offer low margins to channel members and are lacking in promotional appeal. As a general rule, then, the channel manager should attempt to influence product line pricing so as to use low margin products for promotional purposes whenever possible.

Price Points

These refer to specific prices, usually at the retail level, to which consumers have become accustomed. That is, they expect certain products to be available at customary prices. For example, for many years the five-cent candy bar represented a price point that virtually all candy manufacturers selling in the mass market had to meet. Later this increased to ten, then fifteen, and by 1980, thirty cents. As with the candy bar, inflationary forces in the last several years have eroded consumer perceptions of price points for many product categories. Nevertheless, they still exist for some products. Failure to recognize retail price points can create problems for the manufacturer. Consider, for instance, what happened to a toy manufacturer:

A well known manufacturer of pre-school toys decided to drop several products which it felt were obsolete and replaced them with more up to date ones. Little attention was paid to the price slots filled by the old products. The new products were priced according to basic cost considerations, demand, and competition.

Soon after the old products were dropped, however, the manufacturer's field salespeople reported that some of the major accounts were reluctant to handle the new line because it missed two important price points—$2.95 and $7.95. (The lowest priced toy in the new line listed for $4.95.) Moreover, several mass merchandisers who were thought to be on the verge of taking on the toy line for the first time decided not to do so. Failure to meet these price points was cited as one of their reasons for rejecting the line.

As this case suggests, there are times when price points can be an important factor in securing channel member support. The channel manager must, therefore, be sensitive to the existence of price points. If they do exist at various levels in the channel, an attempt should be made to influence the firm's pricing decisions to ensure that products are available at these price points.

Product Variations and Pricing

When a manufacturer attaches prices to the various models within a given product line, it should be careful to associate price differences with differences in product features.[12] If the price differences are not closely associated with visible or identified product features, the channel members will have a more difficult selling job. A sporting goods retailer, for example, handling a line of five models of tennis racquets would like to have an easy "handle" in the form of specific product features which salespeople can use to explain price differences to customers. If, for example, the product differences between the $15.00 and $25.00 models are not made explicit, the retailer is likely to take the course of least resistance— selling mainly the lower priced model or whichever model in the line is easiest to sell. A little extra care by the manufacturer in the form of thinking about the pricing of the product line from the *channel members' perspective* can eliminate this kind of pricing problem.

Other Issues in Channel Pricing

The eight guidelines for channel pricing discussed above deal with a wide range of channel pricing issues. Yet there are several additional channel

---

[12]Ibid., p. 145.

pricing issues that the channel manager is likely to face which require more specific and detailed attention. Four of the most important of these are discussed in the remainder of this chapter.

Pricing Control in the Channel

As alluded to earlier in this chapter, the manufacturer's pricing strategies often require channel member support and cooperation if they are to be implemented effectively. But, as we have also pointed out throughout this text, channel members have "minds of their own" and they often want to do things their way. This is especially true when it comes to pricing. Of all of the elements of the marketing mix, channel members typically view pricing as the area that is most in their domain.[13] They may defer to the manufacturer's claim to knowing how the product should be manufactured, promoted, and even distributed, but when it comes to pricing, channel members believe that they know best and should therefore be free to pursue their own pricing strategies. So long as the manufacturer's pricing policies do not infringe on the channel members' pricing freedom, there is no problem. But as soon as the manufacturer seeks to exercise some control over channel members' pricing strategies, channel members may feel that the manufacturer has stepped out of its proper boundary. Yet, from the manufacturer's point of view, some of the most important pricing policies may call for having some degree of control over the channel members' pricing policies. For example, a manufacturer may want to use pricing strategy to help maintain the quality image of its products and, hence, does not want channel members cutting prices significantly. Or a manufacturer may believe, as many do, that "stable" prices are in the best long run interest of the firm and its channel members because price cutting can lead to fierce price wars which create havoc for the manufacturer and channel members. While outright dictating by the manufacturer of the selling price that channel members can charge their customers is in violation of antitrust legislation since the demise of so-called fair trade laws (see Chapter 3), many manufacturers still do attempt to influence channel members to conform to their pricing policies. In attempting to do so, however, the manufacturer is faced with the difficult and delicate task of enforcing pricing policies without alienating channel members while still staying within the boundaries of antitrust legislation. Needless to say, this is not easy to do. Nevertheless, several guidelines can be offered.

First, any type of coercive approaches to controlling channel member pricing policies should be ruled out immediately. Not only are they likely to increase the probability of alienating the channel members (see the discussion on the use of coercive power in Chapter 4) but they are likely to be illegal as well (see the discussion on price maintenance in Chapter 3).

---

[13] See the discussion in Chapter 4 on decision domain disagreements as a cause of conflict.

Second, encroachment by the manufacturer into the domain of channel member pricing policies should be undertaken only if the manufacturer believes that it is in his vital long-term strategic interest to do so. Such a pricing strategy should never be taken lightly or applied in circumstances which are not of crucial importance.

Finally, if the manufacturer does feel that it is necessary to exercise some control over channel member pricing policies, an attempt should be made to do so through what might be called "friendly persuasion." O.M. Scott's experience in influencing channel member pricing policies illustrates this approach:[14]

O.M. Scott Company, a leading manufacturer of lawn care products, had a long standing policy of having dealers maintain the manufacturer's "suggested" prices. The company expected all of its dealers to conform to that policy. But rather than attempting to use coercion, Scott was able to attain its pricing objectives by persuading dealers that the suggested prices were in their own self-interest. Scott explained that the company's suggested prices were necessary to provide the dealer with adequate margins to cover the high levels of service they offered, such as providing ample stocks and assortments of Scott products, adequate safety stock, and a high degree of personal attention and counseling for lawncare customers. Thus, Scott's approach was to build a strong case for its pricing strategy and then let the dealers decide for themselves whether they wanted to conform to Scott's pricing policies.

Scott's friendly persuasion approach to controlling channel member pricing policies has been very effective in securing channel member cooperation and has also stayed well within the boundaries of the law. In a 1969 court test of Scott's pricing policies, the court could find no evidence of Scott's having to use any coercion, conspiracy, threats, or warnings to enforce its channel pricing policy. Thus, the court concluded that dealers had decided for themselves and of their own free will to abide by Scott's pricing policies and therefore no antitrust violation had been committed by Scott.

Changing Price Policies

Another important channel pricing issue which the manufacturer is almost sure to face at one time or another is dealing with channel member reactions to major changes in the manufacturer's pricing policies and related terms of sale.

Almost certainly, a time will come when the manufacturer feels it necessary to make major changes in pricing policies and terms of sale. This need might spring from cost pressures, competitive factors, or a

[14]William L. Tombetta and Albert L. Page, "The Channel Control Issue Under Scrutiny," *Journal of Retailing*, (Summer, 1978): 46.

variety of other external environmental developments beyond the manufacturer's control.[15] But regardless of the cause, major changes in the manufacturer's pricing policies are bound to affect channel members.

Typically, channel members become very uneasy when they hear about significant changes in manufacturer pricing policies or terms of sale. Channel members become accustomed to dealing with the manufacturer based on a particular set of pricing policies which may have existed in basically the same form for a relatively long period of time. Indeed, their own pricing strategies may be closely tied to the existing pricing policies of the manufacturer. Hence, any change in the status quo becomes a cause for concern. This is especially so when the manufacturer's price policy changes appear to be aimed at toughening channel pricing policies or related terms of sale. A development in the publishing industry provides a good example of the issue:

Harcourt Brace Jovanovich Inc. (HBJ), a major book publisher, initiated new pricing and terms of sale policies in an attempt to solve a serious and growing problem facing book publishers—high returns of unsold books by wholesale and retail channel members. Indeed, for HBJ returns were running between 35 and 50 percent.[16]

The policy of being able to return books for full credit was a long standing tradition in the publishing industry. Basically, publishers would trade off offering relatively modest trade discounts to channel members for these very liberal return privileges.[17]

HBJ's policy change was, in essence, a reversal of the traditional policy; it no longer would allow any returns but would now offer higher trade discounts to its channel members. Under the new pricing policy, the retailers would receive a 40–58 percent discount on the cover price depending on how many books were ordered, compared with the previous range of 25–46 percent. (Wholesaler discounts were to increase to 50–60 percent from 25–50 percent). Figure 10.2 contrasts HBJ's old and new policies.

This change in HBJ's pricing policy, which other book publishers might also follow with similar changes, has set off widespread concern among book distributors and dealers. Liberal return privileges had become a virtual way of life among booksellers. Many booksellers were quite willing to accept the previously lower discount structure in exchange for the return privileges which had enabled them to avoid the disastrous problem of being stuck with heavy inventories of unsalable books. In the face of high interest rates and other increasing costs of carrying inventory, the problem could get even worse.

[15] See for example: Kent B. Monroe and Audis A. Zoltners, "Pricing the Product Line During Periods of Scarcity," *Journal of Marketing*, (Summer, 1979): 49–59.

[16] N. R. Kleinfeld, "Harcourt Bars Book Returns in Key Shift," *New York Times*, (18 November 1980), p. D4.

[17] For a related discussion see: Doreen Mangan, "Book Selling!," *Stores*, (December, 1979): 14–21.

Figure 10.2
Harcourt Brace Jovanovich's Discounts to Retailers

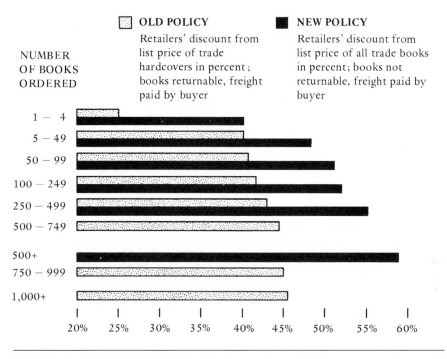

Source: The New York Times/Nov. 18, 1980.

Some industry observers predict that HBJ's new policy and others like it could work against publishers, depending upon the counteractions taken by booksellers. One likely response by booksellers is much more conservative or even timid ordering of books, especially with regard to quantities of books ordered. This might well reduce publishers' sales revenues to a significantly greater extent than the offset to revenues brought about from book returns. Another possible response is "cherry picking" by booksellers. That is, booksellers may zero in on only a relatively few of the publishers' best selling books and avoid buying most of the other books on the publishers' lists.

In any case, HBJ's new approach to book pricing will certainly elicit *some* response from booksellers as they attempt to protect their businesses from the effects of this dramatic policy change. It might have been fruitful for HBJ to have investigated what these responses might be *before* so abruptly announcing the change in policy. Further, it might have also been better (at least according to publishing industry observers) to have phased in the change more slowly in order to give channel members more of an opportunity to adapt to the change. Indeed, these caveats are probably worth considering in most situations involving major changes in channel pricing policies.

Passing Price Increases through the Channel

Price increases by manufacturers are virtually inevitable and during inflationary periods in the economy, which have become a virtual fixture in the United States during the past decade (see Chapter 3), they become steeper and more frequent. So long as each channel member is able to pass manufacturer initiated price increases along to the next channel member, and ultimately to the final user, the price increase issue is not too worrisome. But when increased prices cannot be totally passed through the channel, and hence channel members have to begin absorbing some or all of the price increases by cutting into their margins, price increases become a critical issue.[18] Take, for example, the case of domestic auto manufacturers. During the late 1970s and early 1980s prices were increased on many models every few months so that in some cases as many as four or five price increases would occur in just one year. When dealers found it more and more difficult to pass these price increases on to their customers, their sales and profits plummeted such that in 1980 less than half showed any profit at all, and more than 1,600 went out of business.[19] While this is perhaps an extreme case, it illustrates the very tenuous position in which channel members are placed when faced with rising prices from their suppliers that cannot be passed on.

Added to the direct monetary difficulties arising from such nontransferable price increases is the ill will that they can create as each channel member blames the next for the price increases.

Unfortunately, such price increases are too often simply passed along in rote fashion by the manufacturer (and other channel members) before other possible alternatives or strategies that could help mitigate the effects of the price increase are given adequate consideration. Such alternatives and strategies include the following:

First, before passing on a price increase, manufacturers could give more thought to the long-term and the short-term implications of going through with the price increase vs. attempting to hold the line on prices to the greatest extent possible.[20] There may be cases where the short-term negative effects on the manufacturer's profits of holding the line on prices are more than offset by the long-term benefits, such as a more loyal and viable team of channel members. One wonders how many of those 1,600 domestic care dealers who went out of business in 1980 would still be around if the domestic car manufacturers had made more of an attempt to hold the line on prices. One also wonders how many of those dealers who went out of business selling domestic cars subsequently went back into business selling Japanese or other foreign-made cars. Indeed, one of the largest Chevrolet dealers in the Philadelphia metropolitan area that closed its doors in early 1981 reopened several months later in another loca-

---

[18]John M. Browning, Noel B. Zabriskie, and M. A. Andrews, "Channel Entrapment of a Manufacturer's Price Increase and a Solution," *Proceedings of the Southern Marketing Association,* 1977, pp. 203–206.

[19]"Auto Dealers Try to Hang On," *Business Week,* (4 May 1981): 128–130.

[20]For a method that might help in this analysis see: C. David Fogg and Kent H. Kohnken, "Price-Cost Planning, *Journal of Marketing,* (April, 1978): 97–106.

tion—this time selling Subarus rather than Chevrolets! No doubt the same pattern was repeated in a number of other metropolitan areas across the United States.

Second, if passing on the price increase is unavoidable, the manufacturer should do whatever possible to mitigate the negative effects of the increase on channel members. The domestic auto manufacturers, for example, did take a step in this direction by offering rebates to customers who purchased cars during several periods in 1980 and 1981. Knowledgeable auto industry observers wonder, however, as do many dealers and consumers, how the car manufacturers could afford to offer rebates yet claimed that they could not afford to hold the line on prices in the first place. But such are the mysteries of domestic auto pricing.

Aside from rebates, other price related strategies for mitigating the effects of price increases on channel members include offering financial assistance, more liberal payment terms, and special deals such as allowing the channel members to buy before the price increase goes into effect.

Finally, the manufacturer could change its strategies in the other areas of the marketing mix, particularly product strategy, to help offset the effects of price increases. For example, the product could be improved so that at least the channel members would have a "handle" for justifying the price increase to their customers on the basis of more value in the product. Conversely, the product could be downgraded, not necessarily from a quality standpoint, but in terms of a reduction in certain features or accessories which may not be vital to the appeal and performance of the product. Such a "stripped down" version of the product selling at a lower price may be quite preferable to the "fancier" version selling at a significantly higher price. General Motors decided to pursue such a strategy for its so-called J car (Chevrolet Cavalier and Pontiac J-2000) line, which met with strong consumer price resistance when introduced in 1981. The Cavalier and its J car sister, the Pontiac J-2000, carried high price tags to cover the wide array of features offered as standard equipment. The new versions of the Cavalier and the J-2000 that appeared in the spring of 1982 were stripped of many of the frills such as digital clocks, remote trunk releases (among others), and were priced considerably lower than the original versions. GM dealers were delighted with this strategy—the first time they had been delighted about anything GM had done for quite some time![21]

Using Price Incentives in the Channel

Pricing strategy is frequently used by manufacturers as a promotional tool. A wide range of pricing devices is used to carry out such promotional pricing strategy, including special deals, seasonal discounts, rebates, price reductions, coupons, two for the price of one, and a variety of others.

The purpose of such promotional pricing is, of course, to increase the

[21] See for example: "GM Gambles on 1982 Prices," *Business Week*, (24 August 1981): 29–30.

sales and market share of the product of the manufacturer that is offering the special prices. Among manufacturers of consumer packaged goods, price promotions, particularly cents off and coupons, have become so common and widespread that many consumers regard them as a "birthright" to which they are entitled whenever they buy the product. Indeed, a growing number of consumers will refrain from buying almost any packaged consumer product unless they have a manufacturer coupon for it or a manufacturer sponsored cents off reduction printed on the package.

Such enthusiasm for promotional pricing strategies shown by consumers is not always shared by channel members, however. Retailers, especially supermarkets, drug chains, and mass merchandisers, often complain about the headaches and nuisance involved in handling thousands of coupons, making sure that products which are supposed to be specially reduced actually reflect this when placed on store shelves, and following up on the many details involved in taking advantage of special pricing deals offered by so many different manufacturers.[22] Thus, from the manufacturer's point of view, gaining strong retailer acceptance and follow through on pricing promotions can be a problem. Some of the problem can be solved merely by making pricing promotions as simple and straightforward as possible so that channel members can participate with a minimum of time and effort.

The more significant problem underlying some price promotions, however, stems from the differing price elasticities of consumers vs. retailers (or wholesalers). That is, consumers' responses to price reductions may differ significantly from those of retailers. What consumers might perceive as an attractive price reduction may be perceived by retailers as insignificant and unworthy of the extra effort and risk involved (i.e., if extra inventory has to be purchased). Five or six cents off on a bar of soap, for example, may be sufficient to stimulate consumer demand for the product but the corresponding price incentive offered to retailers for participating in the price promotion may not be sufficient to stimulate *their* desire to get fully involved in the deal. The extra few cents in gross margin available to the retailer for participating may not compensate the store sufficiently for the higher inventory and handling costs involved, as well as the extra display or shelf space that is often called for in such promotions. Consequently, the stores will either refuse to participate in the promotion, or more commonly, accept the promotional allowance from the manufacturer but follow through only half-heartedly on the other aspects of the promotional deal such as providing extra display space, stocking the product on more prominent shelf facings and featuring the product in its advertising. When this happens, the manufacturer does not obtain the full impact of its promotional pricing strategy because low retailer acceptance and follow through undermines the stimulative effects of the strategy.

So, the solution to the problem of getting better mileage out of

---

[22]Charles L. Hinkle, "The Strategy of Price Deals," *Harvard Business Review*, (July–August, 1965): 75–85.

manufacturer-initiated price promotions begins with recognition on the part of the manufacturer of the differing price elasticities between consumers and retailers. Price promotion strategies should be designed to be *at least as attractive to retailers as they are to consumers.* Manufacturers may give a great deal of thought to how much of a price incentive they need to offer to stimulate consumer demand through a price promotion. But if manufacturers expect strong retailer support for their price promotions they also need to make a similar effort to determine just how much of a price incentive they need to offer retailers (or wholesalers) in order to secure it.

Summary

Pricing strategy should incorporate internal cost, target market, competitive, and channel considerations. The channel considerations, however, are often given the least attention in the manufacturer's pricing strategy and are sometimes almost overlooked completely. This is unfortunate because pricing strategy can have a substantial impact on channel member behavior. Specifically, if channel members perceive the manufacturer's pricing strategy as congruent with their own interests, they are more likely to provide a higher level of cooperation. If, on the other hand, the manufacturer's approach to pricing reflects a lack of awareness of channel members' needs, or appears to work against them, a much lower level of cooperation or even conflict is the more likely result. So, the major challenge facing the channel manager in the area of pricing is to foster pricing strategies that promote channel member cooperation and minimize conflict.

In developing pricing strategies, the manufacturer should pay particular attention to the following eight guidelines: (1) profit margins made available to channel members should be adequate to cover costs and provide for reasonable profits, (2) margins offered to different classes of channel members should vary in rough proportion to the functions they perform, (3) margins available to channel members on the manufacturer's products should be competitive with those offered by rival manufacturers, (4) special arrangements between the manufacturer and channel members that result in either an increase or decrease in services rendered should be reflected in the margins available to channel members, (5) whenever possible the manufacturer should try to conform to conventional norms for margins in the trade, (6) variations in margins on different models or styles of the manufacturer's product should be logical and usually not too far off from the conventional margin normal in the trade, (7) if price points exist at the wholesale and/or retail levels they should be recognized and products should be priced so as to meet those price points, and (8) variations in prices by a manufacturer for different products in its line should, whenever possible, be associated with visible or indentifiable differences in product features to help channel members do a more effective selling job.

Four major pricing issues which the manufacturer is likely to face at one time or another were also discussed in this chapter.

The first of these dealt with pricing control in the channel. In general, if a manufacturer seeks to exercise control over channel member pricing policies, it should avoid using coercion and instead use "friendly persuasion" approaches that allow channel members to decide for themselves if they want to conform to the manufacturer's pricing policies.

The second pricing issue discussed dealt with the implementation of major price policy changes on channel member behavior. Whenever possible the manufacturer should attempt to predict channel member reactions to these changes *before* they are undertaken and it is generally preferable to phase in changes slowly rather than spring them suddenly on the channel members.

The third channel pricing issue dealt with the passing of price increases through the channel. When channel members cannot pass on price increases, they must absorb the increases themselves. This results not only in severe financial difficulties in some cases, but in a great deal of ill will as well. Manufacturers could often make more of an effort to consider other options or strategies to mitigate the negative effects of such price increases on channel members.

Finally, the fourth issue in channel pricing dealt with the use of price incentives. While some incentives produce strong stimulative effects on consumer demand for the manufacturer's products, the price elasticity underlying consumer reaction may not be the same for channel members. Hence, channel members may respond much less enthusiastically to the price promotion. Thus, manufacturers should attempt to make price incentives at least as attractive to channel members as they are to consumers if they expect to get strong channel member support.

Discussion Questions

1. The basic factors to consider in developing pricing strategies are market variables, internal cost, and competitive forces. Do you agree or disagree?
2. What should be the role of the channel manager in formulating the manufacturer's pricing policies and strategies?
3. Explain the concept of "buying distribution services" as it applies to channel pricing strategy.
4. How might different classes of channel members, rival brands and special arrangement between the manufacturer and channel members affect pricing strategies?
5. What is meant by conventional norms in margins? How does this affect channel pricing policy?

6. Discuss the issues involved in channel pricing to account for margin variations on different models in a product line, price points, and product variations.

7. Discuss the problems associated with the manufacturer's attempt to exercise price control in the channel. How should the manufacturer deal with these problems?

8. Why might major changes in the manufacturer's pricing policies or terms of sale create havoc for the channel members? How might the manufacturer mitigate the negative effects of such changes?

9. Discuss some alternative strategies available to the manufacturer contemplating the passing of price increases through the channel.

10. What is the underlying factor responsible for possible differing reactions of consumers vs. channel members to a manufacturer-initiated price incentive? Explain.

Chapter 11
Promotion Through the Marketing Channel

In this chapter we examine the third major component of the marketing mix, promotional strategy, from a channel management perspective. *Promotional strategy* may be defined as:

". . . a controlled, integrated program of communications methods and materials designed to present a company and its products to prospective customers; to communicate need-satisfying attributes of products toward the end of facilitating sales and thus contributing to long-run profit performance."[1]

The major tools available to the manufacturer for implementing promotional strategy, according to Engel et al., are:[2]

1. Advertising—*any paid form of nonpersonal presentation of ideas, goods, or services by an identified sponsor, with predominant use made of the media of mass communication*
2. Personal selling—*the process of assisting and persuading a prospect*

---

[1]James F. Engle, Hugh G. Wales and Martin R. Warshaw, *Promotional Strategy* (Homewood, Illinois: Richard D. Irwin, 1975), pp. 4–5.
[2]Ibid., p. 5.

to buy a good or service or to act upon an idea through use of person-to-person communication

3. Selling support by resellers in a channel of distribution—*any form of effort undertaken by a wholesale or retail middleman with the intent of persuading a prospective customer to act favorably upon the goods or services offered by a manufacturer or other seller*

4. Publicity—*any form of nonpaid, commercially significant news or editorial comment about ideas, products, or institutions.*

It is the third of these promotional tools—*selling support by resellers in a channel of distribution*—with which we will be concerned in this chapter.

Because most manufacturers do not sell directly to their ultimate target markets, they must depend upon their channel members to help provide promotion. But as we have emphasized at several points throughout this text, since the channel members are independent businesses, the degree of control the manufacturer can exercise over how products are sold once they are in the hands of the channel members is reduced. Thus, the effectiveness of the manufacturer's overall promotional strategy is highly dependent upon how skillful the manufacturer is in securing cooperation from independent channel members in the promotion of products.

Some manufacturers rely almost entirely on direct promotion, mainly in the form of advertising to their target markets, to "pull" their products through the channel and hence indirectly secure channel member cooperation. The belief underlying this strategy is that by building strong consumer (or industrial user) demand for a product, the manufacturer will force channel members to automatically promote the manufacturer's product because it is in their obvious self-interest to do so. After all, the argument goes, if consumers or other users are "beating down the doors" to buy the manufacturer's product, the channel members would be crazy not to carry the product and be enthusiastic about selling it.

While there is a good deal of merit in this so-called *pull strategy* of promotion, in the long run it is, in many cases, insufficient by itself to secure strong channel member promotional support. Rather, the manufacturer also needs to work more directly with the channel members to develop strong and viable channel member promotional support. This approach to promotion through the marketing channel, sometimes referred to as the *push strategy*, requires more direct involvement by the manufacturer with channel members in the use of promotional strategies. Although the term *push strategy* has come to be an accepted term, it is actually a misnomer because it implies that the manufacturer is forcing promotion programs "down the throats of channel members." Actually, the real idea underlying the so-called push strategy is one of *mutual effort and cooperation* between the manufacturer and channel members in the development and implementation of promotional strategies.[3] In this sense

[3]For related discussion see: James R. Brown and Sherman A. Timmins, "Substructural Dimensions of Interorganizational Relations in Marketing Channels," *Journal of the Academy of Marketing Science,* (Summer, 1981): 168–169.

of the term, then, the manufacturer does not push channel members into promoting its product, but instead *seeks their participation and cooperation* to provide effective promotional strategies that will be mutually beneficial to the manufacturer and the channel members.

In this chapter we discuss a variety of promotional strategies which call for channel member participation. The success of these promotional strategies is influenced greatly by the degree of cooperation the channel manager can secure from the channel members in the implementation of these strategies.

Before discussing these, however, we will take a brief look at some of the major constraints on the channel members that tend to limit the degree of promotional support they can offer to the manufacturer. Armed with this information, the channel manager is then in a better position to appraise the potential effectiveness of the various promotional strategies in terms of gaining channel member promotional support.

Constraints on Channel Member Promotional Support

A number of constraints affect the channel members' capacity to provide promotional support for the manufacturer. In this section we discuss some of the more basic of these at the wholesale and retail levels in the channel.

Wholesale Level

In a major study of manufacturer-wholesaler relations, Warshaw identified four major factors that constrain the kind and level of promotional support which wholesalers can offer to the manufacturer.[4] These are:

1. The wholesaler's product line
2. Character of the market served
3. Service requirements
4. Nature of competition

Product Line.   As a general rule, the broader the line of products handled by the wholesale channel member, the greater the limitation on aggressive promotion of a particular manufacturer's products. Wholesaler product lines composed of many standardized items of low unit value are usually simply catalogued, and any personal selling involved consists mainly of routine order taking. This is because patronage appeals such as avail-

---

[4]Martin R. Warshaw, *Effective Selling Through Wholesalers* (Ann Arbor, Michigan: The University of Michigan Press, 1961), pp. 48–54.

ability, delivery and credit extension are usually more important to the wholesaler's customers than the brand of any particular manufacturer.

On the other hand, for wholesaler product lines consisting of more highly differentiated products, or which have unique features, the likelihood of more aggressive promotion is higher.

Market Served.   The wholesaler's market consists of sales to other resellers (wholesale or retail), or various final users in the industrial market (see Chapter 2). Given the wholesaler's limited promotional resources of personal selling, advertising, and other forms of sales promotion, the diversity of the market faced forces the wholesaler to make choices about how to allocate these resources. For example, a wholesale distributor of chemical products may sell to manufacturers, independent laboratories, hospitals, schools, and other kinds of users.[5] The allocation of promotional effort among these markets is largely a function of their relative importance in generating sales. If a chemical manufacturer's target market is not a large volume segment for the *wholesaler*, it is unlikely that the wholesaler will allocate much promotional effort to that market.

Service Requirements.   Traditionally, the basic array of services provided by the wholesaler to customers was buying, selling, transportation, storage, financing, risk-taking, and providing market information. This traditional list of services, however, may vary for different customers, or for the same customers over time. For example, consider the comment made by a customer of a chemical wholesaler:

"Fifteen years ago you thought of a distributor [chemical wholesaler] as a place where you could get a gallon of something. Now, I think they are thought of as a useful tool for inventory control. . . ."[6]

As this suggests, the chemical wholesaler's customers are demanding more. This may in turn affect the level of promotional support which this wholesaler can offer any particular manufacturer. The channel manager must therefore consider these kinds of influences on wholesalers when looking to them to provide promotional support.

Nature of Competition.   In commenting on the effects of competition on the wholesaler's capacity to provide promotional support Warshaw states:

"The pressures of competition, no matter what their source or type, fall on wholesale margins . . . .

If he is caught in a margin squeeze, the wholesaler, like any other business firm, resists the change in his profit position . . . ."[7]

[5] For an interesting discussion of wholesale chemical distributors see: Peter B. Griffin, "The Chemical Middlemen," *Chemical Marketing Representative*, (25 August 1975): 11, 16.
[6] Ibid., p. 16.
[7] Warshaw, *Effective Selling*, p. 54.

One form of such resistance, according to Warshaw, is in promotional support for the manufacturer. He states:

"... *wholesalers may try adjustments in the selling function. Such changes may be* qualitative *in the early stages.... Eventually, [however], if the margin squeeze continues while competitive pressures remain, the wholesaler may respond by reducing the quantity of selling effort he offers.*"[8]

Just as we pointed out in Chapter 3 of this text, the channel manager must be aware of the effects of competition, not only on his or her own firm, but on channel members as well. It is indeed wishful thinking for the channel manager to expect a higher level of promotional support from wholesalers when competition is forcing their margins down.

Retail Level

The major constraints affecting the retailer's capacity to offer promotional support to the manufacturer parallel those affecting wholesalers.[9] These are:

1. The retailer's product assortment
2. Nature of the market served
3. Type of store
4. Competition

Product Assortment.   If the products in the retailer's assortment are mainly convenience goods subject to heavy price competition, then there is little opportunity for the retailer to engage in nonprice promotion emphasizing a particular manufacturer's brand. On the other hand, if his or her assortment is characterized by shopping and specialty products which are differentiated from those of other manufacturers, the probability of gaining retailer promotional support is much higher. For example, a consumer electronics retailer handling several brands of stereos, tape recorders, video games, etc., may be willing to place substantial promotional support behind the products of a particular manufacturer. A typical discount drug retailer, however, carrying several thousand different items is much less likely to single out the products of any particular manufacturer and offer special promotional support for the line.

Nature of the Market.   Retailers have long engaged in their own brand of market segmentation. Well before the emergence of formal theories and

---

[8]Ibid., p. 54.
[9]See for example: Engel et al., *Promotional Strategy*, pp. 432–435.

sophisticated research techniques, retailers were selecting and position-ing their merchandising strategies at particular market segments. Meet-ing the demands of these market segments, however, puts substantial constraints on retailer promotional strategies. For example, a retailer who emphasizes sales to the price conscious consumer will, of course, tend to emphasize price and deemphasize other forms of nonprice promotion. Prestigious retailers, on the other hand, serving market segments who de-mand quality, have a much greater capacity existing in their pricing struc-tures to emphasize nonprice promotional support for the manufacturer.

Type of Store. In general, the more specialized the store, the greater its capacity for offering promotional support for a particular manufacturer.

For example, a retailer specializing in skiing equipment (highly spe-cialized) is likely to be more eager to promote a particular manufacturer's skis than would a discount department store (much more general). There are, of course, many exceptions to this generalization—particularly if the manufacturer offers strong inducements to secure promotional support from the more general line retailers. We will discuss some of these in the next major section of this chapter.

Competition. Just as the wholesaler is affected by competitive forces, so too is the retailer. In a highly competitive situation, the retailer's margins are very difficult to maintain. This greatly reduces the retailer's capacity to provide strong promotional support for a given manufacturer's prod-ucts. Take for example the fierce competition currently going on in the retailing of automatic drip coffee makers. Price cutting has become fran-tic, with several well-known brands such as Mr. Coffee being used as loss leaders. In the face of this kind of competitive situation, it is difficult in-deed to find a retailer who would be willing to go out on a limb to push a coffee maker which does not sell for less than the already depressed price, but at the same time offers a higher margin.

Promotional Strategies and Channel Member Cooperation

There are a wide variety of strategies which call for the involvement of channel members in the promotion of the manufacturer's products.[10] Be-fore discussing these, however, we should reemphasize an important point discussed in Chapter 8 (Motivating the Channel Members). This is that, in general, any marketing mix strategies calling for channel member coopera-tion should not be haphazard "one shot," or "quick fix" approaches. These are seldom effective. Rather, strategies that involve channel members

---

[10] See for example: Benson P. Shapiro, "Improve Distribution With Your Promotional Mix," *Harvard Business Review*, (March–April, 1977): 115–123.

stand a much higher probability of being favorably received by the channel members when they are *part of an overall program of manufacturer support of channel member needs*. In short, the manufacturer must establish a comprehensive approach for providing support to channel members if *their* cooperation in the promotion of products is expected. Mullin captures this point very succinctly:

"Obtaining distribution support is just like getting interest payments on a savings account. Before you can receive interest payments, you must first deposit the money. Similarly, before you receive distribution cooperation, you must first invest in and cooperate with your distributor."[11]

The approaches discussed in Chapter 8 such as the *cooperative, partnership*, and *distribution programming* (pp. 228–241), if instituted by the manufacturer, can provide the framework for a comprehensive and viable relationship between the manufacturer and channel members. If this kind of relationship exists, specific promotional strategies used by the manufacturer are then likely to have greater impact in terms of fostering channel member cooperation.

With this in mind, we turn to a discussion of some of the specific strategies available to the manufacturer requiring channel member promotional cooperation. These are discussed under the following five headings:

1. Promotional Assistance
2. Training Programs
3. Quotas for Channel Members
4. Missionary Salespeople
5. Special Deals and Merchandising Campaigns

Promotional Assistance

There are a myriad of different forms of promotional assistance. Indeed the variety seems to be limited only by one's imagination. For example, Aspley lists some fifty kinds of promotional assistance to dealers while Weiss has developed a list of some one hundred and thirty.[12] Table 11.1, for example, lists the specific forms of promotional assistance which the Imperial Eastman Corporation, a manufacturer of many types of industrial equipment, offers to its four hundred wholesale distributors. Most forms of promotional assistance, however, may be placed into one of the following categories: (1) cooperative advertising, (2) promotional allow-

---

[11] Roy E. Mullin, "Getting Distributor Support for the Company's Products," in *Building a Sound Distributor Organization* (New York: The National Industrial Conference Board, 1964), p. 43.

[12] See: Steven H. Star, "Obtaining Retailer Support for Marketing Programs," Working Paper P–82 (Cambridge, Mass.: Marketing Science Institute, August, 1973), p. 21.

Table 11.1
Promotional Assistance Offered by the Imperial Eastman Corporation to Its Wholesale Distributors

1. Cooperative Yellow Pages ad program
2. Supply of display material for use in trade shows, open houses and demonstrations
3. Direct mail pieces such as envelope stuffers and self-mailers provided at no cost
4. Ads designed for regional, local, business and purchasing publications, and newspapers
5. Complete catalogue and technical material
6. Signs, end goods, packaging, point-of-sale materials
7. Editorial publicity to business publications
8. Ad insertions listing all distributors in the semi-annual *Fluid Power Handbook & Directory*

Source: Compiled from "Imperial Eastman Outlines Industrial Distributor Plan," *Industrial Marketing*, (December, 1975), p. 25.

ances, (3) displays and selling aids, (4) in-store promotions, and (5) contests and incentives. Each of these is discussed in some detail below.

Cooperative Advertising. One of the most pervasive forms of promotional assistance offered by the manufacturer to channel members is that of cooperative advertising.[13] Although there are many variations, the most common one is for the manufacturer and channel member to share in the cost on a 50-50 basis up to a maximum of 3 percent of the retailer's purchases from the manufacturer. If a channel member made purchases of $100,000 from the manufacturer, the maximum amount of advertising funds available to the retailer would be $3,000.

For the manufacturer, the effectiveness of cooperative advertising as a promotional strategy depends heavily upon the level of support offered by the channel members. Specifically the channel members must: (1) have a sufficient inventory of the advertised product, (2) offer adequate point of purchase display, and (3) provide personal selling support if required. Getting this kind of support, however, requires careful administration of the cooperative program by the manufacturer. Lack of careful administration may result in poor channel member follow-through or even outright abuses, which are common. Consider the following example:

One common ploy of retailers has been around for years. This is the practice whereby a retailer buys newspaper space at the lower local linage rate but bills the manufacturer for its share at the higher national rate, pocketing the difference. In fact some retailers (particularly department stores) have been known to finance the entire advertising expenses for particular departments by billing the supplier at the higher rate.

Abuses are also common among food retailers where cooperative ad-

[13] For some very interesting perspectives on cooperative advertising see: Robert F. Young, "Cooperative Advertising, Its Uses and Effectiveness: Some Preliminary Hypotheses," Working Paper No. 79–112 (Cambridge, Mass.: Marketing Science Institute, October, 1979).

vertising dollars (often referred to as "case allowances") sometimes go, not only for legitimate expenses of store displays and newspaper ads, but also for a fur coat for the store manager's wife![14]

Some manufacturers, such as Procter and Gamble or DuPont, have developed formal and carefully administered cooperative advertising programs to guard against such abuses. In the case of Procter and Gamble, an annual agreement must be signed with its channel members calling for a prescribed number of promotions per year along with stringent requirements for proof of ad spending.[15]

While effective administration by the manufacturer is necessary to avoid abuses and to help secure cooperation from the channel members in a cooperative advertising program, the channel manager must also be sensitive to the channel member's main problem in the use of this kind of promotional assistance. Specifically the channel member may feel that the ads which the manufacturer expects him or her to run will put a disproportionate emphasis on the manufacturer's particular products and not enough on patronage appeals. If this is the case, the channel member is more likely to be reluctant in supporting the program, and may also feel justified in engaging in abuses.[16]

Promotional Allowances. The most common arrangement of promotional allowances is for the manufacturer to offer the channel member a certain percentage of the purchases on particular products if the channel member will agree to perform a promotional activity specified by the manufacturer. This promotional activity is often one of providing space for a specialized display developed by the manufacturer.

Recall from Chapter 8, for example, that the case of the Whitehall Co., makers of Anacin and BiSoDol, involved such an arrangement (see pp. 230–231). In that particular situation, the manufacturer offered a 5 percent rebate on purchases to retailers who would use the special in-store display offered by Whitehall. The problem experienced by Whitehall in getting the retailers to use the display, however, is a common one. This is, that channel members will often accept the promotional allowance but not follow through on using the display, while others will simply reject the allowance and display outright.

Hence, before instituting any type of promotional allowance program, the channel manager must be sure that the capacity exists to supervise the program and that the program is viewed by the majority of channel members as something that is worthwhile rather than being merely a nuisance.

---

[14] Martin Everett, "One Small Step for Co-Op Advertising," *Sales Management*, (3 April 1972): 25.

[15] Ibid., p. 25.

[16] For a discussion of some additional problems in the use of cooperative advertising along with some suggested solutions see: Arthur S. Fay, "How to Get the Most Out of Co-Op as a Tool for Selling," in *Sales and Marketing Management*, (October, 1978): 71–74.

Displays and Selling Aids.   Among the most typical forms of displays and selling aids used by manufacturers to increase promotional support are point of purchase displays, dealer identification signs, promotional kits, special in-store displays, and mailing pieces.

Manufacturers typically have difficulty in getting the retailers to make use of these materials. Consequently, special incentives in the form of promotional allowances are often necessary to encourage their use (see previous section). The reason is that channel members are usually flooded with such promotional material to the point that it is simply thrown away or never even opened. Besides this problem of overabundance, there is also the failure on the part of the manufacturer to take the time to demonstrate the usefulness of this material to channel members. A wide disparity of perceived usefulness of such materials often exists between the manufacturer and channel members. For example, consider the following case:

A major manufacturer of floor coverings designed what it believed to be a spectacular point of purchase display for a group of its floor covering products. The actual display consisted of a rather elaborate and bulky fixture which was shipped to dealers unassembled. Only the high volume dealers were offered this display, which was introduced by the manufacturer with a great deal of fanfare. The retailers who received the display soon came to resent the display and the manufacturer for introducing it because not only did it take a great deal of time and effort to assemble, but the sheer size and bulk of the display took up too much floor space and was virtually impossible to move around once in place. When word of this problem spread through the dealer "grapevine," many of those retailers who had not yet put up the display simply left it in its packing cartons.

So, as this case suggests, care must be exercised in the use of this kind of promotional material. The channel manager must make an effort to see whether the firm's selling aids and displays are serving any useful purpose or whether they are more of a bother than a help.

The most practical and efficient way of doing this is to get feedback from the field sales force. In those cases where the manufacturer's sales force does not call on retailers directly, feedback from a sample of the wholesalers' salespeople will offer some clues about whether the retailers are making good use of this promotional material.

In-store Promotions.   Most in-store promotions are short term events designed to create added interest and excitement for the manufacturer's products. In their quest to create promotional excitement through in-store promotions, some manufacturers have walked a thin line between legitimate promotional events and what some would consider to be ill-conceived nonsense. Consider, for example, an in-store promotion developed by the Coca-Cola Company:

Coca-Cola entombed a popular Kansas City disc jockey in a mountain of Coke cases at a supermarket and had him broadcast an appeal to "Buy me out!" A few hours later the store was a shambles—but the DJ was free, and Coke had pulled off one of the most spontaneous promotions in its history.[17]

The Coca-Cola Company was able to get away with this type of in-store promotion—in fact, it considered this promotion to be quite successful. On the other hand, some might point to the example as indicative of all too many in-store promotions—frivolous, silly, gimmicky, or overblown. This is, of course, a matter of judgement. The important issue for the channel manager, regardless of the actual form of the in-store promotion, is whether the retailers perceive benefits from it. Few retailers will be enthusiastic about cooperating with a manufacturer's in-store promotional event unless doing so yields specific benefits in the form of direct sales and profit increases, and/or increased recognition for their stores. Thus, the planning of a successful in-store promotion should always include considerations of the potential benefits for the retailers involved.

Contests and Incentives.   Contests and incentives are among the most difficult forms of promotional assistance to administer without creating ill will and conflict on the part of channel members. This is because some of these contests and incentives (developed by the manufacturer) can foster behavior by the channel members' salespeople which is detrimental to the channel members. For example, a manufacturer may offer a series of trips to exotic places to the highest volume salespeople employed by the wholesale or retail channel members. Or push money (PM's) may be offered directly by the manufacturer to channel member salespeople for pushing certain products. From the standpoint of the channel members, however, these or similar programs may be seen as conflicting with their (channel members') objectives. Specifically, a wholesaler or retailer with a long established reputation for offering customers the products that they want does not want salespeople to pressure these customers into buying products which may not serve their needs as well, but will help a salesperson to win a contest. In short, many channel members feel that when it comes to contests and incentives it is a one-sided deal—with the manufacturer getting most of the benefits. As a result, some channel members at both the wholesale and retail levels do not permit their employees to participate in manufacturer-sponsored contests or to accept incentive payments from them because they want to maintain control over their selling policies.

Clearly then, in the development of any contest or incentive program, the manufacturer should go out of its way to determine the views of channel members toward such forms of promotion. The potential conflict that can be avoided by doing so is likely to be well worth the effort.

---

[17]Martin Everett, "From Brass to Class," *Sales Management*, (1 November 1971): 23.

Training Programs

Training programs aimed at improving the performance of the channel members' salespeople can be one of the most effective strategies for building channel member promotional cooperation. Such programs can demonstrate in a highly visible way the manufacturer's commitment to helping channel members in an area where many of them need help. At both the wholesale and retail levels, the day to day pressures of doing business leave little room for much in the way of sales training. This is particularly true for many smaller wholesalers and retailers. But even for the larger ones who may have their own programs, the manufacturer's help in this area provides a valuable supplement and helps to offset the cost of the program.

In order to be effective, however, manufacturer sponsored training programs for channel member salespeople must be planned to meet the particular needs of the channel members and must be implemented in a manner that is acceptable to them. Because there are some important differences, we will discuss this topic separately for wholesale and retail level channel members.

Wholesale Level Training Programs.   Training programs at the wholesale level should be aimed at helping the wholesaler's salespeople in three major areas of need: (1) their knowledge of the manufacturer's particular product, (2) their selling techniques, and (3) to help them do a better job of counseling the customers they call on.

The first area is the most obvious one for emphasis from the manufacturer's point of view. Sometimes, however, product training is overemphasized at the expense of the other two areas. In commenting on this problem, Brown politely chides manufacturers to put more weight on the other two areas of sales training, especially the third one. He states:

". . . in the area of sales training, I do not recommend less training on product knowledge, but I do recommend additional training on ways and means of helping the retailer move a product: the kind of training that sends salesmen out prepared to help you sell through *the retailer, not to* him.*"*[18]

As an example of a training program which has been widely recognized as a model one in terms of providing for a good balance between the three areas of training, consider that of the Fafnir Bearing Company:

The Fafnir Bearing Company manufacturers a wide variety of ball bearings, a substantial portion of which are sold through "bearing specialists"—wholesalers specializing in ball bearing products.

[18]R. D. Brown, "Selling Through—Not To—Retailers," in *Marketing Through Retailers*, eds. Malcolm P. McNair and Mira Berman (New York: American Management Association, 1967), p. 61.

Fafnir began its training school for distributor salespeople in the late 1950s and after seven years of operation had trained over 2,000 distributors' salespeople.

The classes are conducted in hotels or motels in the territories of Fafnir distributors. About 20–25 distributor salespeople attend each class. The duration of the classroom instruction is three days.

In commenting on the allocation of class time, Robert W. Powell, Vice President of Sales for Fafnir made the following statement: "The first 20 percent of the total school time covers 'our job together' and deals with the distributor-manufacturer relationship: what the distributor expects from the manufacturer, and, of equal importance, what we, the manufacturer, expect from the distributors. And we emphasize the fact that this must be a two-way proposition if it is to be successful.

"Another 20 percent of the time is spent discussing our own product line—its nomenclature, configurations, functions, and applications with accompanying engineering data. However, we avoid loading the session with continuous plugs for our products. We want it educational. This is not an advertising session.

"The remaining 60 percent of the school time is involved with subjects unique and applicable to the entire ball bearing industry. These include basic bearing history and development, bearing designs, calculations of bearing life, load carrying capacities, and speed limitations. We teach identification and correction of ball bearing failures as well."[19]

Though Fafnir freely admits that the purpose of its training program is ". . . to secure preferential treatment from our distributors' salesmen in an extremely competitive market,"[20] the emphasis of its training program does not stress this. This suggests that training programs that are more subtle about their "bottom-line" objective (such as, by not spending most of the time extolling the virtues of the sponsoring manufacturer's product) may, paradoxically, be the more effective ones in actually attaining the objective of preferential treatment from the distributors.

Retail Level Training Programs.   Training programs aimed at retail salespeople are useful mainly for products which still need a significant level of personal sales assistance. For stores operating mainly on a self-service basis there is little need for sales training.

The areas of sales training need at the retail level mainly parallel the first two at the wholesale level: (1) product knowledge and (2) selling technique. The third area, counseling, also exists but in a much more limited sense. The type of counseling the retail salesperson offers to customers would be in terms of product usage and would not, of course, deal with such issues as how the customer can promote the product or provide management assistance.

[19] Robert W. Powell, "Training Distributor Salesmen," in *Building a Sound Distributor Organization* (New York: The National Industrial Conference Board, 1964), pp. 85–93.
[20] Ibid., p. 86.

Poor personal selling at the retail level has become almost legendary.[21] The reasons for this are too numerous to mention here. Certainly, the poor quality of retail selling cannot be blamed to any great extent on inadequate manufacturer training programs—retailers are far more guilty in this regard. Nevertheless, the manufacturer can have a limited impact on improving the performance of retail sales people by offering training programs aimed at specific and limited objectives. As an example of such programs, the one offered by the Smith-Corona Corporation is instructive:

As part of the overall promotional program to gain retailer cooperation in promoting the Smith-Corona copying machines in the highly competitive market for these products, SCM developed a short training program for the dealers' salespeople (and servicepeople).

As soon as the first shipment of copiers arrived on the dealer's floor, a Smith-Corona service manager and a regional wholesale manager were sent to train the dealer's servicepeople and salespeople in the features of the copier.

In addition, dealers were offered a planning guide for local sales promotions including tips on budgeting.[22]

This example illustrates a relatively simple but effective approach to training at the retail level.[23] Its main purpose was to assure that the retailers' sales and servicepeople had basic knowledge of the products' features from both a sales and service standpoint as soon as the products reached the retailers. This was a modest accomplishment but, nevertheless, an important one. All too often manufacturers do not even provide this kind of rudimentary training at the retail level. It is no wonder then that they complain about the poor selling job done by their retailers.

Quotas for Channel Members

The use of sales quotas for channel members, if used properly, offers another method for improving channel member promotional support. The key to using quotas properly, however, lies in the context in which they are presented to the channel members. If they are presented in a coercive fashion, they may produce ill will and conflict rather than support (i.e., if the manufacturer sets a quota without consulting with the channel members and then holds the quota up as something to be attained—or else). Further, if the manufacturer's line does not make up an important part of the channel member's product mix, the channel member may simply ignore the quota.

---

[21] Bert Rosenbloom, "Improving Personal Selling in Small Retail Stores," (Washington, D.C.: *Small Business Administration Small Marketers Aids* No. 159, November, 1976).

[22] "SCM Copier Promotion Focuses on Selling Dealers and Machines in Competitive Market," *Advertising and Sales Promotion*, (August, 1972): 27–28.

[23] For another approach to retail sales training see: "Learning How to Sell Small Cars," *Business Week*, (27 March 1978): 124–126.

On the other hand, if quotas are developed in conjunction with the channel members, and if they are presented in the context of providing information on the sales potentials in the channel members' territories, they can be a positive force in fostering channel member support. The approach to setting quotas used by the Black and Decker Company in its consumer products division is indicative of this latter approach:

Sales quotas are assigned at the beginning of the year only to those 20 percent of wholesale distributors that represent 80 percent of sales volume. These quotas are closely related to market penetration goals that Black and Decker's marketing department establishes for the specific territories involved and these are then submitted to the distributors for approval. Any differences are worked out between the distributors and Black and Decker's field sales management.[24]

Missionary Salespeople

The term *missionary selling* was first used to describe the activities of manufacturers' salespeople who were sent specifically to convince distributors that they should handle the manufacturer's new products. Because they were attempting to "convert" distributors to handle their products, they were called "missionary salesmen."[25]

Today the term is usually applied to any of the manufacturer's salespeople who are specially assigned to supplement the selling activities of channel members. In the consumer goods industry, missionary salespeople (sometimes called detail men) may be called upon to perform any of the following activities:[26]

1. checking wholesale and retail inventory levels
2. calling on retailers to inform them of new products
3. helping arrange window and in-store displays
4. answering the wholesalers' and retailers' questions and providing advice and training
5. trying to promote goodwill
6. taking orders for merchandise

In the industrial market they are often involved in such activities as these:

1. training distributor salespeople
2. accompanying distributor salespeople on sales calls to assist their selling efforts

[24] Roger M. Pegram, *Selecting and Evaluating Distributors* (New York: National Industrial Conference Board, 1965), p. 138.

[25] Alan B. Huellmantel, "The Use of Missionary and Detail Men," in *Handbook of Modern Marketing*, ed. Victor P. Buell (New York: McGraw-Hill, 1970), pp. 12–133 to 12–152.

[26] See: Engel et al., *Promotional Strategy*, p. 42.

3.   taking initial orders for new products from the final user
4.   providing technical assistance
5.   helping distributors' salespeople to close sales, especially those that require technical knowledge that is beyond the scope of the distributors' salespeople

Perhaps more so than for any of the promotional strategies discussed so far in this chapter, the use of missionary salespeople in building channel member promotional support is a two edged sword.

On the positive side, missionary selling is a useful promotional strategy when the channel members lack the sales capacity or competence to handle tasks assigned to them by the manufacturer, and if the channel members *desire* this kind of assistance.

On the negative side, however, are several significant problems in using missionary salespeople. First, it is expensive, particularly in the industrial market. As Huellmantel points out:

"Missionary selling (in the industrial market) is expensive selling. It requires a highly educated, specially trained salesforce, often with engineering and graduate degrees and these are usually the highest-paid salesmen . . ."[27]

Second, it can lead to serious conflicts in the channel. This may occur when missionary salespeople begin performing many of the wholesaler's tasks. The wholesaler, for example, may perceive this to mean that the manufacturer is on the verge of bypassing the wholesaler altogether and as a result may reduce the level of promotional support given to the manufacturer. A final problem is that many channel members view missionary salespeople as bothersome because they take up too much of the time of their own sales force. This is particularly the case when the products of a manufacturer who uses missionary salespeople play only a small part in the channel member's product mix.

The channel manager must therefore pay careful attention to the attitudes of channel members towards the use of missionary salespeople. They can be an expensive mistake if their use fosters conflict rather than increases promotional cooperation from the channel members.

Special Promotional Deals and Merchandising Campaigns

Special promotional deals or merchandising campaigns take a variety of forms. Almost always, however, they emphasize price incentives to the channel members, consumers, or both. Among the more common ones are large or special displays of products at reduced prices, favorable offers to the consumer to encourage larger volume purchases (e.g., buy two, get

[27] Huellmantel, "Missionary and Detail Men," p. 12–145.

one free; four for the price of three, etc.), percentage or "cents off" offers, rebates, and others.

Though these promotional deal strategies are pervasive, particularly for consumer goods, little has been done in the way of evaluating the role played by retail channel members in the success or failure of these special promotions. An important exception to this is a major study conducted by Hinkle in the food industry.[28] His study examined special deals for some nineteen brands in three product types—regular coffee, cleansing tissues, and frozen dinners—over a five year period. An important part of Hinkle's study dealt with the role played by retailers in providing the kind of cooperation necessary for the success of special promotional deals. One of his major findings was as follows:

"All too often, despite the millions of dollars spent by manufacturers, special promotional and merchandising campaigns fall short of expectations because the programs developed by the manufacturer do not correspond with the needs and requirements of the retailer."[29]

Hinkle argues that a manufacturer must give careful thought to several important questions if it is to improve retailer cooperation in the use of special promotional deals and merchandising campaigns. Four of these are:

1.   Should more emphasis be placed on trade incentives?
2.   Has there been adequate contact and communication with retailers?
3.   Is the profitability being adequately studied?
4.   Who has the inventory?

Each of these questions is discussed in some detail below.

Emphasis on Trade Incentives.   This question deals with the allocation of benefits (in the form of reduced prices) attendant to special deals between the retailer and the consumer. Hinkle found that retailer cooperation is not likely to be forthcoming unless the price incentives allocated to the retailer as part of the deal are perceived as attractive by the retailer. Hinkle recommends that the manufacturer put strong emphasis on the *trade incentive* aspects of price deals. That is, formulating special deals involving price reductions, the manufacturer must see to it that the portion of the total price cut allocated to the retailer will be sufficient to gain cooperation in providing adequate stock of the product, shelf space, and special displays if needed.

Unfortunately, the optimal allocation of price deal benefits between the channel members and consumer varies among product types and

---

[28]Charles L. Hinkle, "The Strategy of Price Deals," *Harvard Business Review*, (July–August, 1965): 75–85.

[29]Ibid., p. 80.

brands, and across different markets. Consequently this must be determined on a case by case basis.

Contact and Communication with Retailers. Hinkle also found that
failures by the manufacturer to contact retailers and to obtain feedback
on their reactions to manufacturer-initiated special promotions were quite
common. This communication failure creates substantial problems because retailers often plan their advertising several weeks in advance, and
display space is allocated sometimes as much as three or four months
ahead of special promotions—and four or five weeks in advance at a minimum. Consequently, retailers may be unable to cooperate in a special promotion due to conflicting prior commitments of space and effort. If this is
the case, even the enticement of a large price allowance is usually inadequate to force a change in the retailer's plans. So whenever possible the
manufacturer should attempt to presell the retailer on the special promotion so that the retailer will know what to expect from the manufacturer.
Indeed, Hinkle argues that some retailers may even offer ideas that will be
helpful in launching promotions. The advance notice also enables the
manufacturer to receive more feedback about the retailer's plans which
may help to develop or modify future special promotions accordingly.

Profitability of Offers. Hinkle makes a strong case about the need for the
manufacturer to evaluate the retailer's profit picture before embarking on
any special promotional deals or offers:

*"It is becoming increasingly apparent that the manufacturer needs to
think in exacting terms of retailer profitability instead of relying on vague
platitudes about how 'good' a particular offer is. Competition for shelf
space is fierce, and when the retailer allocates scarce space and expends
human effort on one brand, others must receive proportionately less selling area and personal attention.*

*In contemplating whether to accept or reject a promotion, the store
operator asks himself if the profit from the deal will offset the loss of
profits from competitive brands and substitute products."* [30]

So, as Hinkle suggests, no matter how excited the manufacturer may be
about the deal being offered, unless it does in fact meet the retailer's margin requirements, the latter is not likely to see it as a wonderful deal.
Thus, the guidelines with respect to channel member margin requirements discussed in Chapter 10 (see pp. 277–282) should not be automatically suspended by the manufacturer when a special promotional deal is
being offered. For surely, the channel members are not going to suspend
these guidelines.

Who Has the Inventory. Given the high carrying costs and risks attendant to holding inventories, most retailers attempt to minimize their in-

[30] Ibid., p. 81.

ventories by shifting them backward in the channel to wholesalers and/ or manufacturers.[31] Merchandise involved in special promotional deals, however, frequently increases the amount of inventory the retailer must carry, leading in turn to an increase in carrying costs. For example, each stock of special deal merchandise may require a different code number and location in the warehouse. Yet even while being asked to hold this special deal merchandise, the retailer must also maintain stock of nondeal merchandise which ties up the retailer's money during the promotion. This added inventory burden has made many retailers reluctant to cooperate in promotional deals which load them up with greater inventories.[32]

To help overcome this problem, the manufacturer must take steps to reduce the retailer's inventory burden when special promotions are offered. This calls for efficient physical distribution to provide the retailer with just enough inventory to meet the anticipated demand but little more. Along with this, some manufacturers have resorted to the practice of sending the retailer a check for the amount of inventory on hand before the start of the promotion and then billing the retailer for it again when the special promotion is over.

Summary

One of the major tools the manufacturer uses for implementing an overall promotional program is selling support by channel members. While some manufacturers feel that they can rely solely on promotion to their target markets to "pull" their products through the channel, in most cases this is not enough. Direct involvement or "pushing" by the manufacturer in a joint approach to promotion with channel members is usually also needed to develop an effective and viable promotional program. Because channel members are independent businesses, however, the degree of control the manufacturer can exercise over how its products are promoted once they are in the hands of the channel members is significantly reduced. Consequently, a manufacturer must carefully administer promotional strategies involving channel members to help assure a high degree of channel member cooperation in the promotion of its products.

In order to increase the odds of attaining this promotional cooperation for the channel members, the channel manager must first recognize the constraints on channel members that tend to limit the degree of promotional cooperation and support they can offer. Among the most important of these are: (1) the nature of their product assortments, (2) types of markets served, (3) type of store (for wholesalers, type of service), and (4) the nature of the competition.

[31] For a theoretical discussion of this issue and related ones see: Louis P. Bucklin, "Postponement, Speculation, and the Structure of Distribution Channels," *Journal of Marketing Research* 2 (February, 1965): 26–31.

[32] For a related discussion see: Michel Chevalier and Ronald C. Curhan, "Temporary Promotions as a Function of Trade Deals: A Descriptive Analysis," Working Paper No. 75–109 (Cambridge, Mass.: Marketing Science Institute, May, 1975).

Armed with an understanding of these limits on channel members' promotional support, the channel manager is then in a better position to develop promotional programs that are both appealing to the channel members and realistic in their requirements for channel member support.

A manufacturer can use one or more of the following five promotional strategies in its channel promotion program: (1) promotional assistance, (2) training programs, (3) quotas, (4) missionary salespeople, and (5) special deals and merchandising campaigns.

Promotional assistance can take many forms; most of them fit into such categories as cooperative advertising, promotional allowances, displays and selling aids, in-store promotions, and contests and incentives. For any of these promotional assistance devices to work well, they must be carefully planned and executed with an emphasis on learning the *channel members'* views and requirements.

Training programs are more common for wholesale channel members than for retail. But in either case, the training programs should not be narrowly confined to being merely a "sales pitch" for the particular manufacturer's product. Rather, training programs worthy of the name should help the channel members to not only sell more of the particular manufacturer's products, but to improve their overall businesses as well.

Quotas are often used by manufacturers as a device to increase channel members' sales effort. The key to using such sales quotas successfully is to present them in a constructive and informative manner rather than in a coercive way.

Missionary salespeople are employed by the manufacturer to help focus channel members' attention on the manufacturer's products and to assist the channel members in their selling efforts. The use of missionary salespeople can be very effective if the channel members want the help they offer, if the missionary salespeople do not take up too much of the channel members' time, and if they do not divert too much of the channel members' salespeople's time from other products.

Finally, special deals and merchandising campaigns are frequently used by manufacturers, especially those selling consumer goods, to heighten interest in the product and to create incentives for channel members to "go all out" in selling the manufacturer's special deal products. In order for these special deals to work successfully, the manufacturer must take into account the channel members' problems in participating in these programs and make them attractive enough to justify the extra effort required of the channel members.

Discussion Questions

1. Explain the rationale for including selling support by resellers in a channel of distribution as a major tool for implementing promotional strategy.

2. Why is the success of a manufacturer's overall promotional strategy dependent to a significant extent on channel member cooperation?

3. Discuss the major constraints on channel members at the wholesale and retail levels which tend to limit the level of cooperation they can offer to the manufacturer.

4. Regardless of what specific promotional strategies the manufacturer uses, a higher level of channel member cooperation is likely to be gained if these strategies are part of an overall program of channel member support. Discuss this statement.

5. Discuss the major problems involved in the use of cooperative advertising from the manufacturer's point of view and from the channel members' perspective.

6. Discuss the pros and cons of the following promotional assistance strategies from the manufacturer's and channel members' viewpoints: (1) promotional allowances, (2) displays and selling aids, (3) in-store promotions, (4) contests and incentives.

7. Since the manufacturer's major objective in instituting a training program for channel member salespeople is to get them to give preferential treatment to the firm's products, the manufacturer should design training programs which are in effect "commercials" for its particular products. Discuss the implications of this statement.

8. Should coercive power be the basis for developing a sales quota program for channel members?

9. How might the use of missionary salespeople foster conflict rather than cooperation in the channel?

10. Discuss the major questions which should be considered when using various promotional deals and special merchandising campaigns.

Chapter 12
Physical Distribution and Channel Management

In this chapter we turn to the final major element needed to foster a cooperative team of channel members—an effective and efficient physical distribution system. *Physical distribution* may be defined as:

"*. . . the broad range of activities concerned with efficient movement of finished products from the end of the production line to the consumer, and in some cases includes the movement of raw materials from the source of supply to the beginning of the production line. These activities include freight transportation, warehousing, materials handling, protective packaging, inventory control, plant and warehouse site selection, order processing, market forecasting, and customer service.*"[1]

Figure 12.1 illustrates these major activity areas of a typical physical distribution system. The need to properly mesh the "cogs" for each of the physical distribution activities to form a smoothly operating physical distribution system is conveyed in the illustration.

Physical distribution (PD) has received increased attention, particularly during the past ten years. This is no doubt due to the great costs in-

[1]Edward W. Smykay, *Physical Distribution Management*, 3rd ed. (New York: Macmillan Co., 1973), p. 5.

Figure 12.1
Activity Cogs in a Physical Distribution System

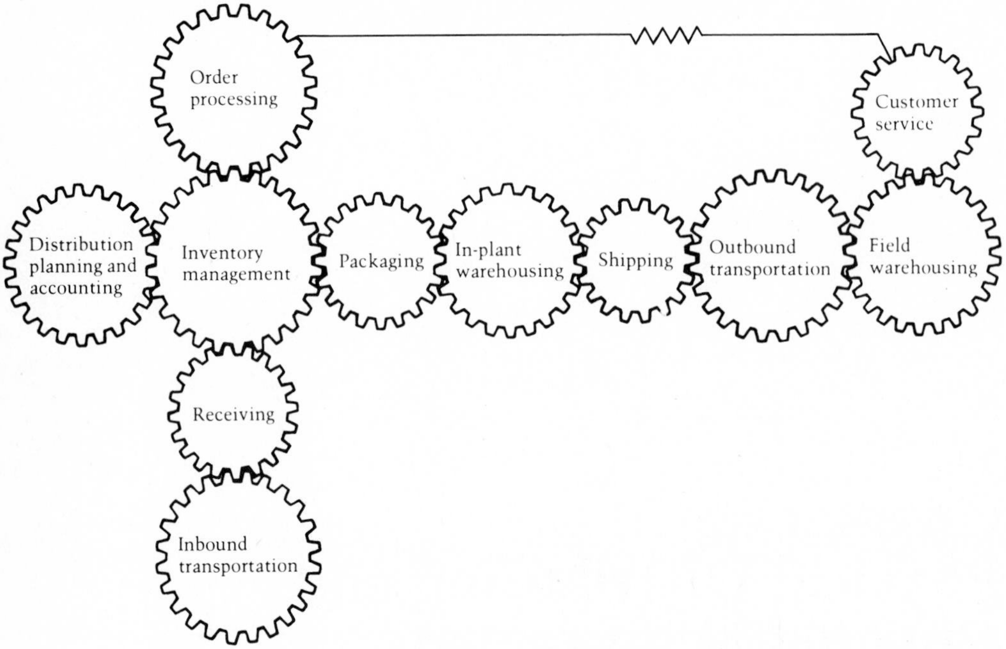

Source: Wendell M. Stewart, "Physical Distribution: Key to Improved Volume and Profits," *Journal of Marketing* 29 (January 1965): 66.

volved in PD activities.[2] For example, a study conducted by the National Council of Physical Distribution Management (NCPDM) estimated costs of physical distribution of goods from producers to final consumer at $400 billion per year. Another NCPDM study found that physical distribution costs account for 13.6 percent of each dollar of sales for all manufacturers and range from a low of 4.4 percent for pharmaceutical companies to a high of 14.1 percent for food manufacturers.[3] Table 12.1 provides a more detailed breakdown. Improved PD systems that can hold down costs while still providing a high level of service hold great potential for improving the productivity and profitability of thousands of business firms.[4]

The modern view of the PD function is that the various activities involved should be managed as an integrated system to provide a defined

[2]Steven B. Oresman and Charles D. Scudder, "A Remedy for Maldistribution," *Business Horizons* 17 (June, 1974): 61.
[3]David P. Herron, "Managing Physical Distribution for Profit," *Harvard Business Review*, (May–June, 1979): 123.
[4]For a related discussion see: James A. Constantin, Ronald D. Anderson and Roger E. Jerman, "Views of Physical Distribution Managers," *Business Horizons*, (April, 1977): 82–86.

Table 12.1
Distribution Costs as a Percentage of Sales Dollar

	Outbound trans-portation	Inventory carrying	Warehousing	Administration	Receiving and shipping	Packaging	Order processing	Total
All manufacturing companies	6.2%	1.3%	3.6%	0.5%	0.8%	0.7%	0.5%	13.6%
Chemicals and plastics	6.3	1.6	3.3	0.3	0.6	1.4	0.6	14.1
Food manufacturing	8.1	0.3	3.5	0.4	0.9	—	0.2	13.4
Pharmaceutical	1.4	—	1.2	0.7	0.5	0.1	0.5	4.4
Electronics	3.2	2.5	3.2	1.2	0.9	1.1	1.2	13.3
Paper	5.8	0.1	4.6	0.2	0.3	—	0.2	11.2
Machinery and tools	4.5	1.0	2.0	0.5	0.5	1.0	0.5	10.0
All other	6.8	1.0	2.9	1.2	1.4	0.4	0.4	14.1
All merchandising companies	7.4%	10.3%	4.2%	1.2%	0.6%	1.2%	0.7%	25.6%
Consumer goods	8.1	8.5	4.0	1.3	0.9	0.9	0.5	24.2
Industrial goods	5.9	13.7	2.9	0.7	0.2	2.0	1.0	26.4

Source: B. J. LaLonde and P. H. Zinszer, *Customer Service: Meaning and Measurement* (Chicago: National Council of Physical Distribution Management, 1976).

level of customer service at the lowest total cost for performing all of the activities necessary to provide that level of service.

In this chapter we will not be concerned with the management of PD per se. Excellent and detailed discussions of this topic appear in many basic marketing texts[5] and several other texts dealing exclusively with physical distribution management.[6] Thus, there is little point in attempting to repeat these materials here. We will be concerned, however, with several important interfaces between PD management and channel management. An awareness of these interfaces is necessary if the channel manager is to play a part in shaping the manufacturer's PD strategy so that it is more likely to foster channel member cooperation rather than conflict. In short, a manufacturer's PD strategy can be instrumental in either fostering or inhibiting channel member cooperation. The channel manager must therefore attempt to influence the firm's PD strategy to help assure that it will promote the more positive effect on the channel members.

Physical Distribution and Channel Management

In Chapter 1 we noted that the distribution component of the marketing mix can be broken down into two major elements: (1) channel management, and (2) physical distribution management. Recall that we discussed channel management as a much broader and more comprehensive element of distribution strategy than physical distribution management. Channel management is concerned with the overall design and administration of distribution channels and involves planning and management of *all* of the major channel flows (product, negotiation, ownership, information, and promotion), whereas physical distribution is concerned mainly with the product flow. But we also noted in Chapter 1 that physical distribution management and channel management are very closely linked and dependent upon each other. A well-designed and administered marketing channel cannot exist without an efficient flow of products to the channel members and final target markets in the right quantities, and at the right times and places. In short, channel management and physical distribution management go together "hand in hand" to provide effective and efficient distribution. But such meshing of channel management and physical distribution requires good coordination. This especially applies

---

[5]See for example: E. Jerome McCarthy, *Basic Marketing: A Managerial Approach*, 6th ed. (Homewood, Illinois: Richard D. Irwin, 1978), pp. 378–399; Philip Kotler, *Principles of Marketing* (Englewood Cliffs, N.J.: Prentice-Hall Inc., 1980), pp. 442–454; Louis E. Boone and David L. Kurtz, *Contemporary Marketing*, 3rd ed. (Hinsdale, Illinois: The Dryden Press, 1980), pp. 257–279.

[6]Donald J. Bowersox, *Logistical Management* (New York: Macmillan Co., 1974); Edward W. Smykay, *Physical Distribution Management*, 3rd ed. (New York: Macmillan Co., 1973); James L. Heskett, Nicholas A. Glaskowsky, and Robert M. Ivie, *Business Logistics*, 2nd ed. (New York: The Ronald Press Co., 1973); Ronald H. Ballou, *Business Logistics Management* (Englewood Cliffs, New Jersey: Prentice-Hall, Inc., 1973); John J. Coyle and Edward J. Bardi, *The Management of Logistics*, 2nd ed. (St. Paul, Minn.: West Publishing Co., 1980).

Figure 12.2
Interfaces between Physical Distribution and Channel Management
Viewed Sequentially

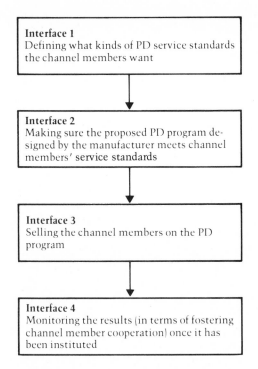

to four major areas of interface between channel management and physical distribution. These are:

1. defining what kinds of PD service standards channel members want
2. making sure that the proposed PD program designed by the manufacturer meets the channel member service standards
3. selling the channel members on the PD program
4. monitoring the results of the PD program once it has been instituted

Figure 12.2 portrays these in a sequential format. The remainder of this chapter discusses each of these areas of PD-channel management interface.

Defining Physical Distribution Service Standards

PD service standards refer to what kinds and levels of service the manufacturer offers to channel members. Heskett et al., for example, list nine common categories of services that are frequently of importance to a broad range of channel members at both the wholesale and retail levels.[7] These are:

1. time from order receipt to order shipment
2. order size and assortment constraints
3. percentage of items out of stock
4. percentage of orders filled accurately
5. percentage of orders filled within a given number of days from receipt of the order
6. percentage of orders filled
7. percentage of customer orders that arrive in good condition
8. order cycle time (time from order placement to order delivery)
9. ease and flexibility of order placement

These PD service standards are usually quantified in some fashion and then the manufacturer's actual performance is measured against these standards. For example, the first standard, time from order receipt to order shipment, might be set at twenty-four hours for ninety percent of all orders received. So, for every one hundred orders received, the manufacturer must have ninety of the orders processed and shipped within twenty-four hours to meet the standard. The second service standard listed above might be set in terms of some minimum quantity of products and certain restrictions might be placed on mixing the various products unless specified minimum quantities of each are ordered. A steel producer, for example, might set the minimum order for various gauges of sheet metal at two tons; to order several gauges in a single order, a certain combined minimum tonnage might have to be met. The third standard, percentage of items out of stock or "stockouts," is almost always set in terms of percent of items ordered during a given period that cannot be filled from inventory. Thus, if a manufacturer wants to fill 95 percent of the items ordered, its stockout percentage can be no higher than five percent to meet the standard. The other six service standards listed above can be quantified and used in a similar fashion as the three discussed here.

In general, the higher the service standards the manufacturer offers, the higher the costs. While well designed PD systems and modern technology can keep these costs under control, it is usually not possible to completely escape this trade off of higher costs for higher service standards.

A manufacturer must cover these costs either indirectly in the price it charges for products, or by passing them along to channel members in the form of service charges. In either case, there is little point in offering PD services that channel members do not want or higher levels of service

---

[7]Heskett et al. *Business Logistics*, pp. 250–251. For a more comprehensive and thorough discussion of PD service see: Martin Christopher, Philip Schary, and Tage Skjott-Larsen, *Customer Service and Distribution Strategy* (New York: John Wiley & Sons, 1979).

than they desire. Types or levels of PD service that go beyond real channel member demands simply increase costs for channel members without providing them with any desired benefits. Thus, the key issue facing the channel manager with respect to defining PD service standards is *to determine precisely the types and levels of PD service desired by the channel members*. To deal with this issue effectively, the channel manager needs to obtain the channel members' views about what kinds of PD service standards *they* want *before* the manufacturer develops a PD service program.

Hutchinson and Stolle suggest the use of survey research for dealing with this problem.[8] The survey should be designed to ask specific questions about what kinds of services the channel members want. For example, do the channel members want such services as toll free telephone ordering, more shipping notices, simplified order forms, special handling systems, etc? Further, such surveys can also help the channel manager to find out whether the channel members would be willing to pay (e.g., through larger orders or higher prices) for improved physical distribution service. Finally, the surveys can provide information from the channel members about the service levels of competitors. Such data will be useful for pinpointing areas where PD can be used to gain a competitive advantage.

Instead of (or along with) surveys of channel members, the approaches discussed in Chapter 8 under *Learning about Channel Member Needs* (pp. 222–227) may be used. In this case, the desires of channel members with respect to PD service could be included as part of the general effort to find out about channel member needs and problems in other areas besides physical distribution.

Perreault and Russ offer yet another approach for learning about channel member PD service demands.[9] They suggest that the channel members be presented with alternative prospective PD service programs. Channel members' preferences on the various alternatives may then be evaluated in terms of what kinds of cost-service trade-offs the channel members would be willing to make. As Perreault and Russ state:

"The dollar trade-off values estimated in this fashion provide the marketing manager an index of what changes the customer considers to be important, and more specifically, whether the additional revenues (due to the possibility of increased prices or increased demand) exceed the additional costs incurred by the higher service level. The result of this type of analysis is the pinpointing of the PDS (physical distribution service) package(s), among all those considered, whose cost increases can best be justified by the potential incremental revenues from its target market."[10]

[8] William M. Hutchinson and John F. Stolle, "How to Manage Customer Service," *Harvard Business Review* 46 (November–December, 1968): 85–96.

[9] William D. Perreault and Frederick A. Russ, "Physical Distribution Service: A Neglected Aspect of Marketing Management" *MSU Business Topics*, (Summer, 1974): 41–44.

[10] Ibid., p. 44.

In sum, the development of PD service standards should not be based solely on the views of the manufacturer. Channel members' views should also be incorporated. If this is done, the set of PD service standards developed by the manufacturer is much more likely to reflect the kinds and levels of service that the channel members actually want rather than what the manufacturer may think they want. Since channel members in one way or another pay for the PD services offered by manufacturers, they should have at least some say in what they are getting for their money.

Evaluating the Proposed PD Service Program

A proposed PD service program may be offered to channel members as a separate entity or be included as a major component of the manufacturer's overall approach for supporting channel member needs. If the latter is the case, the PD service program may, for example, be the keystone feature of a channel "partnership" arrangement or play an important role in a comprehensive distribution programming agreement (see Chapter 8, pp. 228–240). In either case, the PD service program must be carefully developed so that it actually meets the channel members' service requirements within tolerable cost constraints.[11]

A discussion of how to design such a program is far beyond the scope of this chapter. This is a highly technical area which is treated in a number of excellent works on the subject.[12] In practice, the actual design of the program would be done by experts in the field of physical distribution either on the manufacturer's payroll or by outside consultants. Nevertheless, the channel manager should still play a role in this to the extent of making sure that the program does indeed meet the channel members' service requirements. Fortunately, this does not require a high level of expertise in the technical aspects of PD design. What it does require, however, is that the channel manager have a clear understanding of the *objectives* of the proposed PD service program. In short it is the channel manager's job to make sure that the program the PD experts are developing is really what the channel members want. It is all too possible to have a sophisticated PD program incorporating the latest technical advances and still be far off the mark in terms of meeting channel member PD service demands, thus doing little to foster channel member support. For example, consider what happened to the Gillette Co.:

The Gillette Co., makers of the world's largest-selling brand of razor blades and safety razors, was faced with a staggering assortment of changes in its operations. Among these were: diversification into a broad range of toiletry products, a shift of its main distribution channels

---

[11] For a related discussion see: D. L. Bates and John E. Dillard, Jr., "Physical Distribution: Current Application of Theory," *Transportation Journal*, (Winter, 1975): 28–30.

[12] See, for example, Bowersox, *Logistical Management*; Smykay, *Physical Distribution Management*; Heskett, Glaskowsky, and Ivie, *Business Logistics*; and Ballou, *Business Logistics Management*.

from drug and tobacco chains to grocery chains, and the introduction of stainless steel blades by competitors.

Gillette sought to get "one up" on the competition in providing PD service to its thousands of channel members by emphasizing speedy deliveries of its own new blades. The PD program designed to accomplish this was dependent upon the fastest mode of transport—air freight.

It turned out, however, that the cost of this air freight-based PD service was too high. Both Gillette and many of its channel members complained about the high costs and resulting lower profit margins. Gillette quickly dropped this PD program and developed one based on the use of lower cost surface transport.[13]

On the other hand, PD service programs that are carefully designed to focus on meeting customer service requirements can play a major role in promoting channel member support. Consider the following case:

A California based producer of cut flowers wanted to reach the mass consumer markets. This required a channel structure that emphasized retail distribution through department stores and supermarkets rather than the traditional flower shops.

The main problems in doing this, however, were: (1) to convince these retailers that the flowers would use only a minimum of floor space and (2) that a fresh and timely supply would always be available to assure a high rate of turnover.

A high technology PD program was designed to meet these channel member service demands head on.

First, a case that would hold standard trays of cut flowers was designed to minimize the use of floor space. This specifically designed compact case offered the retailers the potential for a very high sales per square foot ratio.

Second, the problem of providing a fresh and timely supply of flowers was solved by using air freight plus a specially designed container that (1) precooled the blossoms as they were cut in the fields, (2) held trays of flowers in different quantities, (3) fitted aircraft dimensions, and (4) had good handling characteristics.

The combination of advanced physical distribution technology made it possible to deliver containers of flowers to almost any retail store in the United States in twenty-four hours or less.[14]

These two examples point out the contrast between a physical distribution service program that did little to foster channel member support for the manufacturer's distribution strategy (Gillette's program) and another that was extremely valuable in doing so (the flower producer's program).

In the case of Gillette, the PD service program was modern and sophisticated but off target in terms of channel member needs—it cost too much

---

[13] "New Strategies to Move Goods," *Business Week*, (24 September 1966): 112.

[14] Smykay, *Physical Distribution*, p. 38.

to implement successfully. From the channel members' standpoint, the fast delivery provided by air freight was not worth the added cost. Perhaps if Gillette had been in a position to absorb all of these added costs itself, the channel members might have been delighted with the system. But this would have been too expensive for Gillette. So what appeared to be a good idea "on paper" turned out to be unworkable when put into practice. A more careful evaluation of the PD program before it was actually implemented would probably have brought this cost problem to light.

In contrast, the PD program developed by the flower producer was very successful because the special and sophisticated technical aspects flowed directly *from channel member* PD service needs. In other words, PD technology was used not for the sake of having an up-to-the-minute PD system but to solve real problems in the distribution of flowers faced by channel members (department stores and supermarkets) who were not experienced or equipped to market fresh cut flowers. The resulting PD service program thus became the key element that enabled the flower producer to implement its overall distribution strategy of marketing fresh cut flowers to the mass market through department stores and supermarkets. In short, the PD service program did what it was supposed to do because it was designed to be consistent with channel member PD service needs.

Selling the Channel Members on the PD Program

Regardless of how good a manufacturer perceives its PD service program to be, it still must convince channel members of its value. As Stewart warns in alluding to this point:

"A word of caution! Changes in [physical] distribution must be palatable to the company's customers [channel members]. Changes which provide cost benefits only to the manufacturer without corresponding benefits to customers may be more difficult to implement than those that offer incentives to customers to change."[15]

Unfortunately there is no "sure fire" way to assure that a proposed PD service program will be palatable to the majority of the manufacturer's channel members. As pointed out in the previous two sections of this chapter, the basis for gaining channel member acceptance is a carefully defined set of PD service standards that are in line with the expressed desires of the channel members. Nevertheless, Stewart does allude to several types of appeals which, if emphasized by the manufacturer in attempting to sell the proposed PD program, may help the manufacturer to be more convincing.[16] Three of these are:

---

[15] Wendell M. Stewart, "Physical Distribution: Key to Improved Volume and Profits," *Journal of Marketing* 29 (January, 1965): 70.

[16] Ibid., p. 68.

1. emphasize the reduction in out-of-stock occurrences which the new PD program will make possible
2. emphasize the reduction in channel member inventories that the PD program will allow
3. emphasize the added manufacturer support for the channel members fostered by the new PD program

Each of these is discussed below.

Minimizing Out of Stock Occurrences.   By minimizing out-of-stock occurrences through an improved PD program, sales lost by the channel members will be reduced. If a manufacturer can convince channel members that the new PD service package will indeed help them to achieve this result, it has a very potent argument for gaining an enthusiastic reception for the program. Of course, this must actually be the case. That is, the new PD program must actually be capable of achieving this result. False, misleading, or exaggerated promises made about a new PD program that are not backed up by facts and that are not borne out when the system is put into operation are likely to create conflict rather than enhance channel member cooperation.[17] No matter how enthusiastic the manufacturer may be about the benefits of a newly developed PD service program, overselling these to channel members should be avoided.

Reduction in Channel Member Inventory Requirements.   A well designed and responsive PD program can mean shortened channel member order cycles which in turn can mean lower inventories carried by the channel members. To the extent that a manufacturer can develop such a PD program to a greater degree than its competitors, the possibility exists for channel members to gain an economic advantage by doing more of their business with this particular manufacturer.[18] Here again, however, the manufacturer must actually be able to deliver on such a claim. One manufacturer that did this was the Norge division of Borg-Warner Co.:

Norge, after conducting a study of its existing physical distribution system, decided to add more regional warehouses. While this increased its costs, which would eventually have to be reflected in higher prices to its dealers, the dealers were still happy with the change. The reason? The shorter order cycle time for shipment of the appliances from the larger number of warehouses to the retailers would enable them to carry smaller inventories and to increase their turnover. This positive result would be more than enough to offset the higher initial costs resulting from the change.[19]

---

[17] For a discussion dealing with this kind of issue see: Warren Blanding, "How Physical Distribution Helps Sales," *Sales and Marketing Management*, (13 September 1976): 95–100.

[18] Stewart, "Physical Distribution," p. 67.

[19] "New Strategies to Move Goods," *Business Week*, (24 September 1966): 115.

Strengthening of Manufacturer–Channel Member Relationship.   A carefully designed PD program aimed at improving service to the channel members can serve as one of the most tangible signs of the manufacturer's concern and commitment to the channel members' success. In presenting a proposed PD program to the channel members, the manufacturer should emphasize that the program was conceived to help them (the channel members) to be more successful. When presented in this light, a newly proposed PD program can be a potent marketing tool for building channel member support. Indeed, the role of better PD management in strengthening the overall marketing efforts of channel members is growing in importance. Thus, it offers manufacturers who can make use of PD management for this purpose an increasingly powerful tool for building channel member support and loyalty. As McClure has pointed out:

"People in distribution should see themselves as viable management consultants to marketing in developing policies, procedures, and approaches to improve the overall effectiveness of the marketing effort.

The expertise residing within the distribution organization, properly utilized, can span the gap between mediocre marketing and marketing excellence.

The biggest need I foresee for the future of the marketing-distribution interface is the need for even more innovative procedures and systems."[20]

As these comments suggest, improved PD management offers great potential as a strategic marketing tool. But it will offer even greater potential to those manufacturers who are able to extend their superior PD capabilities to help channel members to improve *their* PD and marketing capabilities as well.

Monitoring the Physical Distribution System

In referring to the need to continually watch or monitor a PD system, Weeks coined a rule which he calls the "Great Physical Distribution Management Paradox" or GPDMP. The rule is as follows:

Any given PD strategy, carefully thought out, wholeheartedly accepted, honestly implemented, thoroughly de-bugged and scrupulously maintained will be hopelessly inappropriate five years later.[21]

While Weeks' GPDMP rule is not meant to be taken literally, it does point up the difficult problem of keeping PD systems—even well designed up-to-date ones—consistent with channel member needs. As McClure states in referring to this same issue:

[20]Donald McClure, "Costs Force New Relation Between Distribution, Marketing," *Marketing News*, (3 November 1978): p. 1.
[21]Jonathan Weeks, "Planning for Physical Distribution," *Long Range Planning*, (June, 1977): 65.

"The sophistications of the 70's will be forgotten quickly as new technology and resources take over in the 80's. There is need today for an improved monitoring system to measure [PD] service and monitor it on an ongoing basis."[22]

Clearly then, PD systems once put in place cannot be simply left alone with the expectation that they will continue to work well and meet channel member needs indefinitely. Rather, PD systems must be continuously monitored both in terms of how successfully they are performing for the manufacturer and, just as importantly, how well they are meeting changing member needs. Thus, as part of an overall attempt to learn about the needs and problems of channel members (see pp. 220–227 in Chapter 8), the channel manager should continually monitor the channel members' reactions to PD programs. The principal objectives of such monitoring are to appraise the channel members' responses to the program and to find out whether modifications are needed.

The most effective way of doing this is to conduct a survey of a sample of channel members. If the number of channel members is small, it may be feasible to include all of them. The survey dealing with the PD program may be conducted as part of an overall marketing channel audit or separately. In either case, the key areas of customer service at which the PD program was aimed should be examined. The manufacturer must be careful, however, to follow through by actually making improvements in those areas of PD service that channel members feel are deficient. According to a major study of channel member responses to such PD surveys, channel member satisfaction with the manufacturer's PD program tends to *decrease* when surveyed channel members who pointed out deficiencies see no subsequent attempts made by the manufacturer to remedy those deficiencies.[23] In a sense then, PD surveys may open a Pandora's Box by focusing channel members' attention on the manufacturer's PD program and making them more sensitive to its shortcomings. To "close" the box successfully, the manufacturer must make it clear to the channel members that it intends to take prompt and effective action to overcome any shortcomings in the PD program.

A manufacturer is more likely to take such actions if it views the PD program as an *integral part* of the overall marketing program. As Magee states:

"Marketing policy and tactics have a fundamental and controlling influence on the design and operation of physical distribution systems. Marketing requirements establish the servicing limits within which the system must work. Marketing tactics impose loads on the physical distribution system which substantially affect its costs. Marketing man-

---

[22] McClure, "Costs Force New Relation," p. 1.

[23] William D. Perreault, Jr., and Frederick A. Russ, "Physical Distribution Service in Industrial Purchase Decisions," *Journal of Marketing*, (April, 1976): 10.

agement, therefore, has and must accept a substantial responsibility for the design and operating costs of the physical distribution system."[24]

The close ties between PD and marketing management which Magee refers to should exist regardless of where the manufacturer chooses to place the PD function on the organization chart.[25] Thus, whether PD is structured as part of the marketing department, production department, or as a separate department within the total organization, the PD program should still be viewed as a vital component of the manufacturer's overall marketing strategy. As such, PD can play a crucial role in fostering channel member support and cooperation or in undermining such support and cooperation. The channel manager must therefore pay careful attention to the marketing strategy implications of the firm's PD system to assure that it promotes the former outcome rather than the latter.

Summary

The physical distribution function in a manufacturing firm consists of a number of activities concerned with providing product availability in the right quantities, at the right times, and in the right places. These activities include transportation, warehousing, materials handling, packaging, inventory control, order processing and others. Careful management which stresses an integration of these activities is necessary to provide a high level of physical distribution service at an acceptable cost.

Channel management interfaces with PD management in at least four areas: (1) defining channel member service standards, (2) making sure a proposed PD program meets these standards, (3) selling of the program to the channel members, and (4) monitoring the program once instituted to determine if it continues to meet channel members' service needs.

With regard to the first interface, the key issue facing the channel manager is to determine precisely what types and levels of PD service are desired by the channel members. Separate surveys of channel members or surveys conducted as part of an overall effort to learn about channel members' needs and problems (see Chapter 8) offer an effective approach for dealing with this issue. Having channel members react to several alternative prospective PD service programs is another approach which can be used along with, or instead of, channel member surveys.

The second interface, making sure that a proposed PD service program actually meets channel member PD service needs, calls for a careful analysis of the PD service program from the *channel members'* perspective to see if it actually meets the needs it was designed to serve. Many PD systems, though modern and sophisticated from the manufacturer's viewpoint, may still be inadequate from the channel members' standpoint.

[24] John F. Magee, *Physical Distribution Systems* (New York: McGraw-Hill, 1967), p. 25.

[25] For a discussion of the PD function in a firm's organization see: Daniel W. DeHayes, Jr. and Robert L. Taylor, "Making Logistics Work in a Firm," *Business Horizons*, (June, 1972): 37–46.

Turning now to the third interface, selling the channel members on a new PD program, the main task facing the manufacturer is to convince the channel members of the value of the system and thereby secure their cooperation and support in implementing the program. No matter how good a manufacturer thinks the PD program is, it should not assume that the program will sell itself. Channel members must be convinced of its value. If the manufacturer can convince channel members that the PD program will help to: (1) minimize out of stock occurrences, (2) reduce channel member inventory requirements, and (3) strengthen the manufacturer-channel member relationship in a way that benefits the channel members, the manufacturer has a potent set of appeals for selling the PD system to the channel members. Of course, the PD system must actually be able to deliver on these promises.

Finally, interface four, monitoring the PD program, focuses on the need to continually watch a PD program that has been put in place. No matter how well designed and implemented the system is, over time, channel members' changing needs and problems are sure to create shortcomings in the PD system. Careful monitoring of the system should help to spot such deficiencies early before they become severe enough to significantly endanger the effectiveness and efficiency of the PD program and, even more importantly, before they undermine the relationship between the manufacturer and the channel members.

Regardless of how a manufacturer treats the PD function from the standpoint of its own internal organization structure, there is no escaping the PD-marketing interface. Consequently, the channel manager who is concerned with the channels aspects of the manufacturer's overall marketing strategy has an important role to play in influencing the firm's PD strategy.

Discussion Questions

1. Physical distribution is much more than simply shipping products to customers. Explain.
2. Discuss the relationship between channel management and physical distribution management. Is one of these areas more important than the other?
3. Identify and discuss the four major areas of interface between channel management and physical distribution management.
4. Why is the task of defining physical distribution service standards for channel members a channel management issue as well as a PD issue?
5. What role should be played by the channel manager in the design of a PD service program for the channel members?
6. Why might it be necessary to sell the channel members on a proposed PD program? What kinds of appeals might be used?
7. PD programs in recent years have incorporated many sophisticated developments closely associated with computer technology. Some of

these PD programs have been described in the literature in very optimistic terms, to say the least. Discuss the implications of this statement in terms of channel member expectations for proposed PD programs and how these expectations might affect their evaluations of the programs after they have been instituted.

8. Effective monitoring of a newly instituted PD program requires that the PD function be subsumed under the marketing department in the firm's organization structure. Discuss this statement.

Part Four
Appraising the Marketing Channel

This fourth part of the text "steps back" and looks at channel performance and basic changes occurring in marketing channel systems.

Chapter 13 leads off with a comprehensive discussion of the evaluation of channel member performance.

Chapter 14 concludes the text by discussing developments in vertical marketing systems—how they already have affected and how they will continue to affect the management of marketing channels.

Chapter 13
Evaluating Channel Member Performance

The evaluation of channel member performance is just as important as the evaluation of employees working within the firm. For clearly, the success of the firm in meeting its overall long and short-term goals is dependent upon the performance of both groups. The only differences are that in evaluating channel members, the channel manager is dealing with independent business firms rather than employees and the setting of the evaluation process is interorganizational rather than intraorganizational. These distinctions make the evaluation of channel member performance somewhat different from the evaluation of employee performance within the firm.

In this chapter we discuss the evaluation of channel member performance in the interorganizational setting of the marketing channel. Our emphasis will be on pointing out appropriate criteria for performance evaluation and on the application of these criteria for measuring channel member performance.

Before proceeding, however, we will briefly discuss two important background issues related to channel member performance evaluation. These are: (1) factors affecting the scope and frequency of evaluations and (2) the distinction between monitoring channel member performance and comprehensive performance evaluation.

Factors Affecting Scope and Frequency of Evaluations

Four major factors affect the scope and frequency of channel member evaluations. These are:[1]

1. Degree of the manufacturer's control over the channel members
2. Relative importance of the channel members
3. Nature of the product
4. Number of channel members

Degree of Control

The degree of control a manufacturer has over its channel members plays a major role in determining the scope and frequency of its evaluations. If control is based on strong contractual agreements with channel members, the manufacturer is in a position to demand a great deal of information on channel member performance on virtually every aspect of the channel member's operations (sometimes including data on the principal's personal finances). Further, those manufacturers enjoying strong acceptance for their products or a dominant market position have a great deal of leverage over the channel members. This makes it much easier for the manufacturers to demand—and get—extensive channel member performance data that enable them to conduct a more comprehensive evaluation.

On the other hand, a manufacturer who lacks strong channel control based on contractual commitments, and is lacking strong market acceptance for its products, can exert much less control over channel members. Because many channel members do not view the manufacturer's particular brand of products as of great importance to them, they are less likely to be willing to take the time and trouble necessary to provide the manufacturer with comprehensive performance data for a full scale channel member evaluation.

Importance of Channel Members

For the manufacturer who sells all of its output through intermediaries, the evaluation of channel members is likely to be much more comprehensive than for those manufacturers who rely less on intermediaries. This is because the firm's success in the market is so directly dependent on the channel members' performance. A manufacturer of major appliances, for

---

[1]Roger Pegram, *Selecting and Evaluating Distributors* (New York: National Industrial Conference Board, 1965), pp. 103–104.

example, that markets its entire output through distributors and dealers is likely to perform a careful and thorough evaluation of these channel members because they provide the only access to the company's final markets. On the other hand, a tire manufacturer that uses its own company-owned retail stores to market the major portion of its products and relies on independent automotive stores for only a very small percentage of its sales may very well perform only a cursory evaluation of these dealers.

Nature of Product

Generally, the more complex the product, the broader the scope of the evaluation and vice versa. For example, a manufacturer of high-volume products of low unit value requiring little after-sale servicing may settle for routine sales data as the basis for an evaluation of channel members. On the other hand, a channel member handling an expensive and complex machine tool requiring a high degree of after-sales service is likely to be scrutinized by the manufacturer over a much broader range of criteria related to ultimate target market satisfaction. Further, for products of very high unit value, the gain or loss of a single order is important to the manufacturer. In such cases, the manufacturer is likely to evaluate the channel member's performance very carefully, particularly if an order has been lost.

Number of Channel Members

For the manufacturer using intensive distribution, channel member evaluation may be little more than a cursory "once over lightly" look at current sales figures. Some manufacturers find it necessary to use an "evaluation by exception" process whereby a more thorough evaluation is reserved only for those channel members who show sales figures which are unusually out of line.

At the other extreme, manufacturers using highly selective distribution find that their close working relationship with their channel members gives them access to a broad range of data enabling them to conduct very comprehensive performance evaluations.

Performance Evaluation vs. Day to Day Monitoring

In his major study of channel member evaluations used by manufacturers, Pegram identified two basic types of evaluation approaches. He states:

"Though not always clearly separated in practice, two different types of distributor evaluations are in evidence in the procedures of participating manufacturers: (a) appraisals designed to assist management in maintaining current operating control of distributors' efforts, insofar as the sale of the company's products is concerned; and (b) overall performance reviews designed to give management a complete and, hopefully, objective analysis of each distributor's operations."[2]

The first type of evaluation is basically a routine day to day monitoring of the performance of the channel members based almost exclusively on sales criteria. Billings of sales to the channel members, reflected in standard sales analysis reports, furnish the basic data needed for this kind of evaluation.

Pegram goes on to describe the other type of channel member evaluation as follows:

"The second type of evaluation is concerned less with short-term guidance of that part of the company's sales program carried out by distributors than with an overall appraisal of each distributor's conformance to the manufacturer's ideal or established standard for outlets representing him."[3]

The second approach is a much broader and more comprehensive evaluation procedure which usually involves a number of other criteria besides sales. It is this kind of evaluation process with which we will be concerned in this chapter. To clearly distinguish this approach from the day to day monitoring of channel member sales performance, the second and more comprehensive approach will be referred to as a *channel member performance audit* throughout this chapter.

Channel Member Performance Audit

The channel member performance audit refers to a periodic and comprehensive review of channel member performance.[4] The audit may be done for one, several, or all of the channel members at the wholesale and/or retail levels. The frequency of the audit varies (see previous section), but seldom is it done more frequently than once per year, per channel member.

The channel member performance audit consists of three basic phases:

[2]Ibid., p. 102.
[3]Ibid.
[4]For a related discussion see: William G. Brown and E. D. Reiten, "Auditing Distribution Channels," *Journal of Marketing*, (July, 1978): 38–41.

Figure 13.1
Channel Member Performance Audit

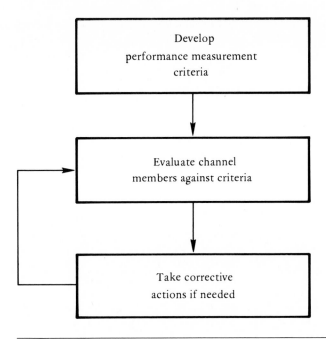

1. Developing criteria for measuring channel member performance
2. Periodically evaluating the channel members' performance against the criteria to measure performance
3. Recommending corrective actions to reduce the number of inadequate performances

Figure 13.1 provides a schematic overview of the channel member performance audit and the process is discussed in the remainder of this chapter.

Developing Criteria

While there are many possible criteria for measuring channel member performance, Pegram found that most manufacturers use a combination of the following:[5]

1. Sales performance of channel members
2. Inventory maintained by channel members

---

[5] Pegram, *Distributors*, pp. 109–125.

3.   Selling capabilities of channel members

4.   Attitudes of channel members

5.   Competition faced by channel members

6.   General growth prospects of the channel members

Sales Performance.   Sales performance is unquestionably the most important and commonly used criterion for evaluating channel member performance. Indeed if the channel member's sales performance is not adequate there may be little else that matters.

In examining the channel member's sales performance the channel manager should be careful to distinguish between: (1) the sales of the manufacturer to the channel member, and (2) the channel member's sales of the manufacturer's products to the channel member's customers. These two are not necessarily the same, and in fact, may be substantially different during a given period. Only in certain cases where there is very rapid turnover such as in the case of perishables do manufacturer-to-channel member sales offer a definitely reliable measure of the channel member's current sales volume. Whenever possible the channel manager should attempt to get sales data from the channel members on their sales of the manufacturer's products to their customers. The manufacturer's ability to get this information, however, is highly dependent on the degree of control exerted over channel members. In a contractual channel where the channel members are franchisees, the manufacturer may have a legal right to such information by virtue of the franchise contract. For example, the Southland Corporation, which franchises 7-Eleven stores, demands and gets detailed sales information from each of its franchised store units whenever it asks for it.[6] On the other hand, in traditional loosely aligned channels, the manufacturer's ability to obtain sales data may be quite limited. In this case, the manufacturer must use data on sales to the channel members as the best approximation of current channel member sales.

Regardless of which of these two types of sales data are used, the channel manager should evaluate sales data in terms of the following three comparisons: (1) the channel member's current sales to historical sales, (2) cross comparisons of a member's sales with other channel members, and (3) comparisons of the channel member's sales with predetermined quotas (if quotas were assigned).

In the case of historical comparisons, the channel manager should look for both total figures as well as specific figures by product line if such data are available. The more detailed the data the better, because the higher level of detail provided in breakdowns by product lines helps the channel manager to spot changing patterns of sales for his or her product line. Figure 13.2, for example, shows a form used by the ARO Corporation, a manufacturer of tool and hoist products, to evaluate the historical sales performance of its distributors. This form provides categories for

---

[6]"Convenience Stores: A $7.4 Billion Mushroom," *Business Week*, (21 March 1977): 61–64.

Figure 13.2
Form for Evaluating Channel Member Sales Performance

DISTRIBUTOR SALES PERFORMANCE
TOOL & HOIST PRODUCTS
197___ to 19____   TERR._____

FOR _____

_____

	PRODUCT CATEGORY	SALES ($000)					
1	FASTENING TOOLS						
2	PORTABLE DRILLS						
3	FIXTURED TOOLS						
4	ABRASIVE TOOLS						
5	HOISTS						
6	POWER MOTORS						
7	SPECIALTY TOOLS						
8	CUSTOM TOOLS						
9	SERVICE PARTS						
10	TOTAL						
11	INFLATION FACTOR						
12	"REAL" TOTAL						

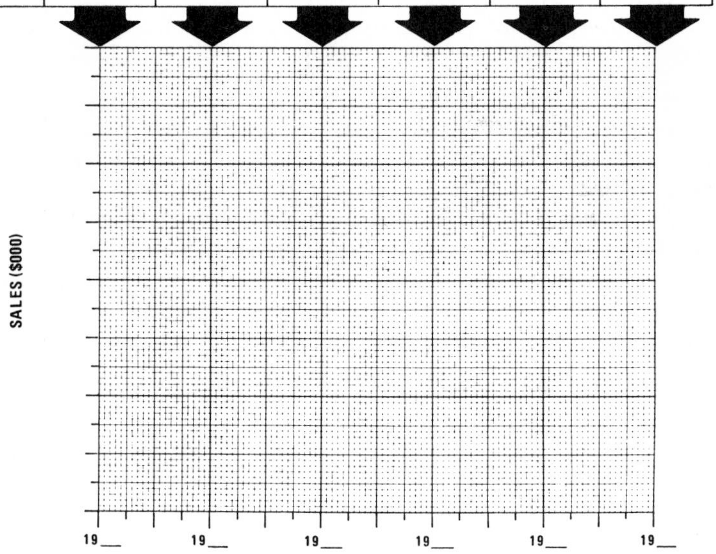

SALES ($000)

19___   19___   19___   19___   19___   19___

Source: Courtesy of Aro Corporation.

Figure 13.3
Small Number of Channel Members Accounting for Major Portion of Sales

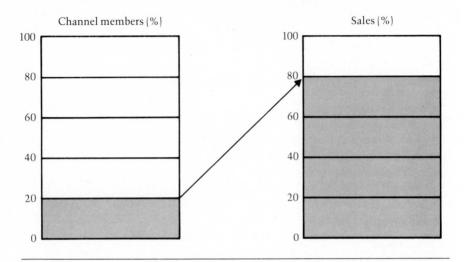

both total sales and sales by particular product. A graphical format is also provided which allows for a pictorial representation of historical sales patterns.

Comparisons of sales among the channel members is also a critically important measure of channel member performance because it is a quite common occurrence for a small number of the channel members to account for a major portion of the sales. One frequently cited ratio is that about 20 percent of the channel members account for 80–85 percent of sales.[7] Figure 13.3 illustrates this pattern.

Quite often this pattern results in a disproportionately high level of marketing costs relative to the sales generated by the low performing channel members with a resultant negative effect on the manufacturer's profit picture. Cross comparisons of channel members' sales performance, made on a regular basis, help to reveal these adverse patterns more readily.

Finally, if the manufacturer has set sales quotas for channel members (see Chapter 11, pp. 308–309), he should evaluate the channel member's actual sales performance in comparison with the quota. If the quota has been broken down by product lines, channel member performance for each category should also be examined. Further, when comparing the channel member's sales performance vs. the quota, the channel manager should look not only at the ratio itself, but also consider it in light of the performances turned in by other channel members on quota attainments.

[7] See for example: Charles H. Sevin, *How Manufacturers Reduce Their Distribution Costs* (Washington, D.C.: Department of Commerce, Marketing Division, Office of Domestic Commerce, Economic Service, No. 72, 1958), p. 1.

If the quota attainment ratio is generally low for a majority of the channel members, the problem is more likely to be a reflection of an unrealistically high quota rather than poor channel member performance.

Inventory Maintenance. Maintaining an adequate level of inventory is another major indicator of channel member performance. Essentially, the manufacturer wants the channel member to live up to the inventory stocking requirements specified in the original agreement between the manufacturer and the channel member. Some of these agreements are quite formal and are manifest in a dealer or distributor contract between the manufacturer and channel members. Figure 13.4, for example, illustrates a comprehensive distributor agreement contract used by Hewitt-Robins Corporation for its distributors. Item 5 (Stocking Requirements) deals with the inventory maintenance responsibilities of the channel members. Based on an agreement such as this, an individualized schedule of inventory requirements is worked out between the manufacturer and channel member based on the sales potential estimated for the territory. The channel member is then expected to abide by this agreement and is evaluated accordingly. Failure by the channel member to live up to the agreement is often viewed as a serious matter by the manufacturer. For example, consider the comment made by an executive of Rockwell Manufacturing Company:

"If a distributor isn't stocking he is asked why. If he continues to carry little, or stock not commensurate with demand among his customers and his marketing area, he may be dropped."[8]

In those cases where agreements on channel member inventories were not originally formalized in a contract, maintenance of inventory is still an important criterion for evaluation. However, in the absence of the formal contract, the manufacturer has less recourse to take action against channel members whose performance is inadequate in this area. Thus, if the manufacturer puts a great deal of weight on inventory maintenance as a criterion of channel member performance, an attempt should be made to include this in a formal agreement with the prospective channel member during the selection phase of channel design (see Chapter 6). Of course, many small and less dominant manufacturers lack the power to get potential channel members to agree to strict inventory stocking requirements. Actually checking on the level of inventory maintained by the channel member may range from being quite simple to very difficult. In the case of manufacturers dealing with a small number of channel members at the wholesale level, a check of channel member inventory levels can often be done by the field sales force as part of their regular sales calls. For those manufacturers selling through a large number of wholesale and/or retail channel members, the job can be much more formidable and

[8]Pegram, *Distributors*, p. 121.

Figure 13.4
Distributor Agreement Used by the Hewitt-Robins Corp.

HEWITT-ROBINS
INCORPORATED
A DIVISION OF LITTON INDUSTRIES

DISTRIBUTOR AGREEMENT

between Hewitt-Robins Incorporated (hereinafter called "Company") and

_____

of _____

(hereinafter called "Distributor.") It is mutually agreed as follows:

1. **PRODUCTS.** Schedule A sets forth the Products covered by this Agreement.

2. **TERRITORY.** Schedule B sets forth the territory for which Distributor is responsible.

3. **PRICES.** Company will sell and Distributor will buy the Products covered hereby at the Company's standard Distributor discount price in effect on the date of Company's acceptance of the order.

4. **PRICE CHANGES.** Company reserves the right to change its prices, transportation allowances and other terms and conditions of sale from time to time. In the event of any price revision, Company will endeavor to notify Distributor two weeks in advance of price change date, but in any event at least 48 hours in advance of price change date by telegraphic or verbal notice.

5. **STOCKING REQUIREMENTS.** Distributor shall maintain an adequate stock of the Products to meet the requirements of the trade in the territory set forth in Schedule B.

6. **TAXES.** Distributor will pay or reimburse Company for all federal, state, or municipal taxes or duties (other than real property, income, and franchise taxes) imposed upon any Product purchased hereunder or upon the manufacture or sale thereof.

7. **ORDER ACCEPTANCE.** All orders placed hereunder shall be in writing, or if placed by telephone or wire, shall be promptly confirmed in writing. Company reserves the right to accept or reject Distributor's orders and the same shall not be covered by this Agreement until accepted in writing by Company.

8. **ORDER CANCELLATION.** Distributor may cancel any order at any time before work is started or any costs are incurred by Company on Products ordered.

9. **ORDER DELAY.** Company shall not be responsible for delay or failure to fill orders in case of fire, labor troubles, war, casualty, emergency or any other cause beyond its control affecting production or delivery.

10. **TERMS.** Terms of payment, transportation allowances, and other terms and conditions of sale for the Products covered hereby as indicated in printed price and or discount sheets provided from time to time by Company and in its standard sales contract shall apply. Company reserves the right to contract with, to bill and to ship Distributor's customers directly and pay Distributor an agreed upon fee as payment in full in those cases where Distributor's financial condition or facilities are disproportionate to the size, value or length and terms of delivery or payment of an order.

11. **ENGINEERED CONTRACTS AND MERCHANDISE PACKAGE ORDERS.** The following types of orders, whether or not including any of the Products, are hereby excepted from the provisions of this Agreement. (a) Engineered Contracts. (b) Merchandise Package Orders. (i e. any order comprised of any combination or grouping of Company's standard products quoted and sold for a special lump sum.) On such orders, Distributor will be allowed an agreed upon discount or paid a fee, if in the opinion of Company, Distributor had made a significant contribution toward securing the order.

12. **DESTINATION BUSINESS.** Whenever a customer, having its main office outside of territory set forth in Schedule B, places an order from said main office, Distributor may be entitled to a fee on such order if Distributor, in the opinion of Company, has made a significant contribution toward securing such order.

13. **RELEASED AND EXCEPTED ACCOUNTS.** Company reserves the right to sell directly to Original Equipment Manufacturers, to federal, state and municipal governments, and to the industrial consumers listed on Schedule C attached hereto, without allowing any sales credit, commission or discount to Distributor. However, it is Company's policy to include such consumers, if any, within the terms of this Agreement when and if the consumer agrees to be serviced by Distributor or Distributor demonstrates that he can serve such consumer in a manner that better promotes the interest of the consumer, Distributor and Company.

14. **LIFE OF AGREEMENT.** This Agreement becomes effective on the date of execution by Company shown below and shall remain in effect until terminated by notice in writing mailed by either party to the other at least 30 days prior to the date of termination specified in the notice.

In the event that Distributor becomes overdue in making payments for Products sold hereunder or otherwise violates any term of this Agreement, Company may terminate this Agreement immediately or decline to make further shipments hereunder.

15. **MISCELLANEOUS.** This Agreement is to be construed under the laws of the State of New York. This memorandum sets forth the entire Agreement between the parties hereto, supersedes any existing agreement related to the subject matter hereto, is personal to the parties and cannot be assigned either voluntarily or by operation of law, without the written consent of Company. The provisions hereof may be altered, waived or modified only by a written instrument signed by a duly authorized officer of each party.

Hewitt-Robins Incorporated

By _____

_____   AUTHORIZED OFFICER
DISTRIBUTOR

By _____   Date _____
AUTHORIZED OFFICER

Source: Roger Pegram, *Selecting and Evaluating Distributors* (New York: The Conference Board, Business Policy Study No. 116, 1965), p. 17.

Table 13.1
Basic Questions for Evaluating Channel Member Inventory Performance

1. What is the total level of the channel member's inventory?
2. What is the breakdown by particular products in units and dollars?
3. How do these figures compare with the channel member's estimated purchases of related and competitive lines?
4. What is the condition of the inventory and inventory facilities?
5. How much old stock is on hand and what efforts have been made to move it?
6. How adequate is the channel member's inventory control and record keeping system?

may require the use of outside market research firms who offer a specialized inventory monitoring service such as the A.C. Nielsen Company, National Retail Trading Index, Inc. or similar firms (see Chapter 9, pp. 257–258). But regardless of whether manufacturers check the channel members' inventories themselves or have it done by an outside firm, they should, at a minimum, consider such inventory-related questions as those shown in Table 13.1.

Selling Capabilities. While channel members' overall sales performance (see above) offers a general idea of their sales capabilities, many manufacturers also believe it to be worthwhile to evaluate channel members' sales capabilities more directly by appraising their salespeople. This is particularly the case for channel members at the wholesale level. If individual sales records for channel members' salespeople can be obtained, the manufacturer has an excellent source of information. These individual ratings enable the manufacturer to discern patterns of sales performance and to develop an overall sales capability rating for each channel member which can then be used for cross comparisons among channel members. Obtaining such information, however, is often a problem because many channel members do not want to reveal or take the trouble to provide this information to the manufacturer.

Assuming the channel members are willing to provide the information, the manufacturer should pay particular attention to such factors as: (1) the number of salespeople the channel member assigns to the manufacturer's product line, (2) the technical knowledge and competence of the channel member's salespeople, and (3) salesperson interest in the manufacturer's products.

The number of salespeople that the channel member is willing to assign to the manufacturer's line provides insight into the exposure and market coverage the manufacturer's products are getting.

Technical knowledge and competence are usually appraised on a judgement basis ranging from excellent to poor. Some manufacturers, however, have developed a quantitative rating by using the amount of extra sales time requested by a channel member as a proxy measure of technical knowledge and competence. The relationship is viewed as being an inverse one—the more extra help requested, the lower the level of competence and vice versa. Whatever the method used, the most useful data result from evaluating the pattern over time. If the channel member's salespeople appear to be growing weaker in technical expertise, this may ultimately be reflected adversely in future sales performance data.

With respect to interest of salespeople, measures which the manufacturer can use include attendance at manufacturer sponsored schools, seminars, and clinics, reports from the channel member's customers, and the opinions of the manufacturer's field sales force. A declining level of interest on the part of the channel member's salespeople may well reflect a declining interest on the part of the channel member's *top management*. If this is the case, the future performance of the channel member is almost sure to be lower.

Attitudes of Channel Members.   The importance of favorable channel member attitudes towards the manufacturer and its product line is captured very well by William T. Young, Chairman of the Board of the Royal Crown Cola Company in referring to the company's 271 franchised bottler-distributors:

". . . the bottler is the key to the success of any soft drink company. The bottler has to be enthusiastic because it is a volunteer system. If he doesn't like the product, then we don't have a chance."[9]

Unfortunately, in practice channel member attitudes are usually not evaluated unless their sales performance is unsatisfactory. As Pegram points out:

"So long as distributor sales are going well, attitudes in themselves may not be closely examined on the assumption that interest and cooperation are probably at acceptable levels. It is when the performance of the distributor account falls short of that expected by the supplier that the latter is apt to start looking into attitudinal factors that may underlie the poor showing."[10]

The problem with this approach to the evaluation of channel member attitudes is, of course, that attitudinal problems will show up only after they have contributed to poor performance as reflected in sales data. In order to spot negative channel member attitudes before they affect performance, attitudes should be evaluated independently of sales data. One approach for doing this is to use the general marketing channel audit suggested by Cox et al.[11] (discussed previously in this text in a different

[9] "Royal Crown Cola Gets a Lot More Fizzy," *Business Week*, (14 March 1977): 85.

[10] Pegram, *Distributors*, p. 123.

[11] Revis Cox, Thomas Schutte, and Kendrik S. Few, "Towards the Analysis of Trade Channel Perception," *Combined Proceedings 1971 Spring and Fall Conference of the American Marketing Association*, ed. Fred C. Allvine (Chicago: American Marketing Association, 1972), pp. 189–193.

context; see Chapter 8, pp. 225–226). If a manufacturer uses this approach, which usually incorporates attitudinal factors, it will have attitudinal data available which may then be reviewed during a channel member performance audit.

Another approach suggested by Foster and Shuptrine is the use of special surveys aimed specifically at measuring channel member attitudes.[12]

Finally, though less satisfactory than the more formal approaches, the channel manager can use informal feedback from the sales force and the grapevine to keep track of channel member attitudes.

Competition.   There are two types of competition that the channel manager should consider when evaluating channel member performance: (1) competition from other intermediaries, and (2) competition from other product lines carried by the manufacturer's own channel members.

An evaluation of a channel member's performance relative to competition from other intermediaries in the same territory or trade area serves two purposes. First, it helps to put the channel member's performance in perspective. That is, by seeing how a particular channel member stacks up against the competition, the other performance criteria become much more meaningful. For example, a particular channel member may have been evaluated as having done poorly on sales volume. However, if it turns out that the territory is characterized by an extraordinary level of competition, that channel member's performance may be seen in a quite different light. Indeed it may be viewed as excellent under the circumstances. Some manufacturers, in fact, will go out of their way to provide extra support to those channel members who are faced with extraordinary competition.

Second, the comparative information obtained can be very useful in the event that the manufacturer decides to expand coverage by adding new channel members or if it is determined that it is necessary to replace some existing ones. While precise and detailed figures on the performance of competitors are difficult to obtain, general information and rank data can often be provided by the manufacturer's salespeople and sales management people. Often it involves simply asking the manufacturer's salespeople, district sales manager, or other sales management personnel to list, in order of importance, competitors of the manufacturer's channel members in particular markets. One large company in the consumer durable goods field, for example, asks for "names of next competitors you rank ahead of your dealer."[13]

The second type of competition, that from competitive lines carried by the manufacturer's own channel members, must also be evaluated very carefully. The main question to evaluate here is, of course, the relative support offered by the channel member for the manufacturer's products vs. the competition (see Chapter 9, pp. 257–260). If the channel

---

[12] Robert J. Foster and Kelly F. Shuptrine, "Using Retailers' Perception of Channel Performance to Detect Potential Conflict," *Proceedings of the American Marketing Association* (August, 1973), pp. 110–123.
[13] Pegram, *Distributors*, p. 126.

Table 13.2
Questions for Evaluating Channel Member Growth Prospects

1. Does the channel member's past performance indicate that sales of the manufacturer's products are likely to keep pace with those projected for the channel member's region, district, or trade area?
2. Has the channel member's overall performance been in keeping with the general level of business activity in the area?
3. Is the channel member's organization expanding or showing signs of improvement in facilities, capitalization, inventory maintained, and quality of lines represented?
4. Are the channel member's personnel not only growing in number but also becoming more highly qualified?
5. Is the channel member, and with it the manufacturer's representation in the area, likely to find itself in jeopardy some day because of the channel member's management, age, health, or succession arrangements?
6. Does the channel member have the adaptability and the overall capacity to meet market expansions that may occur in his area?
7. What are the channel member's estimates of his own medium and long range outlooks?

Source: Compiled from Roger Pegram, *Selecting and Evaluating Distributors* (New York: The Conference Board, Business Policy Study No. 116, 1965), pp. 127–128.

---

member seems to be putting too much support behind the competition and too little on the manufacturer's products, this fact will usually be reflected in other performance criteria evaluated by the manufacturer—particularly sales criteria. However, there is frequently a lag between the channel member's switch to an emphasis on competitive products and when the results show up in lowered sales figures. By spotting this change in emphasis early, the channel manager is in a much better position to take appropriate measures *before* the channel members' actions are reflected in the sales figures.

General Growth Prospects.   This final criterion, general growth prospects, focuses on the future prospects for channel member performance. The basic questions which the manufacturer should seek to answer in this type of evaluation are listed in Table 13.2.

In periodically evaluating most or all channel members in terms of the growth prospect questions presented in Table 13.2, the channel manager will gain a valuable overall view of the total channel system. This will provide highly useful information for formulating realistic objectives for the coming years and particularly to project the role of the channel members in the company's future marketing strategies.[14]

Other Criteria.   Although the six criteria discussed above are the most commonly used and provide coverage of most of the evaluation information needed by most manufacturers, several other criteria are also used in some cases. The most important of these are financial status of channel

---

[14]For further discussion on this see: Fredrick E. Webster, Jr., "The Role of the Industrial Distributor," *Journal of Marketing* 40 (July, 1976): 10–16.

members, their character and reputation, and the quality of service offered by channel members to their customers.

The financial status of channel members is normally carefully considered in the selection of channel members (see Chapter 6) and, if channel members have been paying their bills promptly, there is usually little need for further evaluation. In the face of changing economic and competitive conditions, however, the channel members' financial status can change significantly. So, some manufacturers attempt to make regular reviews of their channel members' financial positions to obtain an early warning of any possible financial deterioration which might adversely affect the manufacturer at a later date.

The character and reputation of channel members are also usually considered carefully before channel members are selected. But here again, this can change over time, especially if there has been a change in ownership or if major changes have occurred in a channel member's operating policies. If such developments have taken place for particular channel members, it may be wise for the manufacturer to investigate whether there has been any substantial change in these channel members' reputations. This can usually be done most effectively by talking with some of the channel members' customers.

Finally, the quality of service offered by the channel members to their customers is ultimately reflected in their sales performances.[15] If their service levels were inadequate, their customers would, in the long run, seek out other suppliers. But in the short run, declines in channel members' service levels may not show up in sales performance data because the channel members' customers may not as yet have found alternative sources of supply. Thus, if it is suspected that particular channel members may be slipping in providing service to their customers, the manufacturer should investigate this problem before it shows up in decreased channel member sales performance.[16]

Applying Performance Criteria

Having developed a set of criteria for channel member performance evaluation (see previous section), the channel manager must turn attention to evaluating the channel members in terms of these criteria. There are essentially three approaches which may be used to do this. These are:

1. Separate performance evaluations on one or more criteria
2. Multiple criteria combined informally to evaluate overall performance qualitatively

[15] See for example: Robert Harlow, "Distributors Are for Us," *Industrial Distribution*, (January, 1978): 87.
[16] For a related discussion see: Leonard J. Konopa, "Are Your Products and Channels Producing Sales?," *Small Business Administration Management Aids No. 203* (Washington, D.C.: Small Business Administration, May, 1974), pp. 5–8.

Table 13.3
Channel Member Performance Evaluation Using Criteria Separately

Criteria	Frequently Used Operational Performance Measures	
1. Sales performance	1. Gross sales 2. Sales growth over time 3. Sales made/Sales quota 4. Market share	No attempt made to combine the operational performance measures within or among the criteria categories.
2. Inventory maintenance	1. Average inventory maintained 2. Inventory/Sales 3. Inventory turnover	
3. Selling capabilities	1. Total number of salespeople 2. Salespeople assigned to manufacturer's product	

3.   Multiple criteria combined formally to arrive at a quantitative index of overall performance

Separate Performance Evaluations.   Separate performance evaluations measure channel member performance against one or more of the criteria discussed in the previous section of this chapter. No attempt is made, however, to combine these performance measures either formally or informally to arrive at an overall measure of performance.

This approach is most commonly used when the number of channel members is very large (as is often the case when intensive distribution is used by the manufacturer) and when the criteria employed are limited to no more than those of: (1) sales performance, (2) inventory maintenance, and (3) possible selling capabilities. This approach to channel member evaluation is portrayed in Table 13.3.

As shown in Table 13.3, the operational measures used to evaluate performance are applied separately. Consequently, when this approach is used, the evaluation of channel member performance consists of little more than a review of each channel member's performance on the relevant criteria.

The main advantage of this approach is that it is simple and fast once the necessary data on channel member performance have been gathered.[17]

A significant disadvantage, however, is that this separate approach offers little insight into overall performance. This is especially true when a channel member's performance is uneven across criteria. For example, it is quite possible for a channel member to show good sales performance but at the same time have a low inventory/sales ratio. This may mean that the channel member has been able to carry a relatively low level of inventory to achieve high sales volume. In effect the channel member

---

[17]For a discussion relevant to the gathering of channel member performance data see: Robert E. Weigand, "The Accountant and Marketing Channels," *The Accounting Review* 38 (July, 1963): 584–590.

may be using the manufacturer as a "warehouse"—by carrying as little inventory as possible and making many small orders. While this situation may be acceptable in the short run, in the longer run such channel member behavior is bound to show up in lower sales as competitive activity increases in the territory, or in ordinately high cost to the manufacturer for servicing this account.

Multiple Criteria Combined Informally.   The multiple criteria approach represents a step forward from separate evaluations of performance criteria in that an attempt is made to combine the various criteria into an overall judgement about channel member performance. The combining of the various performance measures within and among each of the criteria categories is done, however, only in an informal and qualitative manner. That is, the relative importance or weights assigned to each of the performance measures are not made explicit and no formal quantitative index of overall performance is computed. This approach which some may refer to as a "black box" type is portrayed in Figure 13.5.

The major advantages of this approach to evaluating channel member performance are its simplicity and flexibility. It is simple in the sense that no further formal procedures are necessary to combine the particular performance measures on the various criteria once they have been obtained. The channel manager can assign weights and "add" these on the basis of subjective judgement derived from experience. Flexibility exists in this

Figure 13.5
Channel Member Performance Evaluation Using Multiple Criteria Combined Informally

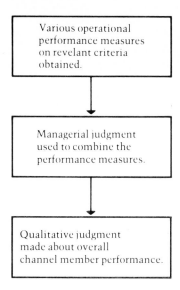

approach because the weights assigned to each criterion can reflect the changing relative importance of criteria.

There are, however, three major problems associated with this approach. The first involves the problem of trade-offs in performance ratings. That is, in a situation where a channel member has done well in terms of some criteria but less so on others, the absence of formal weighting procedures for each criterion can lead to highly arbitrary overall performance ratings.

A second and closely related problem is that of making performance comparisons among channel members. If the relative weights assigned to each criterion are not the same for each channel member, then comparisons of performance ratings among channel members are not valid.

Finally, this approach still does not offer a single quantitative index reflecting overall performance.

Multiple Criteria Combined Formally.   A formal rating using multiple criteria enables the channel manager to arrive at an overall quantitative performance rating for each channel member. The channel members can then be evaluated in terms of this overall performance rating.[18]

This approach consists of the following five steps:

1. Criteria and associated operational measures are decided upon.
2. Weights are assigned to each of the criteria to reflect their relative importance.
3. Each channel member being evaluated is then rated on each of the criteria on a scale of 0–10.
4. The score on each criterion is multiplied by the weight for that criterion. This yields weighted criterion ratings.
5. The weighted criterion ratings are summed to yield the overall performance rating (index) for each channel member.

This method is illustrated in Table 13.4.

If more than one operational measure is used to represent each criterion category, then weights may be assigned to each of the measures and the scoring done on each of the measures. Total scores for each criterion are then added together to arrive at the overall performance score. This is shown in Table 13.5 for the sales criterion with four operational measures used and the sales criterion receiving a weighting of .50.

The major advantages of this approach are that the weights assigned to the criteria and the associated operational performance measures are made explicit and an overall quantitative index of performance is obtained. Thus the major disadvantages associated with the informal approach to combining criteria are resolved. On the other hand, if several

---

[18]This approach is adapted from the Weighted Factor Score Method; see Philip Kotler, *Marketing Decision Making: A Model Building Approach* (New York: Holt, Rinehart and Winston, 1968), pp. 293–294.

Table 13.4
Weighted Criteria Method for Evaluating Channel Member Performance

Criteria	(A) Criteria Weights	(B) Criteria Scores	(A × B) Weighted Scores
		0 1 2 3 4 5 6 7 8 9 10	
1. Sales performance	.50	✔	3.5
2. Inventory maintenance	.20	✔	1.0
3. Selling capabilities	.15	✔	0.9
4. Attitudes	.10	✔	0.4
5. Growth prospects	.05	✔	0.15
		Overall performance rating	5.95

Table 13.5
Weighted Criteria Method for Evaluating Channel Member Performance Using Several Measures per Criterion

Criteria & Associated Operational Measures	(A) Weight	(B) Scores	(A × B) Weighted Scores
1. Sales performance		0 1 2 3 4 5 6 7 8 9 10	
a. Gross sales	.20	✔	1.20
b. Sales growth	.15	✔	1.05
c. Sales made/Sales quota	.10	✔	0.40
d. Market share	.05	✔	0.40
Total score for sales criterion			3.05
Total scores for each of the other criteria added			XX
Overall performance rating			XX

criteria categories are used along with several operational measures per criterion, the method can become cumbersome to use. Nevertheless, the overall performance index produced by this method enables the channel manager to analyze overall channel member performance in a number of useful ways. For example, the overall performance scores for each channel member can be ranked as shown in Table 13.6 or perhaps arranged in a frequency distribution as illustrated in Table 13.7.

There are also many other ways of summarizing these overall rating scores depending upon the information the channel manager needs. For example, the channel manager may be interested in the mean, median, or modal scores, various ranges and/or cross tabulations of the overall scores by the size of channel member, type of outlet (at the wholesale or retail level), or geographical territories.

Table 13.6
Hypothetical Ranking of Ten Channel Members Using the Weighted Criteria Method

Channel Member	Overall Performance Rating Score	Rank
A	6.72	1
B	6.31	2
C	6.00	3
D	5.95	4
E	5.20	5
F	4.97	6
G	4.25	7
H	3.87	8
I	3.01	9
J	2.56	10

Table 13.7
Hypothetical Frequency Distribution of 500 Channel Members' Overall Performance Ratings

Overall Performance Rating Range Categories	Number of Channel Members
8–10*	40
6 but under 8	63
4 but less than 6	234
2 but less than 4	111
below 2	52
Total	500

*Highest possible overall rating

Corrective Actions

In general, manufacturers should try to recommend corrective actions to improve the performance of channel members who are not meeting minimum performance standards. Terminations of these channel members should be used only as a last resort. As Pegram points out in discussing this issue:

"It has been noted that most manufacturers do not regard lightly a change in outlets. . . . Manufacturers emphasize that withdrawal of rec-

ognition is the last step after all attempts to rehabilitate an unsatisfactory outlet have been tried—and failed. (Cases where a 'target' or other superior distributor account, long wanted by the supplier, becomes available constitute the main exception to this attitude.)

Suppliers claim that they hate to drop a distributor (or dealer), not only because of the expense, time, and trouble involved—which may be considerable—but also because numerous terminations may reflect adversely on the manufacturer's business judgement in selecting his resellers."[19]

If corrective actions aimed at rehabilitating are contemplated rather than termination, the channel manager must attempt to find out why these channel members have performed poorly. In order to do this, however, a special effort must be made to learn about the needs and problems of poorly performing channel members to pinpoint the reasons for failure. These may range from basic management inadequacies on the part of the channel members to insufficient support of the channel members by the manufacturer. Indeed, both kinds of problems may exist. To find out, the channel manager must carefully analyze the channel member's needs and problems. Since we discussed this in Chapter 8, we need only recap briefly the major points. First, the channel manager cannot expect to obtain adequate information about channel member needs and problems by passively waiting to receive the information. Rather, the channel manager must develop concrete and practical approaches aimed at actively seeking information on channel member needs and problems.[20] Approaches such as building a formal channel communications network, conducting marketing channel audits, forming distributor advisory councils, and research conducted by outside parties (all of which we discussed in Chapter 8) are indicative of such approaches. Second, programs of channel member support must be congruent with channel member needs and problems. For example, the poor performance of a particular channel member may be traced to a poorly trained sales force. If this is the case, the keystone feature of any rehabilitation program developed by the manufacturer should stress training of the channel member's salespeople. Third, the manufacturer must exercise leadership through the skillful use of power. In the context of a corrective program to improve the effectiveness of a poorly performing channel member, the use of coercive power may have to be carefully avoided even though it may appear to offer quick short-term results. Finally the constraints imposed by the interorganizational setting of the marketing channel (see Chapter 8) must be understood if the channel manager expects to achieve a positive channel member response to the rehabilitation program.

If these principles are followed carefully, the probability of having a

[19] Pegram, *Distributors*, p. 219.
[20] See for example: Peter Craddick, "Distributors Move Aggressively Against Sluggish Sales," *Industrial Distribution*, (March, 1981): 49.

successful corrective program for poorly performing channel members is likely to be significantly higher.

Summary

The success of the firm using independent channel members to serve its target markets is dependent upon effective and efficient performance from its channel members. The evaluation of channel member performance is therefore a critically important part of channel management.

The scope and frequency of channel member performance evaluations are affected by: (1) the degree of the manufacturer's control over the channel members, (2) the relative importance of channel members, (3) the nature of the product, and (4) the number of channel members involved.

The evaluation of channel members can be done on a routine day-to-day basis whereby the evaluation consists essentially of monitoring channel members' sales. But to evaluate channel members thoroughly and effectively, the channel manager must not only monitor day-to-day performance but also periodically conduct a *channel member performance audit*. Such an audit consists of three basic phases: (1) developing appropriate criteria for evaluating performance, (2) applying the criteria to actually measure performance, and (3) recommending corrective actions to reduce the number of poorly performing channel members.

While there are many criteria that can be used to evaluate channel member performance, the most basic and important of these are: (1) sales performance of channel members to *their* customers, (2) the level of inventory maintained by channel members, (3) channel members' selling capabilities, (4) attitudes of channel members, (5) the way channel members deal with competitive product lines and competitors, and (6) the general growth prospects of channel members.

The application of these criteria to evaluate channel member performance can be approached in basically three ways: (1) separate performance evaluations on one or more criteria, (2) multiple criteria combined informally, and (3) multiple criteria combined formally to arrive at a quantitative index.

With separate performance evaluations, channel member performance is measured against one or more of the criteria but no attempt is made to combine these performance measures either formally or informally to arrive at an overall measure of performance.

The multiple criteria approach represents a step forward from separate evaluations in that an attempt is made to combine the various criteria into an overall judgement about channel member performance. The combining of the various performance measures is done, however, only in an informal and qualitative manner.

Finally, with the method of multiple criteria combined formally, criteria are combined through a weighting procedure, and an overall quantitative index of channel member performance is derived. This is the most sophisticated approach for measuring channel member performance.

Corrective action should be taken for those channel members who do not meet minimum performance standards. In order to develop the right kinds of corrective actions, the channel manager should attempt to uncover channel member problems which may underlie the performance problems and try to help the channel member to solve these problems.

Discussion Questions

1. Explain why (or why not) the evaluation of channel member performance is just as important as the evaluation of employees working within the firms.
2. Discuss the major factors affecting the scope and frequency of channel member performance evaluations.
3. Discuss the distinction between channel member performance evaluation and day-to-day monitoring of channel member performance. Is this distinction always clear-cut in practice?
4. Are sales *to* the channel member during a given period typically a good measure of the sales made *by* the channel members during the period? Discuss.
5. What kinds of sales data should the channel manager try to obtain to measure sales performance? What kinds of information are provided by these data?
6. Why should the channel manager be concerned about the failure of channel members to live up to inventory stocking agreements?
7. The only real measure of a channel member's selling capabilities is the sales achieved for the manufacturer's product. Do you agree or disagree? Discuss.
8. Discuss the rationale for including channel member attitudes as a criterion of channel member performance.
9. What kinds of questions should the channel manager seek to answer in appraising the general growth prospects of channel members?
10. Discuss the pros and cons of the three major approaches for applying performance evaluation criteria to measure channel member performance.

Chapter 14
Vertical Marketing Systems and Channel Management

In this final chapter we turn our attention to an analysis of some of the major trends affecting channel management. Rather than present a random collage of channel trends, however, our discussion will be structured around what is perhaps the most fundamental and important development—the growth of *vertical marketing systems*.[1] McCammon has described these as:

". . . professionally managed and centrally programmed networks, pre-engineered to achieve operating economies and maximum market impact. Stated alternatively, these vertical marketing systems are rationalized and capital-intensive networks designed to achieve technological, managerial, and promotional economies through the integration, coordination, and synchronization of marketing flows from points of production to points of ultimate use."[2]

In contrasting vertical marketing systems with conventional channels, Davidson has observed that:

[1] See for example: Johan Arndt, "Domestication of Markets: From Competitive Markets to Administered Interorganizational Marketing Systems," in *Contemporary Issues in Marketing Channels*, ed. Robert F. Lusch and Paul H. Zinzer (Norman, Oklahoma: University of Oklahoma, 1979), pp. 55–61.

[2] Bert C. McCammon, Jr., "Perspectives for Distribution Programming," in *Vertical Marketing Systems*, ed. Louis P. Bucklin (Glenview, Illinois: Scott, Foresman and Co., 1970), p. 43.

"Conventional channels are those fragmented networks in which loosely aligned and relatively autonomous manufacturers, wholesalers, and retailers have customarily bargained aggressively with each other, established trade relationships on an individual transaction basis, severed business relationships arbitrarily with impunity, and otherwise behaved independently.

Vertical marketing systems by way of contrast, consist of networks of horizontally coordinated and vertically aligned establishments which are managed as a system. Establishments at each level operate at an optimum scale so that marketing functions within the system are performed at the most advantageous level or position."[3]

Three types of vertical marketing systems (VMS's) have been identified:[4]

1. Administered
2. Contractual
   a. Retail cooperative organizations
   b. Wholesaler-sponsored voluntary chains
   c. Franchise systems
3. Corporate

Figure 14.1 shows this breakdown of vertical marketing systems schematically.

The accelerated growth of these systems has important implications for the design and management of marketing channels. The channel manager must therefore be familiar with these in order to make effective channel decisions. Accordingly, in this chapter we discuss vertical marketing systems and some of their major implications for the design and management of marketing channels.

Administered Systems

An administered vertical marketing system is in reality a conventional marketing channel that is characterized by effective interorganizational management. That is, it is a conventional channel whose members are more closely aligned than would be the case for the conventional channel. As Stern and El-Ansary point out in referring to administered channels:

"In administered systems, units [channel members] can exist with disparate goals, but a mechanism exists for informal collaboration on in-

---

[3]William R. Davidson, "Changes in Distributive Institutions," *Journal of Marketing*, 34 (January, 1970): 7.

[4]Bert C. McCammon, Jr., "The Emergence and Growth of Contractually Integrated Channels in the American Economy," in *Marketing and Economic Development*, ed. Peter D. Bennett (Chicago: American Marketing Association, 1965), pp. 496–515.

Figure 14.1
A Schematic Representation of Vertical Marketing Systems

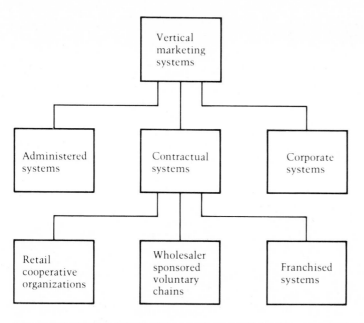

clusive goals. *Decision making takes place by virtue of the effective interaction of channel members in the absence of a formal inclusive structure. The locus of authority still remains with the individual channel members. The latter are structured autonomously but are willing to agree to an ad hoc division of labor without restructuring. As in conventional channels, commitment is self-oriented, but there is at least a minimum amount of system-wide orientation among the members.*"[5]

So, the feature distinguishing the administered marketing channel from the conventional channel is actually one of *degree* rather than a structural difference. The point at which the conventional channel stops and the administered one begins must be made on the basis of judgements about the degree of effective interorganizational management taking place in the channel. Figure 14.2 helps to portray this.

As Figure 14.2 shows, the distinguishing feature between conventional and administered channels is the level of interorganizational management. Thus given a cross-section of marketing channels at some point in time, those characterized by a low level of effective interorganizational management would be categorized as conventional channels, while those with higher levels would be classed as administered channels. For any

[5] Louis W. Stern and Adel I. El-Ansary, *Marketing Channels* (Englewood Cliffs, New Jersey: Prentice-Hall, Inc., 1977), p. 395.

Figure 14.2
Conventional Channels vs. Administered Channels

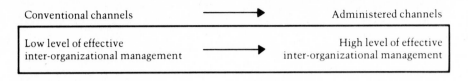

Table 14.1
Examples of Manufacturers Operating Administered Channels

1. Armstrong Cork Co.	Floor coverings
2. Baumritter	Ethan Allen furniture
3. Corning Glass	Cookware and china
4. General Electric	Household appliances
5. Kellogs	Cereal
6. Kraft Co.	Food products
7. Magnavox	Consumer electronics products
8. Scott	Lawn products
9. Sealy	Mattresses
10. Villager	Women's apparel

given channel studied over time, its transition from a conventional channel to an administered one would also be measured by positive increases in interorganizational management occurring during the time period.[6]

While interorganizational management practiced to the extent that it creates an administered channel does at times flow up the channel from the retailer to the manufacturer (e.g., Sears, J.C. Penney, Montgomery Ward, S.S. Kresge, Levitz Furniture), it is more commonly found flowing down the channel from manufacturers of consumer products. Frequently cited examples of the latter groups are shown in Table 14.1.

Channel Management Implications of Administered VMS's

While no precise data exist on the pervasiveness of administered VMS's, they are known to be growing in importance. The overriding implication of this development for the channel manager operating in a conventional channel may be stated as follows:

In order to compete effectively with firms who *are* operating administered channels (or other VM systems), the channel manager must take ac-

[6]For a related discussion see: Michael Etgar, "Differences in the Use of Manufacturer Power in Conventional and Contractual Channels," *Journal of Retailing*, (Winter, 1978): 49–62.

tions which either parallel or offset the advantages of those firms operating administered (or other) VM systems.[7]

If the first course is pursued, that is, if an attempt is made to parallel the actions of existing administered systems, the channel manager will, if successful, effect a transition from a conventional channel to an administered one. For example, the use of the *distribution programming* approach for motivating channel members discussed in Chapter 8 (pp. 233–241), if accepted by the majority of the firm's channel members, would foster the development of an administered channel. Hence one way for the channel manager operating in a conventional channel to compete against administered channels is to work toward creating an administered channel.

This option, however, is far more feasible for the large and powerful manufacturers than for the smaller, less powerful ones. For clearly, in order for manufacturers to operate an administered VMS, they must exercise a relatively high level of control over their channel members. Even excellent strategic plans and skillfully executed programs for motivating channel members are not likely to enjoy much success unless the manufacturer has the power to secure channel member cooperation.

The smaller manufacturer, unable to take a leadership role in developing an administered channel, still has, however, at least two options available for offsetting the differential advantages of administered VM systems:

1. The manufacturer may seek to align itself with large and powerful intermediaries at the wholesale or retail levels who *do* have the power to administer the channel.
2. The manufacturer may attempt to form a contractual marketing channel which will offer a legal power base to help secure channel member cooperation.

Each of these options is discussed below.

Channel Administration by Intermediaries.   Intermediaries at the wholesale and retail levels may be in a position to administer the channel to the advantage of a manufacturer that is unable to assume this position itself.[8]

Some wholesalers, for example, may be quite capable of administering the channel for the manufacturer, especially when a number of wholesalers join together to pool their resources in wholesaler cooperatives. An example of this can be found in the reemergence of the Crosley brand of appliances:

---

[7] For an empirical study lending support to this proposition see: Michael Etgar, "Effects of Administrative Control on Efficiency of Vertical Marketing Systems," *Journal of Marketing Research*, 13 (February, 1976): 12–24.

[8] See for example: Edwin H. Lewis, "Channel Management by Wholesalers," in *Marketing and the New Science of Planning*, ed. Robert L. King (Chicago: American Marketing Association, 1968), pp. 137–41.

Bringing the Crosley brand back is the handiwork of two distributors who found themselves without a refrigerator line when Aeronutronics Ford Corp. (the former Philco-Ford Corp.) bowed out of the business in August of 1976. These two distributors, one located in North Carolina and the other in Illinois, contacted all of the distributors who had previously handled the Philco line in an attempt to persuade them to join a cooperative that would pool their buying power in order to get appliances manufactured for them to be sold under their own private label. The name to be used for this private label brand of appliances would be Crosley, which the cooperative was able to lay claim to because the rights to it had lapsed.

The attempt to create the wholesalers cooperative was highly successful–thirty-five of the forty former distributors of Philco products joined along with eight non-Philco distributors. The buying power of this group was estimated to be about 36 million dollars for the first year with substantial increases expected for future years.

Seeing this high level of buying power, a number of manufacturers were virtually "waiting in line" to supply the wholesale organization with appliances made to its specifications and to be sold under the Crosley name.[9]

As this example suggests, a manufacturer of appliances who feels that it is unable to administer a channel which could compete successfully against the giants such as G.E., Westinghouse, Frigidaire, and Whirlpool may be far better off letting a wholesaler cooperative administer the channel.

Seeking administration of the channel from intermediaries at the retail level may also be a wise move for a manufacturer that lacks the capacity to administer the channel itself. Indeed there are today many large retailers who are quite capable of assuming this role. As Little points out in referring to large retailing organizations:

"They can control resources, buy time by utilizing staff specialists, and employ their resources in a manner to help the channel reduce conflict . . . [they] can employ research personnel to learn more about customers and markets and therefore reduce uncertainty and improve communications throughout the channel. They have the economic power to communicate and enforce a greater recognition of the system's [channel's] common goals. . . . They have the ability to enforce, through economic sanction, a reward and penalty system within the organizational structure. They are thus able to design and administer joint-decision efforts and responsibilities in a manner that can lead to less conflict than would likely be the case without their intervention."[10]

[9] "Distributors Bring Back the Crosley Appliance," *Business Week*, (31 January 1977): 92.
[10] Robert W. Little, "The Marketing Channel: Who Should Lead This Extra-Corporate Organization," *Journal of Marketing*, 34 (January, 1970): 34.

Well-known examples of retailing organizations who have this capacity to administer the channel include Sears, J.C. Penney, Montgomery Ward, K mart, Winn Dixie, Rexall Drugs, and Western Auto Stores. The manufacturer who, because of size or other factors, is unable to administer the channel may attempt to align with a large retailing organization which can.

Developing a Contractual Channel.   Because we will be discussing contractual systems in detail in the next section of this chapter, we need only briefly touch on it here.

Essentially, a manufacturer can substantially increase its power to influence channel members by acquiring a legal basis for the use of power. This can be done by formalizing the channel relationship in a legal contract. That is, if the manufacturer seeks to gain or hold the administrative leadership role in the channel, this posture can be buttressed with a contract that provides a legal power base.

Contractual Systems

Contractual marketing systems exist when the interorganizational relationships among firms are formalized—often with a written contract. Three basic types of contractual marketing systems have been discussed in the literature:

1.   Retail cooperative organizations
2.   Wholesaler sponsored voluntary chains
3.   Franchise systems

Retail Cooperative Organizations

Retail cooperative organizations are created when a group of retailers gets together and agrees to pool its buying power and contribute to the operation of the organization by collectively supporting its own wholesaling operations.

Retailer cooperatives are not a new phenomenon. Some date back to the early 1930's. The size and sophistication of these cooperatives have, however, increased significantly over the years. In several lines of trade they account for a major portion of the total retail sales. For example, in groceries, retailer cooperatives account for over 20 percent of total retail grocery sales in the United States.[11] Other lines of trade where retailer co-

---

[11] Theodore N. Beckman, William R. Davidson, and W. Wayne Talarzyk, *Marketing*, 9th ed. (New York: The Ronald Press, 1973), p. 265.

operatives play a significant role are hardware, drugs, major appliances, office supplies, and stationery.

In all of these fields, the traditional emphasis on group buying as the major advantage of retail cooperatives is increasingly being augmented with such services as group advertising, store engineering, record-keeping systems development, and managerial counseling. Indeed, some retail cooperative organizations now rival or even surpass some corporate chain store systems, not only in sales volume but also in the range of service offered to their members. American Hardware, for example, a cooperative group of hardware stores has some 2,700 hardware dealer members. To help its members compete successfully against the heavy competition in hardware retailing from chains of home centers, mass merchandisers, variety stores, drug stores, and other chain stores selling hardware merchandise, American Hardware developed a comprehensive strategic marketing program for its member dealers. A new name, ServiStar, was coined for the member dealers of American Hardware to convey a strong service image for its traditional hardware store dealers. Detailed strategies have also been developed for its members in such areas as merchandising, store layout, advertising, personal selling techniques, window display formats, and other areas to help convey the image of superior service available from ServiStar hardware stores.[12]

Wholesaler Sponsored Voluntary Chains

Wholesaler sponsored voluntary chains differ from retail cooperative organizations in two respects. First, the initiative for setting up the organization comes from the wholesaler rather than from the retailers themselves. Second, the wholesaler remains under private rather than cooperative ownership.

While wholesaler sponsored voluntary chains vary in some details of operation, the underlying basis is one of mutual cooperation. Generally, the retailers agree to concentrate a major portion of their purchases with the sponsoring wholesaler and each retail member usually agrees to sell all advertised products at the same price as all other members. Because of the concentrated buying power made possible by the voluntary association, the retailers are often able to buy at prices which help them to compete with corporate chain store systems.

Wholesaler sponsored voluntary chains date back to the 1930's, but in more recent years their scope and sophistication in offering a complete range of services to their members have increased significantly as has been the case with retail cooperative organizations (see previous section). Table 14.2, for example, lists some of the services frequently offered by the modern wholesaler sponsored voluntary chain.

As is the case for retail cooperative organizations, wholesaler spon-

---

[12]Bert Rosenbloom, *Retail Marketing* (New York: Random House, 1981), p. 134.

Table 14.2
Typical Services Offered by Wholesaler Sponsored Voluntary Chains to Their Member Retailers

1. Store identification material (such as signs and decals)
2. Model stock plans
3. Seasonal merchandising programs
4. Store location research
5. Store planning services
6. Complete store operations manuals
7. Advertising and sales promotion programs
8. Financial assistance and specialized programs
9. Accounting and management information systems services
10. Use of wholesaler's computer facilities
11. Training for store manager and employees
12. Assistance in the sale of the retailer's business in the event of death or retirement.

Table 14.3
Selected Wholesaler Sponsored Voluntary Associations in the Drug and Hardware Fields

Drugs	Hardware
Associated Druggists	American Wholesale Hardware
Community Shield Pharmacies	Coast-to-Coast
Economost	Farwell, Ozman, Kirk & Co.
Family Service Drug Stores	Gamble-Skogmo
FIP	Pro
Good Neighbor Pharmacies	Sentry
Sell-Thru Guild	Trustworthy
Triple A	Western Auto Stores
United Systems Stores	
Velocity	

sored voluntary chains are most prominent in the grocery trade (e.g., Independent Grocer's Alliance (IGA), Red and White, Spartan, Super Value, Clover Farm, and Super Duper). They are also of growing importance in the drug and hardware fields, however. Table 14.3 lists some of the major wholesaler sponsored voluntary chains in these fields.

To gain additional insight into the operation of the modern wholesaler sponsored voluntary association, consider the case of the Drug Guild:

Drug Guild functions as a wholesaler whose primary goal is to help the independent druggist compete against the chains.

Drug Guild, which supplies independents only, has become one of the top wholesalers in the tough New York–New Jersey Metropolitan

Table 14.4
Franchise Sales in the United States: 1978–1980

Kinds of Franchised Business	1978		
	Total	Company-Owned	Franchisee-Owned
Total–All Franchising	283,362,104	35,608,208	247,753,896
Automobile and truck dealers	145,274,000	1,105,000	146,169,000
Automotive products and services	6,803,045	2,221,505	4,581,540
Business aids and services	5,046,385	688,509	4,357,876
Accounting, credit, collection agencies and general business systems	148,039	6,836	141,203
Employment services	1,113,631	406,834	706,797
Printing and copying services	236,598	14,305	222,293
Tax preparation services	242,142	129,235	112,907
Real estate	3,031,012	81,478	2,949,534
Miscellaneous business services	274,963	49,821	225,142
Construction, home improvement, main-tenance and cleaning services	1,269,384	174,866	1,094,518
Convenience stores	5,012,589	2,886,746	2,125,843
Educational products and services	284,342	60,909	223,433
Restaurants (all types)	21,100,788	6,733,545	14,367,243
Gasoline service stations	60,884,000	12,177,000	48,707,000
Hotels and motels	5,651,477	1,742,812	3,908,665
Campgrounds	112,964	6,386	106,578
Laundry and drycleaning services	244,641	16,163	228,478
Recreation, entertainment and travel	290,882	22,603	268,279
Rental services (auto-truck)	2,526,423	1,561,029	965,394
Rental services (equipment)	236,299	74,888	161,411
Retailing (nonfood)	9,334,697	3,573,041	5,761,656
Retailing (food other than convenience stores)	6,119,548	1,728,747	4,390,801
Soft drink bottlers	10,887,000	762,000	10,125,000
Miscellaneous	283,640	72,459	211,181

*1980 data estimated by respondents.

Source: *Franchising in the Economy 1979–1981* (Washington, D.C.: U.S. Department of Commerce, Bureau of Domestic Commerce), p. 27.

market. Over 270 stores now belong to the association, with some 175 waiting in the wings to join.

In commenting on the success of the Drug Guild organization, Roman Englander, its president, states: "Actually the philosophy behind Drug Guild is very simple and can be summed up in two words–mutual need. We need the independent druggists as much, if not more, than they need us. Through us they get the opportunity to create a chain store image and can save enough in their buying to make it pay. So, in a sense they can have their pill and eat it too–jockeying themselves into a position where they can compete successfully against the chains and make money while they are doing it."

Some of the major services offered by Drug Guild to its members include the following:

	1979			1980*	
Total	Company-Owned	Franchisee-Owned	Total	Company-Owned	Franchisee-Owned
312,187,884	39,546,507	272,641,377	332,952,246	46,811,308	286,140,938
155,738,000	942,000	154,796,000	143,136,000	887,000	142,249,000
7,226,822	2,162,771	5,064,051	7,235,479	2,250,819	4,984,660
6,280,412	871,930	5,408,482	7,018,469	985,243	6,033,226
127,990	5,756	122,234	117,680	6,746	110,934
1,417,001	541,100	875,901	1,586,234	610,605	975,629
302,843	10,684	292,159	348,410	11,989	336,421
255,902	136,852	119,050	292,425	156,505	135,920
3,840,116	122,471	3,717,645	4,281,349	135,008	4,146,341
336,560	55,067	281,493	392,371	64,390	327,981
1,382,273	230,479	1,151,794	1,430,061	223,263	1,206,798
6,131,885	3,604,642	2,527,243	6,908,903	4,100,945	2,807,958
266,548	62,684	203,864	319,398	68,246	251,152
24,765,916	8,076,401	16,689,515	27,715,761	8,921,173	18,794,588
71,894,000	13,660,000	58,234,000	96,338,000	18,304,000	78,034,000
6,625,437	1,971,093	4,654,344	7,380,492	2,334,792	5,045,700
98,558	6,835	91,723	108,428	7,602	100,826
268,283	21,857	246,426	284,915	23,998	260,917
359,573	27,957	331,616	433,312	30,731	402,581
2,889,601	1,762,482	1,127,119	3,070,655	1,832,663	1,237,992
289,485	90,429	199,056	323,160	96,347	226,813
8,901,928	3,294,139	5,607,789	9,461,270	3,679,553	5,781,717
6,512,121	1,871,880	4,640,241	7,175,633	2,033,651	5,141,982
12,194,000	853,000	11,341,000	14,146,000	990,000	13,156,000
363,042	35,928	327,114	466,310	41,282	425,028

1. A 35,000 item inventory to choose from as compared with 20,000 items stocked by the average drug wholesaler.
2. Weekly ads (purchased by Drug Guild and manufacturers) appearing in newspapers, radio, and T.V. promoting the products carried by members.
3. Participation in the distribution of some 10 million circulars per year to the public.
4. Deliveries five times a week.
5. Billing on a twice monthly basis.
6. Guild sponsored seminars on finance, security, merchandising and remodeling.[13]

[13]"Drug Guild: Champion of the Independents," *American Druggist*, (February, 1977): 45–46.

Franchise Systems

Franchising, as the term is used today, refers to a comprehensive method of distributing goods and services. It involves a *continuous and contractual* relationship in which a franchisor provides a licensed privilege to do business plus offers assistance in organizing, training, merchandising, management and other areas in return for a specific consideration from the franchisee.[14] (See appendix at the end of this chapter for an example of a franchise contract.)

Franchise systems, though enjoying spectacular growth in recent years, have been in existence for a long time. Indeed, one of the first companies to make use of franchising was the Singer Sewing Machine Company, which soon after the Civil War established a number of franchised retail outlets. It was not until the advent of the automobile, however, around the turn of the century, that franchised distribution began to have a significant impact on marketing in the United States.

The fledgling automobile industry found that the establishment of franchised dealers provided an ideal means to achieve rapid national distribution for their products. When auto sales created a widespread need for gasoline and lubricating products, the petroleum companies also found franchising to be an effective method of distribution.[15] The dealer networks selling automobiles and petroleum even today continue to dominate franchising, accounting for almost 72 percent of total franchise sales in 1980. When the other early users of franchising, namely soft drink bottlers, are added to this total, the three groups (autos, petroleum and soft drinks) account for over 76 percent of total franchise sales. Table 14.4 offers a more complete breakdown of franchise sales for different product groupings for 1980 and two earlier years.

Table 14.5 shows the percentage of sales growth for each kind of franchised business from 1978 to 1980. As shown in the table, the highest percentages of sales growth (30 percent or over) have occurred for business aids and services, convenience stores, restaurants, gasoline service stations, hotels and motels, recreation, entertainment and travel, equipment rentals, soft drink bottlers, and miscellaneous franchised businesses. The table also shows that auto and truck dealers and campground franchises actually declined in sales over this period. The very high percentage of sales increase for gasoline service stations is quite misleading because much of the increase reflects the almost doubling of gasoline prices between 1978 and 1980. Hence, the increase does not truly reflect real sales growth but rather price inflation. When the number of gasoline service station establishments is compared between 1978 and 1980, a decline is

---

[14] For additional perspectives on defining the modern franchise system see: E. Patrick McGuire, *Franchised Distribution* (New York: The Conference Board Report Number 523, 1971), pp. 4–5; P. Ronald Stephenson and Robert G. House, "A Perspective on Franchising," *Business Horizons,* (August, 1971): 35–42.

[15] McGuire, *Franchised Distribution,* pp. 2–3.

Table 14.5
Comparisons of Rates of Sales Growth for Selected Kinds of Franchises: 1978–1980

Kinds of Franchised Business	Percent of Sales Increase or Decrease
Automobile and truck dealers	−1.5
Automotive products and service	6.5
Business aids and services	39.1
Construction, home improvement, maintenance and cleaning services	12.7
Convenience stores	37.8
Educational products and services	12.3
Restaurants (all types)	31.4
Gasoline service stations	58.2
Hotels and motels	30.6
Campgrounds	−4.0
Laundry and drycleaning services	16.5
Recreation, entertainment and travel	49.0
Rental services (auto-truck)	21.5
Rental services (equipment)	36.8
Retailing (nonfood)	1.4
Retailing (food other than convenience stores)	17.3
Soft drink bottlers	30.0
Miscellaneous	64.4

Source: Derived from Table 14.4

noticed of some 13,760 units (172,300 in 1978 vs. 158,540 in 1980), a decrease of almost eight percent. The only other franchised businesses for which the number of establishments declined between 1978 and 1980 were automobile and truck dealers, automotive products and services, campgrounds, and soft drink bottlers (see Table 14.6).

From the franchisor's point of view, three major reasons are often cited for distributing via the franchise method: (1) capital advantages, (2) potential to reduce distribution costs, and (3) the possible high level of managerial motivation fostered by franchising.[16]

Capital advantages are often cited as *the* most important reason for adopting franchised distribution. The acquisition of funds through franchising does not dilute ownership in the business to the same degree as equity financing through the sale of securities to the public. Further, it does not create the indebtedness attendant to borrowing which may be too burdensome for the firm to carry. A number of newly launched franchise companies, particularly in the fast food field, have thus been able to use the initial fees paid by their franchisees as a major source of working capital. Consider, for example, the case of the Kentucky Fried Chicken Corporation:

[16]McGuire, *Franchised Distribution*, pp. 6–8.

Table 14.6
Numbers of Franchised Establishments: 1978–1980

Kinds of Franchised Business	1978		
	Total	Company-Owned	Franchisee-Owned
Total–All Franchising	453,590	84,817	368,773
Automobile and truck dealers	33,500	250	33,250
Automotive products and services	47,215	4,576	42,639
Business aids and services	38,727	5,606	33,121
Accounting, credit, collection agencies and general business services	3,148	45	3,103
Employment services	3,775	910	2,865
Printing and copying services	2,362	140	2,222
Tax preparation services	8,592	4,225	4,367
Real estate	16,959	162	16,797
Miscellaneous business services	3,891	124	3,767
Construction, home improvement, maintenance and cleaning services	13,300	492	12,808
Convenience stores	14,125	9,479	4,646
Educational products and services	2,313	458	1,855
Restaurants (all types)	55,312	15,510	39,802
Gasoline service stations	172,300	32,737	139,563
Hotels and motels	5,220	986	4,234
Campgrounds	967	18	949
Laundry and drycleaning services	2,678	53	2,625
Recreation, entertainment and travel	4,113	70	4,043
Rental services (auto-truck)	7,202	1,937	5,265
Rental services (equipment)	1,523	153	1,370
Retailing (nonfood)	36,546	11,265	25,281
Retailing (food other than convenience stores)	14,733	969	13,764
Soft drink bottlers	2,096	70	2,026
Miscellaneous	1,720	188	1,532

*1980 data estimated by respondents.

Source: *Franchising in the Economy 1979–1981* (Washington, D.C.: U.S. Department of Commerce, Bureau of Domestic Commerce), p. 31.

John Y. Brown, former president of Kentucky Fried Chicken Corporation, has stated that it would have required $450 million for his firm to have established its first 2,700 stores if they would have been company owned. This sum was simply not available to his firm during the initial stages of its proposed expansion. The use of capital made available from franchisees, however, made the proposed expansion possible.[17]

Obtaining capital through the sale of franchises also offers the franchisor a high level of flexibility in the use of capital, and the capital accumulation can be accomplished rapidly. For example, the franchisor is able to use capital collected from new franchisees for national advertising, franchisee training, and other areas of operations. On the other hand, if the

[17] Ibid., p. 7.

	1979			1980*	
Total	Company-Owned	Franchisee-Owned	Total	Company-Owned	Franchisee-Owned
452,487	85,280	367,207	457,544	86,066	371,478
33,045	200	32,845	32,270	200	32,070
45,089	4,152	40,937	44,298	4,334	39,964
41,013	5,888	35,125	45,154	6,046	39,108
2,983	44	2,939	2,789	47	2,742
4,249	1,119	3,130	4,604	1,179	3,425
2,578	89	2,489	2,700	90	2,610
8,730	4,312	4,418	9,302	4,390	4,813
18,371	215	18,156	21,247	221	21,026
4,102	109	3,993	4,611	119	4,492
14,101	562	13,539	14,905	576	14,329
14,660	9,839	4,821	15,543	10,358	5,185
2,697	508	2,189	3,096	513	2,583
58,936	16,884	42,052	63,001	17,835	45,166
164,790	31,310	133,480	158,540	30,122	128,418
5,339	981	4,358	5,573	1,000	4,573
928	16	912	957	16	941
2,692	56	2,636	2,706	50	2,656
4,267	84	4,183	4,483	89	4,394
7,467	1,884	5,583	7,746	1,890	5,856
1,698	185	1,513	1,845	193	1,652
36,785	11,451	25,334	37,102	11,513	25,589
14,525	1,035	13,490	15,274	1,052	14,222
1,950	75	1,875	1,850	75	1,775
2,505	170	2,335	3,201	204	2,997

firm opts to obtain capital through borrowing or the sale of securities, there are often provisions attached which limit management discretion in the use of funds.

The potential for franchising to reduce distribution costs is particularly important for the firm whose main channel alternative consists of establishing its own network of company-owned outlets. If the firm were to rely on distribution through its own company-owned branch units or stores, it would be burdened with fixed overhead expenses which would have to be met regardless of the sales volume achieved. These high costs of maintaining company-owned business operations in many different locations would have to be borne solely by the firm. By using a franchise channel, however, members would assume much of this overhead cost, and would also pay for the right to market the firm's products or services.

With respect to managerial motivation, franchisees, as independent businesspeople, are more likely to work hard at developing their markets than salaried employees. Further, the franchisee is often better motivated to accomplishment than a company employee because of his or her self-image as a local businessperson who is important in the community.[18]

From the perspective of the potential franchisee, franchising has several strong appeals.

First, the amount of uncertainty involved in going into business is reduced with a franchise. Presumably, the particular business approach being offered by the franchisor has been successfully tested.

Second, the franchisor in many cases offers a well-known trademarked product or service which is likely to already have a high level of consumer acceptance.

Third, as shown in Tables 14.7 and 14.8, many franchisors offer initial and continuing services to their franchisees such as site selection, market surveys, merchandising assistance, operating manuals, advertising, accounting, and many others. Indeed, the extensive services offered by the franchisor are often cited as the main reason for the franchisee's willingness to buy a franchise.[19]

Fourth, in many cases, franchising enables an individual to enter a business which would be prohibitively expensive if he or she tried to go it alone. Being a member of a franchised system may enable the individual to get financial assistance directly from the franchisor, or may put the individual in a better position to secure funds from other sources if it is a respected franchise.

Finally, some prospective franchisees decide to join a franchise organization because the prospects for making adequate returns in a relatively short period of time are often higher than is the case for independent businesses.[20]

Channel Management Implications of Contractual Marketing Systems

Power shifts in the channel resulting from the growth of contractual marketing systems will have an important influence on the structure and management of marketing channels. These are discussed below, first for retail cooperative organizations and wholesaler sponsored voluntary chains, and then, because there are some important differences, for franchise systems.

Retail Cooperatives and Wholesaler Voluntary Chains.   The increasing size and importance of retail cooperatives and wholesale voluntary chains

---

[18]For an analysis and critique of these and several other propositions see: Shelby D. Hunt, "Franchising: Promises, Problems, Prospects," *Journal of Retailing*, (Fall, 1977): 71–84.

[19]For a discussion of promotional services offered by the franchisor to the franchisee see: J. Steven Kelly, J. Irwin Peters, and Robert D. O'Keefe, "Investigating Franchise Advertising and Promotional Support Programs," in *Proceedings of the Southern Marketing Association 1977*, pp. 195–202.

[20]For a related discussion see: Ronald L. Tatham, Ronald F. Bush, and Robert Douglas, "An Analysis of

Table 14.7
Initial Services to Franchisees, as Reported by Franchisors

Type of Service Provided	Franchisors Reporting				
	Total All Companies	Fast-food & Beverage	Nonfood Retailing	Personal Services	Business Products & Services
Operating manuals	100.0%	100.0%	100.0%	100.0%	100.0%
Management training	100.0	100.0	100.0	100.0	100.0
Franchisee employee training	88.3	83.9	83.7	90.9	100.0
Market surveys and site selection	84.4	98.2	93.0	83.6	42.3
Facility design and layout	80.0	100.0	83.7	81.8	26.9
Lease negotiation	62.7	78.5	72.0	58.1	23.0
Franchisee fee financing	37.7	25.0	37.2	47.2	46.1
All other services	21.1	21.4	25.5	20.0	15.3

Note: Based on information reported by 180 franchise companies. Includes 56 franchisors of fast foods and beverages, 43 of nonfood consumer products, 55 of personal services, and 26 of business (or industrial) products and services.

Table 14.8
Continuing Services to Franchisees, as Reported by Franchisors

Type of Service Provided	Franchisors Reporting				
	Total, All Companies	Fast-food & Beverage	Nonfood Retailing	Personal Services	Business Products & Services
Field supervision	96.1%	92.8%	100.0%	100.0%	89.6%
Merchandising and promotion materials	94.5	94.6	100.0	96.3	79.3
Franchisee employee retraining	85.1	78.5	83.3	94.5	82.7
Quality inspections	79.6	98.2	80.9	69.0	62.0
Advertising	66.4	62.5	61.9	83.6	48.2
Centralized purchasing	65.3	64.2	73.8	61.8	62.0
Market data and guidance	62.6	48.2	69.0	67.2	72.4
Auditing and recordkeeping	51.0	48.2	57.1	52.7	44.8
Group insurance plans	48.9	50.0	47.6	58.1	31.0
All other continuing services	13.1	8.9	12.4	12.7	10.3

Note: Based on information reported by 182 franchise companies. Includes 56 franchisors of fast foods and beverages, 42 of nonfood consumer products, 55 of personal services, and 29 of business (or industrial) products and services.

Source: E. Patrick McGuire, *Franchised Distribution* (New York: The Conference Board Report Number 523, 1971), p. 24.

have increased their power relative to that of the manufacturer. Consequently, the dominant role in channel leadership will more than ever be "up for grabs," with the manufacturer in many cases enjoying no special advantages for assuming the leadership role. Many of the marketing tasks which the manufacturer may have felt uniquely qualified to perform in the past may now be well within the capability of retail and wholesaler organizations to offer. Consider, for example, the case of the Drug Trading Co., Canada's largest wholesale drug company, which operates a voluntary chain of retail druggists:

Drug Trading Company offers its members such highly sophisticated marketing services as the following:[21]

1. **Store merchandising and organizational guides, showing the pharmacist precisely what product mix he needs, and how to order and price merchandise to maintain the desired mix and turnover.**
2. **Microfiche—microscopically reduced information along with the reading device. This does away almost entirely with catalogs and other printed reference materials. Indeed Drug Trading Company's complete merchandise catalog is contained on two small strips of fiche.**
3. **A portable electronic order-entry system, using a device which transmits orders directly from the pharmacy to the wholesaler's computer over regular telephone lines.**
4. **Computer-produced price tickets and shelf labels.**
5. **A computerized prescription record system that takes care of patient medication profiles, third party billings, controlled substances records, and the like.**

As this example suggests, a large wholesaler sponsored voluntary chain (or retailer cooperative) can provide its members with a wide range of sophisticated support service that would in most cases not be possible for the independent to match. The manufacturer who must now compete with these organized intermediary systems faces a far more difficult task in attempting to gain a dominant leadership position in the channel. This means that the need for careful planning in the design of marketing channels and effective channel management will be more important than ever for the manufacturer. Evolutionary channel structures and intermittent, ad hoc attempts at channel management can no longer be relied on to achieve distribution objectives.[22]

Franchise Systems.   The contractual basis of the franchised channel offers the manufacturer (supplier) a legal underpinning as a basis for exer-

Decision Criteria in Franchisor/Franchisee Selection Processes," *Journal of Retailing*, 48 (Spring, 1972): 16–21.

[21] "How to Run a Successful Co-op," *American Druggist*, (November, 1975): 45.

[22] One study found that an increasing number of manufacturers *are* engaging in more thorough channel management. See: James R. Moore and Donald W. Eckrich, "Marketing Channels from a Manufacturer's

cising channel control. This has traditionally represented a very important source of power for the franchisor over the franchisee. In recent years, however, there has been a growing tendency by government to examine these powers with a definite bias in favor of limiting them.[23] An important case in point involved the Chicken Delight franchise:

Chicken Delight, franchisor of a well-known fried chicken product, had a tying clause in its franchise contract stipulating that Chicken Delight franchisees must purchase all of their chickens, spices, special flavoring mixes, and paper products from the franchisor. A suit brought against Chicken Delight by one of its franchisees in 1971 claimed that this clause amounted to an illegal tying agreement in violation of the Sherman Antitrust Act. In its defense, Chicken Delight argued that the type of tying clause used was legal because the chickens, spice mixes, and paper products had to be used jointly to produce the Chicken Delight product in the way that the public had come to recognize it. The findings of the court, however, did not support this view. The court argued that all of these components could be secured from other sources, and the quality of the product could be assured through the use of quality control standards developed by Chicken Delight.[24]

This case has set the precedent for far less stringent tying agreements in franchise contracts. Indeed many franchisors fearing unfavorable legal actions have removed tying agreements from their franchise contracts. They have instead replaced them with provisions whereby the franchisor would offer to sell merchandise but at the same time would allow franchisees to buy from other sources if they agree to follow strict guidelines and/or purchase from a list of approved suppliers.

The real significance of this case is not so much the potential revenue lost by the franchisor if franchisees do not buy all of their products from him, for as shown in Table 14.9 the proportion of franchisor revenues attributable to this source is under 5 percent.

What is significant, however, is that this trend reflects a *lessening of the franchisor's legal capacity to excise control over franchisees.* This is true not only with respect to tying agreements but in many other areas as well.[25] Yet, many franchisors believe that this high level of legal control is absolutely necessary to maintain the special competitive advantages and quality features that lie at the heart of the success of their franchises. As

Perspective: Are They Really Managed?" *Marketing 1776–1976 and Beyond*, ed. Kenneth L. Bernhardt (Chicago: American Marketing Association, 1976), pp. 248–255.

[23] See for example: Shelby D. Hunt, "The Socioeconomic Consequences of the Franchise System of Distribution," *Journal of Marketing*, 36 (July, 1972): 32–38; Shelby D. Hunt and John R. Nevin, "Tying Agreements in Franchising," *Journal of Marketing*, 39 (July, 1975): 20–26; Shelby D. Hunt and John R. Nevin, "Full Disclosure Laws in Franchising," *Journal of Marketing*, 40 (April, 1976): 53–62; Ronald Stephenson and Robert G. House, "A Perspective on Franchising," *Business Horizons*, (August, 1971): 35–42; Jack M. Starling, "Franchising," *Business Studies*, (Fall, 1970): 10–16.

[24] "Cramping the Business Style of Franchisers," *Business Week*, (16 June 1975): 82.

[25] See for example: James T. Haverson, "What's in Store at the Federal Trade Commission," *Franchising and Antitrust* (Washington, D.C.: International Franchise Association, 1975), pp. 20–29.

Table 14.9
Principal Sources of Franchisor Revenue

Initial franchise fees	% 22.7
Equipment sales	1.3
Franchise royalties	31.2
Sales of products to franchisees	4.4
Real estate fees	14.0
All other revenue sources	26.4
Total	%100.00

Source: Adapted from: E. Patrick McGuire, *Franchised Distribution* (New York: The Conference Board Report Number 523, 1971), p. 20.

one well-known franchisor commented, "If they [the courts] say franchisees can do anything they want, I can see nothing but failure."[26]

While this statement may be somewhat of an exaggeration, it does convey the concern felt by franchisors about their dwindling legal base for controlling the actions of their franchisees.

The overriding implication of this is that the franchisor will increasingly have to look to power sources other than legal ones to exercise control over franchisees.[27] The franchisor will be less able to point to a line or clause in the franchise contract to control franchisees. Rather, the franchisor will have to depend more on carefully developed programs to motivate the franchised channel members to gain their cooperation in achieving distribution objectives (see Chapter 8).[28]

Corporate Systems

When a particular firm owns and operates organizations at other levels in the distribution system, a *corporate* (vertically integrated) *marketing system* exists. The firm owning and operating the other units may be a manufacturer, wholesaler, or retailer. When it is the manufacturer that owns and operates wholesale and/or retail units, the system is usually described as *forwardly integrated*. Examples of manufacturers operating forwardly integrated marketing systems are shown in Table 14.10

When retailers or wholesalers own and operate their own manufacturing units *backwardly integrated* marketing systems exist. Examples of retailers and wholesalers operating backwardly integrated marketing systems include Sears, Montgomery Ward, Woolworth, Safeway, American

[26] "Cramping the Style," p. 82.

[27] Joseph P. Guiltinan, Ismail B. Rejob and William C. Rodgers, "Factors Influencing Coordination in a Franchise Channel," *Journal of Retailing*, (Fall, 1980): 41–58.

[28] For a related discussion see: Shelby D. Hunt and John R. Nevin, "Power in a Channel of Distribution: Sources and Consequences," *Journal of Marketing Research*, 11 (May, 1974): 186–193.

Table 14.10
Examples of Manufacturers Operating Forwardly Integrated
Marketing Systems

1. Evans Products	Building materials
2. Firestone	Tires and rubber
3. Goodyear	Tires and rubber
4. Hart, Schaffner & Marx	Men's apparel
5. International Harvester	Trucks, agricultural machinery
6. Melville	Shoes
7. Sherwin Williams	Paint
8. Singer	Sewing machines

Hospital Supply, E.M. Jorgenson (steel products), and Grainer (electrical supplies).

A manufacturer or other type of firm may decide to develop a vertically integrated system for a variety of reasons. Sturdivant, for example, points to such factors as the following:[29]

1. Competition from competing systems

2. Changes in market conditions

3. Scale economies

4. Channel conflict

5. Entrepreneurial drive

Competition

If a firm operating a conventional loosely aligned channel finds it increasingly difficult to compete against more tightly knit systems such as those that are administered, contractual, or corporate (vertically integrated) it may consider the possibility of vertical integration as an attractive option. For example, several hospital supply wholesalers and manufacturers upon observing the growth of the vertically integrated American Hospital Supply Company during the 1950's also began to develop vertical systems of their own.

The major increase in manufacturer owned and operated factory outlet retail stores in recent years also reflects the growing competitive pressures on manufacturers. For example, in the clothing field such large manufacturers as Londontown (maker of London Fog coats), V.F. Corporation (Vanity Fair lingerie and Lee jeans) and McDonough Co. (Edicott Johnson shoes) have all opened their own retail factory outlet stores to

[29] Frederick D. Sturdivant, "Determinants of Vertical Integration in Channel Systems," in *Science Technology and Marketing*, ed. Raymond A. Haas (Chicago: American Marketing Association, 1966), pp. 472–479.

compete more effectively with retail discount stores, some of whom are part of backwardly integrated marketing systems.[30]

Changes in Marketing Conditions

Changing market conditions can play a major role in fostering the development of vertically integrated marketing systems. Recall, for example, the case of Evans Products Co., a manufacturer of building materials (primarily plywood and related products) discussed in Chapter 5. Evans, which had been selling through independently owned retail lumber yards, saw a rapidly growing consumer do-it-yourself market to which the independent lumber yards were not adequately adapting. Rather than attempting to get these independent lumber retailers to change, Evans opened up its own stores aimed primarily at the growing do-it-yourself market. This gave Evans the kind of control it needed to successfully exploit this changing market.

Scale Economies

In some cases, vertical integration (backward or forward) may offer scale economies in the manufacture and distribution of products. This will result if the merger of formerly independent units into a vertical system allows them to operate at a level of production output and/or distribution capacity that is greater than they could have achieved on their own. For example, a retailer such as Sears enables many of its vertically linked manufacturers to produce huge quantities and enjoy long standardized production runs because of Sears' enormous capacity to absorb their output.

Channel Conflict

In citing conflict as an important force in fostering vertical integration, Sturdivant points to American Hospital Supply Co. as an illustrative case:

"At least four of American Hospital Supply's manufacturing subsidiaries were acquired or created as a direct result of that company's conflicts with Baxter Laboratories, a major supplier. Although the well-being of both companies was closely interrelated, there were frequent conflicts. The struggles included arguments about profit margins, advertising copy, sales techniques, inventory policies, product quality, and research and development efforts. As a consequence, the two companies took steps to minimize the impact of the other party terminating the distribution

---

[30] "More Companies Open Factory Outlet Stores For Discount Shoppers," *Wall Street Journal,* (24 December 1976): 1, 11.

agreement. American Hospital Supply purchased companies capable of replacing the supply of intravenous solutions normally purchased from Baxter Laboratories just in case Baxter decided to terminate the agreement. Baxter Laboratories countered by building the nucleus of a direct sales force. In effect, the companies fashioned the skeleton of competing systems while still contractually obligated to each other. When the final break did come, the repercussions were felt throughout the industry." [31]

Entrepreneurial Drive

Though little is known about the actions of individual entrepreneurs in fostering the development of vertically integrated marketing systems, Sturdivant believes that it is an important factor. He states:

"The presence of a Richard Sears or an Arthur Spiegel in the mail order industry assures change and if the channels are in a state of disequilibrium they are a likely target for the entrepreneur's creative energy . . . such men are indeed hard to hold down and much extensive merger activity can only be understood in light of an entrepreneurial drive spurred by the vision of organizing and controlling the use of economic resources on a grand scale." [32]

Channel Management Implications of Corporate Systems

From the standpoint of the channel manager in a manufacturing firm, the corporate (vertically integrated) system offers the highest degree of control available over distribution units at the wholesale and retail levels. Since the units are owned by the manufacturer, the channel manager is not operating in an interorganizational system. Instead, the channel manager is dealing with a system that is intraorganizational because all of the entities involved in distribution are employees of the firm rather than independent businesses. In the intraorganizational setting of the vertically integrated channel, the following conditions exist to a much higher degree than would be the case for interorganizational channels:

1. Central direction by an identified authority
2. Formal superior-subordinate relationships
3. More precise reward and penalty systems
4. Centralized planning
5. Centralized coordination
6. Commonality of goals

[31] Sturdivant, "Determinants of Integration," p. 427.
[32] Ibid., pp. 477–478.

These conditions offer the channel manager the potential to operate a very highly controlled distribution system which is unlikely to be matched in the interorganizational setting of other vertical marketing systems or conventional channels.

This high level of control in channel management includes such important areas as: (1) entry into desired markets, (2) control over how the product is sold at different levels in the channel, (3) control over prices at wholesale and retail, and (4) protection of the company and product reputations.

Market Entry.   Manufacturers operating a vertically integrated channel do not have to convince independent middlemen or attempt to sign up franchisees to extend their reach into new markets. Since wholesale and retail units are company owned, they can open up new units whenever and wherever they choose if they have the financial capacity to do so.

Control of Product Sales.   The vertically integrated manufacturers are able to develop sales programs for their products, the implementation of which is subject to their direct control. They do not have to rely on independent middlemen to do the job for them.

Pricing Control.   By virtue of their level of control, vertically integrated manufacturers can restructure their prices to meet changing competitive conditions far more smoothly and rapidly than if they had to deal through independent channel members. Sherwin-Williams, for example, recently instituted a major overhaul of its pricing strategy in a relatively short period of time. Such a major revamping of prices would have been much harder to accomplish if Sherwin-Williams had to convince independent channel members of the virtues of the changes rather than simply issue pricing directives to its company owned retail stores.[33]

Protection of Company and Product Reputation.   One sure way of damaging a manufacturer's reputation for quality products is to have them sold through channel members who do an inadequate job in sales and services, or even worse, disparage the manufacturer's products in order to promote the products of other manufacturers or their own brands. Vertical integration eliminates this possibility.

Limitations on Control and Disadvantages of Vertical Integration.   Some analysts have argued that the high level of control attributable to vertically integrated channels may not materialize. As Sturdivant et al. argue:

"Integrated operations may find that the hoped for advantages of better control prove illusory. The product mix and marketing style of firms on

---

[33] "A Paintmaker Puts a Fresh Coat on Its Marketing," *Business Week*, (23 February 1976): 95–96.

different levels of the channel are, of necessity, quite different. To alter strategy of one level to meet the needs of another level may result in disaster because survival on the annexed level cannot be maintained in that manner."[34]

Along with this caveat, Stern and El-Ansary also point to other disadvantages sometimes associated with vertically integrated channels. Among these are the following:[35]

1. More employees may be needed to serve the various levels of distribution. This can lead to high payroll expenses, and possible involvement with union problems.
2. There may be diseconomies in inventory control. This is particularly the case for the manufacturer who, in many cases, is not equipped to carry high levels of inventory. The integrated manufacturer may need increased warehousing, and storage capacities and showrooms with adequate floor and shelf space to achieve reasonable product exposure.
3. As vertically integrated systems become very large, diseconomies in management's ability to absorb and process information may become a problem.
4. Finally, there may be legal limitations on vertical integration especially when the integration is done through acquisitions or mergers.

Summary

The most fundamental development affecting channel management in recent years has been the growth of vertical marketing systems (VMS's). These systems are characterized by a tight alignment of channel members, a higher degree of central programming by a channel leader, professional management, and scale economies in the performance of distribution tasks. There are three basic forms of VMS's: (1) administered, (2) contractual (which consist of retailer cooperative organizations, wholesaler sponsored voluntary chains, and franchised systems), and (3) corporate systems.

The administered vertical marketing system is a conventional marketing channel that is characterized by effective interorganizational management. Such channels are typically carefully developed and programmed to achieve a very high level of coordination and cooperation in order to meet distribution objectives. More and more firms are becoming members of administered channels. This gives them significant advantages over

[34] Frederick D. Sturdivant, *Managerial Analysis in Marketing* (Glenview, Illinois: Scott, Foresman and Company, 1970), p. 653.
[35] Stern and El-Ansary, *Marketing Channels*, pp. 224–225.

firms who are still operating in conventional loosely aligned marketing channels.

Contractual channels consisting of retailer cooperatives, wholesaler sponsored voluntary chains, and franchise systems are all characterized by a formal legal relationship that binds the channel members together. Both retailer cooperative organizations and wholesale sponsored voluntary chains enable their members to enjoy the advantages of large scale corporate chain systems while still maintaining independent ownership. The growing size and power of retail cooperatives and wholesaler sponsored voluntary chains present a formidable challenge to manufacturers seeking to control the operation of the marketing channel.

Franchise systems also bind the channel members together with a legal contract that often covers a very broad range of operating policies to which the franchisee must adhere. Thus, the franchise contract provides a strong legal underpinning for a high degree of control by the franchisor over the franchisee. Franchise systems have grown significantly in recent years in a wide spectrum of business categories, and are likely to enjoy substantial growth in the future. Franchising can provide the franchisor with: (1) capital advantages, (2) the potential to reduce distribution costs, and (3) a high level of managerial motivation on the part of the individual franchisees who are "their own bosses." From the franchisee's point of view, franchising can (1) reduce the degree of uncertainty involved in going into business, (2) provide the franchisee with a product or service that already enjoys strong consumer acceptance, (3) offer expertise and managerial assistance from the franchisor, (4) provide financial assistance, and (5) shorten the time necessary to make an adequate return on invested capital.

Corporate or vertically integrated systems exist when a firm owns and operates organizations at other levels in the distribution system. The firm owning and operating the other units may be a manufacturer, wholesaler, or retailer. When it is the manufacturer that owns and operates the wholesale and/or retail units, the system is described as forwardly integrated. When a retailer or wholesaler owns and operates manufacturing units, a backwardly integrated marketing system exists. From the standpoint of the manufacturer, forwardly integrated marketing systems provide the highest degree of control available over distribution units at the wholesale and retail levels because the units are owned by the manufacturer. Thus, the manufacturer is operating in an intraorganizational system. All of the entities involved in distribution are employees of the manufacturer rather than independent businesses. So, such factors as central direction, superior-subordinate relationships, rewards and penalties, central planning, central coordination, and common goals are all present to a greater degree than would be the case in an interorganizational system.

All of these forms of VMS's have, and will continue to have, profound effects on the management of marketing channels. The most pronounced effects will be on those firms attempting to compete in the market while still belonging to conventional channels.

Discussion Questions

1. Discuss the distinctions between vertical marketing systems and conventional marketing channels.
2. Is the structure of an administered marketing channel necessarily different from that of a conventional channel? What actually determines whether a channel is characterized as administered or conventional?
3. Discuss the problems the channel manager operating in a conventional channel might face in attempting to compete against an administered channel. What options does he or she have to compete more effectively?
4. Discuss the various types of contractual systems indicating the distinguishing features of each.
5. What kinds of advantages are available to wholesaler sponsored voluntary chains and retailer cooperative organizations as they attempt to compete against corporate chains?
6. What are some of the reasons for entering into a franchise from both the franchisor's and franchisee's points of view?
7. What has happened to the legal basis of power in franchise systems? Is this pattern expected to continue into the future? What are the implications of this development for franchisors, franchisees, and those operating in other forms of vertical marketing systems and conventional channels?
8. Is the corporate marketing system (vertically integrated channel) an interorganizational system? Discuss.
9. What are the general advantages and disadvantages that are usually characteristic of the vertically integrated channel?
10. Discuss the concept of channel control as it applies to the vertically integrated channel.

Appendix 14A
Evelyn Wood Reading Dynamics[1]
A Franchise Contract

Agreement entered into this ____ day of ____, 19__, between DIVERSIFIED EDUCATION AND RESEARCH CORP. (FS), a Delaware corporation, hereinafter referred to as "Franchisor" and _____, whose address is _____, hereinafter referred to as "Sponsor,"

Whereas, Franchisor is engaged in the business of teaching a new and revolutionary system of rapid and perceptive reading under the trade name, "Evelyn Wood Reading Dynamics", said system enabling students to increase their reading speed significantly; and

Whereas, Franchisor is the owner of certain trademarks including "Evelyn Wood", "Reading Dynamics", "Reading Dynamics Institute" and "Knowledge Through Reading"; and

Whereas, Franchisor, by reason of its success in teaching this novel and unusual method of reading and by reason of its maintenance of high standards of quality and performance, has created substantial goodwill and demand for its courses in rapid and perceptive reading known and sometimes hereinafter referred to as "Evelyn Wood Reading Dynamics"; and

[1]Adapted with permission from E. Patrick McGuire, *Franchised Distribution* (New York: The Conference Board Report Number 523, 1971), pp. 63–69.

Whereas, Sponsor is generally familiar with the opportunities and risks of such business and has received no guarantee of profitability from Franchisor but believes that he can carry on such business successfully; and

Whereas, Sponsor therefore wishes upon the terms and conditions herein set forth to obtain a franchise from Franchisor in order to offer courses in Evelyn Wood Reading Dynamics and a license to use Franchisor's trademarks in connection therewith under the supervision of and in accordance with the standards of Franchisor fully appreciating the importance of maintaining those standards in order to protect Franchisor's goodwill; and

Whereas, Franchisor is willing to grant a franchise to Sponsor to conduct courses in Evelyn Wood Reading Dynamics and a license to use Franchisor's trademarks in connection therewith upon the terms and conditions herein set forth, including various options to Sponsor to terminate or limit his obligations;

Now, Therefore, Franchisor and Sponsor, in consideration of the mutual agreements herein contained and for other good and valuable consideration, acknowledged by each of them to be satisfactory and adequate, do hereby agree as follows:

1. Grant of Franchise and License

a. Grant of Franchise

Sponsor requests and Franchisor hereby grants Sponsor a franchise to teach Evelyn Wood Reading Dynamics in the following area, for which Sponsor shall be primarily responsible: _____ Sponsor accepts such franchise, and undertakes to expend his best efforts to develop the potential for conducting Franchisor's system of rapid and perceptive reading in the area described above. Sponsor understands that Franchisor and other Sponsors have expended and will continue to expend substantial efforts and funds to secure and retain public goodwill toward Franchisor's system of reading and its trademarks, and recognizes the vital interest to all franchisees and Franchisor in Sponsor's providing suitable facilities and instructors and in operating its franchise efficiently and reputably. To this end, Sponsor shall use only those methods, systems and techniques as shall have been approved by Franchisor or have been promulgated by Franchisor by manuals, bulletins and memoranda, and shall comply with all other provisions included in Franchisor's manuals, bulletins and memoranda, as they may be reasonably modified by Franchisor from time to time. So long as Sponsor continues faithfully to discharge its obligations under this Agreement, Sponsor will be the only person whom Franchisor will appoint as its franchised Sponsor in Sponsor's area of primary responsibility. Sponsor understands that Franchisor expects to grant other franchises from time to time and that Franchisor cannot and does not assume any responsibility with respect to any advertisements or other operations of existing or future Sponsors in the area of primary responsibility assigned to Sponsor herein.

b. Grant of License

Franchisor hereby grants Sponsor a license to use Franchisor's registered trademarks "Evelyn Wood", "Reading Dynamics", "Reading Dynamics Institute" and "Knowledge Through Reading" within the territory described above upon all the terms and conditions contained herein.

2. Commencement of Operations

Within ninety (90) days of the date of this Franchise and License Agreement Sponsor shall commence operating within the territory described in paragraph 1(a) by offering Evelyn Wood Reading Dynamics courses and during the remainder of the term of the Franchise Agreement Sponsor shall continuously operate its franchise (except if prevented by Act of God or other cause beyond the control of the Sponsor) using Sponsor's best efforts, skills and diligence in the conduct thereof and regulating Sponsor's employees so that they will be courteous and helpful to students and the public.

3. Initial Assistance from Franchisor

Within a period of thirty (30) days following the execution of this Agreement, Franchisor will make the following assistance available to Sponsor.

a. Franchisor will familiarize Sponsor with the business of organizing, offering and conducting courses in Evelyn Wood Reading Dynamics, including furnishing Sponsor with a copy of Franchisor's management manual and other materials.

b. Franchisor will furnish Sponsor with information in Franchisor's possession and will furnish assistance facilitating the successful operation of an Evelyn Wood Reading Dynamics school or institute, including:

 (i) Assistance and advice in selecting the location of Sponsor's school or institute;

 (ii) Assistance and advice in planning the physical layout of Sponsor's school or institute, including advice regarding the proper number of classrooms, suitable furniture, and necessary clerical space and facilities;

(iii) Information and assistance regarding advertising and promotion for the opening of Sponsor's school or institute;

(iv) Information concerning continuing sales promotion, advertising, office techniques, business management and teaching techniques; and

 (v) Assistance in developing a teacher-training course suitable to Franchisor to be given to all instructor-trainees as provided herein in paragraph 4(b).

4. Operating Assistance from Franchisor

a. Franchisor will make available suitable texts and other reading materials and shall maintain current price lists setting forth the prices at which Sponsor may, if it desires, purchase such texts and materials from Franchisor.

   Sponsor shall pay for all texts and materials within thirty (30) days after the date of Franchisor's invoice to Sponsor therefor.

b. Franchisor will certify as qualified instructors of Evelyn Wood Reading Dynamics, such persons selected by Sponsor, as have (a) successfully completed the basic course in Evelyn Wood Reading Dynamics and (b) thereafter successfully completed Sponsor's teacher-training course in accordance with Franchisor's standards. Sponsor shall employ as teachers of Evelyn Wood Reading Dynamics only those persons who are so certified by Franchisor.

c. Franchisor shall provide instructor refresher courses for directors of instruction of Sponsor's school or institute. Sponsor will cause each of Sponsor's directors of instruction to attend such refresher courses as are scheduled by Franchisor. Such refresher courses shall be held at least every three (3) years but not more often than annually.

d. Franchisor will provide assistance to Sponsor in setting up and using accounting methods and procedures acceptable to Franchisor so that Sponsor may maintain complete and accurate books of account and student records, (including records of tuition fees, receipts from sales of textbooks, and other income or remuneration with respect to or from the said course), and such other information as Franchisor may reasonably require on a basis consistent with that provided by other sponsors. Sponsor shall permit a representative of Franchisor at any reasonable time, upon the request of Franchisor and at Franchisor's expense, to inspect or audit Sponsor's books and records (including Federal tax returns) pertaining to organizing, offering and conducting rapid reading courses, for the purpose of assisting Sponsor in the maintenance of its books and records and to assure compliance with Franchisor's requirements. Sponsor shall also provide Franchisor with annual statements of income and expenses certified as accurate by an independent Certified Public Accountant.

e. Franchisor shall furnish Sponsor on its reasonable request, with such advertising and publicity material and advice as Franchisor may have available from time to time, including photo-offsets, booklets, mimeographed letters and releases. Sponsor shall promptly pay Franchisor its reasonable charges in connection therewith.

5. Sponsor's Obligations

a. Sponsor will at all times actively promote the sale of Evelyn Wood Reading Dynamics courses to such an extent that its gross annual sales exceed its annual minimum royalty by at least (*amount specified*).

b. Sponsor shall furnish each new student with a workbook incorporating Franchisor's novel methods, system and techniques of teaching rapid and perceptive reading, said workbook to be either the copyrighted workbook suggested by Franchisor, or a reasonable equivalent.

c. Sponsor shall promptly furnish Franchisor reports as are from time to time reasonably requested by Franchisor for research and analysis.

   (2) In order to enable Franchisor to give appropriate assistance to Sponsor, Sponsor will furnish before the 15th day of each month an accounting statement covering Sponsor's operations for the preceding month. The information regarding Sponsor's operations contained in such accounting statement shall be held in confidence by Franchisor but may be included in compilations of figures and statistics provided that such compilations do not disclose Sponsor's individual figures and statistics. Said accounting statement shall be sent to Franchisor at the address specified for this purpose in Franchisor's management manual. The required form of accounting statement presently in effect is specified in Franchisor's management manual; Franchisor shall have the right to change, modify or amend, without notice, the accounting statement form and the information to be supplied therein.

   (3) In order to enable Franchisor to maintain records necessary to verify the royalty payments mentioned in paragraph 6(a) (1) of this Agreement, and to enable Sponsor to compute his monthly royalty payment, Sponsor will, within the first four (4) days of each month, furnish Franchisor with the number of students enrolled by Sponsor and starting classes during the preceding month.

d. Sponsor shall duly pay any and all debts incurred by him or on his behalf in connection with organizing, offering and conducting of Evelyn Wood Reading Dynamics courses. Sponsor shall not incur any expense or obligation of any nature in or under the name of Franchisor, Evelyn Wood Reading Dynamics or any individual, firm, corporation, association, or other organization with whom or which Franchisor is or may have been associated or succeeded.

e. Sponsor shall not place any advertising, issue any promotional material, or engage in any advertising or promotional campaign that violates any general policy promulgated by Franchisor with respect to the use of Franchisor's trade names or trademarks or that, in the judgment of Franchisor, reflects unfavorably upon Franchisor or the Evelyn Wood Reading Dynamics courses. Sponsor shall at all times conduct its business in accordance with the highest ethical standards of fair dealing with students and the public and shall not make any false or potentially misleading statements, representations or claims (including, without limitation, specific claims as to reading rates and comprehension) in connection therewith or otherwise endanger Franchisor's goodwill.

f. The facilities supplied by Sponsor shall at all times be appropriate, well-ventilated, adequately lighted, safe and convenient for public assembly, and shall at all times be used and maintained in strict conformity with all applicable laws, rules or regulations.

6. Compensation

a. Standard Royalty

(1) Sponsor will pay Franchisor, within the first fifteen (15) days of each month, a royalty of (*amount specified*) for each rapid reading student enrolled by Sponsor and starting classes during the preceding month, including students enrolled on scholarships, at special group rates or in rapid reading courses other than those conducted under the name of or pursuant to the Evelyn Wood Reading Dynamics system but embodying techniques or information Franchisor supplies to Sponsor hereunder. The royalty payments herein specified shall be sent to Franchisor at the address specified for this purpose in Franchisor's management manual.

(2) Franchisor may, at this option, change the royalty rate set forth above, and the place and manner of payment from time to time upon thirty (30) days' written notice to Sponsor, provided, however, that said royalty rate is not increased in any two (2) year period by more than (*amount specified*) of Franchisor's current standard royalty as set forth in this Agreement, except under the extraordinary circumstances provided for in paragraph 17, in which event said royalty rate shall be increased or decreased as provided therein.

b. Minimum Royalties

(1) Initial Period
Sponsor will pay a minimum royalty for each of the first three years of his Agreement of _____ dollars ($____) per annum.
The standard royalty referred to in paragraph 6(a) (1) shall be credited against said minimum royalty, but no part of the franchise fee specified in paragraph 6(c) shall be so credited.

(2) Renewal Periods
In each three (3) year renewal period, the minimum royalty per annum shall be the higher of the following:

(i) the minimum royalty per annum for the past three (3) year term of the Sponsor;

(ii) *(amount specified)* of the average gross receipts of Sponsor for the previous three (3) year term. "Gross receipts" means the gross revenue or total dollar amount received by Sponsor from students, in the form of tuition or otherwise, in connection with Evelyn Wood Reading Dynamics courses.

c. Franchise Fee

Sponsor will pay franchisor a franchise fee of _____ dollars ($___) in cash within ten (10) days of the execution of this Agreement.

d. Sale, Assignment or Transfer of Franchise and License

Sponsor's interest in this Franchise and License Agreement is personal and shall not be assigned, transferred, shared or divided in any manner by Sponsor without prior written consent of Franchisor, which consent shall not be unreasonably withheld.

7. Confidential Information

Sponsor recognizes that by reason of this Agreement he will acquire information of a confidential nature which is of great value to Franchisor. Therefore, Sponsor agrees not to communicate, deliver or surrender material or information designated by Franchisor as confidential, without Franchisor's prior written approval, either before or after the termination or expiration of this Agreement. On the termination or expiration of this Agreement, Sponsor shall promptly return to Franchisor any and all material or information so designated. If Sponsor should, during the term of this Agreement or within a period of three (3) years from the termination or expiration hereof, operate or acquire any financial interest in, directly or indirectly, a school or institute for teaching rapid reading, it shall be presumed, unless Sponsor is able to prove to the contrary, that such materials or information are being communicated to others without Franchisor's approval.

8. Avoidance of Confusion

For the purpose of protecting Franchisor's prestige and goodwill and thereby to benefit Sponsor, Sponsor agrees that during the term of this Agreement, and renewal and extension periods, if any, he shall not for himself or any other person, firm or corporation establish or conduct any business, including without limitation any rapid reading course(s) other than Evelyn Wood Reading Dynamics, under a trademark or trade name or at a location with could confuse or mislead the public into believing that such other business is associated with or is conducted with the authorization of Franchisor.

9. Indemnity

Sponsor shall procure and maintain in full force and effect during the term of this Agreement an insurance policy or policies protecting Sponsor, its officers and its employees against any loss, liability or expense whatsoever, arising out of or in connection with Sponsor's conducting courses in Evelyn Wood Reading Dynamics. Such policy or policies shall be satisfactory to Franchisor as regards the nature and scope of the risks covered, shall be written by a responsible insurance company or companies, satisfactory to Franchisor, and shall include the following: (*amount specified*)

The foregoing kinds of insurance and the limits specified may be reasonably revised by Franchisor upon three (3) months written notice to Sponsor.

Upon commencement of his business, Sponsor shall furnish certificates of insurance complying with the foregoing requirements to Franchisor for approval. Franchisor shall be an additional named insured in the foregoing policy or policies (Workmen's Compensation excepted). The insurance afforded by the policies shall not be limited in any way by reason of insurance maintained by Franchisor. The certificates shall state that the policy or policies will not be cancelled or altered without at least ten (10) days' prior written notice to Franchisor. Maintenance of such insurance and the performance by Sponsor of the obligations of this paragraph shall not relieve Sponsor of his obligations under paragraph 9 of this Agreement.

10. Term

a. The term of this Agreement shall be (*amount specified*) commencing _____, 19__, and ending _____, 19__.

b. At Sponsor's option, this Agreement shall be renewed upon sixty (60) days written notice to Franchisor prior to the end of the period specified in paragraph 10(a) above for an additional term of three (3) years (hereinafter called the "first renewal period"), upon all the terms and conditions herein contained, provided that Sponsor is not in default or breach of any of the terms or conditions of this Agreement, and shall again be renewed, at Sponsor's option, upon sixty (60) days written notice to Franchisor prior to the end of the first renewal period for another term in three (3) years (hereinafter called the "second renewal period"), upon all the terms and conditions herein contained, provided that Sponsor is not in default or breach of any of the terms or conditions of this Agreement.

c. At the expiration of the second renewal period (nine (9) years from the date hereof), this Agreement shall terminate.

11. Default and Termination

a. Right to Terminate
Franchisor shall have the right to terminate this Agreement upon notice in writing to Sponsor upon the occurrence of any one of the following events:

(1) In the event that Sponsor is declared insolvent or bankrupt, or makes an assignment for the benefit of creditors, or in

the event that a receiver is appointed for Sponsor or any proceedings are brought by, for or against Sponsor under any provision of the Federal Bankruptcy Act, or any amendment thereof, or similar act.

(2) In the event that Sponsor defaults in the performance of any provision of this Agreement or fails to make any payment required hereunder and such default shall not be remedied to Franchisor's satisfaction within thirty (30) days after written notice to Sponsor.

(3) Notwithstanding the foregoing, in the event that Sponsor shall fail to pay the franchise fee, as provided in paragraph 6(c) of this Agreement, on three (3) days notice to Sponsor.

(4) In the event that Sponsor's gross annual sales do not exceed the annual minimum royalty by tenfold as provided in paragraph 5(a) of this Agreement, Franchisor may, within the first ten (10) days of the next contract year, elect to terminate this Agreement and on giving notice of said election, this Agreement shall terminate thirty (30) days thereafter. If Franchisor elects to terminate pursuant to this provision, Franchisor shall pay Sponsor fifty percent (50%) of the franchise fee specified in paragraph 6(c) of this Agreement if such termination takes place after Sponsor's first year of operation and before the second year of operation and twenty-five percent (25%) if such termination takes place after Sponsor's second year of operation and before the third year of operation. No payment shall be made thereafter.

b. Effects of Termination

Upon the termination or expiration of this Agreement for any reason:

(1) Sponsor shall immediately discontinue the use of all trade names, trademarks, signs, structures and forms of advertising indicative of Evelyn Wood Reading Dynamics, or any business or products of Franchisor, and shall make, or cause to be made, such changes in signs as Franchisor may direct to effectively distinguish Sponsor's business from its former appearance and from other Evelyn Wood Reading Dynamics operations. If Sponsor shall upon request fail to make, or cause to be made, such changes, the Franchisor shall have the right to enter upon the premises without liability to Sponsor and make, or cause to be made, such changes at Sponsor's expense.

(2) Sponsor shall not after such termination attempt to capitalize on the goodwill of Franchisor or seek to obtain any commercial advantage from the fact that Sponsor has had any previous relation or association with Franchisor unless Sponsor shall have first obtained specific written permission from franchisor to do so.

(3) Sponsor shall offer Franchisor an option to purchase all of Sponsor's right, title and interest in the premises then occupied by Sponsor for conducting Evelyn Wood Reading Dynamics courses and all property used in connection therewith. If upon such offer, Sponsor and Franchisor are unable to agree as to the price and terms of purchase, a fair price and terms shall be determined by three arbitrators, each party selecting one arbitrator, and the two arbitrators so chosen selecting the third arbitrator. In determining a fair price, the arbitrators may include an amount for in-place value of equipment and fixtures but shall not include any amount for the value of any trademarks or other property of Franchisor or for the Sponsor's interest in this franchise and license agreement. The decision of the majority of the arbitrators so chosen shall be conclusive. Franchisor shall have the option at any time within thirty (30) days after being advised in writing of the decisions of the arbitrators to acquire such property at the price and upon the terms so determined, less any amounts then owing to Franchisor by Sponsor.

(4) Sponsor shall pay to Franchisor forthwith all amounts then owing to Franchisor including royalties under this Agreement and outstanding accounts for texts, booklets, and incidental items purchased and delivered. If this Agreement is terminated by Franchisor, pursuant to Paragraph 11, Franchisor shall pay Sponsor all amounts (if any) then owing by Franchisor to Sponsor less any amounts due Franchisor from Sponsor, including without limitation, accrued royalties, and shall purchase from Sponsor all unused current texts, booklets, supplies and incidental items (if any) in Sponsor's possession that were purchased from Franchisor. The price paid by Franchisor shall be the cost thereof to Sponsor less a reasonable handling charge not to exceed twenty-five percent (25%). No payment shall be made for obsolete material. Sponsor shall return to Franchisor without payment all manuals, teaching aids and other material furnished but not debited to Sponsor by Franchisor. Sponsor shall not make any copy or permit any copy to be made or otherwise make use of any said manuals, aids or materials.

Sponsor's obligations under paragraph 7 shall survive termination or expiration of this Agreement.

12. Sponsor's Options: Termination Within 180 Days

Sponsor may elect to terminate this Franchise and License Agreement for any reason within 180 days after the date hereof by written notice to Franchisor. If Sponsor so elects, Sponsor shall be entitled to a partial refund of the franchise fee referred to in this Agreement in accordance with the schedule set forth below. Franchisor shall be entitled to retain the remaining percentage of said franchise fee in consideration of the expenses and obligations undertaken by Franchisor pursuant to this Agreement.

Sponsor shall be entitled to a refund of the following amounts if Sponsor elects to terminate this Agreement pursuant to this provision:

    a. within 60 days after the date hereof—80% of the franchise fee;
    b. between 60 and 120 days after the date hereof—60% of the franchise fee;
    c. between 120 and 180 days after the date hereof—50% of the franchise fee.

This provision shall not release Sponsor from paying all royalties earned prior to termination.

13. Trademarks

Sponsor acknowledges that the words "Evelyn Wood," "Reading Dynamics," "Reading Dynamics Institute" and "Knowledge Through Reading" and various combinations thereof constitute valid registered trademarks owned or licensed by Franchisor, that Franchisor has the sole right, subject to licenses that have been granted, to use such and other trademarks or trade names in the operation of reading classes and that valuable goodwill is attached to such trademarks and to such trade names. Sponsor will use such trademarks or such trade names only in the manner or extent specifically permitted by this Agreement to designate the Evelyn Wood Reading Dynamics courses organized, offered and conducted by Sponsor under this Agreement and shall not use said name for any other purpose, unless Sponsor shall have first obtained specific written permission from Franchisor to do so. Sponsor shall use the words "Evelyn Wood Reading Dynamics" without any unauthorized addition or substitution in organizing, offering and conducting Evelyn Wood Reading Dynamics courses.

Sponsor recognizes that the purpose of the provisions, requirements and restrictions herein relating to the organizing, offering and conducting of regular Evelyn Wood Reading Dynamics courses is solely to protect the goodwill of Franchisor and its franchisees including Sponsor.

14. Independent Contractor

Each of the parties is an independent contractor. Neither party has any authority, express or implied, to act for the other in dealing with others, and neither shall purport to act as the agent or employee of the other. Sponsor shall be responsible for compliance with all laws and regulations governing Sponsor's business, and will hold Franchisor harmless from all claims against Franchisor arising out of conduct of Sponsor.

15. Waiver

This Franchise and License Agreement may not be altered or amended, or any provision hereof waived, except in writing, signed by the parties hereto. This Agreement contains the entire agreement of the parties, and shall inure to the benefit of the successors and assigns of Franchisor.

16. Separability

If any of the provisions of this Franchise and License Agreement shall contravene or be invalid under any applicable laws, such contravention or invalidity shall not invalidate this entire Agreement, but the Agreement shall be construed as not containing the particular provision or provisions held to be invalid, and the rights and obligations of the parties shall be construed and enforced accordingly.

However, if such construction affects Franchisor's rights to any payment herein provided for, this Agreement shall terminate when a final judgment, declaration or finding of contravention or illegality is entered (after appeals, if any) and, in such event, the rights of the parties hereto shall be governed by the provisions of paragraph 12(b) of this Agreement.

17. Governing Law

This Agreement shall be construed in accordance with, and its validity and effect shall be governed by, the laws of the State of Delaware.

In Witness Whereof. Franchisor and Sponsor have caused this Franchise and License Agreement to be duly executed by their respective duly authorized officers and their respective seals to be affixed hereunto, as of the day and year first above written.

[SEAL]   Diversified Education and Research
            Corp. (FS)

Attest: By _____

_____   _____

_____   _____

[SEAL]   Sponsor

Attest: By _____

_____   _____

Part Five
Cases in Marketing Channels

Matrix of Cases and Relevant Chapters

Case (columns) × Relevant Text Chapters (rows)

Relevant Text Chapter	Market Research Associates	R. L. Simpson Company	Airwick Industries Inc.	Catonga Radio Corporation	Tender Lovin Chicken	Green & Company	Carvel Corporation	LaFontaine Potteries Limited	Star Chemical Company	Jayson Guitar Company	Innovative Toys Inc. (A)	The Oliver Corporation	The National Oil Company	Innovative Toys Inc. (B)	The Mass Market Paperback Distribution System	Dunkin Donuts Incorporated	Kelsey Manufacturing Company	Hill Industrial Supply	Wolverine Brass Works	Clarkson Cold Products Company	Hyde-Phillip Chemical Company	Auditing Distribution Channels	Koehring Company	Westron Incorpated	Pepsi-Cola Bottlers Association
1	√	√	√	√		√	√	√	√	√	√	√	√	√	√	√	√				√		√	√	√
2	√	√	√	√		√	√	√	√	√	√	√		√	√	√	√	√			√		√	√	√
3	√	√	√	√	√	√	√	√	√	√	√	√	√	√	√	√	√				√		√	√	√
4	√	√	√	√	√	√	√	√	√	√	√	√	√	√	√	√	√				√		√	√	√
5	√		√			√	√	√	√		√		√	√	√					√	√	√			√
6	√	√	√	√		√			√			√								√	√	√			
7		√				√							√	√	√										
8			√	√	√		√	√		√	√					√	√	√	√					√	√
9		√							√	√						√		√	√	√				√	
10		√									√						√	√	√						
11				√				√		√	√					√	√	√	√	√	√			√	
12		√											√						√						
13			√										√								√	√	√		
14		√				√			√							√		√							√

Case 1
Market Research Associates
Changing Channels of Distribution

Market Research Associates had been asked by a large, nationally prominent manufacturer (Firm X) to make a careful study of some problems in
distribution that had been growing more pronounced. Firm X manufactured all kinds of large and small appliances—it ranked among the 20
largest users of steel in the U.S. Firm X had sold appliances under its
brand for more than 60 years, and during that time it had seen its dealer
network grow to over 1500 outlets. The channels of distribution used by
Firm X are depicted in Exhibit 1.

Note that Firm X used two distinct types of channels—one for serving
industrial/institutional markets, another for serving the appliance needs
of final consumers. Note also that two basic types of retail dealers were
used in X's distribution system: department stores and independent appliance stores. Many of these dealers had been with Firm X for more than
a half century.

The fact that the X dealership network was quite literally full of "old
friends" was at the base of one of the problems confronting the firm.
Since about 1960, the basic mode of distribution for appliances, particularly large appliances, had changed. Distribution of large appliances had
made a dramatic shift to high-capacity channels of distribution and away
from those of low capacity. The high-capacity channel of distribution was
comprised of dealers who:

Exhibit 1
Channels of Distribution—Firm X

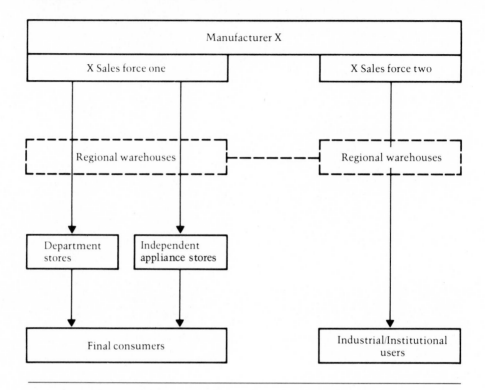

1. were concerned with keeping prices and margins low. "Low margin, high turnover" described their merchandising philosophy. These firms tended to deemphasize services rendered and to emphasize merchandise value.

2. displayed a distinct tendency for a promotional mix that emphasized mass selling techniques. Personal salesmanship skills were subordinated to advertising and point-of-purchase promotional devices.

3. preferred organizational simplicity—with little managerial specialization and few executive positions.

Firm X's dealership network was clearly of the low-capacity type—a type embodying the following traits:

1. an emphasis on nongoods services–a belief that patronage depended *primarily* upon such services.

2. a preference for a promotional mix that emphasized the personal sales effort.

3. a tendency to organization complexity–with a considerable degree of managerial specialization.

To put matters quite bluntly, Firm X needed high-capacity access to markets—their market share had suffered *because* they did not have access to the low-margin, high-turnover type of outlet. Indeed the X dealership network seemed, on balance, to embody a high-margin, low-turnover philosophy of merchandising.

Firm X had been approached on several occasions by retail interests such as K-Mart, Woolco, Target, GEM, and others. Had it not been for the demoralizing effect of such an arrangement on present dealers, X's management would have quickly agreed to additional distribution through that type of firm. Even when X's merchandise fell into the hands of "discounters" in uncontrollable ways (such as through distress sales), the older element in X's dealership network complained.

Discussion Questions

1. What specific courses of action do you believe MRA might recommend to the management of Firm X?
2. Which of these courses of action do you believe is best? Why?

Case 2
R. L. Simpson Company
Policies and Practices of a Distributor

The R. L. Simpson Company is a small firm specializing in the distribution of fire and safety equipment in a large city in the northeast United States. The industrial fire and safety equipment industry has always had a very broad product array. Except in a few special cases, any one type of product is manufactured by several competing manufacturers.

The R. L. Simpson Company has, in the past, made it a practice to carry at least one of each product type offered in their product line, although not every product handled is kept in stock. Negotiations are made with the manufacturers on a contractual basis to determine which distributors will handle which particular products. Each of the manufacturers usually has a different policy for determining distributors and territories. For example, the Ansul Corporation will allow anyone to handle its products regardless of the effects of competition on both the corporation and its distributors. On the other hand, Pyrotronics Corporation has set up specific distributors to act as sole agents within a particular area. The Simpson Company has always made it a practice not to carry competing lines from different manufacturers even though the option is available to it. The manufacturers, however, consider many of their products to be in competition with other products of a different type. For example, Simpson carries a complete line of Ansul dry chemical extinguishers and systems. The Norris Corporation manufactures an array of CO_2 extinguishers and systems that can be used in much the same type of application as dry chemical equipment. The Simpson Company carries a complete line of both, since Mr. Simpson feels that the two products are not in direct competition and each one is best suited to a particular application.

Another important consideration of the product line is the large size (all dimensions) of the various products available to the distributor. For example, in the Ansul line, which specializes in dry chemical equipment, there are over 3000 different combinations of extinguishers. The Davis safety equipment line is as large as that of the Norris Industries (Fyr Fyter) and Pyrotronics, Inc. The preceding four manufacturers make up the largest share of R. L. Simpson's sales. As can be seen, only a small portion of the products available can be carried in inventory at any one time. The decision of which manufacturer and product lines to carry in inventory must be constantly reevaluated.

The sales territory for the entire firm does not have a fixed boundary and varies according to the product and to the marketing policies of the various manufacturers. For example, the Ansul Corporation has set no territorial limits for its distributors nor has it set any maximum number of distributors for any geographical area. For this reason, the Simpson Company is free to go anywhere it is physically able to sell the Ansul line. Conversely, the Pyrotronics Corporation has set very definite limits as to where the Simpson Company may sell the Pyrotronics line so that the various distributors do not compete directly with each other. The other manufacturers have policies that vary between these two extremes. Due to the nature of the flexible sales territory, the territory assignments to Simpson's salespeople are rather loose and flexible. As a minimum, the management of Simpson Company usually considers the entire city to be its major territory. The city is then divided roughly into geographic thirds and is allocated to each of the three salespeople. No attempt is made to break the sales territories down into equal market potential areas. These guidelines are broken in a few cases. All "engineered" (designed from scratch) systems are handled by R. L. Simpson, Jr. He is a registered professional engineer and gets credit for the sale unless there is some reason to split the commission. Another exception is when a sale comes from outside the assigned sales territory, in which case the sale is credited to the house account and there is no commission. The third exception concerns certain well-established accounts that Mr. Simpson handles himself regardless of where the specific sale might be. For example, in dealing with E. I. Du Pont de Nemours, Mr. Simpson will handle all the necessary sales and follow-up work, regardless of the location of the ordering unit.

Mr. Simpson has always felt that service is a major factor in securing sales. However, he also feels that the firm does not make any money from service. So he continues to practice it because he feels it is a necessary evil. The basic premise on which the Simpson Company operates is: "We service what we sell." The servicing of equipment is threefold: (1) the annual inspection, often required by law or insurance rules, of all fire and safety equipment; (2) the refilling, recharging, and reinspection of any equipment that has been used; and (3) the repair of damaged and inoperative equipment. For the annual reinspection of equipment, the Simpson Company has set up a system whereby one year after the date of sale a notice is sent to the purchaser offering this service. If the offer is accepted, the inspection is scheduled. Phase 2, the refilling of equipment, is often done on an emergency basis. The Simpson Company has a 24-hour service for this type of operation. If a firm has had its CO_2 system discharged and its insurance company will not let the firm operate, it can call the Simpson Company, and the system can be put back into operation in a matter of hours. Phase 3, the repair of fire equipment, is done on a component replacement basis. No repairs are ever made to the basic components. If the item cannot be repaired, attempts are made to sell a new item, for in almost all circumstances, no one can repair it to meet the necessary standards. The manufacturers of the various products have no direct control over the servicing policies of the Simpson Company. The servicing of equipment is the most competitive and price sensitive phase of the industry. The servicing firm usually can service all makes of equipment equally well.

Each of the Simpson Company suppliers furnishes a suggested retail price list and has a different policy concerning price maintenance. One of the firms sells to the Simpson Company at 68 percent off list price. The Simpson Company has found that in order to make a profit on any given sale, they must in turn sell their product at about a 40 percent markup on cost. Therefore, they would sell at about 70 percent of list. This price may vary depending on location, costs, and service contracts. Other manufacturers sell to the Simpson Company at 20 percent off list and the Simpson Company has found that they cannot make a profit selling at such a low markup.

The Simpson Company feels it is the most powerful distributor in the area. This premise is based on information received from both customers and suppliers. There are about ten competitors in the area; however, only one or two of these compete directly against Simpson Company in all product markets. For example, the Globe Alarm Company competes with Simpson in the area of fire and smoke alarms. The Wooster Brass Company competes directly in the field of hose and hose equipment. There are only two competitors in the area that carry a multiline, multi-item product array. Simpson Company is the only firm to have a registered professional engineer and Mr. Simpson feels that this gives him a great advantage over the other distributors especially in "engineered" systems and other markets where the customer wants to buy knowledge as well as products.

Discussion Question

What changes, if any, should be made in R. L. Simpson Company's distribution policies and practices?

Case 3
Airwick Industries, Inc.
Changing Channel Strategy to Meet a Changing Environment

In a move which has the business community watching and wondering, Airwick's Professional Products Division recently phased out all of its regional sales offices to further increase an already healthy $30 million-a-year sales volume.

The Professional Products Division is the institutional sales arm of Airwick Industries Inc., which was bought in 1974 by Ciba-Geigy, the $4 billion Swiss chemical company. The division manufactures and markets a variety of disinfectants, cleaning agents, odor counteractants, insecticides, and environmental sanitation products for hospitals, schools, nursing homes, restaurants, hotels/motels, office complexes, airports, government installations, retail stores, and industrial plants.

Airwick's Consumer Products Division is a highly visible manufacturer and marketer of household cleaners and deodorizers. Led by the tremendous successs of its Carpet Fresh and Stick-Ups products, the consumer group expects to ring up $220 million in sales this year.

Although the Professional Products Division receives some "rub off" benefits from the Consumer Division's $25 million-a-year TV ad campaign, it still operates as a financially autonomous unit.

"The institutional supply side of Airwick has always done quite well," said John Updegraph, Professional Products Division president. "We have had a sales rate increase of 5 percent to 10 percent a year.

"But recently, with inflation running at 12 percent to 14 percent annually, we decided there was a need for a change in strategy. It became evident that if we were going to double sales or profits we'd have to do something unorthodox.

"In the beginning our products were marketed exclusively by independent distributors. Then, in the 1970s, we began to buy out the private distributors in the hope of someday dealing totally and directly with our customers through branch offices.

"It progressed to the point where we had a network of 65 distributors and 10 branch offices serving the country. The distributors accounted for 75 percent to 80 percent of total sales volume.

"There was no clear evidence of greater sales penetration in areas where we had our own sales offices. Also, our distributors expressed a growing dissatisfaction with what they considered to be the threat of unfair competition from our direct offices.

"Out of the hard rethinking about the best way to improve support for our distributors, evolved the corporate strategy to divest ourselves of branch offices. We felt it was better to ride one horse successfully rather than risk falling on our faces riding two horses at the same time.

"So all 10 factory sales offices are to be divided into 28 new distributorships. We'll now have a sales force of 93 independent entrepreneurs backed up with every sales aid we can supply."

Updegraph, a Harvard MBA grad and former Procter & Gamble executive, admits there are several disadvantages in the distributorship system. But, he said, in inflationary times the advantages of such a system far outweigh the negative points.

"Sure, you relinquish some control when you have to rely on distributors," Updegraph explains. "It's nice if your company has the money to own every aspect of its business lock, stock, and barrel.

"But there are many favorable things that can be said about the distributorship system. In many industries, such as automobiles and petroleum, the dealer network pattern is the accepted form of doing business.

"In some ways, it is actually better to have the sales of your products handled by private entrepreneurs. These independent distributors run their own businesses and if anyone wants to turn a profit, they do. The more they push our products, the more money they make.

"Also, when you market your products through distributors, you eliminate numerous management headaches. In fact, we've found that Airwick is even stronger now because the distributors know we are behind them 100 percent."

The phase-out of Airwick's field sales offices has been made easier by the creation of a Distributor Development Department within the Professional Products Division.

"It's obvious that the more we help the distributors the more we're actually helping ourselves," Updegraph said. "So we have programs which assist the distributors in managing their businesses."

Supporting the change are programs which help the distributors hire and train salespersons, manage time and territories, control inventory and receivables, increase sales effectiveness, install better accounting systems, and make a computer records conversion.

"Before the phase-out we were not able to do very much in the way of advertising and promotion support for the distributors. But now we can direct more attention to those areas," Updegraph said.

"We've contracted for about 30 insertions in trade journals. There's a direct mail campaign under way, and Airwick will be active in trade shows."

The decision to rely solely on distributors for field sales representation has had several other positive results, Updegraph said.

"Our product line had been developed primarily for the housekeeping needs of the health and hospital field, which we dominated for many years," he said.

"Most of these products also fill the requirements of commercial and industrial housekeeping, but now we can give more research and development attention to heavy duty products for this large segment of the market."

When Airwick divested itself of field sales offices, Updegraph said, the employees in those offices were, quite understandably, alarmed. However, he said, the top field managers were given other jobs in the corporation and many of the sales personnel immediately went to work for the local distributors of Airwick products.

"The products we sell are part of a very fragmented $2.5 billion market," Updegraph explains. "We knew we couldn't buy our way into selling directly, so we made a very strategic move that will give us a larger market share in the future. I think Airwick employees and our competitors realize that we made a smart business decision.

"The competition for the professional housekeeping product market is intense in most geographical areas. We reached the decision that local independent businesses with full factory support are in a better position to give specialized services and meet local competitive conditions than are factory sales offices. I'm sure other national manufacturers will be watching us with interest."

"I think with the current inflation situation, high interest rates, high labor costs, high rents and construction prices, and energy costs many firms will have to reexamine their distribution and service systems."

Discussion Questions

1. Evaluate Airwick's new channel strategy in terms of its appropriateness for meeting the changing environment.
2. Discuss the philosophy underlying John Updegraph's statement: "It's obvious that the more we help the distributors the more we're actually helping ourselves."

Case 4
Catonga Radio Corporation
*Some Legal Issues in
Channel Management*

In the twenty-second year of operation of the Catonga Radio Corporation
(CRC), the brand name Catonga was to most Americans a highly respected synonym for all kinds of electronic gear ranging from radios to
stereo sound equipment to television. CRC had maintained a record of
uninterrupted profits in the face of some extremely difficult price and
quality competition from both domestic and foreign enterprises. When
the competition got tough, the CRC sales force had been able to maintain
inventories with dealers and to show sales increases every year. But it had
not been easy—and on occasion some very curious tactics had been employed. These tactics had proved so successful that they had come to be
identified by Sales Plan numbers, as follows:

Plan 1. The Catonga line of products, like those of almost all manufacturers, embodied both strong and weak products. The strongest elements
within the line literally sold themselves; the weakest elements were extremely difficult to sell. Plan 1, called "full line selling," stipulated, in essence, that a dealer or distributor wishing to buy only the strong elements
in the line had to agree to take other elements as well. Catonga's rationale
was that the firm would be hurt if dealers did not stock their products in
sufficient depth to meet the known diversity of customer preferences.
Catonga argued also that the margin dealers received on the strong ele-

ments of the line was virtually a gratuity—that is, the dealer exerted no special effort to make the sale—so that the special sales effort required in order to sell the less popular items was not inequitable at all. If a dealer became belligerent and insisted on only the stronger elements in the CRC line, the order would be written up, but it was no trade secret that delivery was slow on such orders. Catonga argued that these "partial-line" orders were more difficult to arrange shipment for. There had been instances in which dealers' Christmas stocks had arrived *after* that holiday—and it was believed that those orders had been partial-line.

Plan 2.   This plan was used when new dealers were being sought—for example, when CRC wished to appoint a dealer in a rapidly growing community or when for one reason or another a dealer had been lost. The procedure was as follows. First, a suitable existing radio and/or appliance dealer was located. In this case "suitable" meant that the dealer was financially stable and capable of rendering full appliance service to his customers. When such a dealer had been identified, he was offered the CRC line of products with the unwritten understanding that he should (within one year from the date the agreement began) *cease* to sell competing lines that he might have sold in the past. This procedure had given CRC good established dealers and had helped to make the CRC dealer network the standard of the industry.

Plan 3.   This plan had been developed for sales that CRC made to other manufacturers, who usually used the CRC components in the manufacture of some other product or products. One Japanese manufacturer of subcompact automobiles, for example, used CRC radios (which contained Japanese components), and Plan 3 had been used to secure this international agreement. Plan 3 required that the CRC customer sign an agreement to purchase at least eighty-five percent of their component needs (such as car radios) from CRC.

Plan 4.   Plan 4 was a form of reciprocal purchase agreement, to which CRC had added a special embellishment. CRC had many large industrial customers; indeed, almost every major manufacturer in the U.S. was directly or indirectly a customer of CRC. From time to time, one of these firms would find itself in arrears in payment to CRC. When this happened, and when it was clear that the financial problem was short-term—that is, the debtor company had no serious long-run financial problems—CRC would, if advantageous, negotiate a reciprocal purchase agreement. These reciprocal agreements tended to favor CRC, but CRC management believed that was only as it should be—after all, CRC was the philanthropist in the credit extension.

Discussion Questions

1. Evaluate each of CRC's Sales Plans. Make sure to indicate whether you believe the plans are legal, illegal, or just meet the spirit of the law.
2. What specific federal laws do we have that attempt to control such practices as these?
3. What specific advice would you give the CRC management regarding the continued use of these "Sales Plans"? Why?

Case 5
Tender Lovin Chicken
Abuse of Channel Power?

Tender Lovin Chicken, a New Jersey based producer of chickens, had spent a great deal of effort and money in building the quality image of its product in an attempt to differentiate it from commodity type chickens which were sold in supermarkets without any brand identification. The effort had paid off. Tender Lovin Chicken enjoyed a high degree of consumer acceptance even though it often sold at up to thirty percent higher prices than unbranded chicken. Consumers were willing to pay the higher price for what they perceived to be the superior flavor, texture and overall quality of Tender Lovin whole chickens and chicken parts. Because of this high level of consumer acceptance, supermarkets were eager to carry the product. It sold rapidly, provided a good profit margin and, perhaps most importantly, helped attract patronage. By carrying the Tender Lovin Chicken line, supermarkets enhanced their own reputations for carrying quality products. Further, the Tender Lovin Chicken line was an ideal promotional resource in the intensely competitive supermarket industry. By periodically advertising Tender Lovin Chicken at attractive prices, a supermarket could attract shoppers into the store who otherwise would not have shopped there.

Such high levels of consumer and supermarket acceptance of Tender Lovin Chicken provided the company with a strong power base in the distribution channel. Tender Lovin knew that it had a highly desirable product and the company believed that it was in a position to "call the shots" as to who would get the product and the terms under which it would sell the product to customers.

The channel of distribution Tender Lovin Chicken used in the New York Metropolitan area (one of Tender Lovin's major markets) was through wholesale distributors who then sold the chicken to supermarkets.

In the late 1970s, a development in the New York Metropolitan area market provided a major test of Tender Lovin Chicken's marketing channel power. Tender Lovin heard that several distributors were about to take on another branded line of chicken known as Great Tastin Chicken. Great Tastin Chicken was also heavily advertised to consumers as a superior quality product equal to or better than Tender Lovin Chicken but lower in price. As had been the case for Tender Lovin Chicken, an aggressive advertising campaign conducted by Great Tastin Chicken succeeded in creating strong consumer demand for the product. The company's ads took direct aim at Tender Lovin Chicken, challenging its claim to superior quality and attacking its higher prices. As the campaign took hold, more and more supermarkets wanted to carry the Great Tastin Chicken line. This in turn convinced a growing number of distributors who supplied the supermarkets that they had better start carrying the Great Tastin Chicken line.

When George Perkins, founder and president of Tender Lovin Chicken, heard that some of the distributors were planning to carry Great Tastin Chicken along with Tender Lovin Chicken and indeed some had already done so, he became incensed. He had thought that there was an "understanding" between his company and its distributors that if they wanted to carry Tender Lovin Chicken, they would not carry any other branded line of chickens.

Wasting little time, George Perkins called some of the offending distributors and paid a personal visit to several of them. He minced no words in making it clear to the distributors that if they expected to continue carrying the Tender Lovin Chicken line they had better promptly cease carrying the Great Tastin line.

The distributors' reactions to Perkins' threat were mixed. Some quietly acquiesed to his demand, a few told him, in essence, "where to get off" by saying that they did not need his chicken line anyway. But most protested, arguing that they had a perfect right to sell another branded line of chicken along with the Tender Lovin line. One distributor even threatened to sue Tender Lovin Chicken if it proceeded to act on Perkins' threat.

Within several weeks of delivering his ultimatum to the distributors, Perkins, true to his word, began to act. He slowed down or stopped shipping Tender Lovin Chicken to those distributors who were still handling the Great Tastin line. Also true to his word, the distributor who had promised to sue Tender Lovin Chicken if it acted on Perkins' threat filed suit against Tender Lovin alleging that Tender Lovin had stopped shipping him chickens because he had refused to stop selling Great Tastin chicken.

Discussion Question

Evaluate Tender Lovin Chicken's use of power to control the actions of the distributors in terms of legal ramifications involved, and whether other power bases might have been employed to achieve Tender Lovin's objective without raising legal questions.

Case 6
Green & Company
Conflict in the Channel

Green & Company is the U.S. distributor for Powertreds, a foreign-made brand of athletic shoes. The company has divided the United States into three sales areas, Northwestern, Southwestern, and Eastern, with sales offices in San Francisco and New York in addition to the home office in Salinas, California. The company has annual sales of $1.3 million; its sales have at least doubled each of the eight years of its existence. In 1973, sales by region were Northwest, $150,000; Southwest, $500,000; and East, $650,000.

Mr. Johns, salesman for the California area, has been with the company since 1964. Johns has adhered to the company policies of having only one account in a given geographical area and not opening accounts with direct competitors of existing dealers. Johns receives a 10-percent commission on all sales to dealers, from which he pays his expenses.

Bruno's Sporting Goods, in downtown San Diego, and Jim's Sports Palace, in La Jolla, a northern suburb of San Diego, both carry Powertreds. The sales area can easily handle the volume, and the stores are not in direct competition with each other. Jim's was one of Johns' first accounts for Green & Company, and he has enjoyed a cordial relationship with the owner.

Jim's has been the largest dealer in Johns' area every year. However, since Bruno's Sporting Goods opened an account one year ago, it has taken over as number one in sales on the strength of a large order in the preceding fall. After Johns delivered the order, Bruno announced he was changing his store to a discount sporting goods store and opening a second location in La Jolla in time for the Christmas season.

Jim's Sports Palace learned of Bruno's plan and told Johns that Bruno's must not sell Powertreds in La Jolla or else it would be forced to drop the line and carry a competing brand of athletic shoes. Jim's is a traditional golf, tennis, and hunting equipment store and has developed a sizable team sales department now accounting for 50 percent of store sales. Jim's fall order from Green & Company was $15,000.

Bruno's, on the other hand, concentrates on camping equipment, bowling, and high-volume, low-cost lines of sporting goods. The store's fall order was $20,000; orders the previous year totaled $3,500. Bruno's management believes other low-cost items will attract customers who will purchase Powertreds even if priced at suggested retail list; hence, Bruno's does not object to Jim's being in the same area.

Green & Company executives decided not to intervene but to let Johns settle the problem his own way because Bruno's and Jim's were his clients; besides, they felt the executive committee was too removed from the dispute to understand it fully. This is the first time that Green & Company has experienced such a problem. As a result, Johns' decision could very well become a precedent.

Discussion Questions

1. Should Johns allow Bruno's Sporting Goods to retail Powertreds at the new location?
2. What types of conflict can arise among channel members because of Bruno's action?

Case 7
Carvel Corporation
A Company That Switched Distribution Systems

The Carvel Corporation is a multimillion-dollar franchisor of soft ice cream. The company began its corporate existence as a manufacturer of equipment for producing and distributing soft ice cream. During the latter part of World War II, Carvel became a distributor of soft ice cream at military PX outlets. The company continued to sell a substantial part of its volume through these post exchanges during the period 1945 through 1948.

But management recognized that the PX market was drying up and began to switch the company sales efforts to the civilian market. By early 1949 Carvel had sold dozens of soft ice cream machines to independent businesses throughout the United States. The machines sold for approximately $18,000 apiece and were purchased on an installment basis, the buyer making a small down payment and Carvel taking notes for the balance of the sales price. The business continued to expand until the early 1950s. Then a recession set in and Carvel, which was holding paper on many of its machines, suddenly found itself on the brink of bankruptcy.

The company had previously opened some of its own units. The company-owned stores seemed to be doing very well, whereas the independents were failing at a catastrophic rate. Thomas Carvel, president of the corporation, decided that the "missing ingredients" in the independents' operations were the management experience that Carvel had developed and the reinforcing effect of regional advertising which Carvel was then engaged in. It was at this point that Carvel switched to franchised distribution.

Gradually, the company phased out the company-owned stores and replaced them with those of franchisees. New equipment was sold on a franchise basis, and the owners of the equipment were trained by Carvel and provided with backup advertising and sales promotion support. Carvel management reports that it has never regretted its move, to which it attributes its present position as one of the most successful soft ice cream producers. The company has recently branched out into a variety of other enterprises, including resort development.

Discussion Question

What other alternative might Carvel have used to replace the so-called "missing ingredients"?

Case 8
Lafontaine Potteries Limited
Selecting Channels of Distribution

Founded in 1908, Lafontaine Potteries Limited is Quebec's leading manufacturer of glazed and unglazed giftware. In addition, it has contracted with a local firm to manufacture wrought iron ware which it assembles with its pottery line. There are approximately a hundred product items in each of the company's two product lines. Some of these items are:

1. *Glazed and unglazed giftware:* cups and saucers, tea and coffee pots, mugs and steins, ash trays, planters, tidbit servers, barbecue sets of plates and mugs, fancy flower pots, casseroles, wall plaques, rustic T.V. dinnerware sets, vases and "Habitant" dinnerware sets.
2. *Wrought Iron Ware:* Wrought iron is matched up with the company's pottery items to make smokers, planters, casserole and coffee warmers, cocktail and barbecue sets, and umbrella stands.

Of the company's $8,000,000 sales volume, approximately 65 percent is realized in pottery items. The major portion of Lafontaine's line of products is low-priced and is merchandised primarily in variety stores, department stores, and in independent retail gift shops. Thirty percent of the firm's sales are made through large retail chains.

Organization

The head office and main show room of Lafontaine is located on St. Hubert Street in Montreal. While all the firm's total product line is displayed in the show room, not all items are in stock. The company maintains inventories only of those product items which have proved sales success, and show excellent future market potential. A branch sales office is situated in Toronto.

Lafontaine is family-owned and operated. Mr. Guy Lafontaine is not only president of the company, but also senior sales executive. André Lafontaine, Guy's younger brother, is vice-president in charge of finance and office management. The third and youngest brother, Roland, as vice-president of operations, handles all the firm's manufacturing activities. The sales manager for the province of Ontario is Guy Lafontaine's son-in-law, Sam Stone. Mr. Stone lives in an apartment adjacent to the firm's Toronto show room, and is responsible for it. He is the firm's only salesperson in Ontario and covers the entire province. Roland's son-in-law, Charles Denis, covers the Maritime provinces four times a year assisted by a French-Canadian salesperson who lives in New Brunswick. Both work out of the Montreal office. The Western provinces, including British Columbia, are handled by Thomas Jones, who lives in Vancouver, and Jack Shore, a Winnipeg resident. Both salespeople operate out of the Montreal office, visiting Montreal at least a half dozen times a year. The province of Quebec is supervised by Guy, and accounts for 40 percent of the company's total sales. Six salespeople in Quebec report directly to the president.

The Ontario Situation

Ontario provides 30 percent of the company's total sales volume. Most of these sales are made directly by the Montreal home office to chief buyers of such large companies as T. Eaton Co., Simpsons-Sears, Woolworth, Zellers, Kresge, Henry Morgan Co., and so on. Sam Stone's responsibility is to ensure that these house accounts are satisfactorily serviced. Because Mr. Stone is the only salesperson in Ontario, few sales are made to independent retail stores.

For the past two years, sales expenses have increased dramatically, so much so that Guy has repeatedly expressed concern over Lafontaine's shrinking profit margin. Guy has consistently argued that the problem is two-fold: 1) that expenses are too high and 2) that the company is not maximizing the potential market which could be developed in Ontario by employing more salespeople.

Unlike his brother, Roland does not feel that the solution lies in hiring more salespeople to cover the province of Ontario. He contends such action would involve building or leasing a warehouse in addition to the Toronto showroom to adequately service retailers. The result would be even higher expenses for the company.

On the other hand, Sam Stone argues that the solution would be to employ the services of a regional wholesaler in Toronto who would sell directly to independent Ontario retailers. This wholesaler, with whom Sam is familiar, is a small family-owned organization which has been importing and distributing a few Japanese-made pottery goods but is primarily a jobber for Canadian manufacturers and has a ready-made clientele of small independent stores. Mr. Stone believes that Lafontaine should retain its large house accounts, but let this wholesaler handle all other sales in Ontario.

Guy's reaction to this suggestion is mixed. He thinks the idea should be carefully considered, yet such a radical change in policy might have implications for the company's total operations. For example, might it not be a good idea to employ small wholesalers in all the other provinces too? In this way, costs would be cut down significantly for the simple reason that the salespeople currently serving these areas would no longer be needed. In addition, the company would gain increased market coverage.

André feels that this idea is a good one, but has reservations whether Lafontaine would in fact obtain maximum coverage. How could Lafontaine expect a wholesaler of similar product lines to push Lafontaine's products more than their present line?

Guy's response is that wholesalers not currently in this product line would be the type to approach. However, this raises the question of whether they would have the appropriate captive market of retailers, or the product knowledge to realize effectively Lafontaine's objectives.

According to André: "It is all very fine and dandy to concern oneself with getting maximum market potential. But in return for the assistance of regional wholesalers, what does Lafontaine have to offer in the form of monetary compensation? Do we have the necessary margin to make it attractive for these people not only to handle our products but also to push them? Aren't we putting the cart before the horse? After all, we operate as a wholesaler. How can we expect other wholesalers to operate within our margin, particularly at this moment when it isn't a very profitable one?"

Discussion Questions

1. Evaluate the suggestion that Lafontaine sell through a wholesaler in Ontario.
2. Should Lafontaine consider employing middlemen for the entire Canadian market?

Case 9
Star Chemical Company
Evaluating Alternative
Channel Structures

The Star Chemical Company is an old-line manufacturer of chemicals with annual sales of $100 million. In recent years it has experienced a profit slump, mainly because of excess capacity and severe price competition. Industrial buyers choose their chemical suppliers chiefly on price. They pay some attention to delivery reliability and service, but generally they show little loyalty. Star was more profitable in the past because of superior production efficiency, but competitors had built newer plants and were enjoying equal or lower costs than Star.

A number of stockholders were critical of Star's management for not getting into consumer products. Other chemical companies had integrated forward into making and branding some of the final products that were sold to consumers, thereby capturing the value added and sheltering these products from strict price competition. Star Chemical had not done this, primarily because of its lack of experience in consumer marketing and the lack of any specific product opportunities.

Star's research and development department recently developed a new line of chlorinated organic chemicals that functioned as bleaches, germicides, and oxidants. Ralph Hemstead, the R & D director, suggested that one of the uses of the line could be a germicidal chemical developed for the swimming pool market. He believed that the new chemical would have qualities superior to those of existing swimming pool chemicals. Top management was interested because this offered an opportunity to enter the consumer market on a small scale and gain experience.

A new-products committee consisting of the research director, sales manager, marketing research manager, and advertising manager met to discuss what to do with this new consumer product opportunity. They knew that there were a great number of swimming pools in the United States (residential pools, motel pools, public pools, school pools, etc.). Most of the private residential pools were found in warmer-climate states, although some were found in all big cities. Pools required periodical chemical treatment to keep them safe to use. Pool owners and managers bought their supplies through department stores, hardware stores, garden supply stores, pool specialty supply houses, pool service firms, and so on.

Star Chemical's sales force had no experience selling to wholesale or retail firms in the consumer area. However, the sales manager felt that the sales force should be given a chance to sell the new product to the appropriate channels of distribution. Otherwise the company's salespeople would feel bypassed and demoralized at losing a chance to make commissions on the new product. The other managers, however, felt that the company's sales force should not be diverted from its regular job and that a new sales force or distributor could handle the new task more efficiently.

The new-product committee faced some additional decisions. It had to decide whether to brand the product to sell it in bulk form for private labeling. It had to decide whether to cover a large number of distribution channels and markets or concentrate on certain channels and markets. It had to decide whether to push the brand through with good sales-force effort or pull the brand through with heavy advertising.

The members of the new-product committee realized that there were many alternative approaches to the marketing of this germicidal chemical. They recognized the need for clear criteria to make a choice among distribution alternatives. The members agreed to judge alternative proposals against the following criteria (percentages show the criterion's rated importance):

1. Effectiveness in reaching swimming pool owners (15 percent)
2. Amount of profit if this alternative works well (25 percent)
3. Experience company will gain in consumer marketing (10 percent)
4. Amount of investment involved (lower investment considered preferable) (30 percent)
5. Ability of company to cut short its losses (20 percent)

Discussion Question

Star Chemical has called you in to consult on this problem. Management would like to receive a clear picture of its major distribution alternatives. It would also like you to propose a method for evaluating the major distribution alternatives on a quantitative basis.

Case 10
Jayson Guitar Company
Developing Marketing Channel Strategy

By early 1964 the widespread popularity of folk music had greatly increased the demand for quality acoustical guitars. The few existing domestic manufacturers, Martin, Gibson, and Guild, were unable to meet
this heavy demand. The Martin Guitar Company, for example, was back
ordered by as much as thirty-six months on some of its models. Two imported brands, Goya from Sweden, and Gianini from Brazil, were also unable to meet the heavy demand and were far behind in their shipments.
Music store retailers all over the country were complaining about not
being able to get enough good acoustical guitars to satisfy the demand.

Harry Goldstein, the proprietor of a well established music store in a
suburb of Philadelphia was in somewhat better shape to supply guitars to
his customers because his firm also made its own guitars. He employed
four German craftsmen who produced a limited number of relatively expensive custom made guitars. By April of 1964 Goldstein had decided that
it would be worthwhile to expand his shop facilities into a small factory
for the production of high quality acoustical guitars. He hoped to distribute these guitars to other retailers throughout the country. Five more
craftsmen were added and production at the rate of fifty guitars per week
was projected. Production was scheduled to begin January 1, 1965. Three
basic models were planned: A "concert size" with a list price at retail of
$159.50, a "grand concert" to list at $229.50 and a "dreadnaught" listing

for $299.50. Prototypes of these models were tested against the comparably priced domestic and imported guitars. The consensus of those doing the testing—retail customers, professional local guitarists and folksingers, and several nationally prominent artists, was that the guitars were of very high quality, equal or superior to the competition.

The Channel Problem

Goldstein was convinced that he had a fine product. But he was also well aware of the fact that these guitars lacked the prestige names of most of the other manufacturers. Thus, he believed that his major problem was one of getting the right kind of exposure for the guitar line. The best kind of exposure, he reasoned, would be that which would place these guitars in music stores that carried the well-known brands. This would give these guitars the credibility necessary to get customers to take them seriously. Goldstein firmly believed that once customers would take these guitars into their hands to try them out, the fine tone and playing qualities would provide all the selling necessary. In effect, they would "sell themselves," he believed.

In May of 1964, Goldstein met with his store manager, Jim Johnson, whom he often used as a "sounding board" for his own ideas as well as a source of new ideas. Their conversation proceeded as follows:

Goldstein: "Jim, I think we should try to get our guitars into retailers who handle one or more of the well-known competitive brands. This will enhance the prestige of our product—which is really what we need to get off the ground. This is just the right time to approach these retailers with our line, because almost none of them can get enough of the other brands. I'll bet they would be delighted to get their hands on another quality line of acoustical guitars—they're losing sales like crazy from not having enough good guitars."

Johnson: "I agree with you, Harry, that if we could get our guitars into the retailers who carry the big name products that this would enhance the prestige of our guitars. I also agree that right now and in the immediate future these retailers probably would like to carry another line of quality acoustical guitars to reduce lost sales. This would be especially true if we could better the usual trade discount of 40 percent from list price—perhaps making our discount 50 percent of list. But Harry, what will happen to our line when the supply catches up with demand? This shortage situation is not going to last forever. In fact I just read a trade magazine that reported that all of the major guitar manufacturers are expanding their facilities. It is only a matter of time—probably less than a year—before they start catching up. I have a feeling that when this happens many of these retailers will drop us like a hot potato because in a nonshortage situation they will no longer be willing to purchase our line. We certainly can't compete with the other manufacturers in having a

428   Part Five   Cases in Marketing Channels

widespread brand acceptance or in advertising and promotion to pull our line through the retail stores. I personally think, Harry, that we should concentrate on those retailers who do not presently carry any of the competing guitars. Since most of these retailers have been unable to get the franchise for the other lines, they are more likely to appreciate the opportunity to carry a quality line of acoustical guitars. These are the people who will work for us—pushing our product not only during the shortage but in the longer term as well. These are the kinds of dealers whom we should cultivate."

Goldstein: "You may have a point there, Jim. Let me think about it for awhile."

Discussion Questions

1. Which group of retailers should Goldstein attempt to reach with his new line of acoustical guitars?
2. Can you develop other distribution strategies for the Jayson Guitar Co.?

Case 11
Innovative Toys Inc. (A)
Revamping Channel Strategy

Innovative Toys Inc. is a wholly owned subsidary of a large conglomerate corporation. For a number of years, Innovative enjoyed a reputation for making outstandingly creative and high quality toys, especially for the preschool market. The company's sales and profit picture had, for the most part, been quite good over the years, reflecting a high level of consumer and trade acceptance.

Innovative's channel strategy had traditionally emphasized selective distribution through toy jobbers (wholesalers) who in turn sold to small, independent toy stores and department stores. Innovative did a substantial consumer mail order business and engaged in direct sales to schools as well. Eight company owned retail stores were also used. Innovative specifically avoided sales through mass-merchandisers such as the large volume toy stores and discount department stores.

In 1972 the performance of Innovative Toys suddenly plummeted. Sales had decreased by two thirds and net losses were high. Corporate morale was at an all time low and dealer relations were characterized by the sales force and senior executives as "extremely poor."

The parent corporation wasted no time in replacing Innovative's president with one of its top troubleshooters—Max Shellenberg. The new president's charge was straightforward: He was instructed to turn Innovative around in one year or liquidate the company.

Shellenberg immediately began the task of analyzing Innovative's operations to see if he could salvage what appeared to be a hopeless situation. His analysis of the company's marketing strategy revealed the following findings:

Products

Shellenberg found that Innovative had almost 200 different toy items, many of which were deadwood. He believed that a number of these could be eliminated with no loss of volume.

New product design was lagging. Shellenberg felt this was due to the former top management's failure to recognize that the toy business is a fashion industry requiring continuous and careful attention to changing consumer tastes.

The existing packaging was inadequate and too expensive. An especially acute problem was the failure of the packaging to illustrate the special features of Innovative's toys. Shellenberg believed this defect presented a significant disadvantage for self service merchandising.

Price

Consumer research showed that Innovative toys had a high price image. (In reality most of Innovative's toys were competively priced).

Shellenberg also found a failure by the previous management to be sensitive to particular price points and ranges for toys. Hence Innovative had several price gaps which could not be filled with existing toy items.

Promotion

Promotion was lacking in a sense of direction. This was particularly true for the personal selling effort. Clear policies as to how the company's twenty-member sales force was expected to secure and maintain accounts were not spelled out.

Advertising was sporadic and lacking in focus; i.e., it did not consistently emphasize the competitive advantages of Innovative Toys relative to the competition. Thus, it provided little support for the sales force in its attempts to gain dealer acceptance for Innovative Toys.

Channels

It was in the channels area, however, that Shellenberg found the most extensive and overwhelming problems. He delineated the following:

1. Innovative's selective distribution policy had cut it off from most of the potential toy market. Mail order, school, small independent retailers, and department stores accounted for only about 15 percent of the total toy market.

2. Inadequacies in other areas of the marketing mix (see above) had left Innovative ill-equipped to sell to mass merchandisers.

3. Dealer relations were poor. Not only did Innovative have trouble making deliveries but took a haughty attitude towards its dealers as though it enjoyed a great deal of power which was certainly not the case. Many dealers who had dropped the line were in no mood to take more punishment from Innovative.

4. Little data existed on Innovative's dealers. Thus, the company knew little about the relative performance of its channel members.

5. No strategy existed for broadening the channels to incorporate mass retail merchandisers.

6. Dealer support policies relating to advertising allowances, extra discounts, point of purchase displays, etc. were followed haphazardly.

In late 1972, Shellenberg met with his newly appointed Vice President of Marketing, Donald Morrison, and the sales manager Joe Wilson. Shellenberg believed that the key to salvaging the Innovative Toy Company lay in a complete revamping of the company's channel strategy. Morrison and Wilson agreed but pointed out that changes in the product, price, and promotion variables would be required before the channels strategy could be substantially changed. Shellenberg, who was keenly aware of the interrelationships of the other marketing mix variables to the channel variable, wasted no time in replying to Morrison and Wilson, "Where do you suggest we start?"

Discussion Questions

1. Where should Shellenberg, Morrison, and Wilson begin in devising a strategy to salvage the Innovative Toy Company?
2. How should the channels strategy be revamped?

Case 12
The Oliver Corporation
Finding Prospective Dealers

Oliver Corporation, Chicago-based subsidiary of The White Motor Company, and manufacturer of a wide range of farm and industrial equipment, markets through an independent dealer organization supported by eleven company sales branches and warehouses. Each dealer has a contract with the company giving the dealer sales rights of Oliver products in his or her trading area.

The company has established sales potentials for each of the counties in the United States. On the basis of this information, company area representatives, called territory managers, are assigned "prime target areas" (in their respective territories) where representation of Oliver dealers is considered inadequate, and where new dealers are to be established.

After summarizing the territorial distribution picture, the territory manager, with the agreement of the branch sales manager, selects the top priority target market among prime targets, and sets about locating prospects for an Oliver dealership.

To help in this task, the company has prepared a special manual "Finding . . . Selling . . . Starting a New Dealer—Right!" which outlines the plan the territory manager is to use in finding and establishing a new Oliver dealer.

Finding prospects is essentially a two-step operation: first, the territory manager conducts a market survey; then a "community leaders' meeting" is held.

The Market Survey

The market survey involves a minimum of 100 farm calls (and up to 200 in larger markets). According to the company, "These are necessary to get a cross section of most trade areas, and to give the confidence and conviction necessary to enable the territory manager to enthusiastically present the merits of an Oliver franchise and convince the prospect to accept it. The success of the new dealer will depend in large measure on an accurate knowledge of customer requirements, which can only be had with an inventory of potential sales prospects. It means visiting the farmer, learning his conditions, and building a sales program to fill his needs."

In conducting this market survey, the territory manager assembles a great deal of information on the local market, including the following:

Types and acreages of farms

Principal crops

Number of livestock

Age and condition of equipment used on each farm

Number of farmers living in the market area; their equipment needs and buying habits

Kind of shop facilities, services and programs needed to sell and service this market

Facts on local advertising media (radio, newspapers, etc.)

Capital required, and net profit a dealer in this market might expect

Competition

What kind and how much equipment can be sold annually

This information comes from farmers and a variety of other sources, including vocational-agricultural teachers, the U.S. Bureau of the Census, the Oliver research department in Chicago, and others. More detailed information on the local market is obtained from community leaders, especially from those dealing extensively with farmers.

The Community Leaders' Meeting

A "community leaders' meeting" is the second step in finding Oliver dealer prospects. The five main purposes of this meeting, as stated in the company manual, are to:

1. Sell these businessmen on the Oliver franchise (sometimes it makes one or more of them anxious to sponsor and perhaps finance the dealer prospect)
2. Get leaders in the community helping you to locate the right prospects
3. Building prestige and business for Oliver
4. Help you sell the prospects
5. Multiply your effectiveness.

The groundwork for this meeting, attended by at least six to eight key community leaders—but not more than 12 to 15—is carefully laid in advance. Those invited may include the mayor, county commissioners, high school principals, vocational-agricultural teachers, bankers who lend money to farmers (but not bankers backing competing dealers), chamber of commerce officials, and prominent merchants selling extensively to the farm trade. Known dealer prospects are not invited.

At the meeting itself, an Oliver film is shown that explains the company's philosophy, and the benefits a franchised Oliver dealer brings to the community.

Following the film, a series of about a dozen charts prepared by the territory manager are exhibited, summarizing the results of the market survey. In addition, related information is brought out, such as: capital requirements for establishing a dealership; business and profit opportunities for the Oliver dealer (including the potential sales volume of new and used equipment, repair parts and shop services, based on the volume of the average Oliver dealer in that type of market); and the services available to the farm community through the Oliver dealer. The final step involves asking those present who they think is the right person (or people) in this market area for the Oliver farm implement franchise.

The Follow-Up

After the meeting, the territory manager calls on all prospects whose names have been suggested. The company feels that every suggestion must be followed up, even though the territory manager may already have spotted the party regarded as the best choice—perhaps even before the meeting.

The territory manager then divides the prospects into two groups:

1. Promising prospects, who will be given a franchise presentation
2. Unqualified prospects, who, after being called upon, will be dropped from active consideration

It is then time to choose from among the promising prospects the one the Oliver territory manager wants to interest in signing a franchise agreement.

Discussion Questions

1. Evaluate Oliver's approach to finding prospective dealers.
2. What other approaches can you suggest for finding prospective dealers?

Case 13
The National Oil Company
Evaluation of a Proposal for
a New Type of Station

Max Hunt, marketing manager of a national oil company, had just completed an interview with an independent marketing consultant who had submitted an unsolicited proposal recommending that the company inaugurate the construction and operation of a new type of automotive service station.

The National Oil Company was a regional marketer enjoying a 12.5 percent share of the market. It was an aggressive promoter and advertiser whose basic corporate strategy stressed the development of company-owned service stations. The company's station development program had been highly aggressive, resulting in a high-level density of stations in the major metropolitan areas within the company's area. It was considered a major oil company, and it sold its products at the recognized major price, although certain stations were allowed to shade their prices as much as one or two cents if their location was sufficiently weak that such price cuts were necessary to bring the station's volume past the break-even point.

The consultant's proposal was the outgrowth of a motivational research study he had undertaken for another, nonoil company, plant. One portion of this study disclosed that a great many women were highly reluctant (and frequently adamantly opposed) to having the family automobile gassed or serviced at a service station or garage because of the presence of numerous men in and around the premises. Consequently, consultants had begun investigating the possibilities of developing a specially designed service station located in middle-class to well-to-do neighborhoods, catering exclusively to women and had begun to develop a prototype in which no men at all were allowed on the premises. The station was to be manned by women, and only women could be serviced. Naturally, the women attendants were to be completely trained by the company to perform their duties adequately. The station would be specially designed to appeal to women, not to look like a gasoline station. Special lounges for drinking coffee and the like would be provided.

Hunt was immediately fascinated by the boldness of this concept, and he desired to give it serious consideration. He seriously wondered if such an innovation might not only provide the company with a significant differential advantage but also gain the company a tremendous amount of favorable publicity and improve its image among women drivers. He wondered if a few such stations might have a very favorable carry-over effect into all of the company's chain. However, being an experienced marketing man he was quite certain that there had to be several serious disadvantages to such a development, and so he summoned his assistant and assigned him the task of preparing a report evaluating the feasibility of the consultant's proposal.

Discussion Questions

1. Evaluate the idea.
2. Should the company adopt it?
3. What revisions would you make to the proposal, if any?

Case 14
Innovative Toys Inc. (B)
Consumer Shopping Behavior
and Channel Design

By 1978 Innovative Toys Inc. had developed a new toy line consisting of six high quality toys for infants ranging in price from $1.79 to $2.99. Because of the fierce competition for shelf space in the major retail channels for infant toys (mass merchandisers, discount toy stores, and discount department stores), Innovative was considering the possibility of selling the new infant toy line through supermarkets.

To appraise the feasibility of using supermarkets to distribute the infant toy line, Donald Morrison, Vice President of Marketing, hired an outside research firm to study the question. Excerpts from the findings of the research report are presented below.

Supermarket Channels

Supermarkets have not played a large role in the distribution of infant toys or other classes of toys. In fact it is estimated that only about 2 percent of total industry toy volume is accounted for by supermarkets. But as the 1980's approach, drastic changes may be in store for the distribution of toys through supermarkets. The underlying factor responsible for this change is the heavy push by the supermarket industry to put more emphasis on the sale of nonfoods, particularly general merchandise because of the higher margins available. Toys, particularly infant toys, might play a prominant role in this overall trend towards more emphasis on general merchandise (GM) by supermarkets.

Two basic factors must be present, however, in order to market toys successfully through supermarket channels: (1) supermarket buyers must be favorably disposed toward toys as an important and profitable GM category, and (2) consumers must be willing to purchase toys from supermarkets. An analysis of each of these factors follows:

Disposition of Supermarket Executives toward Toys as a GM Category

Several recent studies show a generally favorable attitude by supermarket executives toward toys as an important GM category. For example, a study of a nationwide panel of supermarket executives reported in the January, 1978 issue of *Progressive Grocer* yielded the results shown in Table 1.

As shown in Table 1, no ratings were less than good, while 54 percent of the supermarket executives rated toys as very good or excellent as a GM category.

Another study conducted by the research division of *Progressive Grocer* developed a comparative rating scale to show how toys are rated by supermarket executives relative to twenty-nine other GM categories. This is shown in Table 2.

As Table 2 indicates, toys do reasonably well, scoring 79 (peg) and 67 (boxed) out of a possible 100. While toys are not rated as highly as light bulbs, disposable lighters, motor oil and other GM categories, peg toys rated ahead of such items as basic soft goods, batteries, and sunglasses, and boxed toys are rated higher than glassware, photo finishing, hardware, etc.

It would appear, then, that toys in general are viewed quite favorably by supermarkets as a potentially important GM category.

Table 1
Sales and Profit Ratings of Toys by a Representative Panel of Supermarket Executives

	Ratings
Excellent	8%
Very Good	46%
Good	46%
Fair/Poor	0

Table 2
How Supermarket Executives Rate Thirty General Merchandise Product Groups

Product	Score
1. Light bulbs	100
2. Disposable lighters	96
3. Pet supplies	91
4. Pantyhose	88
5. School supplies, stationery	88
6. Gloves	87
7. Magazines	86
8. Motor oil	85
9. Housewares	84
10. Photo supplies	80
11. Paperbacks	79
12. Toys (peg)	79
13. Soft goods, basics	78
14. Soft goods, kitchen	76
15. Batteries	75
16. Greeting cards	74
17. Sunglasses	73
18. Softgoods, accessories	73
19. Baby goods	70
20. Toys (boxed)	67
21. Glassware	66
22. Children's books	65
23. Footwear	62
24. Yarn	61
25. Photo finishing	61
26. Party goods	59
27. Hardware, paint supplies	58
28. Sewing notions	58
29. Auto accessories	55
30. Small appliances	51

Index: Highest score = 100
Median score = 75

With respect to supermarket executives' attitudes toward the more specialized category of infant toys, and particularly, Innovative Toys' line of infant toys, no survey data exist. Nevertheless, it is possible at this point to appraise probable supermarket executive attitudes towards Innovative's infant toy line by comparing the line against certain basic criteria commonly used by supermarket buyers when selecting a new GM item. The most important of these criteria are as follows:

1. Margin potential
2. Frequency of sale or repeat factor (turnover)
3. Impulse buying potential

4. Size
5. Degree to which purchased by women
6. Stapleness

Each of these is discussed below in terms of how well Innovative's infant toy line is likely to rate on each criterion.

Margin Potential.   Deteriorating margins on food products and rapidly increasing operating expenses have made supermarket operators highly sensitive to the margin potentials of prospective new GM products. They want margins which are much better than the average 20–21 percent of sales for all products sold by independent and chain supermarkets in 1977. While there is no definite minimum margin requirement for a GM item, if the item is capable of yielding a margin which is approximately 50 percent higher than the 20–21 percent average (i.e. at least 30 percent), it is more likely to be acceptable in terms of margin requirements.

To see how Innovative's infant toys rate in terms of potential margins, Table 3 was prepared.

As shown in Table 3, if these toys could be sold at the prices shown in column 3, the margins generated would be attractive and competitive with many other GM items.

Turnover.   With respect to frequency of sales, the product should be one that can be sold frequently, and to a large percentage of the consumers who shop in supermarkets. Even though supermarkets have high traffic, the shoppers are essentially the same week after week. So, if the product is to be sold over and over again to yield a high turnover, it must be consumed fairly rapidly. It should be pointed out, however, that the turnover figure on GM need not be as high as the 12–14 average stockturns for grocery products. A turnover rate between 6 and 7 is quite acceptable for a

Table 3
Margin Potentials for Innovative Toys' Infant Toys Using Estimated Retail Selling Prices

Toy	Cost	Selling Price	$ Markup	% Margin on Selling Price
Infant Ball	1.75	2.69	.94	34.9
Little Teether	2.00	2.99	.99	33.1
Feel and Look	1.60	2.49	.89	35.7
Fun Rings	1.55	2.29	.74	32.3
Look and Find	1.60	2.39	.79	33.0
Johnny Teething	1.25	1.79	.54	30.1
			Average	33.2

GM product yielding a margin of 30–35 percent. If Innovative Toys could achieve an annual turnover rate of not less than 6 per year it would meet the turnover criteria of many supermarkets.

Impulse Buying.   A good GM product must lend itself to impulse buying. Packaging, price, and quality must be such that the customer does not have to comparison shop other stores. She should be able to decide upon its purchase within a few moments of contact with the product at the point of sale.

Innovative's infant toy line appears to meet this criterion quite well. Packaging, quality, and price are geared to promote impulse purchasing.

Size.   Display space, even in the modern supermarkets of 30,000 sq. feet is limited and, of course, in the smaller supermarkets of 20,000 sq. feet and under, space is even more limited. A good GM product, therefore, must not be overly bulky. On the other hand, given the theft and pilferage problem that exists today, very small items can also present problems.

Innovative's infant toy line appears to present no particular problems on this criterion. But care will have to be given in the future to developing even more effective yet compact prepack displays.

Women Shoppers.   About 80 percent of the supermarkets' customers are women. Accordingly, a GM product must be one which is normally purchased by women. There is no problem here with Innovative's infant toy line because these toys normally would be bought by women.

Stapleness.   A desirable GM product should be relatively staple in the sense that variations in colors, sizes, and styles should be at minimum. Supermarkets do not have the space to offer wide selections and they are very reluctant to handle style or fashion merchandise except for brief in and out promotions.

Innovative's infant toy line scores well on this criterion. The selection is limited and it is not subject to rapid fashion changes.

Consumer Willingness to Purchase Toys in Supermarkets

Even though supermarket operators have a generally favorable disposition toward toys as a GM category, and Innovative's infant toy line should rate highly in terms of meeting basic supermarket purchasing criteria for GM, the ultimate determinant of whether the line will sell successfully in supermarkets lies in the area of consumer shopping habits and patterns. In short, are consumers likely to buy more toys and particularly Innovative's infant toys from supermarkets?

In order to deal with this question, a general profile of supermarket shopping behavior is discussed below in terms of how this shopping behavior is likely to facilitate or inhibit toy sales in supermarkets. Secondly,

Table 4
Preparation for Shopping Trips by Supermarket Shoppers

	Make a List	Read Newspapers	Read Advertising Circulars	Consult Other Family Members
Almost always	65%	64%	52%	20%
Frequently	16%	14%	18%	25%
Occasionally	13%	16%	19%	33%
Almost never	6%	6%	11%	22%
	100%	100%	100%	100%

a preliminary survey was conducted dealing specifically with consumer attitudes toward the purchase of infant toys in supermarkets. The general profile and the survey are discussed in the next two sections.

Supermarket Shopping Behavior and the Purchase of Toys.   Customers shop the supermarket quite frequently. The latest studies show about 2.4 trips per week. Most of these customers are women (about 80 percent) although there is a slight tendency for men to participate more frequently. Children are present on about 17 percent of the trips. In general, during their trips to the supermarket, customers are in a buying mood. Most buy more than they had planned to purchase before visiting the supermarket. With the continuing stigma of inflation, however, recent studies indicate that more careful planning by the shopper is becoming more common as a way of staying within the budget. A recent study conducted by the Home Testing Institute yields the findings shown in Table 4.

As shown in Table 4, preparation or preplanning is done quite frequently by most shoppers.

Because much of the success of supermarket GM marketing stems from frequent shopping and impulse buying, any indication of a decline in shopping frequency and impulse buying could have negative implications for GM sales whether they be toys or other GM products.

Fortunately this does not appear to be the case. Shopping frequency has remained relatively stable over the last five years, and although consumers are becoming more *careful and sharper* shoppers, they are not turning away from impulse buying. They will, however, exercise more care and judgement about which impulse items they buy at the supermarket. More attention will be given to the quality and value of the GM products they buy. Impulse buying in the more extreme sense of haphazardly grabbing a GM item off of the shelf and tossing it into the shopping cart will be replaced by what might be called "point of purchase judgement shopping." That is, new GM products (and new food products for that matter) will be more carefully scrutinized at the point of purchase. If the product passes this more careful scrutiny, then the basic advantages of having a desirable GM item available in the supermarket will prevail.

Customers will be happy to take advantage of the one-stop shopping offered by the supermarket because they will be able to take care of more requirements without making additional stops at the drug store, hardware store, discount department store, toy store or other retail outlets.

Thus, in summary, consumer shopping behavior, while becoming more planned and careful, will still be quite amenable to impulse purchases of GM products of all types, including toys, if these products appear to offer *good values* as well as the *convenience* of buying them in supermarkets.

Survey of Consumer Attitudes toward the Purchase of Infant Toys In Supermarkets. In order to appraise the attitudes and behavior of consumers dealing *specifically* with the purchases of infant toys from supermarkets, a survey of 500 mothers with infant children was conducted. Four hundred sixty usable questionnaires were obtained. The findings are shown in Tables 5 to 13. Analysis of the findings presented in the tables follows.

Table 5 shows that for the sample group of consumers, the overwhelming choice of retail outlet for purchasing infant toys currently is the

Table 5
Types of Retail Outlets from Which Consumers Buy Infant Toys Most Often

	No.	%
Discount toy stores	350	76.1
Discount department stores	40	8.8
Department stores	20	4.3
Variety stores	20	4.3
Supermarkets	8	1.7
Drug stores	12	2.6
Other	10	2.2
Total	460	100%

Table 6
Consumer Ratings of Quality of Infant Toys Sold in Supermarkets

	No.	%
Very high quality	0	0
Good quality	60	13.0
Mediocre quality	100	21.8
Poor quality	180	39.1
Very low quality	120	26.1
Total	460	100%

Table 7
Extent to Which Consumers Plan for the Purchase of Infant Toys before Shopping

	No.	%
Almost always	160	34.8
Frequently	140	30.4
Usually	80	17.4
Seldom	20	4.4
Almost never	60	13.0
Total	460	100%

Table 8
Likelihood of Consumers Buying Infant Toys in Supermarkets in the Future if Such Toys Were of High Quality and Competitively Priced

	No.	%
Extremely likely	80	17.4
Very likely	100	21.8
Somewhat likely	120	26.1
Unlikely	137	29.8
Very unlikely	23	5.0
Total	460	100%

discount toy store. Only 8 (2.6%) mentioned supermarkets. This is not surprising, however, especially in light of consumer perceptions of low quality of infant toys presently sold in supermarkets as shown in Table 6. Hence, at present, it is very rare to find consumers who look to supermarkets as their most likely choice for buying infant toys.

Table 7 shows that the overwhelming majority of consumers plan their purchases of infant toys before shopping. This suggests that consumers are not *at present* heavily inclined toward impulse purchasing when it comes to buying infant toys. This does not mean, however, that they could not become more amenable to impulse buying if quality infant toys were more readily available in highly convenient retail outlets such as supermarkets. This is implied by the findings shown in Tables 8 and 9. Table 8 shows 65.3 percent of the respondents expressed at least some likelihood of buying infant toys from supermarkets if good quality and competitive prices were to become available. Table 9 shows that, for those who would be likely to buy from supermarkets, the most important reasons for doing so are the greater convenience offered by supermarkets (73.3%), and the savings in time (20%). Thus, the heavy trend toward one-stop shopping which fosters impulse buying is evident here.

Table 10 shows the other side of the coin. For those consumers who

Table 9
Reasons Given for Purchasing Infant Toys in Supermarkets by Those Consumers Expressing Any Degree of Likelihood* of Buying Infant Toys from Supermarkets

	No.	%
Greater convenience of supermarkets	220	73.3
Lower prices	17	5.7
Better selection	0	0
Savings in time	60	20.0
Other	3	1.0
Total	300	100%

*somewhat likely, very likely, extremely likely

Table 10
Reasons Given for *Not* Purchasing Infants Toys in Supermarket by Those Consumers Expressing No Likelihood* of Buying Infant Toys from Supermarkets

	No.	%
Lower quality of toys sold in supermarkets	40	25.0
Higher prices charged	0	0
Poor selections offered	60	37.5
Need for planning infant toy purchases	20	12.5
Other	40	25.0
Total	160	100%

*unlikely, very unlikely

expressed no likelihood of buying infant toys in the supermarket (34.7%), the reasons offered were perception of lower quality (25%), poor selection (37.5%) and the need for planning (12.5%). A reasonable inference that may be drawn from Table 10, though, is that if quality and selection of infant toys in supermarkets were improved, a significant portion of the "unlikely to purchase" group might move into the "likely to purchase" group.

Thus, on balance, the data presented in Tables 5–10 suggest that from the standpoint of consumer propensities to shop for infant toys in the supermarkets, the prospects are promising.

Tables 11–13 summarize other information relevant to the marketing of infant toys through supermarkets.

Table 11 shows the maximum amounts that consumers said they would be willing to spend on unplanned purchases of infant toys in supermarkets. The $5.00 amount appears to be the upper limit. No consumers expressed a willingness to spend more than that amount on an unplanned infant toy purchase.

Table 12 shows that the highest percentage of consumers (60.9%) purchased infant toys about twice per year. The next highest percentage (21.7%) made purchases about once per month. It should be pointed out, though, that this frequency of purchase pattern reflects consumer shopping behaviors associated with the types of retail outlets *presently patronized* for infant toy purchases. If quality infant toys were more readily available in supermarkets these patterns could change significantly.

Finally, Table 13 shows the section of the supermarket in which con-

Table 11
Maximum Amount Consumers Are Willing to Spend on *Unplanned* Purchases of Infant Toys in Supermarkets

	No.	%
Under $1.00	47	10.2
1.00–1.49	44	9.6
1.50–1.99	142	30.9
2.00–2.99	151	32.9
3.00–4.99	76	16.5
5.00–6.99	0	0
Total	460	100%

Table 12
Frequency of Infant Toy Purchases

	No.	%
Every 6 months	280	60.9
Every 3 months	40	8.7
Once per month	100	21.7
Every 2 weeks	40	8.7
Total	460	100%

Table 13
Sections of the Supermarket in Which Consumers Expect to Find Infant Toys

	No.	%
Baby department	420	91.3
Section where other toys are sold	36	7.8
Household items section	1	0.2
Check-out counter	3	0.6
Others	0	0
Total	460	100%

sumers would expect to find infant toys displayed. The overwhelming majority (91.3%) expect to find them in the baby department.

Discussion Questions

1. Based on the findings from the market research study, do you think Innovative should attempt to market the infant toy line through supermarkets?
2. What are some of the major obstacles Innovative might face if it does attempt to sell the infant toy line through supermarkets?
3. What other kinds of retail outlets might be appropriate for the infant toy line?

Case 15
The Mass Market Paperback Distribution Systems
An Opportunity for Better Channel Management?

It is estimated that the mass market paperback book industry had annual gross sales of $425,200,000 in 1974. This total amounts to over 600,000,000 paperback books being distributed each year. To obtain this sales volume, a total of 609,000,000 paperback books were introduced into the distribution channels. Two hundred thirty million unsold paperback books were also removed from the retail racks and returned for full credit. Thus at least 839,500,000 paperbacks were handled in 1974. Returns amounted to a staggering 36 percent of gross dollar sales and 38 percent of unit volume sales. To maintain this volume, 350–400 new paperback titles are placed in the distribution channel each month. The limited rack space available to display these books makes competition for rack space fierce. Once rack space is acquired, it is quite important that the books which occupy this space turn over many times during the year.

Evolution of the System

There are four major classes of participants in the distribution of paperbacks to retailers: (1) publishers, (2) national distributors, (3) independent magazine/paperback wholesalers and (4) jobbers. The system as it exists

Exhibit 1
Mass-Market Paperback Distribution System

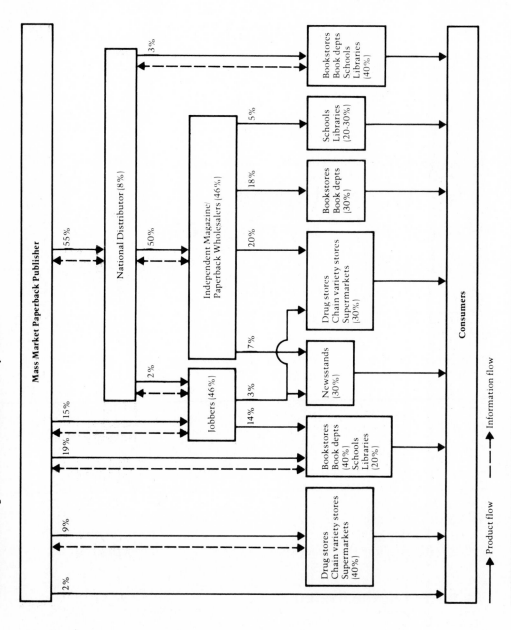

Numbers to right of product flows indicate percentage of total publisher volume.
Numbers in parentheses indicate discounts or fees offered to a given member of the system.

today is the product of a history of evolution beginning in 1939 when Pocket Books introduced in America the forerunner of today's mass market paperback.

When Robert deGraff, the originator of Pocket Books, started out, his idea was to publish a relatively inexpensive (25 cents), small ("pocket" size) novel for a widespread readership. He solved the problem of distribution by engaging the American News Company (ANC) to distribute Pocket Books through its existing network of local newspaper and magazine wholesalers, each of which operated in exclusive geographic territories. By the late 1930s the absolute dominance of the ANC network began to erode as various "independent" magazine distributors and local wholesalers began to appear which fed tens of thousands of retail outlets with newspapers and magazines. The paperback publishers saw the opportunity for widespread distribution and convinced the wholesaler to add paperbacks to his inventory. (During the 1940s and early 1950s a publisher dealt either entirely with ANC wholesalers, or entirely with independent wholesalers.) The agreement, however, called for the publisher to accept the same terms used for magazine sales: full credit for all copies returned.

By 1950 the monopolistic grip of the ANC network was broken. In its place has grown a system of national distributors and local independent magazine/paperback wholesalers (hereafter referred to as wholesalers). Although independent of the ANC organization, these wholesalers still deal in relatively exclusive geographic territories.

The jobber, the fourth class of participant, operates alongside the wholesaler, serving those retailers which the wholesaler has either failed to satisfy or decided not to serve.

The Mass Market Paperback System

Exhibit 1 is the model of the mass paperback book distribution system. The solid lines in Exhibit 1 represent product flows. The dashed lines represent information flows confirmed in questionnaire responses. Down channel information includes promotion for new releases, offers of incentives to encourage greater efficiency and reduce returns, and suggestions for more effective merchandising techniques. Up channel information (feedback) includes sales and returns figures, initial orders for new releases and reorders for existing titles.

The numbers to the right of the solid lines in Exhibit 1 are in all cases the percentage of total publisher volume flowing through the respective channel. The numbers in parentheses in each box are the discounts from cover price generally received by the respective members of the network on volume received through the respective channels. For example, note that a bookstore dealing directly with the publisher will generally receive a 40 percent discount, whereas a bookstore dealing with a wholesaler will generally receive a 30 percent discount. In the case of the national distributor, the number represents a fee based on cover price as opposed to a discount on a purchase.

Elements of the System

There are two general categories of sales by the publishers: those through a national distributor and those directly to jobbers and retailers. The national distributor is shown in Exhibit 1 as independent, although in the cases of five publishers, the national distributor is a wholly-owned division. There are no discernible operational differences between the two methods. One economic difference, of course, is the saving of the 8.0 percent fee for the wholly-owned distributors. In any case, each of the ten more prominent publishers deals exclusively with one national distributor for sales to wholesalers, and typically 55 percent of all business will be through the distributor.

Direct sales to retailers and jobbers account for the other 45 percent of a publisher's business. The percentages shown in Exhibit 1 are derived from the survey results and will differ somewhat from company to company.

Note that nearly all of the volume handled by the national distributor is sold through independent magazine/paperback wholesalers (ID's). Survey results indicate that paperbacks represent 20–35 percent of total volume for most ID's. The greatest share of their sales volume (60 percent or more) is in magazines.

Sales by the publisher to the ID's and jobbers are generally at a discount of 46 percent. Direct sales to retail accounts are at a discount of 40 percent (although 20 percent is more common for schools and libraries). Direct sales activity expanded rapidly in the late 1950s and early 1960s, a period when jobbers began to emerge and gradually increase their share of the market at the expense of the wholesalers. Wholesalers' competitive edge rests on their ability to provide a local source of supply. However, where wholesalers operated within a relatively exclusive territory, jobbers recognized no geographic boundaries. They took over accounts which became dissatisfied with wholesaler service. The jobber could provide central billing for variety store chains where the wholesaler could not.

Another major direct sales customer is the national bookstore chain which purchases directly from the publisher. The growth in chains such as B. Dalton and Waldenbooks has helped to increase direct sales over the years. Wholesalers responded to the erosion of their market share by providing better service, improving their merchandising techniques and emphasizing their responsiveness as local suppliers. They are forced to offer a lower discount, however, in order to cover the additional cost of these improvements. Typically, a wholesaler offers a 30 percent discount to a given retail account as opposed to the 40 percent offered by a publisher.

Estimates for the total number of wholesalers who handle paperbacks vary from 400 to 600, for jobbers from 100 to 200, and for total mass market paperback retailers from 60,000 to 80,000. The number of retail outlets selling paperbacks has dropped from an estimated 110,000 fifteen years ago, although the number of pockets and racks has increased.

The net result of the evolution of the various channels of distribution is that paperbacks are available to the consumer in a wide variety of retail locations. The retailer may at any one time be dealing with a wholesaler who provides immediate delivery of small paperback and magazine orders and complete rack service at a 30 percent discount, a jobber who provides the same service but only for paperbacks and with perhaps less immediate delivery at a 35 percent or 40 percent discount, and a publisher who provides no service and slow delivery at a 40 percent discount.

Discussion Questions

1. How could the channels for mass paperback book distribution be managed to reduce the high levels of returns of books?
2. What role would a better information system play in this?

Case 16
Dunkin' Donuts Incorporated
Channel Member Training

Dunkin' Donuts Incorporated, a fast-food franchisor with an annual sales volume of nearly $100 million, opened its first doughnut and coffee shop in 1950. Ten years later the company had over 430 shops in operation in 31 states and in Canada. The vast majority of its shops are operated by independent franchisees, all of whom have undergone intensive training at "Dunkin' Donuts University," which the company maintains at Quincy, Massachusetts.

The current six-week training program consists of a five-week formal course, broken up into six-day work weeks, and a final week spent on-the-job in a local doughnut shop. Approximately half of the program deals with technical production techniques used in the manufacture of doughnuts and similar products. The other half is concerned with financial, personnel, and management practices to be followed by owner-managers of the retail stores.

The training schedule for each franchisee and the instructional materials for each of his thirty days in training are precisely programmed. Exhibit 1 illustrates a typical daily schedule.

As the trainees proceed through the program, they are tested with a series of exams. These measure both their retention of the material covered and their aptitude in performing the various manual tasks associated

Exhibit 1
Franchisee Daily Training and Classroom Schedule
(Dunkin' Donuts Incorporated)

Place/Time	Instructor	Subject
(Week 1 Day 1)		
Classroom		**Orientation**
8:00 AM 9:30 AM	Staff	1. Introduction and background information on members of the training staff. a. University Organizational Chart 2. Distribution and review of detailed training schedule and associated manuals. 3. Discussion of the training school's requirements, rules and regulations.
9:30 AM	Director of Management Development	4. Review of the objectives, purpose and scope of the 5-week training and classroom schedule. 5. Discussion of the evaluation of franchise owners and other operating personnel during the 5-week training and classroom schedule.
Classroom		**Introduction to Cake Donut Production**
10:00 AM 10:30 AM	Staff	1. Distribution and review of the cake donut production training manual.
Work Area		
10:30 AM 11:00 AM	Staff	2. Introduction to cake donut production equipment and related tools.
11:00 AM 12:30 PM	Staff	3. Demonstration of how to produce and prepare cake donuts.
Lunch		
12:30 PM 1:30 PM		(Not to exceed one hour)

with doughnut production. The trainees are given uniforms, operating manuals, and all the other items required for the course.

During the two and a half weeks they spend on doughnut production, the trainees study subjects ranging from the fermentation process occurring in yeast doughnuts to the correct selection of frying oils, the maintenance of equipment, batch planning, etc. Trainees are required to achieve a certain level of proficiency in doughnut production before they can move on to the management training portion of the program.

During this management training phase, the company attempts to convert what are often blue-collar employees into professional managers. Franchisees are introduced to techniques used in interviewing and selecting employees, in rating their job performances, and in carrying out many other managerial tasks. They also learn how to train employees in the use of supplies and selling techniques.

A record is kept of each trainee's progress in the program. Exhibit 2 illustrates a weekly training report. Copies of such reports are made available to the district manager in whose assigned area the franchisee is to be located.

Exhibit 2
Franchise Weekly Training Report (Dunkin' Donuts Incorporated)

Week Ending_____

Trainee_____   Capacity of Trainee_____
Location_____   Est. Completion Date_____

Area of Training   **Number of Hours**
Donut Production   _____
Sales and Finishing   _____
Financial Management   _____
On-the-job Training   _____
Dunkin' Donuts University Classes   _____
  Total Training Hours   _____

Examination   **Working Donut Examination**
Subject_____   Date Taken_____
Date Taken_____   Score_____
Score_____

Comments on Training

_____
_____
_____
_____
_____
_____
_____

Progress
Below   Above
Average_____ Average_____ Average_____ Outstanding_____
Trainer_____ Date_____

The faculty of Dunkin' Donuts University consists of a director of training and two assistants, augmented by technical, financial, and marketing executives from the nearby corporate headquarters. A local company-owned outlet is used for on-the-job training. Training does not end with graduation from Dunkin' Donuts University. Each franchisee is expected to participate later on in a continuing series of regional and national training seminars scheduled by the company.

A number of Dunkin' Donuts University graduates have gone on to become owners of multiple franchise units. The company, which reports that it has had relatively few franchisee failures, attributes this in large part to the preparation its franchisees receive during the training program.

Discussion Questions

1. Evaluate this training program.
2. What suggestions do you have for improvements?

Case 17
Kelsey Manufacturing Company
Getting Middlemen to Promote
the Manufacturer's Products

The Kelsey Manufacturing Company was one of the largest manufacturers of repair materials for automobile tires and tubes in the United
States. One of the major objectives set by management was for the company to show a continuous growth in sales and profits at a rate of 10 percent a year. In view of this goal, management was greatly concerned by
the fact that Kelsey's annual sales volume had remained at about the
same level for eight years. Some executives labeled the sales volume as
"stable," while others referred to it as "stagnant." Whatever description
was given to this sales situation, management believes it would be improved considerably if the company's wholesalers and retailers could be
persuaded to promote Kelsey's products more aggressively. Consequently,
management was trying to figure out how to "spread the word"—i.e.,
disseminate its product and promotional messages—through the company's rather lengthy channels-of-distribution system, so that the ultimate customer—the retail service station operator—effectively received
these messages.

  The Kelsey Company was founded in the early 1920s as a small,
family-owned company to manufacture cold patches for repairing inner-
tubes. Within a few years hot-patch material was introduced, marking the
beginning of a period of great growth. Tire repair was a service in much
demand during the years of the 1930s depression and World War II. Dur-

ing that war the government took about 90 percent of the production. In 1972 the Kelsey Company was acquired by a large, diversified chemical corporation and was operated as a division of one of that corporation's subsidiary firms.

One key official said, "Once we were just a nice-size family. Now we're really in the mainstream of corporate life. We used to be able to communicate with each other and with our customers on an informal party-line basis. Now we have to pay close attention to the proper channels. As the prison warden said in the movie *Cool Hand Luke,* 'What we've got here is a problem in communication!'"

Kelsey manufactured tire and tube repair materials under three brand names: Lion, which accounted for 54 percent of the sales; Topps, 10 percent of sales; and Air Float, 36 percent. Under the Lion brand the company produced the following products: Chembond patches (a chemical application), rubber cement, liquid buffer and cleaner, Perma Strip patches (outside tire repair), hot vulcanizing patches, clamps, repair gum, cold patches, unitized patches, boot cement, tubeless sealant, tire talc, and rattle stops. In addition, a number of other items were purchased for resale under the Lion name. As a result of the merger with the chemical corporation, Kelsey Manufacturing Company added a new product line consisting of some 280 items in the category of tire valves and accessories.

As the number of products increased, the problem of communicating with the customers was intensified. The sales manager, Mr. Ralph Knott, summed up the problem by saying, "In the old days our sales representatives could carry the entire line in a small briefcase. Now, we'd be hard pressed to get everything in a station wagon. We just aren't able to let the customers know what we really can do for them."

Top executives in the Kelsey Company believed that the firm held about 15 percent of the total tire and tube repair market. The major competitors were H. B. Egan Company, Bowes Seal Fast Company, Monkey Grip Sales Company, Remaco, Inc., and Kex Products Company. Kelsey, however, marketed the most complete line of products in their field.

Kelsey's annual net sales for the years 1965–1973 were as follows:

1965	$4,589,000
1966	4,136,000
1967	4,028,000
1968	4,284,000
1969	4,208,000
1970	4,058,000
1971	4,151,000
1972	4,205,000
1973	3,998,000

During the above period there were no significant fluctuations in the company's gross margin (30–40 percent of sales) or the net profit before taxes (10 percent of sales). While most of Kelsey's sales were to whole-salers who in turn sold to retail service stations, the company also sold in the export market, and under private brands to major oil companies and to chain stores such as Western Auto, Goodrich Tire stores, and Sears.

In recent years there was an increasing demand for the chemical (Chembond) patch at the expense of hot patches. This change in product popularity had enabled competition to make some inroads in the market, since the Kelsey company did not have the advantages productionwise in chemical patches that they had in hot patches.

Looking to the future, Kelsey's management recognized that it faced two problems which were created by technological improvements in other areas: (1) tires are continually being improved, mainly through crea-tion of better rubber and fabric and (2) the highway system is continually being upgraded. These factors tend to produce less tire trouble per mile traveled with less use of repair materials per mile traveled.

However, these points may be offset by the increase in the number of vehicles on the road and the number of miles traveled per vehicle. Also, the two-ply tire, which is standard on most new cars, is more susceptible to punctures than is the four-ply tire. Still another positive factor in this repair-products industry is the large increase in the number of motor-bikes, pneumatic industrial tires, and other inflatable rubber and/or plas-tic items.

The Kelsey Company, like most of its competitors in the industry, dis-tributed its products through manufacturers' representatives (agents) who sold to automotive-parts warehouse distributors. These distributors sold to smaller automotive-parts jobbers who, in turn, sold to service stations. In a sense, the service station sells the product to the individual auto-mobile owner, but by the very nature of the tire repair business, the ulti-mate consumer seldom knows what kind of products have been used to repair his or her tire or tube.

Because of this lengthy channel of distribution, the Kelsey Company was having trouble getting its product story down to the service station. Obviously, no *real* sale occurred until the service station bought the prod-uct. Unless the retailers bought, the jobbers and warehouse distributors, in turn, would not reorder.

In the past, most of Kelsey's manufacturers' agents had handled Kelsey products exclusively. With the increasing difficulty in realizing growth in sales, however, all the representatives now handled other automotive lines, thus dividing their loyalty and decreasing the time available to communicate to the customer about the Kelsey products. Part of the rea-soning behind the addition of the new product line of tire valves and ac-cessories was the hope of rebuilding the agents' loyalty to Kelsey.

As Charles Bronson, the Kelsey vice president, said: "Our real problem right now is getting our story told. We've got to have better contacts with the customers. In the past our reps had to tell the story effectively or they didn't eat. Now, they're handling so many other customers that our story gets lost in the shuffle. As we have traveled across the country and talked with service station operators, we find that they have very little knowledge about the benefits or use of our tire repair materials."

On the other hand, Ray Levine, the manufacturers' representative covering Texas, Oklahoma, and Louisiana, saw the problem this way: "The product line is now so large that you can't possibly do justice to the Kelsey products. I'd have to spend a week with each customer to tell him what the company wants told about each product. There just isn't enough time or money to do what they want."

Discussion Question

What should the Kelsey Company do to get its middlemen to promote the company's products more informatively and aggressively?

Case 18
Hill Industrial Supply
Distribution Programming
through Systems Selling

Mr. Dick Kay, General Manager of Hill Industrial Supply, has become increasingly concerned about Hill's rate of growth. After a 15-year period of solid increases, reflecting the economic expansion of its southern California trading area, Hill's sales slumped—a downturn thought to be due primarily to a decline in the Los Angeles area aerospace contracts and persistent price competition. Actually, Hill's shipment volume had increased slightly.

The industrial supply business, consisting largely of derived demand, is subject to any variation in the level of industrial activity. The local trade association collects business activity reports monthly, which are read with great interest by all suppliers. These reports showed that all business was down. Monthly trade association meetings were rife with discussions of major aerospace contracts, plant relocations, slow collections, increasing imports of low-priced Japanese and European tools, large orders won or lost, and more, a new approach to selling called *systems selling*.

Exhibit 1
Basic Types of Selling Methods Utilized by Hill

1. "Requirements contracts" where the price and terms of items to be sold are agreed upon for supplying a firm's total requirements, usually over a 1-year period. Written bids and letter agreements become the principal selling instruments and quite often prices are very low due to stiff competition. Most requirement contracts specify the expected usage for the items but often the actual purchase volume is much lower than projections.
2. "Bid and buy" or "quote and buy" for larger orders not subject to requirements contracts. This approach covers the bulk of Hill's business and requests for quotes are a substantial part of the telephone call volume to inside salesmen. While price lists and discount sheets are supplied to major customers along with catalogs, price competition is a fact of life and many suppliers are offering additional discounts, especially if they get some encouragement about getting the order.
3. Orders purchased at prevailing published prices and discounts because of the small quantity purchased or the emergency nature of the purchase. Smaller customers tend to buy at prevailing prices because they do not have a strong bargaining position. Rush orders are usually placed with the first supply house that can make immediate delivery from stock. Price in this circumstance is secondary, but because of the high cost of processing rush orders for one or two items and making a special delivery, many supply houses, including Hill, view rush orders as goodwill activity rather than as a profit-making transaction.
4. Counter sales, where small customers in the immediate area buy their needs and pick ups can be delivered. Although technically wholesale, counter sales are very similar to retail hardware sales, and several of Hill's competitors are large hardware stores. Unlike some larger industrial distributors, Hill does not enforce a minimum purchase amount at either the counter or telephone sale. Many counter sales are quite small, but by limiting credit terms and keeping a running invoice for regular small customers, some of the selling expense is minimized. Again, goodwill is emphasized as some of the smaller customers are expected to become major customers someday.

Hill's Selling Methods

Like most industrial distributors, Hill employs outside salesmen who call on large accounts and solicit business from their purchasing department with the aid of a catalog. Hill prides itself on the quality of its catalog. The most comprehensive in Hill's history, it lists about three hundred lines of tools and supplies. While Hill only stocks the main items in about fifty lines, it has access through factory warehouses or other wholesalers to every item in the catalog. The breadth of the catalog gives Hill's six salesmen an opportunity to sell a high proportion of a customer's tool and supply needs, thus increasing the average sale amount and enabling Hill to be a primary supplier for all its customers' industrial supply requirements.

Hill's selling methods fall into four types, depending upon the customer, the quantity of the order, and the urgency of the need. These types of selling methods are illustrated in Exhibit 1.

Hill's outside salesmen are typical of those in the industry and are well described by a composite published by the National Industrial Distributors Association. The average outside salesman makes 6 calls each working day, handles about 125 active accounts and contacts from 10 to

13 individuals at each account. He sells about $300,000 worth of products annually, has been with his present firm 12 years and is 43 years old. The average salesman has attended college and more than one manufacturer's training school. Hill's salesmen are paid a salary that ranges from $400 to $700 per month plus a sales commission of from 1½ percent to 5 percent, depending on the profit margin Hill is able to get on the items sold.

In addition to the outside salesmen, Hill has six inside salesmen who take telephone orders. Routine purchases and price quotes are frequently made by telephone and Hill emphasizes the efficiency of its inside salesmen. Hill also has a small counter-sales area where rush orders can be picked up and walk-in customers served.

Systems Selling

Systems selling appears to be a widely discussed but narrowly understood concept of supply and purchasing. Essentially, it involves contractual agreements between a distributor and user for the total supply of agreed-upon lines of tools and supplies at a predetermined price. The agreement assures a user of a ready source of the tools and supplies it uses, since the distributor agrees to always carry stock. And because of agreed-upon prices and discounts, costs associated with getting bids and quotes and purchasing routines and requirements are substantially reduced. By working closely with customers under the systems selling concept, distributors hope to reduce, if not eliminate, inventories of tools and supplies and traditional purchasing paperwork for customers.

Systems selling appears most similar in concept to requirements contracts, but it is more comprehensive in that it includes all purchases of industrial supplies regardless of the quantity used. Typically, requirements contracts are used only for high-volume items where bidding results in very low prices.

Many alternatives in pricing and coverage are possible under proposed systems selling but two major distinguishing advantages are: (1) a switch from multiple source purchasing to a single source for supplies and (2) the elimination of a traditional purchase requisition and purchase order for each transaction. One case reported in the trade press resulted in cost savings in maintenance, repair, and operation supplies as follows:

TANGIBLE SAVINGS FOR A CUSTOMER USING SYSTEMS SELLING:

85% reduction in present $95,000 inventory × 15% annual carrying cost	= $14,250
Annual volume of $230,000 × 5% guaranteed reduction in total cost of supplies	= $11,500

SAVINGS OF UNDETERMINED VALUE:

Reduction of floor space of 1800 sq. ft.
Elimination of 2300 purchase orders per year
Elimination of 2100 invoices per year
Elimination of 1500 stock record cards

Another potential savings of systems selling is the elimination of sales commissions on purchases under a systems selling plan, since once the arrangements are set up, orders are placed by phone or mail.

In spite of the apparently attractive savings, many firms were expected to resist the changes in the financial controls and purchase authorization that would be required. Also, the purchasing executives of large customers are generally reluctant to use a single source. Multiple sources are often regarded as good insurance against disruption from strikes, fires, and stock-outs and as a guarantee that the benefits of competition on service and price continue to exist. Many distributors stock only some of the items they catalog; to be successful, systems selling requires that increased stocks be carried.

Executive Pondering

A combination of concern about the downturn in sales, its implications for Hill's growth, and the cyclical business pattern led Mr. Kay to give a great deal of thought to systems selling. Mr. Kay was not sure how much of his existing business might be converted into systems selling or what type of purchasing agreements would be replaced with systems selling. A recent trade study had collected information on buyer attitudes, shown in Exhibit 2, which caused him to wonder if systems selling would work at all.

Mr. Kay knew that his customers often purchased from larger competitors and sometimes from local hardware stores. He also was curious about what brands they were buying. To answer these questions, he selected a sample of 100 industrial firms from the *California Manufacturers' Register* and had one of the telephone salesmen call the purchasing departments and ask (without identifying himself) what brand of cutting tools they currently were purchasing and from what company. Many buyers did not have strong brand preference or at least brand recall, and many were reluctant to identify sources of supply. At the end of the calls, forty-five more or less usable responses were obtained, as reported in Exhibit 3.

Since systems selling was relatively new, articles in trade publications stressed the need for a study of costs and a firm proposal to prospective customers. The general recommendations were that the distributors take the offensive in making the necessary arrangements

Mr. Kay was also concerned about the questions and objections that might come up in negotiating systems selling with a prospective account. He wondered how successful Hill might be in pioneering such an approach in its highly competitive market, especially if competitive imitation, if not retaliation, occurred as it had in past years.

To assist him in his evaluations, Mr. Kay collected data from the ac-

Exhibit 2
Buyer Attitudes Concerning Industrial Purchases

How buyers view dividing business among suppliers*

"Good business"	50%
"Keeps suppliers honest"	40
"Good"	10
"Time consuming"	5
"Unnecessary"	5
"Unwise"	1

"In purchasing tools and supplies how important are the following?"

	Very Important	Somewhat Important	Not Too Important
Low price	16%	49%	35%
Quick delivery time	93	7	–
Regular sales calls	18	31	51
Technical advice	22	47	31
Well-known brand	49	46	7

Why firms trade with particular suppliers

Service	80%
Delivery	70
Stock	50
Price	50
Salesmen	10
Miscellaneous	25

Why firms do not trade with particular suppliers

Product quality	75%
Product line	65
Inventory	55
Delivery	50
Order board	35
Salesmen	35
Prices	30
Miscellaneous	30

Importance of distance between buyer and seller

Very important	10%
Somewhat important	60
Not important	30

*Categories sum to over 100 percent because of multiple responses.

counting department on the fixed and variable costs of doing business and other statistics on actual orders. This information is included, along with income statements for 1968 and 1969, in Exhibits 4 through 6.

Exhibit 3
Cutting Tools and Supplies Brands Mentioned (N = 45)

Brands	Number of Mentions	Carried by Hill
Cleveland	8	
Union	6	
Butterfield	6	
Starrett	6	x
National	5	
Sossner	5	
Ace	4	x
Besley	4	
Chicago Latrobe	4	
Whitman & Barnes	3	x
Carbaloy	3	
Greenfield	3	x
Morse	3	x
Illinois	3	
New York	2	
Kennametal	2	
Proto	2	x
Brown & Sharpe	2	x
Vermont	1	
Millers Falls	1	
Momax	1	
Courmet	1	
Quinco	1	
L & F	1	
Holo Krome	1	x
Carborundum	1	
Niagara	1	
Putnam	1	x
Hardinge	1	x
No Preference	4	
Did Not Know	4	

Discussion Questions

1. Should Hill Industrial Supply offer a systems selling program to its customers at the present time? Why or why not?
2. What do you anticipate the competitive response will be if Hill introduces systems selling? If Hill does not introduce it?
3. If the decision is made to introduce system selling, how should the concept be marketed?

Exhibit 4
Analysis Data from the Accounting Department

Order Analysis, March 1979 (Sample N = 100)

	Lines/Order	Orders	Percentage
	1	47	50.5
	2	13	14.0
	3	11	11.8
	4	8	8.6
	5	14	15.1
Total	252	93	100.0
Average Lines/Order	252/93 = 2.7		

Dollar Sales Volume Analysis, March 1979 (Sample N = 100)

Order Size	Orders Number	Percentage	Dollars	Total Sales Percentage	Average Sales/Order
$ 0–$10	24	25.8	$ 146.93	3.1	$ 6.80
$11–$20	18	19.4	287.06	6.0	15.95
$21–$30	12	12.9	300.55	6.3	25.00
$31–$50	12	12.9	469.59	9.8	39.00
$50–$75	7	7.5	422.33	8.8	60.00
>$75	20	21.5	3,170.62	66.0	158.40
	93	100.0	$4,797.08	100.0	$ 51.50

Analysis of Order Processing and Delivery Cost

Duties	
Answering phone	$ .25
Checking catalog for item	.20
Checking stock for item	.50
Writing order	1.25
Checking order	.10
Posting (filing)	.20
Billing	.50
Total	$ 3.00/order

Delivery Truck and Driver	$1000.00/month

$$\frac{\$1000/month}{22\ days/month} = \$45\ day/30\ deliveries/day = \$1.50/delivery$$

Exhibit 5
Hill Supply's Income Data for 1968 and 1969

	1968		1969	
Sales	$2,011,201	100.0%	$1,888,650	100.0%
Cost of goods	1,573,776	78.3	1,492,834	79.0
Gross margin	$ 437,425	21.7%	$ 395,816	21.0%
Expenses:				
Selling	$ 126,206	6.3	$ 118,582	6.3%
Occupancy	7,800	.4	7,800	.4
Warehouse	20,679	1.0	21,752	1.2
Office	113,197	5.6	103,303	1.2
General Administration	86,783	4.3	89,912	4.8
Net operating profit	$ 82,760	4.1	$ 54,467	2.9
Other income	13,010	.6	7,284	.4
Taxes	25,250	1.3	15,566	.8
Net profit	$ 70,520	3.5%	$ 46,185	2.4%

Exhibit 6
Hill Supply's Fixed and Variable Costs for 1968 and 1969

	1968		1969	
	Fixed	Variable	Fixed	Variable
Selling:				
Salaries	$ 34,970		$33,116	
Commissions		$55,549		$55,079
Selling Expenses		6,107		8,821
Travel Expenses	17,000	818	12,176	1,462
Advertising	10,726		5,897	
Miscellaneous		1,036		2,031
Total	$ 62,696	$63,510	$51,189	$67,393
Warehouse:				
Salaries	$ 17,086		$18,454	
Trucking	976		2,160	
Equipment	231		197	
Supplies		$ 1,768		$ 891
Miscellaneous		616		50
Total	$ 18,293	$ 2,384	$20,811	$ 941
Office:				
Salaries	$ 94,838		$83,726	
Equipment	2,788		2,796	
Supplies		$ 6,218		$ 7,604
Credit and Collection	512	920	519	453
Data Processing	1,755		1,794	
Miscellaneous	1,143	5,023	1,143	5,268
Total	$101,036	$12,161	$89,978	$13,325
General Administration:				
Salaries	$ 20,908		$20,908	
Fringe and Bonus		$11,091		$12,783
Expenses		4,109		4,987
Taxes and Licenses	21,433		22,397	
Utilities		14,229		15,301
Miscellaneous	8,182	6,831	7,427	6,109
Total	$ 50,523	$36,260	$50,732	$39,180

Case 19
Wolverine Brass Works
Using the Marketing Mix to Build a Strong Channel

Wolverine Brass Works, a division of The Citation Companies, sells plumbers' brass goods to over twenty thousand quality-conscious builders and contractors. The firm is the only company in its field to sell directly and exclusively to plumbing contractors and other professionals. Its products cannot be bought at retail; nor does the company market through distributors.

The Citation Companies

Individual divisions of The Citation Companies are engaged in various activities related to the home. Its largest operation, Wolverine Brass Works, markets a complete plumbing products line including over two thousand stock items.

Another division, H. B. Sherman, is one of the top two makers of nationally sold lawn sprinklers, hose nozzles, and related accessories. The company sells through manufacturer's representatives. Retail customers

Exhibit 1
Five-Year Summary of the Citation Companies' Financial Statistics

	1977	1976	1975	1974	1973
Operating Results					
Total revenues	$48,669,260	$44,253,409	$37,002,707	$41,873,770	$44,075,095
Operating expenses	43,335,606	40,090,670	35,124,554	38,622,585	40,135,622
Operating income	5,333,654	4,162,739	1,878,153	3,251,185	3,939,473
Interest expense	749,864	703,342	831,337	1,170,384	985,611
Write-off of goodwill	—	—	1,589,417	—	—
Income (loss) before income taxes	4,583,790	3,459,397	(542,601)	2,080,801	2,953,862
Income taxes	2,090,000	1,283,000	549,000	995,000	1,487,000
Net income (loss)	2,493,790	2,176,397	(1,091,601)	1,085,801	1,466,862
Depreciation and amortization of property and equipment	1,239,427	1,043,163	1,006,310	1,036,681	972,700
Capital expenditures, including leased equipment under capital leases	2,011,481	1,561,033	667,824	672,850	1,204,753
Balance Sheet Data					
Current assets	20,889,584	19,871,228	17,874,314	19,931,542	22,652,294
Net property and equipment and leased equipment	9,996,649	9,590,973	9,099,074	9,456,959	9,841,803
Total assets	32,409,320	30,748,981	28,492,722	32,553,215	35,736,855
Current liabilities	7,102,469	7,332,253	5,654,090	7,001,019	11,774,589
Long-term debt, including obligations under capital leases	7,467,607	7,452,500	8,506,500	9,624,422	8,769,809
Stockholders' equity	16,930,691	15,111,908	13,506,593	15,181,306	14,507,460
Working capital	13,797,115	12,538,975	12,220,224	12,930,523	10,877,705
Ratio analysis					
Return on sales	5.1	4.9	(3.0)	2.6	3.3
Revenues per $ of assets	1.50	1.43	1.30	1.29	1.23
Assets per $ of equity	1.91	2.03	2.11	2.14	2.46
Return on assets	7.7	7.1	(3.8)	3.3	4.1
Return on average equity	15.6	15.2	—	7.3	10.5
Current assets to current liabilities	2.9 to 1	2.7 to 1	3.2 to 1	2.8 to 1	1.9 to 1
Debt to equity	.44	.49	.63	.63	.60
Per Share					
Net income (loss) [a]	1.63	1.44	(.71)	.71	.95
Dividends [a]	.43	.34	.32	.26	.25
Payout percentage	26%	23%	—	38%	26%
Stockholders' equity [b]	11.30	11.08	11.35	12.53	11.97
Average shares outstanding [a]	1,532,788	1,516,319	1,530,751	1,539,355	1,542,226

Notes: (a) Restated for stock dividends in 1976 and 1977.
(b) Based on actual number of shares outstanding at the end of each year.

Exhibit 2
Sales and Earnings by Line of Business

Year	Plumbing Products	Consumer Hardware	Builders' Hardware	Other*
	%	%	%	%
1977 Net sales	56.9	30.4	12.7	—
1977 Earnings	49.3	36.1	12.9	1.7
1976 Net sales	54.3	29.9	14.4	1.4
1976 Earnings	52.8	32.8	16.2	(1.3)
1975 Net sales	54.7	28.7	15.3	1.3
1975 Earnings	53.4	28.3	21.5	(3.2)
1974 Net sales	53.7	29.7	14.2	2.4
1974 Earnings	52.9	39.4	13.0	(5.3)
1973 Net sales	48.9	26.4	15.6	9.1
1973 Earnings	68.2	29.9	6.1	(4.2)

*Mobile Home Products discontinued in 1976

include leading hardware chains and co-ops, mass merchandisers, and garden supply outlets.

Handy Things Manufacturing Company, another consumer division, is one of the nation's largest manufacturers of Christmas tree stands. The company also manufacturers household utensils such as potato ricers, kitchen tongs, and fruit presses and a line of housewares including towel racks, soap dishes, and clothes line reels.

In the area of builders' hardware, The Newell Manufacturing division markets pneumatic door closers, door latches, and accessories to retail outlets, mill supply houses, and storm door manufacturers. The firm recently introduced a "WeatherAll," do-it-yourself plastic storm window kit in the retail market.

Glynn-Johnson, another builders' hardware division, specializes in architect-specified products for commercial and industrial construction. Its high styled products, designed to appeal to architects and designers, include overhead door holders, invisible door latches, door catches, bumpers, and special builders' hardware items. The company sells to jobbers through commissioned sales representatives; its retail marketing is insignificant.

Exhibit 1 presents a five-year summary of The Citation Companies' operating and financial statistics. A summary of sales and earnings by line of business is shown in Exhibit 2.

Wolverine Brass Works

Wolverine Brass Works is over eighty years old. Its line of faucets, tubular traps, bronze valves, compression stops, and related specialty items is among the broadest in the industry. Some companies may produce more of a single item, but no competitor serves the plumber's needs with as wide a variety of supplies. Wolverine employs seventy-five full-time sales-men and selected agents who sell to 20,000 contractors in all parts of the country.

The fact that Wolverine Brass Works is the only company in its field to market directly and exclusively to plumbing contractors and other professionals attracts loyal customers. This is one of the firm's principal reasons for staying with this form of distribution. In management's opinion, plumbers' loyalty means reliable sales, an advantage that outweighs the potential sales which might be realized by competing with others in the retail market.

A computerized order entry system enables the company to move with unusual speed, efficiency, accuracy, and low cost. The goal is to fill orders within twenty-four to thirty-six hours of receipt. This goal is designed not only to win customer satisfaction but also to aid production scheduling, inventory control, and trouble shooting in various areas. Management believes its order entry system is a key to profitability and a major reason for success with such a diversified product line and so many individual customers.

The division also makes service fixtures for hospitals and scientific laboratories, including foot-operated and gooseneck faucets, service turrets for controlling and transmitting gases, needle valves, and gas shut-off valves. These products are sold to laboratory furniture manufacturers and scientific apparatus jobbers.

Wolverine Brass sales historically have been stable despite the varying pace of new home construction because, management conjectures, a high percentage of its products are used for remodeling or replacement of plumbing fixtures in existing homes.

Product Areas

Wolverine Brass products are designed and manufactured to assure quality, quick installation, and minimum service. The firm's product offering is divided into six basic areas:

1. Faucets, including necessary accessories, for sinks, showers and tubs, lavatories, laundry, and lawn;
2. valves of all types, including gate, ball, globe, check, relief, and regulating, and valve repair kits;
3. water closet and tank accessories;
4. tubular and cast drainage products;
5. supplies, such as flexible and rigid supply lines and supply valves, tubes, and connections; and
6. miscellaneous plumbing products, including waste disposals, sump pumps, sinks, nuts, bolts, screws, washers, gaskets, and plumbers' supplies and tools.

Advertising

Consistent with its distribution strategy, Wolverine Brass directs its advertising to contractors. Exhibit 3 shows two typical advertisements used in trade publications. The firm also utilizes a series of mailings from the "Wolverine Brass Tacks Department" to inform customers of new products and services. Exhibit 4 gives two examples of such mailings. Advertising specialties such as memo pads, key chains, and coin holders are widely distributed to supplement other advertising efforts.

Current Plans

Wolverine Brass Works sells most heavily to plumbing contractors engaged in repair/remodeling work and builders of custom homes, where quality and service are usually as important or more important than price. As part of the program implemented to attain a stronger position in the larger brass market—especially in speculative multi- and single-family dwellings—Wolverine introduced the competitively priced Encore line of faucets in 1977, planning to add other inexpensive brass products to its line in 1978, keeping cost down by designing simpler products, and still retaining some premium features.

Robert J. MacIntyre, President of Wolverine Brass Works, states:

Wolverine's most important objective, far and away, has been additional strength in the competitively priced field. Our successful introduction of the Encore faucet lines now moves us in that direction. Furthermore, sales of higher priced lines have continued to move ahead, indicating that we're not sacrificing profits in one direction to gain them in another. I should also emphasize that there is a substantial difference between competitive pricing of quality products, which is our program, and the marketing of cheap merchandise on which price is everything and quality means nothing. We'll stay away from that field.

Discussion Questions

1. Discuss the relative advantages of marketing exclusively through plumbing contractors and other professionals as compared to alternative forms of distribution.
2. What marketing recommendations would you make to Wolverine's management? Be specific in terms of distribution, product strategy, pricing, and advertising.

Exhibit 3
Typical Trade Advertisements for Wolverine Brass

When a Plumbing Contractor has something to say to us, we get the message...

through 75 on-the-spot full-time representatives

Wolverine Brass products are sold directly to Plumbing Contractors. The full-time WB man in each marketing area establishes company-to-Contractor communication. He's a customer-oriented man who keeps us sensitive to product and service requirements.

Valves for homes and institutions

WB WOLVERINE BRASS
WOLVERINE BRASS WORKS
Grand Rapids, Michigan 49502

PRODUCTS THAT GIVE AN EXTRA MEASURE OF VALUE

At Wolverine Brass, it's a total effort in behalf of the Plumbing Contractor

Every year we look for new ways to serve our customers

For more than 70 years, our products have been sold exclusively through the Plumbing Contractor, a distribution policy which reflects a company attitude of support for the role of the Plumbing Contractor. Wolverine Brass helps to strengthen the Plumbing Contractor's "complete service" to customers by enabling him to stock and install, with confidence, a recognized quality line of products no other market source can offer.

Wolverine Brass
Concealed Fixtures

WB WOLVERINE BRASS
WOLVERINE BRASS WORKS
Grand Rapids, Michigan 49502

PRODUCTS THAT GIVE AN EXTRA MEASURE OF VALUE

Exhibit 4
Sample Wolverine Brass Tacks Department Mailings

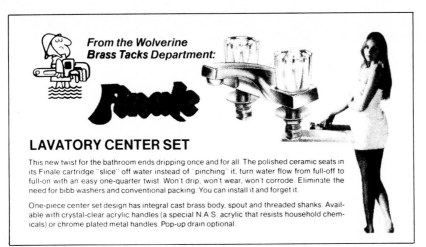

From the Wolverine
Brass Tacks Department:

LAVATORY CENTER SET

This new twist for the bathroom ends dripping once and for all. The polished ceramic seats in its Finale cartridge "slice" off water instead of "pinching" it, turn water flow from full-off to full-on with an easy one-quarter twist. Won't drip, won't wear, won't corrode. Eliminate the need for bibb washers and conventional packing. You can install it and forget it.

One-piece center set design has integral cast brass body, spout and threaded shanks. Available with crystal-clear acrylic handles (a special N.A.S. acrylic that resists household chemicals) or chrome plated metal handles. Pop-up drain optional.

From the Wolverine
Brass Tacks Department:

NEW AQUA-FLO WATER FILTER
for removing rust and sediment
or unpleasant tastes and odors

Here's a new profit maker for you that *keeps on* making profits. One you can quickly and easily install. And give your customers positive removal of rust and sediment or taste and odor from household water. The new Wolverine Aqua-Flo Water Filter has replaceable filter elements for removing either rust and sediment or taste and odor. Elements last from one to six months, depending on conditions, and can be easily replaced by the homeowner (and bought from you, of course). The perfect answer for clearing up discolored, sediment-laden water from private systems. For removing offensive tastes and odors from chemically treated municipal systems, as well. And for making continuous profits for you.

Case 20
Clarkson Cold Products Company
*Channels of Distribution
for a New Product*

The two founders of the Clarkson Cold Products Company, Anthony Clarkson and Everett Iversen, recently developed a new product to add to their line. Now the two men, especially Mr. Iversen, who was in charge of marketing, were wondering what channels of distribution they should use to reach the market for this product.

The Clarkson Company was a small Midwestern firm whose main product was a defrosting unit. The unit was a small device designed to be installed in refrigerators and freezers of all sizes, both domestic and commercial. Its function was to defrost the cooling coils during a defrost cycle. Clarkson held the patents on these units. The company manufactured and marketed them to small and medium-sized manufacturing companies on a contract basis. Clarkson also marketed to jobbers who in turn sold the products to refrigeration service firms. Clarkson's annual sales volume was about $1.4 million.

The new product that was posing a channels problem for Mr. Iversen was a portable cooling unit, popularly called an "ice chest." Rather than using ice to keep the temperature down, however, a cooling coil had been placed in the box. This coil could be connected to, and disconnected from, an automobile air-conditioner compressor. When the air conditioner in the car was turned on, the coils in the box were also charged. With only a one-hour charge, foods and liquids could be kept cold and fresh for 24 hours. A device was also available to allow a person to charge the portable cooling unit without having to run the air-conditioning unit inside the car.

The cooler was 13 inches wide, 22 inches long, and 16 inches high. Its walls were 1 inch thick and were made of aluminum-encased insulating foam. The product was to be priced to the consumer at about 20 percent above competitive models which used ice for cooling. The competition consisted of several branded and unbranded ice chests, with the Coleman brand probably being the best known. Actually, however, Clarkson's marketing studies indicated that brand recognition and brand preference generally were low for portable coolers.

Mr. Iversen believed that the competitive advantages of the Clarkson cooler were many: no more having to locate and buy ice; no more large pieces of ice taking up room in the ice chest; no more having to dump water when the ice begins to melt. The weight of a loaded cooler was reduced because of the no-ice factor. Furthermore, the new Clarkson unit could reach and maintain much lower temperatures than any other unit.

Marketing studies indicated a good market potential for the cooler, and a wide range of potential customers. Increased leisure time in the American market, coupled with a desire to get out in the country, meant that many people were potential users of a portable cooler. Furthermore, the product was considered to be relatively "recession-proof." That is, even during an economic decline, people still engaged in recreational activities such as picnicking, camping, and auto traveling. These activities led to a demand for a portable cooler for food and drinks.

Consequently, the Clarkson executives believed that their new cooler unit would be carried in recreational vehicles and mobile homes. It also would be used in boats, summer cottages, and automobiles. Even the above-market-level price was considered *not* to be a limiting factor, once a potential user had learned of the advantages of the Clarkson unit.

Research further indicated that different buying patterns existed among the segments of the recreation industry that Clarkson hoped to reach. Large manufacturers of recreational vehicles such as campers, vans, and trailers usually preferred to buy their component parts directly from the producers. Once a supplier's sales person had demonstrated and sold a part to the recreational vehicle manufacturer, little servicing of this account was needed. Once a year new bids were made and new purchase contracts were prepared.

Medium-sized manufacturers of recreational vehicles also preferred to deal directly with the producers of equipment and parts. However, the smaller these parts orders became, the more likely it was that the parts manufacturers would prefer to sell through wholesalers, rather than directly to recreational vehicle manufacturers.

Wholesalers played a major role in supplying recreational vehicle parts and supplies to small manufacturers and to retailers of sporting goods. Large retailers preferred to buy directly from manufacturers.

To market its defrosting devices, the Clarkson Company had three salespeople who serviced existing accounts and solicited new accounts. Each salesperson worked in a different part of the United States and reported directly to Iversen. The three did a good job of contacting their manufacturing accounts about once a month and their jobbers about twice a month, if they felt it was necessary. They were on the road about 22 days a month and very seldom got back to the home office. Because of the large number of jobbers, as well as the limits on company funds, however, many potential jobber accounts were not called on at all.

Discussion Question

What channels of distribution should the Clarkson Company use for its new portable cooler?

Case 21
Hyde-Phillip Chemical Company
Alternative Forms of Sales Representation

Michael Claxton, a recent marketing graduate of a well-known college, has been assigned the task of evaluating Hyde-Phillip Chemical Company's methods of selling the firm's products. Hyde-Phillip currently utilizes a mix of company salespersons—merchant wholesalers and agent wholesalers—to present its products to present and potential users. While this combination of selling forces is somewhat unusual, it reflects the orientation of management over time as to the relative values of alternative forms of sales representation. Claxton's challenge is to review the data that have been gathered on the three types of sales efforts, determine if additional information is needed, and make recommendations as to what changes, if any, should be made in the firm's approach to sales representation.

Information on the Company

Hyde-Phillip was formed in the early 1960s through the merger of Hyde Industrial Chemicals and Phillip Laboratories. Both firms had a broad range of experience in the development and production of certain types of chemicals and related supplies for a variety of industrial users. While the two firms had a few overlapping product lines, each brought to the merger some exclusive product offerings. The resulting combination of the two firms yielded a new organization capable of marketing a complete line of chemicals for industrial use.

Prior to the merger, Hyde Industrial Chemicals had utilized a group of industrial distributors (merchant wholesalers) to market its products. Phillip Laboratories, on the other hand, had several manufacturers' agents (agent wholesalers) who sold its product offering. The new firm, after the merger, retained some of the industrial distributors and some of the manufacturing agents and then began to develop its own sales force.

Today, Hyde-Phillip serves 30 sales territories in states east of the Mississippi through its own sales force of 50 individuals (six women and 44 men), nine industrial distributors, and nine manufacturers' agents. The 50 salespeople are about evenly allocated across twelve of the sales territories. Each of the industrial distributors and manufacturers' agents has exclusive selling rights in one of the 18 remaining sales territories. Individual distributors and agents have from five to 30 people working for them and many represent other noncompeting manufacturers. The 30 sales territories were originally established to represent areas of approximately equal sales potential for Hyde-Phillip's products.

Many types of sales support are made available to each sales territory by the company. Individual managers of the territories have the option of using or not using each type of sales support. Sales support items currently available include (1) a variety of descriptive brochures to supplement the information given in the firm's product catalog, (2) study programs with cassette tapes to enable sales representatives to be more familiar with the firm's products and current market situations and developments, (3) a program to provide generous product samples to potential customers for test purposes, and (4) direct-mail programs aimed at prospective customers to solicit inquiries for descriptive materials and product samples.

Data on Sales Territories

As a first step in beginning his analysis, Claxton asked his assistant to compile the available information on each of the 30 sales territories. This information is presented in coded form in Exhibit 1.

In terms of level of sales, nine territories have annual sales in excess of $2 million, fifteen have sales between $1 and $2 million, and six have sales less than $1 million. As already indicated, in twelve of the territories the firm is represented by its own sales force, and industrial distributors and manufacturers' agents each represent the company in nine territories.

Based on estimates provided by the sales support department, twelve

Exhibit 1
Available Data on Sales Territories

Territory Number	Level of Sales	Type of Representation	Use of Sales Support	Geographic Location
1	2	1	2	3
2	3	1	3	3
3	2	2	1	1
4	1	1	1	1
5	2	3	1	1
6	2	1	2	1
7	3	3	2	3
8	1	2	1	1
9	2	1	2	2
10	2	1	2	3
11	1	2	1	1
12	1	1	1	2
13	2	2	2	2
14	2	3	2	1
15	1	1	2	3
16	2	3	2	2
17	2	1	3	1
18	1	2	1	2
19	2	3	2	2
20	3	1	3	2
21	1	3	1	3
22	2	2	1	3
23	3	3	1	1
24	3	1	3	2
25	3	2	3	1
26	1	2	1	2
27	2	1	2	2
28	1	2	1	3
29	2	3	3	3
30	2	3	2	3

Codes: Level of sales: 1 = over $2 million; 2 = $1–2 million; 3 = under $1 million
Type of representation: 1 = company sales force; 2 = industrial distributor; 3 = manufacturers' agent
Use of sales support: 1 = extensive user; 2 = moderate user; 3 = light user
Geographic location: 1 = Northern; 2 = Southern; 3 = Eastern

of the territories make extensive use of the available sales support programs, twelve are moderate users, and six are light users. Each of the firm's sales territories is also divided into one of three geographic divisions, Northern, Southern, or Eastern. As indicated in Exhibit 1, each of these geographic locations includes ten sales territories.

Initial Analysis

Using the information in Exhibit 1, Claxton constructed the cross tabulation of sales versus type of representation as shown in Exhibit 2. He first set up the cross tabulation using raw numbers and then calculated the conditional probabilities for each row and column.

As seen in part B of Exhibit 2, 30.0 percent of Hyde-Phillip's territories with sales over $2 million were ones served by industrial distributors.

Exhibit 2
Cross Tabulation of Level of Sales versus Type of Representation

			Company Salesforce (1)	Industrial Distributor (2)	Manufacturers' Agent (3)	Totals	
Level	Over $2 million	(1)	3	5	1	9	
of	$1–2 million	(2)	6	3	6	15	A
Sales	Under $1 million	(3)	3	1	2	6	
	Totals		12	9	9		

			Company Salesforce (1)	Industrial Distributor (2)	Manufacturers' Agent (3)		
Level	Over $2 million	(1)	33.3	55.6	11.1	100.0	
of	$1–2 million	(2)	40.0	20.0	40.0	100.0	B
Sales	Under $1 million	(3)	50.0	16.7	33.3	100.0	
	Totals		40.0	30.0	30.0	100.0	

			Company Salesforce (1)	Industrial Distributor (2)	Manufacturers' Agent (3)		
Level	Over $2 million	(1)	25.0	55.6	11.1	30.0	
of	$1–2 million	(2)	50.0	33.3	66.7	50.0	C
Sales	Under $1 million	(3)	25.0	11.1	22.2	20.0	
	Totals		100.0	100.0	100.0		

Code: A = raw numbers
     B = row conditional probabilities
     C = column conditional probabilities

Only 11.1 percent of the largest sales territories were represented by manufacturers' agents and 33.3 percent were served by the company sales force. Stated differently, as shown in part C of Exhibit 2, 25.0 percent of territories served by the company's sales force had sales over $2 million, while 55.6 percent of the industrial distributors and 11.1 percent of the manufacturers' agents served territories with sales over $2 million.

Claxton's initial reaction was that the firm should consider replacing part of its own sales force and the manufacturers' agents with more industrial distributors. He was concerned, however, with what other variables should be taken into account to more fully analyze and evaluate Hyde-Phillip's current approach to sales representation.

Discussion Question

What changes, if any, should Hyde-Phillip Chemical Company make in its approach to sales representation?

Case 22
Auditing Distribution Channels
Using Market Research for
Better Channel Management

Simpson Timber's Columbia Door Division, a manufacturing facility for wood flush doors used in home and building construction, is located in southwest Washington. While the major markets for this plant were in California, Oregon, and Washington, it had also penetrated the western areas of the Midwest markets (mostly Mountain States), where no flush door manufacturers existed.

Simpson was realizing major successes in the Midwest market by selling doors to major wholesalers, who supplied many of the retail units and major contractors scattered throughout an eleven-state area. While the wood flush door market was treated by most wholesalers and manufacturers in this area as a commodity market, the wholesalers, given equal treatment by the manufacturers, tended to prefer specific manufacturers like Simpson. This preference presumably arose through "personal" contacts made during the introduction of the products and the contacts made with the wholesalers by the Simpson representatives selling other lines of Simpson specialty products.

Having traditionally treated the flush door market as a commodity market, Simpson had given it minimal attention except for price and delivery. An agent served as the Midwest middleman, providing information to Simpson on competitors' prices and delivery schedules. The agent also took orders from the wholesalers. The agent provided no services to customers other than information processing. The distance between the wholesale centers in the Midwest market and the manufacturing facility made direct visits to these middlemen by Columbia Door marketing personnel an infrequent event. This was deemed unnecessary because the company's share of the product's wholesale market in the region had been substantial, stable, and growing slightly.

New Competition

The period during which this study was conducted was a time of economic weakness for building construction along the West Coast, so competitive manufacturers were attracted to the Midwest market as a temporary outlet for their production capacity. This placed increased strain on the normal market equilibrium; the new suppliers of the commodity door in the market were cutting prices to gain market penetration. A number of the wholesalers recognized this as a temporary condition and attempted to maintain purchases with their regular suppliers, hoping for their support during tighter market conditions.

There was also a new threat in the form of a specialty product. From time to time, new specialty substitute wood flush doors had been introduced in the market by the various manufacturers competing in the Midwest market. Most of the new products were slight modifications of the previous products, and the middlemen quickly identified each of them as just another alternative product, with little or no recognition given to the modification. If the modification had appeal in the market, most of the competitors would quickly provide an equivalent version.

However, one specialty door, produced by Masonite, enjoyed a major market impact. It was recognized by the wholesalers, ultimate buyers, and competition as a product clearly providing final cost and quality benefits that were not associated with the commodity door. Surface material of the door was a special substance that gave it improved scratch and nick resistance. Masonite had a patent on the substance, so competition could not easily copy Masonite's new and successful product. Even though the Masonite flush door had a higher price, it was beginning to achieve broader acceptance among the wholesalers, retailers, contractors, and end users.

Simpson was prepared to introduce its version of the Masonite product using a different surface material at a price lower than the equivalent Masonite door, yet higher than the commodity door. Before introduction, the door division wanted to analyze the market to identify the appropriate middlemen and/or channels for the product.

Marketing Weaknesses

After the decision was made to study the regional market for the commodity product and this specialty substitute, it quickly became apparent that the data Simpson had been using to identify its market share were faulty. Although the company was gaining a larger share of the wholesale market, analysis of the aggregate figures indicated that its share of the entire market might be dropping.

During phone conversations with some of the large Midwest wholesalers, it appeared that the past preferences for the company's commodity product were weakening. Also, it became evident that damage was being done by the agent's failure to provide adequate wholesaler support. This was exemplified by the agent's lack of response to requests for claim settlements for occasional faulty materials. The wholesalers were handling the claims from their buyers with the expectation that the claims would be recognized by the manufacturer. For long term customers, this procedure may have been adequate since they dealt directly with Simpson Timber; but new customers, having placed their orders with the agent, found it difficult to find the correct channel for submitting their claims. This, of course, jeopardized any "goodwill" that had been developed with a new customer.

Further, no one was representing the Simpson flush door products in local and regional home-building shows or conventions attended by the major wholesalers and their customers.

New Class of Middlemen

Another problem in evidence during the initial stages of the study was that a new class of middlemen was entering the market in strong enough force to demand direct negotiations with the competitive manufacturers. Previously Simpson's Columbia Door Division had chosen to ignore other types of middlemen and protect the industry's normal channel relationship (manufacturer → wholesaler → retailer, contractor and industrial builder). This policy probably was appropriate earlier in the company's marketing efforts, when only the wholesaler had order sizes large enough to fill complete carloads (the normal lot size delivered from most building supply manufacturers).

With the advent of major industrialized home builders, major component builders and sizeable chain retail lumber yards, there were increasing pressures for the manufacturers to sell directly to these new middlemen. Statistics had not been prepared to indicate the size and growth potential of this market. Simpson marketing personnel had mistakenly assumed it to be a small and insignificant influence within the entire product market. The results of this study indicated that sales by-passing the wholesalers had grown to 27 percent of the overall market, with the percentage increasing at a rate of up to 8 percent a year: Simpson had an insignificant portion of the new market. This explains why, despite a constant (or slightly increasing) share of the wholesale market, the company's share of the overall market was decreasing.

Simpson Timber, with little information coming from the agent, was having a difficult time tracking the market activities of their competition and potential customers. After a gross picture of the situation was obtained by using many approximations and substantial secondary data sources, management decided to obtain a closer view of the trends and events or conditions that were supporting the trends. Accordingly, a survey was conducted in the market, covering most of the high-volume users.

Need for Data Sources and Analysis

Initially the Columbia Door Division's records were reviewed to develop a list of their customers for the past three years. Volume trends for each of the customers (all of them wholesalers) were established.

Building statistics were obtained from R.C. Mean's Forecasts for home-starts. From these statistics, using standardized conversion multipliers, the number of wood flush doors consumed or to be consumed in the market could be estimated. When these figures were compared with estimates of the number of units handled by wholesalers, they were noticeably larger; and the trend indicated that the gap could become even larger.

Personnel in the door division were concerned as to the accuracy of the secondary sources used in these calculations and wanted confirmation of their initial observations. It became evident that a survey would be necessary to obtain more accurate figures concerning the market impact of the new middlemen purchasing directly from manufacturers. Figures were also needed to obtain better understanding of the impact of new specialty flush doors on the middlemen's purchase intentions. Thus, the survey questionnaire was designed in part to identify the elements of the market most responsive to the specialty type doors.

To identify wholesalers, retailers, major contractors, industrialized home builders, and large component builders who might purchase wood flush doors in sizeable quantities, raw lists were developed from the *Directory of Forest Products Industry; The Bluebook of Major Home-builders; Dun and Bradstreet, Middle Market Directory; The Yellow Pages* of local phone directories; *Lumberman's Redbook;* and Simpson's own accounting records. Best estimates were that these lists included every possible carload lot purchaser in the market. (It was recognized that a number of entries on the lists did not qualify for carload lot purchases so one of the survey's leading questions focused on purchase sizes.) The lists were consolidated into a master list with duplicate entries eliminated.

The questionnaire was developed with the major goals of obtaining information on:

Exhibit 1
Historical Channel Arrangement: Wood Flush Door Suppliers

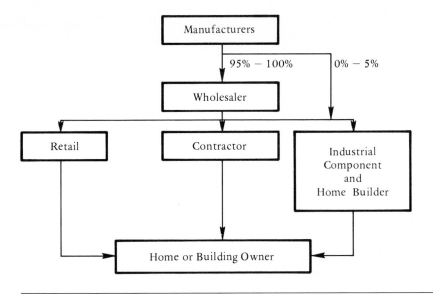

Annual wood flush door volume.

The volume of major door subgroups, such as unfinished and prefinished.

The year-to-year increase in purchases of each such group.

The number of suppliers, volume from each supplier, and breakdown of sales per customer type.

Major competitors.

Any major channel and product volume trends that were occurring, including trends for specialty type subgroups.

Telephone interviews were utilized. The response was better than expected, with approximately 90 percent of the respondents providing data. Many of the respondents were also willing to provide estimates for selected competition, which were helpful in verifying statistics from each respondent and gaining information on the 10 percent who would not reply to the telephone request. Once preliminary data were obtained for each entry on the list, key customers were personally interviewed to verify the findings and to obtain estimates for some of the missing responses.

Responses from the middlemen (wholesalers, retailers, industrial component, and home builders) verified that the historical channel arrangement (until the late 1960s) had been through the wholesaler (see Exhibit 1).

The data also indicated that there had been a substantial shift in the channel arrangement (see Exhibit 2). In particular, further expansion of direct purchases from the industrial sector was to be expected.

Exhibit 2
Current Channel Arrangement: Wood Flush Door Suppliers

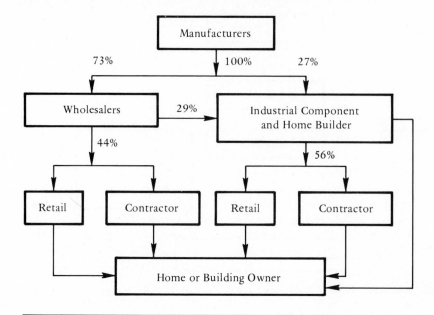

It was also revealed that the specialty product introduced by Masonite was being accepted readily and uniformly throughout the market. No single class of middlemen was providing for the majority of specialty product distribution. Also most of the middlemen, and especially the larger ones, expected to see substantial growth in the specialty market and were looking for new supplier competition in this part of the market.

Changes Instituted

The first change to be considered and instituted was for the company to replace the agent. Simpson feared that the substantial "goodwill" the agent may have created with the company's traditional flush door customers would be endangered.

Also there was concern that the agent's product lines from other manufacturers complemented, in some way, his door offering from Simpson. However, the responses indicated that there was no direct physical connection between the agent's other products and the flush doors. Also, conversations with some of the middlemen who had been cooperative during the questionnaire stages of the project provided data to suggest that these fears should not be of great concern.

Once the decision was made to find a replacement for the agent, it was concluded that the position should be filled internally by opening a sales office in the market. This would mean that there would be a sales position in the region responsible for both the commodity door and the introduction of the new specialty substitute. The company was fortunate to obtain an individual experienced in the geographical market and casually familiar with wood flush door products.

Result: Improved Sales

Missionary work with larger retailers and contractors improved sales to the wholesalers who were serving these markets. There appeared to be an upsurge in demand, primarily to fill inventory in the retail locations where the salesman had substantial influence because of his previous experiences.

The salesman also opened direct negotiations with selected members of the industrial and retail sectors. These visits were limited to industrial and retail customers who had small, if any, flush door purchases from the company's current wholesale customers. Response from these negotiations was favorable, with a number of initial orders. Visible concern by the current wholesale customers was not evident.

Initial response for Simpson's new specialty product was successful. With the dedicated and full support of the salesman, the product was accepted as a competitive substitute for the specialty product previously supplied by a single supplier (Masonite). It is still too early to indicate the long-run impact of Simpson's specialty prefinished door. But if it is successful, as expected, the impact of a competitor's product on Simpson's former market share will have been thwarted. Simpson will have enhanced its ability to attract the new class of direct purchasers with a full line of specialty *and* commodity flush doors.

Discussion Question

Evaluate Simpson's research survey and its channel strategy change in response to the information provided by the survey.

Case 23
Koehring Company
Evaluating Channel Member Performance

The Koehring Company, Milwaukee, manufactures and sells a broad range of construction machinery and other heavy equipment, including industrial machinery and specialty oil well hardware items. The company has eleven domestic operating divisions, each of which is responsible for its own sales, service, and product research and development.

The number of the company's divisions and its annual sales have grown in recent years, and so has the number of distributors selling Koehring products. Complicating the Koehring distribution set-up is the fact that some distributors handle several of the company's construction equipment lines, while others carry only one or two lines of company manufacture.

Several years ago, the company reviewed its methods of distributor evaluation which at the time were "subjective, irregular, and fragmentary." Routine appraisals were not a part of company procedures, and when management asked field salespeople about the performance of an individual distributor, the answer elicited often ran, "Well, they're doing all right," "They could be better," or something equally vague.

Finding this approach to distributor evaluation unsatisfactory, management decided the company needed a better and more comprehensive reporting system—namely, one that would give both the divisions and corporate headquarters better knowledge and control of distributor operations without having to wade through volumes of disorganized, subjective information. One problem of particular concern emanated from the uneven performance of many distributors: they might be doing an excellent job on certain Koehring lines, but a poor one on others. How could intelligence about such performance be effectively communicated to corporate headquarters and between divisions?

In short, an efficient evaluation procedure was called for, one that would uniformly measure distributor performance.

The Dealer Rating Form

The corporate marketing staff hit upon an answer—the "Koehring Dealer Rating Form" (see Exhibit 1) which provides the basis for an annual evaluation system.

The key to the rating system is found in the lower half of the form and is known as the "Penetration Index." This index is computed, as the instruction sheet explains (see Exhibit 2), by dividing the annual dollar value of the dealer equipment sales by the annual equipment sales quota which was assigned to the dealer at the beginning of the year. (Annual quotas assigned to dealers for each Koehring product line they carry are fixed with their advice and consent.) The penetration index is then converted into the dealer rating.

To take a hypothetical example: If a dealer's 1965 annual equipment sales amount to $100,000 and an equipment sales quota was set at $110,000, then $100,000 divided by $110,000 equals 0.909, which falls in the penetration index range of 0.9 to 1.1. A penetration figure in this range equals a dealer rating of 3, which is considered "average" (see Exhibit 2). Dealer ratings range from 1 (excellent) to 5 (poor).

The performance rating developed in this manner is not necessarily the final rating the distributor receives. As described in steps 4 and 5 on the instruction sheet, the computed rating is next evaluated "in terms of the dealer's total performance," so that the rating can be further adjusted if warranted.

An independent rating is prepared on each distributor for every Koehring product line represented. If two or more company lines are carried, the distributor receives independent ratings for each line, and no overall rating, combining performance ratings on each line, is computed.

Ratings and Potentials

A supplementary check on the company's distributor organization is made by matching the dealer's rating with that state's construction-potential classification.

Exhibit 1
Koehring Company Dealer Rating Form

KOEHRING COMPANY DEALER RATING FORM

Division· ....   Fiscal Year: ....

Dealer Name: ....   Dĺr. Code No. ....

MAIN OFFICE AND BRANCHES (List Main Office First) State, City	Number of Employees	Number of Salesmen	Service Facilities Rating	Number of Servicemen	Quality of Service Rendered Ratg.	Parts Stock Rating	Equipment Stock Ratg.	All Product Promotion Rating
Total, All Branches								

Type of Sales Contract or Products Under Sales Franchise

Products	Exclusive	Non Exclusive

Koehring Company Representation

Koeh. Div. ....   Kwik-Mix ....

Schield ....   Johnson ....

Parsons ....   KO-CAL ....

Buf. Spr. ....

Other Major Accounts Handled: ....

Regional Representative (Name) ....   Region or Area No. ....

Credit Rating: ....

Dealer Sales, (All Accounts)   **Profit**   **Net Worth**

1962 _____

1963 _____

1964 _____

1965 _____

Division Dealer Volume

	Equipment A	Parts	Total	$ Volume Quota (Equipment) B	Dealer Percentage		Penetration Index *
					Total Division Dom. Sales	Potential U. S. Sales	
1961							
1962							
1963							
1964							
1965							

Performance Rating:

1961	1962	1963	1964	1965

Action in 1966 _____

_____

_____

*Penetration Index = $\dfrac{\text{Dealer Equipment Sales (Column A)}}{\text{Dealer Equipment Sales Quota (Column B)}}$

Exhibit 2
Instruction Sheet for Koehring Annual Dealer Rating

Instruction Sheet for KOEHRING Annual Dealer Rating

Theoretically, each dealer should be rated annually on his over-all performance in terms of sales volume, penetration, efforts, financing, parts, services, etc. However, in actual practice such ratings tend to become subjective, thereby reducing the comparability and consistency necessary for a continuing program of distributor analysis and review. The following is a guide for making more reliable and valid *objective* judgments:

Method for Computing Rating

1. Fill in the required information for each dealer on the Dealer Rating Forms.

2. Compute the Penetration Index. (Divide the dollar value of column A by the dollar value of column B.)

Formula:

$$\frac{\text{Dealer Equipment Sales} \quad (\text{Col. A})}{\text{Dealer Equipment Sales Quota} \quad (\text{Col. B})}$$

An index of 1.0 indicates the dealer's attainment of his equipment dollar quota. An index value above 1.0 signifies that the dealer has exceeded his quota and any index value below 1.0 expresses the degree to which he has fallen short of his quota.

3. Assign a tentative Performance Rating to each dealer based on his Penetration Index (refer to columns I and II in the table below).

4. Evaluate this rating in terms of the dealer's total performance indicated by his accomplishments of the items listed under the description for that rating in column III.

5. Adjust the rating accordingly if warranted by your evaluation of his total performance.

6. Analyze the situation and record the suggested necessary action for improving his penetration for next year.

I *Penetration Index Ranges*	II *Dealer Rating Code*	III *Description*
1.5 and over	1	Excellent—Performance in sales, penetration, efforts, financing, parts, service, etc.
1.2 to 1.4	2	Good—Performance above average in sales, penetration, efforts, financing, parts, service, etc.
0.9 to 1.1	3	Average—Performance satisfactory or average in sales, penetration, efforts, financing, parts, service, etc.
0.6 to 0.8	4	Fair—Performance below average, weak in all or most of the areas of sales, penetration, efforts, financing, parts, service, etc. and needs improvement.
0.5 or less	5	Poor—Performance unsatisfactory, requiring definite corrective action. Should be considered for cancellation.

Exhibit 3
Koehring Company Construction Equipment Dealers' Performance Ratings

KOEHRING COMPANY
CONSTRUCTION EQUIPMENT DEALERS PERFORMANCE RATINGS

FISCAL 1964

STATE AND DEALER	B-S ROAD EQUIP.		FLAHERTY PRODUCTS		JOHNSON PRODUCTS		KO-CAL PRODUCTS		PARSONS TRENCHERS		PARSONS DUMPTORS		PARSONS LOADER-HOE		PCM M&MH		PCM KA-MO		KOEHRING PRODUCTS		SCHIELD PRODUCTS		THEW CR. & EXCAV.		THEW LOADERS	
	64	63	64	63	64	63	64	63	64	63	64	63	64	63	64	63	64	63	64	63	64	63	64	63	64	63
ALABAMA																										
.... Equip. Co.	3																		2	4						
..... Service									3	1	3	3					4	3								
..... Equip. Co.													3								2	3	2	3		
.... Mach. Co.																										3
.... Tr. Co.			3	3	2	4																				
ALASKA																										
.... Equip. Co.			1	2																						
..... Equipment															3											
..... Equip.						5									5	5	5	3			5	4	5			
..... Equip. Co.					*												4	5	5						
ARIZONA																										
.... Constr. Co.			2	2																						
.... Equip. Co.					*																					
.... Co.							3	3																		
.... Equip. Co.	3	3																	4	5						
.. Machinery Co.									*		*		*		5	5	5	5					2			
..... Machy. Co.																										
ARKANSAS																										
.... Equip. Co. Machy.	4	4	3	2	3	3																				
..... Equip.									4						5	5			4	4	4	3		4		
.... Supp.															1	4										

The classification by state and its use is described in an instruction sheet, as follows:

"To help in reviewing and evaluating the annual dealer performance ratings on a more objective basis, each state has been classified according to its annual potential. The potential for each state is based on dollar volume expressed as a percent of the total U.S. contract awards for engineered construction projects relevant to each Koehring division.

"Alphabetical potential classifications are assigned to each state based on the dollar volume awards expressed as a percentage of total U.S. construction awards for each division's category. The following key shows the range of percentages comprising each potential class:

Potential Classification	Range of the Per Cent of Total U.S. Awards per Class:
A	6% and over
B	5.0%–5.9%
C	4.0 −4.9
D	3.0 −3.9
E	2.0 −2.9
F	1.0 −1.9
G	0.0 −0.9

"Thus, a state classified as having 'A' potential would account for 6% or more of the dollar awards made in the country for projects most likely requiring a particular division's equipment."

Management believes that, while excellent dealers everywhere are of course desirable, states with the heaviest concentration of business should have dealers with superior performance ratings.

Thus, a dealer in an "A" or "B" state achieving a performance rating of 4 or 5 would indicate that a great deal of business in that state remains untapped or, at any rate, is not falling to the company.

Ratings of distributors are carried out by district sales representatives, in conjunction with their sales managers, at least once per year.

Performance Reports

While a number of company reports are drawn, to a greater or lesser extent, from the annual dealer rating process, two are reported to be especially useful to management: a report on "U.S. Construction Equipment Dealers Performance Ratings," and a summary of "Annual Dealer Ratings by Divisions" (see Exhibit 3).

The first gives the performance rating for every domestic and Canadian distributor for every division in the company. The entire annual performance for any distributor may be ascertained at once; and, since the data are arranged by states and provinces, the distributor may also be measured against all colleagues in the same area. Also, the quality of any

Exhibit 4
Annual Dealer Rating Summary for the Schield Bantam Division

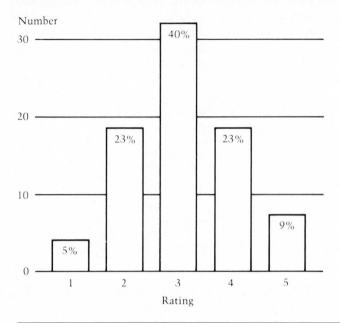

division's representation in any area is immediately apparent. The report is, in effect, a composite of all ratings of all dealers through which the products of Koehring's divisions are sold. Also shown are the two most recent years' ratings for each division on each of its distributors, giving a further quick comparison of distributor performances.

The second report on annual dealer ratings by divisions, in bar-chart form, shows the composite quality of each division's distributor representation during the year. Of 79 dealers rated by the Schield Bantam division, the chart indicates that, in 1964, 5 percent of this division's dealers earned Rating 1 (excellent); 23 percent, Rating 2 (good); 40 percent, Rating 3 (average); 23 percent, Rating 4 (fair); and 9 percent, Rating 5 (poor). (See Exhibit 4.)

The dealer ratings form the basis for supplementary reports that receive limited distribution and are for special internal use. In addition, the ratings are helpful in discussions of problem areas and problem distributors at company-wide sales meetings.

The corporate marketing staff, which is responsible for all statistics, market research and market analyses, including the annual dealer ratings, acts as a clearinghouse for divisional marketing intelligence and prepares the consolidated reports for management.

According to the company, cooperation of the sales force in filling out and sending in dealer ratings has been excellent, and the field sales force is solidly in favor of the dealer rating system.

Commenting on the pros and cons of the approach, a Koehring marketing executive points out: "There are too many variables, of course, to evaluate our distributors completely and with absolute accuracy by this mathematical method. The human element of judgment cannot be eliminated—nor should it be. We do feel, however, that we are on the right track by evaluating in this manner, in that a common denominator is achieved for all distributors by rating them all on the same basis.

"Then, and only then, may the refinements, modifications and exceptions be noted and taken into account. In this way, the 'by gosh and by golly' sort of approach is eliminated. In general, we are most pleased with our evaluation procedures."

Discussion Question

Evaluate Koehring's approach to measuring channel member performance.

Case 24
Westron Incorporated
Administered Vertical Marketing Systems

Westron Incorporated had introduced a complete line of power tools during the pre-Christmas season in 1968. These tools were of very high quality and were priced, on the average, eight to ten percent higher than the highest-priced competitive line. The Westron line of products was *demonstrably* superior to other lines—the power tools were virtually vibrationless, and so the finished results were more precise. One television advertisement had, in fact, demonstrated the Westron line's ultrasmooth operation by running a power drill *unsupported* on an inclined waxed board. The drill did not move—showing, presumably, that the extremely low level of vibration was not sufficient to break the inertia of the drill.

Westron was relatively new to the home power-tool market—indeed, its basic reputation was not in products for final consumers at all. The Westron name was well known and very highly regarded in the realm of industrial markets. Westron had, for over eighty years, manufactured both heavy and light tools for use in industry. These industrial tools were of very high quality and were sold for a premium price. Westron had originally become interested in the home power-tool market when approached by a major general-merchandise chain organization to produce power tools under the name of the chain. Westron had ultimately decided not to produce a line of tools for the private brand, but the management had not dismissed the idea of developing a line of products for home workshops.

When the home power-tool line was finally introduced in 1968, the consumer reaction had not been breathtaking. Dealers had not been easy to find. Many of the stronger dealerships were working under exclusive arrangements with other brands of home power tools. And while promotional support for the new line had been adequate, it was focused *exclusively* on final consumers. The dealers that did take the line often took only part of it; often they wanted only the power drills—the ¼- and ⅜-inch being most popular. The Westron management had wanted full-line "shoppes" to be the dealer norm. These shoppes would display all of the Westron line and provide a demonstration "pit" in which various skills with power tools could be demonstrated and taught. But, in truth, at the end of three years of experience with the product line, very few dealers, even in large metropolitan areas, met this standard.

In the summer of 1971 the Westron management began to develop plans to strengthen their Name Power Tool Division. A complete review of their present power-tool policy showed it to be as summarized in the following list.

1. Dealer margins were set at 35 percent of final selling price. This was thought to be a customary dealer margin in the distribution of hardware.

2. Dealer development included a brochure picturing and describing some of the special uses for Westron power tools.

3. Westron field salespeople were available to dealers–depending on dealer size–at least once every six months. When special problems arose, a Westron representative could be available in a matter of several days.

4. Dealers were encouraged to advertise Westron products. The encouragement took the form of a cooperative advertising program in which Westron would pay fifty percent of the media cost upon receiving satisfactory proof that the ad had been run.

5. A demonstration table, capable of providing a secure mount for all Westron power tools, was provided all Westron dealers. The cost of this table to Westron was almost $50.

6. Dealers were given cash terms of 2/10 net 30–which meant they could deduct a 2 percent cash discount if they paid within 10 days of receipt of a shipment of tools. If they did not wish to pay that quickly, the bill became due at the end of 30 days. In effect, dealers had 30 days in which to generate the money with which to pay their Westron bills.

Several ideas for modifying the present dealer plan had been considered. For example, management had discussed a dealer training program in which one person in each dealership would be appointed a Westron "key man" and trained to demonstrate and sell Westron power tools.

Likewise, the possibility of Westron's leasing departments in some cities had been considered. Under this plan Westron would, in effect, run its own "shoppes"—including staffing, training, and selling. The management of Westron had also developed an interest in something called "vertical marketing systems." These systems included "corporate" systems, "contractual" systems, and "administered" systems. And while the Westron management was not sure exactly what these systems involved, they had heard that the administered system was best suited to their situation.

Discussion Questions

1. What specific changes in the Westron dealer plan would you make? Why? Make sure you consider the addition of wholly new features to the plan as well as deletion or modification of present features.
2. What is a vertical marketing system? How do these vertical marketing systems relate to the Westron case? Which basic type of vertical marketing system is probably best for Westron? Why?

Case 25
Pepsi-Cola Bottlers Association
Organization of a Franchised Channel

Organization of Pepsi-Cola Bottlers Association

Pepsi-Cola is one of the older franchisors with a long-established franchisee association. The Pepsi-Cola Bottlers Association represents all of Pepsi-Cola's independent franchised bottlers. The association was formed in 1948, and its present 500 members include bottlers from each of the 50 states.

A board of directors, consisting of the officers of the association, three immediate past presidents, and the 17 elected district directors, governs the activities of the association. Membership of the board also includes the chairmen of various committees, such as insurance, standardization, marketing, and management education.

The board of directors convenes semiannually and is charged with the responsibility for the management of all affairs, finances, and property of the franchisee association. Between these semiannual meetings, an executive director and an executive committee manage the association's affairs. The latter committee, which is authorized to act on behalf of the board of directors, is made up of officers of the association, the president, executive vice president, treasurer, and immediate past president. Each

Exhibit 1
Franchisee Association District Organizational Structure

Districts (17) and Division(s)

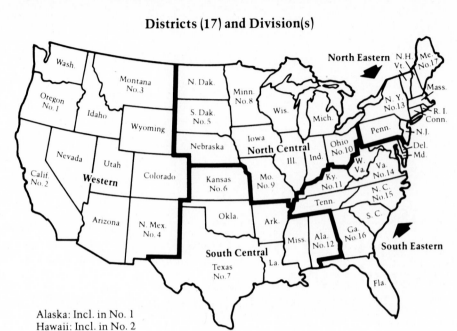

Alaska: Incl. in No. 1
Hawaii: Incl. in No. 2

Marketing Committee Territories

Exhibit 2
Franchisee Organizational Structure (Pepsi-Cola Bottlers Association)

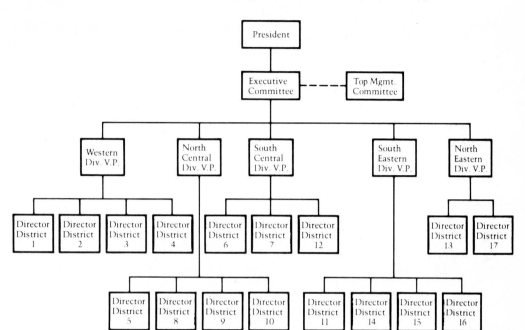

officer is elected for a one-year term by the board of directors during the annual meeting and is selected from candidates suggested by either the board of directors or membership at large.

As shown in Exhibit 1, the association is structured into several districts, each headed by a district director who is elected by the franchisees within the district. A key element in the primary communications of the association, the district director reports to a divisional vice president in his or her region (Exhibit 2).

The standing or permanent committees of the association give close scrutiny to various segments of the franchisees' business operations. The principal standing committees deal with bylaws, finance, insurance, long-range planning, management education, marketing, nominating, and standardization. In addition, the president of the association may also, upon recommendation of the board of directors, appoint special committees intended to fill short-range study needs. In practice, some of these short-range committees have later become standing committees when it was seen that they fulfilled a continuing information or liaison need within the association. All of the committees report through the board of directors or executive committee to the president of the association. The organizational structure of the committees is illustrated in Exhibit 3.

Exhibit 3
Committee Organizational Structure (Pepsi-Cola Bottlers Association)

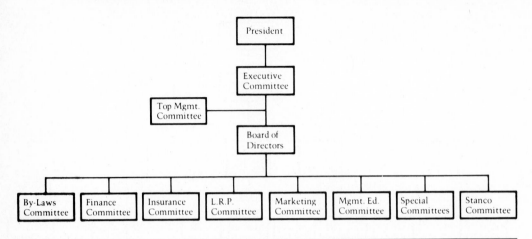

Pepsi-Cola executives are favorably impressed with the results obtained by the franchisee association. A company marketing executive believes that "the association has been an important force in improving franchisee morale and in protecting product quality."

Discussion Questions

1. How does this organization structure help to foster channel member cooperation?
2. Can you suggest improvements?

Index

Name Index

Subject Index

Acknowledgments

Case 1, pp. 401–403, reprinted with permission from Ronald R. Gist, *Cases in Marketing Management*, published in 1972.

Case 2, pp. 404–406, from Ernest B. Uhr, *Marketing Problems: Situations for Analysis*, copyright © 1973. Reprinted by permission of John Wiley & Sons, Inc.

Case 3, pp. 407–409, reprinted with permission from Bernard F. Whalen, "Airwick Drops Sales Offices to Increase Sales," *Marketing News*, published by The American Marketing Association (8 February 1980) p. 6.

Case 4, pp. 410–412, reprinted with permission from Ronald R. Gist, *Cases in Marketing Management*, published in 1972.

Case 7, pp. 418–419, reprinted by permission from E. Patrick McGuire, *Franchised Distribution*, Report No. 523 (New York: The Conference Board, 1971).

Case 8, pp. 420–422, reprinted with permission from Peter M. Banting, *Canadian Marketing: A Case Approach* (Toronto: McGraw-Hill Ryerson Limited, 1977), pp. 182–185.

Case 9, pp. 421–425, from Philip Kotler, *Marketing Management: Analysis, Planning, and Control*, 3rd edition, © 1976, pp. 507–508. Reprinted by permission of Prentice-Hall, Inc., Englewood Cliffs, New Jersey.

Case 12, pp. 432–435, reprinted by permission from E. Patrick McGuire, *Franchised Distribution*. Report No. 523 (New York: The Conference Board, 1971).

Case 13, pp. 436–437, reprinted by permission from Richard H. Buskirk, *Cases and Readings in Marketing*, published in 1970. Copyright 1970 Richard H. Buskirk.

Case 15, pp. 447–453, prepared by Peter G. Betz, Kimberly Knitwear, and Rodger D. Collons, Professor of Business and Administration, Drexel University.

Case 16, pp. 454–456, reprinted by permission from E. Patrick McGuire, *Franchised Distribution*, Report No. 523 (New York: The Conference Board, 1971).

Case 17, pp. 457–460, reprinted from *Fundamentals of Marketing* by William J. Stanton. Copyright © 1975 by McGraw-Hill, Inc. Used with permission of McGraw-Hill Book Company.

Case 18, pp. 461–468, reprinted with permission from W. Wayne Talarzyk, *Contemporary Cases in Marketing*, 2nd ed. (Hinsdale, Ill.: The Dryden Press, 1979), pp. 198–207; modified by David McConaughy, University of Southern California.

Case 19, pp. 469–473, reprinted with permission from W. Wayne Talarzyk, *Contemporary Cases in Marketing*, (Hinsdale, Ill.: The Dryden Press, 1979), pp. 213–221.

Case 20, 476–478, reprinted with permission from William J. Stanton, *Fundamentals of Marketing*, (New York: McGraw-Hill Company, 1981), pp. 369–370.

Case 21, pp. 479–482, reprinted with permission from W. Wayne Talarzyk, *Cases for Analysis in Marketing*, 2nd ed. (Hinsdale, Ill.: The Dryden Press, 1981), pp. 91–95.

Case 22, pp. 483–489, reprinted with permission from *The Journal of Marketing*, published by The American Marketing Association, (July 1978), pp. 38–41.

Case 23, pp. 490–497, reprinted by permission from Roger M. Pegram, *Selecting and Evaluating Distributors*, Business Policy Study No. 116 (New York: The Conference Board, 1965).

Case 24, pp. 498–500, is reprinted with permission from Ronald R. Gist, *Cases in Marketing Management*, published in 1972.

Case 25, pp. 501–504, reprinted by permission from E. Patrick McGuire, *Franchised Distribution*, Report No. 523 (New York: The Conference Board, 1971).